MUCKRAKING!

MUCKRAKING!

The Journalism
That Changed
America

. . . .

JUDITH AND WILLIAM
SERRIN

THE NEW PRESS

NEW YORK

Compilation © 2002 by Judith and William Serrin
All rights reserved.
No part of this book may be reproduced, in any form,
without written permission from the publisher.

Pages 389 through 392 constitute an extension of this copyright page.

Published in the United States by The New Press, New York, 2002
Distributed by W. W. Norton & Company, Inc., New York

ISBN 1-56584-681-8 (pbk.)
CIP data available

The New Press was established in 1990 as a not-for-profit alternative to the large,
commercial publishing houses currently dominating the book publishing industry.
The New Press operates in the public interest rather than for private gain, and is
committed to publishing, in innovative ways, works of educational, cultural, and
community value that are often deemed insufficiently profitable.

The New Press, 450 West 41st Street, 6th floor, New York, NY 10036
www.thenewpress.com

Book design by Lovedog Studio

Printed in Canada

2   4   6   8   10   9   7   5   3

This book is dedicated to our parents,
Alice and George Bruhn
and
Mildred and William Serrin,
who introduced us to libraries in our youths

CONTENTS

THE POOR

THE WORKING CLASS

PUBLIC HEALTH AND SAFETY

WOMEN, THEIR RIGHTS, NOTHING LESS

POLITICS

MUCKRAKING!

FREEDOM

SPORTS

CONSERVATION

AMERICA AT WAR

THE PRESS

CRIME AND PUNISHMENT

AMERICANA

    Herald Holds Its Community
    Together After a Disastrous
    Flood. *Grand Forks Herald,*
    April 27, 1997.

                AN AFTERWORD   387

                PERMISSIONS   389

ACKNOWLEDGMENTS

We wish to thank the following for helping us with this book:

André Schiffrin, publisher of The New Press, whose idea this book was, and who exhibited his usual patience as he pushed us first to start the book, and then to finish it.

Andy Hsiao, who edited the book.

These libraries, which helped us more than they know: the Bethesda, Maryland, branch of the Montgomery County library system; the Library of Congress; the Dr. Martin Luther King, Jr., branch of the Washington, D.C., library system; the Bobst Library of New York University, which has a splendid newspaper and magazine collection, and the Tamiment Collection there; and the New York Public Library at Fifth Avenue and Forty-second Street.

Asjylyn Yoder, Catherine Serrin, and Mary Connolly, who helped us with research, and the following people, who gave suggestions, ideas, or extra help: Barbara Belejack, Tom Bethell, Earl Dotter, Cathleen Dullahan, Moe Foner, Thomas C. Fox, Pat and Tom Gish, Lindsay Goldwert, Don Kennison, Linda Lake, Walker Lundy, Michael Maidenburg, Robert K. Manoff, Anthony Mazzocchi, Gene Miller, Nick Salvatore, Peter Simmons, Matt Witt.

Our daughters, Catherine Serrin and Sara Bigley, who once again have shown interest in and support for our work.

In the course of doing this book we have come in contact with many splendid journalists who make us proud of the journalism profession, and we thank them all.

INTRODUCTION

This is a book about doing journalism and doing good.

It is not common, at the start of the 2000s, to link those two phrases. Journalism has many critics, and correctly so. Journalism is often too superficial, too oriented toward celebrity, too concerned with the doings of high-income readers and viewers. Some publishers and broadcast executives might as well be selling shoes as selling news. They have brought to the newsroom the values of the boardroom and allow Wall Street's idea of the bottom line to be the mark of success. The newsroom can be like an assembly line or an electronic back office: what counts is standardization and productivity more than quality; keystrokes, not content. Some media executives use the news, consciously or unconsciously, to boost their own financial and social interests, or those of their friends. Some reporters and editors buy into this boosterism, seeking to advance themselves with their superiors. Some reporters are lazy, never making five calls when two will do. The Internet has done in the newsroom what the telephone a hundred and more years ago did not: some reporters stay in the newsroom as though they are lashed there. Some reporters are fearful, afraid to speak up when they disagree with a newsroom decision. Some wear ambition like a badge; they will be there for the big story of the moment, only to drop the story when the moment passes. Educational levels and salaries of journalists are the highest they've ever been, and there's a great chance for additional money through television appearances and book con-

tracts. Many journalists, aware of the possibility of riches, are far too interested in improving their own lot, not that of others.

Yet it is also true that journalism has, throughout the centuries, and continuing today, made America better. Journalism, in fact, helped make the United States, with the newsletters of Samuel Adams and others and the essays of Thomas Paine informing and inspiring the colonists during the American Revolution. In the 1800s, journalists such as William Lloyd Garrison and Frederick Douglass helped bring pressure to end slavery, and one abolitionist, Elijah Lovejoy, died for his journalism. An announcement in a small New York weekly newspaper drew surprising crowds to a convention on women's rights in Seneca Falls, New York, in 1848, and over the years journalism was instrumental in assisting suffragists who worked laboriously to help bring greater equality to women in America. During the Civil War, reporters and photographers (modern journalism was in large part invented during the Civil War) committed many errors but brought home to America the horrors and the noble purpose of the Union cause. In the 1940s, a group of young sports reporters, mostly from the black press, led the efforts that eventually broke the color barrier in Major League Baseball. Editorials by a small number of brave Southern journalists during the 1950s helped lead their communities toward equal rights for blacks. In the 1960s and 1970s, a few voices in the press played an important role in causing the country to reconsider its actions in the Vietnam War.

Journalism helped create Yosemite National Park in California, the Boundary Waters wilderness area in northern Minnesota, the Appalachian Trail from Georgia to Maine, the Everglades National Park in Florida, and the C&O Canal park in the District of Columbia and Maryland. Journalism revealed the U.S. government's appalling neglect of black men suffering syphilis in Tuskegee, Alabama, and raised the alarm about inadequate response of the public and private health communities to the onset of AIDS in the early 1980s. Journalism helped bring free public libraries and free public education and unveiled the scandal of Salt Lake City's bidding for the 2002 Olympic Games. Journalism has put people in jail, and journalism has gotten people out of jail, sometimes after their execution date had been set. "More crime, immorality and rascality is prevented by the fear of exposure in the newspapers than by all the laws, moral and statute, ever devised," said Joseph Pulitzer, after taking over the *St. Louis Post* and the *Dispatch* in 1878. Journalism has put people in office and forced people from office, sometimes both. President Richard M. Nixon, Associate Justice Abe Fortas, House Speaker Joe Cannon, Senator George Lorimer of Illinois, Senator Chauncey M. Depew of New York, and assorted sheriffs, city council members, and mayors would have remained in power longer without journalism. Reporters have caused the reform or closing of mental hospitals, the cleaning up of municipal water supplies, new rules for ferry boat operators in San Francisco, and efforts to aid federal workers exposed to plutonium. Journalism helped create the national forests more than a century ago and today is raising the issue of how management of those forests can be strengthened.

Journalism helped bring safer use of fireworks, safer automobiles and meat, and urban renewal. Neither the seventeenth constitutional amendment, calling for direct election of senators, nor perhaps the nineteenth, giving women the vote, would have come about except for reporters.

Working-class families in the early 1900s would probably have paid much more a year for their kerosene if journalism had not exposed the railroad rebate system. Journalism helped reduce child labor, exposed the unnecessary high costs of the American funeral industry, brought to light the dangers of the use of DDT and other pesticides, and led to the recall of automobiles and automobile and truck tires.

Some journalists won prizes for this kind of work. Some did not, but that is fine. Journalism should not be about prizes, and one of its flaws now is that too much work seems to be done more to win journalism prizes than for other purposes. The purpose of journalism, said Peter Finley Dunne, writing as Mr. Dooley in the early 1900s, is to comfort the afflicted and afflict the comfortable. Publisher E. W. Scripps put it this way: "I have only one principle, and that is represented by an effort to make it harder for the rich to grow richer and easier for the poor to keep from growing poorer." When Jacob Riis, New York editor, briefly considered abandoning journalism for the ministry, a minister friend told him, "No, no, Jacob, not that. We have preachers enough. What the world needs is consecrated pens."

The chance to make a difference has historically been, and continues to be, one of the attractions that draws people into journalism. President Theodore Roosevelt was wrong when in 1906 he attacked reporters practicing what was then called the literature of exposure. Taking a phrase from John Bunyon's *Pilgrim's Progress*, Roosevelt accused reporters of raking only the muck of life and never seeing the stars. (Roosevelt later told so many of the crusading reporters, many of them his friends, that his remarks did not refer to *them* personally that it might be suspected that his speech was more about politics than an exercise in criticism of journalism. Whichever, journalists turned Roosevelt's phrase around and attached the name *muckraking* to one of their most cherished practices, the extensive investigating to uncover wrongdoing in private and public life.) The good journalists' retort to Roosevelt and to others who would make similar criticisms today would be along the lines of what George Bernard Shaw said, that it was because journalists could see the stars that they wanted to point out the muck, so that it could be cleaned away and others could see the stars as well. The country's founders had such an idea in mind when, in order to secure passage of the Constitution, they gave a free press special protection in the First Amendment.

Journalists wear disguises, and one of them is the disguise of objectivity. No reporter goes into journalism saying he or she wants to be objective, yet journalists continue to say that they write only what people say and do, that they, professional journalists, have no agendas. This is fiction. All good journalists have agendas. They wish to put the crooked sheriff in jail. They wish to unveil the patent medicine fraud. They wish to free the innocent man from jail. "I could do one thing," Mary Heaton Vorse, the labor journalist, said after the strike of workers in Lawrence, Massachusetts, in 1912 caused her to sidetrack her career of writing women's fiction for journalism. "I could write. I could try to make other people see what I had seen, feel what I had felt. I wanted to make others as angry as I was. I wanted to see wages go up and the babies' death rate go down." The driving force of unobjectivity is not mentioned in journalism schools or newsrooms but it is the truth. The reporters whose work is featured in this book were unobjective and had an agenda. That is why they did such fine work.

Journalists, of course, do not themselves jail the offender or unjail the wrongly accused, set aside the park, fire the official, pass the law, knock down the slum, ban the pesticide, or remove the unsafe car from the road. This may be one reason so little attention is paid to the good that journalism has done. Even journalists often pay little or no attention to the good that they do. Few positive comments are said about journalism in any journalism history, journalism review, or lex-

icon of journalism remarks. One of the few is from the journalist and critic H. L. Mencken, a curious person to say something positive about his profession, given his acerbity. Looking back on his career, Mencken said, "I find myself more and more convinced that I had more fun doing news reporting than in any other enterprise. It really is the life of kings."

Another problem is that historians, disdaining journalists and their work, often ignore them, focusing instead on the politician or the movement that was in at the finish of an episode of change, not on the journalists in at the beginning. Professional jealousy may be involved here, as well as the old feeling, never abandoned in the newsroom or the university, that journalists are somehow inferior creatures, involved in practices akin to, say, poultry or mortuary science, not in a high and honorable calling. The adage, attributed to Philip L. Graham, publisher of the *Washington Post*, is that journalists do the first rough draft of history. By implication, historians then take over and do the important work. Historians are often reluctant to concede that sometimes journalism is history's last draft and also not so rough, and that journalism can be as important as historiography or other crafts or professions. Journalists themselves make the same mistake. Journalism history is often regarded by many journalists and by journalism schools as an inferior history.

Tracking down change that journalism has caused is difficult. Some journalists, particularly in decades gone by, stepped back and forth between writing about problems and working in or heading up groups that tried to deal with the problems. William English Walling, for example, wrote in *The Independent* magazine in 1908 about the race riots in Springfield, Illinois, hometown of Abraham Lincoln, and ended with a call for somebody to do something. Mary Ovington White, a social worker and philanthropist, read the article, invited Walling to a meeting with some of her friends, and he helped form the National Association for the Advancement of Colored People. More often journalists, as probably they should, refrain from taking action. They provide the spark of outrage and citizens and officials take it from there.

Milo Radulovich, of Dexter, Michigan, was an Air Force reserve lieutenant during the 1950s who lost his job because high military officers, in the time of Senator Joseph McCarthy and other anti-Communist officials, said he had continuing contact with people of left political leanings. His father, for example, was receiving Socialist literature from his home country in Eastern Europe. The *Detroit News* brought the case to light and Edward R. Murrow featured it on his *See It Now* broadcast in October 1953. Five weeks later, Radulovich was reinstated. Looking back years later, Radulovich said that he had not recaptured all he lost because of the Air Force's action. But, he said, he was grateful. "I consider myself really lucky. It was only by public opinion that I was able to carry my fight." He continued, "Where else but in this country can you find a free press that is willing to express itself to save a little man?"

In many cases, journalism that causes change has been lost, because it is hidden in the court documents, the legislation, the history writing that follows. This is an effort to bring these important and often courageous acts back to light and to keep them there, in the place they deserve.

In researching this book, we drew upon both of our experiences teaching journalism history, our knowledge of American history, and our view of the world: the idea that, in a democratic, capitalist society, wrongs are exposed and stopped only after public pressure brings them to the forefront. Sometimes this is seen most clearly before

the press picks up an issue. Randy Shilts, who chronicled the onset of AIDS for the *San Francisco Chronicle*, said that when the problem of AIDS first emerged in the early 1980s, "People died and nobody paid attention." This changed, he said, only after the press began to write about the problem. "Without the media to fulfill its role as public guardian, everyone else was left to deal—and not deal—with AIDS as they saw fit." Morton C. Mintz, a longtime *Washington Post* reporter, said much the same thing in his book *At Any Cost.* "The accomplishments of lawyers and legislators can be trees falling unheard in the forest," he wrote, "unless the press, as surrogate for the public, listens."

This book is by necessity subjective, random, and laudatory. The standard throughout was that the pieces could not merely represent good writing or good reporting. Always, they had to, in a substantial way, contribute to change, the kind of change, in the American reform tradition, that we believe makes America a better place. Skeptics may find this hard to believe, but there was much from which to choose.

We realize authors could do a book on the wrongs that journalism has done and continues to do—journalism has ignored problems, maligned races and ethnic groups, taken the side of government and big business, and caused wars. To write about that is someone else's job, if it is decided that enough people have not already done it. What we hope to do is to remind journalists, historians, and the readers and viewers in whose name journalists act that doing journalism is honorable and that honorable journalism can do good.

MUCKRAKING!

THE POOR

JACOB RIIS TELLS HOW THE OTHER HALF LIVES

Theodore Roosevelt, police commissioner of New York City in the 1890s, called the reporter Jacob Riis "the most useful citizen of New York." If there was ever a place that needed a useful person's help, it was the city's Lower East Side. There, in the 1870s and 1880s, hundreds of thousands of newly arrived immigrants, bringing their poverty with them, were crowded into airless and unsanitary tenements thrown up by greedy landlords with political connections. Dozens lived in the same room, thousands lived in basements, others, including children, lived on the streets. Filth, disease, crime, and drunkenness all thrived. Health and happiness did not.

Maybe the problems of the poor attracted Riis's attention because he had been a poor immigrant himself, coming from Denmark in 1870 at the age of twenty-one. Perhaps the reason was the exposure to the Lower East Side he received once he started working as a police reporter for the New York *Tribune* in 1877. Perhaps it was his profound belief that he had almost a religious duty to try to make things better. Perhaps he recognized good stories when he saw them.

Riis campaigned for an end to police lodging houses, basically vagrants' shelters run with terri-

ble laxness by the precincts, and helped bring about a Tenement House Commission charged with improving housing for the poor. He asked New Yorkers commuting to the city to bring flowers with them, so that the flowers could be distributed to the poor; the flowers came by the bunch, the barrel, the wagonsful. Clued by a health department report to possible contamination of the city's water in a time of cholera, he took his camera and documented how towns were dumping sewage into the waterways that led to the reservoirs that provided water for New York City. The Board of Health acted, and new restrictions were placed on the watershed.

In 1890, Riis put all of his knowledge about the city's slums into his first book, *How the Other Half Lives.*

"Introduction," *How the Other Half Lives,* by Jacob Riis. New York: Scribner's, 1890.

Long ago it was said that "one half of the world does not know how the other half lives." That was true then. It did not know because it did not care. The half that was on top cared little for the struggles, and less for the fate of those who were underneath, so long as it was able to hold them there and keep its own seat. There came a time when the discomfort and crowding below were so great, and the consequent upheavals so violent, that it was no longer an easy thing to do, and then the upper half fell to inquiring what was the matter. Information on the subject has been accumulating rapidly since, and the whole world has had its hands full answering for its old ignorance.

In New York, the youngest of the world's great cities, that time came later than elsewhere, because the crowding had not been so great. There were those who believed that it would never come; but their hopes were vain. Greed and reckless selfishness wrought like results here as in the cities of older lands. "When the great riot occurred in 1863," [the New York City draft riot, in July 1863, in which a thousand people, including many blacks, were killed] so reads the testimony of the Secretary of the Prison Association of New York before a legislative committee appointed to investigate causes of the increase of crime in the State twenty-five years ago, "every hiding-place and nursery of crime discovered itself by immediate and active participation in the operations of the mob. Those very places and domiciles, and all that are like them, are to-day nurseries of crime, and of the vices and disorderly courses which lead to crime. By far the largest part—eighty per cent, at least—of crimes against property and against the person are perpetrated by individuals who have either lost connection with home life, or never had any, or whose *homes had ceased to be sufficiently separate, decent, and desirable to afford what are regarded as ordinary wholesome influences of home and family*. . . . The younger criminals seem to come almost exclusively from the worst tenement house districts, that is, when traced back to the very places where they had their homes in the city here." Of one thing New York made sure at that early stage of the inquiry: the boundary line of the Other Half lies through the tenements.

It is ten years and over, now, since that line divided New York's population evenly. To-day three-fourths of its people live in the tenements, and the nineteenth century drift of the population to the cities is sending ever-increasing multitudes to crowd them. The fifteen thousand tenant homes that were the despair of the sanitarian in the past generation have swelled into thirty-seven thousand, and more than twelve hundred thousand persons call them home. The one way out he saw—rapid transit to the suburbs—has brought no relief. We know now that there is no way out; that the "system" that was the evil offspring of public neglect and private greed has come to stay, a storm-centre forever of our civilization. Nothing is left but to make the best of a bad bargain.

What the tenements are and how they grew to what they are, we shall see hereafter. The story is dark enough, drawn from the plain public records, to send a chill to any heart. If it shall appear that the sufferings and sins of the "other half," and the evil they breed, are but as a just punishment upon the community that gave it no other choice, it will be because that is the truth. The boundary line lies there because, while the forces for good on one side vastly outweigh the bad—it were not well otherwise—in the tenements all the influences make for evil; because they are the hot-beds of the epidemics that carry death to rich and poor alike; the nurseries of pauperism and crime that fill our jails and police courts; that throw off a scum of forty thousands human wrecks to the island asylums and workhouses year by year; that turned out in the last eight years a round half million beggars to prey upon our charities; that maintain a standing army of ten thousand tramps with all that that implies; because, above all, they touch the family life with deadly moral contagion. This is their worst crime, inseparable from the system. That we have to own it the child of our own wrong does not excuse it, even though it gives it claim upon our utmost patience and tenderest charity.

What are you going to do about it? is the question of to-day. It was asked once of our city in taunting defiance by a band of political cutthroats, the legitimate outgrowth of life on the tenement-house level. [The band of cutthroats Riis refers to is the Tweed Ring.] Law and order found the answer then and prevailed. With our enormously swelling population held in this galling bondage, will that answer always be given? It will depend on how fully the situation that prompted the challenge is grasped. Forty per cent of the distress among the poor, said a recent official report, is due to drunkenness. But the first legislative committee ever appointed to probe this sore went deeper down and uncovered its roots. The "conclusion forced itself upon it that certain conditions and associations of human life and habitation are the prolific parents of corresponding habits and morals," and it recommended "the prevention of drunkenness by providing for every man a clean and comfortable home." Years after, a sanitary inquiry brought to light the fact that "more than one-half of the tenements with two-thirds of their population were held by owners who made the keeping of them a business, *generally a speculation*. The owner was seeking a certain percentage on his outlay, and that percentage very rarely fell below fifteen per cent., and frequently exceeded thirty.... The complaint was universal among the tenants that they were entirely uncared for, and that the only answer to their requests to have the place put in order by repairs and necessary improvements was that they must pay their rent or leave. The agent's instructions were simple but emphatic: 'Collect the rent in advance, or failing, eject the occupants.'" Upon such a stock grew this upas-tree [a tropical tree that contains poisons used to tip arrows]. Small wonder the fruit is bitter. The remedy that shall be an effective answer to the coming appeal for justice must proceed from the public conscience. Neither legislation nor charity can cover the ground. The greed of capital that wrought the evil must itself undo it, as far as it can now be undone. Homes must be built for the working masses by those who employ their labor; but tenements must cease to be "good property" in the old, heartless sense.

"Philanthropy and five percent" is the penance exacted.

If this is true from a purely economic point of view, what then of the outlook from the Christian standpoint? Not long ago a great meeting was held in this city, of all denominations of religious faith, to discuss the question how to lay hold of these teeming masses in the tenements with Christian influences, to which they are now too often strangers. Might not the conference have found in the warning of one Brooklyn builder, who has invested his capital on this plan and made it pay more than a money interest, a hint worth heeding: "How shall the love of God be understood by those who have been nurtured in sight only of the greed of man?"

• • •

The popularity of *How the Other Half Lives* surprised Riis. The book became a popular topic for ministers' sermons and provided ammunition and inspiration for a cadre of reform groups awakened by Riis and Riis's photographs. Theodore Roosevelt was one of these reformers. After he became police commissioner, he abolished the police lodging houses Riis had fought so long.

Riis also helped establish playgrounds, including one on the site of the notorious Mulberry Bend; helped bring an end to the rear tenements thrown up in what were supposed to be the yards of houses; promoted a style of tenement design that brought more air and light to all rooms; worked for better construction and repair of public schools; pushed for child labor laws, kindergartens, and settlement houses. Whenever efforts to solve a problem lagged, Riis would step up the pressure, through his journalism, his lectures, and his work with reform groups. Some of his crusades went on for a dozen or more years before they saw results. "It takes a lot of telling to make a city know when it is doing wrong," he wrote. "However, that was what I was there for."

EDWIN MARKHAM WRITES OF THE HORRORS OF CHILD LABOR

A California schoolteacher and poet, Edwin Markham was profoundly moved by the painting *The Man with a Hoe* by Jean-François Millet. For several years Markham worked on a poem pondering what the man, a peasant "bowed by the weight of centuries, . . . the emptiness of ages in his face," had gone through, and who was responsible for his plight. On New Year's Eve, 1898, Markham read the poem before a gathering that included the editor of the *San Francisco Examiner*, William Randolph Hearst's first newspaper. The editor was impressed. The *Examiner* and other Hearst newspapers printed the poem, and it became known to millions and a nationwide sensation. Markham had struck a chord that caused people to ponder the problems of poverty.

He went on to do the same as a journalist, particularly in a series on child labor that appeared in the Hearst magazine *Cosmopolitan*.

"The Hoe-Man in the Making," by Edwin Markham. *Cosmopolitan*, September 1906.

Once, so the story goes, an old Indian chieftain was shown the ways and wonders of New York. He saw the cathedrals, the skyscrapers, the bleak tenements, the blaring mansions, the crowded circus, the airy span of the Brooklyn Bridge. "What is the most surprising thing you have seen?" asked several comfortable Christian gentlemen of this benighted pagan whose worship was a "bowing down to sticks and stones." The savage shifted his red blanket and answered in three slow words, "Little children working."

It has remained, then, for civilization to give the world an abominable custom which shocks the social ethics of even an unregenerate savage. For the Indian father does not ask his children to

work, but leaves them free till the age of maturity, when they are ushered with solemn rites into the obligations of their elders. Some of us are wondering why our savage friends do not send their medicine men as missionaries, to shed upon our Christian darkness the light of barbarism. Child labor is a new thing in human affairs. Ancient history records no such infamy. "Children," says the Talmud, "must not be taken from the schools even to rebuild the temple." In Greece and Rome the children of both slave and master fared alike in a common nursery. The trainers worked to build up strong and beautiful bodies, careless of the accident of lineage or fortune. But how different is our "Christian civilization"! Seventeen hundred thousand children at work! Does the enumeration bring any significance to our minds when we say that an army of one million seven hundred thousand children are at work in our "land of the free"? This was the figure in 1900; now there are hundreds of thousands more. And many of them working their long ten or fourteen hours by day or by night, with only a miserable dime for a wage! Can the heart take in the enormity?

Picture the procession of them all—enough to people a modern Babylon—all held from the green fields, barred from school, shut out of home, dragged from play and sleep and rest, and set tramping in grim, forced march to the mills and mines and shops and offices in this our America—the land whose name we have been told is Opportunity! We of the "upper crust" give our children books and beauty by day, and fold them into white beds at night; and we feel all this caretaking to be only the natural order of things. Do we ever think of the over two million children who—in free America—are pushed out as little burden bearers to share the toils and strains and dangers of the world battling men?

Let us glance into the weaving rooms of the cotton mills and behold in the hot, damp, decaying atmosphere the little wan figures flying in hideous cotillion among looms and wheels—children choked and blinded by clouds of lint forever molting from the webs, children deafened by the jar and uproar of an eternal Niagara of machines, children silenced utterly in the desert desolation in the heart of the never-ceasing clamor, children that seem like specter-shapes, doomed to silence and done with life, beckoning to one another across some thundershaken Inferno. . . .

Fifty thousand children, mostly girls, are in the textile mills of the South. Six times as many children are working now as were working twenty years ago. Unless the conscience of the nation can be awakened, it will not be long before one hundred thousand children will be hobbling in hopeless lock-step to these Bastilles of labor. It will not be long till these little spinners shall be "far on the way to be spiders and needles."

Think of the deadly drudgery in these cotton mills. Children rise at half-past four, commanded by the ogre scream of the factory whistle; they hurry, ill fed, unkempt, unwashed, half dressed, to the walls which shut out the day and which confine them amid the din and dust and merciless maze of the machines. Here, penned in little narrow lanes, they look and leap and reach and tie among acres and acres of looms. Always the snow of lint in their faces, always the thunder of the machines in their ears. A scant half hour at noon breaks the twelve-hour vigil, for it is nightfall when the long hours end and the children may return to the barracks they call "home," often too tired to wait for the cheerless meal which the mother, also working in the factory, must cook, after her factory day is over. Frequently at noon and at night they fall asleep with the food unswallowed in the mouth. Frequently they snatch only a bite and curl up undressed on the bed, to gather strength for the same dull round tomorrow, and tomorrow, and tomorrow. . . .

And why do these children know no rest, no play, no learning, nothing but the grim grind of existence? Is it because we are all naked and shivering? Is it because there is sudden destitution in

the land? Is it because pestilence walks at noonday? Is it because war's red hand is pillaging our storehouses and burning our cities? No, forsooth! Never before were the storehouses so crammed to bursting with bolts and bales of every warp and woof. No, forsooth! The children, while yet in the gristle, are ground down that a few more useless millions may be heaped up. We boast that we are leading the commercialism of the world, and we grind in our mills the bones of the little ones to make good our boast. . . .

But not alone upon the South lies the blame of these human hells. Many of the mills of the South are owned by New England capitalists, the machinery having been removed from the North to the South, so as to be near the cotton fields, near the water power, and shame to record, near the cheap labor of these baby fingers, for the brief time before they shall be folded waxenly and forever. It was the New England shipper, greedy for gold at any cost, who carried the blacks to the South, planting the tree of slavery in our soil. And now it is the northern money-grubber who is grafting upon our civilization this new and more terrible white slavery. "South Carolina weaves cotton that Massachusetts may wear silk!" . . .

These little white children often begin work in the mill with no fragment of education. And often after a year of this brain-blasting labor they lose the power to learn even the simple art of reading. There is sometimes a night school for the little workers, but they often topple over with sleep at the desks, after the long grind of the day. Indeed they must not spend too many wakeful hours in the night school, shortening their sleep-time; for the ogre of the mill must have all their strength at full head in the morning. The overseer cannot afford to be sending his mounted "poker-up" to their homes to rout them out of bed day after day, nor can he be continually watching lest they fall asleep on the mill floor while working or eating. Nor can he afford to keep a clerk busy dock-ing the wages of these little sleep-starved workers for the constant mistakes and accidents of the fatigued and fumbling fingers. For these little drudges are fined for their lacks and lapses; and they are sometimes in debt to the concern at the week's end.

But worse than all is the breakdown of the soul in these God-forgetting mills. Here boys and girls are pushed into the company of coarse men who are glib with oaths and reeking jests. Torrents of foul profanity from angry overseers wash over the souls of the children, till they, too, grow hardened in curses of coarseness. Piled on all these are the fearful risks that the young girls run from the attentions of men "higher up," especially if the girls happen to be cursed with a little beauty. . . .

The factory, we are told, must make a certain profit, or the owners (absentee proprietors generally, living in larded luxury) will complain. Therefore the president is goaded on by the directors. He in turn whips up the overseer; the overseer takes it out on the workers. So the long end of the lash cuts red the backs of the little children. Need we wonder, then, that cotton-factory stock gives back portly profits—25, 35, yes, even 50 percent? It pays, my masters, to grind little children into dividends! And the silks and muslins do not show the stain of blood, although they are splashed with scarlet on God's side. . . .

"Rob us of child labor and we will take our mills from your state." This is the frequent threat of the mill owners in the chambers and lobbies of legislation. And, alas! We are in a civilization where such a threat avails. Still, in spite of the apathy of the church, in spite of the assault of the capital, the friends of mercy have in all but four states forced some sort of a protective law: no child under twelve years of age shall work for longer than eight hours, nor any without a common-school education. This reads fairly well; but a law on the statute book is not always a law on the factory-floor. The inspectors are often vigilant and quick with conscience. Some mills desire to keep the law. But others are crooked: they have their forged and perjured certificates, their double payrolls—one for the inspector, another for the countinghouse. They have, also, the device of bringing children in as "mother's helps," giving the mothers a few more pennies for the baby fingers.

Hard masters of mills, shiftless or hapless parents, even misguided children themselves, all conspire to hold the little slaves to the wheel. Yes, even the children are taught to lie about their age, and their tongues are ever ready with the glib rehearsal. Some mills keep a lookout for the inspector, and at the danger signal the children scurry like rats to hide in attics, to crouch in cellars, behind bales of cotton, under heaps of old machinery. But God's battle has begun. Still there must be a wider unification of the bands of justice and mercy, a fusing and forcing of public opinion. Let the women of America arise, unite, and resolve in a great passion of righteousness to save the children of the nation. Nothing can stand against the fire of an awakened and banded womanhood.

• • •

Markham's targets were not just the textile mills, but also the canneries, the cotton fields, the factories, the coal mines. His articles clearly pushed the issue of reform of child labor to the front, wrote Louis Filler, a historian of muckraking. *Cosmopolitan* readers rushed to support the National Child Labor Committee, and the magazine itself formed a Child Labor Federation to press for reform. The articles were included in Markham's 1914 book, *Children in Bondage*. Over the years, both by law and national pressure such as that brought by Markham, child labor was largely eliminated.

MCCLURE'S MAGAZINE TELLS HOW YOUNG WOMEN ARE TURNED TO PROSTITUTION

The waves of poor immigrants who washed into New York and other big cities early in the 1900s found unhospitable ground: crowded conditions, low wages, corrupt police, and politicians disinclined to protect them. As always, the newcomers faced rough choices, and respectability often seemed less important than a good meal. For young women, the options were few.

"The Daughters of the Poor. A Plain Story of the Development of New York City as a Leading Center of the White Slave Trade of the World, Under Tammany Hall," by George Kibbe Turner. _McClure's_, November 1909.

There are now three principal centers of the so-called white slave trade—that is, the recruiting and sale of young girls of the poorer classes by procurers. The first is that group of cities in Austrian and Russian Poland, headed by Lemberg, the second is Paris and the third the city of New York. In the past ten years New York has become the leader of the world in this class of enterprise. The men engaged in it there have taken or shipped girls, largely obtained from the tenement districts of New York, to every continent on the globe; they are now doing business with Central and South America, Africa, and Asia. They are driving all competitors before them in North America. And they have established, directly or indirectly, recruiting systems in every large city of the United States.

The story of the introduction of this European business into New York, under the protection of the Tammany Hall political organization, its extension from there through the United States, and its shipments of women to the four corners of the earth, is a strange one; it would seem incredible if it were not thoroughly substantiated by the records of recent municipal exposures in half a dozen great American cities, by two independent investigations by the United States Government during the past year, and by the common knowledge of the people of the East Side tenement district of New York, whose daughters and friends' daughters have been chiefly exploited by it.

About twenty-five years ago the third great flush of immigration, consisting of Austrian, Russian, and Hungarian Jews, began to come into New York. Among these immigrants were a large number of criminals, who soon found that they could develop an extremely profitable business in the sale of women in New York. The Police Department and the police courts, before which all the criminal cases of the city were first brought, were absolutely in the hands of Tammany Hall, which, in its turn, was controlled by slum politicians. A great body of minor workers among this class of politicians obtained their living in tenement-house saloons or gambling-houses, and their control of the police and police courts allowed them to disregard all provisions of the law against their business. The new exploiter of the tenement-house population among the Jews saw that this plan was good, and organized a local Tammany Hall association to apply it to the business of procuring and selling girls....

The business grew so rapidly under these favoring auspices that the East Side was soon not only producing its own supplies, but was exporting them. The first person to undertake this export trade with foreign countries, according to the verbal history of the East Side, was a man who later became a leading spirit in the Tammany organization of the district; he took one or two girls in 1889 or 1890 to compete with the Russian and Galician kaftan in the Buenos Aires market. This venture was not very successful, and the dealer soon returned to New York. Since that time a few hundred New York girls have been taken to

Buenos Aires, but, generally speaking, it has not proved a successful market for the New York trade.

South Africa, on the contrary, proved an excellent field, as mining districts always are. In the middle of the '90's—during the lean years of Mayor Strong's administration—the stories of the fabulous wealth to be made in the South African gold and diamond fields came to the attention of the New York dealers, and they took women there by the hundred. . . .

It is interesting to see how the picking up of girls for the trade in and outside of New York is carried on by these youths on the East Side of New York, which has now grown, under this development, to be the chief recruiting ground for the so-called white slave trade in the United States, and probably in the world. It can be exploited, of course, because in it lies the newest body of immigrants and the greatest supply of unprotected young girls in the city. These now happen to be Jews—as, a quarter and a half century ago, they happened to be German and Irish.

The odds in life are from birth strongly against the young Jewish-American girl. The chief ambition of the new Jewish family in America is to educate its sons. To do this the girls must go to work at the earliest possible date, and from the population of 350,000 Jews east of the Bowery tens of thousands of young girls go out into the shops. There is no more striking sight in the city than the mass of women that flood east through the narrow streets in a winter's twilight, returning to their homes in the East Side tenements. The exploitation of young women as money-earning machines has reached a development on the East Side of New York probably not equaled anywhere else in the world. . . .

But the largest and most profitable field for exploitation of the girls of the East Side is procuring them for the white slave traffic. This line

of swindling is in itself specialized. Formerly its chief recruiting-grounds were the public amusement-parks of the tenement districts; now for several years they have been the dance-halls, and the work has been specialized very largely according to the character of the halls.

The amusement of the poor girl of New York—especially the very poor girl—is dancing. On Saturdays and Sundays the whole East Side dances after nightfall, and every night in the week there are tens of thousand of dancers within the limits of the city of New York. The reason for all this is simple: dancing is the one real amusement within the working-girls' means. . . .

Contrary to the common belief, intoxicating liquor plays but a small part in securing girls from this particular type of place. These lonely and poverty-stricken girls, ignorant and dazed by the strange conditions of an unknown country, are very easily secured by promise of marriage, or even partnership.

A class very similar to this, but of different nationality and religion, is furnished by a second kind of dance-hall on the East Side. Just north of Houston Street are the long streets of signs where the Polish and Slovak servant-girls sit in stiff rows in the dingy employment agencies, waiting to be picked up as domestic servants. The odds against these unfortunate, bland-faced farm-girls are greater than those against the Galician Jews. They arrive here most like tagged baggage than human beings, are crowded in barracks of boarding-houses, eight and ten in a room at night, and in the morning the runner for the employment agency takes them, with all their belongings in a cheap valise, to sit and wait against for mistresses. Every hand seems to be against such simple and easily exploited creatures, even in some of the "homes" for them. . . .

This is a rough outline of the system of procuring and sending girls out of New York City under the safeguard of political protection. Detectives of the Federal Government, who have made within the past year a special investigation of this business in all of the large cities in this country, estimate that about one half of all the women now in the business throughout the United States started their career in this country in New York. This estimate includes, of course, the women imported into that city, as well as those taken from the population. This estimate may be large, but there can be little doubt, since recent developments, of New York's growth to leadership as the chief center of the white slave trade in the world. . . .

The exploitation of a popular government by the slum politician is a curious thing, always. I sat some time ago with a veteran politician, for many years one of the leading election district captains of the Tammany Bowery organization, conversing sociably in the parlor of his profitable Raines-law hotel.

"The people love Tammany Hall," said my host. "We use 'em right. When a widow's in trouble, we see she has her hod of coal; when the orphans want a pair of shoes, we give it to them."

It was truly and earnestly said. As he spoke, the other half of the political financing was shown. The procession of the daughters of the East Side filed by the open door upstairs with their strange men. It was the slum leader's common transaction. Having wholesaled the bodies of the daughters at good profit, he rebates the widow's hod of coal. . . .

• • •

Besides the political protection of Tammany Hall, Turner wrote, New York procurers were protected because, under a Supreme Court ruling, the federal law that prohibited directly importing girls to work in prostitution did not cover procurers who met up with the young women after they arrived in the country. Such cases would have to be covered under state laws, the Supreme Court said.

Turner's story fell onto the fertile ground of the Progressive movement, of campaigns against Tammany Hall in New York City, and of a vice commission investigation of prostitution in Chicago that had been spurred by a 1907 Turner article on that city. (S. S. McClure, the editor, had been disappointed by the lack of action in response to Lincoln Steffens's "Shame of the City" stories and had suggested that Turner try again to show how government corruption injured the lives of a city's residents. It worked.) Two months after "Daughters of the Poor" appeared, New York City appointed a grand jury to investigate. It was headed by John D. Rockefeller Jr., whose father had been stung by Ida Tarbell's earlier muckraking articles in *McClure's*. Similar vice commissions were established in Minneapolis, Portland, Oregon, and Hartford, Connecticut. The uproar caused a number of states to pass laws dealing with "white slave" traffic.

About the same time, U.S. Representative James Mann of Chicago introduced an act to make it a felony to transport or aid in the transportation of women in interstate commerce for immoral purposes. The Mann Act passed in 1910.

JOHN STEINBECK INTRODUCES AMERICA TO THE PLIGHT OF CALIFORNIA MIGRANTS

In the mid-1930s, migrants displaced by dust storms and failed farms headed for California in search of work picking fruits and vegetables for the large growers who dominated the state. When the Okies got there, they found little work, little money, no housing, and much competition and resentment. One of the few efforts to help them was the federal Resettlement Administration, which experimented with migrant camps. Tom Collins, a former teacher and social worker, was setting up the second camp in the state in the summer of 1936 when the agency asked him to help out a writer doing a series on the migrants for the *San Francisco News*. The writer, who was starting to gain attention as a novelist, was John Steinbeck.

Collins let Steinbeck stay in the camp and examine his reports and took him to nearby farms and shanty settlements. The series ran in the *San Francisco News* from October 5 through 12.

The squatters' camps are located all over California. Let us see what a typical one is like. It is located on the banks of a river, near an irrigation ditch or on a side road where a spring of water is available. From a distance it looks like a city dump, and well it may, for the city dumps are the sources for the material of which it is built. You can see a litter of dirty rags and scrap iron, of houses built of weeds, of flattened cans or of paper. It is only on close approach that it can be seen that these are homes.

Here is a house built by a family who have tried to maintain a neatness. The house is about 10 feet by 10 feet, and it is built completely of corrugated paper. The roof is peaked, the walls are tacked to a wooden frame. The dirt floor is swept clean, and along the irrigation ditch or in the muddy river the wife of the family scrubs clothes without soap and tries to rinse out the mud in muddy water. The spirit of this family is not quite broken, for the children, three of them, still have clothes, and the family possesses three old quilts and a soggy, lumpy mattress. But the money so needed for food cannot be used for soap nor for clothes.

With the first rain the carefully built house will slop down into a brown, pulpy mush; in a few months the clothes will fray off the children's bodies while the lack of nourishing food will subject the whole family to pneumonia when the first cold comes.

Five years ago this family had fifty acres of land and a thousand dollars in the bank. The wife belonged to a sewing circle and the man was a member of the grange. They raised chickens, pigs, pigeons and vegetables and fruit for their own use; and their land produced the tall corn of the middle west. Now they have nothing.

If the husband hits every harvest without delay and works the maximum time, he may make four hundred dollars this year. But if anything happens, if his old car breaks down, if he is late and misses a harvest or two, he will have to feed his whole family on as little as one hundred and fifty.

But there is still pride in this family. Wherever they stop they try to put the children in school. It may be that the children will be in a school for as much as a month before they are moved to another locality.

Here, in the faces of the husband and his wife, you begin to see an expression you will notice on every face; not worry, but absolute terror of the starvation that crowds in against the borders of the camp. This man has tried to make a toilet by digging a hole in the ground near his paper house and surrounding it with an old piece of burlap. But he will only do things like that this year. He is a newcomer and his spirit and decency and his sense of his own dignity have not been quite wiped out. Next year he will be like his next door neighbor.

This is a family of six; a man, his wife and four children. They live in a tent the color of the ground. Rot has set in on the canvas so that the flaps and the sides hang in tatters and are held together with bits of rusty baling wire. There is one bed in the family and that is a big tick lying on the ground inside the tent.

They have one quilt and a piece of canvas for bedding. The sleeping arrangement is clever. Mother and father lie down together and two children lie between them. Then, heading the other way, the other two children lie, the littler ones. If the mother and father sleep with their legs spread wide, there is room for the legs of the children.

There is more filth here. The tent is full of flies clinging to the apple box that is the dinner table, buzzing about the foul clothes of the children, particularly the baby, who has not been bathed nor cleaned for several days. This family has been on the road longer than the builder of the paper house. There is no toilet here, but there is a clump of willows nearby where human feces lie exposed to the flies—the same flies that are in the tent.

Two weeks ago there was another child, a four year old boy. For a few weeks they had noticed that he was kind of lackadaisical, that this eyes had been feverish. They had given him the best place in the bed, between father and mother. But one night he went into convulsions and died, and the next morning the coroner's wagon took him away. It was one step down.

They know pretty well that it was a diet of fresh fruit, beans and little else that caused his death. He had no milk for months. With this death there came a change of mind in his family. The father and mother now feel that paralyzed dullness with which the mind protects itself against too much sorrow and too much pain.

And this father will not be able to make a maximum of four hundred dollars a year any more because he is no longer alert; he isn't quick at piece-work, and he is not able to fight clear of the dullness that has settled on him. His spirit is losing caste rapidly.

The dullness shows in the faces of this family, and in addition there is a sullenness that makes them taciturn. Sometimes they still start the older children off to school, but the ragged little things will not go; they hide in the ditches or wander off by themselves until it is time to go back to the tent, because they are scorned in the school.

The better-dressed children shout and jeer, the teachers are quite often impatient with these additions to their duties, and the parents of the "nice" children do not want to have disease carriers in the schools.

The father of this family once had a little grocery store and his family lived in back of it so that even the children could wait on the counter. When the drought set in there was no trade for the store any more.

This is the middle class of the squatters' camp. In a few months this family will slip down to the lower class. Dignity is all gone, and spirit has turned to sullen anger before it dies.

The next door neighbor family of man, wife and three children of from three to nine years of age, have built a house by driving willow branches into the ground and wattling weeds, tin, old paper and strips of carpet against them. A few branches are placed over the top to keep out the noonday sun. It would not turn water at all. There is no bed. Somewhere the family has found a big piece of old carpet. It is on the ground. To go to bed the members of the family lie on the ground and fold the carpet up over them. . . .

The husband was a share-cropper once, but he couldn't make it go. Now he has lost even the desire to talk. He will not look directly at you for that requires will, and will needs strength. He is a bad field worker for the same reason. It takes him a long time to make up his mind, so he is always late in moving and late in arriving in the fields. His top wage, when he can find work now, which isn't often, is a dollar a day.

The children do not even go to the willow clump any more. They squat where they are and kick a little dirt. The father is vaguely aware that there is a culture of hookworm in the mud along the river bank. He knows the children will get it on their bare feet. But he hasn't the will nor the energy to resist. Too many things have happened to him. This is the lower class of the camp.

This is what the man in the tent will be in six months; what the man in the paper house with its peaked roof will be in a year, after his house has washed down and his children have sickened or died, after the loss of dignity and spirit have cut him down to a kind of subhumanity. . . .

This is the squatters' camp. Some are a little better, some much worse. I have described three typical families. In some of the camps there are as many as three hundred families like these. Some are so far from water that it must be bought at five cents a bucket.

And if these men steal, if there is developing among them a suspicion and hatred of well-dressed, satisfied people, the reason is not to be sought in their origin nor in any tendency to weakness in this character.

• • •

"Steinbeck used the camp manager's experiences for real-life material, the grist of a writer's mill," wrote Charles Wollenberg, a professor of history, in his introduction to *Harvest Gypsies*, a reprint of the Steinbeck articles (Berkeley: Heyday Books, 1988). "And Collins used Steinbeck to publicize a deeply felt cause, to awaken the citizenry to the migrants' plight."

Two groups to aid the migrant workers made use of the Steinbeck articles, although they could do little in the face of the power of the growers.

Steinbeck also used his camp reporting, plus a second trip with Collins, as the basis for *The Grapes of Wrath*. The book and the movie defined the Dust Bowl experience for all time in the same way that *The Jungle*, the work of another journalist-novelist, Upton Sinclair, defined the meatpacking industry in Chicago a quarter of a century before.

The manager of the government "Wheatpatch Camp" in *The Grapes of Wrath*, the only modern and hospitable place the Joad family encountered, was based on Tom Collins.

THE *DAYTONA BEACH MORNING JOURNAL* SPOTLIGHTS THE ILLS OF CITY'S SLUM HOUSING

In the segregated 1950s, with Florida cities like Daytona Beach making a big pitch for tourists and retirees, city leaders were motivated even more than usual to ignore the problems of housing for the poor. A new reporter in town, Aaron Epstein, was struck by the nineteenth-century conditions in which people, most of them black, were living. He proposed a series on slum conditions, and did much of the work on his own time.

"The Truth About Our Slums: One Dwelling in Five Is Substandard," by Aaron Epstein. *Daytona Beach Morning Journal,* **June 18, 1957.**

Chances are tourists coming to Daytona Beach don't get to see our vast housing decay. Neither are the slums mentioned officially to inquiring businessmen seeking new locations, nor are they included in the C. of C. tour for prospective retirees.

Furthermore, the city is fortunate in having the shabby side of its map well hidden from the cursory view of its vacationing visitors seeking breathtaking sights of another sort.

Naturally, tourists have no reason to care. But Daytonans—and other contributors to public funds expended here—should know something about their housing blight, where large chunks of their tax money pay for an excessive amount of crime, filth, fires and general poverty.

And low slum tax assessments assure the community of little in return.

Most city dwellers may not be aware of the extent of deficient housing here. Daytona Beach had 2,746 housing units rated substandard in 1950, according to the Census Bureau. That was 22 percent of all units in the city at that time.

A 1951 survey of five Florida cities made by the regional office of the U.S. Dept. of Commerce placed Daytona Beach third behind Jacksonville and Lakeland in the percentage of units rated substandard, with Orlando and West Palm Beach fourth and fifth.

Practically nothing has been done to lower Daytona Beach's total of substandard houses.

What is a substandard dwelling unit? The Public Housing Administration defines it as either dilapidated or lacking these facilities: Flush toilet and bath inside each structure for each unit's exclusive use, and hot running water.

Absence of hot running water is usually evidence of a poor quality unit, but the PHA admits "there may be some locations in which the absence of hot running water is not deemed to be a sufficient indication by itself of poor quality."

Of Daytona Beach's 2,746 substandard dwelling units in 1950, 59 percent were occupied by Negroes and 41 percent by Whites.

White substandard dwellings, with no social barriers confining their inhabitants to specified sectors, are scattered over nearly all older parts of the city.

On the other hand, the city's substandard Negro houses are concentrated. They form two virtual ghettos, separated by a strip bordering U.S. 92. They are the focal points of this series.

Inadequate incomes and high rents guarantee an undiminished population living in sub-par conditions. Other factors—such as large families, poor economy and disabilities—contribute heavily.

Of the 2,055 primary families—two or more persons, all related to the head of the household—living in Daytona Bach's substandard units in 1951, 26.5 percent earned $999 or less a year, including three times as many Negroes as Whites.

And 11.1 percent earned $1,000 to $1,249, 8.2 percent made $1,250 to $1,499, 8 percent made $1,500 to $1,749 and 6.6 percent made $1,750 to $1,999.

Most families rented, and 21.7 percent of these paid 35 percent or more of their income for rent.

The monthly gross rent of 64.2 percent of them was between $15 and $34.

They didn't—and don't—get much for their money. Here are further breakdowns of Daytona Beach's 2,746 substandard housing units seven years ago.

- Inhabitants' status: 57.4 percent were rented; 42.6 percent were occupied by owners.

- Condition: 35.9 percent were dilapidated. But more than half of the Negro dwellings were dilapidated.

- Water supply: 62.6 percent had only cold piped water inside structures; 23.9 percent had no piped running water inside.

- Toilet facilities: 52.8 percent had exclusive use of flush toilets inside structures, 12.5 percent shared flush toilets inside structures, and 34.7 percent had other toilet facilities, including privies (43.5 percent of the Negro units fell into this last category).

- Bathing facilities: 50.8 percent had no installed bathtub or shower inside structures. The Negro percentage again was higher— 67.1.

- Persons per unit: One person, 19.7 percent; two persons, 33.4 percent; three, 18.6 percent; four, 11.9 percent; five, 7 percent; six, 4.2 percent; seven, 2.4 percent; eight, 1.3 percent; and nine, 1.6 percent.

Of course, these statistics alone can't tell the story of a part of Daytona Beach that State Supreme Court Justice Glenn Terrell described as looking like "a dilapidated turpentine still or saw mill 'quarters,' abandoned by the owner and preempted by bats, bedbugs and Billy goats."

"He lives in 19th Century Relic," by Aaron Epstein. *Daytona Beach Morning Journal,* June 19, 1957.

Sonny Carter is one of Florida's thousands of retirees. But unlike most of the others, Carter's migration to a life of leisure covered only a few blocks.

He moved from one section of Daytona Beach's slums to another.

Carter lives in a two room, wooden shack— 558 Greet St.—on a short, dismal lane one block south of Second Ave. between Walnut and Pine Sts. Pieces of its timbers, covered with the etchings of rot, can easily be broken, crumbled and blown away like dust. The roll roof sags. Floor planks rock with each step.

The age of Carter's "home" isn't known, but it contains nearly all the residential conveniences of the mid-19th century: Kerosene lamp, kerosene stove, cold running water from a spigot next door, a pail on the floor serving as a lavatory.

No electricity, no inside water, no plumbing of any kind.

Carter, 58, came to Daytona Beach more than 30 years ago from Georgia. He was "a common laborer" until a few years ago, when a "light stroke" rewarded him with an old wooden cane and $60 monthly checks from Florida's Dept. of Public Welfare.

Usually he can be found during the day sitting quietly on his porch with Mrs. Rosalie Smith, whose husband died about 10 years ago. Carter and Mrs. Smith are never apart.

She has one eye, and cataracts are expected to claim the other soon. She can't remember her age, but Carter says she's about 60. She wears a dirty flannel nightgown; he, worn overalls.

Carter's sole entertainment, he says, is reading. Relaxing beneath cobwebs hidden in the eaves, he reads about the Kingdom of Heaven. One of his books is titled: "With God All Things Are Possible."

Inside, a double bed piled with clothes, on a mattress slowly extruding its stuffing, nearly fills one tiny room. In the kitchen—boxes and bottles of pills atop the icebox, the old kerosene stove, a heavily laden eating table, a stench from the unemptied pail.

In the back—baskets full of rags, a storeroom strewn with ladders, old window frames and other slum landlord's indispensables.

"The project? I just never thought about it," Carter says.

The couple accumulates $105 a month in welfare funds. It is welfare funds which combine with abnormally low wage scales to keep the city's slums a thriving operation.

Out of their income, $5 a week goes to the landlady, Mrs. Minnie Massey, who lives in a shabby two-story, 11-room building next door, 245 Pine St. (assessed valuation: $1,460).

Carter's rented shack is valued by the County Tax Assessor at $200, a figure which probably exceeds its selling price if anyone would buy it.

Mrs. Massey, claiming homestead exemption, pays only $39.96 a year for her land and the two income-producing buildings. That means her annual total tax for the 558 Greet St. property improvement is about $4, or less than one week's rent.

Depreciation, of course, is negligible or nil. Maintenance is foolhardy. (Carter says she did put some tarpaper on the room last year to cover the holes.) Rent is regular—welfare cases, especially the disabled, are sound risks.

Mrs. Massey's profit on the shack alone, then, is in the neighborhood of $250, with no worries attached. Many slum landlords in Daytona Beach net much more, but few give less.

Carter and Mrs. Smith spend, in addition to the $5 weekly rent, about $2 a week for kerosene and $2 a week for ice. The remainder pays for food, medical treatment and taxi fares to the doctor and to church.

"Sometimes we go downtown for a walk," Mrs. Smith says proudly.

Their living conditions particularly are striking, but these tenants aren't an isolated case in Daytona Beach.

Like Sonny Carter and Mrs. Smith, most of the city's blight enveloped citizens live on the outskirts of the downtown area, earn less than $2,000 a year, and spend from a fifth to a third of what they earn on housing characterized—in varying degrees—by overcrowding, no heating equipment, deficient plumbing or none at all, defective wiring, inadequate ventilation, leaking roofs and massive rat-termite infestation.

• • •

Other parts of Epstein's series, which went on for fifteen days, always on the front page, focused on the profits made by slum landlords, the city's failure to use powers it had to tackle the housing problem, and the practice of listing shacks as renovated homes on city rolls.

Although it seems hard to imagine that officials in Daytona Beach were unaware of housing problems of such magnitude, it took this series, and several hundred follow-up stories, to stir them to action. City commissioners ordered a survey of slum conditions, citizen committees were set up, a professional planner was hired, and a savings and loan bank put up $250,000 in low-income loans. By the end of the year, construction of a 100-unit public housing project was begun, and Daytona Beach was moving toward the first comprehensive urban renewal plan in the state of Florida. Not until 1965, however, were the final legislative and court fights over and the urban renewal project started.

THE OTHER AMERICA: MICHAEL HARRINGTON REMINDS THE COUNTRY OF THE HIDDEN POOR

Much of America, white America at least, considered the 1950s a time of prosperity and complacency. Dwight Eisenhower was in the White House, and the nation stood at ease. This bothered Michael Harrington, a leftist writer and activist who had been a part of Dorothy Day's Catholic Worker movement. As he traveled across the country, giving lectures and talking to people, he determined that there was a large group of 40 to 50 million poor Americans who had faded from public attention. *The Other America* was published in 1962. This excerpt is from Harrington's first chapter.

The Other America, by Michael Harrington. New York: Macmillan, 1962.

There is a familiar America. It is celebrated in speeches and advertised on television and in the magazines. It has the highest mass standard of living the world has ever known.

In the 1950's this America worried about itself, yet even its anxieties were products of abundance. The title of a brilliant book was widely misinterpreted, and the familiar America began to call itself "the affluent society." There was introspection about Madison Avenue and tail fins; there was discussion of the emotional suffering taking place in the suburbs. In all this, there was an implicit assumption that the basic grinding economic problems had been solved in the United States. In this theory the nation's problems were no longer a matter of basic human needs, of food, shelter, and clothing. Now they were seen as qualitative, a question of learning to live decently amid luxury.

While this discussion was carried on, there existed another America. In it dwelt between 40,000,000 and 50,000,000 citizens of this land. They were poor. They still are.

To be sure, the other America is not impoverished in the same sense as those poor nations where millions cling to hunger as a defense against starvation. This country has escaped such extremes. That does not change the fact that tens of millions of Americans are, at this very moment, maimed in body and spirit, existing at levels beneath those necessary for human decency. If these people are not starving, they are hungry, and sometimes fat with hunger, for that is what cheap foods do. They are without adequate housing and education and medical care.

The Government has documented what this means to the bodies of the poor, and the figures will be cited throughout this book. But even more basic, this poverty twists and deforms the spirit. The American poor are pessimistic and defeated, and they are victimized by mental suffering to a degree unknown in Suburbia. . . .

The millions who are poor in the United States tend to become increasingly invisible. Here is a great mass of people, yet it takes an effort of the intellect and will even to see them. . . .

There are perennial reasons that make the other America an invisible land.

Poverty is often off the beaten track. It always

has been. The ordinary tourist never left the main highway, and today he rides interstate turnpikes. He does not go into the valleys of Pennsylvania where the towns look like movie sets of Wales in the thirties. He does not see the company houses in rows, the rutted roads (the poor always have bad roads whether they live in the city, in towns, or on farms), and everything is black and dirty. And even if he were to pass through such a place by accident, the tourist would not meet the unemployed men in the bar or the women coming home from a runaway sweatshop.

Then, too, beauty and myths are perennial masks of poverty. The traveler comes to the Appalachians in the lovely season. He sees the hills, the streams, the foliage—but not the poor. Or perhaps he looks at a run-down mountain house and, remembering Rousseau rather than seeing with his eyes, decides that "those people" are truly fortunate to be living the way they are and that they are lucky to be exempt from the strains and tensions of the middle class. The only problem is that "those people," the quaint inhabitants of those hills, are undereducated, underprivileged, lack medical care, and are in the process of being forced from the land into a life in the cities, where they are misfits.

These are normal and obvious causes of the invisibility of the poor. They operated a generation ago; they will be functioning a generation hence. It is more important to understand that the very development of American society is creating a new kind of blindness about poverty. The poor are increasingly slipping out of the very experience and consciousness of the nation.

If the middle class never did like ugliness and poverty, it was at least aware of them. "Across the track" was not a very long way to go. There were forays into the slums at Christmas time; there were charitable organizations that brought contact with the poor. Occasionally, almost everyone passed through the Negro ghetto or the blocks of tenements, if only to get downtown to work or to entertainment.

Now the American city has been transformed. The poor still inhabit the miserable housing in the central area, but they are increasingly isolated from contact with, or sight of, anybody else. Middle-class women coming in from Suburbia on a rare trip may catch the merest glimpse of the other America on the way to an evening at the theater, but their children are segregated in suburban schools. The business or professional man may drive along the fringes of slums in a car or bus, but it is not an important experience to him. The failures, the unskilled, the disabled, the aged, and the minorities are right there, across the tracks, where they have always been. But hardly anyone else is.

In short, the very development of the American city has removed poverty from the living, emotional experience of millions upon millions of middle-class Americans. Living out in the suburbs, it is easy to assume that ours is, indeed, an affluent society.

This new segregation of poverty is compounded by a well-meaning ignorance. A good many concerned and sympathetic Americans are aware that there is much discussion of urban renewal. Suddenly, driving through the city, they notice that a familiar slum has been torn down and that there are towering, modern buildings where once there had been tenements or hovels. There is a warm feeling of satisfaction, of pride in the way things are working out: the poor, it is obvious, are being taken care of.

The irony in this (as the chapter on housing will document) is that the truth is nearly the exact opposite to the impression. The total impact of the various housing programs in postwar America has been to squeeze more and more people into existing slums. More often than not, the modern apartment in a towering building rents at $40 a room or more. For, during the past decade and a half, there has been more subsidization of middle- and upper-income housing than there has been of housing for the poor.

Clothes make the poor invisible too: America

has the best-dressed poverty the world has ever known. For a variety of reasons, the benefits of mass production have been spread much more evenly in this area than in many others. It is much easier in the United States to be decently dressed than it is to be decently housed, fed, or doctored. Even people with terribly depressed incomes can look prosperous.

This is an extremely important factor in defining our emotional and existential ignorance of poverty. In Detroit the existence of social classes became much more difficult to discern the day the companies put lockers in the plants. From that moment on, one did not see men in work clothes on the way to the factory, but citizens in slacks and white shirts. This process has been magnified with the poor throughout the country. There are tens of thousands of Americans in the big cities who are wearing shoes, perhaps even a stylishly cut suit or dress, and yet are hungry. It is not a matter of planning, though it almost seems as if the affluent society had given out costumes to the poor so that they would not offend the rest of society with the sight of rags.

Then, many of the poor are the wrong age to be seen. A good number of them (over 8,000,000) are sixty-five years of age or better; an even larger number are under eighteen. The aged members of the other America are often sick, and they cannot move. Another group of them live out their lives in loneliness and frustration: they sit in rented rooms, or else they stay close to a house in a neighborhood that has completely changed from the old days. Indeed, one of the worst aspects of poverty among the aged is that these people are out of sight and out of mind, and alone.

The young are somewhat more visible, yet they too stay close to their neighborhoods. Sometimes they advertise their poverty through a lurid tabloid story about a gang killing. But generally they do not disturb the quiet streets of the middle class.

And finally, the poor are politically invisible. It is one of the cruelest ironies of social life in advanced countries that the dispossessed at the bottom of society are unable to speak for themselves. The people of the other America do not, by far and large, belong to unions, to fraternal organizations, or to political parties. They are without lobbies of their own; they put forward no legislative program. As a group, they are atomized. They have no face; they have no voice.

Thus, there is not even a cynical political motive for caring about the poor, as in the old days. Because the slums are no longer centers of powerful political organizations, the politicians need not really care about their inhabitants. The slums are no longer visible to the middle class, so much of the idealistic urge to fight for those who need help is gone. Only the social agencies have a really direct involvement with the other America, and they are without any great political power.

To the extent that the poor have a spokesman in American life, that role is played by the labor movement. The unions have their own particular idealism, an ideology of concern. More than that, they realize that the existence of a reservoir of cheap, unorganized labor is a menace to wages and working conditions throughout the entire economy. Thus, many union legislative proposals—to extend the coverage of minimum wage and social security, to organize migrant farm laborers—articulate the needs of the poor.

That the poor are invisible is one of the most important things about them. They are not simply neglected and forgotten as in the old rhetoric of reform; what is much worse, they are not seen.

• • •

As powerful as Harrington's book was, it might not have come to great attention had it not been for a thirty-page review of books on poverty by Dwight Macdonald in the January 19, 1963, issue of *The New Yorker*. "The extent of our poverty has suddenly become visible," Macdonald wrote. It certainly had. Harrington, thirty-five at the time, told of being on vacation in Europe and being approached by traveling Americans who recognized him and asked to shake his hand.

President John F. Kennedy, who had been looking for a new, large initiative, asked for copies of the book for his staff, then instructed them to put together a coordinated antipoverty program. He was assassinated before the program could be sent to Congress, but his successor, Lyndon B. Johnson, adopted it. Food stamps, Medicare, Medicaid, expanded Social Security, community action programs, VISTA, and Head Start were all part of the effort.

Harrington remained a leftist activist until his death in 1989.

VOICE FROM THE HOLLOWS: HOMER BIGART WRITES OF POVERTY IN APPALACHIA AND SETS OFF A WAR ON POVERTY

Coal country always has a boom-or-bust economy, and the booms are never so high as the busts are low. In 1963, things were looking bad.

"Kentucky Miners: A Grim Winter," by Homer Bigart. *New York Times,* October 20, 1963.

WHITESBURG, Ky, Oct. 19—In the Cumberland Mountains of eastern Kentucky, tens of thousands of unemployed coal miners and subsistence farmers face another winter of idleness and grinding poverty.

This region was an early victim of automation. Replaced by machines, the miners can find no work. They are forced to live on Government handouts.

Escape to the cities is not easy, for the average miner has no skill for another job. He is deficient in education. His native clannishness makes adjustment to urban life painfully difficult.

So the mountains have become a vast ghetto of unemployables. Sociologists, fearing that automation may bring the biggest upheaval since the Industrial Revolution, are watching the effects of a blight that threatens to spread.

The few tourists who venture into the area seldom see the pinched faces of hungry children, the filth and squalor of cabins, the unpainted shacks that still serve as schoolhouses. These dramatic manifestations of want and governmental neglect are usually tucked away in narrow valleys, the "hollows," off the main road.

Sticking to the highway, hurrying through a region that offers few attractive motels and even fewer good restaurants, the tourist sees only the usual disorder of coal country.

Creeks are littered with garbage, choked with boulders and silt dislodged by strip-mine operations. Hillsides that should be a solid blaze of autumn color are slashed with ugly terraces, where bulldozers and steam shovels have stripped away the forest to get at the coal beneath.

If the tourist is a conservationist, he is likely to feel momentary anger at the ravaging of a once-magnificent landscape that now looks dour and malevolent.

But to the sociologist, the erosion of the character of the people is more fearsome than the despoiling of the mountains.

The welfare system has eroded the self-respect of the mountain people. Gone is the frontier bravado, the sense of adventure, the self-reliance that once marked the Kentucky mountaineer. Three generations of living on handouts have resulted in a whipped, dispirited community.

Sociologists say the welfare system seems deliberately calculated to corrode morals and hasten degeneracy.

"Folks don't aim to work if they can get a handout," said Dr. Randall D. Collins, health officer for Letcher County. "They are becoming a kept people."

He called for work relief projects like those undertaken by the Public Works Administration during the Depression. In that way, he said, people could regain self-respect by earning pay checks through labor performed in the public welfare.

The present system has encouraged the break-up of families, according to Harry M. Caudill, Whitesburg lawyer, whose book "Night Comes to the Cumberland" has been hailed by critics as a definitive study of the region. It was published by Atlantic–Little, Brown of Boston.

No matter how hungry his wife and children may be, an able-bodied man cannot get on the relief rolls, Mr. Caudill explained. In desperation, the man deserts his family so they can qualify for relief checks and get food.

Mr. Caudill said Leslie County was averaging 100 desertion cases a year. One village was known as "Widowsville" because of the exceptional number of women whose husbands had conveniently vanished so the family could eat.

"We are promoting illegitimacy," said Leslie County Judge George Wooton.

"We sure are," added Mayor William C. Da-wahare of Hazard. "A widow can go out and have as many illegitimate children as she likes and get paid for it." The dole provides $23.48 a month for each dependent child.

To get relief, able-bodied men resort to ruses to become certified by a welfare board as eligible. "The usual complaint is rheumatism or a slipped disk," said Dr. Collins.

One man found he could simulate blindness by diluting snuff and dripping it into his eyes. It fooled the welfare board, so he tried it on his wife with equal success.

But when he brought in his daughter to claim a third relief check for blindness, the board became suspicious and the ruse was exposed.

Perley F. Ayer, a sociologist of Berea College, disputed the theory that the relief system encouraged illegitimacy.

"These people can't look nine months ahead," he said. "The illegitimate offsprings are not products of maliciously planned adventures, but symbols of a chaos of cultural values."

Crowds of listless, defeated men hang around the county courthouses of the region. In this situation the county school superintendent, or the person in charge of welfare, has assumed unusual power.

The school superintendent controls the county's biggest payroll. The welfare director decides about food.

Schools in eastern Kentucky are among the poorest in the nation. The low educational standards of the people are a major obstacle to the location of new industries.

Last week Judge Wooton took a visitor on a tour of some of the worst schools in Leslie County. The county has no railroad and has only 67 miles of blacktop road. It is desperately poor, the median family income being only $1,838. A family often has eight or more children.

Truck mines and lumbering provide a few jobs, but most of the county's population, variously estimated at 10,000 to 20,000, tries to scrounge a living off the soil.

There is no distribution of Government surplus foods in Leslie because the county government is too poor to fetch and distribute them.

In other counties such foods are essential to stave off hunger for most of the population. Leslie gets nothing except some supplies to support the school lunch program. . . .

The road to Gilbert's Creek is so bad, he [Judge Wooton] explained, that school buses could not reach the settlement and bring the children to a consolidated school.

Mrs. Stone, on the verge of tears, pleaded for a new stove and some tarpaper.

"If I were school superintendent, I could never go to sleep and leave children in this condition," Judge Wooten said. He promised to see to it that this road was improved so the school bus could get in.

In another forlorn hollow, Phillipp's Fork, the Judge hailed Foster Caldwell, a farmer who said he had not "seen a dime in months."

"I got rheumatism so bad I can't put my shoes

on," Mr. Caldwell complained, "but they turned me down (for relief)." A former miner, he had not worked since January, 1962.

"If you were President and lived on this creek, you wouldn't make enough to have gravy for breakfast," he added, walking off.

At the settlement school, another unpainted one-room building of rough lumber, Asher Sidemore, the teacher, said his 16 pupils seemed to be getting enough to eat. Only one boy was barefoot.

"There isn't a soul in this hollow making a dime," Judge Wooton said. "I don't see how people can get along without the free foods."

Children of Phillipp's Fork seemed better off than many in the desolate coal camps of Letcher and Pike counties. At Hellier, a dying community in Pike, the principal of the high school, Paul L. Owens, said:

"We had to tighten up on the free-lunch program because last month the school ran $86 in the red. We are getting less food from the Government. I had to tell one father: 'Look, you have four kids eating free. You'll have to pay for two of them.'"

The school charges 25 cents a lunch for those able to pay. Last month 70 children received free lunches because they came from desperately poor homes. This month Mr. Owens had to reduce the number to 50.

"It's very difficult to tell a child he can't eat," Mr. Owens said.

Hellier, once a flourishing trading center for surrounding coal camps on Marrowbone Creek, was left stranded three years ago when the Blue Diamond Coal Company abruptly closed the mines and demolished the coke ovens. . . .

Despite a modest boom in coal production, unemployment remains high because of automation. At Lyrich, in Harlan County, one-third of the city is being demolished by United States Coal and Coke, a subsidiary of the United States Steel Corporation.

The company no longer wants most of the 3,800 population it had in 1960. Whole streets have been torn down. All that remains in the upper part of the city are forlorn rows of chimneys, standing like artifacts from a forgotten culture.

The company had strip-mined the steep slopes of Big Black Mountain behind the town. Deprived of the protective cover of forest, the mountainside is exposed to erosion. Last March part of the town was inundated by mud slides that ruined homes and company facilities and choked Looney Creek.

"I just don't think this would be tolerated in a civilized country," Mr. Caudill said.

The plight of children growing up in hopeless poverty is a greater national disgrace than soil erosion, observers declared.

"I've seen children who are pot-bellied and anemic," remarked Dr. Collins, the Letcher County health officer. "I've seen children eat dirt out of chimneys. Of 8,200 children in Letcher County, 75 to 85 per cent are underweight."

Dr. Mary P. Fox, health officer for Leslie and Knott Counties, estimated that 75 percent of the children had intestinal parasites. One of ten in the village of Stinnett, in Leslie, has hookworm disease, she added.

Dr. Fox and Dr. Collins warned that considerable quantities of worm medicines were needed. The state provides free vitamin pills, Dr. Fox said, but the demand exceeds the supply—"We can always use more."

Despite the hopelessness of an area that seems consigned to permanent poverty, there appears little evidence that the people are embracing political extremism.

Community leaders see little hope that the Administration will press for a program bold enough to solve the region's problem.

Mr. Caudill believes only a vast Federal power project, similar to the Tennessee Valley Authority, will end poverty.

He stresses the need for Federal control because he fears the continued growth of local political dynasties.

"The massive doling out of Federal welfare money has financed, and now sustains, a dozen or more crafty, amoral, merciless and highly effective countywide political machines," he told a recent meeting of the Council of the Southern Mountains, a philanthropic organization that is undertaking a drive against illiteracy in the mountains.

"They thrive on the present economic malaise and are powerful because the people are helpless." . . .

•   •   •

President John F. Kennedy, who already had his staff at work drawing up proposals to fight poverty, in part after reading Michael Harrington's *The Other America*, also saw Bigart's story. In October 1963, Kennedy gave the go-ahead for inclusion of the antipoverty program in the next year's legislative efforts. Bigart's story may have triggered the action, James L. Lundquist wrote in *Politics and Policy*, a study of presidential decision making. "At the least," Lundquist said, "the article led Kennedy to initiate a 'crash' program to mobilize federal resources to alleviate conditions in that region during the coming winter."

THE WORKING CLASS

LABOR JOURNALIST JOHN SWINTON DEMANDS JUSTICE FOR WORKING PEOPLE AND KEEPS THE IDEA OF UNIONS ALIVE

In the mid-1880s, labor was demanding its rights against capital. It was a tumultuous time. Strikes were conducted by spinners in Fall River, Massachusetts, stovemakers in Troy, New York, cigar makers in Cincinnati, coal miners in the Hocking Valley of Ohio, Buffalo brickmakers and longshoremen, New York brownstone carvers, Pittsburgh miners, and Philadelphia carpet weavers. But except for a strike against the Jay Gould railroad system in the Middle West and on the Plains in 1885, almost all the strikes failed. Labor was looking for a new weapon, and found one in the boycott.

A major supporter of the boycott was the labor journalist John Swinton. Swinton, born in 1830 in Scotland, emigrated at the age of thirteen. He moved to Montreal, where he learned the printing trade. In 1850, he came to New York City. He soon moved from the composing room to the editorial office. During the Civil War, Swinton was managing editor of Henry J. Raymond's *New York Times*. (A Swinton brother, William, was a noted Civil War reporter who, after the war,

wrote the classic book *The Army of the Potomac*, which Civil War historians consult to this day.) In 1870, Swinton joined Charles A. Dana's New York *Sun*, and, in 1871, he became the paper's chief writer.

Following the Tompkins Square riot of unemployed workers on January 13, 1874, after a year of severe depression, Swinton entered politics and was nominated for mayor of New York on a workingman's ticket. But politics was not his calling; he received only a few hundred votes.

In 1883, Swinton resigned from his position as managing editor of the New York *Sun*—the position was highly lucrative for Swinton—to start *John Swinton's Paper*, a four-page weekly labor newspaper, with a goal, Swinton said, of warning "the American people against the treasonable and crushing schemes of Millionaires, Monopolists and Plutocracy."

In was a bold thing to start a labor paper at that time, but Swinton was unafraid and put much of his life's savings into the publication. He began to applaud the use of boycotts, a weapon that the emerging Knights of Labor was using with much success. Boycotts were to become in the mid-1880s what sit-down strikes became in the 1930s—something of a national pastime. Boycotts were conducted against newspapers, including the New York *Tribune*; cigar makers; dry goods manufacturers; hotels; steamboat excursion companies; makers of stoves, ranges, and pots; hatters; brewers; makers of pianos and organs. By the mid-1880s, the labor historian John R. Commons was to write early in the twentieth century, the boycott had assumed "the nature of an epidemic." Swinton called the boycott "a new force in hand."

"The Boycotters." *John Swinton's Paper,* May 11, 1884.

One of the main things of interest in New York during the past half year has been the action of the *Boycotters*—the adoption of the system of *Boycotting* those business firms and newspapers who are especially obnoxious on account of their hatred of Trade Unions, or who have otherwise proved themselves the enemies of the rights of the working people. To boycott a concern simply means to refrain from having anything to do with it. You boycott a dry goods firm by refusing to deal with it; you boycott a newspaper by ceasing to buy it; you boycott a cigarmaker by avoiding his cigars. Organized boycotting of a concern is carried out when the Trade Unions unite in refusing to purchase any of its wares, or to have any dealing with it; and thus attempt to break down the business of the concern which is antagonistic to them. The Trades Unions and the rest of the working classes whom they influence are a mighty power everywhere; and there is no doubt that, if they can be brought to combine upon the vigorous boycotting of any given enemy, it will not, in most cases, take them long to reduce the enemy's works. In many instances, it has told with crushing effect; and we have repeatedly chronicled the surrender of the men and the newspapers upon whom its power has been brought to bear.

For sometime past, we have been desirous of finding out exactly how far the boycotters of this city have made themselves felt. Some of the parties boycotted have boasted that under the influence of boycotting their business was heavier than ever; and, according to the boycotted *Tribune*, its circulation has steadily swelled under the attacks of the Trade Unions, led by Typographical Union No. 6.

We determined to make an attempt to find out the facts, if they could be got; and, in doing so, reporters were sent to the headquarters of both sides, to procure the statements of both the boycotters and the boycotted. The result is that we now have a bundle of the most contradictory interviews that were ever brought together in a newspaper. . . .

There are many solid reasons for believing that Rogers, Peet & Co., the clothiers, have suffered at the hands of the boycotters. Thousands of men who are in the habit of dealing with the house have pledged themselves not to purchase a single article of clothing there; and they have used all their influence to induce countless others to follow their example. The establishment itself does not display that activity which ought to be seen at this season of the year; and there is information from a source which Rogers, Peet & Co. would themselves acknowledge to be well informed, that their business is between ten and twenty per cent less than it would be but for the boycotting; and their losses on that account for the past half year have been at least $1,000 a month.

The reporter, having ascertained these facts, called at their establishment. Mr. Chambers, of the firm of Rogers, Peet & Co., was interviewed, and asked if he could give any information concerning the boycotting movement. He replied: "I was waited upon, in the early part of the struggle, by a committee of the Typographical Union, which asked me to cease advertising in the New York *Tribune*. I could not, on general principles, accede to the demand. Since then the sales in our retail department for the month of April this year have exceeded by about $3,000 those of the same month last year. . . . The effect of the boycotting on our business has been imperceptible."

•   •   •

Swinton continued to push the boycott as a means of labor power. The boycott, he said, was based on the principle of " 'an eye for an eye' and a 'tooth for a tooth'—the law as laid down by Moses." He wrote. "The employers say, 'we will blacklist you,' whereupon the men reply, 'we will boycott you.' That is the whole story." But Swinton believed that the boycotts had to be done properly. All boycotts needed to be approved in an organized fashion by union committees and officials, he said, and handbills urging boycotts should take care to state the organization calling for the action.

By December 1885, Swinton reported 237 boycotts in more than fifty cities. "Not very far from one-half have been successful," he said, "while but one-tenth have been failures, and the rest are yet unsettled. With such a display of acts, no one can doubt that the American boycott is a menacing weapon, and it seems to have been successful in far more than half of the cases in which it was founded in reason, pushed with energy, and backed by a large organized force."

But Swinton, despite his enthusiasm and the fact he was putting out an outstanding paper, faced difficulties. *John Swinton's Paper* was to last only four years, folding on August 21, 1887, and costing Swinton $40,000. The paper, the labor historian Philip S. Foner said, "had the faults of every free-lance enterprise, lacking real organic links with the trade union organizations of the day." Furthermore, for a worker to subscribe to a labor paper at that time was courageous, as *John Swinton's Paper* reported: "Several men think it safer to get the paper in roundabout ways or at post-offices distant from their homes. To be caught with it in some of the slave-mills of New England would cost a man as much as his wages are worth." Still, Foner said, the paper was "well edited, excellently written and interesting throughout" and "constantly responsive to the needs of trade unionists of New York and the rest of the country."

In the late 1880s, the boycott weapon was to fizzle, as had the strikes before them, and working-class people and the emerging labor movement were to face enormous difficulties, among them the injunction, the yellow dog contract, and the truncheon, gun, and bayonet. But it was Swinton and people like him who kept the flame of labor alive. Finally, in the 1930s, a strong labor movement was to emerge.

After the death of his paper, Swinton remained a journalist and a champion of working-class people and the labor movement. He wrote two books, *Striking for Life* and *Live, Burning Questions*, and campaigned for working-class people and the labor movement well into the 1890s. Swinton died in 1901.

OLD AGE AT FORTY: JOHN A. FITCH ATTACKS STEEL'S TWELVE-HOUR DAY AND TWENTY-FOUR-HOUR TURN

For steelworkers at the beginning of the twentieth century, the hard work, long hours, and dangers of working in the mill were an accepted fact. To complain would be to quit; plant owners believed in their right to run their operations the way they wanted.

Although most industries and occupations had gone to the ten-hour day before 1890, steel company executives insisted that making steel required twenty-four-hour operations and that three shifts of workers would be too expensive. But in the early 1900s, the steel industry was under uncommon public scrutiny, partly because the government was looking into the immense size of the newly formed United States Steel Corporation, partly because of the beginnings of union activity and several protracted strikes.

Using its groundbreaking magazine, *Survey,* the Charity Organization Society of New York set out to make use of the opportunity and improve conditions in the steel mills. Its main, though not only, focus was ending the twelve-hour day.

Charles Cabot, a prominent Boston lawyer, asked John A. Fitch, one of the researchers for The Pittsburgh Survey, a pioneering sociological study, to explore conditions in the plants.

"Old Age at Forty," by John A. Fitch. *American Magazine,* March 1911.

The story of steel is a story of men. It is a story, not of tens or of hundreds, but of tens of thousands. If the steel workers of Pittsburg* and Allegheny County should go with their families to Nebraska and build a new city, they would have one that for size would equal Omaha. But if, instead of that, everyone in the United States who is dependent on the steel mills for his living should migrate to Nevada, that state would be immediately entitled to five Congressmen, at least, instead of one. And the steel workers themselves would have four representatives in Congress, instead of none at all.

For of course you understand that no one represents the steel workers in Congress now. The industry is represented there, and that is supposed to be sufficient. It is at least in accordance with some of the prevalent theories of the rights of labor.

Certain types of capitalists in this country believe it their right to control industry; and by that they mean, not the inanimate things of industry alone, not alone stocks and bonds, but men—the workmen who make industry possible. With this theory in mind, let us consider some things that have occurred in the last two decades in America. . . .

After nearly a year spent among the Pittsburg steel workers in 1907 and 1908 three phases of the labor policies of the steel companies stand out in my mind as overshadowing all others; they are the factors that enter most deeply into the lives of the men: a daily and weekly schedule of hours, both shockingly long; a system of speeding that

*Note: Fitch spells "Pittsburg" the old way, without the *h*.

adds overstrain to overtime; and, crowning all, a system of repression that stifles initiative and destroys healthy citizenship.

There are workmen in the Pittsburg mills who have an eight-hour day. Before 1892 there were many of them, but to-day you can find them only after persistent search. In 1907, before the panic began, there were about 120 eight-hour workmen among the 17,000 men employed in Allegheny County by the Carnegie Steel Company, and that is a proportion which is fairly typical of the whole industry.

To-day a large majority of the steel workers in Allegheny County work 12 hours out of each 24. . . .

The working time per week is not regular because the shifts change from day to night at the week ends. The steel works run continuously 23 hours a day and the work is divided between two shifts of men, one working days, the other nights. The hours at night are the longer, because the 24 hours are not usually divided evenly into two twelve-hour shifts, but into 10 and 14, or 11 and 13. The latter is the more general, I think, and on that schedule a man will work 11 hours every day for one week and then change about and work 13 hours every night. I asked them why they worked the longer hours at night, since the men often fix the time of changing to suit themselves and their "buddies." They all gave me the same answer: "When a man works night turn, he can't do anything but work, eat and sleep anyhow, and so he might as well work a long time and have a little freedom when he is on the day turn." . . .

To be strictly accurate, though, it is but striking an average to say that these men work seven days a week. Some of them do, but fully half of the 13,000 men work six days in one week and eight days in the next. Some people can't understand how there can be eight days in a week, but men who work at the blast furnaces know all about it. Every alternate week they have the "long turn" so as to "change the shift." On Sunday morning at six or seven o'clock, the men from the night shift begin to file through the big gates, and as they go they meet the last contingent of the last week's day shift coming in. There is indisputable evidence that it is Sunday, the day that the legislature of Pennsylvania has denominated as belonging to the Lord, for some of the men entering carry two dinner pails each, or a package of lunch double the usual size. Incoming workers then tend the furnaces until Monday morning, a full 23 hours without rest. That puts them onto the night shift for the week and the others change to the day.

Can you conceive of what it means to work twelve hours a day? Twelve hours every day spent within the mill walls mean thirteen or fourteen hours away from home, for the skilled men often live at least a half hour's ride from the mills. It means early hours for the wife, if breakfast is to be on time, and late hours too, if the supper dishes are to be washed. It doesn't leave much time for family life either, when the husband begins to doze over his paper before the evening's work in the kitchen is done, and when necessity inevitably drives him early to bed so that he may get up in time for the next day's routine. It doesn't leave much chance to play with the children when a man's job requires one week of heavy toil, during ten or eleven hours of daylight, six or seven days, and then an overturning of things and another week of night work, each shift thirteen or fourteen hours long, with the "mister" working while the children sleep, and sleeping while they play. But that is the regular round of events in the typical mill family while the weeks stretch to months and the months mount to years. "Home," said many a steel worker to me with grim bitterness, "is just the place where I eat and sleep."

On top of the hour question comes the question of strain. Twelve hours a day inside a mill, whether a man is in a position demanding constant activity or whether he has a "waiting job," is a long time. But its effect may be more serious

if his work is heavy. At the blast furnaces and open-hearth furnaces there can be little speeding. The iron takes its own time and few of the positions require constant labor. At the big up-to-day rolling mills, however, the men work steadily. In these positions there is a speeding system unparalleled in its effectiveness. . . .

Perhaps you are wondering now why the steel workers don't refuse to accept these conditions. Perhaps, though, there wouldn't be many American citizens with fighting blood left anywhere, if everybody worked twelve hours a day, and one out of every five had to work seven days in the week. Then, too, if all the men with families were absolutely dependent on one particular job for bread and butter and the children's education, perhaps they wouldn't say much that would make them run the risk of losing that job. These are the factors that make possible the system of repression, that binds together the labor policies of the steel companies. . . .

Holding meetings is not the only dangerous pastime in the western Pennsylvania mill towns either. Talking is generally admitted to have dangerous possibilities anywhere, but around the steel mills the danger is not only possible but probable. I called one day at the home of a skilled steel worker, an employee of the United States Steel Corporation, and he sent his wife to the door to tell me that he couldn't talk with me because the company had "given orders that the men shouldn't talk about mill work!" Nowhere in America, I think, will one find so suspicious a body of men as the steel workers. They are always on guard, for they never know who may be a spy. Perhaps the man on the next job, perhaps the next-door neighbor, is one. The only way to be safe is not to talk. . . .

So this "business" control of labor has gone far toward determining for the steel worker all the details of his living. In the face of a twelve-hour day, Carnegie libraries are a cruel joke. The church, lacking vigor to fight for industrial justice, is losing its hold on the workingmen. Home influences are trampled upon and the better forms of social life are made impossible by the ever-present and ever-dominant industrial power. . . .

The great steel companies had an opportunity, when unionism was destroyed, to lay foundations of a new and better order, where more of justice should prevail and more of harmony than under the old regime. Of them all the United States Steel Corporation has had the greatest opportunity, for it has dealt with the largest number of employees, and as it is larger than other companies, it could afford to be generous.

And, as this article is written there is reason to hope that the Steel Corporation will lead the way toward a broader and better policy, and set a standard for all other employing corporations. The papers have been full, of late, of the labor policies of the Steel Corporation. First came the news of the order sent out from the offices of the corporation in New York that all unnecessary Sunday work must be done away with. Then followed in rapid succession the announcements of a compensation scheme for victims of industrial accidents, of an increase in wages and the establishment of a pension fund. These are movements of utmost importance, but little can be said of them until they have been tried. . . .

The question before us just now is this: Have the steel companies made good in the eighteen years that they have been practically free to manage their "own business" in their "own way"? It was a responsibility staggering in its magnitude that they assumed when they took absolute control of labor conditions. Have they discharged that responsibility well or ill?

The manufacturers have made good from the standpoint of tonnage—they have beaten the world. They have made good from the financial standpoint. United States Steel preferred is selling considerably above par. But they have inaugurated labor policies that are undemocratic and destructive. They have taken more and more of the day from their workmen; they have demanded more and more of their strength; they have taken from them individual freedom; they have robbed the home of a father's time and care, and from the citizenship of the mill towns they have sapped the virility and aggressiveness necessary to democracy.

• • •

Cabot's original plan, one to which Judge Elbert H. Gary, the chairman of U.S. Steel, had surprisingly agreed, was to send a copy of Fitch's report to all of the corporation's preferred stockholders. When Gary saw the article, however, he was furious that Fitch raised issues other than hours. Only a scaled-back article went to stockholders.

Too late. The *American Magazine* version spread, and "old age at forty" became, said David Brody, a labor historian, "a rallying cry for critics." The Pittsburgh Survey researchers were called to testify before the congressional committee investigating U.S. Steel, and the committee eventually censured the corporation's labor practices. Reporters elsewhere went to other steel plants and found much the same conditions.

The steelmakers fought back, organizing do-nothing committees, putting out publicity of their own, and arguing that the work was not as hard as portrayed. The industry was able to hold off change through World War I, but gradually the pressure of publicity made steelmakers realize that, unless they cut the hours, legislation was likely. President Warren G. Harding and Secretary of Commerce Herbert Hoover also demanded action. Beginning in the summer of 1923, most steel mills put their workers on eight-hour shifts and ended the dreaded "long turn" that Fitch had done so much to spotlight.

WILLIAM G. SHEPHERD OF UNITED PRESS DESCRIBES THE HORRORS OF THE TRIANGLE SHIRTWAIST FIRE

The Triangle Shirtwaist fire was such a horrific event—resulting in the deaths of 146 workers, most of them teenaged women—that it was almost certain to have an impact on America. But even greater tragedies have at times slipped beneath the surface of history and been forgotten. The Triangle Company, a manufacturer of popular women's blouses, however, was in New York City, a block from crowded Washington Square, not far from the center of the city's newspapers. The horror of the day was captured by reporters and by photographs and drawings. Decades later, the story William G. Shepherd dictated by telephone to his office still brings anguish to the reader.

"Eyewitness at Triangle," by William G. Shepherd. United Press, May 27, 1911.

I was walking through Washington Square when a puff of smoke issuing from the factory building caught my eye. I reached the building before the alarm was turned in. I saw every feature of the tragedy visible from outside the building. I learned a new sound—a more horrible sound than description can picture. It was the thud of a speeding, living body on a stone sidewalk.

Thud-dead, thud-dead, thud-dead, thud-dead. Sixty-two thud-deads. I call them that, because the sound and the thought of death came to me each time, at the same instant. There was plenty of chance to watch them as they came down. The height was eighty feet.

The first ten thud-deads shocked me. I looked up—saw that there were scores of girls at the windows. The flames from the floor below were beating in their faces. Somehow I knew that they, too, must come down, and something within me—something that I didn't know was there—steeled me.

I even watched one girl falling. Waving her arms, trying to keep her body upright until the very instant she struck the sidewalk, she was trying to balance herself. Then came the thud—then a silent, unmoving pile of clothing and twisted, broken limbs.

As I reached the scene of the fire, a cloud of smoke hung over the building . . . I looked up to the seventh floor. There was a living picture in each window—four screaming heads of girls waving their arms.

"Call the firemen," they screamed—scores of them. "Get a ladder," cried others. They were all as alive and whole and sound as were we who stood on the sidewalk. I couldn't help thinking of that. We cried to them not to jump. We heard the siren of a fire engine in the distance. The other sirens sounded from several directions.

"Here they come," we yelled. "Don't jump; stay there."

One girl climbed onto the window sash. Those behind her tried to hold her back. Then she dropped into space. I didn't notice whether those above watched her drop because I had turned away. Then came that first thud. I looked up, another girl was climbing onto the window sill; others were crowding behind her. She dropped. I watched her fall, and again the dreadful sound. Two windows away two girls were climbing onto the sill; they were fighting each other and crowding for air. Behind them I saw many screaming heads. They fell almost together, but I heard two distinct thuds. Then the flames burst out through the windows on the floor below them, and curled up into their faces.

The firemen began to raise a ladder. Others took out a life net and, while they were rushing to the sidewalk with it, two more girls shot down. The firemen held it under them; the bodies broke it; the grotesque simile of a dog jumping through a hoop struck me. Before they could move the net another girl's body flashed through it. The thuds were just as loud, it seemed, as if there had been no net there. I seemed to me that the thuds were so loud that they might have been heard all over the city.

I had counted ten. Then my dulled senses began to work automatically. I noticed things that it had not occurred to me before to notice. Little details that the first shock had blinded me to. I looked up to see whether those above watched those who fell. I noticed that they did; they watched them every inch of the way down and probably heard the roaring thuds that we heard.

As I looked up I saw a love affair in the midst of all the horror. A young man helped a girl to the window sill. Then he held her out, deliberately away from the building and let her drop. He seemed cool and calculating. He held out a second girl the same way and let her drop. Then he held out a third girl who did not resist. I noticed that. They were as unresisting as if he were helping them onto a streetcar instead of into eternity. Undoubtedly he saw that a terrible death awaited them in the flames, and his was only a terrible chivalry.

Then came the love amid the flames. He brought another girl to the window. Those of us who were looking saw her put her arms about him and kiss him. Then he held her out into space and dropped her. But quick as a flash he was on the window sill himself. His coat fluttered upward—the air filled his trouser legs. I could see that he wore tan shoes and hose. His hat remained on his head.

Thud-dead, thud-dead—together they went into eternity. I saw his face before they covered it. You could see in it that he was a real man. He had done his best.

We found out later that, in the room in which he stood, many girls were being burned to death by the flames and were screaming in an inferno of flame and heat. He chose the easiest way and was brave enough to even help the girl he loved to a quicker death, after she had given him a goodbye kiss. He leaped with an energy as if to arrive first in that mysterious land of eternity, but her thud-dead came first.

The firemen raised the longest ladder. It reached only to the sixth floor. I saw the last girl jump at it and miss it. And then the faces disappeared from the window. By now the crowd was enormous, though all this had occurred in less than seven minutes, the start of the fire and the thuds and deaths.

I heard screams around the corner and hurried there. What I had seen before was not so terrible as what had followed. Up on the [ninth] floor girls were burning to death before our very eyes. They were jammed in the windows. No one was lucky enough to be able to jump, it seemed. But, one by one, the jams broke. Down came the bodies in a shower, burning, smoking—flaming bodies, with disheveled hair trailing upward. They had fought each other to die by jumping instead of by fire.

The whole, sound, unharmed girls who had jumped on the other side of the building had tried to fall feet down. But these fire torches, suffering ones, fell inertly, only intent that death should come to them on the sidewalk instead of in the furnace behind them.

On the sidewalk lay heaps of broken bodies. A policeman later went about with tags, which he fastened with wires to the wrists of the dead girls numbering each with a lead pencil, and I saw him fasten tag no. 54 to the wrist of a girl who wore an engagement ring. A fireman who came downstairs from the building told me that there were at least fifty bodies in the big room on the seventh floor. Another fireman told me that more girls had jumped down an air shaft in the rear of the building. I went back there, into the narrow court, and saw a heap of dead girls. . . .

The floods of water from the firemen's hose that ran into the gutter were actually stained red with blood. I looked upon the heap of dead bodies and I remembered these girls were the shirtwaist makers. I remembered their great strike of last year in which these same girls had demanded more sanitary conditions and more safety precautions in the shops. These dead bodies were the answer.

• • •

Investigators soon found that several doors in the building did not open, either jammed or locked to make sure girls stayed at their jobs or did not take any material home. The company owners were tried for manslaughter but acquitted, the jury unsure whether the doors had been ordered locked. New York City established an overdue Bureau of Fire Investigation, tightened the laws—the Triangle building had passed fire codes before the disaster—and stepped up inspection. The State of New York set up a Factory Investigation Commission that for several years looked at the broader range of working conditions. Its recommendations led to scores of new laws that improved safety conditions, reduced the work week for women from sixty to fifty-four hours, limited night work, and banned employment of children under fourteen. Other states followed New York's lead. The garment-workers union, recently formed, had a surge of recruits.

No one who was at the scene, or who worked in the aftermath of the fire, ever forgot what he or she experienced. In that group were a number of people who went on to spur reform movements for workers in the state and the country, including Alfred E. Smith, Robert F. Wagner, and Frances Perkins.

EDWARD LEVINSON LETS A STRIKEBREAKER CONVICT HIMSELF IN HIS OWN WORDS

Workers in America started banding together to exert pressure on their bosses—that is, to form unions—in the 1840s. The efforts were sporadic and fiercely resisted by employers, a pattern that continues today. The sides were rarely equal.

Workers could agitate, complain to the boss, or go on strike. The bosses could, and often did, hire spies, fire suspected union leaders, eject striking workers and members of their families from company housing, run organizers out of town, ask the governor (usually their friend) to send in the state militia. When all else failed, the bosses could hire professional strikebreakers. Allan Pinkerton was perhaps the first of these strikebreakers, putting the organization he had assembled for the Union army during the Civil War into the service of whatever employer would rather put out the money than face the possibility of dealing with unionized workers.

Edward Levinson grew up with the American labor movement. Born at the turn of the century, Levinson, at age eighteen, obtained his first newspaper job with the *New York Call,* a socialist newspaper. He then worked at papers in Denver and San Francisco and for the socialist weekly, the *New Leader.* Then, in 1932, Levinson managed the presidential campaign of Norman Thomas, the Socialist Party candidate. The combination of journalism and leftist, labor-oriented issues made Levinson a perfect person to become chief labor correspondent for the New York *Post,* then a liberal paper.

Levinson was interested in equalizing conditions between workers and bosses. "One of the topics Levinson followed closely was professional strikebreaking," said historian Robert Zieger of the University of Florida. That put him onto following Pearl L. Bergoff, an anti-labor businessman who broke his first strike in 1907 and kept up his strikebreaking for almost three decades. Levinson cozied up to Bergoff and won his confidence. In 1934 he interviewed Bergoff and wrote two revealing articles on him, each, in the manner of the time and all the more sensational because they were, in Bergoff's words.

"I Break Strikes," by P. L. Bergoff.
New York *Post,* October 25, 1934.

The profits of strikebreaking have been large. The work is always of an emergency nature. It calls for handling large numbers of men under perilous circumstances.

My biggest job was for the Erie Railroad in the shopmen's strike of 1920. For four and a half months I supplied the company with 6,000 to 7,000 men. The Erie paid about $2,000,000 for that job. The exact figures are the property of the railroad.

Theodore Shonts, president of Interborough Rapid Transit Company, and Frank Hedley, general manager, paid my organization over $1,000,000 to break the 1916 subway strike.

The Brooklyn-Manhattan Transit Company cheerfully paid us $700,000 for our work during their 1920 strike. The City of New York claimed my services during two street-cleaners' strikes. The United States Government has used our bureau. The nature of that work I cannot divulge.

I started in the detective business during the Harry K. Thaw case. Stanford White, who was later shot by Thaw, retained me to help guard him. After the murder I was employed by the District Attorney's office in New York County in connection with the case.

About 1907 I decided there was more money in industrial work. I had worked with "Jim" Farley—not the present Postmaster-General—who was known as king pin among the strike-breakers. My first large job was in the New York longshoremen's strike of that year. The French and Italian lines, the White Star, Munson and Scandinavian lines were among my clients.

My work on the waterfront won me a retainer by MacDonald Cravan, New York Street Cleaning Commissioner in 1907, when the sweepers walked out. The same year the Postal Telegraph Company found use for us.

By that time, although a young man, I had accumulated almost half a million dollars. In those days my charge for a strike-breaker was $5 a day. In addition, the companies paid the wages of the strike-breakers or guards, usually $5 a day. Sometimes they would go on the company pay roll, sometimes we would handle that end through the bureau.

The cost of men for industrial service has naturally gone up. Today the rate for the bureau runs as high as $12 a day for each man supplied.

After a two-year trip around the country, I was back on the firing line in New York in 1909. Pretty soon I ran into one of the largest jobs I handled. Trouble was brewing on the Philadelphia Transit system. Before the strike started, I supplied the general manager, later president, Charles O. Kruger, with a number of men.

Kruger adopted a slightly different technique. He wrote me at the time:

"I am only going to place these men at the rate of two a day, although, of course, I am perfectly willing to pay them for full time. I do not wish to do anything that is going to create comment at the different barns."

Soon I got an order for 5,000 motormen, conductors and guards. I was appointed dictator of the railroad. I had 1,500 men in Philadelphia in twenty-four hours. I housed the men in three big circus tents, with full commissary and sleeping equipment.

The first day of the strike two of our men were killed. I buried one at our expense. He was a man with a family. In that strike, our men fought hard. There were three or four killed and fifty wounded before the strike was over.

The company had agreed to indemnify the men against all injuries, but at the end we found a number of chiselers. With the help of Fred Johnson, then claim agent for the P.R.T., we paid off the wounded men first. The other claims were then investigated and we succeeded in weeding out a number who had tried to fake injuries.

McKees Rock, Pennsylvania, was the next scene of our operations. I am skipping the smaller strikes. In McKees Rock I had an agreement with James Ryder, general manager of the Pressed Steel

Car Corporation, which he asked me to keep confidential at the time.

I supplied the steel company with 4,000 men in the bloodiest strike I have ever seen. The strike lasted forty-nine days. Twenty-two men were killed on both sides and 216 wounded. Three box cars were converted into hospitals.

In recruiting the help, we had advertised for American workers. We found the foreigners a violent crowd, especially when they were egged on by their women-folk. I have seen foreign women with babies in their arms in the midst of battle urging strikers on to kill the guards.

We paid four or five thousand dollars for each of our men killed. The income was so large that this expense made no difference. . . .

I was in the field nine times out of ten then. Some newspaper man dubbed me "the Red Demon" because of my hair and my reputation in strikes. I deserved the title in those days. I look gentle but when I'm directing 1,000 men in the midst of a mob of strikers I'm a different man. . . .

Frequently we have had to equip our guards with weapons of defense and offense. Our activities in this connection today must be treated as a "trade secret."

In the old days we maintained an arsenal. We had 2,500 rifles with plenty of ammunition.

A couple of thousand nightsticks and clubs were always on hand. We had two men to keep the equipment in shape ready for any call. Today we keep pace with the modern requirements.

We sent tear gas by airplane to Georgia in the recent textile strike. There, however, our work was hampered by Governor Talmadge, who was playing both sides against the middle. Our men were sent at the request of W. D. Anderson of the Bibb Manufacturing Company. He said he preferred one of our men to ten of the National Guard.

But Governor Talmadge interfered. To please the mill owners he declared martial law. Then to curry favor with the strikers he turned on us and ordered us out of the State. My men were guards, not strikebreakers. They felt badly about the Governor's action.

We ran into trouble with Mayor Daniel W. Hoan of Milwaukee in the recent utilities strike. He is a Socialist and he might have been expected to take the course he did. He had about 150 of our men, sent by airplane, locked up. We succeeded, however, in forcing their release.

I want to emphasize again that strikebreaking is only one of our specialties. We concentrate now on strike-prevention work. The job is to instill confidence in the conservative workers and discredit the radical and the agitator. We have put men among employees who can match any agitator in eloquence.

• • •

Levinson expanded his two articles into a book, *I Break Strikes!*, published in December 1935. With the book, wrote Jerold S. Auerbach, a historian of labor in that era, "Levinson nearly did for strikebreaking what Upton Sinclair had done for the meat-packing industry by publishing *The Jungle*." The articles and the book exposed the extent of organized strikebreaking that had thwarted the efforts of unions and the intent of Section 7(a) of the National Industrial Recovery Act, which, for the first time in American history, had given government support to union organizing. In 1936, in response to the book and to the general labor turmoil of the time, Senator Robert M. La Follette, Jr., a Progressive from Wisconsin, obtained Senate approval to investigate "violations of the rights of free speech and assembly and undue interference with the right of labor to organize and bargain collectively."

What came to be called the La Follette Civil Liberties Committee did not achieve the passage of new legislation, but the committee put on record the espionage, strikebreaking, and use of armed guards and munitions employed by companies. In the process, said Auerbach, the committee "dis-

pelled the aura of respectability surrounding unethical antilabor practices," encouraged automobile
workers and miners to organize, and "contributed
to the increase of public tolerance of unions."

Levinson followed the labor movement
wherever it went for two more decades. Then
he joined the staff of the United Automobile
Workers.

Because of Levinson's work and the investigations that followed, the use of strikebreakers
faded. In the 1970s, strikebreaking companies reemerged, this time with focus on legal and public
relations apparatuses. But the guns remain.

THE *NEW MASSES* REVEALS DEATHS FROM SILICOSIS IN HAWK'S MOUNTAIN TUNNEL PROJECT

The Hawk's Nest Tunnel near Gauley Bridge,
West Virginia, was an engineering marvel. Three
miles long, a mile of it through solid rock, the tunnel diverted the New River and harnessed it for
electricity, enough to light the city of Charleston.

Nearly 5,000 men worked at building the tunnel, more than 3,000 of them blacks. At the time
tunnel construction started, 1930, the men were
easy to find, even in that sparsely populated area.
Word of work spread around the Southeast, and
unemployed workers got to Gauley Bridge any
way they could. Pay for laborers was fifteen to
thirty cents an hour. The job was hard, a ten-hour
cycle of drilling, dynamiting, clearing rock, then
drilling again. But it was a job.

Through an accident of geology, the rock at
Hawk's Nest was more than 90 percent silica.
Workers had no respirators. Within months, the
men started to get sick and to die. They filed for
state compensation, they filed lawsuits against
Union Carbide, the project owner, but they got
little help.

The disaster at Hawk's Nest first came to national attention in *New Masses* in 1935, first in

"Man on a Road," a fictionalized account by Albert Maltz, and then in a two-part report by
someone who had been there.

"Two Thousand Dying on a Job," by Bernard Allen. *New Masses,* January 15, 1935.

The story back of Albert Maltz's description of
the tortured shell of a man he picked up on the
Gauley road in West Virginia which was published
in the issue of *The New Masses* for January 8, is
the story of a major industrial tragedy involving
2,000 men. Two thousand workmen, according to
the estimated figures of the contractors, were employed for over a period of two years in drilling
a three and three-quarter mile tunnel under a
mountain from Gauley's Junction at Hawk's Nest
in Fayette County, West Virginia. The rock
through which these men bored was sandstone of
a high silica content (in tunnel number one it ran
from 97 percent pure silica to as high as 99.4
percent) and the contracting company neglected
to provide any safety devices.

Almost as soon as the tunnel was started, men
began dying. They were robust, hard-muscled
men. Many of them had lived all their lives near
Gauley where the rock cropping out on the roads
is sandstone, largely made up of silica. Yet they
were unaware of the risk they ran in blasting into
the rock without the safeguard of masks and wet
drills. With every breath they were inhaling a massive dose of microscopic silica dust.

Silica dust is deadly in large doses. Proof of
this is that every man who worked in the tunnel
any length of time and who had been examined
recently by a doctor was found to have developed
a lung disease that cannot be stopped once it has
started. Finally these men must strangle to death
from silicosis.

For several reasons it is impossible to tabulate
the number of men who have died:

Before it was generally known just what disease
was killing the men, the company doctors diag-

nosed the cause of numerous deaths as pneumonia (to which silicosis-infected lungs are highly susceptible because of a greatly lessened power of resistance).

An undertaker who handled many of the burials said his records had been "destroyed."

And finally, after law suits were started and everyone knew that it was the rock dust which was actually killing the men, the tunnel laborers left their jobs and scattered over the country looking for other work. Exactly how many of them have died elsewhere since, it would be a vast job to determine. The known medical fact, which points out their fate clearly, is that silicosis, once it has taken hold of a victim, is incurable and that death by strangling is only a matter of time.

The tunnel is part of a billion-dollar water-power project begun in 1929 by the New-Kanawha Power Company. This company was formed ostensibly to develop public water rights for public sale. In reality, however, the company was formed to sell all the power manufactured to a single corporation. Proof of this is that in 1933 the Electro-Metallurgical Company (a subsidiary of the Union Carbide & Carbon Company, one of the largest holding companies in America) was allowed to buy up the New-Kanawha Power Company, lock, stock and barrel. You will find it in the Acts of the Legislature of West Virginia, 1933, Regular Session, on page 296. An outright steal of the public water rights made lawful by an act of the West Virginia Legislature!

Jack Pitckett, Albert Maltz's "Man on the Road," commented when writing to his wife about his "death sickness":

Hit comes frum the time the mine was shut down and I worked in the tunel nere Gauley Bridge when the govinment is turnin the river inside the mounten.

More literate men than he are confused by the fact that state "govinment" and big corporations work so neatly hand in hand.

Jack Pitckett is only one of hundreds of men who are still dying like flies in the vicinity of Gauley Bridge. Men who "ginerally follow the mines" for a trade, but who found steadier work drilling in the tunnel.

Out of the 2,000 men employed over a period of nearly three years, many hundreds of men have been examined by private doctors and were found to have the disease. Men were succumbing to it a year—two, three—after they had quit work; and there seems little doubt that few of the 2,000 men will escape it.

No one, it seemed, knew the danger of the dusty tunnel until the first of the $6,000,000 worth of lawsuits were filed by victims or victims' widows against the Rinehart & Dennis Company of Charlottesville, Virginia, the contractors, and against the New-Kanawha Power Company who allotted to them the task of drilling the tunnel. All of the suits, some two hundred of which are still pending, charged that men were either dead or dying because they had worked in the tunnel.

The first suits, tried in the spring of 1933, were settled out of court after a disagreement. The lawyers representing 300 men, compromised upon payment of a total sum of $130,000. As the lawyers had undertaken to try the cases upon a 50 percent contingent basis, they pocketed one-half of the total after paying court costs of $1,000. This left a very small sum to be divided among a large number of men. . . .

The trial uncovered the following facts concerning working conditions in the tunnel:

The dust was so thick in the tunnel that the atmosphere resembled a patch of dense fog. It was estimated on the witness stand in the little court room at Fayetteville where the suits against the builders of the tunnel were tried, that workmen in the tunnel could see only ten to fifteen feet ahead of them at times. Man after man—drillers, drill helpers, nippers, muckers, dinkey runners and members of the surveying crew who were the plaintiff's witnesses—told of this dusty condition.... Dust got in the men's hair, on their face, in their eyebrows; their clothing was thick with it. Raymond Johnson described how men blew dust off themselves with compressed air in the tunnel; if they did not, they came out of the tunnel white, he said. One worker told how dust settled on top of the drinking water, "so I took milk in the tunnel with me and drank it instead."

What caused this dusty condition? The use of dry drills, the workmen said. J. J. Huffman told the court that he asked the foreman if a little water couldn't be used in the hole when the bit became "hung up" and that the foreman's reply was, "Hell, no!" Milledge Venson said that the foreman stopped the dry drilling while the mine safety inspector was in the tunnel.

And Sam Butner testified that he was stationed at the scaling tower which was several hundred (600) feet from the heading, and directed to hurry information to the heading foreman of the approach of the mine inspector, so that the dry drilling could be stopped before the inspector got there. Not only Sam, but Laird King and others told how they had acted as lookouts and warned the foreman when they saw the inspector coming....

Another witness for the contractors was Robert M. Lambie, former chief of the state mines department, who said that the tunnel was practically dust-free when he made inspections in 1930 and 1931....

Throughout the court trails the witnesses for the contractors gave the flimsiest testimony. O. M. Jones, chief engineer of the New-Kanawha Power Company, "never saw dust, or at least enough to say it was dusty." He saw fog and mist in the tunnel: but "the air was as clear as it was in the court room, except on foggy days."

Under cross-examination O. M. Jones admitted that he had received a letter from Lambie, mine safety inspector, on May 18, 1931, saying that the heavy concentration of silica dust in the tunnel was highly dangerous and ordering the workers to use respirators.

The contractors tried to show in court that they had not been negligent in making arrangements to care for the safety of men on a construction job of this sort. Engineers from other contracting companies were called to testify that their companies made a practice of drilling "dry"; that respirators were not necessary. But regardless of the legal facts, many hundreds of these West Virginia miners are paying for their jobs with their lives....

It was Mrs. Jones who first discovered what was killing the tunnel workers.

Mrs. Jones had three sons—Shirley, 17 years old, Owen, 21, and Cecil, 23—who worked in the tunnel with their father. Before they went into the tunnel, Mr. Jones and Cecil and Owen worked in a coal mine. But it was not steady work because the mines were not going much of the time. Then one of the foremen of the New-Kanawha Power Company learned that the Joneses made home-brew, and formed a habit of dropping in of an evening to drink it. It was he who persuaded the boys and their father to give up their jobs in the coal mine and take on this other work which would pay them better. Shirley, the youngest son and his mother's favorite, went into the tunnel, too.

Mrs. Jones began to be suspicious when she saw the amount of sediment that was left on the bottom of the tub after she had washed their clothes. She asked the foreman about the dust and he said that it was just ordinary dust and would not hurt anybody. Then one day Shirley came home and complained, "Ma, I'm awfully short-winded." She said to him, "Well, if you feel no better, you'll not work no more." This took place in September of 1931 and he died in June, 1932. ... She told us the boy's last wish. He said, "Mother, after I'm dead, have them open me up and see if I didn't die from the job. If I did, take the compensation money and buy yourself a little home." Within thirteen months of Shirley's death, Cecil and Owen died.

• • •

"Bernard Allen" was in truth Phillippa Allen, a New York social worker who had heard the rumors of death on the tunnel project and in the summer of 1934 went to West Virginia to investigate. It took a while for Maltz's and Allen's stories to have an effect. Maltz told the editor of the *People's Press,* a radical labor tabloid in Detroit, who sent a photographer to what the editor called "the village of walking skeletons." A reporter with the *Pittsburgh Press* saw the *People's Press* story, went to Gauley Bridge himself, and wrote about it.

Eventually the articles were seen by Representative Vito Marcantonio of New York, a leftist known for his interest in worker rights. Marcantonio arranged for a congressional subcommittee to hold hearings. Allen testified, as did the *Pittsburgh Press* and *People's Press* reporters.

The somewhat abbreviated hearings did little to help the victims at Gauley Bridge or to fix responsibility on the companies, wrote Martin Cherniak, a physician and occupational health researcher, in his definitive book, *The Hawk's Nest Incident.* But, he said, "The hearings indirectly achieved an objective of immense significance in awakening recognition of the need to protect workers exposed to silica."

The national press, including the newsreels, started to pay attention, although accounts varied widely between being sensational or dismissive. Secretary of Labor Frances Perkins called a national conference on the dangers of silicosis. No federal legislation resulted, but by the end of 1937, forty-six states had included workers suffering from silicosis under their workers' compensation laws. As a result of Hawk's Nest, Cherniak wrote, the medical profession first recognized acute silicosis as a disease.

No final death toll was ever obtained, but Hawk's Nest is regarded as the most deadly American industrial tragedy.

THE *ST. LOUIS POST-DISPATCH* ASSIGNS BLAME FOR THE CENTRALIA MINE DISASTER

Mining coal underground has always been dangerous work. Too much trouble can happen— explosions, fires, collapse of the mine roofs and walls—and when trouble happens in the mines, the escape routes are few. Moreover, the mine owners and operators are often economic and political powers in their communities who are given all the benefit of their power. Safety inspections can be accordingly lax.

Miners at the Centralia mine in southern Illinois were well aware of the special dangers there, largely from the potentially explosive coal dust that hung everywhere in the air. Something's going to happen, one miner told his wife, to kill us all. In early 1945, four members of the United Mine Workers local at Centralia wrote to Illinois Governor Dwight Green beseeching him for help. His state mine inspectors, friends of industry, did not enforce the safety rules, the miners said. "Please save our lives," they begged the governor.

When the explosion finally came, on March 25, 1947, it went pretty much the way the worried men expected. One hundred eleven miners were trapped and died before they could be rescued, an operation that took days. The pocket of men deepest in the mine had time to write notes to their families before they were overcome.

The nearby *St. Louis Post-Dispatch*, under Joseph Pulitzer, second-generation publisher, decided even before the mine had been cleared that its reporters were going to pursue the story and pin blame.

A twenty-four-page special section on April 30, 1947, set the scene of the tragedy. Harry Wilensky wrote the main story.

The clock in the office of the Centralia Coal Co.'s Mine No. 5 ticked toward quitting time on the afternoon of March 25. As the hands registered 3:27 and the 142 men working 540 feet underground prepared to leave the pit at the end of their shift, an explosion occurred.

The blast originated in one of the work rooms in the northwestern section of the working. Fed by coal dust, it whooshed through the labyrinth of tunnels underlying the town of Wamac, Ill., on the southern outskirts of Centralia. Thirty-one men, most of whom happened to be near the shaft at the time, made their way to the cage and were brought out alive, but the remaining 111 were trapped. Fellow workmen who tried to reach them shortly after the explosion were driven back by poisonous fumes.

As rescue crews with special equipment hurried from Belleville, West Frankfort, Herrin, DuQuoin, Eldorado and other Illinois mine towns, relatives of the trapped miners gathered in tense, silent groups around the tipple. It was a raw day, and an icy wind shipped the coal dust through the air, begriming faces and clothing; but the wives, sons and daughters stayed on, hour after hour.

Here and there a woman wiped tears from her eyes, but few broke down. After darkness fell, many of the relatives retired to a washhouse where they sat on the benches the miners had used in changing their clothes. Overhead, suspended on chains and pulleys, hung the street clothing of the men who had failed to come up. In some cases wives recognized their husbands' garments and selected their places for the long vigil.

It rained. Then it snowed. Still most of the wan, tight-lipped relatives stayed on, refusing to go home "until we can find out." The Red Cross and the Salvation Army set up canteens which served coffee and sandwiches.

It was 27 hours before the rescue crews brought the first trapped miner to the surface. An eerie hush fell over the crowd, held back by police, as the first stretcher was carried from the cage to the line of waiting ambulances. When it

was observed that the blanket in which the huddled form was wrapped covered the face, some women turned their heads and wept. Sixteen other victims followed out of the shaft, but all were dead.

The next day, after 18 additional bodies were brought out, those in charge began to refer to their work as "recovery operations" instead of rescue activities, and hopes for the men still unaccounted for faded.

Penetration of the underground passageways was a laborious as well as extremely hazardous operation involving removal of debris, sealing off of side tunnels and partial restoration of the mine's ventilating system.

On March 28, the rescue volunteers threatened to quit when Robert M. Medill, director of the Illinois Department of Mines and Minerals, sought to turn the electric power on in the blast-torn mine to "speed the work." Driscoll Scanlan, state mine inspector who had been overruled in repeated efforts to close the mine as unsafe months before the explosion occurred, upheld the workers' contention that this might result in a new explosion.

A chemical test of the air in the mine disclosed the presence of a mixture of gases that could be ignited by an electric spark, and Medill conceded he was wrong.

The day-and-night operations proceeded with mules instead of power-driven equipment, and on March 29 the farthest corner of the mine was penetrated, disclosing that all of the remaining miners were dead.

The victims left 99 widows and 76 children under the age of 18.

The toll of 111 dead made the Centralia explosion the nation's worst mine disaster in 23 years. Only once before had Illinois experienced a mining tragedy of such proportions; this was at Cherry in 1909, when 259 men were killed.

After an intensive study, a team of five experts from the United States Bureau of Mines reported the Centralia explosion "was caused by coal dust raised into the air and ignited by explosives fired in a dangerous and non-permissible manner."

The inspectors found explosives had been tamped with combustible coal dust, in violation of regulations. They pointed out the mine was not using electric detonators, as had been recommended. State and federal experts agreed the explosion was spread from the point of ignition to distant reaches of the mine by excessive quantities of coal dust blown into the air and ignited.

Both Scanlan and federal mine inspectors had notified the management prior to the disaster that accumulations of coal dust in the mine were excessive, and had recommended use of rock dust. When blown into the air by an explosion, rock dust lessens the combustibility of coal dust, thereby localizing and smothering the blast.

In his inspections reports on Mine No. 5, Scanlan time and again had cited the danger of a dust explosion and had urged rock-dusting, thereby resisting pressure from higher-ups in the State Department of Mines who considered his concern for the miners' safety excessive. On one occasion the inspector had risked the loss of his job by forcing the Centralia mine partially to suspend production until it corrected the dust hazard.

Conditions in the mine remained safe for only a short time, however, Scanlan reported, and soon his official complaints and his recommendations for corrective steps were resumed.

At the conclusion of the recovery operations, which Scanlan had directed personally, going down into the mine with the volunteers, the weary inspector made this bitter comment:

"Every one of my recommendations could have been complied with, could have saved the company money, and could have saved these men's lives."

• • •

The *St. Louis Post-Dispatch* distributed the special section free throughout the southern Illinois coal region and continued its reporting. Seven reporters were detailed to dig into Governor Green's role in the disaster. Stories detailed how he ordered state mine inspectors to lean on the mine operators for campaign donations, and how he had ignored complaints about mine safety. Medill, the head of the state department of mines, resigned. But Green ran for reelection.

Pulitzer ran an editorial challenging the Green machine, then bought space in Illinois newspapers and ran an advertisement based on the editorial. Green was defeated by Adlai E. Stevenson, a Chicago lawyer who had been a federal official and a member of the United States delegation to the beginning session of the United Nations.

Illinois stepped up its mine inspections and gave the inspectors indefinite tenure, to free them from political pressures. The state also made it a crime for inspectors to solicit campaign funds from the coal industry. Federal mine regulations were also strengthened.

The Centralia Coal Co., indicted for willful neglect in the mine disaster, pleaded no defense and was fined.

MARY HEATON VORSE EXPOSES CORRUPTION ON THE NEW YORK WATERFRONT

Rackets, corruption, and violence were for decades as much a part of the New York waterfront as the sound of water splashing against the sides of the great cargo ships. Neither the ship owners, the stevedore companies that loaded and unloaded the ships, the International Longshoremen's Association, the union that supposedly represented dock workers, nor the longshoremen themselves could change matters, for a certain proportion of each was involved in the corruption. Many of the rest were unconcerned—or scared. In such a situation, public pressure was the necessary tool.

Mary Heaton Vorse was a pioneer labor reporter of the early twentieth century, to be found

at all of the most contentious of the early labor battles—Lawrence, Massachusetts; the Iron Range of
Minnesota; Gastonia, North Carolina; the Monongahela Valley of Pennsylvania; Flint, Michigan. She
reported from Europe before and during both
World War I and World War II, focusing on the effect of war on ordinary citizens. She was in Russia
after the revolution. She was a suffragette, sometimes a union organizer and publicist, a writer of
profitable women's fiction.

By the middle of the century, Vorse, born in
1874, felt somewhat out of step. The labor movement she had been so devoted to, and indeed the
whole country, was moving away from radicalism.
The kind of writing she liked to do fell out of
favor. Three book manuscripts in a row never
found publishers. Although somewhat disillu-
sioned, Vorse then turned her reporting skills to
other arenas. In 1952, when Vorse was seventy-
eight, *Harper's* magazine published her investigation of waterfront crime in New York.

"Pirate's Nest of New York," by Mary Heaton Vorse. *Harper's,* April 1952.

"When Johnny Cockeye Dunn went to the chair
for the murder of Andy Hintz, before he died,
they found he'd done at least thirteen murders,"
said Father Corridan.

"Didn't Johnny Cockeye use the concrete?"
asked the longshoreman, an old-timer. He was
talking to two Jesuit priests about the New York
docks, where the convenient way to get rid of
embarrassing corpses is to dump a man in a barrel, fill it with concrete, and drop it down to the
twelve-foot ooze at the bottom of the harbor.

"No, no," said Father Corridan. "Johnny
Cockeye never used concrete. He used what is
called the Chinese method entirely—a quick bullet in the back of the head and the car radio
turned up."

"Didn't he put Peter Pan in the concrete, Father?" asked the other priest gently.

"You have it all confused, Father. Peter Panto
didn't go in the concrete at all. They found him
in the lime and garroted nearly a year after he
disappeared. To this day, the police say they don't
know who got to him, although the Anastasia
mob has been suspected." Father Corridan turned
to me. "Peter Panto was a hiring boss who
couldn't stand the waterfront rackets, so he protested. He was called in and told the boys he
didn't like what he was doing. Four days later he
disappeared."

We were in the office of Father John M. Corridan, S.J., assistant director of the Xavier Institute
of Industrial Relations. His organization offers instruction to New York City laboring men on the
techniques of union activity—classes in parlia-
mentary procedure, union organization, labor
journalism, public speaking, and the like. In the
course of learning to do their own jobs the Jesuits
have had to find out a great deal about the city
and the ways in which its work is done. Father
Corridan has become an authority on the waterfront. He talks of murder in a quiet, matter-of-
fact voice. The two priests might have been
discussing a change in their students' schedules
instead of sudden death.

The twenty-five-day longshoremen's strike of
October–November 1951 had ended spectacu-
larly at one o'clock the night before. A billion
dollars' worth of cargo lay on the piers. The strike
was estimated to have cost millions in spoilage
and demurrage, and $300,000 daily in wages—
$40,000,000 in all. The immediate cause of it had
been discontent with their contract, which the
longshoremen claimed was "a phony" and which
they said put back the clock twenty-five years in
loading procedure, even though their international
union leadership accepted it. They showed their
discontent in the most eloquent way they knew—
"voting with their feet," which means walking out
on a wildcat strike.

"The strike is over," Father Corridan said, "but
the disturbance behind it is not." From a nearby

room came the voice of another priest, telephoning: "This wasn't a strike. It was a revolt!"

"You heard Father Dobson?" asked Father Corridan. "The causes of the strike were deeper than resentment about a contract. There'll be trouble on the waterfront as long as there are union officials with long criminal records, as long as stevedoring companies use criminals for hiring bosses. The strike was a revolt against mob rule. The men on the docks are living for the day when they'll be out from under it."

There is no concentration of power and might and beauty in any port on earth like that of New York City. Its exports and imports are worth over $7,000,000,000 a year. Yet this magnificent harbor, with its shoreline in many cities, is a pirates' nest. Violence and theft are as much taken for granted as they were in Morocco during the boisterous days of the gaudy bandit, Raisuli, forty years ago—or as they are today in many ports of the Orient. Murder is common on the waterfront. New York District Attorney Frank S. Hogan says that there are more murders here per square yard than anywhere else in the world. Death comes quickly to men like Andy Hintz or Peter Panto who protest against "the system."

The "system" is an informal, fourfold understanding between certain union officials, business men, gangsters, and politicians....

Among the many complex reasons why this port of unsurpassed splendor is the most expensive in the world for shippers, why its business is steadily ebbing away to other cities, is the existence of organized pilferage, a polite word for piracy. It is reflected in the insurance rate—25 percent additional on cargoes consigned to New York. Each year gangsters are believed to rob ships alone (not including the warehouses) of between 65 and 100 million dollars' worth of property, maybe more. Loading itself, under the local arrangement called "public loading," is so much a

racket that it costs $15 million annually. The overcharges for loading are about 20 per cent more than if the same goods were shipped elsewhere on the Atlantic seaboard. Another major source of illegal income is the incredibly profitable smuggling of narcotics; so is extortion, which sent Socks Lanza—until then the waterfront boss on the East Side—to jail. Among the many minor ones which affect the longshoremen are loan-sharking, kickbacks, "short" gangs, "voluntary" contributions, and gambling rackets....

Joseph P. Ryan, president for life of the International Longshoremen's Association, insists that Communists played an important part in the unauthorized walkout. Father Corridan, who opened a strike meeting with a prayer, denies this. Yet, in spite of the opposition of their union chief, there was a moment when the "insurgents" trembled on the edge of success. "You might say that the men had the ball on the five-yard line," one striker put it. "Anyway, they had walked out on Joe Ryan and the only ones he had with him were the gangsters."

Joe Ryan has expressed the belief that the method of hiring longshoremen best suited to the port of New York is the shape-up, an archaic system long since abandoned in the great ports of Europe....

"The 'shape' is a real experience," one longshoreman told me. "The men stand around and tell dirty jokes and talk about sports and girls. The dock is chilly and it gets in your bones, and all the time everyone is waiting for the 'shape.' At five minutes to eight on any dock in New York a whistle blows, and the men who have been waiting form a circle around the hiring boss. Unless you're on the inside track with him, you don't know until that moment whether you're going to get the brass check, which means you're hired. No matter how long he's worked on the docks, every man is hired fresh every day. There are always more men than they want and many who are not hired wait in a saloon for another 'shape.' "

Under this system the hiring boss has the power of life and death over the longshoremen. He controls their economic life and sometimes their physical life, for many of the hiring bosses have criminal records. Some stevedoring companies prefer such men. "If you squawk you leave the docks, most likely in the fruit wagon," said one longshoreman. (The "fruit wagon" is the ambulance.) "If you don't leave in a barrel of cement," added another.

The "shape" and favoritism are inseparable, and they keep alive the threat of unemployment. . . . Not only is the longshoreman the victim of perpetual insecurity but his employment itself is hazardous. According to the Bureau of Labor Statistics, a longshoreman has one chance in five hundred of being killed or disabled for life, one in forty of permanent impairment. One man in every four has lost thirty-four days annually because of temporary injury.

The longshoremen themselves can best tell you how the "system" affects their lives. There is not one who has not suffered, not one who has security. . . .

At Harry's they were looking at a fine television set. The little cold-water flat had recently been done over as pretty as a bird's nest. It costs as much to heat as it does to rent and the bath is outside, but the kitchen is a housewife's dream.

Like his father, Harry is a cooper, or cargo repairman, and he has worked eleven years on the waterfront. We were talking about the difficulties for the ordinary worker in the ILA. "Take me," Harry said. "I was overseas twenty-three months, and when I came back they'd let a lot of longshoremen work as coopers who'd never learned the trade, so I was out of work eight months. My wife had to go to work. That's how it is when there's no seniority in a union." . . .

When I climbed up the tenement stairs to Andy Dubrow's place, it seemed as though the hand of time had turned back thirty years, when the whole swarming East Side lived in tenements like this one. It smelled of dirt and bad toilets. Mrs. Dubrow let me in.

"Excuse this place," she said. "With all the children, you know how it is." The shades were broken; paper was peeling from the wall; there was a baby in a high chair near the table. Two other children played quietly on the worn and dirty linoleum floor. There were two more children in school, and the Dubrows were worried about their boy of sixteen, who "never seems to work steady."

"One time we lived nice. We had a different sort of place; it was after Andy got a smashed leg we began to have bad luck. He used to work good—always on the same pier. He made fifty and sixty dollars. He stood in with the boss." Mrs. Dubrow pushed back her hair with a hopeless kind of gesture that took in everything, the hopeless way the housework had got beyond control, Andy's bad luck, the boy they were worried about. "When he went back, there didn't seem to be no work for him. The boss had changed. He don't get more than two or three days a week, sometimes not that. We couldn't live without welfare. Oh, how I wish we didn't have to take it." . . .

At present no fewer than five investigating groups are fishing in the waters around the docks. . . . With the public indignant as never before about crime in high places, this may be the psychological moment to clean up the waterfront and to put an end to these monstrous conditions. It will not be an easy task. Over the years a way of life has been established, through which ships are loaded fast enough to satisfy their owners, and everyone but the longshoremen becomes rich. Before now, in part because of the code of silence, no complete investigation of the waterfront has ever been made. Perhaps the many grand juries and crime committees between them will at last succeed in making one. Arrests will help, as will the unmasking of those politicians who profit from the waterfront rackets. The partnership of politicians and gangsters can be broken if drastic enough measures are taken—and if they *are* taken, it will be because the public has demanded them. . . .

Meanwhile the men who suffer most, the thousands of anonymous longshoremen on the docks, are ripe for "revolt against mob rule." They are living, as Father Corridan had said, for the day of liberation from it.

• • •

The drama and detail of the article had a big popular impact and drew national attention. Connected with the work of other reporters, such as Murray Kempton of the New York *Post* and Malcolm Johnson of the New York *Sun*, Vorse's article helped bring about hearings of the New York State Crime Commission, beginning in December 1952. After that, both Governor Thomas E. Dewey of New York and the American Federation of Labor felt under public pressure to take action. In September 1953, the AFL expelled the International Longshoremen's Association and replaced it with a new union on the docks. New York and New Jersey set up a joint waterfront commission to oversee the docks. Among the commission's requirements were registration of longshoremen, replacing the shape-up with employment centers, and restricting the role ex-convicts could play on the docks and in the unions. No one claimed that waterfront corruption was eliminated, but for a time conditions improved.

Vorse was greatly pleased by the attention she received from the article, which turned out to be one of her last. She died in 1966 at the age of ninety-two.

UNITED MINE WORKERS JOURNAL FORCES FEDERAL GOVERNMENT TO NAME A NEW MINE SAFETY OFFICIAL

Like other sponsored papers, the labor union press has historically served two masters, theoretically representing the interests of the union members and their families while answering also to the union officials who appoint the editors and usually want to use internal publications as a tool of power. Matt Witt, a labor journalist, described the *United Mine Workers Journal* in the early 1970s: "Thirty-two-page issues included as many as thirty-two photos of W.A. 'Tony' Boyle, then union president. A contract negotiated by Boyle was portrayed as the greatest document since the Ten Commandments, and criticism of the high command, widespread though it was, did not find its way into the *Journal*'s pages."

Criticism of union leaders was so widespread that, in December 1972, Arnold Miller, a candidate of the Miners for Democracy, was elected union president. One of his promises was to reform the *Journal*, open it to critics of the officers, and make it a voice of the ordinary miner. Witt and another young labor journalist, Don Stillman, were given the job and, against considerable opposition from union officials accustomed to the magazine's kept ways, succeeded for a time in making the *Journal* a true investigative organ popular with the membership.

An example of the *Journal*'s work was a story in the July 1–15, 1974, issue, examining the career of James Day, acting chief of the federal mine safety team, who was facing confirmation hearings by the U.S. Senate.

• • •

"Sabotaging Safety," by Matt Witt.
United Mine Workers Journal,
July 1–15, 1974.

Betty Duckworth could tell you about James Day. Or you could ask Louise May Hyer. Or her four, fatherless children.

In fact, if James M. Day goes before the U.S. Senate Labor and Public Welfare Committee this month for hearings on his nomination as administrator of the U.S. Mining Enforcement and Safety Administration (MESA), the widows of William Duckworth and Lawrence Hyer will probably be watching very closely. Although for them, it's really too late.

It wasn't too late last January, though. James Day still had a chance then to listen to the pleas of the UMWA Safety Division and save Bill Duckworth's life. But he didn't listen, and now, hundreds of miles from Day's comfortable office in Washington, D.C., another coal miner's family just has to learn to live with its loss as best it can.

Bill Duckworth worked at Consolidation Coal Co.'s Loveridge mine in northern West Virginia. He ran a special kind of continuous miner called a "heli-miner," which was in use at a number of Consol mines. The machine is equipped with cutting wheels on the sides which produce slightly rounded corners on the sides of the roof. Consol said these rounded corners form a self-supporting arch which will prevent roof falls without any additional roof supports, even when as much as 200 feet of roof is exposed at one time.

The UMWA Safety Division did not agree that the heli-miner made roof supports unnecessary. Union officials were well aware that three men had previously been killed in a roof fall on a heli-mining section at Eastern Associated's Federal No. 2 mine. As fearful complaints from miners poured in to the Safety Division last fall, UMWA President Arnold Miller and Safety Director John Sulka went to personally inspect Consol's heli-mining system. They concluded that it was unsafe, and demanded that Consol begin to provide roof supports. Consol flatly refused.

The union took its case to James Day, acting MESA administrator. Day has the power to approve or disapprove roof control plans for the mines where heli-mining was being used. A simple order from Day and the danger could have been avoided permanently.

Day and his assistants issued no such order, however. They upheld the company position and refused to take any action.

On Jan. 24, Bill Duckworth paid with his life for James Day's inaction. As Duckworth was operating his machine, he either saw or heard the roof begin to give way. He tried to escape, but there were no supports to slow or prevent the fall, and he was crushed.

Supports were set up so that the body and the machine could be recovered from the area, but the supports were removed—with MESA approval—when mining operations resumed.

The UMWA went back to James Day, and again asked him to require roof supports in the roof control plans for heli-mining sections.

"How many more men need be slaughtered before MESA's position changes?" wrote the UMWA's Sulka to Day on Feb. 4. . . .

On May 17, Lawrence Hyer became the next victim of the song-and-dance routine coming from James Day and the MESA team. A miner operator at the Four States mine, Hyer was killed in a roof fall. The roof bolts supposedly required three months before were not there to protect him. . . .

But James Day does not seem to understand these dangers, and part of the reason is that he does not understand coal mining. He may have worked hard to get his present job, but that hard work wasn't in a coal mine, or anywhere near one. Day rose through the ranks—not of the mining industry—but of the Republican party. A Nixon campaign worker, a lawyer, and a former CIA employee, Day came to the U.S. Interior Department in 1970 not knowing the difference between a heli-miner and a helicopter. . . .

The Interior Department was a natural place for him to start. Rogers Morton, the Interior Secretary, had been chief Republican fund-raiser in 1968, and the department had generally served as a dumping ground for campaign workers and industry lobbyists. Lewis Helm, who worked with Day in both the 1964 and 1968 campaigns, had become Interior's Deputy Assistant Secretary for Programs. In case he needed other recommendations, top Nixon aides Peter Flanigan and William Timmons also knew Day's work from past campaigns.

And so, on July 1, 1970, Day was installed as director of the Office of Hearings and Appeals. . . . It was a program which assessed $28.7 million in fines against coal companies, but which was only able to collect about $5 million of that total by April, 1973, when a federal court decision forced creation of a new system. . . .

Just the slow pace of the work in Day's office was enough to stall any effective use of the Act's penalty sections to improve safety. But apparently Day felt he could do more to insure fairness to the coal companies.

Among the rules Day issued for OHA—which are still in use today—was one which could allow a company which had been issued a violation to continue the unsafe practice until a final decision had been reached at Interior, months or even years later. This rule, according to UMWA safety lawyer Davitt McAteer, appears to be in direct conflict with the letter of the 1969 Act, which said that orders would remain in effect while being appealed.

But despite his share in the assessment mess and other failures, James Day's performance was apparently just what the Nixon Administration wanted. In the spring of 1973, the Interior Department was looking for a boss in the new Mining Enforcement and Safety Administration which had been set up to take over safety enforcement from the Bureau of Mines. . . .

Although few coal miners would have agreed that Day was qualified at all for the job, he did seem to have the skills the Nixon Administration has admired in many of its staff appointments. He was, like Nixon's closest advisors, a man who cared more about how programs appeared than how they worked. He was quick with the press release and talked tough on mine safety, but a close look at what was actually accomplished revealed—behind the reassuring statements—the same old pro-industry, bureaucratic farce to which the miner had become accustomed.

Winter alert. With great fanfare, Day announced a special effort to have all inspectors on the job during the winter period when mine explosions are most likely to occur. "Non-enforcement activities by mine inspectors will be curtailed from Oct. 1, 1973 through March 1, 1974," Day's news release said.

Then, with no fanfare at all, Day pulled in 74 inspectors from their field jobs to do non-enforcement work in the assessment office—beginning Oct. 1, 1973. The 74 inspectors remained in the assessments office during the dangerous winter months, so that Day's "winter alert" turned out to be a reduction in the inspection force and not an increase.

Assessment office. Day called the assessment program a "mess" when taking over and promised to put it in order. In fact, only $2 million has been received in fines in the last year, while nearly $16 million more was assessed. . . .

New regulations. Under Day, MESA officials have talked about safety training as the key to mine safety, claiming that miners and not coal companies cause accidents. Yet regulations requiring safety training programs are no closer to being put into effect today than they were one year ago, when Day was appointed. . . .

Criminal prosecutions. Day has encouraged press coverage of the hiring of new staff members to step up prosecution of coal companies for criminal violations of the 1969 Act. The figures are still easily available for how many new investigators have been added, or how many cases are being considered. But the figures on how many cases have actually gone to trial are pathetic. Only two criminal cases have ever been pursued in court, and none of those were brought in the last 12 months. MESA blames the Justice Department, which serves as MESA's lawyer, and the Justice Department blames MESA for failing to provide strong enough evidence. Probably both are right, and meanwhile the companies get away with murder. . . .

For Day himself, a defeat [at his confirmation hearing] will not, after all, be too devastating. He apparently has substantial outside income, and he can always go back to practicing law until it's time for him to resume his real line of work in the 1976 Republican presidential campaign.

Most of the coal miners MESA is supposed to protect, on the other hand, are not likely to leave their jobs for some political assignment, and for them it could be devastating if Day is allowed to stay on. If the killings of the William Duckworths and the Lawrence Hyers and dozens of others are to be stopped, then, the next move is up to Congress.

• • •

The *Journal* article, along with other criticism, caused several additional senators to oppose Day's appointment, and President Gerald R. Ford eventually let Day's nomination lapse. Instead, said Witt, Ford nominated a man with actual mining and mine enforcement experience.

Other stories in the *Journal* of that time, often picked up by the commercial press in coal communities, also brought changes. Senator Howard Baker Jr. of Tennessee sold land after the *Journal* pointed out he would benefit from a new national recreation area being created in the vicinity. A story on how schoolchildren in coalfield communities learned about labor and mining led to new programs in several communities. A story and photograph revealing an attempted bribe to striking union officials helped keep up pressure on the company and led to a union win. Stories on racial discrimination in West Virginia coal mines drew action from the state Human Rights Commission. In 1975, the *UMW Journal* won a National Magazine Award for specialized journalism, the first labor union publication to be so honored.

After four years, however, facing a strong challenge to his reelection, Arnold Miller began to long for the old publication as a way to, he hoped, influence miners to support him. "I haven't used it that way in the past, and where has it gotten me?" Witt recounted Miller saying. A public relations company hired by the union wrote the story on the 1977 contract negotiations; Miller was pictured on the cover three times in five months. Witt, by then the editor, resigned.

PUBLIC HEALTH
AND SAFETY

FRANK LESLIE'S ILLUSTRATED NEWSPAPER ATTACKS THE SWILL MILK THAT WAS KILLING NEW YORK CHILDREN

Like most large cities, New York in the mid-1800s was filthy, garbage-strewn, and manure-laden, with rats, hogs, horses, and cows sharing the crowded streets with humans. The cows were there out of necessity: without refrigeration, milk would spoil if there was too much distance between the cow and the customer. Still, cities obviously did not provide the pasture and grain needed for healthy milk production. Unscrupulous producers often located their dairies next to distilleries, and directed the swill, a waste product of fermentation, directly to the cows' troughs. Swill had nutritional value, as Edwin Burrows and Mike Wallace noted in their comprehensive history, *Gotham*, but the cows needed hay and grain in addition, which many owners did not provide. The result was a thin, blue milk that was doctored with magnesia or chalk to be more palatable. Thousands of infants became sick and died. Meanwhile, the wealthy ordered their milk from the country.

Reformers pressed for city inspection, but the city council was reluctant to interfere with the powerful dairy owners.

In 1858, an exposé in *Frank Leslie's Illustrated Newspaper* gave the reformers crucial help. Leslie, an engraver, had come to New York from England a decade before. After success with a fashion gazette and a "journal of romance," he began his illustrated newspaper, a pictorial news weekly, in December 1855.

"The Swill Milk Trade of New York and Brooklyn." *Frank Leslie's Illustrated Newspaper,* May 8, 1858.

For the midnight assassin we have the rope and the gallows; for the robber the penitentiary; but for those who murder our children by the thousands we have neither reprobation nor punishment. They are not penal villains, but licensed trades, and though their traffic is literally in human life the Government seems powerless or unwilling to interfere. It has become a byword among the great rogues of the country that conviction is impossible where the culprit has wealth, and the existence of so high a misdemeanor in our midst as the vending of that liquid poison, swill milk, is another damning fact in support of the prevailing belief of the nullity of our laws, or the criminal inertness of our constituted authorities for protecting the rights of the citizens. If it is deemed necessary that the dispensers of narcotic drugs should distinctly mark upon them "poison," how much more necessary, nay imperative, is it that every swill milk can should be branded in its front with the word "poison" in characters of fire! The evil is not of recent date, neither is the honor of its conception due to America; but so far we can claim, that in the gigantic scheme for the legal destruction of human life we have outstripped all competitors, and the New York and Brooklyn milkman stands forth as the great modern Herod, the wholesale slaughterer of the innocents!

The nefarious swill milk business once took root in Germany, and it flourished with other festering sores upon the body corporate while the authorities looked calmly on, but the inhabitants of one town near Elberfeld, on the Rhine, in 1818, took the matter in hand, judged the facts, and administered the chastisement; they destroyed the establishment by fire, and drove out the owners from among them. This fact will show how vast these philosophical Germans deemed the evil to be, and how terribly this law-abiding people punished the miscreants who deliberately trafficked in the lives of their fellow-beings, and grew fat and then purse-proud upon the wages of death.

During the last few years we have once and again been thrown into an ecstasy of horror and astonishment by the detailed crimes of some monster who has been detected in removing to a better world some few individuals by the means of some subtle poison. A shout of execration has gone up from every Christian nation when the terrible revelations were made known, but the tens of thousands of milk murders that creep into our lists of mortality under the heads of marasmus and cholera infantum are passed over in silence, and the swill poison enders of New York and Brooklyn, like their German compeers, grown fat and purse-proud; but unlike them go unscathed of justice, and walk erect among the survivors of their yearly massacres.

The attention of the community has been called from time to time to the subject of distillery

milk. It has been brought before the public with vigor; it has been treated with earnest sincerity; but for want of sustained and combined efforts the agitation has been allowed to subside just as public attention is about to concentrate upon the active consideration of the matter. There are many reasons assigned for these unhappy failures, but there are only two which we think worthy of notice, and these tell the whole tale: First, the moneyed opposition of those so summarily arraigned at the bar of public opinion—the golden reason which convinces the judge on his bench and the editor in his sanctorum; and second, the want of means and influence of the hearty workers in a good cause, who are necessarily unable to keep the subject before the public.

The circumstances are now changed. We will supply the means and the organ to work out the salvation of our city by banishing the distillery milk manufactories from our homes and surroundings, and perchance from off the face of the land. . . .

As soon as we determined to thoroughly sift this matter, we paid a visit to Husted's distillery, situated on Skillman st. and Franklin ave., Brooklyn. The approach to it is through a collection of miserable hovels, containing, apparently, the offscourings and dregs of the foreign population, with here and there a fair-sized mansion inhabited by respectable Americans, who groan in spirit over their pestiferous surroundings. When we find ourselves in a strange neighborhood we generally inquire of the residents for the place we want, but on this occasion we had no need of this precaution, for we had only to "follow our nose"—to use an old proverb—and we arrived at the Vesuvius which belched forth the intolerable and stinking stench. The sight which greeted our eyes was detestable to our visit as was the palpable stench to our nostrils. The distiller building of Husted and Wilson, which are represented in our engraving on page 368, are wretched ramshackle hovels, blackened by the fume of the poisoning liquid which corrupts and rots everything with which it comes in contact. . . .

The stables, as we have said, are filthy in the extreme. They are long, rude wooden shanties, with roofs so low that we can touch them by extending our arms, and so thickly hung with cobwebs that we could assert that no cleansing operation had ever been carried on since the stables were erected. Our large drawing . . . gives a faithful and most accurate idea of the arrangements of the interior of the cow stables, but it is impossible by mere engraving to give the faintest conception of the dirt, the filth and the stench that abides above, below, around—that lingers lovingly in every corner and makes the atmosphere of the interior thick with revolting and life-killing miasma. The cows are ranged in double rows, their heads to the swill troughs, and their tails—or rather the remnants of tails—towards each other, and so close that sometimes one cow actually lies on the other. The space between can be better imagined than described. The distillery stuff, or swill, comes rushing and foaming down into the troughs from an upper duct connected with a tank, which is again connected with the distillery; boiling hot and reeking with subtle poison it splashes into the troughs, and the cows, at the risk of scalding their mouths, thrust their heads into it. At first the cows revolt against the swill, but after a week or two they begin to have a taste for it, and in a short time we find them consuming from one to two, and even three barrels of swill in a day. . . .

When the milk enters the human stomach its first change is coagulation, the second assimilation. If, herefore, a quantity of milk should refuse to coagulate it remains as an indigestible substance in the stomach; and we should suppose would produce the effects usual to children when their stomachs are loaded with improper food—*producing convulsions, vomiting and purging.*

We have brought the subject down to that point where its gravest consideration commences,

namely, its results upon our weekly list of deaths. This part of the subject received the closest attention of the Academy of Medicine, and the report emanating from that scientific body declares that swill milk is the principal cause of cholera infantum and marasmus, to say nothing of other diseases.

Upon examining the report of the City Inspector of New York for 1843 (before the distemper prevailed in the cow stables around New York), we find the number of deaths reported—

Under five years of age 4,588
Over five years of age 8,693

In 1856, we find the number of deaths reported—

Under five years of age 13,373
Over five years of age 8,285

Or nearly *five-eighths* of the deaths were infants under five years of age, an increased percentage of infant mortality in the past ten years that is startling to the mind of every thinking man.

From the bills of mortality in European cities, the committee find that infant mortality in New York is eight per cent above Glasgow, ten percent above Liverpool, and nearly thirteen per cent greater than London; and the per centage in those cities is decreasing, whilst it is increasing in New York. But it must be remembered that cholera infantum and the distemper that prevails in our cow stables are unknown there.

• • •

Leslie also followed half a dozen swill milk deliverers leaving their stables and published the routes of their deliveries. In the next week's issue, he proudly reported that all the routes he had published had gone out of business, and that the one dairy he had named was selling off its swill milk cows and had contracted with country dairies for healthful milk. "Is not the good work begun? May we not hope for the future?" *Leslie's* said.

The city council, though reluctant to challenge

the power of the dairy owners, ordered an investigation, but not much came from it. Four years later, the state legislature passed a law banning swill milk. The law had loopholes, but the grossest violations were eliminated.

The swill milk campaign won *Leslie's* new readers and helped guarantee the paper's survival in its rocky early years. The paper went on to cover the Civil War and the settlement of the American West and to bring a new kind of pictorial journalism to America.

THE *SAN FRANCISCO EXAMINER* HAS A REPORTER JUMP OVERBOARD TO BRING HARBOR FERRY SAFETY

In 1887, at age twenty-four, William Randolph Hearst took over the *San Francisco Examiner* from his father, a mining millionaire who had just become a United States senator. The younger Hearst assured his father that he was going to make the paper pay and he was going to change journalism on the West Coast. His father was more interested in the first, he in the second.

William Randolph Hearst quickly increased the *Examiner*'s national and international news. He spent money, his father's, on new presses and printing equipment. He increased the number of reporters and editors and paid well. He made more use of drawings. Sports stories appeared on the front page. He more than doubled the amount of space given to crime news. Writing improved; the news was presented in ways that were more personal and more like short stories. Reporters were set on the trail of corruption and incompetence in all government agencies. "*Examiner* reporters are everywhere," an editorial said in Hearst's first year. "They are the first to see everything, and the first to perceive the true meaning of what they see."

Certainly they were the first to test the lifesaving equipment on the municipal ferries. It will be clear that the writer, who was not named, was a man of much good humor.

"Overboard. An 'Examiner' Man Tests the Life-Saving Gear of the Ferry. Invisible Life Buoys. The General Public Are Recommended Not to Fall Overboard Too Often." *San Francisco Examiner,* **September 2, 1888.**

One day last week the Sad Sub-Editor, whose task it is to gather literary roses from thorny manuscript for the adornment of the *Examiner*'s Sunday supplement, was assailed by a persistent poet. All ordinary methods of defense proved unavailing, and, in his anguish, the Sad Sub-Editor devised a new formula. "I regret, sir," he said, "that your 'Ode Inspired by the Approach of Admission Day' is not available for publication in our columns, but there is something else you might do for the Sunday supplement."

"Is it fiction you want?" asked the poet. "I have in hand a love story based upon tariff reform which would make a good newspaper serial."

"No," said the sufferer, "but it occurs to me that if you would accidentally fall overboard from an Oakland ferryboat, in order to test the lifesaving appliances furnished by the company, you might make a readable story out of the incident." And the speaker chuckled within himself, thinking that he had found the panacea for poets at last.

"Sir," said the poet, "my life has a certain value. I am a bard. I have a gap in literature to fill. Why don't you do it yourself?"

For a poet, this was not bad; and as the author of the ode bowed himself out the Editorial Fifth-Wheel realized that the gun of flippancy had kicked him in its recoil. He didn't want to catch cold, spoil his clothes and be jeered at. On the other hand he didn't want to be bluffed. And at 9 o'clock the next morning, accompanied by two artists, a time-keeper, an old sailor and a sinking sensation at the pit of his stomach, he boarded the good ship *Oakland* at the foot of Market street. The artists had been chosen from the *Examiner*'s staff with great care. One was the gentleman who does flattering portraits, and the specialty of the other is water; his marine sketches fairly drip, so realistic is his touch. The timekeeper was selected because he knew where he could borrow a stop-watch, and the old salt was taken along to supply nautical terms.

The boat struck the *Oakland* slip with a dull, sickening thud—or what would have been a dull, sickening thud if the executions reporter had been present—and then started on its return journey. The Sad Sub-Editor seated himself on the rail and prepared for accidents. He knew that it would not be right to jump overboard with malice aforethought, but if he could Fill a Long-felt Public Want, and experiment on the ferryboat's ability to pick up a man, by *falling* overboard, he was ready to assist chance to any reasonable extent. He had provided himself with one of his own manuscripts—a pleasant idyl of summer resort life which he hopes some day to publish—and after reading over a few sheets of it he felt a delicious drowsiness steal over him. He dreamed that an organ-grinder, a proof-reader and the baby at his boarding-house were being burned at the stake, and was preparing to add to the company a Carson man who writes illegibly, when he awoke with a distinct impression that he was under water. The next discovery he made was that the wake of a steamboat does not afford desirable swimming-water. The keep when it has passed leaves a hole in the water (not to be too scientific), and the water behind rushes into the hole, carrying down with it empty bottles, orange peel, sub-editors, or other refuse matter with which it is encumbered. It took pretty solid swimming to overcome this undertow, and by the time he reached the surface he was so indifferent about the niceties of decorum that he took off his coat and kicked off his shoes. They sank. This is the only tragic incident of the affair, and it is to be regretted that the sub-editor cannot write verse; the coat deserves an epitaph.

By this time the boat was half a mile off (or so the old salt says—the sad-eyed one had forgotten his tape measure), and he looked round for a life buoy, not because he wanted it, of course, but because it seemed the conventional thing to do, and then he made his first Note. The life buoys are not much use, because they cannot readily be seen. The foam in the wake of the boat and the light and water in the swimmer's eyes make it almost impossible to find a small flat object on the surface of the water. Each buoy should carry a little stick with a flag on it. The writer saw one buoy and swam toward it, but subsequently saw another one nearer. The average "faller-overboard" would probably not have seen either of them, because he would have been confused and bewildered.

About this time a boat was lowered, and the details of this part of the business are furnished by the old sailor before mentioned, who watched the operation closely, and speaks with authority. First and foremost, the officers and crew of the boat deserve every possible credit. They were prompt, efficient and courteous. They must have thought the sub-editor was a confirmed fool, as a man who goes to sleep on the rail of a boat certainly would be if he had no good reason for doing so—perhaps he is anyhow, for that matter—but they treated him with the utmost consideration.

The boat, according to the timekeeper, was in the water three minutes and forty seconds after the cry of man overboard, which is excellent time. But, one or two matters require the attention of the ferry people. The boat davits are so rusty that it requires a sharp effort to turn them. The rust ought to be chipped off them and they ought to be oiled. The davit tackle falls are in such bad shape that if it had been a rainy day the boat could not have been lowered at all. The rope is three and a half inches thick and stuck in the block so much that it took a man's whole weight to overhaul the forward fall, and the boat went into the water so far down by the stern that she was nearly swamped;

this, too, when the rope was dry. If a wet day had swollen it, it would have been sticking there yet. . . . No great blame attaches to the officers; the boats are seldom required, and it is a natural blunder to neglect them—but still they ought to be looked after, and if the *Examiner*'s little expedition accomplishes this much, it will have been of public service. A smaller boat would be far more easily launched, too.

When the boat was in the water, the men began to row. This, the old salt says, was natural and proper. But one of the oars broke, which was neither natural nor proper. For no living man can break a stout oar, and this one must have been old and half decayed. The ferry authorities certainly ought to try their boats from time to time.

Notwithstanding the little hitches mentioned the boat approached the writer before he had been in the water more than six minutes, and he clambered over the side, hatless, coatless, bootless, cold and clammy. Then came the unpleasant part of the performance. To have a thousand people look at you is sometimes agreeable, if you think you are a thing of beauty. But the writer, under the most auspicious circumstances, is not a shapely man, inclining to lankiness and roundness of the back, and when he is bedraggled and wet he looks about as unlovely as a man well can. The boat was hauled up. He heard one man say, "I guess he won't get drunk again in a hurry," and a lady's voice murmured, "I think he wanted to commit suicide. I wonder if it was a love affair!" This was not pleasant. Then about a dozen men rushed at him with glasses of whisky, and he began to feel like a sneak. He was cold, and he took some of the whisky. . . .

• • •

The San Francisco city government held hearings on ferryboat safety and rules were tightened.

Stunts like the ferryboat test were a popular staple of Hearst journalism—on the *Examiner*, in New York on the *Journal*, and throughout the newspaper chain he built.

THE *CHICAGO TRIBUNE* BRINGS SAFER FOURTH OF JULY CELEBRATIONS

From the signing of the Declaration of Independence, which was then printed and dispatched by riders to be read in town squares throughout the colonies, Americans have considered the Fourth of July a special holiday. Along the way it got to be a noisy and dangerous one.

On July 4, 1899, James Keeler, managing editor of the *Chicago Tribune*, was sitting home with an ill daughter and became angered that the noise from explosions outside seemed to keep her from falling asleep. He telephoned his secretary at the *Tribune* office—they could barely hear each other because of the loud noises on each end—and ordered reporters to call thirty cities for reports on deaths and injuries from fireworks. Ten minutes later he called her back and said, Make it a thousand cities. By deadline, the *Tribune* reporters had numbers from sixty-two cities.

"Havoc of the 'Fourth.' " *Chicago Daily Tribune,* July 5, 1899.

Three Known Killed, 1,074 injured, Fire Loss, $149,105

Statistics Showing Casualties Reported in Chicago and Other Principal Cities—Toy Cannons Fatal to One and Maim 115—Firecrackers Wound 627—Explosions of Power Burn 60—Stray Bullets Catch 15—Skyrockets Claim Victims—The Lists

The foregoing is a tabulated list of the dead and injured and the losses by fire marking the celebration of the Fourth of July in the principal cities of the nation. The number of those fatally injured is large. The cannon firecracker and the toy cannon, as a rule through premature explosion, claimed the most victims. Guns and revolvers, through bursting or stray bullets, show a far less number of casualties.

In Chicago the explosion of a toy cannon caused the death of Joseph Swedek. At Hebron, Ind., the bursting of a gun, heavily loaded with dynamite, took the life of Carl King, while carelessness in handling firecrackers resulted in the dress of Katie Halley, a child 6 years of age, catching fire. Death ensued from the burns received.

The greatest loss by fire was recorded in New York City, where the flames, started in almost every instance by firecrackers and rockets, consumed property valued at $100,000. In Chicago, the Fire Department was busy, several fires breaking out in the downtown district. The damage was, however, kept within the limit of $14,000, a result due largely to the heavy rain which beat down upon the city during the morning.

Despite Mayor Harrison's proclamation forbidding the use of small cannon, firearms, dynamite crackers and other dangerous forms of fireworks on the Fourth of July, and the subsequent orders to the police to enforce the ban, one person was killed in Chicago yesterday and many injured by the use of these and other forms of explosive goods in celebrating the day.

In Oak Park and Austin accidents were particularly numerous, the number hurt in those suburbs being nearly half as many as in the entire City of Chicago outside of Austin.

Several persons were arrested during the day for violations of the law, one man being taken into custody after a child had been seriously injured by the explosion of a huge firecracker he had lighted. In general, offenders against the restrictions imposed by the Mayor escaped the notice of the police and were not arrested. Most of those hurt were children who received injuries while playing with toy cannon or firecrackers.

Chief Kipley at 6 o'clock said he had heard of numerous accidents, many of which he thought were caused by persons placing tin cans over large firecrackers. He at that hour ordered the police to arrest summarily all persons seen igniting firecrackers and placing tin cans over them.

Herewith is given a record of the day's casualties, so far as reported:

THE DEAD

Swedek, Joseph, 15 years old, 176 Bunker street, killed by explosion of a toy cannon.

THE INJURED

Alters, John, 14 years old, 666 Addison avenue; hand lacerated by explosion of giant firecracker.

Beaman, Jesse, 14 years old, South Home avenue, Oak Park, face burned by firecracker.

Bly, Lou, 26 years old, 431 Clark street; hand lacerated by exploding cannon cracker; taken to Mercy Hospital; not serious.

Brewer, Harry, 14 years old, 9–5 Fifty-first place; blinded for five hours by explosion of two cannon crackers while examining them to see if their fuses were still burning, and face badly burned; taken home. . . .

Foss, Charles, 14 years old, 975 North Robey street; badly burned about the face by the explosion of a firecracker; taken to St. Elizabeth's Hospital. . . .

Goettel, Daniel, policeman of Canalport Avenue Station, hands burned rescuing Otto Webber from live wire broken by skyrocket shaft. . . .

Jessen, Elmer, 14 years old, Humboldt boulevard and Rockwell street; burned about face by explosion of toy cannon. . . .

Lambson,—, 2-year-old daughter of W. Lambson, 416 North Walter avenue, Austin; seriously ill from eating firecrackers. . . .

Lippert, Lorene, 7 years old, 418 North Park avenue, Austin; head cut by piece of flying tin can put over firecracker. . . .

McCoy, Frank, 6 years old, 1211 Milwaukee avenue; right ear blown off and face burned by a cannon cracker thrown by Louis Daum; taken to St. Elizabeth's Hospital . . .

Olsen, Benjamin, 24 years old, 647 Humboldt street; fingers of right hand blown off by explosion of cannon cracker. . . .

Scanlon, William, 13 years old, 100 Willow avenue, Austin; left hand injured by wadding from a blank cartridge. . . .

Yellow, John, 27 year old, Thirty-first and Wallace streets, right knee cap shattered by explosion of a toy cannon; injury is serious.

Wazmy, Frank, 10 years old, 1279 Maplewood avenue, hands and face burned by explosion of toy cannon.

Wazmy, Victoria, 22 years old, 1279 Maplewood avenue; dress ignited from explosion of toy cannon; hands burned while extinguishing flames.

Wazmy, Leon, 12 years old, 1279 Maplewood avenue; burned on face and hands by explosion of toy cannon.

Webber, Otto, 12 years old; seized live electric wire which had been broken by skyrocket shaft; left arm burned, necessitating amputation.

The body of Joseph Swedek, with a deep wound in the right breast, lies at the house of his parents. The face and arms are black from powder burns.

A small toy cannon was the instrument of death. The boy had been waiting eagerly for the arrival of the Fourth, for with pennies he had saved he had purchased the cannon, with which he expected to enjoy the day's celebration. His parents had warned him against using the toy, and in the morning for awhile he amused himself with firecrackers, caps, and other small explosives.

Finally a companion suggested that the cannon be brought from the house. Joe brought it to the sidewalk. Gunpowder was secured and, surrounded by numerous children, the boy filled the cannon, placed a fuse in the powder, and applied a match.

Instantly there was a flash, a puff of black smoke, and a loud report. Most of the children had run to places of safety. After the explosion of the cannon they came running to find Joe lying on the sidewalk, his face and arms burned severely and blood flowing from a wound in the right side.

A physician was called and the boy was carried

into the house. An examination showed that the cannon had burst and a piece of it had penetrated the boy's right lung. Death was instantaneous.

The death of the boy put a damper on the celebration in Bunker street. Throughout the day groups of sad children and women stood before the house and in low tones discussed Joe's death. Children refused to handle explosives of any kind, and few more accidents were reported in that vicinity. . . .

• • •

The next day, the *Tribune* ran a more complete list, from 250 towns—reporters did not fulfill the managing editor's goal of 1,000 cities—and reported a total of 33 dead and 1,730 injured, with $233,070 of property destroyed. The accidents included ones involving frightened horses, frightened crowds, fights at holiday picnics, and men falling from balloon rides, but firecrackers were the greatest cause. "The figures of the dead, maimed and injured," the paper said, "read like the list of the casualties after a bloody battle."

After every Fourth of July for nearly thirty years, the *Tribune* kept up the list of firecracker casualties, often against opposition from readers, until the states starting passing laws restricting fireworks. It was one of the paper's few nonpolitical crusades, said John Tebbel, a journalism historian, and saved countless lives.

THE *READER'S DIGEST* BREAKS THE SILENCE ON CIGARETTES AND DEATH

Because in its early years it took no advertising, the *Reader's Digest* was immune to the considerable pressures of tobacco company advertisements, and became the only mainstream periodical to crusade against smoking. A December 1941 article signed by Gene Tunney, the retired heavyweight champ and head of the Navy's fitness program, warned that serious smokers would smell bad, cough in their sleep, and die young. In 1942, in "Cigarette Advertising Fact and Fiction," the magazine reported that tests of two dozen cigarettes revealed only a minute difference in irritation properties, prompting complaints against four cigarette manufacturers from the Federal Trade Commission. The companies dragged things out, however, and by the time the matter was settled, they had stopped using the claims in advertising.

In 1952, the *Digest* broadened its attack, reflecting new findings reported in the scientific and medical journals.

"Cancer by the Carton," by Roy Norr. *Reader's Digest,* December 1952 (Condensed from *Christian Herald*).

For three decades the medical controversy over the part played by smoking in the rise of bronchiogenic carcinoma, better known as cancer of the lung, has largely been kept from public notice. More than 26 years ago the late Dr. James Ewing, distinguished pathologist and leading spirit in the organization of the American Association for Cancer Research (now the American Cancer Society), pleaded for a public educational campaign.

"One may hardly aim to eliminate the tobacco habit," he wrote in his famous essay on cancer prevention, "but cancer propaganda should emphasize the danger signs that go with it."

No one questions that tobacco smoke irritates the mucous lining of the mouth, nose and throat, or that it aggravates hoarseness, coughing, chronic bronchitis and tonsillitis. It is accepted without argument that smoking is forbidden in cases of gastric and duodenal ulcers; that it interferes with normal digestion; that it contracts the blood vessels, increases the heart rate, raises the blood pressure. In many involvements of heart disease, the first order from the doctor is to cut out smoking immediately.

But what gives grave concern to public-health leaders is that the increase in lung-cancer mortality shows a suspicious parallel to the enormous increase in cigarette consumption (now 2500 cigarettes per year for every human being in the United States).

The latest study, which is published in *The Journal of the American Medical Association* (May 27, 1952), by a group of noted cancer workers headed by Dr. Alton Ochsner, former president of the American Cancer Society and director of the famous Ochsner Clinic in New Orleans, discloses that, during the period 1920 to 1948, deaths from bronchiogenic carcinoma in the United States *increased more than ten times*, from 1.1 to 11.3 per 100,000 of the population. From 1938 to 1948, lung-cancer deaths increased *144 percent*. At the present time cancer of the mouth and respiratory tract kills 19,000 men and 5000 women annually in the United States.

"It is probable that bronchiogenic carcinoma soon will become more frequent than any other cancer of the body, unless something is done to prevent its increase," is Dr. Ochsner's conclusion. "It is frightening to speculate on the possible number of bronchiogenic cancers that might develop as the result of the tremendous number of cigarettes consumed in the two decades from 1930 to 1950."

A survey recently published by the United Nations World Health Organization cites the conclusion of an investigation carried out by the Medical Research Council of England and Wales that "above the age of 45 the risk of developing the disease increases in simple proportion with the amount smoked, and may be 50 times as great among those who smoked 25 or more cigarettes daily as among nonsmokers."

A study of 684 cases, made by Ernest L. Wynder and Evarts A. Graham for the American Cancer Society and published in the AMA *Journal,* May 27, 1950, stated this conclusion: "Excessive and prolonged use of tobacco, especially cigarettes, seems to be an important factor in the induction of bronchiogenic carcinoma."

More recently Wynder, now associated with Memorial Cancer Center in New York, expanded the statement: "The more a person smokes the greater is the risk of developing cancer of the lung, whereas the risk was small in a nonsmoker or a light smoker."

In his summary *Some Practical Aspects of Cancer Prevention*, Wynder lists tobacco as the *major factor* in cancer of the larynx, the pharynx, the esophagus and the oral cavity. "In 1926," he points out, "Ewing wrote that 'though a great body of clinical information shows that many forms of cancer are due to preventable causes there has been little systematic research to impress this fact on the medical profession or to convey it to the public.' This was true then, as it is today."

After a study of world-wide medical opinion, Wynder reaches the same conclusion arrived at by Ewing 26 years ago. "Cancer of the lung," he reports, "presents one of the most striking opportunities for preventive measures in cancer."

Cancer workers want something done, and done now on the basis of present clinical knowledge, to alert the smoking public.

• • •

"Although it offered no fresh findings," wrote Richard Kluger in his monumental history of the tobacco industry, *Ashes to Ashes*, "the article induced chills by charging the cigarette industry with covering up the real peril of smoking through all its advertising claims of mildness and references to such relatively benign side effects of the habit as throat irritation and 'cigarette hangover.' The far graver worry was lung cancer, a disease never mentioned or alluded to in the cigarette ads. The *Digest* had taken the unmentionable subject out of the medical journals and laid it bare for the masses."

The silence of other magazines, particularly women's magazines, on the subject of the dangers of smoking undeniably caused more damage than the *Digest*'s boldness helped. Still, the article became a touchstone in the antismoking battle, which went on for decades but eventually cut the proportion of smokers from one in two adults in mid-century to one in four adults fifty years later.

RALPH NADER AND *THE NATION* OPEN THE FIGHT FOR AUTOMOBILE SAFETY

For decades, anyone who questioned the American automobile industry about car safety was told that bad drivers and bad highways caused accidents, not the cars. Besides, the companies said, they were only responding to customers' wishes: safety features cost money, and safety didn't sell. What sold was style.

But in the late 1950s, a number of safety experts, most of them based at universities, started investigating how much of the blame for automobile accidents rested in the design of the cars. One of the first accounts of this work appeared in 1959 in *The Nation*, a magazine better known for its political reportage, under editor Carey McWilliams. "The Safe Car You Can't Buy" was by a young lawyer named Ralph Nader.

"The Safe Car You Can't Buy," by Ralph Nader. *The Nation*, April 11, 1959.

The Cornell Aeronautical Laboratory has developed an exhibition automobile embodying over sixty new safety concepts which would enable an occupant to withstand a head-on collision at 50 mph with at most only minor scratches. In its design, six basic principles of crash protection were followed:

1. The car body was strengthened to prevent most external blows from distorting it against the passengers.

2. Doors were secured so that crash impacts could not open them, thereby saving passengers from ejection and maintaining the structural strength of the side of the car body.

3. Occupants were secured to prevent them from striking objects inside the car.

4. Interior knobs, projections, sharp edges and hard surfaces have been removed and the ceiling shaped to produce only glancing blows to the head (the most vulnerable part of the body during a crash).

5. The driver's environment was improved to reduce accident risk by increasing visibility, simplifying controls and instruments, and lowering the carbon monoxide of his breathing atmosphere.

6. For pedestrian safety, dangerous objects like hood ornaments were removed from the exterior.

This experimental car, developed with funds representing only a tiny fraction of the annual advertising budget of, say, Buick, is packed with applications of simple yet effective safety factors. In the wrap-around bumper system, for instance, plastic foam material between the front and rear bumpers and the back-up plates absorbs some of the shock energy; the bumpers are smoothly shaped to convert an increased proportion of blows from direct to glancing ones; the side bumpers are firmly attached to the frame, which has been extended and reinforced to provide support. Another feature is the installment of two roll-over bars into the top of the car body as added support.

It is clear that Detroit today is designing automobiles for style, cost, performance and calculated obsolescence, but not—despite the 5,000,000 reported accidents, nearly 40,000 fatalities, 110,000 permanent disabilities and 1,500,000 injuries yearly—for safety.

Almost no feature of the interior design of our current cars provides safeguards against injury in the event of collision. Doors that fly open on impact, inadequately secured seats, the sharp-edged rear-view mirror, pointed knobs on instrument panels and doors, flying glass, the overhead structure—all illustrate the lethal potential of poor design. A sudden deceleration turns a collapsed steering wheel or a sharp-edged dashboard into a bone- and chest-crushing agent. Penetration of the shatterproof windshield can chisel one's head into fractions. A flying seat cushion can cause a fatal injury. The apparently harmless glove-compartment door has been known to unlatch under impact and guillotine a child. Roof-supporting structure has deteriorated to a point where it provides scarcely more protection to the occupants, in common roll-over accidents, than an open convertible. This is especially true of the so-called "hardtops." Nor is the automobile designed as an efficient force moderator. For example, the bumper does not contribute significantly to reduction of the crash deceleration forces that are transmitted to the motorist; its function has been more to reflect style than absorb shock.

These weaknesses of modern automobile construction have been established by the investigation of several groups, including the Automotive Crash Injury Research of the Cornell University Medical College, the Institute of Transportation and Traffic Engineering of the University of California and the Motor Vehicle Research of Lee, New Hampshire. . . .

The remarkable advances in crash-protection knowledge achieved by these research organizations at a cost of some $6 million stands in marked contrast to the glacier-like movements of car manufacturers, who spend that much to enrich the sound of a door slam. This is not due to any dearth of skill—the industry possesses many able, frustrated safety engineers whose suggestions over the years invariably have taken a back seat to those of the stylist. In 1938, an expert had this to say in *Safety Engineering*:

The motor industry must face the fact that accidents occur. It is their duty, therefore, to so design the interiors of automobiles that when the passenger is tossed around, he will get an even break and not suffer a preventable injury in accidents that are today taking a heavy toll.

In 1954, nearly 600,000 fatalities later, a U.C.L.A. engineer could conclude that "There has been no significant automotive-engineering contribution to the safety of motorists since about the beginning of World War II. . . ." In its 1955 annual report, the Cornell crash-research group came to a similar conclusion, adding that "the newer model automobiles [1950–54] are increasing the rate of fatalities in injury-producing accidents."

In 1956, Ford introduced the double-grip safety-door latch, the "dished" steering wheel, and instrument panel-padding; the rest of the industry followed with something less than enthusiasm. Even in these changes, style remained the dominant consideration, and their effectiveness is in doubt. Tests have failed to establish, for example, an advantage for the "deep-dish" steering wheel compared with the conventional wheel; the motorist will still collapse the rim to the hub.

This year, these small concessions to safety design have virtually been discontinued. "A square foot of chrome sells ten times more cars than the best safety-door latch," declared one industry representative. . . .

Prevailing analyses of vehicular accidents circulated for popular consumption tend to impede constructive thinking by adherence to some monistic theory of causation. Take one of the more publicized ogres—speed. Cornell's findings, based on data covering 3,203 cars in injury-producing accidents, indicate that 74 per cent of the cars

were going at a *traveling* speed under 60 mph and about 88 per cent involved *impact* speeds under 60 mph. The average impact speed on urban roads was 27 mph; on rural roads, 41 mph. Dangerous or fatal injuries observed in accidents when the traveling speed was less than 60 mph are influenced far more by the shape and structure of interior car components with which the body came into contact than by the speed at which the cars were moving. . . .

In brief, automobiles are so designed as to be dangerous at any speed.

Our preoccupation has been almost entirely with the cause of accidents seen primarily in terms of the driver and not with the instruments that produce the injuries. Erratic driving will always be characteristic, to some degree, of the traffic scene; exhortation and stricter law enforcement have at best a limited effect. Much more significant for saving life is the application of engineering remedies to minimize the lethal effects of human error by designing the automobile so as to afford maximum protection to occupants in the event of a collision. In a word, the job, in part, is to make accidents safe.

The task of publicizing the relation between automotive design and highway casualties is fraught with difficulties. The press, radio and television are not likely to undertake this task in terms of industry responsibility when millions in advertising dollars are being poured into their coffers. Private researchers are reluctant to stray from their scholarly and experimental pursuits, especially when cordial relations with the industry are necessary for the continuation of their projects with the maximum of success. Car manufacturers have thought it best to cooperate with some of these programs and, in one case, when findings became embarrassing, have given financial support. The industry's policy is bearing fruit; most investigators discreetly keep their private disgust with the industry's immobility from seeping into the limelight. . . .

———

By all relevant criteria, a problem so national in scope and technical in nature can best be handled by the legislative process, on the federal level, with delegation to an appropriate administrative body. It requires uniformity in treatment and central administration, for as an interstate matter, the job cannot be left to the states with their dissimilar laws setting low requirements that are not strictly enforced and that do not strike at the heart of the malady—the blueprint on the Detroit drawing board. The thirty-three-year record of the attempt to introduce state uniformity in establishing the most basic equipment standards for automobiles has been disappointing.

Perhaps the best summation of the whole issue lies in a physician's comment on the car manufacturer's design policy: "Translated into medicine," he writes, "it would be comparable to withholding known methods of life-saving value."

• • •

The Nation article was a preview of Nader's 1965 book, *Unsafe at Any Speed*, which was particularly critical of the Chevrolet Corvair, a General Motors car with a tendency to overturn. The book was selling nicely but drawing little major attention until it was revealed, by James Ridgeway in the March 12, 1966, issue of *The New Republic*, that Nader was being investigated by private agents. It soon became the unhappy task of an executive in the General Motors headquarters in Detroit to tell James M. Roche, the president of the company, that, yes, GM had put detectives on Nader's trail.

A Senate subcommittee under Abraham Ribicoff of Connecticut, Nader's home state, and Robert F. Kennedy of New York summoned Roche to testify. Roche, wisely, apologized. But he still maintained that the corporation had a right to check out Nader, and the testimony of the private detective GM had hired only angered some senators more. The incident rallied the politicians, government staffers, and safety experts who had been working to set federal standards for automobiles. Congress passed the Traffic and Motor

Vehicle Safety Act of 1966 overwhelmingly. President Lyndon B. Johnson signed it on September 9. Federal rules regarding seat belts, air bags, manufacturers' recalls, crash tests, and other safety factors can be traced to that act.

Nader emerged from the hearings a public figure, and he used his constituency to keep the pressure on the automobile industry and to press for changes in meatpacking, poultry processing, airlines, coal mines, air pollution, and occupational safety, among other areas. He went on to become a watchdog not only of corporations, but of government agencies and Congress. In 1970, using part of the $425,000 settlement from his lawsuit against General Motors, Nader founded the Public Interest Research Group in Washington, D.C., which has since spread throughout the country. In 1996 and 2000, Nader was, unsuccessfully, the Green Party candidate for the presidency of the United States.

NICK KOTZ OF THE *DES MOINES (IOWA) REGISTER* FINDS LOOPHOLES IN FEDERAL MEAT LAWS

The name seemed so reassuring to the stomach of a nation that had been appalled by the wrenching conditions in stockyards and packinghouses revealed in Upton Sinclair's powerful novel *The Jungle*. Surely under the "Pure Food and Drug Act" and the "Federal Meat Inspection Act," both passed in 1906, the problem would be solved.

But the federal meat inspections covered only the meat that moved in interstate commerce. By the 1960s, that left out about one in four pounds of meat purchased in supermarkets and butcher shops. State standards and inspection varied widely. An Iowa congressman, Neal Smith, trying to win publicity for an effort to tighten inspection, tipped a *Des Moines Register–Minneapolis Star-Tribune* reporter, Nick Kotz, to the problem of "dirty meat." Sympathetic officials at the U.S. Department of Agriculture provided the key documents.

"Ask Tighter Law on Meat Inspections," by Nick Kotz. *Des Moines Register,* July 16, 1967.

The vast majority of American meat products are federally inspected to insure wholesomeness, but a confidential nation-wide investigation has revealed shocking abuses in some segments of the non-regulated meat industry.

The investigation was made five years ago by the United States Department of Agriculture (USDA), to find out conditions in non-federally regulated plants which slaughter 20 million cattle and process 8.7 billion pounds of meat.

This amounts to about 15 per cent of all cattle slaughtered in the United States and about 25 per cent of all the meat processed in the nation.

The investigation convinced USDA officials and a few congressmen, including Representative Neal Smith (Dem., Ia.), that the 1906 meat inspection law badly needs overhauling.

The Johnson administration and Smith tried two years ago for enactment of a strong law which would have required states to meet federal inspection standards or else have the federal government expand its inspection to cover intrastate slaughtering and processing.

The bill was buried in committee because of opposition from most of the meat industry and the National Association of State Departments of Agriculture (N.A.S.D.A.)

This year the administration and Smith have obtained a house subcommittee hearing for two much weaker bills which they regard as at least a start toward more comprehensive meat inspection.

Details of the USDA investigation, the only data collected on the condition of federally uninspected meat plants in the nation, are coming to light for the first time now that congressional action appears possible.

Iowa adopted a mandatory inspection law in 1965 and is among 25 states providing inspection of both slaughtering and processing. A total of 147,000 animals were slaughtered in 1966 without federal inspection. All of this meat must be sold within Iowa.

Smith says he became interested in the meat inspection issue after noticing at Iowa cattle auctions "that whenever they would sell a cancer-eye cow or diseased hog" the purchaser inevitably was a packer who is not covered by federal inspection.

One packer who Smith has observed buying diseased animals for Iowa use was also described by federal investigators as the operator of an unsanitary plant in Nebraska.

Only meat sold in inter-state commerce is covered by the 1906 federal inspection law—a law virtually unchanged since Upton Sinclair provoked it with his shocking book about the meat industry.

Most USDA experts believe conditions have not changed substantially since a federal meat inspector five years ago reported these conditions in a Minnesota meat packing plant:

"Both the saw and the inspection truck were sterilized with a hot water hose with the result that pus from abcesses and other disease-carrying media was splashed on nearby carcasses."

At another uninspected plant in Minnesota, the federal inspector reported:

"Hooks and racks in the cooler were not clean. I feel that they had at least a week's accumulation of tissue and meat juice."

At yet another Minnesota plant exempt from federal inspection, the investigator reported:

"In checking a meat grinder, it was determined that—although the piece of equipment had been used this day, here was an accumulation of tissue which had been from some previous day's operation."

At still another Minnesota plant, an inspector reporting watching a carcass being washed with a high pressure hose which "resulted in manure and urine being washed on the open brisket and neck."

At a South Dakota plant exempt from federal inspection, an investigator reported:

"The carcass splitting saw was dirty, with accumulated grease, fat and oil. The general sanitation of the plant was such that it was inexcusably dirty.

"All walls and doors were splattered with blood, fat, and grease. I noticed sausages on trees that were dragging through puddles of water on the floor, which is gross contamination."

At a Nebraska processing plant of the owner who also operates in Iowa the federal investigator reported:

"In the beef boning room, one's attention was first called to the odor of putrid meat product. A good many flies were observed in the sausage manufacture room and, of course, crawl upon and contaminate meat products." . . .

At another uninspected Nebraska plant, the investigator reported moldy sausage products were observed in the holding cooler.

At both Nebraska plants, the inspector reported that products labeled "all-meat" wieners actually contained 6 per cent filler products, a practice which would be forbidden under federal inspection.

Similar conditions were found throughout the nation in the USDA investigation.

The investigation showed many federally inspected plants or non-inspected plants were meeting federal standards, but it also revealed abuses at some plants in almost every state.

State and local inspection laws vary widely as does the quality of non-federal inspection.

Minnesota and South Dakota are among nine states which do not provide for state inspection of meat.

In 1966, a total of 206,000 Minnesota animals and 80,000 South Dakota animals were slaughtered without federal inspection.

Nebraska and North Dakota are among 13 other states which only provide for voluntary in-

spection of slaughtering. Neither state has any inspection of meat processing. In 1966, 162,000 Nebraska animals and 28,900 North Dakota animals were slaughtered without federal inspection.

The following list shows the total number of slaughtering and processing plants in Iowa and the upper midwest and the number undergoing federal inspection. The Nebraska figures show only slaughter plants.

STATE	TOTAL PLANTS	FEDERALLY INSPECTED
Iowa	847	41
Minnesota	887	46
Nebraska	345	51
South Dakota	232	9
North Dakota	98	9
Wisconsin	701	43

The vast majority of meat production in each of these states is conducted by the large national companies in the relatively few federally inspected plants.

National firms, along with smaller companies, also operate plants not federally inspected in order to compete in local and state markets.

Consumers can identify processed meat products inspected by the federal government by a circle on the package with the wording "U.S. Department of Agriculture Approved for Wholesomeness" and raw meat by a purple stamp reading "USDA Approved."

The administration's proposed Wholesome Meat Act, sponsored by Smith, would:

Provide federal-state agreements under which the federal government would pay 50 per cent of the cost and supply technical assistance to states willing to establish and enforce federal inspection standards.

Provide tools of enforcement not presently authorized by the federal government to checkmate the distribution of unwholesome and adulterated meat products. Controls would be placed upon animal food manufacturers and their distributors to guarantee that their products do not find their way into channels of human consumption.

Broaden the authority of federal coverage to include all meat "capable of" human consumption. At present federal control is limited to meat "intended for" human consumption, which has permitted unscrupulous operators in contaminated meat to escape federal inspection.

Provide the federal government with powers of detention, injunctions, and federal court actions to cope with contaminated meat discovered in transit or outside of federally-inspected establishments. At present, the USDA cannot detain such meat, except by getting assistance from other federal, state or local agencies.

In addition, Smith has introduced another bill which would broaden coverage of federal inspection to include large intrastate plants which are covered by provisions of the Taft-Hartley law, but not the meat inspection act.

Noting the inadequacy of state inspection, Rodney Leonard, deputy assistant secretary of agriculture, testified before the House subcommittee:

"Inspection under state programs is generally well below federal standards. Yet, these products are intermingled in many retail stories with federally inspected products for sale to the unknowing public.

"Administrators of state meat inspection programs generally admit they have neither the money nor managers to conduct an intensive, continuous inspection service for both slaughtering and processing operations."

He added that variations between federal standards and those in many states permit use of "excessive water and extenders, chemicals that mask the true conditions of products, and misleading or deceptive labeling."

Leonard stressed that modern technology, in addition to providing a wide variety of better products, has made it easier for unscrupulous operators to disguise the true condition of meat.

Thus, he said, far more sophisticated methods of inspection and analysis are needed to protect the consumer.

"We are dealing with problems not conceived by those who drafted the original legislation 60 years ago," said Leonard.

"The act is becoming increasingly inadequate to deal with the problems of today's modern aggressive industry."

Calling for federal or state control over dealers in unwholesome meat products, he said:

"It is far too easy for dealers in dead animals, renderers, animal food handlers and others to divert unfit meat into human channels."

Leonard and Smith stress that the main hope of the legislation is that states will accept federal assistance to improve or institute their own inspection programs.

The bill has a few strong allies, including the Amalgamated Meat Cutters and Butcher Workmen (A.F.L.-C.I.O).

Arnold Mayer, legislative representative for the union, called for even stronger legislation and testified:

"Live cattle which obviously cannot pass inspection are sent to uninspected plants. This is done not only by the small number of get-rich-quick operators but also by some highly reputable firms.

"The very competitive situation in the industry currently leaves them no alternative. Only Congress can break this cycle by extending meat inspection and by providing the same rules for all."

Mayer also emphasized that even an expert often has a difficult time determining whether good or diseased meat has gone into ground hamburger or processed salami.

The National Farmers Organization and the National Livestock Feeders Association have testified for the bill. Companies who have their products federally inspected are quietly supporting the bill.

The bill also has numerous opponents. The National Farm Bureau Federation opposes it as a further intrusion of federal control into state affairs.

The National Meat Institute, representing the large national firms, and the Independent Meat Packers Association, representing smaller companies, both are professing neutrality, except for proposing changes which supporters feel would weaken the bill.

The National Association of State Departments of Agriculture (N.A.S.D.A.) also proposes changes, which the USDA feels would eliminate the needed new authority to control operations or renderers and dog-cat food manufacturers.

After long years of seeking increased regulation, supporters are wary about what the N.A.S.D.A. and the Meat Association may be doing behind the scenes.

• • •

The meat industry reacted vehemently, as it had against Sinclair and *The Jungle*, and marshaled its considerable political power to downplay what it was doing and delay congressional action. But the story spread and the cause was taken up by consumer advocates. At the end of the year, in part because the industry wanted to head off something worse, the Wholesome Meat Act was passed, giving federal help to states that would bring their inspection standards up to federal levels. One of President Lyndon B. Johnson's guests at the signing was Upton Sinclair, eighty-nine and in a wheelchair.

Even with the act, slow movement by the states, political pressure, and budget cuts meant that abuses continued. More importantly, the technology of the large packing plants that soon became the norm made the traditional "poke-and-sniff" method of inspection inadequate. Several outbreaks of bacterial inspection that led to deaths in the 1990s brought the issue back to attention. In January 2000, the magazine *Meat and Poultry*, an industry publication, ran a cover article

called "The Jungle Revisited," examining new problems in the industry and illustrating the need for continuing vigilance of the nation's food supply.

BLACKS AS GUINEA PIGS: THE ASSOCIATED PRESS UNCOVERS THE TUSKEGEE SYPHILIS STUDY

Macon County, Alabama, was a very poor, mostly rural county in the 1930s, with about 27,000 residents, four-fifths of them black. It also had a syphilis infection rate of 36 percent, the highest in the nation, with the rate for blacks nearly twice that for whites. And it had a medical center, at the Tuskegee Institute, where doctors from the U.S. Public Health Service could conveniently work. The three conditions made the county a logical choice—an "unparalleled opportunity," the founding doctors put it—for the Tuskegee Study of Untreated Syphilis in the Negro Male, a shocking experiment in which black men with syphilis were regularly tested so that the effects of the disease could be tracked. The men were not told what was wrong with them, and a portion of them never received any treatment, even after the mid-1940s, when penicillin was proven to be an effective treatment of syphilis.

Clearly the men did not realize what was going on. Clearly, too, the scientists involved lost sight of the implicit moral questions and their doctors' pledge to "first, do no harm." Not until the mid-1960s did a few doctors start raising questions. Even then, the Public Health Service's response was to convene a panel, which approved of the study's being continued, and to consult with the local Alabama medical society, and black doctors, who also approved.

In early 1972, Peter Buxton, a frustrated former interviewer for the Public Health Service, told the story about the experiment to a friend who worked for the Associated Press. The assignment went to Jean Heller in the Washington bureau. Surprisingly, she said, the story was easy to get, for the Public Health Service answered all her questions quickly.

"Syphilis Patients Died Untreated," by Jean Heller. Associated Press, July 25, 1972.

For 40 years the U.S. Public Health Service has conducted a study in which human guinea pigs, not given proper medical treatment, have died of syphilis and its side effects.

The study was conducted to determine from autopsies what the disease does to the human body.

PHS officials responsible for initiating the experiment have long since retired. Current PHS officials, who say they have serious doubts about the morality of the study, also say it is now too late to treat syphilis in any of the study's surviving volunteers.

But PHS doctors say they are rendering whatever other medical services they can give to the survivors while the study of the disease's effects continues.

The experiment, called the Tuskegee Study, began in 1931 with about 600 black men, mostly poor and uneducated, from Tuskegee, Ala., an area which had the highest syphilis rate in the nation at the time.

One-third of the group was free of syphilis; two-thirds showed evidence of the disease. In the syphilitic group, half were given the best treatment known at the time, but the other half, about 200 men, received no treatment at all for syphilis, PHS officials say.

As incentives to enter the program, the men were promised free transportation to and from hospitals, free hot lunches, free medicine for any diseases other than syphilis and free burial after autopsies were performed.

The Tuskegee Study began 10 years before

penicillin was discovered to be a cure for syphilis and 15 years before the drug became widely available. Yet even after penicillin became common, and while its use probably could have helped or saved a number of the experiment subjects, the drug was not given to them, according to Dr. J. D. Millar.

He is chief of the venereal disease branch of the PHS's Center for Disease Control in Atlanta and is now in charge of what remains of the Tuskegee Study. Dr. Millar said in an interview he has serious doubts about the program.

"I think a definite moral problem existed when the study was undertaken; a more serious moral problem was overlooked in the post-war years when penicillin became available but was not given to these men; and a moral problem still exists," Dr. Millar said.

"But the study began when attitudes were much different on treatment and experimentation. At this point in time, with our current knowledge of treatment and the disease and the revolutionary change in approach to human experimentation, I don't believe the program would be undertaken," he said.

Syphilis, a highly infectious disease spread by sexual contact, can cause, if untreated, bone and dental deformations, deafness, blindness, heart disease and central nervous system deterioration.

No figures were available on when the last death occurred in the program. And one official said that apparently no conscious effort to halt the program was made after it got underway.

A 1969 Center for Disease Control study of 276 treated and untreated syphilitics who participated in the Tuskegee Study showed that seven had died as a direct result of syphilis. Another 154 died of heart disease. CDC officials say they cannot determine at this late date how many of the heart disease deaths were caused by syphilis or how many additional deaths could be linked to the disease.

Don Prince, another official of the Center for

Disease Control, said that he does not know the names of PHS officials who initiated the study.

Like Dr. Millar, he said he believes the study should have been concluded with penicillin treatment after World War II.

"I don't know why the decision was made in 1946 not to stop the program," Prince said. "I was unpleasantly surprised when I first came here and found out about it. It really puzzles me."

At the beginning of 1972, according to center data, 74 of the untreated syphilitics were still living. All of them, Dr. Millar said, were men who did not suffer any potentially fatal side effects from their bouts with the disease.

Some of them received penicillin and antibiotics in past years for other ailments, Prince said, but none has ever received treatment for syphilis. Now, both men agree, it's too late.

Recent reviews of the Tuskegee Study by CDC indicate that treatment now for survivors is medically questionable, Dr. Millar said. Their average age is 74 and massive penicillin therapy, with possible ill side effects, is deemed too great a risk to the individuals, particularly for those whose syphilis is now dormant.

However, Dr. Millar added, there was a point in time when survivors could have been treated with at least some measure of success.

"The most critical moral issue about this experiment arises in the post-war era, the years after the end of World War II when penicillin became widely available.

"Looking at it now, one cannot see any reason they could not have been treated directly for syphilis at that time."

For survivors of the Tuskegee Study, the PHS is currently providing the best medical treatment it can, Prince said.

"We see to it that they get a complete physical at least every two years," he said. "We can't treat them for syphilis but we can treat them for her-

nias and arthritis and any other problems they have. I guess you'd say we're doing all we can."

• • •

When one reads the story now, it seems unusual that relatively little is made of the fact that the subjects of the study were black, for that has come to be the strongest legacy of the study. To this day, blacks shy away from participation in medical studies and many believe that any new medical problem, such as AIDS, is just an indication that white society is out to get them. Why do they think that? Time and again, the answer is Tuskegee. "No scientific experiment inflicted more damage on the collective psyche of black Americans," said James Jones, author of *Bad Blood*, a history of the experiment.

Responding to the uproar caused by the Heller story, the government announced an investigation, and, this time, its own commission called the experiment ethically unsound. The remaining participants were tracked down and, finally, given health care. The men sued. In December 1974, the government agreed to a $10 million out-of-court settlement, including $37,500 to each of the approximately 120 men whose syphilis had gone untreated all those years.

Tuskegee also showed the need for tough new regulations on human experiments, with special attention to the conditions under which a person could give informed consent to participation. Hospitals, universities, states, and the federal government now have ethical review procedures governing medical experiments.

In May 1997, President Bill Clinton had five of the eight remaining survivors of the Tuskegee experiment to the White House and, on behalf of the country, apologized to them. "What was done cannot be undone, but we can end the silence," he said, adding, "What the United States did was shameful, and I am sorry."

"PINTO MADNESS": *MOTHER JONES'S* MARK DOWIE SAYS FORD MOTOR COMPANY PUTS COSTS ABOVE SAFETY

Trying to counter the enormous popularity of the Volkswagen Beetle and small Japanese imports in the late 1960s, American automakers abandoned their cherished fondness for big cars and focused on developing new subcompacts. Ford Motor Company entered this market in the 1971 model year with the Ford Pinto, shepherded by the company president, Lee Iacocca, who had had major success with the sporty Ford Mustang. The Pinto sold well, its $2,000 price putting it within reach of many new buyers, and became the most popular American make. But problems were quickly obvious: when hit from behind, the car tended to leak fuel and explode. Lawsuits were being filed by victims and their families. Ford defended itself aggressively and was largely able to keep its problems quiet. Then the Pinto came to the attention of *Mother Jones,* a progressive weekly founded in 1976 and named for Mary Harris Jones, a pioneer labor organizer and radical agitator.

"Pinto Madness,"
by Mark Dowie.
Mother Jones, September–October 1977.

One evening in the mid-1960s, Arjay Miller was driving home from his office in Dearborn, Michigan, in the four-door Lincoln Continental that went with his job as president of the Ford Motor Company. On a crowded highway, another car struck his from the rear. The Continental spun around and burst into flames. Because he was wearing a shoulder-strap seat belt, Miller was unharmed by the crash, and because his door didn't jam he escaped the gasoline-drenched, flaming wreck. But the accident made a vivid impression on him. Several months later, on July 15, 1965, he recounted it to a U.S. Senate subcommittee

that was hearing testimony on auto safety legislation. "I still have burning in my mind the image of that gas tank on fire," Miller said. He went on to express an almost passionate interest in controlling fuel-fed fires in cars that crash or roll over. He spoke with excitement about the fabric gas tank Ford was testing at that very moment. "If it proves out," he promised the senators, "it will be a feature you will see in our standard cars."

Almost seven years after Miller's testimony, a woman, whom for legal reasons we will call Sandra Gillespie, pulled onto a Minneapolis highway in her new Ford Pinto. Riding with her was a young boy, whom we'll call Robbie Carlton. As she entered a merge lane, Sandra Gillespie's car stalled. Another car rear-ended hers at an impact speed of 28 miles per hour. The Pinto's gas tank ruptured. Vapors from it mixed quickly with the air in the passenger compartment. A spark ignited the mixture and the car exploded [Gillespie died in the hospital]. Her passenger, 13-year-old Robbie Carlton, is still alive; he has just come home from another futile operation aimed at grafting a new ear and nose from skin on the few unscarred portions of his badly burned body. (This accident is real; the details are from police reports.)

Why did Sandra Gillespie's Ford Pinto catch fire so easily, seven years after Ford's Arjay Miller made his apparently sincere pronouncements— the same seven years that brought more safety improvements to cars than any other period in automotive history? An extensive investigation by *Mother Jones* over the past six months has found these answers:

• Fighting strong competition from Volkswagen for the lucrative small-car market, the Ford Motor Company rushed the Pinto into production in much less than the usual time.

• Ford engineers discovered in preproduction crash tests that rear-end collisions would rupture the Pinto's fuel system extremely easily.

• Because assembly-line machinery was already tooled when engineers found this defect, top Ford officials decided to manufacture the car anyway—exploding gas tank and all—*even though Ford owned the patent on a much safer gas tank.*

• For more than eight years afterwards, Ford successfully lobbied, with extraordinary vigor and some blatant lies, against a key government safety standard that would have forced the company to change the Pinto's fire-prone gas tank.

By conservative estimates Pinto crashes have caused 500 burn deaths to people who would not have been seriously injured if the car had not burst into flames. The figure could be as high as 900. Burning Pintos have become such an embarrassment to Ford that its advertising agency, J. Walter Thompson, dropped a line from the end of a radio spot that read "Pinto leaves you with that warm feeling."

Ford knows the Pinto is a firetrap, yet it has paid out millions to settle damage suits out of court, and it is prepared to spend millions more lobbying against safety standards. With a half million cars rolling off the assembly lines each year, Pinto is the biggest-selling subcompact in America, and the company's operating profit on the car is fantastic. Finally, in 1977, new Pinto models have incorporated a few minor alterations necessary to meet that federal standard Ford managed to hold off for eight years. Why did the company delay so long in making these minimal, inexpensive improvements?

Ford waited eight years because its internal "cost-benefit analysis," *which places a dollar value on human life*, said it wasn't profitable to make the changes sooner.

Before we get to the question of how much Ford thinks your life is worth, let's trace the his-

tory of the death trap itself. Although this particular story is about the Pinto, the way in which Ford made its decision is typical of the U.S. auto industry generally. There are plenty of similar stories about other cars made by other companies. But this case is the worst of them all.

The next time you drive behind a Pinto (with over two million of them on the road, you shouldn't have much trouble finding one), take a look at the read end. That long silvery object hanging down under the bumper is the gas tank. The tank begins about six inches forward of the bumper. In late models the bumper is designed to withstand a collision of only about five miles per hour. Earlier bumpers may as well not have been on the car for all the protection they offered the gas tank.

Mother Jones has studied hundreds of reports and documents on rear-end collisions involving Pintos. These reports conclusively reveal that if you ran into that Pinto you were following at over 30 miles per hour, the rear end of the car would buckle like an accordion, right up to the back seat. The tube leading to the gas-tank cap would be ripped away from the tank itself, and gas would immediately begin sloshing onto the road around the car. The buckled gas tank would be jammed up against the differential housing (that big bulge in the middle of your rear axle), which contains four sharp, protruding bolts likely to gash holes in the tank and spill still more gas. Now all you need is a spark from a cigarette, ignition, or scraping metal, and both cars would be engulfed in flames. If you gave that Pinto a really good whack—say, at 40 mph—chances are excellent that its doors would jam and you would have to stand by and watch its trapped passengers burn to death.

This scenario is no news to Ford. Internal company documents in our possession show that Ford has crash-tested the Pinto at a top-secret site more than 40 times, and that *every* test made at over 25 mph without special structural alteration the car has resulted in a ruptured fuel tank. Despite this, Ford officials denied under oath having crash-tested the Pinto. . . .

Whether Ford should manufacture subcompacts at all was the subject of a bitter two-year debate at the company's Dearborn headquarters. The principals in this corporate struggle were the then-president Semon "Bunky" Knudsen, whom Henry Ford II had hired away from General Motors, and Lee Iacocca, a spunky Young Turk who had risen fast within the company on the enormous success of the Mustang. Iacocca argued forcefully that Volkswagen and the Japanese were going to capture the entire American subcompact market unless Ford put out its own alternative to the VW Beetle. Bunky Knudsen said, in effect: let them have the small-car market; Ford makes good money on medium and large models. But he lost the battle and later resigned. Iacocca became president and almost immediately began a rush program to produce the Pinto.

Like the Mustang, the Pinto became known in the company as "Lee's car." Lee Iacocca wanted that little car in the showrooms of America with the 1971 models. So he ordered his engineering vice president, Bob Alexander, to oversee what was probably the shortest production planning period in modern automotive history. The normal time span from conception to production of a new car model is about 43 months. The Pinto schedule was set at just under 25. . . .

Design, styling, product planning, advance engineering and quality assurance all have flexible time frames, and engineers can pretty much carry these on simultaneously. Tooling, on the other hand, has a fixed time frame of about 18 months. Normally, an auto company doesn't begin tooling until the other processes are almost over: you don't want to make the machines that stamp and press and grind metal into the shape of car parts until you know all those parts will work well together. *But Iacocca's speed-up meant Pinto tooling went on at the same time as product development.* So when

crash tests revealed a serious defect in the gas tank, it was too late. The tooling was well under way.

When it was discovered the gas tank was unsafe, did anyone go to Iacocca and tell him? "Hell no," replied an engineer who worked on the Pinto, a high company official for many years, who, unlike several others at Ford, maintains a necessarily clandestine concern for safety. "That person would have been fired. Safety wasn't a popular subject around Ford in those days. With Lee it was taboo. Whenever a problem was raised that meant a delay on the Pinto, Lee would chomp on his cigar, look out the window and say, 'Read the product objectives and get back to work.'"

Heightening the anti-safety pressure on Pinto engineers was an important goal set by Iacocca known as "the limits of 2,000." The Pinto was not to weigh an ounce over 2,000 pounds and not to cost a cent over $2,000. "Iacocca enforced these limits with an iron hand," recalls the engineer quoted earlier. So, even when a crash test showed that that a one-pound, one-dollar piece of plastic stopped the puncture of the gas tank, it was thrown out as extra cost and extra weight.

People shopping for subcompacts are watching every dollar. "You have to keep in mind," the engineer explained, "that the price elasticity on these subcompacts is extremely tight. You can price yourself right out of the market by adding $25 to the production cost of the model. And nobody understands that better than Iacocca."

Dr. Leslie Ball, the retired safety chief for the NASA manned space program and a founder of the International Society of Reliability Engineers, recently made a careful study of the Pinto. "The release to production of the Pinto was the most reprehensible decision in the history of American engineering," he said. Ball can name more than 40 European and Japanese models in the Pinto price and weight range with safer gas-tank positioning. Ironically, many of them, like the Ford Capri, contain a "saddle-type" gas tank riding over the back axle. *The patent on the saddle-type tank is owned by the Ford Motor Co.*

Blame for Sandra Gillespie's death, Robbie Carlton's unrecognizable face and all the other injuries and deaths in Pintos since 1970 does not rest on the shoulders of Lee Iacocca alone. For, while he and his associates fought their battle against a safer Pinto in Dearborn, a larger war against safer cars raged in Washington. One skirmish in that war involved Ford's successful eight-year lobbying effort against Federal Motor Vehicle Safety Standard 301, the rear-end provisions of which would have forced Ford to redesign the Pinto.

Pinto lawsuits began mounting fast against Ford. Says John Versace, executive safety engineer at Ford's Safety Research Center, "Ulcers are running pretty high among the engineers who worked on the Pinto. Every lawyer in the country seems to want to take their depositions." ...

When the Pinto liability suits began, Ford strategy was to go to a jury. Confident it could hide the Pinto crash tests, Ford thought that juries of solid American registered voters would buy the industry doctrine that drivers, not cars, cause accidents. It didn't work. It seems that juries are much quicker to see the truth than bureaucracies, a fact that gives one confidence in democracy. Juries began ruling against the company, granting million-dollar awards to plaintiffs.

"We'll never go to a jury again," says Al Slechter in Ford's Washington office. "Not in a fire case. Juries are just too sentimental. They see those charred remains and forget the evidence. No sir, we'll settle."

... Until recently, it was clear that, whatever the cost of these settlements, it was not enough to seriously cut into the Pinto's enormous profits. The cost of retooling Pinto assembly lines and of

equipping each car with a safety gadget like that $5.08 Goodyear bladder was, company accountants calculated, greater than that of paying out millions to survivors like Robbie Carlton or to widows and widowers of victims like Sandra Gillespie. The bottom line ruled, and inflammable Pintos kept rolling out of the factories.

In 1977, however, an incredibly sluggish government has at last instituted Standard 301. Now Pintos will have to have rupture-proof gas tanks. Or will they?

Whether the new American Pinto fails or passes the test, Standard 301 will never force the company to test or recall the more than two million pre-1977 Pintos still on the highway. Seventy or more people will burn to death in those cars every year for many years to come. If the past is any indication, Ford will continue to accept the deaths.

According to safety expert Byron Bloch, the older cars could quite easily be retrofitted with gas tanks containing fuel cells. "These improved tanks would add at least 10 mph improved safety performance to the rear end," he estimated, "but it would cost Ford $20 to $30 a car, so they won't do it unless they are forced to." Dr. Kenneth Saczalski, safety engineer with the Office of Naval Research in Washington, agrees. "The Defense Department has developed virtually fail-safe fuel systems and retrofitted them into existing vehicles. We have shown them to the auto industry and they have ignored them."

Unfortunately, the Pinto is not an isolated case of corporate malpractice in the auto industry. Neither is Ford a lone sinner. There probably isn't a car on the road without a safety hazard known to its manufacturer. And though Ford may have the best auto lobbyists in Washington, it is not alone. The anti-emission control lobby and the anti-safety lobby usually work in chorus form, presenting a well-harmonized message from the country's richest industry, spoken through the voices of individual companies—the Motor Vehicle Manufacturers Association, the Business Council and the U.S. Chamber of Commerce.

Furthermore, cost-valuing human life is not used by Ford alone. Ford was just the only company careless enough to let such an embarrassing calculation slip into public records. The process of willfully trading lives for profits is built into corporate capitalism. Commodore Vanderbilt publicly scorned George Westinghouse and his "foolish" air brakes while people died by the hundreds in accidents on Vanderbilt's railroads.

The original draft of the Motor Vehicle Safety Act provided for criminal sanction against a manufacturer who willfully placed an unsafe car on the market. Early in the proceedings the auto industry lobbied the provision out of the bill. Since then, there have been those damage settlements, of course, but the only government punishment meted out to auto companies for non-compliance to standards has been a miniscule fine, usually $5,000 to $10,000. One wonders how long the Ford Motor Company would continue to market lethal cars were Henry Ford II and Lee Iacocca serving 20–76 year terms in Leavenworth for consumer homicide.

• • •

Seeking to get his investigation before a larger audience than *Mother Jones* typically provided, Dowie took the unusual step of holding a news conference in Washington, D.C., with Ralph Nader, the consumer advocate, in attendance.

"Dowie's expose was the most important factor in triggering a crusade against Ford's 'Pinto madness,'" conclude Francis T. Cullen, William J. Maakestad, and Gray Cavender, the authors of *Corporate Crime Under Attack*. Ford angrily denied Dowie's charges, but the article, with its sensational internal documents, helped convince the National Highway Traffic Safety Administration to investigate the Pinto's safety. In May 1978, NHTSA told Ford it had found a serious safety defect in the Pinto. Seeking to blunt a public hearing, Ford announced a recall of 1.5 million Pintos,

made between 1971 and 1976, and Mercury Bobcats, made in 1975 and 1976, which had similar design flaws. The cars would be equipped with a shield and a longer filler pipe to help protect the gas tank. Ford denied any wrongdoing, however.

Among the people who read Dowie's article was Neil Graves, an Indiana state trooper. In August 1978, he was called to investigate a terrible crash north of Goshen, in which three teenage girls riding in a 1973 yellow Pinto were burned to death after their car had been struck from behind by a slow-moving van. Graves contacted Dowie, who put him in touch with some of his sources. With Graves's help, the prosecutor of Elkhart County filed criminal homicide charges against the Ford Motor Company, an unheard-of action. Although Ford was acquitted, the case opened the possibility of holding corporations criminally responsible for faulty products.

In July 1980, four months after the end of the trial, the Pinto was phased out. More than 2.9 million of the cars had been sold. The Ford Motor Company continued to settle lawsuits from families of people killed in Pinto crashes.

LARRY KRAMER ISSUES A CALL FOR ACTION AGAINST AIDS

The first U.S. cases of what would come to be called AIDS were reported in 1979 in New York City, San Francisco, and Los Angeles. The disease did not have a name. What doctors were seeing were uncommon numbers of cases of Kaposi's sarcoma, a skin cancer typically found in older men, and Pneumocystis carinii pneumonia, a lung infection usually seen only in cancer or transplant patients taking drugs to suppress their immunities. The link seemed to be that the patients were young gay men. The diseases were fast moving, and there was no cure.

The overwhelming response of the gay community, battered in many ways, was to keep things quiet, lest they hand the broader public another excuse to discriminate against gays. The mainstream media, then less attuned to homosexual issues, provided little coverage.

At the same time, the toll of the sick and dead, and the toll of knowing the sick and dead, became an incredible burden on the gay community. Early attempts at organizing to increase resources in the fight against the disease often fractured because of personalities and politics. In March 1983, Larry Kramer—writer and gay activist—decided to speak out. Here are excerpts from his piece.

"1,112 and Counting," by Larry Kramer. *New York Native,* March 14–27, 1983.

If this article doesn't scare the shit out of you we're in real trouble. If this article doesn't rouse you to anger, fury, rage, and action, gay men may have no future on this earth. Our continued existence depends on just how angry you can get.

I am writing this as Larry Kramer and I am speaking for myself and my views are not to be attributed to Gay Men's Health Crisis.

I repeat: our continued existence as gay men upon the face of this earth is at stake. Unless we fight for our lives we shall die. In all the history of homosexuality we have never been so close to death and extinction before. Many of us are dying or dead already.

Before I tell you what we must do, let me tell you what is happening to us.

There are now 1,112 cases of serious acquired immune deficiency syndrome. When we first became worried, there were only 41. In only 28 days, from January 13 to February 9, there were 164 new cases—and 73 more dead. The total death tally is now 418. Twenty percent of all cases was registered this January alone. There have been 195 dead in New York City from among 526 victims. Of all serious AIDS cases, 47.3 percent are in the New York metropolitan area.

These are the serious cases of AIDS, which means Kaposi's sarcoma, Pneumocystis carinii

pneumonia, and other deadly infections. These numbers do not include the thousands of us walking around with what is also being called AIDS: various forms of swollen lymph glands and fatigues that doctors don't know what to label or what they might portend.

The rise in these numbers is terrifying. Whatever is spreading is now spreading faster as more and more people come down with AIDS.

And, for the first time in this epidemic, leading doctors and researchers are finally admitting they don't know what's going on. I find this terrifying too—as terrifying as the alarming rise in numbers. For the first time, doctors are saying out loud and up front, "I don't know."

For two years they weren't talking like this. For two years we've heard a different theory every few weeks. We grasped at the straws of possible cause: promiscuity, poppers, back rooms, the baths, rimming, fisting, anal intercourse, urine, semen, shit, saliva, sweat, blood, blacks, single virus, new virus, repeated exposure to a virus, amebas carrying a virus, drugs, Haiti, voodoo, Flagyl, constants bouts of amebiasis, hepatitis A and B, syphilis, gonorrhea.

I have talked with the leading doctors treating us. One said to me, "If I knew in 1981 what I know now I would never have become involved with this disease." Another said, "The thing that upsets me the most in all of this is that at any given moment one of my patients is in the hospital and something is going on with him that I don't understand. And it's destroying me because there's some craziness going on in him that's destroying him." A third said to me, "I'm very depressed. A doctor's job is to make patients well. And I can't. Too many of my patients die."

After almost two years of an epidemic, there still are no answers. After almost two years of an epidemic, the cause of AIDS remains unknown. After almost two years of an epidemic, there is no cure.

Hospitals are now so filled with AIDS patients that there is often a waiting period of up to a month before admission, no matter how sick you are. And, once in, patients are now more and more being treated as lepers as hospital staffs become increasingly worried that AIDS is contagious.

Suicides are now being reported of men who would rather die this way than face such medical uncertainty, such uncertain therapies, such hospital treatment, and the appalling statistic that 86 percent of all serious AIDS cases die after three years' time.

If all of this had been happening to any other community for two long years, there would have been, long ago, such an outcry from that community and all its members that the government of this city and this country would not know what had hit them. Why isn't every gay man in this city so scared shitless that he is screaming for action? Does every gay man in New York *want* to die?

Let's talk about a few things specifically.

—Let's talk about which gay men get AIDS.

No matter what you've heard, there is no single profile for all AIDS victims. There are drug users and non-drug users. There are the truly promiscuous and the almost monogamous. There are reported cases of single-contact infection.

All it seems to take is the one wrong fuck. That's not promiscuity—that's bad luck.

—Let's talk about AIDS happening in straight people.

We've been hearing from the beginning of this epidemic that it was only a question of time before the straight community came down with AIDS and when that happened AIDS would suddenly become high on all agendas for funding and research and then we would finally be looked after and all would then be well.

I myself thought when AIDS occurred in the first baby, that would be the breakthrough point. It was. For one day the media paid an enormous amount of attention. And that was it, kids.

There have been no confirmed cases of AIDS in straight, white, non-intravenous drug-using, middle-class Americans.... Why isn't AIDS hap-

pening to more straights? Maybe it's because gay men don't have sex with them.

Of all serious AIDS cases, 72.4 percent are in gay and bisexual men.

—Let's talk about various forms of treatment.

It is very difficult for a patient to find out which hospital to go to or which doctor to go to or which mode of treatment to attempt.

Hospitals and doctors are reluctant to reveal how well they're doing with each type of treatment. They may, if you press them, give you a general idea. Most will not show you their precise numbers of how many patients are doing well on what and how many failed to adequately respond.

Because of the ludicrous requirements of the medical journals, doctors are prohibited from revealing publicly the specific data they are gathering from their treatments of our bodies. Doctors and hospitals need money for research and this money (from the National Institutes of Health, from cancer research funding organizations, from rich patrons) comes based on the performance of their work (i.e., their tabulations of their results of their treatment of our bodies); this performance is written up as "papers" that must be submitted to and accepted by such "distinguished" medical publications as the *New England Journal of Medicine*. Most of these "distinguished" publications, however, will not publish anything that has been spoken of, leaked, announced, or intimated publicly in advance. Even after acceptance, the doctors must hold their tongues until the article is actually published. Dr. Bijan Safai of Sloan-Kettering has been waiting for over six months for the *New England Journal*, which has accepted his interferon study, to publish it. Until that happens, he is only permitted to speak in the most general terms of how interferon is or is not working.

Priorities in this area appear to be peculiarly out of kilter at this extreme moment of life or death.

—Let's talk about hospitals.

Everybody's full up, fellows. No room in the inn.

Part of this is simply overcrowding. Part of this is cruel.

Sloan-Kettering still enforces a regulation from pre-AIDS days that only one dermatology patient per week can be admitted to that hospital. (Kaposi's sarcoma falls under dermatology at Sloan-Kettering.) But Sloan-Kettering is also the second-largest treatment center of AIDS patients in New York. You can be near to death and still not get into Sloan-Kettering. . . .

Most hospital staffs are still so badly educated about AIDS that they don't know much about it, except that they've heard it's contagious. (There have been no cases in hospital staff or among the very doctors who have been treating AIDS victims for two years.) Hence, as I said earlier, AIDS patients are often treated as lepers. . . .

If three out of four AIDS cases were occurring in straights, instead of in gay men, you can bet all hospitals and their staffs would know what's happening. And it would be this city's Health Department and Health and Hospitals Corporation that would be telling them.

—Let's talk about health insurance and welfare problems.

Many of the ways of treating AIDS are experimental, and many health insurance policies do not cover most of them. Blue Cross is particularly bad about accepting anything unusual.

Many serious victims of AIDS have been unable to qualify for welfare or disability or Social Security benefits. There are increasing numbers of men unable to work and unable to claim welfare because AIDS is not on the list of qualifying disability illnesses. (Immune deficiency is an acceptable determining factor for welfare among children, but not adults. Go figure that one out.) There are also increasing numbers of men unable to pay their rent, men thrown out on the street with nowhere to live and no money to live with, and men who have been asked by roommates to

leave because of their illnesses. And men with serious AIDS are being fired from certain jobs.

The horror stories in this area, of those suddenly found destitute, of those facing this illness with insufficient insurance, continue to mount. (One man who'd had no success on other therapies was forced to beg from his friends the $16,600 he needed to, as a last resort, try plasmapheresis.)

Finally:

—Let's talk about our mayor, Ed Koch.

Our mayor, Ed Koch, appears to have chosen, for whatever reason, not to allow himself to be perceived by the non-gay world as visibly helping us in this emergency.

Repeated requests to meet with him have been denied us. Repeated attempts to have him make a very necessary public announcement about this crisis and public health emergency have been refused by his staff. . . .

With his silence on AIDS, the mayor of New York is helping to kill us.

Enough. I am told this is one of the longest articles the *Native* has ever run. I hope I have not been guilty of saying ineffectively in 5,000 words what I could have said in five: we must fight to live.

I am angry and frustrated almost beyond the bounds my skin and bones and body and brain can encompass. My sleep is tormented by nightmares and visions of lost friends and my days are flooded by the tears of funerals and memorial services and seeing my sick friends. How many of us must die before *all* of we living fight back?

I know that unless I fight with every ounce of my energy I will hate myself. I hope, I pray, I implore you to feel the same.

I am going to close by doing what Dr. Ron Grossman did at GMHC's second Open Forum last November at Julia Richman High School. He listed the names of the patients he had lost to AIDS. Here is a list of 21 dead men I knew:

Nick Rock
Rick Wellikoff
Jack Nau
Shelly
Donald Krintzman
Jerry Green
Michael Maletta
Paul Graham
Toby
Harry Blumenthal
Stephen Sperry
Brian O'Hara
Barry
David
Jeffrey Croland
Z
David Jackson
Tony Rappa
Robert Christian
Ron Doud
And one more, who will be dead by the
time these words appear in print.

If we don't act immediately, then we face our
approaching doom.

• • •

Randy Shilts, the *San Francisco Chronicle* reporter
who covered AIDS first and most extensively,
wrote in *And the Band Played On*: "Larry Kramer's
piece irrevocably altered the context in which
AIDS was discussed in the gay community and,
hence, in the nation." Shilts called the article "in-
arguably one of the most influential works of advocacy journalism of the decade," and said it
"swiftly crystallized the epidemic into a political
movement for the gay community." Kramer, with
an abrasive personality, also antagonized a number of gay leaders, as he would do with the foundation in March 1987 of ACT UP (the AIDS
Coalition to Unleash Power), an assertive civil dis-
obedience organization. Letters flooded into the
Native accusing Kramer of being unduly alarmist

and, in his way, a prude trying to limit homosexual sex.

Knowing the article was coming, the New
York AIDS Network quickly demanded new city
services, warning of the increasing anger of the
gay community and vaguely threatening protests.
(Kramer had spoken of sit-ins and traffic tie-ups.)
Two days later, Mayor Edward Koch and the city
health commissioner announced the formation of
an Office of Gay and Lesbian Health Concerns.

The article also spurred education efforts about
safe sex.

Kramer further helped alert people to AIDS
through his playwriting, especially *The Normal Heart*.

RANDY SHILTS REVEALS THAT ROCK HUDSON HAS AIDS AND THE PUBLIC ATTITUDE TOWARD THE DISEASE BEGINS TO CHANGE

The story of the public's interest in the fight
against AIDS had two phases, Randy Shilts, the
San Francisco Chronicle reporter who covered it
best, wrote in his book *And the Band Played On*.
One was before Rock Hudson got AIDS, and the
other was after. By the end of May 1984, Shilts
said, more than 2,000 Americans had been killed
by AIDS, and another 2,600 were diagnosed and
awaiting death. But the tragedy of the numbers
"had not moved society toward mobilizing its resources against the new epidemic."

Hudson was diagnosed with Kaposi's sarcoma
on June 5, 1984. In September, already suffering
weight loss, he went to the Pasteur Institute in
Paris to try an experimental drug treatment. It
seemed to remove traces of the AIDS virus from
his blood, and Hudson thought he was cured. He
returned to the United States and went to a White
House state dinner at the invitation of his old
Hollywood friends, President Ronald Reagan and
his wife, Nancy.

It was soon apparent that the drugs had only a temporary effect. He lost weight and grew fatigued, the sarcoma progressed, and in July 1985 he was diagnosed with another cancer, lymphoblastic lymphoma. Only a handful of friends knew.

On July 15, Hudson kept a promise to tape a television segment with Doris Day for her show on the Christian Broadcasting Network. He looked terrible, but told people he had the flu. The next week Hudson returned to Paris, where he intended to retake the experimental drug treatment. He collapsed walking across the hotel lobby. News organizations began tracking the rumors that Hudson had AIDS. Some gay groups hoped to use Hudson's masculine image as a way to convince the world that "AIDS is not a gay disease," in the hopes of increasing public interest and funding.

"Why Rock Hudson Kept Quiet About Being Gay," by Perry Land and Randy Shilts. *San Francisco Chronicle,* July 25, 1985.

Even as Rock Hudson played the traditional role of a cinematic sex symbol in Hollywood, his gay friends in San Francisco were quietly urging him to publicly acknowledge his homosexuality.

Hudson toyed with the idea briefly, friends said yesterday, but refrained from any public pronouncements, deciding instead to play by the rules of the entertainment industry, which has yet to produce any openly gay stars.

"Rock had learned his lesson well in Hollywood," said Armistead Maupin, a former *Chronicle* columnist and a friend of the movie idol. "And he played by the rules.

"Those rules say that you keep quiet about (being gay) and everyone will lie about it for you," he said. "The gossip columnists will make up girlfriends for you and everyone in Hollywood will know you're gay—except the public."

The years of evasion ended tragically in Paris on Monday when doctors revealed that Hudson was being tested for AIDS and seeking treatment from specialists at the Pasteur Institute, one of the world's pioneering AIDS research and treatment centers.

Hudson's publicist said he will announce today the outcome of the tests for acquired immune deficiency syndrome.

"Rock loved San Francisco and was coming here for years," recalled another friend, Ken Maley. "We never went out to gay places with Rock in Los Angeles, but in San Francisco, it was different. He was more relaxed about it."

During one 1976 visit, Maupin recalled, he suggested to Hudson that he publicly discuss being gay.

"Rock seemed to take to the idea and said, 'One of these days I'm going to have a lot to tell,'" Maupin said. "I thought it would be a good idea because he was exactly the same in private life as on the screen, very masculine and natural."

However, Maupin added, "You could tell the idea would be difficult for someone of his generation. . . . He could never bring himself to go public about it."

Aside from attending private dinner parties and dining at some of the city's better-known restaurants on his visits here, Hudson and his entourage often patronized two of the city's popular gay discos, the I-Beam and the Trocadero Transfer, Maley said.

For all his reservations about coming out publicly, the 59-year-old actor harbored substantial resentment for the decades during which he was forced to cloak his sexuality, friends said. They pointed to his marriage to a secretary, shortly after a fan magazine privately threatened to expose his homosexuality, as a source of particular bitterness.

The studio arranged the whole wedding—the publicity, the honeymoon, everything, said Maley. "He frequently said he was bitter about it. That was in the days when the studios ran the star's lives. They'd set up all these dates with the starlets and do all the phony stuff for publicity."

Less than two years after Hudson's 1955 marriage, the couple separated. His wife, Phyllis Gates, charged in her divorce suits, in 1958, that Hudson had caused her "grievous mental distress, suffering and anguish."

Hudson's press spokesman, Dale Olson, would neither confirm nor deny reports of Hudson's homosexuality yesterday. He said the topic never arose in the years he has worked for the movie star.

"He is a very private person," said Olson, "He feels that his private life is not a part of his public life and therefore of no real concern to the public. I've never discussed it with him."

• • •

The *Chronicle* story, Shilts wrote, relieved other news organizations of the awkward problem of explaining how Hudson had contracted AIDS, and they quoted the paper on the actor's homosexuality. Hudson's illness became a reason for media attention to all aspects of the AIDS crisis, brought an increase in donations to AIDS groups, and moved AIDS to the front of the public policy debate. "It took a square-jawed, heterosexually perceived actor like Rock Hudson to make AIDS something people could talk about," Shilts said.

Shilts died, of AIDS, in 1994, at the age of forty-two.

GUINEA PIGS OF THE ATOMIC AGE: A NEW MEXICO REPORTER BREAKS GOVERNMENT SILENCE

The scientists working on the crash project to build the atomic bomb during World War II knew that the plutonium they were working with was a dangerous material. What they did not know was how dangerous. Finding that out, the scientists concluded, would be important for establishing standards for plutonium exposure for the coming atomic age. Tests on dogs, mice, rats, and rabbits had been conducted. To the scientists, the logical next step was tests on humans.

"The Plutonium Experiment," by Eileen Welsome. *Albuquerque Tribune,* November 15, 1993.

The experiment began in the hot, fretful dawn of the Atomic Age in quiet hospitals far removed from the New Mexico desert where scientists were putting the finishing touches on a "gadget" that would alter the course of history.

In the wards of the sick and dying, syringes were loaded with an ingredient so secret it was known only as "the product." Then, in quick succession, the needles were plunged into the veins of an auto accident victim in Tennessee, a cancer patient in Chicago, a house painter in San Francisco.

The product was plutonium, the highly radioactive substance that would power the brilliant mushroom cloud over Alamogordo three months later. But what did plutonium—the ingredient in a weapon that President Truman would boast harnessed the power of the universe—do in the human body? How long did it circulate in the blood? Where did it lodge in the bone? How quickly was it excreted?

The experiment was approved by the U.S. Army's Manhattan Project, the wartime machine that developed the atomic bomb. Some contemporary scientists compare the project to the human experiments conducted in Nazi Germany. Others defend it.

In all, scientists injected 18 people with plutonium between 1945 and 1947. Even as the plutonium was being administered, the Army colonel listed in documents as primarily responsible for the experiment was describing plutonium as the "most poisonous chemical known."

The patients were ordinary people with one thing in common: life-threatening illnesses that made survival beyond 10 years "highly improbable." They included a boy of slight build who was just two months shy of his fifth birthday, a malnourished alcoholic, an 85-pound woman suffering from widespread cancer.

With the possible exception of one patient, *The Tribune* found no written evidence that any of the patients were informed of the nature of the experiment or gave consent. Most of them probably went to their graves not knowing they had been injected with one of the most potent cancer-producing chemicals on Earth.

One patient received "many times the so-called lethal textbook dose" of plutonium. That patient and five others received radiation doses to the bone that a scientist 30 years later calculated as being high enough to cause tumors.

One-third of the patients outlived their doctors' grim predictions, and in the early 1970s, four still were living when a follow-up study began. Scientists took urine, blood and stool samples from three to measure the plutonium remaining in their bodies. Scientists also sought exhumations of deceased patients.

Neither the survivors nor the relatives of the deceased plutonium patients initially were told the real reason for the government's interest. In some cases, the relatives were lied to when permission for exhumation was sought.

"This is one of the great, dark stories of the nuclear era," said Arjun Makhijani, president of the Institute for Energy and Environmental Research in Washington, D.C., a non-profit group that studies nuclear issues. "The public is not aware of the depths to which many universities, doctors and scientists descended."

Los Alamos National Laboratory played a major role in the experiment's first phase. The lab analyzed the excretion samples of the patients injected in a Rochester, N.Y., hospital and later published a classified report that has become the definitive source document on the experiment.

The data, some scientists say, helped protect thousands of workers at nuclear facilities from being overexposed to plutonium and did not harm the patients or contribute to their deaths. Others say the experiment was unethical and bad science because, among other reasons, the sample size was too small.

The experiment itself has received limited attention in the media. But to this day, the patients' identities have been known by numbers only.

Six years ago, *The Tribune* began a search to find them. We thought they deserved to be remembered as something more than numbers, something more than laboratory animals who contributed to science a wealth of data on how plutonium is deposited in the human body—its heart, skeleton, even its ashes.

Working with scant data from scientific reports and a few clues from government documents, we determined the identities of five of the 18 patients.

In the next few days, *The Tribune* will tell you how these ordinary Americans unwittingly were swept up by the hot winds of the Atomic Age. We also will tell you about how their families weren't told the truth for almost 50 years.

The first patient we found was a railroad porter named Elmer Allen, identified in records as "Cal-3." Elmer was injected with plutonium in the left calf, and three days later, his leg was amputated for what was thought to be a pre-existing bone cancer.

The second patient was a California house painter named Albert Stevens, known as "Cal-I." Albert received a massive dose of plutonium four days before undergoing surgery for stomach cancer. But he didn't have stomach cancer. Specimens of his spleen, rib and body tissues later show up in a report titled "A Comparison of the Metabolism of Plutonium in Man and the Rat."

The third patient was "HP-6," a man named John Mousso who suffered from Addison's disease and struggled to make ends meet in a small town outside Rochester, N.Y.

The fourth was Eda Schultz Charlton, identified as "HP-3" in official records. Eda's condition was monitored for almost 35 years by the University of Rochester's Strong Memorial Hospital. She underwent dozens of diagnostic tests ranging from X rays to biopsies and barium enemas, and she developed an obsessive fear of cancer.

And finally, there was "HP-9," a man named Fred C. Sours, a political official in a Rochester suburb whose body was exhumed 31 years after his death and sent to a national laboratory near Chicago. His remains were kept there for more than three years.

Who are the others? The malnourished alcoholic? The auto accident victim in Tennessee?

We don't know. And the government won't say.

We've filed two legal requests under the Freedom of Information Act with the Department of Energy, the sprawling agency that eventually took over many functions of the wartime Manhattan Project.

The first was filed in 1989. The second, filed more than a year ago, was a seven-page request based on the DOE's own documents—including a 1974 report detailing an internal inquiry into the experiment conducted by its predecessor agency, the Atomic Energy Commission.

We've received some documents from the DOE, but it is still withholding many of the most important records, such as medical files and other correspondence that would identify the other patients. The DOE said it doesn't even have a copy of the findings of its own investigation—an investigation that involved teams of officials who reviewed numerous records, conducted interviews with scientists in 14 cities and returned to Washington with 250 documents.

The plutonium experiment began in the hubris of a new age. Among its advocates and architects were some of the brilliant young scientists from Los Alamos who, from behind protective lenses, watched on the morning of July 16, 1945, when a man-made explosion outshone the New Mexico sun.

A half-century has elapsed. The Cold War is over, and the bombs are being dismantled. Still, the DOE refuses to relinquish the identities of the victims of one of its darkest secrets.

• • •

Coincidentally, the secretary of energy in the Clinton administration, Hazel O'Leary, had by late 1993 become upset by what she saw as the department's culture of secrecy and had embarked on a policy of declassifying agency documents. Three weeks after the first *Journal* article, at a news conference that had been scheduled before publication, O'Leary conceded that radiation experiments on humans had been carried out. She said she had been appalled and shocked to find out about them, a stance that angered many radiation scientists, who regarded the tests as necessary for the nation's atomic program. President Clinton directed federal agencies to make public any records dealing with radiation experiments and appointed an Advisory Committee on Human Experiments to investigate.

The records released made clear the names of all but one of the people who received plutonium injections. They also contained previously secret information that was almost astounding. "It became apparent that the story was much bigger than anyone had imagined," even she, Eileen Welsome wrote in her book, *The Plutonium Files* (New York: The Dial Press, 1999). "It turned out that thousands of human radiation studies had been conducted during the Cold War." Prisoners, mentally retarded schoolchildren, pregnant women, soldiers, nursing mothers, hospital patients—all received, unknowingly, traces of radiation so that the researchers for the Atomic Energy Commission or the military could trace radiation's effects.

The advisory committee heard angry testimony from scores of people whose family members suffered from, or had died of, diseases they felt were related to radiation exposure. In the end, however, the committee said that most of the experiments, while deplorable, were harmless. No one was blamed specifically, no medical follow-up was recommended, no compensation was proposed.

The federal government did adopt new rules covering the subjects of classified research. A lawsuit was filed in sixteen of the eighteen cases of plutonium injection, and eventually the federal government settled out of court, for several hundred thousand dollars for each.

Welcome was disappointed in the commission's timid work, and so were many of the experimental subjects. Nonetheless, she wrote, the vast amount of information made public as a result "will serve as a cautionary tale about the corrupting power of secrecy, the danger of special interest groups, the excesses of science and medicine, and the need to monitor closely the activities of civilian and military weapons makers."

A HOUSTON TELEVISION STATION REVEALS THE PATTERN OF FORD-FIRESTONE DEATHS

Ford Motor Company had been using Firestone tires on its vehicles since Henry Ford made his first tire purchase from his friend Harvey Firestone in 1906. So it was business as usual in 1990 when Ford put Firestone ATX radials on its new, family-sized Explorer sports utility vehicle. The SUV market boomed and millions of Explorers, with millions of Firestone tires, were put on the road during the model's first decade.

Gradually, a few customers, insurance agents, mechanics, and lawyers started complaining of accidents caused after the tread peeled off the tire and the Explorer rolled over. The complaints were handled quietly by Ford and Bridgestone/Firestone and filed away at the National Highway Traffic Safety Administration, the federal agency that is supposed to oversee automobile safety.

In November 1999, Anna Werner, a reporter on the "Defenders" investigation unit of television station KHOU in Houston, was making calls to a lawyer she knew, just to see if he had any story ideas. The lawyer alerted her to an accident case in which the tread had come off a Firestone tire. One source led to another.

"Blow-Outs and Roll-Overs," by reporter Anna Werner, photographer Chris Henao, and producer David Raziq. Television station KHOU in Houston. February 7, 2000.

Houston—It was a new marriage for Cynthia and C.J. Jackson.

Jackson: We were just two middle-aged people trying to start over and to have fun.

So one June day this choir teacher and her husband packed up her Ford Explorer.

Jackson: He says, let's just take a ride.

And they took off for Galveston.
But as Jackson drove back north something went horribly wrong.

Jackson: As I went to change lanes, I heard a pop.

What she heard was the tread coming off a back tire, a Firestone Radial ATX that came with the car.

Jackson: I yelled at my husband, "Hey, baby, wake up! The truck is shaking!"

Then the car began to roll.

Jackson: Next thing I remember waking up in the hospital.

And she was facing bad news. Both of her legs would have to be amputated below the knee.
But worst of all, her husband of a year and a half was dead . . . leaving her with one haunting memory.

Anna Werner: So the last time you remember seeing C.J. was when he looked up. . . . Do you find youself thinking about that?

Jackson: (whispered) Yes. . . .

Now, she does the best she can with a life that's very different than the one she had planned.

(Choir singing)

Jackson: Even after three years, it's still pretty hard.

But Cynthia Jackson isn't alone.

Cathy Taylor: "Jessica LeAnn Taylor . . ."

Cathy and Jim Taylor's daughter loved being a cheerleader.

Cathy Taylor: She liked to see people happy. . . .

That afternoon in October of 1998, the 14-year-old was heading to a homecoming pep rally.

Cathy Taylor: . . . and a big smile on her face . . . she said, "Mom, I love you and I'll see you tomorrow."

But there was no tomorrow for Jessica. Minutes later, a terrifying crash. Police say one of the car's tires, a Firestone ATX, came apart at highway speed. The Explorer flipped three times. Jessica was killed.

Cathy Taylor: She was prepared for her trip to homecoming. We just didn't know it was the final homecoming.

Anna Werner: But as it turns out, those are just two of many similar cases the Defenders found all over Texas, as many as a dozen over the past few years. And all of them have a familiar combination: a Ford Explorer and a Firestone ATX tire with what's called tread separation, where the tread literally peels off the tire. . . . When that happens, experts say that with some vehicles, it can mean a devastating roll-over crash.

Perhaps the most famous case is that of KTRK-TV reporter Stephen Gauvain. He was on the job and on the road when the tread separated from one of his Explorer's tires. He was thrown and killed.

But as we discovered, it's not just happening in Texas. We found cases in Florida, New Mexico, and all over the country. As many as 30 deaths that victims blame on Ford Explorers with Firestone Radial ATX tires.

Joan Claybrook/Public Citizen: I think it calls for an investigation and to me, it's very, very strong evidence for a recall.

Joan Claybrook is head of Public Citizen, a consumer watchdog group famous for its oversight of the auto industry.

Claybrook: When you have this number, almost 30, then you've got a very, very large number. I'm sure that this number is not all of them.

And she should know.

As the head of the National Highway Transportation Safety Administration in the 1970s, she forced a landmark recall of another tire, the Firestone 500.

That's why Claybrook says she can't believe she's seeing this problem.

Claybrook: I am totally shocked that in the year 2000 or leading up to the year 2000, tires could be manufactured and have this problem.

Grogan: I am seeing a lot of these, and they're coming thicker and faster now.

He's Rex Grogan, considered by many to be the dean of tire failure analysis and an expert witness who testifies against tire companies.

Grogan: I have had since the beginning of the year nine new cases total—five of them are Firestone ATXs.

He says those tread separations can be incredibly dangerous, because they can make it extremely hard to control some vehicles.

Grogan: That's why they're so dangerous, the driver is panic-stricken, doesn't know what to do. In fact, there's very little he can do.

The manufacturers say otherwise.

For example, take a video produced by Ford. It supposedly shows that when the tread comes off a tire, the driver can easily remain in control of the vehicle.

But Grogan points out:

Grogan: The driver is an experienced driver; he is expecting something to happen. This isn't the same as Joe Public who's driving along, not anticipating danger.

But why are the tires coming apart?

Alan Hogan/Former Bridgestone-Firestone employee: I didn't like building bad tires, I didn't like it, didn't like it at all. . . .

He's former Firestone employee Alan Hogan.

Hogan: . . . knowingly building bad tires. But it's somewhat acceptable; within the walls of the plant, it's acceptable.

Hogan used to work at a Firestone plant in North Carolina. It was there he claims workers were under constant pressure to make their quotas.

Hogan: When you come up short and you've only got a couple hours left in the day, me as well as other people, might have to cut corners.

Hogan says one of the things done was to use rubber stock that was too old, or what tire builders call "dry."

Anna Werner: When you would encounter dry stock, what would happen to that stock?

Hogan: I would reject it. But if that's all they had, that's what you're gonna use.

In fact, the Defenders obtained a court deposition of one of Firestone's plant supervisors. In it, he confirms that workers were sometimes told to use old rubber stock to make tires.

And what does Firestone say? The company would not answer our questions about the use of older rubber stock and declined an on-camera interview.

But officials gave this statement, saying the company has "full confidence in the performance of Firestone Radial ATX tires." And company officials point out that although 12 million have been manufactured, that "no court or jury has ever found any deficiency in these tires."

But Alan Hogan says that doesn't matter.

Hogan: Somebody from Firestone needs to tell them that they're sorry.

Especially, Hogan says, in the case of Daniel Van Etten. He was a 22-year-old from Florida with hopes of a pro football career, whose family claimed he died after the tread separated from a Firestone ATX tire. It's the case in which Hogan testified.

Anna Werner: So what do you think you would say to the Van Ettens if you met them now?

Hogan: I'm sorry you lost your son. Sorry people like me were building rags your son [was] driving on.

And what about Ford Motor Company, who for six years issued the Firestone ATX tires with its new Explorers? Ford also turned down an on-camera interview but sent us a statement. In it, the company declined to answer questions about tires, but said tread separation accidents were the driver's fault—that they, quote, "clearly resulted from driver error."

Ford again cited its tread separation tests and called the 20 to 30 accidents we documented "isolated" incidents. Something Rex Grogan takes issue with.

Grogan: What you're saying is, it's all right to kill a few people so long as you don't kill too many. Is that moral?

And Joan Claybrook believes both manufacturers need to do something.

Anna Werner: So you believe that both Ford and Firestone have responsibility in this matter.

Joan Claybrook/Public Citizen: Absolutely no question about it, because these are original equipment tires. Ford ordered these tires to put on these vehicles.

Meanwhile, crash victims like Cynthia Jackson struggle to put their lives back together again. . . .

She says only now, after three long years, that she can finally sing a favorite song of faith.

Jackson: And it goes, "You don't have to worry, and don't you be afraid. Joy comes in the morning, trouble it don't last always."

The tires discussed in the story were original equipment on Explorers from 1990 to 1996.

Now a word about those 30 deaths we mentioned. We should point out that not all those cases have gone to trial yet, and the manufacturers dispute those claims. However, some of the cases have been settled out of court.

· · ·

After the story had been aired, KHOU received a number of calls from people who had had similar experiences, and one stern letter from Bridgestone/Firestone, accusing the station of "falsehoods and misrepresentations." The National Highway Traffic Safety Administration saw a jump in official complaints about Firestone tread separation, many from Texas. Firestone and the Ford Motor Company continued to deny there was a problem.

A few other stations across the country and the *Chicago Sun-Times* did similar stories about crashes caused by tread separation, according to the *American Journalism Review*'s reconstruction of events. But for months there was no national uproar, al-

though in early May the NHTSA began a preliminary investigation. Then, in late July, KHOU learned that Ford had voluntarily replaced Firestone tires on Explorers sold in Venezuela, Colombia, and Ecuador, a fact that federal officials in the United States did not know. In early August, *USA Today* weighed in. The paper, with its 1.6 million circulation, put Firestone and the Ford Explorer in an uncomfortable national spotlight.

At congressional hearings, Jacques Nasser, chief executive officer of Ford, said of the KHOU team: "They deserve a medal, actually. . . . They started everyone to think: 'Well, wait a minute. Maybe there really is something there.'" Ford and Firestone announced a recall of 6.5 million tires, at a cost of $1.3 billion. Although the two corporations at times traded charges about which was responsible for the problem, Firestone took the biggest hit. Its stock price dropped by two-thirds. Legal suits were expected to continue for years. As of 2001, Firestone had stopped selling tires to Ford and announced the closing of one of its tire factories.

Continued investigations showed that both companies, and the federal government, had received early clues that could have alerted them to the problem, and did nothing. In October, Congress acted to give the transportation safety agency more power, and upped its budget by $9 million. The agency promised to change its procedures so that future complaints would be acted upon more quickly.

At the middle of the year 2001, the death toll from accidents involving Firestone tires was about 175. More than 500 people had been injured.

WOMEN, THEIR RIGHTS, NOTHING LESS

A MEETING IS CALLED, AND THE FIGHT FOR WOMEN'S SUFFRAGE BEGINS

Early in 1848, the women's rights activist Elizabeth Cady Stanton and Lucretia Mott, a Quaker and another women's rights activist, decided the time was ripe to begin a campaign in America for women's rights.

The two were friends and a formidable pair. Stanton, born in Johnston, New York, in 1815, was educated at the Johnston Academy and then Emma Willard's Female Seminary in Troy, New York. For a time she studied law with her father, but left her studies when she became interested in reform, particularly women's rights and the antislavery movement. She married an abolitionist, Henry Brewster Stanton.

Mott, born on Nantucket, in Massachusetts, in 1793, was educated at a Quaker boarding school near Poughkeepsie, New York, and then became a teacher there. It was as a teacher that Mott became interested in women's rights, when she realized that female and male students paid the same tuition but that women teachers received lower salaries than men teachers. Mott became a minister in the Society of Friends and began to work for education reform, assistance for the working class and the poor, and abolition. In 1833

she was the only woman to participate in the national antislavery convention in Philadelphia and that year helped found the Philadelphia Female Anti-Slavery Society and worked for the participation of women in the antislavery movement. In the 1840s, she was active in founding the Philadelphia Association for the Relief and Employment of Poor Women and for years was its president.

Stanton and Mott met in 1840 at the world antislavery convention in London, which was to be a seminal event in the antislavery movement. Women were barred from the floor for the ten days of the convention and forced to sit in a gallery behind a curtain.

The two, who became lifelong friends, were indignant. In the years that followed they worked aggressively for women's equality, becoming leaders in that movement. In the spring of 1848, the two—with a handful of other reformers, among them Mary McClintock—returned to an idea they had long talked about, a convention of women's rights advocates. With Stanton and Mott leading, the reformers decided to hold the convention in July in Seneca Falls, New York, where Stanton lived, a hamlet between Seneca and Cayuga Lakes in the Finger Lakes area of the northwestern part of the state.

Unlike the men in London eight years before, the women said that men could attend.

The women encountered problems. William Lloyd Garrison, editor of the abolitionist newspaper *The Liberator,* refused to print the convention news item, contending that a women's rights movement would detract from the abolitionist movement. But an eighty-two-word news item appeared July 14, 1848, in the local paper, the *Seneca County Courier,* a semi-weekly, and, the same day, in abolitionist Frederick Douglass's *The North Star* in nearby Rochester.

A Convention to discuss the Social, Civil and Religious Condition and Rights of Women, will be held in the Wesleyan Chapel at Seneca Falls, New York, on Wednesday and Thursday, the 19th and 20th of July instant.

During the first day, the meetings will be exclusively for women, which all are earnestly invited to attend. The public are generally invited to be present on the second day, when Lucretia Mott, of Philadelphia, and others, both ladies and gentlemen, will address the Convention.

• • •

The convention, the first women's rights convention in the United States, was a success. On the first day Mott urged the women present to throw aside the status their education might give them and join in debates at the convention and in the women's rights movement. Stanton read a Declaration of Sentiments, a bill of rights demanding equal rights for women, including suffrage. It was then reread, paragraph by paragraph. On the second day the declaration, with some changes made the day before, was read again and was approved by the delegates, who included thirty-five women and thirty-two men (the men who attended risked being called "hermaphrodites" or "Aunt Nancy Men").

The women's rights movement in America had begun.

A report on the convention was soon published by Douglass's newspaper and widely distributed.

The convention also brought an alliance between Stanton and another suffragist, Susan B. Anthony. Anthony had not attended the convention but was impressed with what Stanton had accomplished, and by 1852 she and Stanton became friends and keen advocates of women's rights. The two, says one biographer, "formed one of the most productive intellectual partnerships in American history."

In 1868 Stanton and Anthony founded *The Revolution,* a weekly newspaper devoted to women's rights. That same year Stanton became president of the National Woman's Suffrage Association. She served in that position until 1890, when she became head of the National American Women's Suffrage Association, which she headed until 1902. Together Stanton and Anthony wrote *History of Woman Suffrage,* a massive, masterly account of the women's rights movement. Stanton was also largely responsible for *Woman's Bible.*

Mott continued her work for abolition and made her home in Philadelphia a sanctuary for runaway slaves and a center for other reform activities. Along with Anthony and Stanton, she supported the Civil War, despite their normal opposition to war.

Suffrage, the centerpiece of the advocates' plans, came on August 18, 1920, when the Nineteenth Amendment to the U.S. Constitution, giving nationwide suffrage to women, was ratified. The amendment reads: "The right of citizens of the United States to vote shall not be denied or abridged by the United States or by any State on account of sex."

SUSAN B. ANTHONY AND ELIZABETH CADY STANTON'S *THE REVOLUTION* SAVES A WOMAN ACCUSED OF INFANTICIDE FROM THE GALLOWS

In 1867, while campaigning in Kansas for the enfranchisement of blacks and white women, women suffragists Susan B. Anthony and Elizabeth Cady Stanton met George Francis Train, a rich, eccentric Democrat, Fenian, and Copperhead. Train offered to finance a suffrage newspaper, and his offer was accepted. Train gave the women $3,000. David Melliss, editor of the New York *World*, contributed $7,000. *The Revolution*'s motto would be: "Men, their rights, and nothing more; women, their rights, and nothing less." The paper would sell for two dollars a year. Anthony would be the paper's proprietor, Stanton and Parker Pillsbury, former editor of the *Anti-Slavery Standard,* the editors.

The suffragists faced huge obstacles. During the Civil War, Anthony and Stanton had broken with William Lloyd Garrison and other abolitionists because suffrage was to be extended only to black men. Horace Greeley in the New York *Tribune* refused to print any notice of the paper, as did Wendell Phillips's *The Liberator*. Some members of the Equal Rights Association attempted to block the suffragists from obtaining a room on Park Row, the newspaper row in lower New York City. But the suffragists persevered, and on January 8, 1868, *The Revolution* brought out its first number.

While it had a circulation of only 3,000 and a small amount of advertising, *The Revolution* was a militant paper for "strong-minded women." At one point it condemned Garrison, the abolitionist, who had fallen out of favor with many suffragists because of his prickly arrogance and his belief that the radicals should concentrate on the abolition of slavery. Garrison was infuriated; *The Revolution*

did not care. The paper said, "If there are people who cannot come over to our broad, catholic ground and demand suffrage for all—even negro suffrage, without distinction of sex—why, let them have another association until they are educated for the higher platform the present [National Woman's Suffrage] Association proposes."

The Revolution was concerned about issues other than suffrage, as shown by this excerpt from the paper in 1869.

Then came the tug of war for Hester Vaughan, as every other woman who, from what cause soever, finds herself compelled to fight the battle of life alone. This of this young girl, a stranger in a strange land, with neither friend nor relative to advise or comfort. For several weeks she lived out as servant in a family at Jenkintown; was then recommended as dairy maid to another family, and here misfortune befell her. Overcome, not in a moment of weakness and passion, but by superior strength—*brute force*—Hester Vaughan fell victim to lust and the gallows. The man also went his way. Three months after this terrible occurrence, Hester moved to Philadelphia and hired a room there. She supported herself by little odd jobs of work from different families always giving the most perfect satisfaction. During one of the fiercest storms of last winter she was without food or fire or comfortable apparel. She had been ill and partially unconscious for three days before her confinement and a child was born to Hester Vaughan. Hours passed before she could drag herself to the door and cry out for assistance, and when she did it was to be dragged to a prison.

• • •

Vaughan's child died before she could find assistance and she was charged with murder. To look into Vaughan's health and investigate her story, Anthony and Stanton found the finest female doctors to examine her. Anthony and Stanton also began to raise money to support Vaughan legally and financially. But Vaughan was found guilty of murder and sentenced to death.

Anthony and Stanton then took their campaign for Vaughan to the governor of Pennsylvania. The governor told Stanton he did not believe Vaughan was a bad woman, but, Kathleen Barry wrote in *Susan B. Anthony: A Biography of a Singular Feminist*, a jury had found her guilty and thus he could do nothing. The governor said, "You have no idea how rapidly the crime of 'infanticide' is increasing. Some woman must be made an example of it. It is for the establishment of a principle, ma'am." Stanton was infuriated. " 'Establishment of a principle,' indeed! I suggest you inaugurate the good work by hanging a few women."

Anthony and Stanton were, as usual, formidable. They continued their work in defense of Vaughan, including more pieces in *The Revolution*, and brought enough pressure on the governor that Vaughan was released from prison. With money Anthony and Stanton raised, Vaughan returned to England.

The Revolution was not to last long. By early 1870, it was clear that *The Revolution* could not be kept solvent. Still, Anthony and Stanton would not cut back and continued to use the highest-quality paper and the best typesetters, and had, Barry wrote, "light, airy offices . . . a matter of womanly pride, a reflection of her esteem for her sex." Stanton refused to accept her salary; Anthony accepted only expenses, and others, while spending long hours putting out the paper, drew only a part of their salaries. Anthony insisted, "My paper must not, shall not go down." She received a loan of $4,000 from a cousin. It was not enough. The paper was sold for a dollar and transformed into a genial literary and society journal, which its founders lamented. In May 1870, the paper was killed. Anthony was in debt for paper for $10,000. It took her six years to pay off the bill from the small lecture fees she received.

The paper had lasted thirty months, but, against great odds and with strong enemies, it had made an enormous contribution to women rights. In a court action that followed her attempt—illegal at the time—to vote, Anthony gave the paper a proper benediction. The "sole object" of the paper, she said, was to "educate all women to do precisely as I have done, rebel against your man-made, unjust, unconstitutional forms of law, which tax, fine, imprison and hang women, while denying them the right of representation in the government. . . ."

THE *NEW REPUBLIC* TAKES UP MARGARET SANGER'S CRUSADE FOR BIRTH CONTROL

Until 1914, the term "birth control" did not exist, although knowledge of ways to limit births was available among some groups, particularly the wealthy. The term is attributed to Margaret Sanger, a public health nurse motivated by the poverty, health problems, and physical burdens she saw in families with many children in New York City. As she and a group of supporters met to consider an organization that would spread knowledge of contraceptives, they debated names: "voluntary parenthood," "voluntary motherhood," "family limitation," "neo-Malthusian," "family control," and "birth rate control." Then someone said to drop "rate," Sanger wrote in her autobiography, and they knew they had their name.

Sanger made birth control her cause, working aggressively against the mores and laws of the time. The first of her writings to be labeled obscene was an answer to a letter to her "What Every Girl Should Know" column in the New York *Call,* a radical weekly. She had used the words "gonorrhea" and "syphilis," and the U.S. Post Office, which had the power to bar obscene material from the mails, objected. The federal and state Comstock laws, named after Anthony Comstock, a self-proclaimed anti-vice crusader, also defined material about birth control as obscene.

Sanger was arrested for some of the content in her short-lived magazine, *Woman Rebel,* and harassed for her pamphlet, *Family Limitation.*

In that climate, it took courage for a mainstream magazine to write about birth control. The *New Republic* was one of the first to do so, in a cover article on March 6, 1915, shortly after it was founded.

"The Control of Births." *New Republic,* March 6, 1915.

Few intelligent people would still maintain that it is better to have been born an imbecile than not to have been born at all, or say in the genial language of Luther, "If a woman becomes weary, or at last dead, from bearing, that matters not; let her only die from bearing. She is there to do it." Yet this hideous doctrine is to-day an American policy enforced whenever possible by long imprisonment. The time is at hand when men and women must denounce it as a conspiracy by the superstitious against the race, when public opinion must compel the amendment of laws which make it a criminal offense to teach people how to control their fertility.

Harmless methods of preventing conception are known. The declining birth-rate shows that they are in use by the upper classes of all countries, including the United States. They are widely distributed in Europe and Australia. In Holland the society which instructs the poorer classes through the agency of medical men and midwives has had the approval of ministers of state, and has since 1895 been recognized by royal decree as a society of public utility. Yet Holland has not been going to the dogs. The death rate and infantile mortality have been falling rapidly, the excess of births over deaths is increasing, and according to the recent Eugenics congress, the stature of the Dutch people has improved more rapidly than that of any other country.

But what so many of the well-to-do and the educated practice, the poor are prevented from learning. The law in effect insists that where conditions are worst, breeding shall be most unregulated, that those who can care for children least shall stagger under a succession of pregnancies, that the race shall be replenished by ignorance and accident, that the diseased, the weak-minded, the incompetent, shall by law be compelled to fill the world with horror. Men and women pay for it. They pay for it by a high infant mortality, that monument of tragic waste. They pay for it by the multiplication of the unfit, the production of a horde of unwanted souls. They pay for it in the health of women, the neglect of children, and the fierce burden of destitution. They pay for it in late marriages and their complement of prostitution and disease, in the widespread practice of abortion, in illegitimate births, in desertions and adulteries. There is no one of these miseries which cannot be largely reduced by the extension to all classes of inventions already the property of the educated.

What are the objections to the use of a knowledge which is defended by so few and practiced by so many? The root of them is the tendency to shudder at anything which seems to interfere with God's plan. Added to it is the theory that sex is sin, that whatever reduces its terror increases its joy. In his scheme of things the child is a threat against unchastity, a punishment, as they say, for "getting caught." It is the view of life which makes men fight prophylaxis as an inducement to immorality, which terrorizes the unmarried mother, and insists that the wages of sin shall be expiated in the death of infants, in thwarted childhood, in hospitals, insane asylums, and prisons.

But the clean good sense of mankind is through with that black inversion, and wherever intelligent people meet, the doctrine is accepted that the child shall not be considered the punishment of sin but the vessel of the future. All decency to-day insists that no one shall be born until there is a home anxious to receive him, that nothing is to be gained by the bearing of undesired and unforeseen children. It is argued that contraception is injurious. No doubt some methods are injurious, but that there is a simple method innocuous enough seems to be amply proved. It has been claimed that there is a subtle psychic injury in the use of mechanical preventives, but it has not been demonstrated, and against this possibility must be weighed the crushing effects on the health of the race which clearly result from chaotic breeding.

Among reasoning people the argument from superstition is no longer heard, and the supposed injury to health is urged less and less. The ground of the discussion to-day is moral. It is said that if sexual intercourse is severed from childbearing, a great increase of promiscuity will result. Reduced to accurate terms, it is believed that more unmarried women will have sexual relations. On this ground the existing law is defended. But what is the actual situation? The fact that contraceptives are not widely known is the greatest cause of late marriages, because it is the cost of children which makes men postpone their marriages. This leaves an increasing population of unmarried men and women. The great majority of men live an illicit sexual life with the minority of women who are prostitutes. The other women remain abstinent or they take a lover and either bear an illegitimate child or undergo an abortion. The use of contraceptives would undoubtedly diminish the real evils of illegitimacy and abortion. There would remain the women who prefer celibacy, the women who are condemned to it, the women who honestly prefer to wait for a husband, and the women who are afraid not to wait. These last are the ones whom the moralists have in mind. They are thinking of a vaguely defined but real class who preserve a technical virginity for fear that they will become pregnant. The defenders of the law are afraid, too, that a general relaxation would follow, that this class would grow at the expense of the women who now believe in a really monogamous life.

This, as we understand it, is the case as it stands in the minds of most people to-day. There is an honest conviction that ignorance of preventives is the safeguard of chastity. It would be folly to deny that it is a safeguard, though it is certainly not the only one. The question is whether earlier marriages, the reduction of illegitimacy and abortion, the prevention of too frequent pregnancy with its disastrous effect on the health of the wife and the morale of the husband, the lightening of economic burdens, the decrease in the birth of the unfit, are not reasons which far outweigh the importance attached to the personal chastity of a minority among women. Is everything to wait for them? Are we to balk at measures which will do more than any step we can take to solidify the family, to make it sane, tolerable, and civilized, because we are afraid that some women cannot be trusted with the conduct of their own lives? Is society to set all its machinery in operation to make a terrifying darkness, for fear that the light of knowledge may tempt a few?

Surely the cost is monstrous and the method ridiculous. For after all, ignorance can be enforced only upon those wives of the poor who suffer from it most. The young woman of the middle class who really wishes to know can find out, but it is the poor and the illiterate who need to know and cannot find out. It is the business of society to enlighten them, to allow physicians and district nurses and mothers' clubs to spread the needed information. It should not be necessary for brave women like Mrs. Sanger to risk their liberty. The knowledge need not be published in the newspapers. It should be circulated quietly and effectively. What society cannot afford to do is to enforce the ignorance because of a timidity about the potentially unchaste. A mature community would trust its unmarried women, knowing that the evil of unchastity is greatly exaggerated. Our society does not seem to have attained such self-confidence; it still seems to regard virginity and not child life as the great preoccupation of the state.

It has been claimed that the knowledge of how to limit births is the most immediate practical step that can be taken to increase human happiness. The relief which it would bring to the poor is literally incalculable. The assistance it would lend all effort to end destitution and fight poverty is enormous. And to the mind of man it would mean a release from terror, and the adoption openly and frankly of the civilized creed that man must make himself the master of his fate; instead of natural selection and accident, human selection and reason; instead of a morality which is fear of punishment, a morality which is the making of a finer race. Fewer children and better ones is the only policy a modern state can afford. If there are fewer children there will be better ones. A nation must care for its young if they are precious. It cannot waste them in peace or war with that insane prodigality which is characteristic of the great spawning and dying nations where the birth-rate and the death-rate are both exorbitant, where men breed to perish.

•   •   •

The *New Republic*'s article encouraged Sanger and others, but the fight was to be a long one.

Sanger opened the first birth-control clinic in the United States in 1916. She was arrested for that, too. She went on to found the American Birth Control League, which became Planned Parenthood.

Not until 1965 did the Supreme Court strike down state laws prohibiting use of contraceptives by married couples. That decision, a Planned Parenthood publication says, "resulted in the immediate liberalization of family planning legislation in 10 states and paved the way for the nearly unanimous acceptance of contraception that now exists in this country."

BETTY FRIEDAN WRITES OF LIMITED ROLES FOR WOMEN AND BEGINS A REVOLUTION

The 1950s in the United States have gone down in lore and in television, wrongly, as a time of great domestic satisfaction. Men home from the war took their brides to the new suburbs, where they could make a down payment and get a house. They had babies and more babies, and their lives revolved around their families. New appliances, unleashed by the end of wartime shortages, flooded the markets and became matters of neighborhood status. Yet the husbands and wives lived very separate, and unequal, existences. The men went off to work in the morning; the women stayed home, took care of the children, carpooled, did laundry, did the shopping, made sure everything was ready for the main event of the day: Father's walking through the door at night. The mother would likely not have talked to another grown-up all day, certainly not about anything other than recipes or toilet-training problems. The situation applied equally for college-educated women. "Never in history had educated women married so young and had so many babies," one of them, Betty Friedan, was to write later. Friedan, a promising Smith College graduate, gave up her writing job to move with her husband and children to a suburb outside New York City. Although she continued to freelance for women's magazines, she did not consider that her main occupation. She considered herself a housewife. Gradually, she understood that was not enough.

•   •   •

The Feminine Mystique, by Betty
Friedan. New York: W. W. Norton &
Company, 1963.

THE PROBLEM THAT HAS NO NAME

The problem lay buried, unspoken, for many years
in the minds of American women. It was a strange
stirring, a sense of dissatisfaction, a yearning that
women suffered in the middle of the twentieth
century in the United States. Each suburban wife
struggled with it alone. As she made the beds,
shopped for groceries, matched slipcover material,
ate peanut butter sandwiches with her children,
chauffeured Cub Scouts and Brownies, lay beside
her husband at night—she was afraid to ask even
of herself the silent question—"Is this all?"

For over fifteen years there was no word of this
yearning in the millions of words written about
women, for women, in all the columns, books and
articles by experts telling women their role was to
seek fulfillment as wives and mothers. Over and
over women heard in voices of tradition and of
Freudian sophistication that they could desire no
greater destiny than to glory in their own femininity. Experts told them how to catch a man and
keep him, how to breastfeed children and handle
their toilet training, how to cope with sibling rivalry
and adolescent rebellion; how to buy a dishwasher,
bake bread, cook gourmet snails and build a swimming pool with their own hands; how to dress,
look, and act more feminine and make marriage
more exciting; how to keep their husbands from
dying young and their sons from growing into de-
linquents. They were taught to pity the neurotic,
unfeminine, unhappy women who wanted to be
poets or physicists or presidents. They learned that
truly feminine women do not want careers, higher
education, political rights—the independence and
the opportunities that the old-fashioned feminists
fought for. Some women, in their forties and fifties, still remembered painfully giving up those
dreams, but most of the younger women no longer

thought about them. A thousand expert voices applauded their femininity, their adjustment, their
new maturity. All they had to do was devote their
lives from earliest girlhood to finding a husband
and bearing children.

By the end of the nineteen-fifties, the average
marriage age of women in America dropped to
20, and was still dropping, into the teens. Fourteen million girls were engaged by 17. The
proportion of women attending college in comparison with men dropped from 47 per cent in
1920 to 35 per cent in 1958. A century earlier,
women had fought for higher education; now girls
went to college to get a husband. By the mid-
fifties, 60 per cent dropped out of college to
marry, or because they were afraid too much education would be a marriage bar. Colleges built
dormitories for "married students," but the students were almost always the husbands. A new
degree was instituted for the wives—"Ph.T."
(Putting Husband Through).

Then American girls began getting married in
high school. And the women's magazines, de-
ploring the unhappy statistics about these young
marriages, urged that courses on marriage, and
marriage counselors, be installed in the high
schools. Girls started going steady at twelve and
thirteen, in junior high. Manufacturers put out
brassieres with false bosoms of foam rubber for
little girls of ten. And an advertisement for a
child's dress, sizes 3-6x, in the *New York Times* in
the fall of 1960, said: "She Too Can Join the Man-
Trap Set."

By the end of the fifties, the United States
birthrate was overtaking India's. The birth-control
movement, renamed Planned Parenthood, was
asked to find a method whereby women who had
been advised that a third or fourth baby would
be born dead or defective might have it anyhow.
Statisticians were especially astounded at the fantastic increase in the number of babies among college women. Where once they had two children,
now they had four, five, six. Women who had
once wanted careers were now making careers out

of having babies. So rejoiced *Life* magazine in a 1956 paean to the movement of American women back to the home.

In a New York hospital, a woman had a nervous breakdown when she found she could not breast-feed her baby. In other hospitals, women dying of cancer refused a drug which research had proved might save their lives: its side effects were said to be unfeminine. "If I have only one life, let me live it as a blonde," a larger-than-life-sized picture of a pretty, vacuous woman proclaimed from newspaper, magazine, and drugstore ads. And across America, three out of every ten women dyed their hair blonde. They ate a chalk called Metrecal, instead of food, to shrink to the size of the thin young models. Department-store buyers reported that American women, since 1939, had become three and four sizes smaller. "Women are out to fit the clothes, instead of vice-versa," one buyer said.

Interior decorators were designing kitchens with mosaic murals and original paintings, for kitchens were once again the center of women's lives. Home sewing became a million-dollar industry. Many women no longer left their homes, except to shop, chauffeur their children, or attend a social engagement with their husbands. Girls were growing up in America without ever having jobs outside the home. In the late fifties, a sociological phenomenon was suddenly remarked: a third of American women now worked, but most were no longer young and very few were pursuing careers. They were married women who held part-time jobs, selling or secretarial, to put their husbands through school, their sons through college, or to help pay the mortgage. Or they were widows supporting families. Fewer and fewer women were entering professional work. The shortages in the nursing, social work, and teaching professions caused crises in almost every American city. Concerned over the Soviet Union's lead in the space race, scientists noted that America's greatest source of unused brainpower was women. But girls would not study physics: it was "unfeminine." A girl refused a science fellowship at Johns

Hopkins to take a job in a real-estate office. All she wanted, she said, was what every other American girl wanted—to get married, have four children and live in a nice house in a nice suburb.

The suburban housewife—she was the dream image of the young American women and the envy, it was said, of women all over the world. The American housewife—freed by science and labor-saving appliances from the drudgery, the dangers of child-birth and the illnesses of her grandmother. She was healthy, beautiful, educated, concerned only about her husband, her children, her home. She had found true feminine fulfillment. As a housewife and mother, she was respected as a full and equal partner to man in his world. She was free to choose automobiles, clothes, appliances, supermarkets; she had everything that women ever dreamed of.

In the fifteen years after World War II, this mystique of feminine fulfillment became the cherished and self-perpetuating core of contemporary American culture. Millions of women lived their lives in the image of those pretty pictures of the American suburban housewife, kissing their husbands goodbye in front of the picture window, depositing their stationwagonsful of children at school, and smiling as they ran the new electric waxer over the spotless kitchen floor. They baked their own bread, sewed their own and their children's clothes, kept their new washing machines and dryers running all day. They changed the sheets on the beds twice a week instead of once, took the rug-hooking class in adult education, and pitied their poor frustrated mothers, who had dreamed of having a career. Their only dream was to be perfect wives and mothers; their highest ambition to have five children and a beautiful house, their only fight to get and keep their husbands. They had no thought for the unfeminine problems of the world outside the home; they wanted the men to make the major decisions. They gloried in their role as women, and wrote proudly on the census blank: "Occupation: housewife."

For over fifteen years, the words written for

women, and the words women used when they talked to each other, while their husbands sat on the other side of the room and talked shop or politics or septic tanks, were about problems with their children, or how to keep their husbands happy, or improve their children's school, or cook chicken or make slipcovers. Nobody argued whether women were inferior or superior to men; they were simply different. Words like "emancipation" and "career" sounded strange and embarrassing; no one had used them for years. When a Frenchwoman named Simone de Beauvoir wrote a book called *The Second Sex*, an American critic commented that she obviously "didn't know what life was all about," and besides, she was talking about French women. The "woman problem" in America no longer existed.

If a woman had a problem in the 1950's and 1960's, she knew that something must be wrong with her marriage, or with herself. Other women were satisfied with their lives, she thought. What kind of a woman was she if she did not feel this mysterious fulfillment waxing the kitchen floor? She was so ashamed to admit her dissatisfaction that she never knew how many other women shared it. If she tried to tell her husband, he didn't understand what she was talking about. She did not really understand it herself. For over fifteen years women in America found it harder to talk about this problem than about sex. Even the psychoanalysts had no name for it.

• • •

Soon the problem had a name: The Feminine Mystique. Friedan was tapping into a dissatisfaction that was more widely spread, or soon came to be more widely spread, than perhaps even she—or her editors—knew. The book had a first printing of 3,000 copies, but in 1964, when it came out in paperback, it was the top-selling nonfiction paperback that year. The letters starting pouring in, Friedan wrote in her second book, which took its title from the common response she received, *It Changed My Life.*

Friedan became one of the main founders of the National Organization for Women, the National Women's Political Caucus, and the National Abortion Rights Action League. Although her view of middle-class feminism was before long eclipsed by more radical versions, and, she long felt, by the more photogenic Gloria Steinem, and although she was at times too argumentative and pushy to help her own cause, she gave many women, for the first time, the comfort that they were not alone in their dissatisfactions. Women did many things with their unleashed energies. They formed feminist collectives, went to business school, obtained divorces, sought jobs, went to law school, pressured politicians and became politicians themselves, seized the possibilities of the world without apology—and, unfortunately, gradually forgot the role of Friedan's book.

A NEW KIND OF WOMEN'S MAGAZINE BRINGS THE KAREN SILKWOOD STORY TO THE PUBLIC

Into the 1970s, about the only articles to be found in magazines aimed at women had to do with lipstick, movie stars, getting and keeping a boyfriend, losing weight, and the latest fashion. Then came *Ms.*, where the fashion was feminism. The magazine grew out of the early feminist movement, with Gloria Steinem as one of its founders. It was published as an insert in *New York* magazine in December 1971, then launched as a magazine on its own in July 1972. That issue included a piece on welfare, an article calling for desexing the English language, and a stunning story, "We Have Had Abortions," which featured fifty-three women calling for reproductive rights. *Ms.* printed 300,000 copies of that issue, and they sold out in ten days.

The magazine brought a new range of issues to public attention, legislation for women, domestic violence, sexual harassment, date rape, and the problems women faced in the workplace. One of its most noted covers, capturing the way women were excluded from many matters, was a Christmas issue in the 1970s with the line, "Peace on Earth, Good Will to People." Sometimes *Ms.* was criticized as being too middle-class and ignoring the problems of blue-collar and poor women. But *Ms.* was often on the mark.

In April 1975, for example, *Ms.* published a story that suggested that a blue-collar worker in the nuclear power industry, Karen Silkwood, had been exposed to radiation, had then begun to investigate her employer, Kerr-McGee, and had died in mysterious circumstances. The article also raised questions about the safety of all of the nation's nuclear power industry. This, clearly, was not a piece about upper-class women.

"The Case of Karen Silkwood," by B. J. Phillips. *Ms.,* April 1975.

The small white car going toward Oklahoma City on State Highway 74 would never travel farther than a few hundred yards past a small crossroads. In seconds, the car lay on its side, the front end crumpled into the concrete wing of a drainage culvert, its driver—the sole occupant—dead of massive injuries. Half an hour later, a truck would drive by, slow, and come to a stop. A man would peer into the wreckage, then hurry to alert the police.

A mystery was beginning, a mystery that has enveloped in controversy a powerful corporation and a labor union. It is a mystery yet to be solved. There are no answers, only questions, the most important of which is whether or not this country could suffer a nuclear catastrophe not through the madness of war but from the peaceful use of atomic energy to heat and light our homes, offices, and factories.

Karen Gay Silkwood, age 28, a laboratory worker in a plant that manufactured highly radioactive plutonium fuel for nuclear reactors, died in the wreck on November 13, 1974. She was traveling to meet a *New York Times* reporter and an official of the Oil, Chemical, and Atomic Workers International Union to document alleged irregularities in the plant where she worked, the Kerr-McGee Corporation's Cimarron Facility.

A six-months-long chain of events brought her to her journey. But in a real sense, it began before she was born with the detonation of atomic bombs over two Japanese cities. What Tacitus had said of the ancient Roman legions, "They make a desert and call it peace," had taken on a terrifying technological reality. Mankind had unleashed a power from which it could only recoil in horror. Or turn to benefit. So the dream of "harvesting the atom for peaceful purposes"—a catch-phrase of the pre-energy-crisis fifties when Arab oil was still cheap—started to take shape.

The Atomic Energy Commission (AEC) was created in 1946 to oversee the development of these goals, principally the building of reactors to generate electricity. A multibillion-dollar industry sprang up: uranium mining and processing, reactor manufacturing with its myriad of components ranging from special wiring to 750-ton containment vessels. At the forefront in the fledgling industry was an Oklahoma-based company, Kerr-McGee. Founded in 1929 to drill for oil, the company was a perfect blend of two gifted men, the late Senator Robert S. Kerr, "the uncrowned king of the Senate," and Dean A. McGee, often acknowledged to be one of the most technically brilliant and visionary men in the energy industry. Political clout and the long view. Kerr-McGree began to explore for, mine, and process uranium—first for the nuclear weapons program, then for reactors. When planning began in the late sixties on the Liquid Metal Fast Breeder Reactor—the ultimate dream, a power source that creates, "breeds," more fuel than it consumes—the company contracted to produce plutonium fuel pins for the test version of the LMFBRs. In 1970, a plutonium-processing plant went up alongside a uranium plant near Crescent, Oklahoma, thirty miles north of Oklahoma City. The plant took its name, Cimarron Facility, from the nearby river.

It is doubtful that Karen Silkwood knew more

about the background of the nuclear-power industry than the average American—which is to say very little—when she went to work for Kerr-McGee in the summer of 1972. It was a job certain to attract her, for it involved laboratory work, her forte since her high school days. Born on February 19, 1946, in Longview, Texas, she had grown up in Nederland, a town halfway between Port Arthur and Beaumont. Nederland is in the heart of the Texas petrochemical region and, as in its larger neighboring cities, the night sky is lit by the floodlights and tall torches of oil refinery stacks burning off gaseous waste. A maze of pipes and storage tanks stretches across the flat terrain. Her grandfather worked in one of the refineries and was the family's first member of the Oil, Chemical, and Atomic Workers union. . . .

After her first year in college, Karen went to Kilgore, Texas, to spend the summer with her grandmother. There she met Bill Meadows and they eloped. They had three children. Meadows worked for one of the oil companies, and the young family moved from one town to another across Texas and Oklahoma oil fields. There were financial difficulties leading to bankruptcy, and marital problems that led to separation. Their marriage broke down after six years, and Karen left with the children to begin life on her own, working in hospitals. When her husband decided to remarry, he filed for divorce, citing incompatibility. She gave him custody of the children while retaining visiting privileges, telling her parents and friends that she felt it was better for the children to grow up in the more stable atmosphere of her former husband's new marriage. She was alone now. She moved to Oklahoma City and went to work for Kerr-McGee.

Compared to the final months of her life, the first 20 months or so at Kerr-McGee were rather uneventful for Karen. Unlike the majority of workers, she joined the union, perhaps out of memory of her grandfather's stories about the early organizing days of the OCAW. When the

union went out on strike in the fall of 1972, she walked the picket lines. The strike was brief, nine weeks, and, from the union's viewpoint at least, difficult. The picket lines were crossed; production wasn't stopped; and, in the end, the union was forced to accept Kerr-McGee's original offer, the one they had struck against. Around that time, she met Drew Stephens, a fellow laboratory analyst who was among the plant's original employees. Stephens was married when they met, but was sued for divorce a few months later. His relationship with Karen was a factor in the end of his marriage.

The couple began to draw one another into their respective enthusiasms. Stephens was a sports-car freak. He taught Karen to drive in competitions and rallies; she went on to earn trophies. She was an excellent driver. They collected records—rock, and country and western. And they shared an ardent interest in union activities. In the late spring of 1974, Karen was elected one of three governing committee members of the OCAW local. It was at this point that Karen's life began to change sharply. As would the plutonium fuel she helped to manufacture, Karen Silkwood began to implode, to turn inward a concentrated power, a power intense enough to set off a chain reaction.

What held Karen's concentration was the health and safety of herself and her co-workers who handled plutonium at Kerr-McGee. There is no substance which more deserves concern, for plutonium is the most toxic substance known. It is 20,000 times more lethal than cobra venom, and in very small amounts—a single particle the size of a grain of pollen—it has been shown to cause cancer in laboratory test animals. Furthermore, plutonium retains its radioactivity for 250,000 years. Exposure to high levels of radiation can sicken and kill; in small doses, radioactive particles can lie latent for years with the possibility of triggering cancer.

As the summer of 1974 opened, Karen and some of her co-workers started to notice what they considered to be a production speedup and a concomitant decline in standards and safety. Additionally, there was a rapid personnel turnover, certainly attributable in part to long work shifts (often 12 hours) and changes from day- to night-work on short notice. Whatever the cause for the high turnover (99 of 287 workers left between January 1 and October 31, 1974, 35 percent of the payroll), it seems axiomatic that such a turnover would cause the experience and skill levels of the workforce to decline. Karen began to take notes on occurrences inside the plant. She started to become obsessed with the Cimarron Facility.

On the night of July 31/August 1, 1974, Karen was working a 4 P.M. to 4 A.M. shift in the Emission Spectrography Laboratory. When the two air sample filter papers from the room in which she worked were analyzed on August 1, they indicated that radioactive material has escaped into the room between 4 P.M. and midnight. When urine samples collected from Karen during the following week were analyzed, they showed that she had received some contamination. A full awareness of the implications had not yet come to Karen.

By the end of September, the ramifications were quite real, and Karen had fallen into the spiral of events that led to her death. With two other union committee members, she flew to Washington, D.C., on September 26 to meet with national officials of the OCAW. A contract was coming up for renewal on December 1, and the union local was locked into a struggle for survival. A campaign to decertify the OCAW at Cimarron had begun; an election to determine whether or not the union would continue to represent workers was scheduled for October 16. There was no love lost on either side. Kerr-McGee had a hard-line history on unionization. A strike of OCAW miners at its major uranium mines in New Mexico the previous year had lasted six long, bitter months. But the three union officials from Cimarron came with other worries as well: a series of allegations about health and safety conditions and falsification of quality-control information.

The allegations were based largely on notes taken by Karen Silkwood. The OCAW has a record of vigorous concern for occupational safety, and officials in Washington viewed the charges with alarm. Steve Wodka, a member of the Washington staff, recalled their reaction. He feared that if the charges were true, "the consequences here were very deep and very grave, not only for the people in the plant, but for the entire atomic industry and the welfare of the country. If badly made pins were placed into the reactor without deficiencies being caught, there could be an incident exposing thousands of people to radiation." . . .

Karen kept up her note-taking. On Tuesday, November 5, she returned to work after four days off. She started work at 1:20 P.M. in the Metallography Lab, performing a number of operations. At approximately 6:30, she took her hands out of a glovebox (a sealed box in which one handles radioactive materials with built-in gloves). She checked her hands on a monitoring instrument, and the machine read out contamination. A health physics technician was called and found contamination on her coveralls up to 20,000 disintegrations per minute. (Kerr-McGee's limit is set at 500 d/m. If the limit is exceeded, decontamination procedures are begun.) She was taken to a shower for decontamination, a procedure that calls for scrubbing three times with a mixture of Tide and Clorox. Her left hand, right wrist, upper arm, neck, face, and hair showed levels above 500 d/m. According to an AEC report, kits for taking urine and fecal samples were prepared, marked with her name and left unattended on a rack outside the shower for an hour. Finally, she showed safe levels again, went back to work for a few more hours, and left at 1:10 A.M. When the glovebox in which she had worked was checked, the reading was positive contamination.

That morning, Wednesday, she came to work at 7:50 A.M. An hour later, she was scheduled to attend a contract negotiating meeting, but once again a check with a monitor revealed contamination. She went back to the health physics department, and this time there were indications of exposure on her right forearm, neck, and face. She went through another scrubbing. Wodka recalls her relating the procedure. "The most eloquent line in this whole sad thing," he said, "was when she was telling the AEC investigators about the decontamination procedure with these harsh chemicals. She said, 'By Thursday, it hurt to cry because the salt in my tears burned my skin.'"

Fecal and urine samples taken Tuesday night and Wednesday morning showed the presence of new levels of plutonium in her body. On Thursday, November 7, she brought in additional samples that reached extremely high levels. The AEC, in a report issued after her death, concluded that some unknown person, for some unknown reason, had added plutonium to key samples after the urine was excreted. How that came to pass and by whose hand remain two of the unanswered questions of the case. The AEC's inability to reach a conclusion as to how the adulteration occurred—while understandably a conclusion cannot be found in test tubes and radiation counters but in the minds of people—has left the field open to two diametrically opposed theories: that Karen contaminated the sample herself to embarrass the company or that someone else did it to frighten or discredit her.

By Thursday noon, it was decided to check her apartment for contamination. Health physics personnel went to the apartment she shared with Sherri Ellis (another Kerr-McGee employee), took preliminary reading in street clothes, then rushed back to the plant to don overalls, cloth booties, and respirators. Her apartment was hot with contamination. . . .

• • •

Silkwood's death in a car accident came six days later. A co-worker who was at a union meeting with her before she left to drive to meet the OCAW official and the *Times* reporter said that she had a manila folder and a notebook with her, presumably containing documentation on incidents of contamination at Kerr-McGee. The material was never found. The Oklahoma Highway Patrol said that Silkwood had fallen asleep while driving and that her death was an accident. Her family and supporters believed that she had been deliberately forced off the road by someone who then took the Kerr-McGee material.

Anthony Mazzocchi, then a top official of the chemical workers union who had been involved in the dealings with Silkwood, said that the *Ms.* article accomplished what Silkwood had wanted to achieve by talking to a reporter. It made the Silkwood case into a national story (which became the subject of the movie *Silkwood*) and highlighted what Mazzocchi and other authorities said were suspect safety practices at Kerr-McGee and other companies in the plutonium industry.

In 1976, a U.S. House of Representatives subcommittee held investigations into the Silkwood case and safety lapses at Kerr-McGee. Silkwood's family won $1.38 million from Kerr-McGee for her radiation injuries. The plant where Silkwood worked was later closed.

Ms. magazine flourished for a time, reaching a circulation of 500,000 by 1983, but, given its stands and outspokenness, ran into trouble because of low advertising revenues. In addition, other magazines began taking up some of the feminist issues that once could be found only in *Ms.* After several ownership changes, *Ms.* was revived in 1999 by Steinem and a group of other women investors and continues as an advertisement-free magazine.

POLITICS

THE *NEWPORT (VIRGINIA) MERCURY* PUBLISHES THE VIRGINIA RESOLVES AND SETS AMERICA ON THE COURSE TO INDEPENDENCE

In 1765, at the end of the Seven Years' War, the English treasury was exhausted. On February 6, English Prime Minister George Grenville proposed legislation imposing a stamp act, a tax on newspapers, legal documents, advertisements, and nearly every other kind of written or printed matter in the American colonies. The English Parliament approved the act, and on March 22, 1765, the king approved the measure.

On its face, the stamp tax seemed ingenious, for under the act, as Fred Anderson writes in *Crucible of War: The Seven Years' War and the Fate of Empire in British North America, 1754–1766*, no "excisemen would ever enter American workplaces or homes to extract money from American purses." Instead, Anderson writes, the "tax would be both unintrusive and virtually self-collecting" in that before any piece of paper could be printed on a press or used in a court of law it would have to have a stamp affixed showing that the duty on the paper had been paid. Court clerks could not enter unstamped paper into court records, vendors of newspapers or pamphlets could not sell unstamped wares without facing arrest, and vessels could be seized if their masters used unstamped bills of lading. Moreover, revenues from the taxes would, theoretically, increase as colonial commerce and population increased.

News that Parliament had passed the Stamp Act reached America in April 1765. Reaction was immediate, especially in Virginia, where Patrick Henry, a burgess from Hanover County, introduced a set of resolves opposing the act. The House of Burgesses eliminated some phrasing that was regarded as inflammatory. But Henry's supporters spread the full version of the resolves to the press. The editor of the *Virginia Gazette*, a Royalist, refused to print them, but on June 24, 1765, the *Newport (Virginia) Mercury* printed the full text, including the following language that was regarded as too incendiary by more moderate members of the House of Burgesses:

> Resolved, That his Majesty's liege People, the Inhabitants of this Colony, are not bound to yield Obedience to any law or Ordinance whatever, designed to impose any Taxation whatsoever upon them, other than the Laws or Ordinances of the General Assembly aforesaid.
>
> Resolved, That any Person, who shall, by speaking or writing, assert or maintain, that any Person or Persons, other than the Gen-

eral Assembly of this Colony, have any Right or Power to impose or lay any Taxation on the People here, shall be deemed an Enemy to his Majesty's Colony.

Historians differ as to what precisely occurred in the debates in the House of Burgesses. But Anderson says that the two most inflammatory resolves were false, and had not been adopted. No matter. Other newspapers soon also printed the Resolves, either the version printed by the *Mercury* or a version published July 4 by Baltimore's *Maryland Gazette*, and between August and December of 1765, opposition to the Stamp Act began to spread through the American colonies. On July 8 in Boston, Benjamin Edes, a printer and a member of a group of artisans and merchants known as the "Loyal Nine," later to be known as the "Sons of Liberty," published this in his paper, the *Boston Gazette*:

The People of Virginia have spoke very sensibly.... Their spirited Resolves do indeed serve as a perfect Contrast for a certain tame, pusillanimous, daub'd insipid Thing, delicately touch'd up and call'd an Address; which was lately sent from this Side of the Water, to please the Taste of the Tools of Corruption on the other.... We have been told with an insolence the more intolerable, because disguis'd with a Veil of Public Care, that it is not prudence for us to assert our Rights in plan and Manly Terms: Nay, we have been told that the word RIGHTS must not be once named among us! Curs'd Prudence of interested designing Politicians!

• • •

Colonial assemblies acted with moderation against the Stamp Act, but thousands of patriots, far more radical than their representatives, took to the streets. In November in Boston, a mob burned the Boston stamp office and demolished the interior of the home, carriage, and privy of the stamp tax collector and forced him to renounce his commission. The house of the royal governor, Thomas Hutchinson, was destroyed. Riots against the act then spread to Rhode Island, Virginia, and other colonies. On August 20 in Newport, a mob demolished the home of two supporters of the act and forced the local stamp distributor to take refuge on a British man-of-war in the harbor. Under pressure, stamp distributors in New York, New Jersey, and New Hampshire renounced their commissions.

Sons of Liberty chapters were now established throughout the colonies, and many colonial printers joined the group, among them Benjamin Edes of the *Boston Gazette*, Isaiah Thomas of the *Massachusetts Spy*, John Holt of the *New York Journal*, William Goddard of *Philadelphia's Pennsylvania Chronicle* in Philadelphia and the *Maryland Journal* in Baltimore, and Solomon Southwick of the *Newport Mercury*. On November 1, when the Stamp Act took effect, only Georgia among the colonies enforced it and then only briefly.

On October 7, 1765, twenty-seven colonial delegates met as the Stamp Act Congress at City Hall in New York, and, meeting through October 25, sent memorials to the king and the House of Commons saying that the English government had no right to tax Americans or attempt to remove colonists' rights to trials by jury.

News of the Virginia Resolves reached the English government in London in July 1765. On March 17, 1766, the Stamp Act was dissolved.

In May, ships arriving in the colonies from London brought news that the act had been repealed. Colonists, Fred Anderson writes, celebrated with bonfires, banquets, and barrels of beer. Most important, the resistance that forced repeal of the Stamp Act demonstrated to colonists that they could overcome colonial divisions and stand united against the English crown. The crown remained in debt, and its army in the colonies, because it was dispersed, remained ineffectual and, in addition, widely despised. The English government dispatched additional regiments to the colonies, but this only caused additional anger. An economic depression caused by the Stamp Act and resistance to it continued. The interior of North America, Anderson says, remained ungoverned. Many colonists and their leaders remained opposed to the Crown. Animosities continued; patriots called for continued resistance to the Parliament and the king; newspapers fanned this discontent.

The Boston Massacre occurred in 1770, the Boston Tea Party in December 1773 when patriots dumped tons of tea into Boston Harbor, blackening the shore with tea for miles. The Intolerable Acts were passed. Benjamin Edes in the *Boston Gazette* continued to oppose the English government. John Holt of the *New York Journal* reprinted these pieces and in turn distributed them to papers in Baltimore, Charleston, South Carolina, and other cities. Other printers-publishers weighed in, demanding liberty. On April 19, 1775, patriots fought British soldiers at Lexington and Concord. The American Revolution had begun.

"KING OF FRAUDS": THE NEW YORK *SUN* EXPOSES THE CREDIT MOBILIER

America's westward dream has been one of its sinews. So it was that within months of the building of the country's first steam locomotive in 1830, a train limited to thirteen miles of track in Maryland, a dreamer was already putting forth the idea of a rail route from the Atlantic to the Pacific. The idea rose and fell with the western movement, the state of the national economy, and the state of people's belief in whether problems of geography, topography, and finance could be defeated. Gradually financiers, politicians, and railroad men came to believe that the project would be not only doable, but, with the help of government subsidies of money and land, immensely profitable. In 1863 the Union Pacific Railroad started laying track west from Omaha and the Central Pacific Railroad Company started laying track east from Sacramento.

Officials of the Union Pacific soon took steps to guarantee their profits. Several of the railroad's top stockholders, including Oakes Ames, a businessman and congressman, and Thomas C. Durant, railroad promoter and builder, organized the Credit Mobilier of America as a construction company. Then the insiders essentially made contracts with themselves for railroad work, at terms that guaranteed them millions and ate through the government grants. When rumors of the slick dealing spread through Washington, Ames headed off investigation by spreading the wealth: he sold discounted Credit Mobilier shares to other members of Congress, often keeping their names off the books for ethical concerns. The stock went "where it will produce the most good for us," Ames wrote an associate, Henry S. McComb. There was no congressional interference into the work of the railroad. The two lines met at Promontory Point, Utah, in 1869.

Within months, the Credit Mobilier plotters were fighting among themselves. McComb, angered that he had not received all the stock he thought he was due, sued Credit Mobilier and its officers. In the middle of the presidential election campaign of 1872, Charles A. Dana, editor of the New York *Sun*, got the story.

> **"The King of Frauds. How the Credit Mobilier Bought its Way Through Congress. Colossal Bribery. Congressmen who Have Robbed the People, and who now Support the National Robber. How Some Men Get Fortunes." New York *Sun*, September 4, 1872.**

PHILADELPHIA, Sept. 3—The revelations contained in the sworn testimony accompanying this need no explanatory introduction. It is the most damaging exhibition of official and private villainy and corruption ever laid bare to the gaze of the world. The Vice-President of the United States, the Speaker of the House of Representatives, the chosen candidate of a great party for the second highest office in the gift of the people, the chairman of almost every important committee in the House of Representatives—all of them are proven, by irrefutable evidence, to have been bribed. Surely, after this exposure, no man who has any respect for the honor of his country— any love for our institutions—will by his vote aid to maintain these men in place and power. If there was room for a doubt in this case, I for one would be in favor of giving these men the benefit of it, for it is almost beyond belief that our public men could have fallen so low. But there is no escaping the conclusion that they are guilty.

The public has long known, in a vague sort of way, that the Union Pacific Railroad was a gigantic steal. The subsidies in bonds alone given it by the Government were sufficient to build and equip the road. Yet, in addition to this, Congress passed an act allowing the company to issue first mortgage bonds, and compelling the Government to accept a second mortgage as security for the millions of bonds guaranteed by it. Nor was this all. Tens of millions of acres of the public domain were thrown in as another nice bequest to this corporation. The evidence printed below shows into whose hands all this plunder fell; how it enriched a favored few, who still continue to grow richer and richer as the valuable lands lying along the line of the road are thrown upon the market.

A half dozen men, by buying up a Pennsylvania corporation known as the Pennsylvania Fiscal Agency, and changing its name to the Credit Mobilier of America, got control of the Union Pacific Railroad, and made millions upon millions of dollars in building and equipping it. They still control it, and, as Mr. McComb says below, the stockholders outside the Credit Mobilier of America "have not and never will receive a cent of dividend." The history of the suit which is the means of giving this exposure to the public is somewhat curious. It seems that Henry S. Mc-

Comb, who has filed a bill in equity in the Supreme Court of Pennsylvania against the Credit Mobilier, was one of the original corporators of the Union Pacific Railroad Company, as well as one of the favored few who got into the inside ring. He was an active manipulator of both the railroad company and the Credit Mobilier, and, as will be seen by his testimony, he made piles of money out of both. But some of his good friends, it seems, were not willing that he should have all that rightfully belonged to him. He had subscribed for 250 shares—$25,000 worth—of the stock of the Credit Mobilier of America for one H. G. Fant, then of Richmond, Va., now of Washington, D.C. He gave his draft on Fant to the treasurer of the company in payment of this stock; but Fant failed to honor the draft, and thus threw the load on McComb. Mr. McComb knew there was a big thing in it, and he had the cash to spare, so he agreed to take Fant's stock. But there was some difficulty at the time about an imperfect power of attorney from Fant, and when that was corrected the President was out West and there was no certificate signed. Before the President returned he had been deposed by another faction headed by Ames [Oakes, a congressman], and the stock had become so valuable that they determined to cheat McComb out of his stock. He demanded it time and again, but the Ames faction would not let him have it. He then threatened to bring suit. This made them tremble and promise fair, but never brought them to terms. They explained to him that it had been necessary to use all of his 250 shares and a great deal more to keep certain members of Congress right, and told him that he had been benefited thereby and ought to bear his proportion of the loss. This explanation seems only to have increased McComb's determination to force them to settle with him. He had adroitly drawn two letters and several verbal statements from Oakes Ames, explaining how he had distributed the stock among the prominent members of Congress, and he determined to use this information to bring Ames and his faction, who are still controlling the company, to terms. Accordingly, in 1869, he filed his bill in equity in the Supreme Court of Pennsylvania. After a great deal of maneuvering, the counsel for McComb applied for an examiner to take testimony in the case. A Wilson Norris of Philadelphia was appointed, and the testimony of McComb has thus far been taken. By the most singular chance this testimony has been placed in my hands, and I hasten to lay it before The *Sun*'s million of readers.

(The testimony goes on for two closely set pages of the paper, laying out McComb's complaint against the Credit Mobilier. Some of the most sensational material did not come until the end, when McComb is asked about letters from Oakes Ames, and produces them.)

OH MY COUNTRY!

The following is in pencil on the Ames letter:

Oakes Ames's list of names, as shown to-day to me for Credit Mobilier, is:

	SHARES
Blaine of Maine	3,000
Patterson of New Hampshire	3,000
Wilson, Massachusetts	2,000
Painter (Pep.) for Quigley	3,000
S. Colfax, Speaker	2,000
Scofield and Kelley, Pa.	2,000 each
Eliot, Massachusetts	3,000
Dawes, Massachusetts	2,000
Fowler, Tennessee	2,000
Boutwell, Massachusetts	2,000
Bingham and Garfield, O	2,000 each

Endorsed: Oakes Ames, Jan. 30, 1868

Q.—This writing in pencil on the letter dated Jan. 28, 1863, whose handwriting is that? A.—It is mine.

Q—Where were you when Oakes Ames wrote this letter? Where were you when you received it? A.—I think in Wilmington, Del. I have here the other letter dated Jan. 25, 1868. This letter is as follows:

PROOF UPON PROOF OF THE CORRUPTION OAKES AMES'S LETTER, JANUARY 25, 1868.

Washington, January 25, 1868

H. S. McCombs, Esq.:

DEAR SIR: Yours of the 23d is at hand, in which you say Senators Bayard and Fowler have written you in relation to their stock. I have spoken to Fowler but not to Bayard. I have never been introduced to Bayard, but will see him soon. You say I must not put too much in one locality. I have assigned as far as I have given to—four from Massachusetts, one from New Hampshire; one, Delaware; one, Tennessee; one-half, Ohio; two, Pennsylvania; one, Indiana; one, Maine; and I have three to place, which I shall put where they will do the most good to us. *I am here on the spot, and can better judge where they should go.* I think after this dividend is paid we should make our capital $4,000,000 and distribute the new stock where it will protect us. Let them have the stock at par and profits made in the future. The 50 per cent increase on the old stock I want for distribution here, and soon. . . .

Judge Carter wants a part of it. At some future day we are to surrender a part to him. Yours, truly, Oakes Ames

Mr. MrMurtle here closed his examination.

• • •

Dana, who had campaigned relentlessly against what he saw as the corruption of the administration of President Ulysses S. Grant, saw confirmation in these accusations, even though the events of the scandal occurred during the administration of President Andrew Johnson. Almost every day for two months, David Howard Bain wrote in *Empire Express* (New York: Viking, 1999), Dana reprinted the list of the thirteen congressmen Ames had named. Other papers picked up the story, although their enthusiasm depended on their political leanings.

The congressmen quickly denied the charges, sometimes with the carefully crafted wording that, in the Watergate days of a century later, came to be known as a "non-denial denial." Although the voters paid little attention during the November election, the scandal would not go away. When Congress resumed afterward, Speaker of the House James G. Blaine, one of those named, surprisingly moved for a House committee to investigate the matter. Three months of hearings produced dramatic testimony and more charges about other members. At the end, Ames and Representative James Brooks of New York were censured, but not prosecuted. Blaine was cleared. The rest of the members charged were found to be indiscreet but not accused of taking bribes. In the atmosphere of gross public corruption of the time, such indiscretion was not seen as a crime. It also was helpful for those cleared that they were all members of the majority Republican party.

The Credit Mobilier scandal, along with the Whisky Ring of internal revenue agents and distillers and the frauds involving the Post Office's Star Routes, gave a taint of corruption to the years after the Civil War.

PRESIDENTIAL CAMPAIGN OF JAMES G. BLAINE FALTERS ON RUM, ROMANISM, AND REBELLION

Which is more important for a presidential candidate—his public or private behavior? How much should the press print about a candidate's private life if it doesn't affect what he does in office? Is it responsible for a newspaper to try to determine the outcome of a campaign?

The issues may sound twenty-first century, but they have marked almost every presidential campaign in American history. A prime example is the 1884 contest between James G. Blaine of Maine, a former speaker of the U.S. House, senator, and secretary of state in the Republican administration, and Grover Cleveland, the Democratic governor of New York.

A magnetic campaigner who charmed his way past allegations of being in the pocket of railroad owners, Blaine was favored in the last days of the campaign, helped by Cleveland's concession that he had fathered a child out of wedlock. In New York, a key battleground, Blaine was helped immensely by his Irish ancestry and, thus, the loyalty of Catholic voters. But Joseph Pulitzer had arrived in New York the year before, and he saw the election as a way to continue his circulation-building attacks on the rich and to make his New York *World* the leading Democratic paper in the nation.

Although all the newspapers had reporters following Blaine on Wednesday, October 29, 1884, only the *World* realized the implications of an anti-Catholic comment made by a minister greeting Blaine, plus Blaine's attendance at a glittery fundraising dinner at Delmonico's during a period of economic hard times. Even though the *World* had been banned from the dinner, its reporters characteristically found out all that happened.

The banquet story ran the next day under the headline "The Royal Feast of Balshazzar Blaine and the Money Kings." Under it was a seven-column cartoon by the talented Walt McDougall, showing the financiers partaking of "lobby pudding," "patronage cake," and "monopoly soup" while a poor family begged for crumbs. The story about the minister followed, with the headlines "His Black Wednesday . . . Dr. Burchard's References to 'Rum, Romanism and Rebellion.'"

LEWISTON, Me., Oct. 29—On account of the shutting down of the mills in this city there is considerable distress among the discharged operatives. The Overseers of the Poor report that applications for assistance have increased rapidly of late. Forty persons left for Canada yesterday.

Delmonico's was filled with millionaires last evening. A marvellously elaborate banquet was served there. The expenses were born by 200 gentlemen who are prominent in the councils of the Republican party and all of whom are personally and peculiarly interested one way or another in preventing a change of administration at Washington. The object of the banquet was two-fold—nominally to honor Mr. James G. Blaine, but really to raise a corruption fund of $500,000 with which to attempt to defeat the will of the people. The managers of the G.O.P. are in desperate straits. They almost admit that they cannot win by fair means. "Their standard-bearer," said one of their number, "is long-headed and an expert in practical politics." He realizes where his weakness is and knows that a "golden stream" will be more effective in certain quarters than the most picturesque orators, or the artificial enthusiasm created by the magnetism of his own presence.

Every gentleman who was invited to Delmonico's was expected to bring with him a check to be used for the benefit of the guest of the evening. The rain came in torrents, the wind sighed mournfully through the trees in Madison Square and the air was raw and chilly. It was just such a night as one would like to pass within doors. Two hundred of the monopolists of the metropolis, representatives of the Republican party, who on election day would not venture out of doors in such weather, went to Delmonico's and paid homage to James G. Blaine.

It was probably the most remarkable gathering ever held in the city—remarkable specially for the enormous amount of wealth it represented, and incidentally for the semblance of respectability given to it by the presence of a few well-known public spirited citizens. . . .

The banqueting hall was gorgeously decorated, and with its warmth and flood of gas-light, its green tropical plants and banks of cut flowers, its glittering cut-glass chandeliers and its gold-framed mirrors made a dazzling picture on the like of which ordinary mortals—such as dwell in the Hooking Valley or build houses in Washington—are not permitted to gaze. There was everything there that art could suggest and that a limitless supply of money could provide. But it is doubtful if, after all, the guest and his hosts were happy. The former did not look contented. It is possible that his mind was disturbed by the ever present dread of the defeat which he is to experience at the polls next Tuesday.

The gallery in which Bernstein's orchestra discoursed inspiring national airs to raise the spirits of the banqueters was festooned with flags, their folds being looped with evergreens and amilax. Banners were hung about the walls.

A large portrait of honest George Washington was suspended back of the seat reserved for the writer of the Mulligan letters, who hoped to sit in his chair. There was a stand of the national colors at either side. The guests' table was on the platform at the end of the hall and the seven tables at which the hosts sat were arranged at right angles. There was on each a profuse display of palms and other tropical plants in bloom, and at intervals there were huge baskets of cut flowers, which filled the room with their sweet fragrance. The flowers and plants alone had cost a small fortune. The menu was printed on heavy bristol board, two national flags, with their staffs crossed, being painted upon the front. A crimson ribbon bound the staffs at the point where they crossed and the streaming ends of the ribbon turned upward formed the initials "J.G.B."

(The story then goes on to list all the guests who attended, under such subheads as "The Company He Keeps," "Monopolists of the Lower Order," and "The Jay Gould Corner." In most cases, a suggestion was made of the benefit the guest expected from a Blaine election: "looking for a second term," "one of

the heaviest monopolists in the city," "from whom a check for a large amount was expected," "a reward for what he did in the way of 'boodle raising.' " The complete menu was given, including foie gras, filet de bouf a la Clarendon, canvasback ducks, terrapene à la Maryland, then an account of the introduction of Blaine and his comments. But what the World recognized was that the importance of the event was not what was said, but the occasion.

(Although the banquet got the leading story in the World, *a phrase from a speech made by a Blaine supporter earlier in the day is the one that has gone down in history as a reflection of the campaign.)*

James G. Blaine arose about 9 o'clock yesterday morning. He breakfasted in company with Mrs. Blaine, Miss Margaret and Messrs. Emmons and Walker Blaine. Shortly after 10 o'clock a delegation of pastors, representing churches in New York, Brooklyn and other cities in the vicinity, gather in Parlor F. Word was sent to Mr. Blaine that his presence was desired in the grand salon, and before Mr. Blaine made his appearance several hundred pastors of churches and divinity students were assembled. Mr. Blaine was greeted with cheers, as was his wife. Mr. Blaine was attired in a plain black Prince Albert suit. Upon his left hand he wore a glove of brown kid. The mate was carried in his hand. He appeared exceedingly haggard, giving unmistakable evidence that the recent forty days of hippodroming had told severely upon his health. He was introduced to the clergy by the Rev. Dr. King, and the Rev. Dr. Burchard, the chairman of the delegation, delivered an address of welcome. He said:

"We are very happy to welcome you to this circle. You see here a representation of all the denomination of this city. You see the large number that are represented. We are your friends, Mr. Blaine. Notwithstanding all the calumnies that have been waged in the papers against you, we stand by your side. We expect to vote for you next Tuesday We have a higher expectation, which is that you will be the President of the United States, and that you will do honor to your name, to the United States and to the high office you will occupy. We are Republicans, and don't propose to leave our party and identify ourselves with the party whose antecedents have been RUM, ROMANISM and REBELLION. We are loyal to our flag, we are loyal to you."

The Rev. Drs. Spier, MacArthur and Roberts, and Mr. Halliday also delivered short addresses.

Mr. Blaine seemed affected by the reception and the sentiments illustrated by the addresses. When these were ended he replied as follows:

"This is altogether a very remarkable assemblage—remarkable beyond any which I have known in the history of political contests in the United States, and it does not need my personal assurance that you should know I am very deeply impressed by it. I do not feel that I am speaking to these hundreds of men merely. I am speaking to the great congregations and the great religious opinion which is behind them, and as they represent the great Christian bodies, I know and realize the full weight of that which you say to me, and of the influence which you tender to me. Were it to me personally confess that I should be overcome by the compliment and the weight of confidence which it carries, but I know it is extended to me and the representative of the party whose creed and whose practice are in harmony with the churches."

At no time did Blaine challenge or contradict the remarks made by the minister. In case any voters, especially New York's 500,000 Irish, missed the point, Pulitzer hammered away in an editorial:

How do the Democrats, and especially those of Irish birth and descent who are said to be willing to support Mr. Blaine, relish this picture of the party to which they have adhered for years? How do they like the idea of an association with hypocrites and bigots who denounce the faith of their fathers as ROMANISM and place it on a par with RUM and REBELLION?

Mr. Blaine and his friends, in their eagerness to clutch at every chance of making political capital, have not hesitated to inflame religious prejudices and to drag creeds into politics. They have appealed to all religions and to all nationalities in their reckless struggle for votes. But their ingrained intolerance speaks out through the voices of the less trained and politic adherents.

• • •

In a time when newspapers, more than now, shaped their coverage according to their editorial positions, none of the other big newspapers in New York City carried the "rum, Romanism, and rebellion" line. But the story was picked up by the wire services, and Democrats distributed copies of the McDougall cartoon. The *World* kept hammering at the issue for the few remaining days of the campaign. The presidential vote was so close that it took three days for the final count. New York made the difference: Cleveland won the state, and its needed electoral votes, by a margin of 1,149. "He would have lost had Pulitzer been missing," said Pulitzer biographer W. A. Swanberg.

MUCKRAKER DAVID GRAHAM PHILLIPS TELLS HOW THE U.S. SENATE HAS BEEN BOUGHT BY THE MONIED INTERESTS

The writers of the U.S. Constitution, concerned about giving too much power to the people, specified that members of the Senate would be elected not by popular vote, but by each state's legislature. That would, the founding fathers thought, ensure that good men would be picked by other good men who knew them. Sometimes things worked out that way, but, it became increasingly clear in the late 1800s, the system also made it easy for powerful political and financial figures in a state to dictate, and then control, the legislatures' choice. This became particularly true in the

robber-baron years and the early years of the twentieth century. In 1905, for example, Senator John Mitchell of Oregon and Senator Joseph Burton of Kansas were both convicted on charges of land and postal fraud and sent to prison.

Among the people campaigning for direct election of senators was William Randolph Hearst, newspaper publisher, son of a senator from California, and ambitious politician in his own right. Hearst marshaled the editorial pages of his newspapers, particularly the *San Francisco Examiner* and New York *Journal*. "The people will never be protected against the trusts by a Senate in which the trusts occupy many seats and control a majority," Hearst thundered. In 1905, correctly foreseeing a boom time for American general-interest magazines, Hearst purchased *Cosmopolitan*. One of his first editorial decisions was to order up a series on corruption in the Senate. The job fell to David Graham Phillips, a veteran newspaper and magazine writer who had also written a number of popular novels with an anticorruption theme.

The first installment, widely promoted in true Hearstian style, ran in March 1906. On the cover was a picture of Senator Chauncey Depew of New York and the words, "Depew's joviality and popularity, according to Mr. Phillips, have cost the American people at least one billion dollars."

"New York's Misrepresentatives," by David Graham Phillips. *Cosmopolitan,* March 1906.

One morning, during this session of the Congress, the Senate blundered into a discussion of two of its minor disreputables, Burton [Joseph, Republican of Kansas] and Mitchell [John, Republican of Oregon], who had been caught with their fingers sliding about in the change pocket of the people. The discussion on these change-pocket thieves was a fine exhibition of "senatorial dignity and courtesy," which means, nowadays, regard for the honor and dignity of the American people smugly sacrificed to the Senate's craftily convenient worship of the Mumbo-Jumbo mask and mantle of its own high respectability. In closing the brief debate over his fellow-senators who had been so unluckily caught, Senator Lodge [Henry Cabot, R-Mass.] said,

"There is too much tendency to remember the senators, and to forget the Senate."

A profound criticism—profounder far than was intended, or realized, by the senator from the "interests" that center in Massachusetts.

Let us take Mr. Lodge's hint. Let us disregard the senators as individuals; let us for the moment "remember the Senate."

The treason of the Senate!

Politics does not determine prosperity. But in this day of concentrations, politics does determine *the distribution of prosperity*. Because the people have neglected politics, have not educated themselves out of credulity to flimsily plausible political lies and liars, because they will not realize that *it is not enough to work, it is also necessary to think,* they remain poor, or deprived of their fair share of the products, though they have produced an incredible prosperity. The people have been careless and unwise enough in electing every kind of public administrator. When it comes to the election of the Senate, how describe their stupidity, how measure its melancholy consequences? The Senate is the most powerful part of our public administration. It has vast power in the making of laws. It has still vaster power through its ability to forbid the making of laws and in its control over the appointment of the judges who say what the laws mean. It is, in fact, *the final arbiter of the sharing of prosperity*. The laws it permits or compels, the laws it refuses to permit, the interpreters of laws it permits to be appointed—these factors determine whether the great forces which modern concentration has produced shall operate to distribute prosperity equally or with shameful inequality and cruel and destructive injustice. The United States Senate is a larger factor than your labor or your intelligence, you average American, in determining your income. And the Senate is a traitor to you!

The treason of the Senate! Treason is a strong word, but not too strong, rather too weak, to characterize the situation in which the Senate is the eager, resourceful, indefatigable agent of interests as hostile to the American people as any invading army could be, and vastly more dangerous; interests that manipulate the prosperity produced by all, so that it heaps up riches for the few; interests whose growth and power can only mean the degradation of the people, of the educated into sycophants, or the masses toward serfdom.

A man cannot serve two masters. The senators are not elected by the people; they are elected by the "interests." A servant obeys him who can punish and dismiss. Except in extreme and rare and negligible instances, can the people either elect or dismiss a senator? The senator, in the dilemma which the careless ignorance of the people thrusts upon him, chooses to be comfortable, placed and honored, and a traitor to oath and people rather than to be true to his oath and poor and ejected into private life.

Let us begin with the state which is first in population, in wealth, in organization of industries. As we shall presently see, the nine states that contain more than half the whole American people send to the Senate eighteen men, no less than ten of whom are notorious characters, frankly the servants of the interests the American people have decided must be destroyed, unless they themselves are to be crushed down. And of these servants of the plutocracy none is more candid in obsequiousness, in treachery to the people, than are the two senators from the state which contains one-tenth of our population and the strong financial citadel-capital of the plutocracy.

Thomas Collier Platt! Chauncey Mitchell Depew!

Probably Platt's last conspicuous appearance will have been that on the witness stand in the insurance investigation, where he testified that he had knowingly received thousands of dollars of the stolen goods of the insurance thieves. . . .

Platt cannot live long. His mind is already a mere shadow. . . .

Let us turn to the other of the two representatives whom the people of New York suffer to sit and cast the other of their two votes in the body that arbitrates the division of the prosperity of the country, the wages and the prices. At this writing Depew has just given out a flat refusal to resign. "Why should I resign?" he cried out hysterically. "Has anybody put forward any good reason why I should resign?" And he added, "As soon as I have completed my resignation from certain companies, I shall give all my time to my senatorial duties."

What are his senatorial duties? What does he do in the body that is now as much an official part of the plutocracy as the executive council of a Rockefeller or a Ryan? No one would pretend for an instant that he sits in the Senate for the people. Indeed, why should he, except because he took an oath to do so—and among such eminent respectabilities as he an oath is a mere formality, a mere technicality. Did the people send him to the Senate? No! The Vanderbilt interests ordered Platt to send him the first time; and when he came up for a second term the Vanderbilt-Morgan interests got, not without difficulty, Harriman's O.K. on an order to Odell to give it to him. . . .

It was . . . when Depew was but thirty-two years old that he took "personal and official" service with the Vanderbilt family. And ever since then they have owned him, mentally and morally; they have used him, or rather, he, in his eagerness to please them, has made himself useful to them to an extent which he does not realize nor do they. So great is his reverence for wealth and the possessors of wealth, so humble is he before them, that he probably does not appreciate how much of the Vanderbilt fortune his brain got for that family. The successive heads of the family have been, like the old commodore, typical plutocrats. The plutocrat sees something he wants; he had not the brains to get it, only the appetite for it and the determination to gratify that appetite. He hires a brain, a lawyer, to tell him how to get what he wants. Depew's public front of light-hearted, superficial jester and buffoon, and his private reputation, and character, of spineless sycophant have combined to make him mentally underestimated both by others and by himself. . . .

Depew's popularity with the public so loath to believe that "one may smile and smile, and be a villain," his "pull" with the too good-natured editors and reporters throughout the state have gracefully cloaked the ignorant and greedy and criminal policy which the Vanderbilts have always pursued, and which, by the way, has cost them many more millions than they put in the bag. Our history offers no more striking instance of one-man power than the wide paralyzing effect and the vast and sinister economic results of the studied and shallow geniality of this sycophant to a plutocratic family.

And, for reward, the Vanderbilts have given him scant and contemptuous crumbs. After forty years of industrious, faithful, and, to his masters, enormously profitable self-degradation he has not more than five millions, avaricious and saving though he has been. And they tossed him the senatorship as if it had been a charity. Of all the creatures of the Vanderbilts, none has been more versatile, more willing or more profitable to his uses than Depew. Yet he has only five million dollars and a blasted name to console his old age, while his users are in honor and count their millions by the score.

Besides the Vanderbilts, he has served one other member of the plutocracy—the famous, the curious, the posthumously exposed and disgraced Henry B. Hyde. Hyde discovered Depew's genius for giving "good" advice away back in the late seventies—in 1877. Depew, on the witness stand last December, told the shameful story. He said,

"I came in close touch with Mr. Hyde because a revolution was taking place in life insurance largely through the instrumentality of Mr. Hyde."

This revolution was, he went on to explain, the "deferred dividend plan," which means, though he did not admit it, a scheme by which the managers of a life insurance company accumulate in their own hands an enormous sum to be used in gambling and stockjobbing and in a variety of ingenious ways for adding vastly to their own personal fortunes, while the owners of the risked wealth get only the meagerest, if any, interest on their money. . . .

Depew was a director of the Equitable from 1877, and an enthusiastic and even noisy public advocate of insurance. Yet he had no insurance himself, seeker of safe, conservative investments though he was. From 1888 he drew twenty thousand dollars a year as counsel—to give the Hydes and Alexanders advice on the "vast and intricate problems" which the Hyde "revolution" of life insurance, from an honorable and even public-spirited business to a swindling scheme, had created. And he took this salary graft—though the law forbids life-insurance directors to make money for themselves out of their trust funds. He did more and worse. As a member of the executive committee he voted to authorize a loan of two hundred and fifty thousand dollars to the Depew Improvement Company, an enterprise in which he was interested to the extent of one hundred thousand dollars of stock and whose total properties were appraised by the insurance department at one hundred and fifty thousand dollars. He went still further and did still worse. . . .

Last spring, before the quarrel which is still raging in Wall Street over the great life insurance

bone, Depew was urged to "pay up" by friends of his, who knew what was coming. He was warned that disgrace was imminent for him. But he has one further characteristic which his mask of geniality has hid. He is stingy. . . . It is his stinginess that has prevented him from getting enormously rich, despite the niggardliness of the Vanderbilts—his stinginess and that utter lack of courage to act for himself which is best revealed in his adoring admiration of very rich men who have the courage to risk real money. This admiration seems the quainter when it is considered that no one knows better than he that those "bold captains of industry" put their money down only when they have marked the cards and loaded the dice; and that, if by some strange chance they should lose in an enterprise, they make the people, as passengers or freight shippers or policy holders, bear the loss. Depew's stinginess made it impossible for him to settle up his Equitable "loan" loot, which, as he was forced to admit on the stand, he had, as a member of the executive committee, voted to himself and his associates. He went away to Europe—and the blow fell. And now he is back where he was thirty years ago in the matter of reputation. With this difference— the world judges youth leniently, but not maturity, especially not such experienced maturity as Depew's.

As the financial result of Depew's shortsighted stinginess in failing to get himself off the black list of the insurance investigating committee, suits for seven hundred and fifty thousand dollars are now pending against him—seven hundred and fifty thousand dollars of the money of the Equitable policy holders whose trustee he was for twenty-eight years.

• • •

The Senate was understandably touchy about the charges that had been made against its members, and Phillips's popular articles—*Cosmopolitan*'s editors said that circulation jumped by 50 percent because of the nine-part series—did not improve its mood. Although many of the facts had been known previously, it was their accumulation in a national magazine and the intensity and lack of restraint of Phillips's writing that caused a sensation. Still, no senator sued.

The series cannot be directly credited for bringing about the passage of the Seventeenth Amendment, for pressure had been building for several years in state legislatures and minor parties. But the "Treason" articles increased the attention paid to Senate corruption and brought the issue to the forefront, said George Mowry and Judson Grenier, two historians, in their introduction to a 1964 collection of the articles. They also found that the public scrutiny of the Senate as a result of the articles led to an unusual burst of Senate activity in 1906 and freed a number of progressive bills that had been stalled, including passage of a pure food bill, Oklahoma statehood, meat inspection, railroad rate regulation, and an employers' liability act.

President Theodore Roosevelt, worried about the fate of his party (most of the senators profiled were Republicans) and angered by what he saw as an unrelenting tendency of some progressive journalists to focus on the bad, responded in a speech before the Gridiron Club, a group of Washington journalists, and at the dedication of the cornerstone of the House Office Building about two months after the Depew article appeared. His target was not just Phillips but the whole group of reporters who had aggressively exposed social and economic problems.

"It is very necessary that we should not flinch from seeing what is vile and debasing," Roosevelt said. "There is filth on the floor, and it must be scraped up with the muckrake; and there are times and places where this service is the most needed of all services that can be performed. But the man who never does anything else, who never thinks or speaks or writes save of his feats with the muckrake, speedily becomes, not a help to society, not an incitement to good, but one of the most potent forces of evil."

Though Roosevelt had intended criticism, the reporters adopted the name "muckrakers" proudly and for a century it has stood to represent one of the finest journalistic traditions.

Direct election of senators passed Congress, and in 1913 the amendment was ratified. By that year, because of the pressure of investigations, retirement, defeat, or death, only four of the twenty-one senators Phillips profiled were still in office.

COLLIER'S MAGAZINE HELPS BREAK THE POWER OF SPEAKER JOE CANNON

For more than forty years, beginning in 1873, Joseph Gurney Cannon represented his southern Illinois district in the U.S. House of Representatives. He was a small-town politician writ large, Republican to the core, protectionist, against what he considered government interference with business, and against expanding government into such areas as conservation. ("Not one cent for scenery," he proclaimed.)

Cannon was blunt and crude, smoking cheap cigars, spitting tobacco juice freely, and sprinkling his language with curses. His first hiatus from Congress came in 1890, after Cannon, in a debate about compound lard, used a vulgarism to describe a congressional colleague.

Such things were not done in official circles. The New York *Sun* took Cannon to task, running a drawing of what it considered Cannon's most notable feature, his mouth.

"A Campaign Picture." New York *Sun,* September 4, 1890.

We print herewith an accurate and lifelike portrait of the mouth of Joseph G. Cannon, who misrepresents in the Fifty-first Congress, the gentleman of the Fifteenth district of Illinois:

———

This mouth has achieved for its owner the celebrity of infamy, and it is the only physical feature of Joseph G. Cannon that needs to be considered by the voters of the Fifteenth district during his canvass for reelection.

We advise every pure-minded man and woman in Cannon's district, every self-respecting citizen, whether Democrat or Republican, to study the picture. It is a campaign portrait, and it should enter largely into the canvass now beginning in the Fifteenth district of Illinois.

Let the picture of the dirty mouth of Joseph G. Cannon be reproduced in the columns of the local press. Let it be distributed throughout the counties of Champaign, Coles, Douglas, Edgar, and Vermilion, on posters and handbills, and presented in enlarged form on transparencies and lantern screens wherever the voters of the district assemble for political instruction. Then every constituent whom Cannon's mouth has insulted and humiliated will have a chance to scan its foul outlines.

It is a speaking likeness of the dirty mouth that has recently spoken what are perhaps the vulgarest and vilest words ever publicly uttered on the floor of the House of Representatives.

•   •   •

The *Sun's* harsh words had an effect. The story was reproduced in Cannon's district, and he was defeated in 1890. But Cannon rallied in the next election and was back in Washington in 1893. By working hard, giving and keeping track of favors, and accumulating seniority, he rose in power. He became chairman of the appropriations committee and then, in 1903, was elected speaker of the House. His iron control, arbitrary manner, and refusal to concede any ground to the reform movement won him enemies. Cannon "concluded that only by crushing the reformers could he save his America," wrote Blair Bolles in his biography, *Tyrant from Illinois.* The speaker manipulated rules to control legislation and, Bolles said, the House "enacted only the laws that Cannon deigned to

have enacted." Cannon was known as "Czar" and "Iron Duke," and relished the titles.

Dissident congressmen trying to break Cannon's power got help from the press beginning in the spring of 1908. Cannon adamantly favored high tariffs and ignored President Theodore Roosevelt's recommendation that the tariff be abolished on newsprint and wood pulp. "Then we shall destroy you," Cannon claimed Herman Ridder, head of the American Newspaper Publishers Association, told him. From the spring of 1908 onward, Bolles wrote, publishers "portrayed Cannon to every newspaper reader in the United States as a mulish, narrow, mean, self-seeking Czar."

Magazines joined in. One of the more effective pieces was in *Collier's* in May 1908.

"Uncle Joe" Cannon, by William Hard. *Collier's,* May 23, 1908.

Mr. Cannon, in his capacity as "Uncle Joe," laid an admonitory arm across the shoulders of the reporter from *Collier's* and, after having earnestly remarked "My boy," paused. In a moment, with deepened earnestness and with that old camp-meeting, mourning-bench tone of voice which often makes his most unnecessary oaths sound as if they were pious denunciations of the unconverted, "God damn," he solemnly ejaculated, "the article that's fulsome on the one hand or libelous on the other. Get in between, my boy, get in between."

In order to get in between at the very start, it may be conceded that Mr. Cannon's career is not the most glorious in the history of American politics nor yet the most heinous. Nevertheless, on middle ground, it may be safely claimed for it that it deserves a superlative adjective all of its own. It is absolutely and undeniably the most persistent.

The old Fourteenth Congressional District of Illinois, lying in the east centre of the State, sent Mr. Cannon to Congress in 1872, when he was thirty-six years old.

A very limited number of years in the national capital is likely to finish a man with ideas. His ideas get superseded. The innovator and roaring lion of to-day becomes the reactionary and dead dog of to-morrow. But politics remains forever and the pure politician, who flexibly accommodates himself to a succession of ideas, survives.

Mr. Cannon has survived thirty-six years and a thousand ideas in Washington. And at the end of that time, instead of sinking exhausted and discredited into private life, he is observed emerging buoyantly into his first serious candidacy for the Presidential office. It has been a marvelous exhibition of political *and physical* vitality. It has been the greatest second-wind career in the political annals of the United States. The physical element in it rivals the political in importance.

Two years ago Mr. Cannon, being then seventy years old, and seeking reelection to Congress for the eighteenth time, went out to make a speech at the shops of the Chicago and Eastern Illinois Railway Company, at Danville, his hometown. He encountered, just outside the shops, a platform, which had been provided for his convenience. Four high steps led up to it. He climbed them sedately.

"You see," he cried, turning to the crowd, "how an old man would do it. Now I'll show you how a young man does it."

Sedately he descended. Ten or twelve feet off he swung on his heel, executed a prance or two, and leaped from the ground to the middle of the platform without touching a step.

It startles and almost horrifies the casual visitor in Mr. Cannon's office at Washington to hear this old man, who ought to be conserving his health for public effect in the approaching campaign if for no other purpose, shout into the telephone: "All right. I'll drop in about eleven-thirty. I can't come to your dinner. I've got to meet some of the boys at the Willard. But I'll drop in before I go to bed."

And, night after night, whenever he pleases, he will drop in at eleven-thirty and make a little speech at twelve, and get to bed at one and hand out an interview at half-past eight the next morning, and his slim, solid, nervous body, composed of equal parts of granite and whipcord, will be just as elastic and just as erect the next morning as it was the night before, and his complexion will be just as pink and clear, and his restless teeth will still be biting off large, untidy sections from the near end of a maltreated cigar, till his wet lips, from one side of his large mouth to the other, are strewn with sodden, shredded tobacco leaves, and the neglected, fitful smolder at the cigar's far end seems to be in greater danger from flood than from fire.

The American Federation of Labor, in 1906, undertook to secure Mr. Cannon's defeat at the hands of the common people in the Eighteenth Congressional District of Illinois. The result was: Cannon, Republican, 22,801; Taylor, Democrat, 12,777; Walker, Socialist and Labor, 1,551.

Some people, however, were not surprised. They had expected it all the time. "Mr. Cannon," they said, "is a farmer. His constituents are farmers. He boldly slaps the working class and then goes back to a district where there isn't any working class and gets endorsed for it. Anybody could do that. He's just a farmer representing the prejudices of farmers."

It happens that the drift of the actual situation is almost precisely the other way. Mr. Cannon, no matter how earnestly bucolic he may be in speech and dress, is not now and never has been, a real farmer, and the main sinews of his strength do not run among the real farmers of his district. In fact, he maintains his personal residence and his central political garrison in an industrial trade union town.

Danville is filled with industrial enterprises in which trade unions flourish. It is an important railway junction and division point. It has large railway repair shops. It has iron works, brickyards, tile factories, overalls factories, glass factories, lumber mills and mills for the manufacture of corn foods.

In 1905, with a population of 22,000, the United States census found 2,000 employees in its manufacturing establishments.

Danville also has coal mines. The Illinois coal report of 1906 credits 1,900 coal miners to the Danville post-office. All these men are controlled by the United Mine Workers, John Mitchell's organization. And Mr. Walker, the Socialist and labor candidate against Mr. Cannon, was a prominent district officer in that organization.

Danville is a little piece of modern industrial America. It has interurban electric railways, rows of linotype machines in its newspaper offices, Greek fruit stores, all-night restaurants, and nickel theatres. Mr. Cannon's primitive personality is an anachronism on the streets of Danville almost as glaring as in the streets of Boston, and "Uncle Joe" is a "quaint character" to the young men on Vermilion Street almost as striking as to the young men in the press gallery at Washington.

Living, then, in an industrial town and being apparently out of harmony with it in appearance and in legitimate record. How did Mr. Cannon commend himself to his laboring class constituents? In this way:

He went to the railway shops and to the brickyards and to all the other places where he could find large numbers of working men, and shook his left fist at them and yelled:

"I'm against Mr. Gompers and his anti-injunction bill. You want that bill. But it's a bad bill. Now, if you still want it, you'd better elect somebody else. I won't vote for it. I'll see Mr. Gompers there and back first."

Now, Mr. Cannon is not in the habit of going straight at the point in his way. He usually roams and rambles. But in the last campaign he struck viciously at the centre of the target.

The fact is that the working men of Mr. Cannon's district like him. The final proof of the fact was seen in Westville. Westville was the home town of the labor candidate. It is peopled almost exclusively by members of the miners' union. The vote there was:

Cannon, 289. Walker, 209.

It was a marvelous victory, particularly so because Mr. Cannon has never really done anything for the laboring class. No labor measure owes either its original conception or its final passage to the fiery enthusiasm and undaunted championship of "Uncle Joe." His labor record contains many anti-labor features, and that part of it which is favorable to labor consists only of occasional perfunctory affirmative votes on measures urged and carried by the energy of others. His labor record, concisely, amounts to just nothing. But he understands human beings, including those who work for wages and in the gentle art of leading the proletariat by the nose through the desert there are many labor leaders who might profitably take counsel from the "Farmer of Danville."

It is sometimes hopefully asserted by Mr. Cannon's enemies that his well-known antipathy to new legislative projects is an indication of advancing years. The old man is congealing on the outside. No amount of massage can rub a new idea, like the Appalachian National Forest, in through his pores. He is petrifying.

All of which is a complete misapprehension of Mr. Cannon's character. He was just as hardened thirty years ago as he is now. In fact, he was born waterproof and impervious.

• • •

Even conservative publications, such as the *Wall Street Journal*, joined the criticism. The press attacks helped bring Cannon's enemies together and emboldened them. In 1910, a coalition of Democrats and insurgent Republicans was able to break Cannon's power. They amended the rules of the House to kick the speaker off the powerful Rules Committee, which controlled what legislation came to the floor. Committee membership was enlarged, and members were to be elected by their colleagues, meaning the speaker could no longer pull the strings of his lackeys.

Cannon remained in the weakened speakership until 1911. He lost a reelection bid in 1912, but bounced back two years later and served as a congressman until he retired in 1923.

YOUNG JOURNALIST EDGAR SNOW VISITS THE CHINESE COMMUNISTS' RURAL STRONGHOLDS AND INTRODUCES THE CHINESE COMMUNISTS TO THE WEST

For centuries, concern about foreign intervention had been a hallmark of Chinese life, and understandably so, considering the country's history. Western powers interested in trade forced a slight opening in the early 1900s, and a small commercial, missionary, and diplomatic Western presence was established in the 1920s and 1930s. The few Westerners who came to China were largely confined to the coastal cities and trade ports, where they lived protected lives and had contact mostly with each other. That left most of the vast country unknown to the West. For the most part, the West did not care.

In those years, China was undergoing internal political turmoil. The end of the rule of the emperors led to a republic in 1912, but the change was followed by fighting between the warlords and the Kuomintang party, which first allied with, then fought the Communists, led by Chou En-lai and Mao Tse-tung. The Japanese saw the internal fighting as a chance to seize Manchuria and to move south from there. Chiang Kai-shek, leader of the Kuomintang, seemed more concerned about defeating his Communist opponents, who were based in fragmented soviets in the interior, than in defeating the Japanese.

As an exotic, unknown country, China had always attracted a remarkable group of Western adventurers, beginning perhaps with Marco Polo. In the twentieth century, one of these adventurers was Edgar Snow, the son of a Kansas City printer,

who in 1928, at age twenty-two, took a deck-hand's job and set off to see the world. He arrived in Shanghai, where he hooked on with an English-language weekly, intending to stay a short while to earn extra money. First he was an advertising salesman, but he soon was able to try his hand at reporting. Unlike most Westerners, Snow took every chance he could to travel throughout China. Also unlike most Westerners, he was appalled at the special privileges they received and concerned about the poverty, famine, and the trouble-plagued life of ordinary Chinese people. He began writing widely, ranging to Burma, Vietnam, and India as well as China, and he gained popular standing and a reputation for objectivity and courage. He learned to speak Chinese and became familiar with Chinese intellectual and student critics of the Nationalist government. He wrote a book, *Far Eastern Front*, about Japanese aggression and edited a collection of modern Chinese short stories, *Living China*.

Yet, for all of his adventuresomeness, Snow had not been able to report on the Chinese Communists, who were scattered in rural strongholds under attack by Nationalist forces. The last Western journalists visited the Communists in 1927. After that, the little news that came out of China was often colored by Nationalist sources. Whether the movement, or even Mao, was alive or dead depended upon which source one believed. As a reporter whose strength was in the details of being a witness, Snow kept pressing for passage to Red China. In 1936, he was the right person in the right place at the right time.

After defeat by the Nationalists in 1934, Mao Tse-tung (names are as they were used then) led his Red Army forces to the northwest provinces of China, an arduous yearlong trip of more than 6,000 miles, which left tens of thousands of casualties. The Long March came to be seen as a remarkable venture, one that showed the strength of the Communist forces. Once established in the caves of Yenan, Mao reached out to tell the story of his movement. The logical person to tell it to was Edgar Snow, for he was an American, he wrote for mainstream, popular publications, and his work was regarded as fair by the Chinese Communists.

"We all knew that the only way to learn anything about Red China was to go there," Snow wrote after his trip. "We excused ourselves by saying '*Mei yu fa-tzu*'—'It can't be done.' A few had tried and failed. It was believed impossible. People thought that nobody could enter Red territory and come out alive."

But in June 1936, Snow got word from a Chinese friend that a trip to Red territory might be possible. "The opportunity was not to be missed," Snow said. "I decided to take it and attempt to break a news blockade nine years old."

Working in secret, traveling with a letter of introduction, he slipped through the Nationalist blockade and reached Chou En-lai and Mao at their headquarters. It was a journalistic adventure as remarkable in its way as New York *Herald* reporter Henry Morton Stanley's two-year search in Africa for Dr. David Livingstone in the 1870s.

Snow spent four months in Communist territory, freely taking notes, interviewing Mao and Chou and scores of other Red Army officials, and traveling widely. He spent time with the army, in peasant villages, in schools. He played tennis and taught army leaders rummy and poker. Then he came out. He brought back dozens of diaries and notebooks and the first still and moving pictures taken of the Chinese Red Army. He told of his trip in articles, interviews, and, finally, in 1937, his book, *Red Star Over China*. As he was finishing writing the book, he could hear the sounds of Japanese gunfire in Peking. In a run-up to world war, Japanese forces killed hundreds of thousands in Shanghai and Nanking. Mao had told Snow that the Communists would agree to join Chiang Kai-shek in fighting the Japanese, and that somewhat unlikely united front came about. "There could hardly have been a better scenario for the book Snow was writing," wrote John Maxwell

Hamilton, a Snow biographer. "Everyone, it seemed, was interested in China."

Snow's reporting changed the way the Western world looked at the Chinese revolutionaries. Perhaps the most remarkable information was Snow's portrait of Mao. Even Mao's wife gathered around during the interviews, Snow said, for she knew nothing of the story of his early life.

Red Star Over China, by Edgar Snow. New York: Random House, 1937; New York: Grove Press, 1973.

FROM PART THREE, "IN 'DEFENDED PEACE.' " SECTION 1, "SOVIET STRONG MAN."

Small villages were numerous in the Northwest, but towns of any size were infrequent. Except for the industries begun by the Reds it was agrarian and in places semipastoral country. Thus it was quite breathtaking to ride out suddenly on the brow of the wrinkled hills and see stretched out below me in a green valley the ancient walls of Pao An, which means "Defended Peace."

Pao An was once a frontier stronghold, during the Chin and T'ang dynasties, against the nomadic invaders to the north. Remains of its fortifications, flame-struck in that afternoon sun, could be seen flanking the narrow pass through which once emptied into this valley the conquering legions of the Mongols. There was an inner city, still, where the garrisons were once quartered; and a high defensive masonry, lately improved by the Reds, embraced about a square mile in which the present town was located.

Here at last I found the Red leader whom Nanking had been fighting for ten years—Mao Tse-tung, chairman of the "Chinese People's Soviet Republic," to employ the official title which had recently been adopted. The old cognomen, "Chinese Workers' and Peasants' Soviet Republic," was dropped when the Reds began their new policy of struggle for a united front.

Chou En-lai's radiogram had been received and I was expected. A room was provided for me in the "Foreign Office," and I became temporarily a guest of the soviet state. My arrival resulted in a phenomenal increase of the foreign population of Pao An. The other Occidental resident was a German known as Li The T'ung-chih—the 'Virtuous Comrade Li.' Of Li The, the only foreign adviser ever with the Chinese Red Army, more later.

I met Mao soon after my arrival: a gaunt, rather Lincolnesque figure, above average height for a Chinese, somewhat stooped, with a head of thick black hair grown very long, and with large, searching eyes, a high-bridged nose and prominent cheekbones. My fleeting impression was of an intellectual face of great shrewdness, but I had no opportunity to verify this for several days. Next time I saw him, Mao was walking hatless along the street at dusk, talking with two young peasants and gesticulating earnestly. I did not recognize him until he was pointed out to me—moving along unconcernedly with the rest of the strollers, despite the $250,000 which Nanking had hung over his head.

I could have written a book about Mao Tse-tung. I talked with him many nights, on a wide range of subjects, and I heard dozens of stories about him from soldiers and Communists. My written interviews with him totaled about twenty thousand words. He told me of his childhood and youth, how he became a leader in the Kuomintang and the Nationalist Revolution, why he became a Communist, and how the Red Army grew. He described the Long March to the Northwest and wrote a classical poem about it for me. He told me stories of many other famous Reds, from Chu The down to the youth who carried on his shoulders for over 6,000 miles the two iron dispatch boxes that held the archives of the Soviet Government.

The story of Mao's life was a rich cross-section of a whole generation, an important guide to understanding the sources of action in China, and I have included that full exciting record of personal history, just as he told it to me. But here my own impressions of him may be worth recording.

There would never be any one "savior" of China, yet undeniably one felt a certain force of destiny in Mao. It was nothing quick or flashy, but a kind of solid elemental vitality. One felt that whatever there was extraordinary in this man grew out of the uncanny degree to which he synthesized and expressed the urgent demands of millions of Chinese, and especially the peasantry. If their "demands" and the movement which was pressing them forward were the dynamics which could regenerate China, then in that deeply historical sense Mao Tse-tung might possibly become a very great man. Meanwhile, Mao was of interest as a personality, apart from his political life, because, although his name was as familiar to many Chinese as that of Chiang Kai-shek, very little was known about him, and all sorts of strange legends existed about him. I was the first foreign newspaperman to interview him.

Mao had the reputation of a charmed life. He had been repeatedly pronounced dead by his enemies, only to return to the news columns a few days later, as active as ever. The Kuomintang had also officially "killed" and buried Chu The many times, assisted by occasional corroborations from clairvoyant missionaries. Numerous deaths of the two famous men, nevertheless, did not prevent them from being involved in many spectacular exploits, including the Long March. Mao was indeed in one of his periods of newspaper demise when I visited Red China, but I found him quite substantially alive. There were good reasons why people said that he had a charmed life, however; although he had been in scores of battles, was once captured by enemy troops and escaped, and had the world's highest reward on his head, during all these years he had never once been wounded.

I happened to be in Mao's house one evening

when he was given a complete physical examination by a Red surgeon—a man who had studied in Europe and who knew his business—and pronounced in excellent health. He had never had tuberculosis or any "incurable disease," as had been rumored by some romantic travelers. His lungs were completely sound, although, unlike most Red commanders, he was an inordinate cigarette smoker. During the Long March, Mao and Li The had carried on original botanical research by testing out various kinds of leaves as tobacco substitutes.

Ho Tzu-ch'en, Mao's second wife, a former schoolteacher and a Communist organizer herself, had been less fortunate than her husband. She had suffered more than a dozen wounds, caused by splinters from an air bomb, but all of them were superficial. Just before I left Pao An the Maos were proud parents of a new baby girl. He had two other children by his former wife, Yang K'ai-hui, the daughter of his favorite professor. She was killed in Changsha in 1930 at the order of General Ho Chien, warlord of Hunan province.

Mao Tse-tung was forty-three years old when I met him in 1936. He was elected chairman of the provisional Central Soviet Government at the Second All-China Soviet Congress, attended by delegates representing 9,000,000 people then living under Red laws. Here, incidentally, it may be inserted that Mao Tse-tung estimated the maximum population of the various districts under the direct control of the Soviet Central Government in 1934 as follows: Kiangsi Soviet, 3,000,000; Hupeh-Anhui-Honan Soviet, 2,000,000; Human-Kiangsi-Hupeh Soviet, 1,000,000; Kiangsi-Hunan Soviet, 1,000,000; Chekiang-Fukien Soviet, 1,000,000; Hunan-Hupeh Soviet, 1,000,000; total, 9,000,000. Fantastic estimates ranging as high as ten times that figure were evidently achieved by adding up the entire population in every area in which the Red Army or Red partisans had been reported as operating. Mao laughed when I quoted him the figure of "80,000,000" people liv-

ing under the Chinese soviets, and said that when they had that big an area the revolution would be practically won. But of course there were many millions in all the areas where Red partisans had operated.

The influence of Mao Tse-tung throughout the Communist world of China was probably greater than that of anyone else. He was a member of nearly everything—the revolutionary military committee, the political bureau of the Central Committee, the finance commission, the organization committee, the public health commission, and others. His real influence was asserted through his domination of the political bureau, which had decisive power in the policies of the Party, the government, and the army. Yet, while everyone knew and respected him, there was—as yet, at least—no ritual of hero worship built up around him. I never met a Chinese Red who drooled "our-great-leader" phrases, I did not hear Mao's name used as a synonym for the Chinese people, but still I never met one who did not like "the Chairman"—as everyone called him—and admire him. The role of his personality in the movement was clearly intense.

(Snow enthusiastically described the discipline and idealism of the insurgents, and he described them as having much more support among the peasants than had been previously thought. He also suggested that the Communists were likely to be victorious, saying in his last paragraph:)

The movement for social revolution in China might suffer defeats, might temporarily retreat, might for a time seem to languish, might make wide changes in tactics to fit immediate necessities and aims, might even for a period be submerged, be forced underground, but it would not only continue to mature; in one mutation or another it would eventually win, simply because (as this book proves, if it proves anything) the basic conditions which had given it birth carried within themselves the dynamic necessity for its triumph.

• • •

Snow had scooped the world. Before his trip, neither China experts nor the bulk of Chinese themselves had any knowledge of the personalities and the operations of the Chinese Communists. Now they did. "His report that they were not mere 'Red Bandits,' as Nationalists depicted them, but a coherent force with a loyal peasant following, was news not only abroad but in China itself," Hamilton wrote. With sympathy for China's plight growing, and with America anxiously looking for antifascist and anti-Japanese allies, *Red Star* caused many to rethink Chinese options and view the Communists in a more favorable light.

The reviews were stunning; in a not uncommon reaction, Malcolm Cowley called it "the greatest single feat performed by a journalist in our own century." The Chinese read it to learn more about Mao. Government officials, professors, and diplomats read it. The Communists printed Snow's interviews with Mao into a pamphlet. Even Snow's critics showed the measure of the work. The Nationalist Chinese, outraged at Snow's not-unfavorable portrayal of the Red army, denounced his reporting as a communist-inspired hoax and tried to keep the book out of the country. At the same time, Moscow communists and the American Communist Party, which followed the Moscow line, criticized Snow because of his view that the Chinese Communists were operating independently of Moscow.

The book also had an effect on individual readers. A Harvard student, Theodore White, read it and set out for China to write about it himself; two decades later, another Harvard student, Orville Schell, did the same. A cartoonist, Milton Caniff, read *Red Star* and used it as needed background for his new *Terry and the Pirates* strip, set in China. Snow later reported that he was told by individual rebels in at least four countries that

they had learned about how to fight their own revolutionary movements by reading his book.

Snow did not rest on his fame. He covered the Soviet western front in World War II, writing for the *Saturday Evening Post,* was the second American reporter into Riyadh, Saudi Arabia, and covered Indian independence.

Given the work he did in China, and later in the Soviet Union, it was not surprising that Snow's name came up during congressional and FBI investigations of supposed Communists after the Communist Revolution in China succeeded in 1949 and the People's Republic of China was proclaimed on the mainland.

Snow was never called to testify before legislative committees, but he was mentioned in numerous reports. He also started encountering problems getting his work published. In 1951, Snow resigned from the *Saturday Evening Post,* which was under considerable pressure from its conservative supporters about his employment. Snow felt his editors were not supporting him. For the rest of the decade, he wrote relatively little. "American views of China have swung in pendulum fashion between reality and illusion," and Snow's career tracked that swing, Seymour Topping, former foreign editor and managing editor of the *New York Times*, a man with substantial reporting experience in China, wrote in 1989. As American policy and public opinion returned to support of Chiang Kai-shek and the Nationalists, headquartered in Taiwan, Americans wanted only bad news about the Communists. Snow was out of sync.

But China would not leave his life. In 1960, he was invited to return, the first American reporter with previous experience in China to visit the People's Republic. He talked with old friends, many of them now government officials, and again met with Chou En-lai and with Mao Tse-tung. It was Mao's first interview with a Western reporter since 1949. Snow's book after that trip, *Red China Today,* was full of rare firsthand reporting, but its reception reflected American anti-

Communism and ignorance about China. *Look* magazine ran only one of the three articles for which it had contracted.

Snow returned to China again in 1964–65, and in 1970 he was the first American journalist admitted after the Cultural Revolution. Snow again saw Chou, and he was invited to stand with Mao at Peking's central square as thousands of Chinese trooped past to celebrate the twenty-first anniversary of the People's Republic. The invitation to Snow was, it was later learned, part of a Chinese effort to signal to America a desire for closer relations.

In 1972, President Richard M. Nixon made a break with his and the U.S. past by making a trip to China. In preparation, he read Snow's writings. Snow had hoped to be among the journalists covering the trip but was diagnosed with cancer in the months before. Snow died at his home in Switzerland in February 1972, at age sixty-six, less than a week before Nixon left on the historic trip.

Snow's ashes were placed at the campus of Peking University.

COLUMNIST DREW PEARSON TURNS THE TABLES ON A MCCARTHYITE CONGRESSMAN

Although the name of Senator Joseph McCarthy is most associated with the anti-Communist furor that swept Washington after World War II, Rep. J. Parnell Thomas of New Jersey was widely regarded as even more vehement and mean-tempered in his pursuit of communists, former communists, friends of communists, and people who ever had even neutral thoughts about communism. As head of the House Committee on Un-American Activities, and bolstered by large Republican victories in the 1946 midterm elections, Thomas organized a series of hearings to air charges of communist support in government and, most famously, in Hollywood.

Watching Thomas with a well-honed news-man's instincts, Drew Pearson, the investigative columnist, kept pressing his staff to get something on the congressman. As Pearson's colleague, Jack Anderson, wrote in *Confessions of a Muckraker*, "That Thomas was likely to have committed such acts was clear to Drew. The Branch of Americanism that went in for public inquisitions into the political notions of movie actors was bound to attract the dishonest man, the cheat looking for a patriotic cover."

Finally, with the help of Thomas's longtime secretary, the effort paid off.

The story was reported mostly by Anderson and written by Pearson.

August 4, 1948: WASHINGTON—One congressman who has sadly ignored the old adage that those who live in glass houses shouldn't throw stones is bouncing Rep. J. Parnell Thomas of New Jersey, Chairman of the UnAmerican Activities Committee.

If some of his own personal operations were scrutinized on the witness stand as carefully as he cross-examines witnesses, they would make headlines of a kind the Congressman doesn't like.

It is not, for instance, considered good "Americanism" to hire a stenographer and have her pay a "kickback." This kind of operation is also likely to get an ordinary American in income tax trouble. However, this hasn't seemed to worry the Chairman of the UnAmerican Activities Committee.

On Jan. 1, 1940, Rep. Thomas placed on his payroll Myra Midkiff as a clerk at $1,200 a year with the arrangement that she would then kick back all her salary to the Congressman. This gave Mr. Thomas a neat annual addition to his own $10,000 salary, and presumably he did not have to worry about paying income taxes in this higher bracket, because he paid Miss Midkiff's taxes for her in the much lower bracket.

The arrangement was quite simple and lasted for four years. Miss Midkiff's salary was merely deposited in the First National Bank of Allendale,

N.J., to the Congressman's account. Meanwhile she never came anywhere near his office and did not work for him except addressing envelopes at home for which she got paid $2 per hundred.

This kickback plan worked so well that four years later, Miss Midkiff having got married and left his phantom employ, the Congressman decided to extend it. On Nov. 16, 1944, the House Disbursing Officer was notified to place on Thomas's payroll the name of Arnette Minor at $1,800 a year. Actually Miss Minor was a day worker who made beds and cleaned the room of Thomas's secretary, Miss Helen Campbell. Miss Minor's salary was remitted to the Congressman. She never got it.

This arrangement lasted only a month and a half, for on Jan. 4, 1945, the name of Grace Wilson appeared on the Congressman' payroll for $2,900.

Miss Wilson turned out to be Mrs. Thomas's aged aunt, and during the year 1945 she drew checks totaling $3,467.45, though she did not come near the office, in fact remained quietly in Allendale, N.J., where she was supported by Mrs. Thomas and her sisters, Mrs. Lawrence Wellington and Mrs. William Quaintance.

In the summer of 1946, however, the Congressman decided to let the country support his wife's aunt, since his son had recently married and he wanted to put his daughter-in-law on the payroll. Thereafter, his daughter-in-law, Lillian, drew Miss Wilson's salary, and the Congressman demanded that his wife's aunt be put on relief.

• • •

Not settling to merely print the story, Pearson took the supporting information to the Justice Department and pressured officials there to prosecute. Thomas called the charges dirty politics and then stalled; his trial was postponed five times on grounds of his illness. Thomas served out his term, but did not run for reelection. The case finally went to court in late 1949. In the middle of the trial, Thomas pleaded no contest. He was

fined $10,000 and sentenced to eighteen months. He served his time at the Danbury State Prison in Connecticut, where a fellow prisoner was Ring Lardner, Jr., one of the Hollywood Ten jailed for refusing to cooperate with Thomas's committee.

The Thomas exposé was not Pearson's first nor last. In the 1930s he had brought about the conviction of many top members of the state government of Louisiana; in the 1940s he broke the news, which other reporters had purposely kept quiet, that General George S. Patton had slapped a soldier; in the 1950s, he reported that Sherman Adams, an Eisenhower White House aide, had received gifts, including a vicuna coat; in the 1960s his reports led to the expulsion of U.S. Representative Adam Clayton Powell and the censure of U.S. Senator Thomas Dodd. "It is the job of a newspaperman to spur the lazy, watch the weak, expose the corrupt," Pearson said. He was still working at his column when he died September 1, 1969.

BREAKING FROM THE "SILENT PRESS," THE *SEATTLE TIMES* FIGHTS ANTI-COMMUNISM AND SAVES A PROFESSOR'S JOB

Before there was a Joseph R. McCarthy, there was McCarthyism without the name. The nation had experienced what was a first "Red Scare" immediately following World War I. In June and November of 1919, widely publicized raids were conducted in New York City, and several thousand radicals and immigrants were arrested. In December of that year, 249 radicals and aliens, without benefit of trial and with the approval of the New York press, were deported on the ship S.S. *Buford* to the Soviet Union.

A second Red Scare began in the 1930s, abated during World War II, and exploded upon America in the ten years and more after the war. As early as 1944, U.S. Representative Claire Booth Luce, a Republican, said that the Communist Party "has gone underground, after the fashion of termites, into the Democratic Party." With the end of the war, almost no profession was safe from anti-Communism: teachers and university professors; labor union members and leaders; Hollywood actors, directors, and producers; scientists; authors; newspapermen; municipal workers and state and federal government employees; lawyers; and ordinary citizens.

In June 1946, the national chairman of the Republican Party said the fall elections offered a choice between Communism and Republicanism and that the "policy-making force of the Democratic Party" was now committed to the Soviet Union. That fall, Joseph R. McCarthy, running for the U.S. Senate from Wisconsin, accused his Democratic opponent, a professor, of being "Communistically inclined" and fabricated a *Daily Worker* reference to his opponent as a Communist symphathizer. The same year, Richard M. Nixon, campaigning in California for a U.S. congressional seat, said a vote for him was a vote against Communism.

Through all this, and through the ardent anti-Communism that would follow, most of the press applauded the anti-Communist hysteria, editorially and in news columns. In 1949, Robert R. McCormick's *Chicago Tribune* described Dean Acheson, secretary of state, as a "striped-pants snob" and a "lackey of Wall Street bankers, British lords, and Communistic radicals from New York." David Caute wrote in his book *The Great Fear:* "Without the assistance of the right-wing press, Red-baiting would have yielded much lower dividends for the politicians and prosecutors, just as a more principled resistance by supposedly liberal newspapers might have stiffened the spine of the Jeffersonian tradition." The anti-Communism occurred in big chains like Hearst, in the New York *Daily News*, the Washington *Times-Herald*, and the *Chicago Tribune*, and, Caute said, in hundreds of local papers that saw anti-Communism as a way to increase circulation.

In such an atmosphere, the case of Melvin Rader, a philosophy professor at the University of Washington, was typical. An admitted Communist charged that Rader had been with him at a Communist Party training school in New York state in 1938. Rader was called before the Washington State Un-American Activities Committee, where he denied the charges. But the committee believed its witness. The university fired Rader. Then Edwin Guthman, a reporter for the *Seattle Times*, took a look at the case. After five months of reporting, Guthman backed Rader's account.

An October 21, 1949, story detailed Guthman's findings:

The *Times* checked Rader's story and found it could be corroborated by documentary evidence and testimony of reputable citizens.

Dr. Carl Jensen, a prominent Seattle eye specialist, had tested Rader's eyes and given him a prescription for new glasses on August 15, 1938.

Rader said he had broken his glasses while at Canyon Creek and had gone to Seattle to get new ones. The record of his treatment was in Dr. Jensen's files.

Rader voted in the primary election of September 13, 1938, city records disclosed.

The two dates, plus university records showing that Rader taught summer school until July 20, and had signed for a book at the university library July 29, made it highly improbable that Rader had traveled to New York that summer.

The Communist school was reported to have lasted six weeks. Hewitt [George Hewitt, a former Communist who had accused Rader] definitely established that it was in the summer of 1938 that he assertedly saw Rader at the Communist school.

Rader said he and Mrs. Rader and their daughter went to Canyon Creek July 30 or 31 and stayed until about September 5.

Weighing most heavily against Rader was the small typewritten card that Canwell Committee investigators took from the files of Canyon Creek Lodge two days after Hewitt testified before the committee.

The card bore Mrs. Rader's name and listed her address as 6017 30th Avenue, N.E. A date "8-16-40" and "(40)" had been penned on the card, plus the notation "Prof. at U. of Washington, guest for 1 month."

The Canwell Committee assumed that the card meant the Raders had been at Canyon Creek in 1940, not 1938. The address was the tip-off that the committee was wrong.

An examination of the 1938, '39, and '40 telephone books and city directories showed that the Raders lived at the address on the card in 1938, had moved to 1402 E. 63rd Street in 1939, and were living at 1750 E. 62nd Street in 1940.

Mrs. Quincy Mueller, elderly former owner of the Canyon Creek resort, told this reporter that the card did not indicate when the Raders stayed at the lodge, but was from an index she had used for correspondence purposes.

Shown a photostatic copy of the card, Mrs. Mueller declared that the notation "8-16-40" referred to the date when she last wrote to the Raders. At that time, she recalled, she offered to sell them a lot near the resort.

Further indication that the Raders had been at the lodge in 1938 came from Mrs. Ida Kirby, who had been housekeeper at Canyon Creek.

Mrs. Kirby remembered that after the Raders' vacation was over she drove them to their home in Seattle. It was on 30th Avenue, their 1938 address.

Mrs. Mueller and Mrs. Kirby, who both still live near the lodge, had given affidavits to the committee investigators within four days after Hewitt testified. On that occasion they remembered the Raders, but were uncertain of the date the Raders had been at the lodge, because neither woman had had occasion to think about the Raders' visit during the intervening years.

Later, after recalling incidents of the Raders' visit, both women were certain it was in the summer of 1938.

The main lodge building burned in February 1938, and Mrs. Mueller remembered showing Mrs. Rader the charred wreckage. The ruins were removed later in 1938 or the next spring, Mrs. Mueller said.

Both women believed that Rader or Mrs. Rader had signed the lodge's loose-leaf register. According to Thomas J. Grant, present owner of the lodge, pages from the register were given to the Canwell committee's investigators.

The committee never has disclosed whether Rader's signature was or was not on the register.

• • •

Reacting to the *Times*'s reporting, the president of the University of Washington cleared Rader and reinstated him in October.

Guthman and the *Seattle Times* had scored a signal victory but it was, given the era and the press's pusillanimity, a rare one, for the press remained largely silent on the abuses of anti-Communism. In September 1949, President Harry S. Truman had revealed the Russians had exploded an atomic weapon. In February 1950, in a speech to a dinner meeting of the Ohio County Women's Republican Club in Wheeling, West Virginia, Senator Joseph McCarthy said, "I have here in my hand a list of 205 . . . a list of names that were known to the Secretary of State and who nevertheless are still working and shaping the policy of the State Department." All on the list, he said, were Communists. McCarthy had no list and later changed the numbers, once using 57 and another time using 207, but the press bought what he was saying and reported it. A senator had said it, after all, so it was, by journalistic definitions and conventions, news.

Although he often attacked the press, McCarthy "was able to generate the massive publicity that made him the center of anti-Communism because he understood the press, its practices and its values; he knew what made news," wrote Edwin R. Bayley, a *Milwaukee Journal* reporter, in *Joe McCarthy and the Press*. Journalistic convention, the practice of reporting straight what a high official said, whether or not the reporter thought the statement was true, enabled McCarthy and his colleagues to escape accountability. The protection of senatorial privilege, meaning that a senator, or a paper that reported his words, could not face libel charges for statements made on the floor of Congress, made it difficult for those attacked to respond.

Only a few papers, particularly the Madison, Wisconsin, *Capital-Times* and the *Milwaukee Journal*, both in McCarthy's home state, were diligent about trying to point out the falseness in McCarthy's charges. The *Journal* regularly inserted in brackets the facts about what McCarthy had said; one story, Bayley said, contained fifteen paragraphs of such facts. Now and again, individual reporters would, like Guthman, investigate individual cases, as I. F. Stone did in his weekly paper, Anthony Lewis did for the *Washington Daily News*, and Edward R. Murrow, near the end of the new Red Scare, did for CBS. But for the most part, the performance of the press—*the silent press*—during the era was flawed, damaging, and wrong.

EDWARD R. MURROW DEFENDS AN AIR FORCE LIEUTENANT UNJUSTLY TARRED IN ANTI-COMMUNIST ATTACKS

Television was in its infancy, or at least toddlerhood, in the early 1950s, technologically possible since the 1920s, on air commercially beginning in 1941, but frozen during World War II. Like radio, television broadcasting began by emphasizing music, comedy, and other entertainment. Regular television news began at CBS, where an unusually talented, war-trained group of radio announcers made the transition. Edward R. Murrow, who gained such fame for his reporting in World War II, was their dean. Working with Fred Friendly, an innovative newsman and producer who had put *I Can Hear It Now* on NBC radio, Murrow started the *See It Now* series on CBS on November 18, 1951.

Senator Joseph R. McCarthy of Wisconsin was in his prime in the early 1950s, seizing upon the uneasy mood of the time, the Korean War, and the country's fear of communism, the Soviet Union, and China to build an anti-Communist campaign that bullied people with innuendo and exaggeration. The campaign won McCarthy national prominence, the enthusiastic support of conservative groups, and the fear of many liberals. McCarthy prized all three.

Given Murrow's background of concern for civil liberties and freedom of speech, his experience covering World War II, and his awareness of the loyalty oaths and blacklisting in the broadcast and entertainment industries, a clash between Murrow and McCarthy was probably inevitable. But Murrow knew enough about the way television worked to know that he had to tell a story to win over the audience. In his voracious reading of the nation's newspapers, he found a story in the *Detroit News* that he thought might make a case history of the chilling ways the government was trampling on the freedom of average citizens. The subject was Lieutenant Milo Radulovich, a World War II veteran, a meteorologist in the Air Force Reserve, and a University of Michigan student.

The Air Force refused to comment for the broadcast, and sent a general and lieutenant colonel to New York to try to steer Murrow, who had narrated Defense Department films, in another direction. CBS did not step in to try to stop production, but its backing was hardly enthusiastic; the network refused to publicize the program and Murrow and Friendly paid $1,500 of their own money to take an advertisement, which did not mention the network's name, in the *New York Times*.

See It Now, the Columbia Broadcasting System, October 20, 1953. Edited by Edward R. Murrow and Fred W. Friendly.

EDWARD R. MURROW: Good evening. A few weeks ago, there occurred a few obscure notices in the newspaper about a Lieutenant Milo Radulovich, a lieutenant in the Air Force Reserve, and also something about Air Force Regulation 35–62. That is a regulation which states that a man may be regarded as a security risk if he has close and continuing association with Communists or people believed to have Communist sympathies. Lieutenant Radulovich was asked to resign. He declined. A Board was called and heard his case. At the end, it was recommended that he be severed from the Air Force, although it was also stated that there was no question whatever as to the lieutenant's loyalty. We propose to examine, in so far as we can, the case of Lieutenant Radulovich. Our reporter, Joe Wershba. Cameraman, Charlie Mack.

JOE WERSHBA: This is the town of Dexter, Michigan, population, 1,500.

MURROW: This statue is at the head of Ann Arbor Street: "Erected by the citizens of Dexter to the heroes who fought and the martyrs who died that the Republic might live." This is the story of Milo Radulovich—no special hero, no martyr. He came to Dexter one year ago, after ten years in the Air Force, won a general commendation for working on a secret weather station in Greenland. Now he is a senior at the University of Michigan eight miles away. His wife works nights at the telephone company. They live at 7867 Ann Arbor Street. This is Milo Radulovich.

MILO RADULOVICH: The Air Force does not question my loyalty in the least. They have reiterated that on several occasions. They have presented me with allegations against my sister and father— that they have—to the effect that my sister and dad have taken—have read what are now called subversive newspapers, and that my sister and father's activities are questionable. That's the specific charge—or allegation, I prefer to call it— against them. Against me, the actual charge against me is that I had maintained a close and continuing relationship with my dad and my sister over the years. I had spent the last seven years studying or actually working in meteorology— that is, weather forecasting—and now for the past approximately year and a half or two I have been studying physics at the University of Michigan. Well, I think I am being a realist about it. Anybody that is labeled with a security risk in these days, especially in physics or meteorology, simply won't be able to find employment in his field of work. In other words, I believe that if I am labeled a security risk—if the Air Force won't have me, I ask the question, who else will?

MURROW: This is Selfridge Field, Headquarters of the Tenth Air Force, where the Radulovich hearing took place. There was a Board made up of three colonels, whose recommendation was that Radulovich be separated from the service as a bad security risk "for having maintained a close, continuing association with your sister and your father." The Board also stated: "No question as to your loyalty is involved." No reporters were permitted at the hearing, and the Air Force refused to provide us with a transcript of the hearing. It was unclassified, however. Lietutenant Radulovich was defended by Attorney Charles C. Lockwood, and this is his report on the hearing.

CHARLES C. LOCKWOOD: When this case started, the president of the Hearing Board placed a sealed envelope in front of him and said: "These are the allegations. Now proceed to exonerate yourself." There were twelve charges made by the Air Force— eight of them against the sister and four of them against the father. We put in several disinterested witnesses, who testified definitely and positively upon the allegations made by the Air Force. These witnesses gave unchallenged testimony and they gave it under oath. The Air Force did not produce a single witness. We were not told who the accusers were. We have no right to confront them or cross-examine them. But at the conclusion of the trial, although we had met the allegations; the Air Force made findings at the conclusion of the hearing that every single allegation was true. They disregarded every bit of testimony we introduced and the statements of all our witnesses. As a matter of fact, we have had no hearing at all. We have had no day in court. In all the thirty-two years that I have been a practicing attorney in Detroit, I have never witnessed such a farce and travesty upon justice as this thing has developed. Now this whole theory of guilt by relationship is something that was adopted back in the thirteenth and fourteenth century and then abandoned as being inhuman and cruel. It was later revived in Germany under Hitler and Himmler, and it died when they died. Now the Air Force, for some unknown reason, has revived this intolerable guilt by relationship, and the whole country is shocked by reason thereof.

MURROW: Dexter has been a town for over one hundred years—has had no spectacular news stories, no causes célèbres. But they are vitally concerned with the case of Milo Radulovich, and they are willing to discuss it. This is John Palmer, chief marshal of the town. He has known Radulovich a year.

JOHN PALMER: I find him to be a good fellow here, and the people were quite shocked in Dexter when they found out about it—and as I read about it more in the papers. Why, it's still a mystery to me why they are condemning him for something that his father did. Certainly he can't condemn his father and cast him aside just because he read a paper that he wasn't supposed to read. I couldn't do that. Neither could any other boy who had a father....

———

MURROW: Milo Radulovich's father lives at 3953 Nottingham Street [in Detroit]. He owns his own house. According to Milo, his father denied subscribing to the *Daily Worker* and said he subscribed to the Serbian-language newspaper, which was pro-Tito, because he liked their Christmas calendars. This week John Radulovich and his wife decided to send a letter to the President of the United States.

JOHN RADULOVICH: Here's a letter I write to the President. I want to read to you. "Dear Mr. President: I writing to you with heavy heart. I am an American citizen who come here thirty-nine years ago from Serbia. I serve America in the Army in the first world war. My boy Milo was in this last war. My whole life, my whole family, is American. Mr. President, I writing to you because they are doing a bad thing to Milo. They are wrong. The things they say about him are wrong. He has given all his growing years to his country. He is good for this county. Mr. President, I am an old man. I have spent my life in this coal mine and auto furnaces. I ask nothing for myself. All I ask is justice for my boy. Mr. President, I ask your help."

MURROW: This is the sister, Margaret Radulovich Fishman. She neither defends nor explains her political activities.

MARGARET RADULOVICH FISHMAN: I do feel very personally, I feel very badly about the thing. I feel that he is being forced to undergo a strain for a very unjust cause. I feel that my activities, be what they may—my political beliefs are my own private affair; and I feel that the charges leveled against me, and by reason of which they are trying to purge him from the Army are—you know—just seem to me to be a fantastic trend in this country. It's—I mean, you know, since when can a man be adjudged guilty, which is in effect what's happened to him, because of the alleged political beliefs or activities of a member of his family.

MURROW: Back in Dexter, we returned to the wooden frame house on Ann Arbor Street and talked to Milo's wife.

WERSHBA: Nancy, considering you are a mother with two kids—deep down, wouldn't you have preferred that Milo would have kept sort of quiet about this and maybe it would have passed over? And nobody would have known about it?

NANCY RADULOVICH: Well, no, I wouldn't want him to take it lying down. If he did, he would be admitting to something that we aren't guilty of, and I don't see how this should have happened to us when we have done nothing to warrant it.

WERSHBA: Do you think you might have avoided all trouble if Milo would have said, "Well, I will resign; I'll quit!"?

NANCY: No. No, I wouldn't want him to do that. As far as the publicity is concerned, it makes the rest of the country know what's happening, and they all feel for us and want to help us. I don't regret anything—him coming forward and fighting it.

WERSHBA: Well, Milo, what about this close and continuing relationship that the Air Force talked about, in terms of you and your father and sister?

MILO: That charge is defined by the Air Force as visiting frequently, writing frequently, or living at the same address as the accused. In my case—I don't mean to apologize or anything like that for my relationships or my relatives—but I have maintained throughout this entire hearing that what my sister does, what political opinions or activities she engages in, are her own affair. Because they certainly do not influence me. She is a woman, married, about to have a child; twenty-nine years of age, perfectly capable of making her own decisions: a mature adult. The close association I have maintained in the hearing—and this is what the Air Force hung its removal decision on—I told them

in the hearing that I felt that, yes, I was close to my sister and my father, and that I was born into it. I mean, she is my sister and he is my father. I am his son and I am her brother, and I certainly can't cut the blood tie nor do I wish to cut the blood tie; and they quoted me directly those words in their findings. In other words, the implication seemed—to me, at least—to be that if I had said, "I will cut the blood ties, et cetera," everything would have been beautiful with the Air Force.

————

MURROW: We have told the Air Force that we will provide facilities for any comments, criticism, or correction it may wish to make in regard to the case of Milo Radulovich. The case must go through two more Air Force Boards, routine and channels, before it reaches Secretary Talbott, who will make the final decision. We are unable to judge the charges against the lieutenant's father or sister, because neither we, nor you, nor they, nor the lieutenant, nor the lawyers know precisely what was contained in that manila envelope. Was it hearsay, rumor, gossip, slander, or was it hard, ascertainable fact that could be backed by creditable witnesses? We do not know.

There is a distinct difference between a loyalty and a security risk. A man may be entirely loyal, but at the same time be subjected to coercion, influence, or pressure, which may cause him to act contrary to the best interest of national security. In the case of Lieutenant Radulovich, the Board found that there was no question of his loyalty, but he was regarded as a security risk. The security officers will tell you that a man who had a sister in Warsaw, for example, might be entirely loyal, but would be subjected to pressure as a result of threats that might be made against his sister's security or well-being. They contend that a man who has a sister in the Communist Party in this country might be subjected to the same kind of pressure; but here again, no evidence was adduced to prove that Radulovich's sister is a member of the party, and the case against his father was certainly not made.

We believe that "the son shall not bear the iniquity of the father," even though that iniquity be proved; and in this case, it was not. But we believe, too, that this case illustrates the urgent need for the Armed Forces to communicate more fully than they have so far done, the procedures and regulations to be followed in attempting to protect the national security and the rights of the individual at the same time. Whatever happens in this whole area of the relationship between the individual and the state, we will do it ourselves—it cannot be blamed upon Malenknov, or Mao Tse-tung, or even our allies. And it seems to us that—that is, to Fred Friendly and myself—that that is a subject that should be argued about endlessly.

• • •

Five weeks later, the secretary of the U.S. Air Force, Harold E. Talbott, called Murrow and asked him to send a cameraman to the Pentagon to film a statement. Technology was different, and slower in these days; it was several hours later, in New York, that Murrow saw what Talbott had said: Upon reviewing the case, the secretary had concluded that Radulovich was not a security risk and directed that the lieutenant be allowed to remain in the Air Force. A cheer went up, and, A. M. Sperber, one of Murrow's biographers, said, even though it was morning, Murrow broke out the Scotch for a toast "To Milo."

Television critics and much of the public praised Murrow, although a number of CBS affiliates and some in the corporate hierarchy were lukewarm about any discussion of the controversial issue of anti-Communism. Murrow nonetheless was emboldened to produce more programs on civil liberties and the hysteria of the McCarthy era: "An Argument in Indianapolis," between the American Legion and the American Civil Liberties Union; a report on "Annie Lee Moss Before the McCarthy Committee," about a Defense Department file clerk accused of being a Communist; and, finally, on March 9, 1954, "A Report on Senator Joseph R. McCarthy," mostly in McCarthy's

own words, which ended with Murrow's call for citizens to speak up against McCarthy's tactics. Although that program has in retrospect become more famed, Murrow himself thought it came a little late in the game, that he had only realized before others that McCarthy was in a slide and therefore vulnerable. Joseph Wershba, Murrow's longtime *See It Now* reporter, said it was the Radulovich story that remained special to Murrow: "Ed was more pleased about this than anything else. It was clean. No rough edges. A victory."

The Radulovich broadcast, however, angered McCarthy. In November, a McCarthy investigator gave the reporter, Wershba, a copy of a 1935 newspaper story noting that Murrow had worked for the Institute for International Education, an exchange group that had held a seminar at Moscow University. The investigator described this as proof "Murrow was on the Soviet payroll in 1934." To Wershba, "The implication was clear. Murrow was now a full-fledge McCarthy target for having dared to broadcast the Radulovich story."

Radulovich never graduated from college, but went on to become a meterologist for the National Weather Service. The Air Force attack, he said in the 1960s, "stopped me from achieving some of the goals I wanted to attain." But, he said, "I consider myself really lucky. It was only by public opinion that I was able to carry my fight."

THE *LOS ANGELES TIMES* REPORTS ON THE JOHN BIRCH SOCIETY AND TAKES A STEP TOWARD BECOMING A MAJOR AMERICAN NEWSPAPER

At the end of the 1950s, in conservative southern California and the newspaper that built it, the *Los Angeles Times*, the John Birch Society understandably expected to find a comfortable home for its strongly anti-Communist views. After all, when

Colonel Harrison Gray Otis bought into the infant paper in 1882, he had set it on an antilabor, antireform, anti-immigrant, prodevelopment course that stuck. Harry Chandler, Otis's son-in-law and successor, who took control of the paper in 1917, added the Bolsheviks to the paper's list of enemies, although he was not adverse to joining into a profitable oil deal with agents of Lenin. Norman Chandler, Harry's son, who became publisher in 1944, kept up the anti-Communism, which naturally led to the paper's support of Senator Joseph McCarthy of Wisconsin and of a hometown politician, Richard Milhous Nixon. The *Times* was the "information bible" of the radical right, wrote Robert Gottlieb and Irene Wolt in *Thinking Big* (New York: G. P. Putnam, 1977), "a means by which the Southern California upper-class recognized itself and its politics."

The Birchers were also comforted by the fact that, in a little more than two years after the society's founding in December 1958, it had nearly 100,000 members across the country. Southern California was a stronghold, with several thousand members, including Norman Chandler's brother, Philip, executive vice president of the paper, and Philip's wife, Alberta. This fact was apparently unknown to Otis Chandler, who became publisher in April 1960 at the age of thirty-two.

Chandler took over one of the country's most profitable papers, but he had a vision of adding another value to it: making it one of the country's best papers. His editor, Nick Williams, and day managing editor, Frank McCulloch, hired from *Time* magazine, prepared to reshape the paper. New, aggressive reporters were hired, and old-timers fired. Editorial budgets were increased, and travel expenses paid. In-depth series and interpretive articles began to appear. Progress was gradual, however, with the forces of the old ways still strong in the newsroom.

The story that tipped the balance was the *Times*'s profile of the John Birch Society. During 1960 and 1961, David Halberstam wrote in *The Powers That Be*, great bundles of hate mail began pouring into the *Times* demanding that Chief Justice Earl Warren, a former governor of California, be impeached for what were called his procommunist, prodesegregation leanings. The mail became more and more abusive, and the *Times* was one of the targets.

Williams recognized that the Birchers were having a national impact and that little was known about them. He had seen the small, nearby *Santa Barbara News-Press* take a look at the society, a courageous act for a small paper and one that would win it a Pulitzer Prize for editorial writing. Still, Williams wanted to move cautiously. He assigned Gene Blake, a veteran reporter whose courtroom experience gave him the strictly objective tone Williams was looking for.

"The John Birch Society: What Are Its Purposes?" by Gene Blake. *Los Angeles Times,* March 5, 1961.

On a wintry day a little over two years ago, a dozen men gathered in Indianapolis at the invitation of a retired Massachusetts candy manufacturer, Robert Welch.

They were influential, busy men. One came from Oregon, one from Kansas, one from Missouri, two from Wisconsin, one from Illinois, one from Indiana, one from Tennessee, one from Virginia and two from Massachusetts.

These men weren't exactly sure why they were there, except that they all shared the same concern over the menace of international communism, its influence in America and the fate of this nation.

For two full days they listened to Robert Welch set forth his views of the problem and what he thought should be done about it. Out of that meeting of Dec. 8 and 9, 1958, came the John Birch Society.

Within a year there were working chapters in New Hampshire, Massachusetts, Connecticut, New York, Virginia, South Carolina, Florida, Tennessee, Michigan, Illinois, Wisconsin, Iowa, Louisiana, Texas, California and Washington. There were also members of the home chapter—sort of "at large" members in about 40 states.

Now, after another year, the list of states with from one to more than 100 working chapters has grown to 34, plus the District of Columbia, and there are home chapter members in all 50 states.

Organized and developed quietly at first—almost secretly—the society is now making its voice heard and no longer shuns the spotlight. By the end of the year the national membership is expected to reach 100,000. The goal is a million.

There are several thousand members in scores of chapters throughout Southern California today, according to Paul H. (Tex) Talbert, Beverly Hills insurance executive who is a member of the society's national council.

They are hard at work attacking the Communist menace as they see it on the home front, either directly or through other organizations— PTAs, social and civic groups, study clubs, church societies.

Talbert won't hazard a guess as to how many working, hard-core, live Communists there are in Southern California. But he and his fellow John Birchers do not believe that is the crux of the problem.

"Even though there are relatively only a few Communists," Talbert said, "for every one there are 10 people standing behind ready to do their bidding and for each of these there are another 10—the do-gooder type—willing to go along with them.

"It would take only a few hundred Communists to upset the balance from a political standpoint. In Russia, less than 3% of the 200 million people are Communists and in any country they have taken over there have been no more."

Talbert sees Communist influences working directly here in front organizations, infiltrating political organizations and college campuses. But more than that he sees Communist objectives be-

ing furthered by certain newspaper writers, in motion pictures, in church pulpits and in all levels of government.

"It it sometimes necessary to differentiate between Socialism and Communism, although their aims are the same—leading to the destruction of our constitution and private enterprise," Talbert said.

"There are a lot of things going on in city, country, state and federal government that are certainly driving us into the arms of Socialism. If we continue on the road to Socialism, it will be just an overnight shift to Communism."

John Birchers in Southern California and throughout the country are trying to alert the public, according to Talbert, through concentrated letter-writing campaigns, circulating petitions, speaking before various groups, showing anti-Communist films and distributing anti-Communist literature—under the over-all leadership of founder Robert Welch.

Who is the man who brought this about and what is his purpose?

Detractors are quick to point out that Robert Welch is the man who wrote several years ago, in a manuscript called "The Politician" by some and the "black book" by others, that former President Eisenhower and top members of his administration were Communist or tools of the Communists. . . .

Others listed by Welch in "The Politician" as part or tools of the Communist conspiracy included former Presidents Roosevelt and Truman, Chief Justice Warren, the late Secretary of State John Foster Dulles and his brother Allen, head of the Central Intelligence Agency. . . .

This gives a clue to the general tenor of the society's charges: communists have been and still are in control of high places in the U.S. government, the armed forces, the courts, the schools and universities, the press, radio, television and motion pictures, unions, the United Nations, the private foundations and the churches.

Unless the public wakes up, the society fears, it is only a question of time before the United States falls without a struggle into the world-wide Communist dominion ruled from the Kremlin.

Welch, of course, is just one of many who have preached this doctine of imminent Communist domination to some degree for years. One was the late Sen. Joseph McCarthy, who has become almost a patron saint of the John Birch Society.

But Welch appears to have had success greater than any other man in welding his followers into a cohesive force with a program of action. It is a program of fighting fire with fire, openly using some of the tactics that have proved successful for the enemy....

For five years he has edited and published a monthly magazine, *American Opinion*. In 1957 he gave up most of his other business responsibilities to devote nearly all his time and energy to the anti-Communist cause.

Welch chose the subject of one of his books as the name for his society because he felt this young man symbolized all that the society should stand for.

John Birch was a fundamentalist Baptist preacher from Georgia who became a missionary in China and then an intelligence officer with Gen. Claire Chennault's forces during World War II. He helped Gen. James Doolittle escape from China after the famous raid on Tokyo.

But 10 days after V-J Day, Capt. Birch was shot and killed in a Chinese village near Hsuchow. Five years later, former Sen. Knowland charged in a Senate speech that he was murdered in cold blood by Chinese Communists.

Welch's book purports to be a documentation of that charge, as well as an exposé of a "cover-up" by the U.S. government in a policy of "appeasement" toward Red China.

"It is clear that the Communists, high and low, recognized John Birch as standing for America, for Christianity, and as the very embodiment of those qualities and forces which were in their way," Welch wrote.

• • •

"The Blake series was the first investigative story by a major news medium, and from it flowed the national attention focused on the Birch Society," wrote Jack R. Hart in *The Information Empire* (University Press of America, 1981). Wire services and other papers followed up. The governor of California announced a probe, and a few conservative politicians denounced the group for its secretive ways.

In truth, the *Times*'s articles on the Birch Society were moderate. But that, in itself, was a sea change for the paper. The five-part series, supported by a front-page Sunday editorial, "Peril to Conservatives," running under Otis Chandler's name, resulted in an intense attack on the paper. There was pressure from advertisers and more than 15,000 people canceled their subscriptions, an amazing number. With its preeminence in the Los Angeles area, however, the paper was not seriously injured.

Executives were made nervous by the reaction. For a time, the *Times* overcovered anti-Communist events. The series also exacerbated a family feud, and in November, Philip Chandler, whose Birch Society membership was never mentioned in the series, was asked to resign.

Most important, the John Birch series was a coming-out for a new, less deferential, more balanced kind of journalism at the *Times*. "Ultimately," said Gottlieb and Wolt, "the most profound impact of the Bircher series was its effect on local journalists. A *Los Angeles Times* reporter, Don Neff, recalled, 'By God, when I saw that series, my eyes popped, and I realized that this was going to be a serious newspaper.' "

The *Los Angeles Times*, which became part of Tribune Publishing in 2000, routinely makes lists of the country's great papers. The John Birch Society has dwindled to a few thousand members.

LIFE MAGAZINE BRINGS DOWN A U.S. SUPREME COURT JUSTICE

Abe Fortas was the prototype of a liberal, New Deal lawyer. He was educated at Southern University in Memphis, Tennessee, his hometown, and at Yale University Law School, where he was graduated first in his class. He worked in various positions in Washington from 1937 to 1946, gaining valuable knowledge of the federal government that served him well as a private lawyer. He also became a trusted adviser of Lyndon B. Johnson, whom he successfully represented in a disputed U.S. Senate primary election in 1948.

In 1965, Johnson, by then president, appointed Fortas an associate justice on the U.S. Supreme Court. Fortas was somewhat reluctant to accept the appointment—though not as concerned as his wife, who was upset by the loss of income. In 1968, Chief Justice Earl Warren resigned, and Johnson nominated Fortas as chief justice. The nomination faced a filibuster, however, given Fortas's continuing alliances with Johnson and outside fees he had received for teaching a university course. Fortas asked that the nomination be withdrawn, but he remained on the court.

The next year, Fortas's habit of seeking extra money came again to public attention in an article in *Life* magazine.

"The Justice . . . and the Stock Manipulator," by William Lambert. *Life,* May 9, 1969.

On Tuesday, April 1, the Supreme Court of the United States shut the door on an appeal by financial manipulator Louis Wolfson and his long-time associate, Elkin "Buddy" Gerbert. It was very nearly the last hope of the two men to set aside the first of two convictions for violating U.S. securities laws. In the announcement of denial of the writ, one of the Justices, Abe Fortas,

was noted as "recused," a lawyers' expression meaning he declined to take part in the decision.

On the surface, the recusal seemed usual and proper, for it was widely known that the Justice's former law firm—Arnold, Fortas & Porter—had represented a Wolfson company, New York Shipbuilding Corp., while Fortas was a member of the firm. Moreover, after Fortas had ascended to the bench and his name had been scraped off the law firm's door, Arnold & Porter had represented Gerbert in his two criminal trials with Wolfson. Actually, quite apart from the actions of his former firm, Justice Fortas had reason to abstain from judging Louis Wolfson.

In an investigation over a period of several months, LIFE found evidence of a personal association between the Justice and Wolfson that took place *after* Fortas was seated as a member of the nation's highest tribunal.

The basic facts are simple: While a member of the High Court, Fortas was paid $20,000 by the Wolfson Family Foundation, a tax-free charitable foundation set up by Wolfson and his brothers. Ostensibly, Justice Fortas was being paid to advise the foundation on ways to use its funds for charitable, educational and civil rights projects. Whatever services he may or may not have rendered in this respect, Justice Fortas' name was being dropped in strategic places by Wolfson and Gerbert in their effort to stay out of prison on the securities charge. That this was done without his knowledge does not change the fact that his acceptance of the money, and other actions, made the name-dropping effective.

Justice Fortas ultimately refunded the money to the foundation—but not until nearly a year after receiving it. By that time Wolfson and Gerbert had been twice indicted on federal criminal charges. . . .

From Lyndon Johnson's days as a congressman through his term as President of the United States, Fortas was his counsel and close confidant. In 1964, when Johnson aide Walter Jenkins ran afoul of the law, it was Fortas (along with Clark Clifford) who tried to get the newspapers to suppress the story. If a person had to see the President, Fortas was the man who could arrange it. If the President wished to fend off influential tormentors—including the press—Fortas frequently was dispatched to do the fending.

Fortas continued to advise and do favors for President Johnson after he took his seat on the Supreme Court in October, 1965. That extrajudicial activity finally got him in trouble and cost him the job of Chief Justice. . . .

Fortas' personal association with Wolfson appears to have begun about four years ago. Wolfson himself recalls that Milton Freeman, a partner in Arnold, Fortas & Porter and a highly skilled securities lawyer, was active in his behalf as early as December 1964 in regard to his growing difficulties with the Securities and Exchange Commission. Fortas himself says that apart from the firm's representation of one of Wolfson's companies since May or June 1965, his "only 'association' with Mr. Wolfson had to do with conversations beginning when I first met him in 1965, in which he told me of the program of the Wolfson Family Foundation. . . ." This statement is contained in a letter to LIFE written in response to a request for a meeting when he would be given an opportunity to explain any information in LIFE's possession that might be construed in any way as an impropriety on his part. The request was turned down. "Since there has been no impropriety, or anything approaching it, in my conduct, no purpose could be served by any such meeting," Fortas wrote.

It is not easy to pin down the exact extent of the Wolfson-Fortas relationship, nor has LIFE uncovered evidence making possible a charge that Wolfson hired Fortas to fix his case. But the conflicting accounts of participants (some of whom refuse to tell all or anything), compiled with the findings of LIFE's independent investigation, yield certain facts.

On Jan. 3, 1966, three months after Fortas was sworn in as Associate Justice, a check for $20,000 was drawn to him personally on a Jacksonville, Fla. bank account of the Wolfson Family Foundation, and signed by Gerbert as foundation treasurer. It was endorsed with the Justice's name and deposited in his personal—not his old law firm's—bank account.

In February, Alexander Rittmaster, a Wolfson business associate who later was to be indicted with him, asked Wolfson what he was doing about the Securities and Exchange Commission's investigation, then at least 15 months in progress. Rittmaster said Wolfson told him it was going to be taken care of "at the top," and that the matter wouldn't get out of Washington. He also said that Fortas was joining the foundation.

On March 14, the SEC forwarded a report to the Justice Department in Washington and to U.S. Attorney Robert Morgenthau in New York. The report, highly classified, recommended criminal prosecution of Wolfson and Gerbert. The charge was that they conspired to unload secretly their control shares in the Wolfson-dominated Continental Enterprises, Inc., by failing to publicly register their proposed stock sales. (The SEC investigation showed they realized $3.5 million from the sale, after which the remaining stockholders found their shares had dropped from $8 to $1.50.) . . .

On June 14, the day after the Supreme Court had gone into a week's recess, Justice Fortas flew to Jacksonville. Gerbert met him at the airport and drove out to Wolfson's elegant Harbor View Farm, near Ocala, where Wolfson owns one of the largest thoroughbred horse-breeding spreads in the country.

On June 15, while Fortas was a house guest at Harbor View, the SEC's long-feared investigation finally came to public attention. . . .

On Sept. 19, Wolfson and Gerbert were indicted in the Continental Enterprises case. . . .

On Dec. 22, Fortas drew a personal check for $20,000 on his own bank account, payable to the Wolfson Family Foundation, thus paying back the money he had received from the Wolfson foundation more than 11 months earlier. . . .

The question arises: Aside from legal advice, what manner of counseling service could Fortas perform for the foundation that would justify a $20,000 fee? In the light of other recorded foundation expenditures, the amount seems generous in the extreme.

In its 1966 fiscal year, the foundation's gross income from capital investment was $115,200. Its outlay for expenses was $9,300 and included taxes, interest and $415 in miscellaneous costs. Its total grants for charity, scholarships and gifts came to $77,680. . . .

Wolfson's reputation and his troubles with the SEC were well known in financial and legal circles. Fortas' questionable association with such a man was rendered even more serious by the fact that money passed between them. . . .

• • •

The *Life* article caused a firestorm. Fortas's statement in response to the charges was, as so often happens in Washington, incomplete. Congress and the press howled. The Justice Department, working for President Nixon, who sorely wanted to have the opportunity to appoint a conservative to the Supreme Court, investigated. In documents subpoenaed from Wolfson, officials found a copy of an agreement that Fortas was to get $20,000 a year for life from the Wolfson Foundation. On May 14, as the *Los Angeles Times* was preparing to run an article disclosing the annuity agreement, Fortas sent his resignation to President Richard Nixon. Fortas admitted "no wrongdoing" but said he wanted to spare the Supreme Court "extraneous stress."

With Chief Justice Earl Warren already having announced his retirement, Nixon had two vacancies to fill. He nominated federal Judge Warren Burger to be chief justice of the United States and then Henry Blackmun, a federal appeals court judge, to replace Fortas as associate justice. Both were more conservative than their predecessors, and the era of the Warren Court was over.

Fortas returned to corporate law, though not at his old firm, and quickly was back among Washington's big players. The American Bar Association later rewrote its canons of ethics to explicitly forbid conflicts like that involving Fortas.

TWO YOUNG *WASHINGTON POST* REPORTERS FOLLOW THE MONEY AND FORCE THE RESIGNATION OF A PRESIDENT

By the early 1970s, President Richard M. Nixon's White House had become a center of paranoia and contempt for American values. In Nixon's mind, there were no cordial disagreements of policy; a person was with him or against him. Illegal investigations were ordered. Wire taps were made. An enemies' list was assembled.

With a second presidential campaign coming in November 1972, the Nixon forces established the Committee to Re-elect the President, which later became known as CREEP, headed by Attorney General John N. Mitchell. This was a highly secret organization with vast amounts of money at its disposal. Some of the money was used to pay burglars to enter the Watergate Hotel on a Saturday night in June 1972, apparently in search of information from the offices of the Democratic National Committee that would damage possible Democratic opponents.

Two young reporters on the metro staff of the *Washington Post*, Carl Bernstein and Bob Woodward, were assigned to the burglary story. It shortly became apparent to Woodward and Bernstein and some of their editors that the story was more than a simple burglary—that the White

House was somehow deeply involved in the crime. It also became apparent that the goings-on at the Watergate were just one example of the illegal activities engaged in by White House and campaign committee operatives.

For a long time, the *Washington Post* was alone in following the trail of the burglary. In many newsrooms, reporters and editors scoffed at what the *Post* was doing. Within the *Post*, some editors wanted to take the story away from Woodward and Bernstein and give it instead to seasoned political reporters. But Woodward and Bernstein and their editors—especially Howard Simons, Barry Sussman, and Ben Bradlee—persevered.

Here is a story, among hundreds, the two wrote on Watergate and related matters. (The order of their names in the byline was alternated.) This is the first story that linked the reelection committee and the burglary, and is a prime example of the reporting rule: follow the money.

"Bug Suspect Got Campaign Funds," by Carl Bernstein and Bob Woodward. *Washington Post,* August 1, 1972.

A $25,000 cashier's check, apparently earmarked for President Nixon's re-election campaign, was deposited in April in a bank account of one of the five men arrested in the break-in at Democratic National Headquarters here June 17.

The check was made out by a Florida bank to Kenneth H. Dahlberg, the President's campaign finance chairman for the Midwest. Dahlberg said last night that in early April he turned the check over to "the treasurer of the Committee (for the Re-election of the President) or to Maurice Stans himself."

Stans, formerly Secretary of Commerce under Mr. Nixon, is now the finance chief of the President's re-election effort.

Dahlberg said he didn't have "the vaguest idea" how the check got into the bank account of the real estate firm owned by Bernard L. Barker, one of the break-in suspects. Stans could not be reached for comment.

Reached by telephone at his home in a Minneapolis suburb, Dahlberg explained the existence of the check this way:

"In the process of fund-raising I had accumulated some cash . . . so I recall making a cash deposit while I was in Florida and getting a cashier's check made out to myself. I didn't want to carry all that cash into Washington."

A photostatic copy of the front of the check was examined by a *Washington Post* reporter yesterday. It was made out by the First Bank and Trust Co. of Boca Raton, Fla., to Dahlberg.

Thomas Monohan, the assistant vice president of the Boca Raton bank, who signed the check authorization, said the FBI had questioned him about it three weeks ago.

According to court testimony by government prosecutors, Barker's bank account in which the $25,000 was deposited was the same account from which Barker later withdrew a large number of hundred-dollar bills. About 53 of these $100 bills were found on the five men after they were arrested at the Watergate.

Dahlberg has contributed $7,000 to the GOP since 1968, records show, and in 1970 he was finance chairman for Clark MacGregor when MacGregor ran unsuccessfully against Hubert M. Humphrey for a U.S. Senate seat in Minnesota.

MacGregor, who replaced John N. Mitchell as Mr. Nixon's campaign chief on July 1, could offer no explanation as to how the $25,000 got from the campaign finance committee to Barker's account.

He told a *Post* reporter last night: "I know nothing about it . . . these events took place before I came aboard. Mitchell and Stans would presumably know."

MacGregor said he would attempt this morning to determine what happened.

Powell Moore, director of press relations for the Committee for the Re-election of the President, told a reporter that Stans was unavailable for comment last night. Mitchell also could not be reached for comment.

In a related development, records made available to the *Post* yesterday show that another $89,000 in four separate checks was deposited during May in Barker's Miami bank account by a well-known Mexican lawyer.

The deposits were made in the form of checks made out to the lawyer, Manuel Ogarrio Daguerre, 68, by the Banco Internacional of Mexico City.

Ogarrio could not be reached for comment and there was no immediate explanation as to why the $89,000 was transferred to Barker's account.

This makes a total of $114,000 deposited in Barker's account in the Republic National Bank of Miami, all on April 20.

The same amount—$114,000—was withdrawn on three separate dates, April 24, May 2 and May 8.

Since the arrest of the suspects at 2:30 A.M. inside the sixth floor suite of the Democratic headquarters in the Watergate, Democrats have tried to lay the incident at the doorstep of the White House—or at least to the Nixon re-election committee.

One day after the arrests, it was learned that one of the suspects, James W. McCord Jr., a former FBI and CIA agent, was the security chief to the Nixon committee and a security consultant to the Republican National Committee. McCord, now free on bond, was fired from both posts.

The next day it was revealed that a mysterious White House consultant, E. Howard Hunt Jr., was known by at least two of the suspects. Hunt immediately dropped from sight and became involved in an extended court battle to avoid testimony before the federal grand jury investigating the case.

Ten days ago it was revealed that a Nixon re-election committee official was fired because he had refused to answer questions about the incident by the FBI. The official, G. Gordon Liddy,

was serving as financial counsel to the Nixon committee when he was dismissed on June 28.

In the midst of this, former Democratic National Chairman Lawrence F. O'Brien filed a $1 million civil suit against the Nixon committee and the five suspects charging that the break-in and alleged attempted bugging violated the constitutional rights of all Democrats.

O'Brien charged that there is "a clear line developing to the White House" and emphasized what he called the "potential involvement" of special counsel to the President, Charles Coulson.

Coulson had recommended that the White House hire Hunt, also a former CIA agent and prolific novelist, as a consultant.

While he was Nixon campaign chief, Mitchell repeatedly and categorically denied any involvement or knowledge of the break-in incident.

When first contacted last night about the $25,000 check, Dahlberg said that he didn't "have the vaguest idea about it... I turn all my money over to the (Nixon) committee."

Asked if he had been contacted by the FBI and questioned about the check, Dahlberg said: "I'm a proper citizen. What I do is proper."

Dahlberg later called a reporter back and said he first denied any knowledge of the $25,000 check because he was not sure the caller was really a reporter for the *Washington Post*.

He said that he had just gone through an ordeal because his "dear friend and neighbor," Virginia Piper, had been kidnapped and held for two days.

Mrs. Piper's husband reportedly paid $1 million ransom last week to recover his wife in the highest payment to kidnappers in U.S. history.

Dahlberg, 54, was President Nixon's Minnesota finance chairman in 1968. The decision to appoint him to that post was announced by then-Rep. MacGregor and Stans.

• • •

The money link made it clear that Watergate was not merely a burglary story, no matter what the

White House said. By the time events were over, about forty administration officials, including top White House aides, had been imprisoned.

On November 7, 1972, Richard Nixon was re-elected. On August 9, 1974, facing impeachment, Nixon resigned.

THE *MIAMI HERALD* FINDS VOTER FRAUD AND FORCES A MAYOR FROM OFFICE

In some ways, it's almost surprising that anyone wanted to be mayor of Miami in 1997. A number of people were not even sure Miami—poor, mismanaged, almost perpetually in crisis—should be a city of its own. A proposal to merge Miami with surrounding Dade County was brought to a vote in September 1997. Miami voters rejected that. The November 4 mayoral election went ahead, pitting the incumbent, Joe Carollo, against Xavier Suarez, who had been mayor from 1985 to 1993. The race was excruciatingly close. Carollo won 49.6 percent of the vote, and Suarez 46.8 percent, including a two-thirds advantage in absentee votes. Since neither man won more than 50 percent of the votes, a runoff was required. Suarez won that.

By the time Suarez took office, state officials were investigating vote fraud and had seized more than 5,000 absentee ballots from the first election, saying the votes had been bought. Also investigating was the *Miami Herald.*

"Dozens Cast Votes in Miami Mayoral Race—For $10 Each," by Joseph Tanfani and Karen Branch. *Miami Herald,* January 11, 1998.

A flood of absentee ballots proved decisive in the November race for Miami mayor. Former Mayor Joe Carollo would have won outright on Nov. 4 were it not for Mayor Xavier Suarez's lopsided advantage in absentees.

Now, the Florida Department of Law Enforcement is investigating allegations of widespread absentee vote fraud. There have been two arrests: a part-time Suarez volunteer, on charges of agreeing to buy phony ballots from an undercover agent, and a 92-year-old former produce peddler who gathered dozens of questionable ballots.

In its continuing investigation of possible election fraud, the *Herald* has reported that:

• The produce peddler witnessed a ballot case in the name of a dead man—Manuel Yip, who died four years ago and is buried in a pauper's grave.

• At least 40 possibly fraudulent absentee votes came from homes linked to supporters of Miami Commission Chairman Humberto Hernandez in Little Havanna and the Roads.

• Some inner-city voters were paid $10 apiece to vote absentee.

One day before the Miami mayoral runoff election, a stream of poor and homeless people flowed to a back lot at St. John Baptist Church in Overtown. They weren't there to pray.

A man with a wad of cash was paying for votes. As word spread, dozens of people boarded vans, headed downtown and cast absentee ballots—in exchange for $10 each.

Thomas Felder took the money.

"I had no choice. I was hungry that day," said Felder, who is out of work and broke.

"You wanted the money, you were told who to vote for—212, Suarez." That was Miami Mayor Xavier Suarez's number on the runoff ballot.

"I did it to get paid, that's all," said Mary Ludlow, 32, who lives in a run-down apartment building on Northwest First Place that overlooks a flooded and trash-strewn roof.

She said she was told to vote for Suarez, and did.

A dollars-for-votes operation was in full swing

in Miami's inner city during last November's mayoral election, a *Herald* investigation shows.

In independent interviews with the *Herald*, 14 voters and witnesses outlined the same basic vote-buying operation at the church lot in Overtown, though not all said they were told to vote for Suarez.

Voters were driven in white vans and beat-up cars to County Hall, where the Miami-Dade elections department was accepting absentee ballots in the Nov. 13 runoff between Suarez and former Mayor Joe Carollo.

When they came back to the church lot, they got their payoff: a $10 bill peeled off the top from a stack stashed in a recruiter's pocket.

The operation was hard to miss, witnesses said.

"It was about 300 or 400 people. God, yeah, they were coming all day," said Ellis S. Dunning Jr., who lives in an apartment that overlooks the church lot. He said he, too, took the $10.

The *Herald* located five people who said they received $10 to vote during the operation at 1328 NW Third Ave.

Three voters said they were told to vote for Suarez, although one of them declined to say whether he pocketed any cash.

One woman said she learned about the absentee operation from a Carollo operative and voted for Carollo—although she would not say whether the vote-buyer at the church gave her instructions.

The two other $10 voters said they don't recall receiving instructions on how to vote.

Five witnesses identified a man they said was handing out cash or taking down names: Jeffrey "Pop" Hoskins, 34. Hoskins admitted he has participated in "two or three" $10-a-vote operations in the past—but denied any involvement in November's vote-buying scheme.

A basketball coach for the Overtown Optimists, Hoskins said he was at adjoining Gibson Park that day. He said he didn't see anybody trading cash for votes....

————

Both the Suarez and Carollo campaigns said they had nothing to do with the vote-buying operation....

State law makes it a third-degree felony to pay someone to vote for a candidate. It's a misdemeanor violation for a voter to sell his or her vote.

The Overtown vote-buying operation came a day before the Nov. 13 runoff, at a time when the mayoral campaigns were desperate to drum up support in Miami's black neighborhoods.

Campaign professionals said many black voters lost interest in the elections the week before, when veteran politician Arthur E. Teele Jr. easily won election to a seat on the Miami City Commission. Teele represents predominantly black District 5, which includes Overtown.

Both Suarez and Carollo are white Cuban Americans.

"The people in this community didn't care, not at all," who won the mayoral election, said McKnight, the political consultant who spearheaded Suarez's campaign in Overtown. "A lot of people said, 'I'm not going to vote for anybody but Teele.' It didn't matter who was mayor."

Despite that apathy, the number of absentee votes from Overtown rose in the mayoral runoff.

On Nov. 4, when Teele and opponent Pierre Rutledge were on the ballot, 48 people living within a half-mile of the St. John church voted absentee, election results show.

For the Nov. 13 race, that number rose to 75.

Election records show that none of the five who sold their votes cast ballots in the Nov. 4 primary. Several told the *Herald* they turned out only because of the $10 offer.

"You're trying to make 10 bucks, you know?" said Dunning, the man who lives in an apartment overlooking the church lot. "Ten bucks is ten bucks." He said he took the money but received no instructions on how to vote.

For years, the elections department has set up

a number of early voting sites around Miami-Dade where people can cast ballots a week or more before Election Day.

Those votes are counted as absentees, since they are cast outside a voter's home precinct.

James Kohanek, assistant elections supervisor, said campaigns are "abusing" that system by busing in voters who could easily vote at the polls.

All of the sites except the county building will be shut down in future elections, he said.

"It was set up as a convenience for the voter, and all it turned out to be was an abuse by candidates," Kohanek said.

Miami-Dade election administrators have long heard reports of vote-buying in Dade.

"You always hear it, but you never see it, and no one has ever brought any proof," Kohanek said. . . .

Most of the voters said two men seemed to be running the operation: a stocky, well dressed white man who carried documents, possibly a voting roll, and talked on a cellular phone, and a black man who checked voter cards and doled out the $10 bills.

Shown his photo, two voters—Felder and Lola Chapman, 55—identified Hoskins—the Overtown Optimists basketball coach—as the man who gave them the money.

Hoskins at first said he didn't work for either Carollo or Suarez.

"I didn't work for any campaign," he said Tuesday, in an interview at his dilapidated apartment complex on Northwest Second Avenue. "People make accusations every day."

He later said he volunteered one morning for Suarez during the nine-day runoff campaign in November. Hoskins also was paid for one day's work on the Carollo campaign on the Miami primary election day, Nov. 4.

Hoskins, shaken after a first visit by *Herald* re-

porters, said he called Mayor Suarez's chief of staff and campaign manager, Jorge Alvarez. He said he did not know Alvarez but got his name and number from a friend, whom he would not identify. . . .

"This has been very unsettling for me. I got Jorge Alvarez because I wanted to get in touch with someone to get some names [of those involved in the vote-buying operation]," Hoskins said. "Alvarez hung up on me. He said he knew nothing about it."

Alvarez said he did not know Hoskins and did not remember getting such a phone call. . . .

In an era when Hispanic votes dominate Miami politics, Hoskins said vote-buying in black precincts has become passe.

"These 50 votes you get out of Overtown, they don't really count for s———," Hoskins said. "Nineties politics doesn't really dictate it. It's real dirty now.

"Do what you got to to win—that's what Miami politics is about."

• • •

Suarez was not fond of the *Herald*'s stories. At one point he left a voice-mail message on the phone of the paper's advertising manager, threatening to pull the city's $200,000 in annual advertisements unless the paper became "a lot nicer to me, my people, my citizens, and my city."

In February, a Florida grand jury recommended revamping the system of absentee voting. In March, a circuit court judge, citing a "pattern of fraudulent, intentional and criminal conduct" in absentee ballots, voided the election and ordered another vote held. A Florida appeals court said that a new election was not necessary, given that without the tainted ballots, Carollo clearly won. He was returned to office. About three dozen people, including a city commissioner, were charged in the vote scheme.

MUCKRAKING!

HELEN HUNT JACKSON WRITES IN DEFENSE OF NATIVE AMERICANS WHEN FEW OTHERS CARE

From the beginning, European settlers of what became the United States largely regarded the natives who greeted them as a problem, one best resolved by distance or by death, meaning killing the Indians. Of course, the settlers thought it was the natives who had to move, whether they wanted to do so or not. The land was needed, whites argued, for farms, railroads, for rumored gold. Since the American Indians were widely seen as heathens and barbarians, government officials were able to justify to themselves the extreme, dishonest, cruel deals that moved the Indians off their lands and interfered in their established way of life.

Few whites cared about the plight of the Native Americans. Most of those who did were church-based; for a time, in reaction to the corruption of the government-appointed Indian agents, Quakers chose the people who ran reservation trading posts. Even the abolitionists, mostly based in the East, did not link the issue of ending slavery with granting equality to Native Americans. After the Civil War, a certain exhaustion set in among reformers. Financial reconstruc-tion and aid for the freed blacks took up what energies they had left.

By the 1870s, however, reform interest in tribal problems was increasing, spurred by outraged individuals and several outrageous events: the U.S. Army's chase of Chief Joseph of the Nez Perce tribe, the slaughter of Northern Cheyenne who fled military confinement, the attempt by the Ponca Indians in 1877 to return to Nebraska after their forced removal to Indian Territory. T. H. Tibbles, an editor of the *Omaha Daily Herald*, took up the Poncas' cause and won, through the courts, their right to stay in Nebraska. Then Tibbles took the Ponca leader, Standing Bear, on a national lecture tour exposing the government's abuse of the natives.

Helen Hunt Jackson, a poet and travel writer, heard Standing Bear at a lecture in Boston. She had not previously been involved in, or even known about, the treatment of the tribes. With the determination of a zealot, she devoted the rest of her life to trying to obtain better treatment for Indians.

A Century of Dishonor, by Helen Hunt Jackson. New York: Harper & Brothers, 1885.

CONCLUSION

There are within the limits of the United States between two hundred and fifty and three hundred thousand Indians, exclusive of those in Alaska. The names of the different tribes and bands, as entered in the statistical tables of the Indian Office Reports, number nearly three hundred. One of the most careful estimates which have been made of their numbers and localities gives them as follows: "In Minnesota and States east of the Mississippi, about 32,500; in Nebraska, Kansas, and the Indian Territory, 70,650; in the Territories of Dakota, Montana, Wyoming, and Idaho, 65,000; in Nevada and the Territories of Colorado, New Mexico, Utah, and Arizona, 84,000; and on the Pacific slope, 48,000."

Of these, 130,000 are self-supporting on their own reservations, "receiving nothing from the Government except interest on their own moneys, or annuities granted them in consideration of the cession of their lands to the United States."

This fact alone would seem sufficient to dispose forever of the accusation, so persistently brought against the Indian, that he will not work.

Of the remainder, 84,000 are partially supported by the Government—the interest money due them and their annuities, as provided by treaty, being inadequate to their subsistence on the reservations where they are confined. In many cases, however, these Indians furnish a large part of their support—the White River Utes, for instance, who are reported by the Indian Bureau as getting sixty-six percent of their living by "root-digging, hunting, and fishing"; the Squaxin band, in Washington Territory, as earning seventy-five percent, and the Chippewas of Lake Superior as earning fifty percent, in the same way. These facts also would seem to dispose of the accusation that the Indian will not work.

There are about 55,000 who never visit an agency, over whom the Government does not pretend to have either control or care. These 55,000 "subsist by hunting, fishing, on roots, nuts, berries, etc., and by begging and stealing"; and this also seems to dispose of the accusation that the Indian will not "work for a living." There remains a small portion, about 31,000 that are entirely subsisted by the Government.

There is not among these three hundred bands of Indians one which has not suffered cruelly at the hands either of the Government or of white settlers. The poorer, the more insignificant, the more helpless the band, the more certain the cruelty and outrage to which they have been subjected. This is especially true of the bands on the Pacific slope. These Indians found themselves of a sudden surrounded by and caught up in the great influx of gold-seeking settlers, as helpless creatures on a shore are caught up in a tidal wave. There was not time for the Government to make treaties; not even time for communities to make laws. The tale of the wrongs, the oppressions, the murders of the Pacific-slope Indians in the last thirty years would be a volume by itself, and is too monstrous to be believed.

It makes little difference, however, where one opens the record of the history of the Indians; every page and every year has its dark stain. The story of one tribe is the story of all, varied only by differences of time and place; but neither time nor place makes any difference in the main facts. Colorado is as greedy and unjust in 1880 as was Georgia in 1830, and Ohio in 1795; and the United States Government breaks promises now as deftly as then, and with an added ingenuity from long practice.

One of its strongest supports in so doing is the wide-spread sentiment among the people of dislike to the Indian, of impatience with his presence as a "barrier to civilization," and distrust of it as a possible danger. The old tales of the frontier life, with its horrors of Indian warfare, have gradually, by two or three generations' telling, produced in the average mind something like an hereditary instinct of unquestioning and unreasoning aversion which it is almost impossible to dislodge or soften.

There are hundreds of pages of unimpeachable testimony on the side of the Indian; but it goes for nothing, is set down as sentimentalism or partisanship, tossed aside and forgotten.

President after president has appointed commission after commission to inquire into and report upon Indian affairs, and to make suggestions as to the best methods of managing them. The reports are filled with eloquent statements of wrongs done to the Indians, of perfidies on the part of the Government; they counsel, as earnestly as words can, a trial of the simple and unperplexing expedients of telling truth; keeping promises, making fair bargains, dealing justly in all ways and all things. These reports are bound up with the Government's Annual Reports, and that is the end of them. It would probably be no exaggeration to say that not one American citizen out of ten thousand ever sees them or knows that they exist, and yet any one of them, circulated throughout the country, read by the right-thinking, right-feeling men and women of this land, would be of itself a "campaign document" that would initiate a revolution which would not subside until the Indians' wrongs were, so far as is now left possible, righted.

In 1869 President Grant appointed a commission of nine men, representing the influence and philanthropy of six leading States, to visit the different Indian reservations, and to "examine all matters appertaining to Indian affairs."

In the report of this commission are such paragraphs as the following: "to assert that 'the Indian will not work' is as true as it would be to say that the white man will not work.

"Why should the Indian be expected to plant corn, fence lands, build houses, or do anything but get food from day to day, when experience has taught him that the produce of his labor will be seized by the white man to-morrow? The most industrious white man would become a drone un-

der similar circumstances. . . . Every crime committed by a white man against an Indian is concealed or palliated. Every offence committed by an Indian against a white man is borne on the wings of the post or the telegraph to the remotest corner of the land, clothed with all the horrors which the reality or imagination can throw around it. Against such influences as these the people of the United States need to be warned."

To assume that it would be easy, or by any one sudden stroke of legislative policy possible, to undo the mischief and hurt of the long past, set the Indian policy of the country right for the future, and make the Indians at once safe and happy, is the blunder of a hasty and uninformed judgment. The notion which seems to be growing more prevalent, that simply to make all Indians at once citizens of the United States would be a sovereign and instantaneous panacea for all their ills and all the Government's perplexities, is a very inconsiderate one. To administer complete citizenship of a sudden, all round, to all Indians, barbarous and civilized alike, would be as grotesque a blunder as to dose them all round with any one medicine, irrespective of the symptoms and needs of their diseases. It would kill more than it would cure. . . .

However great perplexity and difficulty there may be in the details of any and every plan possible for doing at this late day anything like justice to the Indian, however hard it may be for good statesmen and good men to agree upon the things that ought to be done, there certainly is, or ought to be, no perplexity whatever, no difficulty whatever, in agreeing upon certain things that ought not to be done, and which must cease to be done before the first steps can be taken toward righting the wrongs, curing the ills, and wiping out the disgrace to us of the present condition of our Indians.

Cheating, robbing, breaking promises—these three are clearly things which must cease to be done. One more thing, also, and that is the refusal of the protection of the law to the Indian's rights of property, "of life, liberty, and the pursuit of happiness."

When these four things have ceased to be done, time, statesmanship, philanthropy, and Christianity can slowly and surely do the rest. Till these four things have ceased to be done, statesmanship and philanthropy alike must work in vain, and even Christianity can reap but small harvest.

• • •

At her own expense, Jackson sent a copy of the book, with its bloodred cover, to every member of Congress. She was criticized as being hasty, emotional, and overdrawn. But her passion came through clearly, and she was appointed to a commission investigating the condition of the Mission Indians in California. She used that knowledge in a novel, *Ramona*, which sold widely. The two books created a more sympathetic view of Native Americans than the country was used to and brought uncommon attention to the government's shoddy policies.

Jackson was one of a handful of individual reformers who kept the cause of better treatment of Native Americans alive during a drought of interest. By the 1890s, organized groups took up the issues that Jackson had triumphed, and that might have faded without her.

NELLIE BLY SPENDS TEN HARROWING DAYS IN A MAD-HOUSE

Although American newspapers had engaged in crusades from their beginning, no editor developed the crusade as an art as effectively as did Joseph Pulitzer, editor and publisher of, first, the *St. Louis Post and Dispatch,* and then the *World* in New York City. Pulitzer believed in *making* news— that his newspapers, every day, should have one cause to be triumphed, one bit of corruption to attack, or, at least, one stunt that would capture the interest of readers, increase circulation, and make his papers more attractive to advertisers.

He found perhaps the perfect reporter in Nellie Bly, real name Elizabeth Cochrane, who after a year on the *Pittsburgh Dispatch* talked her way onto the *World* with her willingness to tackle any assignment. Her first: get herself committed to one of the city's Asylums for the Insane, so she could write about the treatment there. She checked herself into a temporary home for women and, pretending to have forgotten her identity, fooled four doctors into declaring her insane. She spent ten days on Blackwell's Island before, as previously arranged, a lawyer came to arrange for her release.

The resulting articles gave a rare view of a tortured world little seen by the public.

"Ten Days in a Mad-House," by Nellie Bly. New York *World,* October 16, 1887.

As the wagon was rapidly driven through the beautiful lawns up to the asylum my feelings of satisfaction at having attained the object of my work were greatly dampened by the look of distress on the faces of my companions. Poor women, they had no hopes of a speedy delivery! On the wagon sped, and I, as well as my comrades, gave a despairing farewell glance at freedom as we came in sight of the long stone buildings. We passed one low building, and the stench was so horrible that I was compelled to hold my breath, and I mentally decided that it was the kitchen. . . .

The wagon stopped and the nurse and officer in charge told us to get out. The nurse added: "Thank God they came quietly." We obeyed orders to go ahead up a flight of narrow stone steps, which had evidently been built for the accommodation of people who climb stairs three at a time. I wondered if my companions knew where we were, so I said to Miss Tillie Mayard: "Where are we?" "At the Blackwell's Island Lunatic Asylum," she answered sadly. "Are you crazy?" I asked. "No," she replied, "but as we have been sent here we will have to be quiet until we find some means of escape. They will be few, though, if all the doctors, as Dr. Field, refuse to listen to me or give me chance to prove my sanity." We were ushered into a narrow vestibule and the door was locked behind us.

In spite of the knowledge of my sanity and the assurance that I would be released in a few days, my heart gave a sharp twinge. Pronounced insane by four expert doctors and shut up behind the unmerciful bolts and bars of a madhouse! Not to be confined alone, but to be a companion, day and night, of senseless, chattering lunatics; to sleep with them, to eat with them, to be considered one of them, was an uncomfortable position. Timidly we followed the nurse up the long uncarpeted hall to a room filled by so-called crazy women. We were told to sit down, and some of the patients kindly made room for us. They looked at us curiously and one came up to me and asked: "Who sent you here?" "The doctors," I answered. "What for?" she persisted. "Well, they say I am insane," I admitted. "Insane!" she repeated incredulously. "It cannot be seen in your face." . . .

We were taken into a cold, wet bathroom and I was ordered to undress. Did I protest? Well, I never grew so earnest in my life as when I tried to beg off. They said if I did not they would use force and that it would not be very gentle. At this I noticed one of the craziest women in the ward standing by the filled bathtub with a large discolored rag in her hands. She was chattering away to herself and chuckling in a manner which seemed to me fiendish. I knew now what was to be done with me. I shivered. They began to undress me and one by one they pulled off my clothes. At last everything was gone excepting one garment. "I will not remove it," I said vehemently, but they took it off. I gave one glance at the group of patients at the door watching the scene, and I jumped into the bathtub with more energy than grace.

The water was ice-cold, and I again began to protest. How useless it all was. I begged, at least, that the patients be made to go away, but was ordered to shut up. The crazy woman began to scrub me. I can find no other word that will express it but scrubbing. From a small tin pan she took some soft soap and rubbed it all over me, even all over my face and my pretty hair. I was at last past seeing or speaking, although I had begged that my hair be left untouched. Rub, rub, rub, went the old woman, chattering to herself. My teeth chattered and my limbs were goose-fleshed and blue with cold. Suddenly I got, one after the other, three buckets of water over my head—ice-cold water, too—into my eyes, my ears, my nose and my mouth. I think I experienced some of the sensations of a drowning person as they dragged me, gasping, shivering and quaking, from the tub. For once I did look insane, as they put me, dripping wet, into a short canton flannel slip, labeled across the extreme end in large black letters, "Lunatic Asylum, B.I.H.6" The letters meant Blackwell's Island, Hall 6. . . .

I was taken to room 28 and left to try and make an impression on the bed. It was an impossible task. The bed had been made high in the centre and sloping on either side. At the first touch my head flooded the pillow with water and my wet slip transferred some of its dampness to the sheet. When Miss Grupe came in, I asked if I could not have a night-gown. "We have no such things in this institution," she said. "I do not like to sleep without," I replied. "Well, I don't care about that," she said. "You are in a public institution now, and you can't expect to get anything. This is charity, and you should be thankful for what you get." "But the city pays to keep these places up," I urged, "and pays people to be kind to the unfortunates brought here." "Well, you don't need to expect any kindness here, for you won't get it," she said, and she went out and closed the door. . . .

———

Just as morning began to dawn I went to sleep. It did not seem many moments until I was rudely awakened and told to get up, the window being opened and the clothing pulled off me. My hair was still wet and I had pains all through me, as if I had the rheumatism. Some clothing was flung on the floor and I was told to put it on. I asked for my own but was told to take what I got and keep quiet by the apparently head nurse, Miss Grady. I looked at it: one underskirt made of coarse dark cotton goods and a cheap white calico dress with a black spot in it. I tied the strings of the skirt around me and put on the dress. It was made, as are all those worn by the patients, into a straight tight waist sewed to a straight skirt. As I buttoned the waist I noticed the underskirt was about six inches longer than the upper, and for a moment I sat down on the bed and laughed at my own appearance. No woman ever longed for a mirror more than I did at that moment.

I saw the other patients hurrying past in the hall, so I decided not to lose anything that might be going on. We numbered forty-five patients in Hall 6, and were sent to the bathroom, where there were two coarse towels. I watched crazy patients who had the most dangerous eruptions all over their faces dry on the towels and then saw women with clear skins turn to use them. I went to the bathtub and washed my face at the running faucet and my underskirt did duty for a towel. . . .

I was never so tired as I grew sitting on those benches. Several of the patients would sit on one foot or sideways to make a change, but they were always reproved and told to sit up straight. If they talked they were scolded and told to shut up. If they wanted to walk around in order to take the stiffness out of them, they were told to sit down and be still. What, excepting torture, would produce insanity quicker than this treatment? Here is a class of women sent to be cured? I would like the expert physicians who are condemning me for my action, which has proven their ability, to take a perfectly sane and healthy woman, shut her up

and make her sit from 6 A.M. until 8 P.M. on straight-back benches, do not allow her to talk or move during these hours, give her no reading and let her know nothing of the world or its doings, give her bad food and harsh treatment, and see how long it will take to make her insane. Two months would make her a mental and physical wreck.

I have described my first day in the asylum, and as my other nine were exactly the same in the general run of things it would be tiresome to tell about each. In giving this story I expect to be contradicted by many who are exposed. I merely tell in common words, without exaggeration, of my life in a mad-house for ten days. The eating was one of the most horrible things. Excepting the first two days after I entered the asylum there was no salt for the food. The hungry and even famishing women made an attempt to eat the horrible messes. Mustard and vinegar were put on meat and in soup to give it a taste, but it only helped to make it worse. Even that was all consumed after two days, and the patients had to try to choke down fresh fish, just boiled in water, without salt, pepper or butter; mutton, beef and potatoes without the faintest seasoning. The most insane refused to swallow the food and were threatened with punishment. In our short walks we passed the kitchen where food was prepared for the nurses and doctors. There we got glimpses of melons and grapes and all kinds of fruits, beautiful white bread and nice meats, and the hungered feeling would be increased tenfold. . . .

A Mrs. Cotter told me that for speaking to a man she was sent to the Retreat. "The remembrance of that is enough to make me mad. For crying the nurses beat me with a broom-handle and jumped on me, injuring me internally so that I will never get over it. Then they tied my hands and feet and, throwing a sheet over my head, twisted it tightly around my throat, so I could not scream, and thus put me in a bathtub filled with cold water. They held me under until I gave up every hope and became senseless. At other times they took hold of my ears and beat my head on the floor and against the wall. Then they pulled my hair out by the roots so that it will never grow in again."

Mrs. Cotter showed me proofs of her story, the dent in the back of her head and the bare spots where the hair had been taken out by the handful. I give her story as plainly as possible: "My treatment was not as bad as I have seen others get in there, but it has ruined my health, and even if I do get out of here I will be a wreck. When my husband heard of the treatment given me he threatened to expose the place if I was not removed, so I was brought here. I am well mentally now. All that old fear has left me, and the doctor has promised to allow my husband to take me home."

I made the acquaintance of Bridget Mc-Guinness, who seems to be sane at the present time. She said she was sent to Retreat 4 and put on the "Rope gang." "The beatings I got there were something dreadful. I was pulled around by the hair, held under the water until I strangled, and I was choked and kicked. The nurses would always keep a quiet patient stationed at the window to tell them when any of the doctors were approaching. It was hopeless to complain to the doctors for they always said it was the imagination of our diseased brain, and besides we would get another beating for telling. They would hold patients under the water and threaten to leave them to die there if they did not promise not to tell." . . .

The Insane Asylum on Blackwell's Island is a human rat-trap. It is easy to get in, but once there it is impossible to get out. I had intended to have myself committed to the violent wards, the Lodge and Retreat, but when I got the testimony of two sane women who could give it, I decided not to risk my health—and hair, so I did not get violent.

I had towards the last been shut off from all visitors, and so when the lawyer, Peter A. Hendricks, came and told me that friends of mine were willing to take charge of me if I would rather be with them than in the Asylum, I was only too glad to give my consent. I asked him to send me something to eat immediately on his arrival in the city, and then I waited anxiously for my release.

It came sooner than I had hoped. I was out "in line" taking a walk, and had just gotten interested in a poor woman who had fainted away while the nurses were trying to compel her to walk. "Good-bye; I am going home," I called to Pauline Moser as she went past with a woman on either side of her. Sadly I said farewell to all I knew as I passed them on my way to freedom and life, while they were left behind to a fate worse than death. "Adios," I murmured to the Mexican woman. I kissed my fingers to her, and so I left my companions of hell.

I had looked forward so eagerly to leaving the horrible place, yet when my release came and I knew that God's sunlight was to be free for me again, there was a certain pain in leaving. For ten days I had been one of them. Foolishly enough, it seemed selfish to leave them to their sufferings. I felt a Quixotic desire to help them by sympathy and presence. But only for a moment. The bars were down and freedom was sweeter to me than ever.

Soon I was crossing the river and nearing New York. Once again I was a free girl after ten days in the mad-house on Blackwell's Island.

• • •

The problems of Blackwell's Island were hardly unknown. Charles Dickens had compared the institution to London's Bedlam in the 1840s, and about the same time, Margaret Fuller had attacked it in the New York *Tribune*. Early mental-health reformers were raising questions. But Bly's firsthand account of the appalling conditions galvanized city officials. A grand jury was convened. By the time Bly visited the island with officials two weeks later, the worst conditions had been cleaned up and the most brutal nurses transferred. Still, the jury issued a report calling for reforms, and the city council gave a $1 million budget increase to the city department of hospitals, with a considerable sum earmarked for Blackwell's Island. Bly did not do it by herself, said a biographer, Brooke Kroeger, but she could deservedly take pride in her accomplishments.

Bly wrote a book, *Ten Days in a Mad-House*, which sold well, and went on to use the same investigative, first-person techniques to attack Albany lobbyists, working-class abuses, and prison conditions. What came to be called "stunt journalists"—or, when they were women, "sob sisters"—were quickly hired by many big-city newspapers.

Unfortunately, providing proper care for the mentally and emotionally troubled proved an unending challenge. Time and again, in state after state, journalists have needed to bring attention to abuses, with the knowledge that corrective action tends to be temporary.

LINCOLN STEFFENS EXPOSES THE SHAME OF A CITY

Lincoln Steffens, reporter and editor at the *New York Evening Post* and the *Commercial Advertiser*, reformer, friend of Theodore Roosevelt, backer of the anticorruption efforts in New York in the late 1890s, had been editor at *McClure's* magazine only four months when S. S. McClure, the owner, recognized Steffens was getting restless behind a desk. "Get out of the office," McClure told Steffens. "Meet people, find out what's going on, and write yourself." This was a luxury few magazine reporters had, but McClure, who was selling about 360,000 copies a month, wanted his reporters to be experts on the topics they wrote about. Steffens jumped at the opportunity, and traveled the country, interviewing businessmen, city officials, and political bosses and deciding that he wanted

to do a series of articles on municipal misgovernment.

The first, "Tweed Days in St. Louis," appeared in October 1902 and the second, "The Shame of Minneapolis," in January 1903.

"The Shame of Minneapolis," by Lincoln Steffens. *McClure's,* January 1903.

Whenever anything extraordinary is done in American municipal politics, whether for good or for evil, you can trace it almost invariably to one man. The people do not do it. Neither do the "gangs," "combines," or political parties. These are but instruments by which bosses (not leaders; we Americans are not led, but driven) rule the people, and commonly sell them out. But there are at least two forms of the autocracy which has supplanted the democracy here as it has everywhere democracy has been tried. One is that of the organized majority by which, as with the Republican machine in Philadelphia, the boss has normal control of more than half the voters. The other is that of the adroitly managed minority. The "good people" are herded into parties and stupefied with convictions and a name, Republican or Democrat; while the "bad people" are so organized or interested by the boss that he can wield their votes to enforce terms with party managers and decide elections. St. Louis is a conspicuous example of this form. Minneapolis is another. Colonel Ed Butler is the unscrupulous opportunist who handled the non-partisan minority which turned St. Louis into a "boodle town." In Minneapolis "Doc" Ames was the man.

Minneapolis is a New England town on the upper Mississippi. The metropolis of the Northwest, it is the metropolis also of Norway and Sweden in America. Indeed, it is the second largest Scandinavian city in the world. But Yankees, straight from Down East, settled the town, and their New England spirit predominates. They had

Bayard Taylor lecture there in the early days of the settlement; they made it the seat of the University of Minnesota. Yet even now, when the town has grown to a population of more than 200,000, you feel that there is something Western about it too— a Yankee with a round Puritan head, and open prairie heart, and a great, big Scandinavian body. The "Roundhead" takes the "Squarehead" out into the woods, and they cut lumber by forests, or they go out on the prairies and raise wheat and mill it into fleet-cargoes of flour. They work hard, they make money, they are sober, satisfied, busy with their own affairs. There isn't much time for public business. Taken together, Miles, Hans, and Ole are very American. Miles insists upon strict laws, Ole and Hans want one or two Scandinavians on their ticket. These things granted, they go off on raft or reaper, leaving who so will to enforce the laws and run the city.

The people who were left to govern the city hated above all things strict laws. They were the loafers, saloon keepers, gamblers, criminals, and the thriftless poor of all nationalities. Resenting the sobriety of a staid, industrious community, and having no Irish to boss them, they delighted to follow the jovial pioneer doctor, Albert Alonzo Ames. He was the "good fellow"—a genial, generous reprobate. Devery, Tweed, and many more have exposed in vain this amiable type. "Doc" Ames, tall, straight, and cheerful, attracted men, and they gave him votes for his smiles. He stood for license. There was nothing of the Puritan about him. . . .

Had he been wise or even shrewd, he might have made himself a real power. But he wasn't calculating, only light and frivolous, so he did not organize his forces and run men for office. He sought office himself from the start, and he got most of the small places he wanted by changing his party to seize the opportunity. His floating minority, added to the regular partisan vote, was sufficient ordinarily for his useless victories. As time went on he rose from smaller offices to be a Republican mayor, then twice at intervals to be a Democratic mayor. He was a candidate once for Congress; he stood for governor once on a sort of Populist-Democrat ticket. Ames could not get anything outside of his own town, however, and after his third term as mayor it was thought he was out of politics altogether. He was getting old, and he was getting worse.

Like many a "good fellow" with hosts of miscellaneous friends downtown to whom he was devoted the good Doctor neglected his own family. From neglect he went on openly to separation from his wife and a second establishment. The climax came not long before the election of 1900. His wife died. The family would not have the father at the funeral, but he appeared—not at the house, but in a carriage on the street. He sat across the way, with his feet up and a cigar in his mouth, till the funeral moved; then he circled around, crossing it and meeting it, and making altogether a scene which might well close any man's career.

It didn't end his. . . . Minneapolis got its old mayor back, and he was indeed "reformed." Up to this time Ames had not been very venal personally. He was a "spender," not a "grafter," and he was guilty of corruption chiefly by proxy; he took the honors and left the spoils to his followers. His administrations were not worse than the worst. Now, however, he set out upon a career of corruption which for deliberateness, invention, and avarice has never been equaled. It was as if he had made up his mind that he had been careless long enough, and meant to enrich his last years. He began promptly.

Immediately upon his election, before he took office (on January 7, 1901), he organized a cabinet and laid plans to turn the city over to outlaws who were to work under police direction for the profit of his administration. He chose for chief his brother, Colonel Fred W. Ames, who had recently returned under a cloud from service in the

Philippines. But he was a weak vessel for chief of police, and the mayor picked for chief of detectives an abler man, who was to direct the more difficult operations. This was Norman W. King, a former gambler, who knew the criminals needed in the business ahead. King was to invite to Minneapolis thieves, confidence men, pickpockets and gamblers, and release some that were in the local jail. They were to be organized into groups, according to their profession, and detectives were assigned to assist and direct them. The head of the gambling syndicate was to have charge of the gambling, making the terms and collecting the "graft," just as King and a Captain Hill were to collect from the thieves. The collector for women of the town was to be Irwin A. Gardner, a medical student in the Doctor's office, who was made a special policeman for the purpose. These men looked over the force, selected those men who could be trusted, charged them a price for their retention, and marked for dismissal 107 men out of 225, the 107 being the best policemen in the department from the point of view of the citizens who afterward reorganized the force. John Fitchette, better known as "Coffee John," a Virginian (who served on the Jefferson Davis jury), the keeper of a notorious coffee-house, was to be a captain of police, with no duties except to sell places on the police force.

And they did these things that they planned— all and more. The administration opened with the revolution on the police force. The thieves in the local jail were liberated and it was made known to the Under World generally that "things were doing" in Minneapolis. The incoming swindlers reported to King or his staff of instructions, and went to work, turning the "swag" over to the detectives in charge. Gambling went on openly, and disorderly houses multiplied under the fostering care of Gardner, the medical student. . . .

The revenue from all these sources must have been large. It only whetted the avarice of the mayor and his Cabinet. They let gambling privileges without restriction as to location of "squareness"; the syndicate could cheat and rob as it would. Peddlers and pawnbrokers, formerly licensed by the city, bought permits now instead from the mayor's agent in this field. Some two hundred slot machines were installed in various parts of the town, with owner's agent and mayor's agent watching and collecting from them enough to pay the mayor $15,000 a year as his share. Auction frauds were instituted. Opium joints and unlicensed saloons, called "blind pigs," were protected. Gardner even had a police baseball team, for whose games tickets were sold to people who had to buy them. But the women were the easiest "graft." They were compelled to buy illustrated biographies of the city officials; they had to give presents of money, jewelry, and gold stars to police officers. But the money they still paid direct to the city in fines, some $35,000 a year, fretted the mayor, and at last he reached for it. He came out with a declaration, in his old character as friend of the oppressed, that $100 a month was too much for these women to pay. They should be required to pay the city fine only once in two months. This puzzled the town till it became generally known that Gardner collected the other month for the mayor. The final outrage in this department, however, was an order of the mayor for the periodic visits to disorderly houses, by the city's physicians, at from $45 to $200 per visit. The two physicians he appointed called when they willed, and more and more frequently, till toward the end the calls became a pure formality, with the collections as the one and only object.

In a general way all this business was known. It did not arouse the citizens, but it did attract criminals, and more and more thieves and swindlers came hurrying to Minneapolis.

Burglaries were common. How many the police planned may never be known. Charles F. Brackett and Fred Malone, police captains and detectives, were active, and one well-established crime of theirs is the robbery of the Pabst Brewing Company office. They persuaded two men, one an employee, to learn the combination of the safe, open and clean it out one night, while the two officers stood guard outside.

The excesses of the municipal administration became so notorious that some of the members of it remonstrated with the others, and certain county officers were genuinely alarmed. No restraint followed their warnings. Sheriff Megaarden, no Puritan himself, felt constrained to interfere, and he made some arrests of gamblers. The Ames people turned upon him in a fury; they accused him of making overcharges in his accounts with the county for fees, and, laying the evidence before Governor Van Sant, they had Megaarden removed from office. Ames offered bribes to two county commissioners to appoint Gardner sheriff, so as to be sure of no more trouble in that quarter. This move failed, but the lesson taught Megaarden served to clear the atmosphere, and the spoliation went on as recklessly as ever. It became impossible.

Even lawlessness must be regulated. Dr. Ames, never an organizer, attempted no control, and his followers began to quarrel among themselves. They deceived one another; they robbed the thieves; they robbed Ames himself. His brother became dissatisfied with his share of the spoils, and formed cabals with captains who plotted against the administration and set up disorderly houses, "panel games," and all sorts of "grafts" of their own.

It was at this juncture, in April, 1902, that the grand jury for the summer term was drawn. An ordinary body of unselected citizens, it received no special instructions from the bench; the county prosecutor offered it only routine work to do. But there was a man among them who was a fighter— the foreman, Hovey C. Clarke. He was of an old New England family. Coming to Minneapolis when a young man, seventeen years before, he had fought for employment, fought with his employers for position, fought with his employees,

the lumber Jacks, for command, fought for his company against competitors; and he had won always, till now he had the habit of command, the impatient, imperious manner of the master, and the assurance of success which begets it. He did not want to be a grand juryman, he did not want to be a foreman; but since he was both, he wanted to accomplish something.

Why not rip up the Ames gang? Heads shook, hands went up; it was useless to try. The discouragement fired Clarke. That was just what he would do, he said, and he took stock of his jury. Two or three were men with backbone; that he knew, and he quickly had them with him. The rest were all sorts of men. Mr. Clarke won over each man to himself, and interested them all. Then he called for the county prosecutor. The prosecutor was a politician; he knew the Ames crowd; they were too powerful to attack.

"You are excused," said the foreman.

There was a scene; the prosecutor knew his rights.

"Do you think, Mr. Clarke," he cried, "that you can run the grand jury and my office, too?"

"Yes," said Clarke, "I will run your office if I want to, and I want to. You're excused."

Mr. Clarke does not talk much about his doings that summer; he isn't the talking sort. But he does say that all he did was to apply simple business methods to his problem. In action, however, these turned out to be the most approved police methods. He hired a lot of local detectives who, he knew, would talk about what they were doing, and thus would be watched by the police. Having thus thrown a false scent, he hired some other detectives whom nobody knew about. This was expensive; so were many of the other things he did; but he was bound to win, so he paid the price, drawing freely on his own and his colleagues' pockets. (The total cost to the county for a long summer's work by this grand jury was $259.) With his detectives out, he himself went to the jail to get tips from the inside, from criminals who, being there, must have grievances. He made the acquaintance of the jailer, Captain Alexander, and Alexander was a friend of Sheriff Megaarden. Yes, he had some men there who were "sore" and might want to get even.

• • •

The remainder of the article detailed the grand jury's success in winning convictions, including those of Irwin Gardner, the medical student who collected fees from the "women of the town"; Fred Ames, police chief and the mayor's brother; and Norman King, the chief of detectives. "Doc" Ames, indicted for bribery, extortion, and conspiracy, left the state on the night train, and later resigned, Steffens reported. The president of the city council became acting mayor. And the people of Minneapolis, and the newspapers of Minneapolis, lost interest in the scandal.

Steffens's article reinvigorated the citizenry. "When I went there, the men who had led the reform movement were 'all through,'" Steffens wrote in the introduction to *The Shame of the Cities*, a collection of his *McClure's* articles published in 1904. "After they had read the 'Shame of Minneapolis,' however, they went back to work, and they have perfected a plan to keep the citizens informed and to continue the fight for good government. They saw, these unambitious, busy citizens, that it was 'up to them,' and they resumed the unwelcome duties of their citizenship." Mayor Ames was brought back after being tracked down in New Hampshire, convicted of accepting a bribe, and sentenced to prison.

Steffens's other articles looked at municipal government and corruption in Pittsburgh, Chicago, Philadelphia, and New York. He reported receiving invitations from a number of other cities "to come and show us up; we're worse than they are."

Tangible results were few, Steffens lamented a year later, although he took some heart in the fact that the ordinary voters of the cities responded to corruption once their pride was hurt by public exposure.

The Steffens articles did give a boost to the various good-government movements that emerged with early Progressivism, and political scientists and government reformers praised Steffens's work for its clear view of American municipal government and the role of interest groups. Justin Kaplan, in his 1974 book *Lincoln Steffens: A Biography*, concluded that *The Shame of the Cities* "effectively demolished a number of cherished beliefs held by reformers from the Civil War on: that corruption came from the bottom of the economic and social order, not the top; that it was part of the growing pains of young cities; that it accompanied an immigrant population who in a strange land reverted to innate lawlessness; and that the businessman was the good citizen and the politician the bad citizen. All of these, according the Steffens, were 'hypocritical lies that save us from the clear sight of ourselves.'"

By happenstance, Steffens's article on Minneapolis appeared in the same issue of *McClure's* that contained a part of Ida M. Tarbell's history of Standard Oil and "The Right to Work," by Ray Stannard Baker, an investigation of the pressures on nonstriking miners in the Pennsylvania anthracite fields. McClure ordered up an editorial commenting on the connection: together, he said, the three stories were different looks at a common theme, the American contempt of law. "We are all doing our worst and making the public pay," the editorial said. The issue sold out and stoked an indignant public's demand for more looks at corruption. McClure's rivals in the magazine world took note and jumped into the exposure business themselves, leading to one of the most storied eras of magazine publishing and building support for progressive political crusades.

MUCKRAKER IDA M. TARBELL TAKES ON JOHN D. ROCKEFELLER AND THE STANDARD OIL COMPANY

Just after the turn of the century, the journalist Ida M. Tarbell, at the behest of her boss, S. S. McClure, was casting about for a topic that would address the increasing public concern over the powerful industrial trusts that had emerged in America. Tarbell, then in her forties, had been born in Erie County, Pennsylvania, and grew up in Titusville, in the heart of the Pennsylvania oil fields. She was graduated from Allegheny College in Meadville, Pennsylvania, where she was one of five female students. She had worked for eight years at the *Chautauquan,* a monthly magazine, then gone to Paris to write, where she came to the attention of McClure, the founder and editor of *McClure's*. In 1894, he hired her to write a life of Napoleon. The work was highly successful and the increased circulation helped ensure the magazine's survival. Tarbell followed with a similarly successful twenty-part biography of Abraham Lincoln.

Then Tarbell turned her attention to Standard Oil, spending two years with the help of an assistant, John Siddall. The first installment of Tarbell's work appeared in *McClure's* in November 1902, and her articles continued until 1904. The nineteen parts of the *McClure's* series were then published as a book. Tracing the development of Standard Oil, the work detailed the business practices that had built the company and driven out its competitors. But Tarbell also wrote with a moral perspective, as was shown in this excerpt from the conclusion to her work.

"The History of the Standard Oil Company," by Ida M. Tarbell. *McClure's,* 1904.

Very often people who admit the facts, who are willing to see that Mr. Rockefeller has employed force and fraud to secure his ends, justify him by declaring, "It's business." That is, "it's business" has come to be a legitimate excuse for hard dealing, sly tricks, special privileges. It is a common enough thing to hear men arguing that the ordinary laws or morality do not apply in business. Now, if the Standard Oil Company were the only concern in the country guilty of the practices which have given it monopolistic power, this story never would have been written. Were it alone in these methods, public scorn would long ago have made short work of the Standard Oil Company. But it is simply the most conspicuous type of what can be done by these practices. The methods it employs with such acumen, persistency, and secrecy are employed by all sorts of business men, from corner grocers up to bankers. If exposed, they are excused on the ground that this is business. If the point is pushed, frequently the defender of the practice falls back on the Christian doctrine of charity, and points that we are erring mortals and must allow for each other's weaknesses!—an excuse, which, if carried to its legitimate conclusion, would leave our business men weeping on one another's shoulders over human frailty, while they picked one another's pockets.

One of the most depressing features of the ethical side of the matter is that instead of such methods arousing contempt they are more or less openly admired. And this is logical. Canonise "business success," and men who make a success like that of the Standard Oil Trust become national heroes! The history of its organisation is studied as a practical lesson in money-making. It is the most startling feature of the case to one who would like to feel that it is possible to be a commercial people and yet a race of gentlemen. . . .

The effects on the very men who fight these methods on the ground that they are ethically wrong are deplorable. Brought into competition with the trust, badgered, foiled, spied upon, they come to feel as if anything is fair when the Standard is the opponent. The bitterness against the Standard Oil Company in many parts of Pennsylvania and Ohio is such that a verdict from a jury on the merits of the evidence is almost impossible! A case in point occurred a few years ago in the Bradford field. An oil producer was discovered stealing oil from the National Transit Company. He had tapped the main line and for at least two years had run a small but steady stream of Standard oil into his private tank. Finally the thieving pipe was discovered, and the owner of it, after acknowledging his guilt, was brought to trial. The jury gave a verdict of Not guilty! They seemed to feel that though the guilt was acknowledged, there probably was a Standard trick concealed somewhere. Anyway it was the Standard Oil Company and it deserved to be stolen from! The writer has frequently heard men, whose own business was conducted with scrupulous fairness, say in cases of similar stealing that they would never condemn a man who stole from the Standard! Of course such a state of feeling undermines the whole moral nature of a community.

The blackmailing cases of which the Standard Oil Company complain are a natural result of its own practices. Men going into an independent refining business have for years been accustomed to say: "well, if they won't let us alone, we'll make them pay a good price." The Standard complains that such men build simply to sellout. There may be cases of this. Probably there are, though the writer has no absolute proof of any such. Certainly there is no satisfactory proof that the refinery in the famous Buffalo case was built to sell, though that it was offered for sale when the opposition of the Everests, the managers of the Standard concern, had become so serious as later to be stamped as criminal by judge and jury, there is no doubt. Certainly nothing was shown to have been done or said by Mr. Matthews, the owner of the concern which the Standard was fighting, which might not have been expected from a man who had met the kind of opposition he had from the time he went into business.

The truth is, blackmail and every other business vice is the natural result of the peculiar business practices of the Standard. If business is to be treated as warfare and not as a peaceful pursuit, as they have persisted in treating it, they cannot expect the men they are fighting to lie down and die without a struggle. If they get special privileges they must expect their competitors to struggle to get them. If they will find it more profitable to buy out a refinery than to let it live, they must expect the owner to get an extortionate price if he can. And when they complain of these practices and call them blackmail, they show thin sporting blood. They must not expect to monopolise hard dealings, if they do oil.

These are considerations of the ethical effect of such business practices on those outside and in competition. As for those within the organisation there is one obvious effect worth noting. The Standard men as a body have nothing to do with public affairs, except as it is necessary to manipulate them for the "good of the oil business." The notion that the business man must not appear in politics and religion save as a "standpatter"—not even as a thinking, aggressive force— is demoralising, intellectually and morally. Ever since 1872 the organisation has appeared in politics only to oppose legislation obviously for the public good. At that time the oil industry was young, only twelve years old, and it was suffering from too rapid growth, from speculation, from rapacity of railroads, but it was struggling manfully with all these questions. The question of railroad discriminations and extortions was one of the "live questions" of the country. The oil men as a mass were allied against it. The theory that the railroad was a public servant bound by the spirit of its charter to treat all shippers alike, that fair play demanded open equal rates to all, was generally held in the oil country at the time Mr. Rockefeller and his friends sprung the South Improvement Company. One has only to read the oil journals at the time of the Oil War of 1872 to see how seriously all phases of the transportation question were considered. The country was a unit against the rebate system. Agreements were signed with the railroads that all rates henceforth should be equal. The signatures were not on before Mr. Rockefeller had a rebate, and gradually others got them until the Standard had won the advantages it expected the South Improvement Company to give it. From that time to this Mr. Rockefeller has had to fight the best sentiment of the oil country and of the country at large as to what is for the public good. He and his colleagues kept a strong alliance in Washington fighting the Interstate Commerce Bill from the time the first one was introduced in 1876 until the final passage in 1887. Every measure looking to the freedom and equalisation of transportation has met his opposition, as have bills for giving greater publicity to the operations of corporations. In many of the great state Legislatures one of the first persons to be pointed out to a visitor is the Standard Oil lobbyist. Now, no one can dispute the right of the Standard Oil Company to express its opinions on proposed legislation. It has the same right to do this as all the rest of the world. It is only the character of its opposition which is open to criticism, the fact that it is always fighting measures which equalise privileges and which make it more necessary for men to start fair and play fair in doing business.

Of course the effect of directly practising many of their methods is obvious. For example, take the whole system of keeping track of independent business. There are practices required which corrupt every man who has a hand in them. One of the most deplorable things about it is that most of the work is done by youngsters. The freight clerk who reports the independent oil shipments for a fee of five or ten dollars a month is probably a young man, learning his first lessons in corporate morality. If he happens to sit in Mr. Rockefeller's church on Sundays, through what sort of a haze will he receive the teachings? There is something alarming to those who believe that commerce should be a peaceful pursuit, and who believe that the moral law holds good throughout

the entire range of human relations, in knowing that so large a body of young men in this country are consciously or unconsciously growing up with the idea that business is war and that morals have nothing to do with its practice.

And what are we going to do about it? For it is *our* business. We, the people of the United States, and nobody else, must cure whatever is wrong in the industrial situation, typified by this narrative of the growth of the Standard Oil Company. That our first task is to secure free and equal transportation privileges by rail, pipe and waterway is evident. It is not an easy matter. It is one which may require operations which will seem severe; but the whole system of discrimination has been nothing but violence, and those who have profited by it cannot complain if the curing of the evils they have wrought brings hardship in turn on them. At all events, until the transportation matter is settled, and settled right, the monopolistic trust will be with us, a leech on our pockets, a barrier to our free efforts.

As for the ethical side, there is no cure but in an increasing scorn of unfair play—an increasing sense that a thing won by breaking the rules of the game is not worth the winning. When the business man who fights to secure special privileges, to crowd his competitor off the track by other than fair competitive methods, receives the same summary disdainful ostracism by his fellows that the doctor or lawyer who is "unprofessional," the athlete who abuses the rules, receives, we shall have gone a long way toward making commerce a fit pursuit for our young men.

• • •

The book was a huge success, as measured by critical reaction and sales.

Rockefeller said little publicly about the book, but he was furious. He was particularly incensed to find that Tarbell and her assistant had come to a church service in Cleveland to observe him and that she had described him in unsavory detail, implying that his disease, alopecia, which caused him to lose all facial hair, including his eyebrows, was a result of moral turpitude.

"Before she was done, Ida Tarbell turned America's most private man into its most public and hated figure," said a Rockefeller biographer, Ron Chernow. Rockefeller refused to strike back, in part because he did not want to dignify, or answer, her charges. Still, Chernow said, "While Tarbell's articles were running, Rockefeller, his wife, his son, and two of his three daughters were afflicted by serious medical problems or nervous strain."

Rockefeller and the company's reputation were severely damaged. Tarbell's portrait of Rockefeller as cunning, ruthless, and soulless "is a picture which not even a subsequent half-century of Rockefeller philanthropy has successfully dispelled," David M. Chalmers wrote in his introduction to a 1966 edition of Tarbell's book.

Some critics said Tarbell's contempt for Rockefeller was largely personal, in that she believed he had wronged her father and other relatives, who had been early oil men in western Pennsylvania. Defenders of Rockefeller, including Allan Nevins, the historian, pointed out errors she had made and suggested that her "great-man" approach to history had unfairly made Rockefeller the face of Standard Oil and let his colleagues off the hook.

In 1911, the United States Supreme Court ordered Standard Oil broken up.

Rockefeller learned a lesson from the public relations debacle that Tarbell caused. In 1914, after the national guard attacked striking coal miners at Ludlow, Colorado, Rockefeller and his family hired the publicist Ivy Lee and others to burnish the family name. The decision created the profession of business public relations.

Tarbell left *McClure's* in 1906, in part because she found McClure crotchety and unpredictable. With other muckrakers, she purchased *American* magazine, where she continued her exposés. But she was stung by President Theodore Roosevelt's denunciation of muckrakers as destructive critics.

As the years went by, she became increasingly conservative. She wrote in praise of welfare capitalism, scientific management, and "modern" corporation executives such as Elbert H. Gary of United States Steel and Owen D. Young of General Electric. She also praised the social welfare programs of Mussolini. Tarbell died on January 6, 1944.

For all that she did, her reporting on Standard Oil is remembered as the centerpiece of her life's work and is a highlight of American muckraking.

MCCLURE'S MAGAZINE BRINGS INCREASED REGULATION OF AMERICA'S RAILROADS

The fight against the railroads came roaring out of the West, because that is where, in the late 1800s, the railroads had the greatest power. Railroads determined how much a farmer or rancher had to pay to ship his crops. Railroads set land values. Railroads made a town boom, by laying tracks there, or dry up, by bypassing it. Railroads cut special deals with shippers, meaning some would prosper and others would fail. Railroads routinely bribed politicians. Railroad magnates cut deals with one another, and the lack of competition meant that freight rates jumped. Accidents and passenger deaths were common, because the railroads did not want to invest in safety devices.

The states tackled railroad regulation first, within decades of the completion of the cross-continental railroad. But the state laws were declared unconstitutional, because they dealt with interstate commerce. Congress first stepped in with a deliberately weak Interstate Commerce Act of 1887. That bought some time, but by the turn of the century there was even greater pressure to do something about the railroads. Muckraking articles in magazines such as *Collier's, The Arena, Leslie's,* and *McClure's* kept the issue before the public. Readers were urged to write their congressmen, and did.

One of the key journalistic players in the debate was Ray Stannard Baker, a former Chicago reporter, who joined *McClure's* in 1898. He became known for his capacity to immerse himself in a topic, then write balanced, detailed, but fresh stories.

"Railroad Rebates," by Ray Stannard Baker. *McClure's,* December 1905.

It is not exaggeration to say that the railroads of this country have infinitely more to do with the happiness and success of the people than the United States Government itself. They touch more people more intimately. "In America," says Acworth, the eminent British authority on transportation, "the railroad rate is a matter of life and death."

In its essence a freight-rate is a tax levied upon the people: a tax upon every mouthful of food we eat, every garment we wear, every timber in the house we live in, every shovelful of coal we burn. "A railroad," says President Mellen of the New York, New Haven & Hartford Railroad, "lives by a tax upon the community."

No other sort of taxation is so universal or so heavy as the freight-rate. In America each person pays about $7 annually for the expenses of the Federal Government, and this supports the army, the navy, pays the post-office deficiency, builds the Panama Canal, and provides for the entire machinery of government: president, congress, and supreme court; but the railroad tax in freights averages each year over $26 for every man, woman and child, nearly four times the government tax.

Now, taxation is an elemental function of government; it is, indeed, the foundation of government.

No money, no state.

One of the chief purposes of taxation is to build and maintain roads. The old Romans levied enormous taxes for roadbuilding—and conquered the world. All governments levy taxes in some form (road taxes, poll-taxes, toll-gate taxes, etc.) for maintaining highways. It is recognized as an essential function of government to keep open the public roads. President Roosevelt strikes this fundamental note in his message:

"Above all else, we must strive to keep the highways of commerce open to all on equal terms."

The railroad, by all the laws of the nation, is quite as much a highway as is a wagon road. But instead of levying direct taxes for keeping up the rail-highways (as do the people of Prussia, Austria, Switzerland and other countries) we Americans "farm out" the power of taxation to private individuals organized as a railroad corporation. The old kings farmed out the power of ordinary taxation to their favorite barons in the same way. The instrument that conveys this power upon a railroad company is a "charter." It gives the railroad company the right to operate the rail-highways and to charge a freight-rate (a tax) for doing it. Railroad presidents and directors are thus by appointment made the tax-collecting representatives of the people. For railroads are not now, and never were, private property, like a farm or a grocery store. They are *highways*.

The first essential of a tax is that it shall be just. To establish that point the Anglo-Saxon people have shed rivers of blood: our English ancestors revolted against the old barons who taxed both unequally and extortionately. Our American progenitors tossed the British tea into Boston Harbor and fought from Lexington to Yorktown to establish the principle of fair taxation.

In the present railroad agitation, the old, old question of equal taxation and the right of representation in levying taxes, is squarely before us again. The cry arises from every part of the country that the railroad "baron" does not tax fairly and equally. He is charged with making the taxes low and easy for his rich favorites—the Rockefellers, the Armours, and their like, and he is charged with making the taxes high and hard for the farmer, the small struggling manufacturers and shippers, and all the vast unorganized mass of producers and consumers. He is charged with using his great power to practice extortion. He is charged with secretly paying back part of the taxes to his rich favorites by a device called the "rebate." Let the city of New York secretly rebate part of the taxes of its wealthy citizens and see what a commotion would arise! And yet the railroad corporation, which by virtue of its charter stands in the place of the government, is charged with committing exactly that offense. In other words, these railroad representatives of ours, appointed by us as tax-collectors, do not represent us—but work for their own personal interests. Strangely like some of our political representatives! The present demand for rate-legislation by the government is nothing more nor less than the old demands for "taxation with representation." ...

By this system of discrimination the men who dominate the Chicago beef trust, for example, have by rebates and special favors closed up small, prosperous meat-packing establishments all over this country, concentrated the business in a few unsanitary slaughter-houses in the great cities, and by underpaying the cattle-raisers on the one hand and overcharging the meat consumers on the other, are laying up for themselves large fortunes. ...

Quite the most astonishing thing about the railroad rebate is the unanimity with which we agree that it is wrong, wrong morally, wrong economically, wrong legally. ... Next to the unanimity of the railroad presidents in declaring last winter that rebates are wrong was their surprising unanimity in declaring that rebating no longer exists, that it has, in reality, disappeared—or "nearly disappeared." ...

But in spite of this testimony to the nonexistence of rebates, public charges of injustice, unfairness, and favoritism were never more vehement or widespread than they have been since the passage of this excellent Elkins law [which forbade rebates].

What is right then, as to the facts, the railroad presidents or the people? Is this public agitation wholly unfounded, or is it really warranted? It is, after all, a question not of principle—we are all Americans here—but of downright *facts*.

A good deal of the present confusion arises from a quibbling (or legal) use of terms. The difficulty lies in our various applications of the words "rebate" and "discrimination" as in politics it lies in the use of the word "bribery." What is a rebate? Strictly speaking, a rebate is a sum of money secretly paid back by a railroad company to a favored shipper as a refund upon his freight-rate. And in this narrow sense, rebating is undoubtedly much less common than formerly.

But the people, who are unaccustomed to making close distinctions—to whom stealing of any one of the seventeen kinds known to the law is still plain stealing—use the word "rebate" in a much wider sense. It means any sort of favoritism to one shipper that is not given to all shippers.

But the fact that cash rebating has decreased in volume is by no means evidence that the *principle* of railroad discrimination has been changed. New ways of rebating were devised, but the thing itself—the injustice, inequality and favoritism—continued with uninterrupted vigor.

As a single example, the Elkins law, as I have said, applied only to interstate business. Accordingly, the Wisconsin investigators found that the railroads sometimes divided their interstate shipments so as to pay the rebate only on the Wisconsin or Illinois end of it. In one instance a railroad made out a "mem-bill" and shunted the carload across the state line where a new bill of lading was made out and stamped "Purely State Business"—and the rebate was then paid without fear. Innumerable other ways were devised. I saw a most remarkable statement of the amounts paid by one railroad to "encourage new industries." This is one of the points upon which railroad companies commend themselves—very often justly; they help establish infant industries, "develop the country." So this particular list was most impressive. Such evidence of activity in new industries along this line of road seemed a tribute to a most enterprising industrial agent. But the investigators looked into some of the new industries so greatly encouraged by contributions of cash. One was established in 1873—an infant thirty-two years old. But others were really younger, scattered through the 80's and 90's mostly—and the cash they received were old-fashioned rebates.

After I had examined a few dozen of such devices I was inspired with a new respect for the genius displayed in railroad bookkeeping. Some one should write a book on the "Marvels and Possibilities of Astute Accounting." . . .

Another device shows how the passenger and freight departments of a railroad work together in giving rebates. It has long been known that the favored shipper could often get a pass not only for himself, but for his entire family. This is, of course, a true rebate, for it saves the shipper just so much money. But it is more or less public, therefore undesirable. Accordingly, one Wisconsin railroad, among others, has been employing a much shrewder device. Certain large concerns in Wisconsin who employ traveling men, purchase the ordinary passenger mileage-books, upon the cover of which, when the mileage is used, the railroad will refund $20. But it was discovered that in the case of certain favored shippers, when the cover was sent back, the railroad refunded $20 in the ordinary way, and then afterwards and secretly they rebated the *entire original cost of the book*—or $60. In other words, these favored Wisconsin industries were able to send out their entire force of traveling men without paying one cent of railroad fare—while their competitors paid full fares. A good many business men of Wisconsin do not know, to-day, of this insidious and despicable competition which is undermining their business. This article may give them the first news of it! . . .

One of the very worse results of the payment of rebates to favored shippers has been the corroding growth of suspicion and distrust throughout the railroad business. It is a hard thing to say, but one cannot look into the question at all closely without reaching the conclusion that the honor of a promise, "the word of a man," has disappeared in the railroad freight business. A promise—even a signed contract—will not stand for one moment, if by breaking it a railroad agent can secure one car more of freight. These are strong words, but every man in the service, down in his heart, knows that they are true. I have listened to these men telling with absolute glee how they got together—all promising, even swearing—a "gentleman's agreement" not to give a rebate to a certain shipper, and how, the moment they got out of the meeting, every man used his best wits to break his oath as quickly as possible. Surely, a system which produces such dishonesty is wrong, wrong from the bottom to the top. . . .

• • •

Shortly after Baker's five-part series began, President Theodore Roosevelt—a man who read the muckraking magazines to keep a finger on the public pulse—called on Congress to pass a bill regulating railroads.

The Hepburn bill passed the House easily. The real fight came in the Senate, where special interests like rail, steel, and oil had their acknowledged representatives. Baker's series had a direct influence on the furious debates, Louis Filler, a historian of muckraking, said, and created a public climate that meant the senators would have to do something about the railroads.

Roosevelt fought his own party to get the bill through, and it passed in 1906. The Interstate Commerce Commission received new powers, including the power to set maximum railroad rates. On the other hand, and Roosevelt had intended this result as well, passage of the bill put the brakes on public sentiment for government ownership of railroads.

Baker left *McClure's* for *American* magazine, another muckraking stronghold, in 1906. His progressive instincts then led him to politics and to enthusiasm for Woodrow Wilson. Over more than two decades, Baker wrote an eight-volume Wilson biography and edited six volumes of Wilson's papers. He also wrote three autobiographical books, including *American Chronicle*. Baker died in 1946.

THE *WORLD-TELEGRAM AND SUN* DOES THE IMPOSSIBLE AND STOPS POWER BROKER ROBERT MOSES

For half a century beginning in the 1930s, through six governors and five mayors, Robert Moses was the man who built New York City, and much of the state of New York. With billions of dollars of public money under his control, Moses ordered up hundreds of miles of highways, state parks that set the standard for the country, urban renewal projects that reshaped vast areas, the Lincoln Center for the Arts, the United Nations, university campuses, stunning bridges, power dams, playgrounds. His efforts were admired and copied across the country. "In the twentieth century," said the urban critic Lewis Mumford, "the influence of Robert Moses on the cities of America was greater than that of any other person."

All this was possible because of Moses's success at seizing early on new federal programs; his mastery of the concept of the public authority, which, despite its title, enabled him to keep his contracts and records private; his accumulation and unstinting wielding of power; and his carefully cultivated reputation for being efficient, prudent, and above politics. It also helped that he spread round lavish contracts and that the people he displaced when he wanted to build—Robert Caro, in his magesterial biography, *The Power Bro-*

ker, estimated there were nearly half a million—were typically poor and minorities. And that the press, particularly the publishers and editorial writers, thought Moses could do no wrong. Even at the *New York Times*, Gay Talese wrote in *The Kingdom and the Power*, reporters believed Moses had to be "more delicately handled than other important newsmakers."

In the early 1950s, some chinks started to appear in Moses's armor, but they received little attention. A few maverick city officials and good-government groups spoke out against the way Moses was running the Title I urban renewal program. The *New York Post* gave voice to the hundreds of Bronx families being kicked out of their homes for the Cross-Bronx Expressway, but no one of power cared. Then Moses tried to use his typical rough-shod methods to knock out a part of Central Park to expand a parking lot for the fancy Tavern on the Green restaurant. The mothers who used the park were angry, wealthy, and media savvy. Their protests drew the kind of headlines Moses was not used to seeing: "Moms-vs-Moses," "Fighting Park Moms," the "Battle of Central Park." Following a practice he had used in other disputes, Moses sent park department workers and bulldozers in after midnight to knock down some trees and start construction. Bad move. By the time Moses had to, uncharacteristically, retreat, his aura of infallibility and incorruptibility, Caro wrote, was gone. The press was ready to take a serious look at his empire, and Gene Gleason and Fred J. Cook of the *World-Telegram and Sun* were first.

"Few Homes Built by Title 1 Billion," by Gene Gleason and Fred J. Cook. *World-Telegram and Sun,* July 30, 1956.

The world's most ambitious plan to create new and glowing neighborhoods from slums has cost federal and local taxpayers more than $1 billion in seven years of effort—and so far has been almost a complete flop.

This is the inescapable conclusion drawn from a three-month study of all facets of the Title I slum clearance program by members of the staff of the *World-Telegram and Sun.*

Even after the passage of those seven years and the expenditure of that $1 billion, just two slum clearance projects in the entire United States have been completed, FHA officials admit.

And in some cases, this newspaper's survey showed, the program actually had a reverse effect, creating new slums instead of abolishing old ones.

The story is one of infinite complexity, tangled in the rarified realms of multi-million-dollar finance, snafued in bureaucratic red tape that has seen projects stagnate for two to three years while men with titles wrote letters to men with titles.

In New York City, 10 projects are under contract, but only one is nearing completion. In some instances, tenements which did, at least, represent homes have been torn down and replaced with parking lots—a displacement of human beings by cars that has led to bitter criticism.

It is a system under which neighborhoods actually have deteriorated; under which the number of apartments, already inadequate, has been reduced for years to come. It is a system under which many families have been forced to double up with relatives, beginning again the cycle of overcrowding and bad housing that creates slums.

This is the broad picture of the vast Title I program that seemed, when it was born in Congress seven years ago, to have so much to offer in lifting the faces of America's cities and providing a better future for urban dwellers.

The idea was that slum-blighted areas would be reborn through public and private enterprise. Government would acquire slum areas so vast that the land cost would be prohibitive to the private investor. Then the area would be turned over at a much lower cost to a private developer. The loss on the land would be borne two-thirds by the federal government, one third by the municipal. Then private capital would do the rest, developing each area as a neighborhood unit complete with modern stores, businesses and apartments.

That was the vision, and this is the way it has worked, according to the FHA's own figures:

The federal government has paid out or has earmarked for the program a total of $1 billion. Municipal governments have put up or committed themselves for roughly another half-billion. This prodigious expenditure embraces 375 projects now on the drafting boards in about 220 municipalities across the nation. Of these, only two, one in Philadelphia and one in Baltimore, have been completed. Only 17 are actually under construction.

In this city, the program has dragged since its inception. A graphic idea of just how badly it has lagged may be obtained by studying a recent progress report. This shows that, while some projects were approved as early as February, 1952, and were supposed to be completed by now, construction work stands at an absolute zero.

Robert Moses, chairman of the Mayor's Committee on Slum Clearance, blames federal officials for the long delay. Testifying last fall before a Congressional committee, he submitted voluminous correspondence to show that FHA officials dilly-dallied two and one-half years on applications for loans to finance projects.

Mr. Moses declared bluntly that the city program had been stymied because FHA officials, made jittery by the windfall scandal in housing developments, wouldn't say yes and wouldn't say no when confronted with applications for Title I slum clearance loans.

He told the Congressional committee that the city's most advanced project, Corlears Hook on the lower East Side—now listed officially as 82 percent complete, though to the eye it looks finished—had got under way only after attempts to get an FHA loan had been abandoned and private financing arranged. The FHA, Mr. Moses testified, had wanted to saddle an extra $4 million in costs on the project by requiring refinements that "wouldn't be applied on Park Ave. or Fifth Ave."

There is, of course, another side to the story. The fact is that New York City, under the guidance of Mr. Moses, handles its Title I projects differently from any other city in the nation.

Elsewhere, municipal authorities acquire the land, relocate the tenants and demolish slum buildings. The cleared area is then turned over to the private developer, who has no choice, if he wants to made a profit, except to build as expeditiously as possible.

In New York, however, the area to be redeveloped is turned over to private interests with buildings intact. The developer is given the job of relocating the tenants and clearing the land, and for this he is recompensed. But he need not hurry. He is permitted to reap a profit up to 10 percent annually from rentals on the area just as it stands, and he can go on collecting this for years, on a relatively small initial cash outlay, until ultimately he gets around to building.

Federal housing officials in Washington say the unique New York system was approved because Mr. Moses wanted it that way, but they confess they're not happy about it. They feel that the New York method could lead to corruption, to another windfall scandal, and that it breeds delay by permitting the private developer to milk the property for rents and parking lot fees over a long period before he begins construction.

Whether this dissatisfaction with the New York plan helps to explain FHA tardiness in processing loan applications, the city's own statistics make it clear the FHA alone isn't to blame for the muddle. For the indisputable fact is this: many private developers here, given vast areas to play with, have not yet made applications for loans for all the buildings contemplated in blueprints more than four years old.

The Godfrey Nurse Housing development in Harlem, for instance, was approved in February, 1952. Construction is only 10 percent complete, and FHA loans have been sought, more than four years later, for only 287 housing units out of the projected 1716.

Similarly, the Manhattantown development was initiated in February, 1952, and was supposed to have been completed by Aug. 29, 1958. But construction hasn't even started. FHA backing was sought only a few months ago—and then for only 861 apartments instead of the 2583 originally scheduled to be built.

● ● ●

With the Gleason-Cook stories opening the possibility of press criticism of Moses, scores of tips started coming in from city employees, outraged private citizens, and others eager to demonstrate the way Moses worked. Still, Moses held his power. For many months, Cook and Gleason were the only reporters criticizing the way Moses operated urban renewal in New York City. Gradually, with the help of other young, aggressive reporters on other New York papers, and with the help of some rare miscues on Moses's part, Moses's public image began to crumble. In 1962, when Moses issued one of his periodic threats of resignation, intending to cower Governor Nelson Rockefeller, Rockefeller accepted. It was another six years before Rockefeller maneuvered Moses out of the last of his power, but by the time that happened, the public little cared.

JESSICA MITFORD PUTS FUNERAL DIRECTORS UNDER NEW SCRUTINY

Funerals are one of the largest purchases of one's life, and purchases made under the worst circumstances: emotional pressure, time pressure, lack of experience, lack of information about competition, smooth salesmanship, peer pressure, guilt. No wonder most people neither seek help nor talk about their experiences, feeling that if they were unsatisfied, it was their own fault.

Robert Treuhaft, a labor lawyer in California, became interested in the funeral industry in the 1950s, because he saw funeral homes raking in the death benefits of workers in unions he represented. In an attempt to get good, simple, inexpensive funerals, Treuhaft helped organize the Bay Area Funeral Society. "I am sorry to say I rather mocked these good folks, calling them the Necrophilists and teasing them about their Layaway Plan," wrote Treuhaft's wife, the writer Jessica Mitford.

Mitford would atone herself, although somewhat accidentally. Looking for a topic, she wrote an article, "St. Peter, Don't You Call Me," that appeared in a small California magazine, *Frontier*. But that led to her appearance on a debate on television, and that debate led the *Saturday Evening Post* to assign Roul Tunley to write "Can You Afford to Die?" in June 1961. Mitford was quoted in the story. After Tunley said he was too busy to do a book on the topic, Mitford did.

The American Way of Death, by Jessica Mitford. New York: Simon and Schuster, 1963.

"How long, I would ask, are we to be subjected to the tyranny of custom and undertakers? Truly, it is all vanity and vexation of spirit—a mere mockery of woe, costly to all, far, far beyond its value; and ruinous to many; hateful, and an abomination to all; yet submitted to by all, because none have the moral courage to speak against it and act in defiance of it."

—LORD ESSEX

O Death, where is thy sting? O grave, where is thy victory? Where, indeed. Many a badly stung survivor, faced with the aftermath of some relative's funeral, has ruefully concluded that the victory had been won hands down by a funeral establishment—in disastrously unequal battle.

Much has been written of late about the affluent society in which we live, and much fun poked at some of the irrational "status symbols" set out like golden snares to trap the unwary consumer at every turn. Until recently, little has been said about the most irrational and weirdest of the lot, lying in ambush for all of us at the end of the road—the modern American funeral.

If the Dismal Traders (as an eighteenth-century English writer calls them) have traditionally been cast in a comic role in literature, a universally recognized symbol of humor from Shakespeare to Dickens to Evelyn Waugh, they have successfully turned the tables in recent years to perpetrate a huge, macabre and expensive practical joke on the American public. It is not consciously conceived of as a joke, of course; on the contrary, it is hedged with admirably contrived rationalizations.

Gradually, almost imperceptibly, over the years the funeral men have constructed their own grotesque cloud-cuckoo-land where the trappings of Gracious Living are transformed, as in a nightmare, to the trappings of Gracious Dying. The same familiar Madison Avenue language, with its peculiar adjectival range designed to anesthetize sales resistance to all sorts of products, has seeped into the funeral industry in a new and bizarre guise. The emphasis is on the same desirable qualities that we have all been schooled to look for in our daily search for excellence: comfort, durability, beauty, craftsmanship. The attuned ear will recognize too the convincing quasi-scientific language, so reassuring even if unintelligible.

So that this too, too solid flesh might not melt, we are offered "solid copper—a quality casket which offers superb value to the client seeking long-lasting protection," or "the Colonial Classic Beauty—18 gauge lead coated steel, seamless top, lap-jointed welded body construction." Some are equipped with foam rubber, some with innerspring mattresses. Elgin offers "the revolutionary 'Perfect-Posture' bed." Not every casket need have a silver lining, for one may choose between "more than 60 color matched shades, magnificent and unique masterpieces" by the Cheney casket-lining people. Shrouds no longer exist. Instead, you may patronize a grave-wear couturier who promises "handmade original fashions—styles from the best in life for the last memory—dresses, men's suits, negligees, accessories." For the final, perfect grooming: "Nature-Glo—the ultimate in cosmetic embalming." And, where have we heard that phrase "peace of mind protection" before? No matter. In funeral advertising, it is applied to the Wilbert Burial Vault, with its ⅜-inch precast asphalt inner liner plus extra-thick, reinforced concrete—all this "guaranteed by Good Housekeeping." Here again the Cadillac, status symbol par excellence, appears in all its gleaming glory, this time transformed into a pastel-colored funeral hearse.

You, the potential customer for all this luxury, are unlikely to read the lyrical descriptions quoted above, for they are culled from *Mortuary Management* and *Casket and Sunnyside*, two of the industry's eleven trade magazines. For you there are ads in your daily newspaper, generally found on the obituary page, stressing dignity, refinement, high-caliber professional service and that intangible quality, *sincerity*. The trade advertisements are, however, instructive, because they furnish an important clue to the frame of mind into which the funeral industry has hypnotized itself.

A new mythology, essential to the twentieth-century American funeral rite, has grown up—or rather has been built up step by step—to justify the peculiar customs surrounding the disposal of our dead. And, just as the witch doctor must be convinced of his own infallibility in order to maintain a hold over his clientele, so the funeral industry has had to "sell itself" on its articles of faith in the course of passing them along to the public.

The first of these is the tenet that today's funeral procedures are founded in "American tradition." The story comes to mind of a sign on the freshly sown lawn of a brand-new Midwest college: "There is a tradition on this campus that students never walk on this strip of grass. This tradition goes into effect next Tuesday." The most cursory look at American funerals of past times will establish the parallel. Simplicity to the

point of starkness, the plain pine box, the laying out of the dead by friends and family who also bore the coffin to the grave—these were the hallmarks of the traditional funeral until the end of the nineteenth century.

Secondly, there is the myth that the American public is only being given what it wants—an opportunity to keep up with the Joneses to the end. "In keeping with our high standard of living, there should be an equally high standard of dying," says the past president of the Funeral Directors of San Francisco. "The cost of a funeral varies according to individual taste and the niceties of living the family has been accustomed to." Actually, choice doesn't enter the picture for the average individual, faced, generally for the first time, with the necessity of buying a product of which he is totally ignorant, at a moment when he is least in a position to quibble. In point of fact the cost of a funeral almost always varies, not "according to individual taste" but according to what the traffic will bear.

Thirdly, there is an assortment of myths based on half-digested psychiatric theories. The importance of the "memory picture" is stressed—meaning the last glimpse of the deceased in open casket, done up with the latest in embalming techniques and finished off with a dusting of makeup. A newer one, impressively authentic-sounding, is the need for "grief therapy," which is beginning to go over big in mortuary circles. A historian of American funeral directing hints at the grief-therapist idea when speaking of the new role of the undertaker—"the dramaturgic role, in which the undertaker becomes a stage manager to create an appropriate atmosphere and to move the funeral party through a drama in which social relationships are stressed and an emotional catharsis or release is provided through ceremony."

Lastly, a whole new terminology, as ornately shoddy as the satin rayon casket liner, has been invented by the funeral industry to replace the direct and serviceable vocabulary of former times. Undertaker has been supplanted by "funeral director" or "mortician." (Even the classified section of the telephone directory gives recognition to this; in its pages you will find "Undertakers— see Funeral Directors.") Coffins are "caskets"; hearses are "coaches," or "professional cars"; flowers are "floral tributes"; corpses generally are "loved ones," but mortuary etiquette dictates that a specific corpse be referred to by name only— as "Mr. Jones"; cremated ashes are "cremains." Euphemisms such as "slumber room," "reposing room," and "calcination—the *kindlier* heat" abound in the funeral business.

If the undertaker is the stage manager of the fabulous production that is the modern American funeral, the stellar role is reserved for the occupant of the open casket. The décor, the stagehands, the supporting case are all arranged for the most advantageous display of the deceased, without which the rest of the paraphernalia would lose its point—*Hamlet* without the Prince of Denmark. It is to this end that a fantastic array of costly merchandise and services is pyramided to dazzle the mourners and facilitate the plunder of the next of kin.

Grief therapy, anyone? But it's going to come high. According to the funeral industry's own figures, the *average* undertaker's bill in 1961 was $798 for casket and "services," to which must be added the cost of a burial vault, flowers, clothing, clergy and musician's honorarium, and cemetery charges. When these costs are added to the undertaker's bill, the total average cost for an adult's funeral is, as we shall see, closer to $1,450. [In 2001, the Funeral Society of America said the cost was often $5,000 or more.]

The question naturally arises, *is* this what most people want for themselves and their families? For several reasons, this has been a hard one to answer until recently. It is a subject seldom discussed. Those who have never had to arrange for a funeral frequently shy away from its implications, preferring to take comfort in the thought that sufficient unto the day is the evil thereof. Those who have acquired personal and painful knowledge of the subject would often rather forget about it. Pioneering "Funeral Societies" or "Memorial Associations," dedicated to the principle of dignified funerals at reasonable cost, have existed in a number of communities throughout the country, but their membership has been limited for the most part to the more sophisticated element in the population—university people, liberal intellectuals—and those who, like doctors and lawyers, come up against problems in arranging funerals for their clients.

Some indication of the pent-up resentment felt by vast numbers of people against the funeral interests was furnished by the astonishing response to an article by Roul Tunley, titled "Can You Afford to Die?" in *The Saturday Evening Post* of June 17, 1961. As though a dike had burst, letters poured in from every part of the country to the *Post*, to the funeral societies, to local newspapers. They came from clergymen, professional people, old-age pensioners, trade unionists. Three months after the article appeared, an estimated six thousand had taken pen in hand to comment on some phase of the high cost of dying. Many recounted their own bitter experiences at the hands of funeral directors; hundreds asked for advice on how to establish a consumer organization in communities where none exists; others sought information about pre-need plans. The membership of funeral societies skyrocketed. The funeral industry, finding itself in the glare of public spotlight, has begun to engage in serious debate about its own future course—as well it might.

Is the funeral inflation bubble ripe for bursting? A few years ago, the United States public suddenly rebelled against the trend in the auto industry towards ever more showy cars, with their ostentatious and nonfunctional fins, and a demand was created for compact cars patterned after European models. The all-powerful auto industry, accustomed to *telling* the customer what sort of car he wanted, was suddenly forced to *listen* for a change. Overnight, the little cars became for millions a new kind of status symbol.

Could it be that the same cycle is working itself out in the attitude towards the final return of dust to dust, that the American public is becoming sickened by ever more ornate and costly funerals, and that a status symbol of the future may indeed be the simplest kind of "funeral without fins"?

• • •

The first 20,000 copies of Mitford's book sold out on publication day. At public event after public event, Mitford's readers told her their own stories about what they considered the callousness and greed of funeral homes. Newspapers used the book as a reason to investigate their local funeral homes and CBS television did its own national report. Mitford was attacked by the funeral industry, in magazines such as *Casket and Sunnyside* and *Concept: The Journal of Creative Ideas for Cemeteries.* The industry was angered by her humorous style and occasionally brought up her leftist leanings. She never lost either of them.

The Federal Trade Commission investigated the funeral industry for two years. In 1975, the agency announced proposed rules that would help protect buyers dealing with morticians, including requiring itemized bills, forbidding undertakers from misleading customers about whether embalming was required, requiring that prices be given over the telephone, and requiring that the cheapest casket be displayed with the others. The industry reacted vehemently, and the rules were scaled back before final adoption in 1984. Between 1984 and 1995, Mitford wrote in *The American Way of Death Revisited* (New York: Alfred A. Knopf, 1998), only thirty-eight cases were formally filed against funeral directors. Fines for violation, she said, ranged between $10,000 and $100,000.

The bigger change was in the minds of Americans. Increasing numbers became determined to take control of their last purchase. Membership in nonprofit funeral homes and memorial societies grew exponentially; today there are about 125 with more than a million members. Cremation

likewise increased dramatically. In 1961, when she was writing her book, 3.75 percent of American dead were cremated, Mitford said. By 1995, when she was writing *Revisited,* the share was 21 percent and rising. Moreover, consumer magazines began writing stories on funeral planning.

Jessica Mitford died of cancer in 1996.

SEYMOUR M. HERSH REVEALS ILLEGAL C.I.A. SPYING IN AMERICA

When Congress set up the Central Intelligence Agency in 1947, it explicitly prohibited the agency from doing work within the United States. Any suspicions of espionage were to be the province of the Federal Bureau of Investigation. Publicly, both C.I.A. officials and presidents honored the distinction. Privately, they occasionally found it to be a nuisance that could be ignored in the interest of what they considered a larger evil, such as the rise of an antiwar movement during the 1960s. One of the most avid believers in the C.I.A.'s right—to him it was a need—to do what it wanted was James Angleton, who started spying during World War II and became the agency's powerful head of counterintelligence in 1954.

"Huge C.I.A. Operation Reported in U.S. Against Antiwar Forces, Other Dissidents in Nixon Years," by Seymour M. Hersh. *New York Times,* December 22, 1974.

WASHINGTON, Dec. 21—The Central Intelligence Agency, directly violating its charter, conducted a massive, illegal domestic intelligence operation during the Nixon Administration against the antiwar movement and other dissident groups in the United States, according to well-placed Government sources.

An extensive investigation by *The New York*

Times has established that intelligence files on at least 10,000 American citizens were maintained by a special unit of the C.I.A. that was reporting directly to Richard Helms, then the Director of Central Intelligence and now the Ambassador to Iran.

In addition, the sources said, a check of the C.I.A.'s domestic files ordered last year by Mr. Helms's successor, James R. Schlesinger, produced evidence of dozens of other illegal activities by members of the C.I.A. inside the United States, beginning in the nineteen-fifties, including break-ins, wiretapping and the surreptitious inspection of mail.

Mr. Schlesinger was succeeded at the C.I.A. by William E. Colby in September, 1973.

Those other alleged operations, in the fifties, while also prohibited by law, were not targeted at dissident American citizens, the sources said, but were a different category of domestic activities that were secretly carried out as part of operations aimed at suspected foreign intelligence agents operating in the United States.

Under the 1947 act setting up the C.I.A., the agency was forbidden to have "police, subpoena, law enforcement powers or internal security functions" inside the United States. Those responsibilities fall to the F.B.I., which maintains a special internal security unit to deal with foreign intelligence threats.

Mr. Helms, who became head of the C.I.A. in 1966 and left the agency in February, 1973, for his new post in Teheran, could not be reached despite telephone calls there yesterday and today.

Charles Cline, a duty officer at the American Embassy in Teheran, said today that a note informing Mr. Helms of the request by *The Times* for comment had been delivered to Mr. Helms's quarters this morning. By late evening Mr. Helms had not returned the call.

The information about the C.I.A. came as the Senate Armed Services Committee issued a report today condemning the Pentagon for spying on the White House National Security Council. But the report said the Pentagon spying incidents in 1970 and 1971 were isolated and presented no threat to civilian control of the military.

The disclosure of alleged illegal C.I.A. activities is the first possible connection to rumors that have been circulating in Washington for some time. A number of mysterious burglaries and incidents have come to light since the break-in at Democratic party headquarters in the Watergate complex on June 17, 1972.

Throughout the public hearings and courtroom testimony on Watergate, Mr. Helms and other high-level officials said that the C.I.A. had been "duped" into its Watergate involvement by the White House.

As part of its alleged effort against dissident Americans in the late nineteen-sixties and early nineteen-seventies, *The Times*'s sources said, the C.I.A. authorized agents to follow and photograph participants in antiwar and other demonstrations. The C.I.A. also set up a network of informants who were ordered to penetrate antiwar groups, the sources said.

At least one avowedly antiwar member of Congress was among those placed under surveillance by the C.I.A., the sources said. Other members of Congress were said to be included in the C.I.A.'s dossier on dissident Americans.

The names of the various Congressmen could not be learned, nor could any specific information about domestic C.I.A. break-ins and wiretappings be obtained.

It also could not be determined whether Mr. Helms had had specific authority from top officials to initiate the alleged domestic surveillance, or whether Mr. Helms had informed the President of the fruits, if any, of the alleged operations.

These alleged activities are known to have distressed both Mr. Schlesinger, now the Secretary of Defense, and Mr. Colby. Mr. Colby has reportedly told associates that he is considering the possibility of asking the Attorney General to institute legal action against some of those who had been involved in the alleged domestic activities.

One official, who was directly involved in the initial C.I.A. inquiry last year into the alleged domestic spying, said that Mr. Schlesinger and his associates were unable to learn what Mr. Nixon knew, if anything.

Mr. Colby refused to comment on the domestic spying issue. . . .

Mr. Schlesinger, who became Secretary of Defense after serving less than six months at the C.I.A., similarly refused to discuss the domestic spying activities.

But he was described by an associate as extremely concerned and disturbed by what he discovered at the C.I.A. upon replacing Mr. Helms.

"He found himself in a cesspool," the associate said. "He was having a grenade blowing up in his face every time he turned around."

The associate said one result of Mr. Schlesinger's inquiries into Watergate and the domestic aspects of the C.I.A. operations was his executive edict ordering a halt to all questionable counterintelligence operations inside the United States.

When confronted with *The Times*'s information about the C.I.A.'s domestic operations earlier this week, high-ranking American intelligence officials confirmed its basic accuracy, but cautioned against drawing "unwarranted conclusions."

Those officials, who insisted on not being quoted by name, contended that all of the C.I.A.'s domestic activities against American citizens were initiated in the belief that foreign governments and foreign espionage may have been involved.

"Anything that we did was in the context of foreign counterintelligence and it was focused at foreign intelligence and foreign intelligence problems," one official said.

Beyond his briefings for Senator John C. Stennis, Democrat of Mississippi, and Representative Lucien N. Nedzi, Democrat of Michigan, the respective chairmen of the Senate and House Intelligence subcommittees of the Armed Services Committees, Mr. Colby apparently had not informed other Ford Administration officials as of yesterday of the C.I.A. problems.

"Counterintelligence!" one high-level Justice Department official exclaimed upon being given some details of the C.I.A.'s alleged domestic operations. "They're not supposed to have any counterintelligence in this country."

"Oh, my God," he said, "oh my God."

A former high-level F.B.I. official, who operated in domestic counterintelligence areas since World War II, expressed astonishment and then anger upon being told of the C.I.A.'s alleged domestic activities.

"We had an agreement with them that they weren't to do anything unless they checked with us," he said. "They double-crossed me all along."

He said he had never been told by his C.I.A. counterintelligence colleagues of any of the alleged domestic operations that took place. . . .

The C.I.A. domestic activities during the Nixon Administration were directed, the source said, by James Angleton, who is still in charge of the Counterintelligence Department, the agency's most powerful and mysterious unit.

As head of counterintelligence, Mr. Angleton is in charge of maintaining the C.I.A.'s "sources and methods of intelligence," which means that he and his men must ensure that foreign intelligence agents do not penetrate the C.I.A.

The Times's sources, who included men with access to first-hand knowledge of the C.I.A.'s alleged domestic activities, took sharp exception to the official suggestion that such activities were the result of legitimate counterintelligence needs.

"Look, that's how it started," one man said. "They were looking for evidence of foreign involvement in the antiwar movement. But that's not how it ended up. This just grew and mushroomed internally."

"Maybe they began with a check on Fonda," the source said, speaking hypothetically. "But then they began to check on her friends. They'd see her at an antiwar rally and take photographs. . . .

"This wasn't a series of isolated events. It was highly coordinated. People were targeted, information was collected on them, and it was all put on [computer] tape, just like the agency does with information about K.G.B. [Soviet] agents.

"Every one of these acts was blatantly illegal."

Another official with access to details of C.I.A. operations said that the alleged illegal activities uncovered by Mr. Schlesinger last year included break-ins and electronic surveillance that had been undertaken during the fifties and sixties.

"During the fifties, this was routine stuff," the official said. "The agency did things that would amaze both of us, but some of this also went on in the late sixties, when the country and atmosphere had changed."

The official suggested that what he called the "Nixon antiwar hysteria" may have been a major factor in the C.I.A.'s decision to begin maintaining domestic files on American citizens. . . .

Along with assembling the domestic intelligence dossiers, the source said, Mr. Angleton's department began recruiting informants to infiltrate some of the more militant dissident groups.

"They recruited plants, informers and doublers [double agents]," the source said. "They were collecting information and when counterintelligence collects information, you use all of those techniques.

"It was like a little F.B.I. operation."

This source and others knowledgeable about the C.I.A. believe that Mr. Angleton was permitted to continue his alleged domestic operations because of the great power he wields inside the agency as director of counterintelligence. . . .

Dozens of other former C.I.A. men talked in recent interviews with similar expressions of fear and awe about Mr. Angleton, an accomplished botanist and Yale graduate who once edited a poetry magazine there.

He was repeatedly described by former C.I.A. officials as an unrelenting cold warrior who was convinced that the Soviet Union was playing a major role in the antiwar activites. . . .

Despite intensive interviews, little could be learned about the procedures involved in the alleged domestic activities except for the fact that the operation was kept carefully shielded from other units inside the C.I.A. . . .

Mr. Angleton, also reached by telephone this week at his suburban Washington home, denied that his Counterintelligence Department operated domestically.

"We know our jurisdiction," he said.

Mr. Angleton told of a report from a United States agent in Moscow who was relaying information to the C.I.A. on the underground and radical bombings in the United States during the height of the antiwar activity.

"The intelligence was not acquired in the United States," Mr. Angleton declared, "it came from Moscow. Our source there is still active and still productive; the opposition still doesn't know."

Mr. Angleton then described how the C.I.A. had obtained information from Communist sources about the alleged demolition training of black militants by the North Koreans. He also told of recent intelligence efforts involving the K.G.B. and Yasir Arafat, chairman of the Palestine Liberation Organization. . . .

Other officials closely involved with United States intelligence expressed amazement and dismay that the head of counterintelligence would make such random suggestions during a telephone conversation with a newsman.

"You know," said one member of Congress who is involved with the monitoring of C.I.A. activities, "that's even a better story than the domestic spying."

• • •

The support and fear that C.I.A. directors gave to Angleton varied depending on their views of the world and their willingness to pick a fight they might not win. By 1974, however, troubled by some of Angleton's activities and his paranoid tendencies, C.I.A. director William Colby was trying to oust him. Angleton did not take the hint. After being interviewed for Hersh's story, Colby called in Angleton and fired him. Several other top officials resigned.

Contrary to previous C.I.A. scandals, in which presidents and Congress expressed outrage but took little action, this time the pressure was on. A commission headed by Vice President Nelson A. Rockefeller and hearings by Senate and House committees found even more widespread domestic spying than Hersh had indicated. The hearings also revealed other questionable C.I.A. practices, including its involvement in assassination plots against foreign leaders. Reflecting public outrage, new laws were passed requiring that C.I.A. activities come under more careful scrutiny of Congress.

SECRETS OF THE PARISH: THE *NATIONAL CATHOLIC REPORTER* UNVEILS THE HIDDEN STORY OF PRIESTS MOLESTING CHILDREN

When the *National Catholic Reporter*, an independent weekly reporting on the news of the Catholic Church, was founded in 1964, the opening editorial warned readers to expect "the putting of awkward questions and the printing of awkward facts."

NCR kept its word. In the early 1980s, staff members started hearing reports about priests having sexual relations with young boys, often altar boys. "Knowing we would catch a lot of flack were we to write about it, we were not eager to cover the story," said Thomas C. Fox, then the editor. But he decided that if *NCR* did not do the story, no one would: "No chance the Catholic press would pick it up; the secular press was staying clear as well, not wanting to be labeled as being 'anti-Catholic.' "

The story, Fox said, soon became twofold: abuse was occurring, and, by and large, local church officials were covering up, sometimes merely transferring the victimizing priest to another parish. All the cases used in the *NCR*'s first report were in the court, usually because the victims and their families were frustrated by the lack of response from church officials.

"Priest child abuse cases victimizing families; bishops lack policy response," *National Catholic Reporter*, **June 7, 1985.**

In cases throughout the nation, the Catholic church is facing scandals and being forced to pay millions of dollars in claims to families whose sons have been molested by Catholic priests.

These are serious and damaging matters that have victimized the young and innocent and fuel old suspicions against the Catholic church and a celibate clergy. But a related and broader scandal seemingly rests with local bishops and a national episcopal leadership that has, as yet, no set policy on how to respond to these cases. As the articles in this issue show:

- *All too often, complaints against the priest involved are disregarded by the bishops, or the priest is given the benefit of the doubt.*

- *Frequently, local bishops exhibit little concern for the traumatic effects these molestations have on the boys and their families—even though mental disturbances and, in one recent case, suicide, have followed such molestations.*

- *Only legal threats and lawsuits seem capable of provoking some local bishops into taking firm actions against the priests. In some cases reported here, the priests, once identified for their offenses, have been moved to other parishes and again placed in positions of responsibility. . . .*

By ARTHUR JONES
Washington Bureau Chief

Between 1972 and 1983, Father Gilbert Gauthe committed hundreds of sexual acts with dozens of boys in four south Louisiana Catholic parishes. He also took hundreds of pornographic photographs, which have disappeared. The priest, suspended by the Lafayette diocese in 1983, is now in a Connecticut mental facility.

The situation has no real precedent in American case law. The criminal trial expected this fall is thought to be the first of a priest for such felonies, one of the largest single cases of pedophilia on record. A Lafayette diocese defense attorney has entered a plea of not guilty by reason of insanity. Millions of dollars in damage claims are at stake, and millions have already been paid.

When a Catholic priest in Thousand Oaks, Calif., 45 miles northwest of Los Angeles, pleaded no contest to three charges of child molestation, the event sent shock waves across this small community of condominiums, ranch-style homes and shopping centers. The priest, Father Donald Roemer, then an assistant pastor, was widely praised for this work among youth and enjoyed a reputation as being "kind," "energetic" and "caring." But, according to court records, after he admitted to psychologists and probation authorities that he had molested at least 15 youngsters, he was committed to a state mental hospital for 22 months. Roemer, now 40, is serving a strictly supervised 10-year probationary period.

In February 1984, the parents of three boys Roemer allegedly molested filed a civil suit against Roemer's superiors, claiming they knew of his inclinations but still allowed him to work with children. Named as defendants are the Catholic Archdiocese of Los Angeles, the local parish and the local pastor. A California judge ruled Sept. 15, 1984, that the Los Angeles archdiocese is liable because church authorities knew about the priest's tendencies.

The suit stems from a complaint by a mother who informed the pastor that Roemer had molested her son during a religious retreat the pre-

vious May. The pastor assured her the matter would be "investigated and remedied." But a month later, two other alleged victims claimed that, within a month of the original complaint, they had also been molested. That led to Roemer's arrest and his subsequent admissions.

Three months after meeting with the pastor, the mother wrote to Los Angeles Cardinal Timothy Manning to describe her son's behavioral changes after the alleged molestation and to request money, explaining the costs of her son's subsequent therapy. Until that point, she said, "the only time the church contacted me was to request I not speak with the news media."

The woman received a reply from Manning's secretary, Monsignor Clement J. Connolly: "We perfectly understand the financial burdens which have beset you in those difficult days." He enclosed a check for $500. Connolly told *NCR* he could make no further comment, because the matter is in litigation; Roemer's pastor was hospitalized for stress and has retired permanently to his native Ireland.

The civil suit against Roemer and the archdiocese could drag on for months, even years. Yet, according to the plaintiffs' attorney, "I hate to sound harsh about it, but had they (the church authorities) shown a caring attitude, the parents would never have been interested in filing a lawsuit."

For years, the altar boys at one Portland parish church and pupils at the local school passed along a whispered message never heard by their parents: Never go anywhere alone with Father Thomas Laughlin.

Laughlin, a diocesan priest for more than 37 years, onetime teacher in an all-boys high school, pastor in a middle-class parish, was a man of influence in the local chancery until 1983. Twenty-two months ago, he was convicted of two sexual abuse misdemeanor counts involving boys under 18 and was sentenced to five months in jail. When arrested, the 57-year-old priest admitted he had been sexually involved with boys for 15 to 20 years; he now is reportedly at Villa Louis Martin, a New Mexico treatment center operated by the Servants of the Paraclete religious community.

The issue for the many parents who have come forward and discussed this case with *NCR* is their worry that Laughlin will one day have the powers and privileges of his Roman collar restored. . . .

An associate pastor said he had told Auxiliary Bishops Waldschmidt and Kenneth Steiner in 1979 that parents had approached him with suspicions about Laughlin. The pastor, Laughlin, was called in for a meeting but denied any problems, Waldschmidt told *NCR*. "If he denies it, you sort of take him at his word," said Waldschmidt. "After all, he's a priest, and you figure he wouldn't lie to you." . . .

In Idaho, in January this year, Father Mel Baltazaar was sentenced to seven years in the state penitentiary after pleading guilty to a reduced charge of lewd behavior with a minor in Boise, Idaho. Before sentencing, the judge ordered an investigation of Baltazaar's personnel records, which reveal a history of illegal sexual contacts with youths dating back 20 years.

The priest reportedly had been discharged as a naval chaplain in 1979 for homosexual conduct and was dismissed from hospital chaplaincy work "for his involvement with a dying youth on a dialysis machine." The investigation revealed the priest's superiors knew of other complaints but had taken no action. . . .

The difficulties of the families and the boys are shown in interviews . . . (their real names are not used).

Rod Ward, a strapping man in his late 30s, had been an altar boy and encouraged his son to be one. In time, however, the youth grew disenchanted and said he no longer wanted to serve at mass. "You gotta be involved, m'boy," Ward said he told his son. Today, Ward says, "Bless his little

heart. He wanted to get away from Gauthe, and we couldn't understand."

Ward said that when word leaked through the community in 1983 that Gauthe had molested altar boys, Ward commented to himself, "Not my son." But then he began to brood. One day when he and his son were working together he gently asked the teenager whether Gauthe had ever played with his body. The youngster, said Ward, put his head down and said, "Yes."

Ward said he swallowed hard and replied, "That's all right, m'boy. It's not your fault." Then he stepped outside and stared at the sky, filled with rage.

The Wards were one of the first families to negotiate a settlement with the Lafayette diocese. The youth had undergone months of therapy by the time the settlement of $270,000 was negotiated.

—Betty Smith and her husband said that when Gauthe was arrested, their son began to sleep soundly every night for the first time in months because he knew the priest was behind bars. According to the parents, when the priest left Louisiana, the boy asked his parents, "How do you know where he is? How do you know he won't come back?"

Jack Hawkins said he is finding it tougher to forgive Portland's chancery officials than he is the priest who sexually abused his son while the boy was a parochial school student. Hawkins described his frustrations in obtaining money for counseling costs from the archdiocese and claimed diocesan officials violated a verbal promise made at a meeting between parents and officials to pay.

Ultimately, the archdiocese's refusal so angered Hawkins and others that they switched lawyers and threatened a lawsuit. That led to a recent Portland settlement for three victims; Hawkins' son received the largest settlement, based on a professional assessment of the psychological damage. Hawkins said he thinks his son is slowly recovering, but he worries about how well his son might handle the financial settlement when he turns 18.

Hawkins noted his son is no longer a church-going Catholic. "The last thing we discuss in our family right now is religion," he said. . . .

How should the institutional church safeguard itself against pedophile priests or identify them? . . .

Obtaining professional information about pedophilia is difficult, said one priest-psychiatrist, Father Michael Petersen of St. Luke's Institute, outside Washington, D.C. "Where do you look as far as its history?" he asked. "Most (child sexual) abuse is in families, and if you take the sheer numbers, it's hard to get data.

"Our whole view as a profession is skewed to the population of prisoners who are sex offenders. So, suddenly, in the last two years, sexual abuse of children has emerged as a national issue. The church is as perplexed as the people in the society.

"This is so completely new. I remember a priest (accused of) robbing a bank in Maryland. No bishop is equipped to deal with something like that. Imagine if you're a bishop, and a parent says, 'Your priest did this to my child.' He's thinking, 'My God, I can't believe it.' It's that kind of milieu they're coming out of."

Los Angeles psychotherapist Father David Cousineau said, "I think (bishops) are getting more and more careful in handling cases, because they are in the press. The hierarchy needs to realize that they have some resources to draw on. They're afraid, sometimes, to deal with the problem before it's too late." . . .

Petersen sees pedophilia as a "problem rooted in childhood; the person may not be aware of the proclivity until much later. I'm quite sure (there are) probably biological as well as environmental factors involved. Psychological testings don't pick these things up. You can't predict it. Celibacy is not the issue. I don't see it as a pressure leading to pedophilia."

The Portland archdiocese's reaction to the suits has been to expand the health panel for clerics to include sex abuse problems, to disperse information about the subject to priests and to initiate sex-abuse education in Catholic schools.

After Laughlin's arrest, priests began talking about expanding the code of ethics for priests to deal with this sort of problem. Griffin admitted that interest waned after Laughlin's case dropped from the headlines and said it could be a "form of denial" about the problem.

The U.S. Catholic Conference, secretariat to the national bishops' conference, reports that, at this stage, it is just trying to find out what the facts about priests and sexual abuse with children actually are.

• • •

NCR came back to the story of pedophiles in the priesthood again and again. It was nearly two years before the national media stepped in, and pedophilia became a topic for the covers of the national news magazines. By that time, Fox had survived an attempt by a Jesuit priest on the *NCR* board of directors to oust him; the priest did not get a second to his motion and left the board.

"Our coverage made the subject more acceptable in the wider press," Fox said. "It also allowed victims the encouragement to speak up." Eventually the National Conference of Catholic Bishops gingerly took up the subject and devised policies to deal with such situations. Unfortunately, said Fox, who became *NCR* publisher in 1996, "our coverage has not yet led church authorities to the point where they are willing to deal frankly with the deeper causes of pedophilia."

FREEDOM

WILLIAM LLOYD GARRISON ANNOUNCES PUBLICATION OF ABOLITIONIST PAPER AND SAYS "I WILL BE HEARD"

Sometimes the very existence of a publication, more than any article that it publishes, makes a difference. Before William Lloyd Garrison, a reformer and printer, founded *The Liberator* in 1831, the voices against slavery were scattered and little heard in the mainstream press. Garrison united the abolitionists, rallied them, and gave them shared information and arguments on behalf of their cause.

He proclaimed what he intended to do in his first issue, January 1, 1831.

In the month of August, I issued proposals for publishing *The Liberator* in Washington City; but the enterprise, though hailed in different sections of the country, was palsied by public indifference. Since that time, the removal of the *Genius of Universal Emancipation* to the Seat of Government has rendered less imperious the establishment of a similar periodical in that quarter.

During my recent tour for the purpose of exciting the minds of the people by a series of discourses on the subject of slavery, every place that I visited gave fresh evidence of the fact that a greater revolution in public sentiment was to be effected in the free States—and *particularly in New England*—than in the South. I found contempt more bitter, opposition more active, detraction more relentless, prejudice more stubborn, and apathy more frozen, than among slave-owners themselves. Of course, there were individual exceptions to the contrary. This state of things afflicted, but did not dishearten me. I determined at every hazard to lift up the standard of emancipation in the eyes of the nation, *within sight of Bunker Hill and in the birthplace of liberty*. That standard is now unfurled; and long may it float, unhurt by the spoliations of time or the missiles of a desperate foe—yea, till every chain be broken, and every bondman set free! Let Southern oppressors tremble—let their secret abettors tremble—let their Northern apologists tremble—let all enemies of the persecuted blacks tremble.

I deem the publication of my original Prospectus unnecessary as it has obtained a wide circulation. The principles therein inculcated will be steadily pursued in this paper, excepting that I shall not array myself as the political partisan of any man. In defending the great cause of human rights, I wish to derive the assistance of all religions and of all parties.

Assenting to the "self-evident truth" maintained in the American Declaration of Independence, "that all men are created equal, and endowed by their Creator with certain inalienable rights—among which are life, liberty, and the pursuit of happiness," I shall strenuously contend for the immediate enfranchisement of our slave population. In Park Street Church, on the Fourth of July, 1829, in an address on slavery, I unreflectingly assented to the popular but pernicious doctrine of *gradual* abolution. I seize this opportunity to make a full and unequivocal recantation and thus publicly to ask pardon of my God, of my country, and of my brethren, the poor slaves, for having uttered a sentiment so full of timidity, injustice and absurdity. A similar recantation, from my pen, was published in the *Genius of Universal Emancipation* at Baltimore, in September, 1829. My conscience is now satisfied.

I am aware that many object to the severity of my language: but is there not cause for severity? I *will* be as harsh as truth, and as uncompromising as justice. On this subject, I do not wish to think, or speak, or write, with moderation. No! no! Tell a man whose house is on fire to give a moderate alarm; tell him to moderately rescue his wife from the hands of the ravisher; tell the mother to gradually extricate her babe from the fire into which it has fallen;—but urge me not to use moderation in a cause like the present. I am in earnest—I will not equivocate—I will not excuse—I will not retreat a single inch—AND I WILL BE HEARD. The apathy of the people is enough to make every statue leap from its pedestal and to hasten the resurrection of the dead.

It is pretended that I am retarding the cause of emancipation by the coarseness of my invective and the precipitancy of my measures. *The charge is not true.* On this question my influence—humble as it is—is felt at this moment to a considerable extent, and shall be felt in coming years—not perniciously, but beneficially—not as

a curse, but as a blessing; and posterity will bear witness that I was right. I desire to thank God that He enables me to disregard "the fear of man which bringeth a snare," and to speak his truth in its simplicity and power.

And here I close with this fresh dedication:

Oppression! I have seen thee, face to face.
And met thy cruel eye and cloudy brow;
But thy soul-withering glace I fear not now—
For dread to prouder feelings doth give place
Of deep abhorrence! Scouring the disgrace
Of slavish knees that at thy footstool bow,
I also kneel—but with far other vow
Do hail thee and thy herd of hirelings case:—
I swear, while life-blood warms my throbbing veins,
Still to oppose and thwart, with heart and hand,
The brutalizing sway—till Africa's chains
Are burst, and Freedom rules the rescued land,—
Trampling Oppression and his iron rod:
Such is the vow I take—SO HELP ME GOD!

• • •

Garrison saw himself as being somewhat of an Old Testament prophet. Although the thirty-five years of *The Liberator*'s publication never brought Garrison a large circulation—Garrison said circulation never exceeded 3,000—his constant prodding helped make the public ready to address the issue of ending slavery. In 1870, when the Fifteenth Amendment to the Constitution, giving blacks the right to vote, was adopted, Garrison marveled at the transformation he had seen, of blacks moving from "the auction-block to the ballot box."

ILLINOIS EDITOR ELIJAH LOVEJOY ATTACKS SLAVERY AND IS SHOT TO DEATH

Elijah Lovejoy was born in Maine in 1802, the son of a minister, but he did not turn to religion himself until he was an adult and had spent some time as a schoolteacher and editor of a Whig newspaper in St. Louis, Missouri. Then he went to the Princeton Theological Seminary, much to his parents' delight. When he returned to St. Louis in 1833, he was put in charge of the *St. Louis Observer*, the paper for Presbyterians in Missouri and Illinois.

No rabble-rouser, Lovejoy favored gradual emancipation for slaves and their colonization, and he showed sympathy for the slave masters who had grown up in the old ways. But in the hot flames of the debate over slavery, moderation was no refuge. Public reaction to the rumor that Lovejoy was distributing abolitionist newspapers, to his criticism of a judge's leniency after an African American was burned to death, and to other events led him to think it wise to move his press to Alton, Illinois, across the Mississippi River, in June 1836. Before he could do so, a mob broke into his office, destroyed the press, and dumped it into the river. But antislavery supporters in Alton raised the money for a new press. For about ten months, things were relatively calm. Then Lovejoy published an article urging the formation of a state antislavery association.

"Illinois State Anti-Slavery Society," by Elijah Lovejoy. *Alton (Illinois) Observer*, July 6, 1837.

Is it not time that such a society should be formed? There are many, very many, friends of the cause in this State, and their number is daily increasing. Ought not measures to be taken to embody their influence so as to make it tell with the greatest possible effect upon the holy cause of emancipation?

We would do nothing rashly, but it does seem to us that the time to form such a society has fully come. There are a number of local societies already existing in the State, and it would be every way better that their influence should be concentrated. If it be decided that such a society ought to be formed, when and where shall the convention meet to form it? Shall it be at this place, or at Jacksonville, or Springfield, or elsewhere?

We take the liberty to throw out these questions for the consideration of our friends, and we suggest the propriety of their giving to them a speedy and candid consideration. Let as many as are in favor of the measure here proposed, send us their names, for the purpose of having them attached to the call of the proposed convention, and let each one indicate the time and place of his preference for the meeting of the convention, with the express understanding that that place shall be selected which has the most votes in its favor.

We shall hope to have a response from the friends of the slave without delay. Every day do we feel more and more the necessity of action, decided and effective action, on this subject. With many, we are already a 'fanatic' and an 'incendiary' as it regards this matter, and we feel that we must become more and more vile in their eyes.

We have never felt enough, nor prayed enough, nor done enough, in behalf of the perishing slave.

This day (the 4th) reproaches our sloth and inactivity. It is the day of our nation's birth. Even as we write, crowds are hurrying past our window, in eager anticipation, to the appointed bower, to listen to the declaration that 'all men are born free and equal'; to hear the eloquent orator denounce, in strains of many indignation, the attempt of England to lay a yoke upon the shoulders of our fathers, which neither they nor their children could bear. Alas! What bitter mockery is this. We assemble to thank God for our own freedom, and to eat and drink with joy and gladness of heart, while our feet are upon the necks of nearly three millions of our fellow-men! Not all our shouts of self-congratulation can drown their groans—even that very flag of freedom that waves over our heads is formed from materials cultivated by slaves, on a soil moistened by their blood, drawn from them by the whip of a republican task-master!

Brethren and friends, this must not be—it can not be—for God will not indure it much longer. Come, then, to the rescue. The voice of three millions of slaves calls upon you to come and 'unloose the heavy burdens, and let the oppressed go free!' And on this day, when every freeman's heart is glad, let us remember that—

Wearily every bosom pineth,
    Wearily, oh! wearily, oh!
Where the chains of slavery twineth,
    Wearily, oh! wearily, oh!
There the warrior's dart
    Hath no fleetness,
There the maiden's heart
    Hath no sweetness.
Every flower of life declineth,
    Wearily, oh! wearily, oh!
Wearily—wearily—wearily—
Wearily—wearily—wearily, oh!
    Wearily, oh! wearily, oh!

• • •

The good citizens of Alton, a city of about 4,000, convened a public meeting and condemned Lovejoy for "incendiary publications." Across the river, the *Missouri Republican* argued editorially that something be done to get rid of Lovejoy, that "minister of mischief." On August 21, 1837, a mob broke into Lovejoy's office and destroyed the press and type. Ministers and other sup-porters put up the money for another press, but that too was destroyed when it arrived in September. Friends of free speech and foes of slavery put up the money for a fourth press. When it arrived in early November, Lovejoy and nineteen friends stayed up all night to guard it. They were not enough. Attackers tried to set fire to the warehouse, and when Lovejoy went outside to try to fight them off, he was shot and killed.

The killing of Lovejoy shocked the anti-slavery community, and stirred people to action around the country. The abolitionist Wendell Phillips gave a eulogy in Boston. In an editorial in *The Liberator*, William Lloyd Garrison said, "Lovejoy died the representative of philanthropy and justice, liberty and Christianity; well, therefore, may his fall agitate all heaven and earth." Henry Tanner, one of Lovejoy's colleagues, said, "No single event in the early history of the anti-slavery contest in the United States produced a more profound impression." The Rev. Edward Beecher, president of Illinois College and a member of the prestigious Beecher family of intellectuals and preachers, said, "Ten thousand presses, had he employed them all, could never have done what the simple tale of his death will do."

The historian Stephen B. Oates said that after hearing of Lovejoy's death, at a meeting in Hudson, Ohio, the radical John Brown arose and vowed before God that he would consecrate his life to eliminating slavery.

No one was ever charged in the killing. The city of Alton, at that time the same size as Chicago, suffered from the reputation of the "Lovejoy Riots" and many antislavery men moved away. Lovejoy's brother, Owen, became a leading abolitionist in Congress.

THE MOST RESPECTED BLACK MAN IN AMERICA DEMANDS THAT SLAVERY MUST END AND SAYS BLACKS MUST SERVE IN UNION ARMY. JUNE 2, 1854, OCTOBER 1862, APRIL 1863.

Frederick Douglass was born Frederick Augustus Washington Bailey in February 1817, and as a slave was a house servant, a shipyard worker, and a farm laborer. So incorrigible was he that his master sent him to a slave breaker to be trained, worked into submission, or beaten to death—which mattering little to his master. But on September 3, 1838, Douglass escaped from slavery, fleeing from Baltimore and coming to freedom in Philadelphia wearing a borrowed sailor suit and carrying false protection papers. He married a freedwoman, Anna Murray, and settled in New Bedford, Massachusetts, where he adopted his new surname.

As a freedman, Douglass tended furnaces. Sometimes, a biographer says, Douglass, who had learned to read and write while a house servant, nailed a newspaper to a post near his bellows so he could read while working.

Douglass began to write for newspapers, and between 1842 and 1847 he published several pieces in William Lloyd Garrison's *The Liberator*. An autobiography, the first of two, was published in 1845, to substantial success. For a time Douglass edited *The Ram's Horn,* an antislavery paper. Then, on November 1, 1847, in Rochester, New York, Douglass began publishing *The North Star,* a paper devoted to abolition, free public education, and women's suffrage. Its slogan was, "Right is of no Sex—Truth of no Color—God is the Father of us all, and we are all Brethren." The paper's circulation quickly rose to 3,000 and it circulated in the United States, the West Indies, and Europe. Like other abolitionists, Douglass was attacked; his home in Rochester was burned, and his papers destroyed.

The North Star was vigorous and possessed high literary merit but always faced substantial financial difficulties, with Douglass at one point mortgaging his home to keep the paper going. In 1851, Douglass merged the paper with the *Liberty Party Paper*, published by the abolitionist Gerrit Smith. That combined paper took the name *Frederick Douglass' Paper* and lasted until the mid-1860s.

In his journalism Douglass promoted job training, the mechanical arts, and farming for black Americans. His was an uncompromising moral voice during the turbulence that marked the years before the Civil War. During the war, Douglass supported President Abraham Lincoln, helped the government enlist Negro soldiers, and continued to push for black emancipation.

Here are some examples.

In June 1854, after a slave catcher had been killed in Boston, Douglass reacted to criticism of those who opposed the Fugitive Slave Law.

Frederick Douglass' Paper, June 2, 1854.

There is not a citizen of Rochester worthy of the name, who would not shoot down any man in defence of his own liberty—or who, if set upon, by a number of robbers, would not thank any friend who interposed, even to the shedding of blood, for his release.—The widow and orphans are far better off with such a wretch in the grave, than on the earth. Then again, the law which he undertook to execute, has no tears for the widows and orphans of poor innocent fugitives, who make their homes at the North. With a hand as relentless as that of death, it snatches the husband from the wife, and the father from his children, and this for no crime.—Oh! that man's ideas of justice and of right depended less upon the circumstance of color, and more upon the indestructible nature of things. For a white man to defend his friend unto blood is praiseworthy, but for a black man to do precisely the same thing is crime. It was glorious for Patrick Henry to say, "Give me liberty or give me death!" It was glorious for

Americans to drench the soil, and crimson the sea with blood, to escape the payment of three-penny tax upon tea; but it is crime to shoot down a monster in defence of the liberty of a black man and to save him from a bondage "one hour of which (in the language of Jefferson) is worse than ages of that which our fathers rose in rebellion to oppose." Until Mr. Mann [who wrote an article that Douglass criticized] is willing to be a slave—until he is ready to admit that human legislation can rightfully reduce him to slavery, by a simple vote—until he abandons the right of self defence—until he ceases to glory in the deeds of Hancock, Adams, and Warren—and ceases to look with pride and patriotic admiration upon the sombre pile at Bunker Hill, where the blood of the oppressor was poured out in torrents making thousands of widows and orphans, it does not look graceful in him to brand as murderers those that killed the atrocious Turckman [the slave catcher] who attempted to play the blood-hound on the trace of the poor, defenceless [slave] Burns.

Douglass' Monthly, October 1862

Common sense, the necessities of the war, to say nothing of the dictation of justice and humanity have at last prevailed. We shout for joy that we live to record this righteous. Abraham Lincoln, President of the United States, Commander-in-Chief of the army and navy, in his own peculiar, cautious, forbearing and hesitating way, slow, but we hope sure, has, while the loyal heart was near breaking with despair, proclaimed and declared: "That on the First of January, in the Year of Our Lord One Thousand, Eight Hundred and Sixty-three, All Persons Held as Slaves Within Any State or Any Designated Part of a State, The People Whereof Shall Then be in Rebellion Against the United States, Shall be Thenceforward and Forever Free." "Free forever" oh! long enslaved millions, whose cries have so vexed the air and sky, suffer on a few more days in sorrow, the hour

of your deliverance draws nigh! Oh! Ye millions of free and loyal men who have earnestly sought to free your bleeding country from the dreadful ravages of revolution and anarchy, lift up now your voices with joy and thanksgiving for with freedom to the slave will come peace and safety to your country. President Lincoln has embraced in this proclamation the law of Congress passed more than six months ago, prohibiting the employment of any part of the army and naval forces of the United States, to return fugitive slaves to their masters, commanded all officers of the army and navy to respect and obey its provisions. He has still further declared his intention to urge upon the Legislature of all the slave States not in rebellion the immediate or gradual abolishment of slavery. But read the proclamation for it is the most important of any to which the President of the United States has ever signed his name.

"Why Should a Colored Man Enlist?" Douglass' Monthly, April 1863.

This question has been repeatedly put to us while raising men for the 54th Massachusetts regiment during the past five weeks, and perhaps we cannot at present do a better service to the cause of our people or to the cause of the country than by listing a few of the many reasons why a colored man should enlist.

First. You are a man, although a colored man. If you were only a horse or an ox, incapable of deciding whether the rebels are right or wrong, you would have no responsibility, and might like the horse or the ox go on eating your corn or grass, in total indifference, as to which side is victorious or vanquished in this conflict. You are however no horse, and no ox, but a man, and whatever concerns man should interest you. He who looks upon a conflict between right and wrong, and does not help the right against the wrong, despises and insults his own nature, and invites the contempt of mankind. As between the North and South, the North is clearly in the right and the South is flagrantly in the wrong. You should therefore, simply as a matter of right and wrong, give your utmost aid to the North. In presence of such a contest there is no neutrality for any man. You are either for the Government or against the Government. Manhood requires you to take sides, and you are mean or noble according to how you choose between action and inaction.—If you are sound in body and mind, there is nothing in your color to excuse you from enlisting in the service of the republic against its enemies. If color should not be a criterion of rights, neither should it be a standard of duty. The whole duty of a man, belongs alike to white and black. . . .

• • •

Douglass's rationale continued for eight other reasons, and many other issues of his paper. Two sons were among the hundreds of black men from upstate New York who enlisted in the 54th Massachusetts. The regiment fought bravely throughout the war, including an assault on Fort Wagner, an artillery post on an island off South Carolina where hundreds died.

In March 1864, Douglass attended President Abraham Lincoln's second inauguration (as did John Wilkes Booth, who stood on the right buttress of the east portico) and was spied in the audience by Lincoln. That evening, Douglass went to the White House for an inaugural reception, but was barred entrance by the police because he was black. Hearing this, Lincoln had him shown in. "I saw you in the crowd today, listening to my address," Lincoln said. "I want to know what you think of it."

Douglass said he believed it was a "sacred effort."

"I am glad you liked it," Lincoln said. "There is no man in this country whose opinion I value more than yours."

It was, writes the historian Stephen B. Oates in *With Malice Toward None: The Life of Abraham Lincoln,* "the first inaugural reception in the history of the Republic in which an American president had greeted a free black man and solicited his opinion."

In 1871 Douglass returned to journalism, for four years running the *New National Era,* a paper devoted to the "defence and enlightenment of the newly emancipated and enfranchised" black residents of Washington. A third book on his life, *The Life and Times of Frederick Douglass, Written by Himself,* was published in 1881. From 1888 to 1891 Douglass was minister to Haiti. The Douglass family home, in Washington, D.C., is now a national monument. Douglass died February 20, 1895.

SOLITARY VOICE: IDA B. WELLS ATTACKS LYNCHINGS

On May 21, 1892, the Memphis, Tennessee, *Free Speech,* a 2,000-circulation newspaper serving the Afro-American community, ran the following editorial:

Eight negroes lynched since last issue of the "Free Speech" one at Little Rock, Ark., last Saturday morning where the citizens broke (?) into the penitentiary and got their man; three near Anniston, Ala., one near New Orleans; and three at Clarksville, Ga., the last three for killing a white man, and five on the same old racket—the new alarm about raping white women. The same programme of hanging, then shooting bullets into the lifeless bodies was carried out to the letter.

Nobody in this section of the country believes the old thread bare lie that Negro men rape white women. If Southern white men are not careful, they will over-reach themselves and public sentiment will have a reaction; a conclusion will then be reached which will be very damaging to the moral reputation of their women.

Outraged at the implications, the leading citizens of the city called a meeting in the Cotton Exchange Building, where more threats of lynching were heard, this time directed toward the paper. The business manager, one of the owners of the *Free Speech,* fled Memphis. The other owner—and the author of the inflammatory editorial—was on vacation in New York when her editorial was printed. Friends warned Ida B. Wells not to return. A mob destroyed the furniture in the newspaper office and posted a death threat. Creditors took over the paper, and Wells was out of work.

At the age of twenty-nine, Wells, the daughter of slaves and a former schoolteacher, had a national reputation in the African-American press. She was forceful, argumentative, and interested in writing about public affairs, not the more traditional women's topics. The editor of the *New York Age,* another black newspaper, quickly hired her. Her first story elaborated on the themes raised in the Memphis editorial. It was a bold and sensational argument for the times: that often sex between black men and white women was consensual. Wells listed many examples, drawing on incidents reported in the white press, which she presumed would be more trusted.

From the *New York Age,* reprinted in *Southern Horrors, Lynch Law in All Its Phases,* 1892

Hundreds of such cases might be cited, but enough have been given to prove the assertion that there are white women in the South who love the Afro-American's company even as there are white men notorious for their preference for Afro-American women.

There is hardly a town in the South which has not an instance of the kind which is well-known, and hence the assertion is reiterated that "nobody in the South believes the old thread bare lie that negro men rape white women." Hence there is a growing demand among Afro-Americans that the guilt or innocence of parties accused of rape be fully established. They know the men of the section of the country who refuse this are not so desirous of punishing rapists as they pretend. The utterances of the leading white men show that with them it is not the crime but the *class.* Bishop Fitzgerald has become apologist for lynchers of the rapists of *white* women only. Governor Tillman, of South Carolina, in the month of June, standing under the tree in Barnwell, S.C., on which eight Afro-Americans were hung last year, declared that he would lead a mob to lynch a *negro* who raped a *white* women. So say the pulpits, officials and newspapers of the South. But when the victim is a colored woman it is different. . . .

. . . the South is shielding itself behind the plausible screen of defending the honor of its women. This, too, in the face of the fact that only *one-third* of the 728 victims to mobs have been *charged* with rape, to say nothing of those of that one-third who were innocent of the charge. A white correspondent of the *Baltimore Sun* declares that the Afro-American who was lynched in Chestertown, Md., in May for assault on a white girl was innocent; that the deed was done by a white man who had since disappeared. The girl herself maintained that her assailant was a white man. When that poor Afro-American was murdered, the whites excused their refusal of a trial on the ground that they wished to spare the white girl the mortification of having to testify in court.

This cry has had its effect. It has closed the heart, stifled the conscience, warped the judgment and hushed the voice of press and pulpit on the subject of lynch law throughout this "land of liberty." Men who stand high in the esteem of the public for christian character, for moral and physical courage, for devotion to the principles of equal and exact justice to all, and for great sagacity, stand as cowards who fear to open their mouths before this great outrage. They do not see that by their tacit encouragement, their silent acquiescence, the black shadow of lawlessness in the form of lynch law is spreading its wings over the whole country.

Men who, like Governor Tillman, start the ball of lynch law rolling for a certain crime, are powerless to stop it when drunken or criminal white toughs feel like hanging an Afro-American on any pretext.

Even to the better class of Afro-Americans the crime of rape is so revolting they have too often taken the white man's word and given lynch law neither the investigation nor condemnation it deserved.

They forget that a concession of the right to lynch a man for a certain crime, not only concedes the right to lynch any person for any crime, but (so frequently is the cry of rape now raised) it is in a fair way to stamp us a race of rapists and desperadoes. They have gone on hoping and believing that general education and financial strength would solve the difficulty, and are devoting their energies to the accumulation of both.

The mob spirit has grown with the increasing intelligence of the Afro-American. It has left the out-of-the-way places where ignorance prevails, has thrown off the mask and with this new cry stalks in broad daylight in large cities, the centres of civilization, and is encouraged by the "leading citizens" and the press. . . .

The strong arm of the law must be brought to bear upon lynchers in severe punishment, but this cannot and will not be done unless a healthy public sentiment demands and sustains such action.

The men and women in the South who disapprove of lynching and remain silent on the perpetration of such outrages, are particeps criminis, accomplices, accessories before and after the fact, equally guilty with the actual law-breakers who would not persist if they did not know that neither the law nor militia would be employed against them.

In the creation of this healthier public sentiment, the Afro-American can do for himself what no one else can do for him. The world looks on with wonder that we have conceded so much and remain law-abiding under such great outrage and provocation.

To Northern capital and Afro-American labor the South owes its rehabilitation. If labor is withdrawn capital will not remain. The Afro-American is thus the backbone of the South. A thorough knowledge and judicious exercise of this power in lynching localities could many times effect a bloodless revolution. The white man's dollar is his god, and to stop this will be to stop outrages in many localities.

The Afro-Americans of Memphis denounced the lynching of three of their best citizens (Editor: The three were friends of Wells, and had fired their guns when a group of whites attacked their grocery store. Before they could be tried, a mob broke them out of the jail and killed them.), and urged and waited for the authorities to act in the matter and bring the lynchers to justice. No attempt was made to do so, and the black men left the city by thousands, bringing about great stagnation in every branch of business. Those who remained so injured the business of the street car company by staying off the cars, that the superintendent, manager and treasurer called personally on the editor of the "Free Speech," asked them to urge our people to give them their patronage again. Other business men became alarmed over the situation and the "Free Speech" was run away that the colored people might be more easily controlled. . . .

Of the many inhuman outrages of this present year, the only case where the proposed lynching did *not* occur, was where the men armed themselves in Jacksonville, Fla., and Paducah, Ky., and prevented it. The only times an Afro-American who was assaulted got away has been when he had a gun and used it in self-defense.

The lesson this teaches and which every Afro-American should ponder well, is that a Winchester rifle should have a place of honor in every black home, and it should be used for that protection which the law refuses to give. When the white man who is always the aggressor knows he runs as great risk of biting the dust every time his Afro-American victim does, he will have greater respect for Afro-American life. The more the Afro-American yields and cringes and begs, the more he has to do so, the more he is insulted, outraged and lynched.

The assertion has been substantiated throughout these pages that the press contains unreliable and doctored reports of lynchings, and one of the most necessary things for the race to do is to get these facts before the public. The people must know before they can act, and there is no educator to compare with the press. . . .

Nothing is more definitely settled than he must act for himself. I have shown how he can employ the boycott, emigration and the press, and I feel that by a combination of all these agencies can be effectually stamped out lynch law, that last relic of barbarism and slavery. "The gods help those who help themselves."

• • •

If the white leaders of Memphis had hoped to silence Wells, they miscalculated. The *New York Age* distributed 10,000 copies of her story. A group of African-American women in Brooklyn and New York invited Wells to speak. She, in turn, used her $500 fee to publish the article as a pamphlet. Two other pamphlets on southern lynching and a series of lectures, including some in England, encouraged the antilynching movement and led to the formation of several antilynching groups.

The fight was extremely slow, and efforts to pass a federal antilynching law failed repeatedly. Yet Wells's active writing and lecturing kept the issue before the nation. "With her leadership," wrote Linda O. McMurry in a biography, "lynching was named a national crime. While lynchings did not end during her lifetime, their numbers were significantly reduced from 1892 to 1900,

during the height of Wells' campaign." The attention that Wells brought to Memphis, particularly in England, a valuable partner in the cotton trade, helped that city avoid another lynching for more than twenty years. Not until 1953 did a complete year pass without a lynching being recorded in the United States.

A REPORT ON A RACE RIOT IN ILLINOIS BRINGS FOUNDING OF THE NATIONAL ASSOCIATION FOR THE ADVANCEMENT OF COLORED PEOPLE

Despite some gains, most African Americans were feeling politically deserted during the early 1900s. Booker T. Washington's influence was waning, among both blacks and whites. President Theodore Roosevelt's treatment of black troops in Brownsville, Texas, after a shooting fight in which whites were killed—the president dishonorably discharged a battalion of blacks without a trial—soured many African Americans on the Republican Party, their home since the Civil War. Lynchings continued and, in September 1906, white mobs rioted against blacks on the streets of Atlanta. Two years later, whites rioted against blacks in Springfield, Illinois. The event showed that blacks were not safe outside the South, not even in the hometown of Abraham Lincoln.

"The Race War in the North," by William English Walling. *The Independent,* September 1908.

"Lincoln freed you, we'll show you where you belong," was one of the cries with which the Springfield mob set about to drive the negroes from town. The mob was composed of several thousand of Springfield's white citizens, while other thousands, including many woman and children, and even prosperous business men in automobiles, calmly looked on, and the rioters proceeded hour after hour and on two days in succession to make deadly assaults on every negro they could lay their hands on, to sack and plunder their houses and stores, and to burn and murder on favorable occasion.

The American people have been fairly well informed by their newspapers of the action of that mob; they have also been told of certain alleged political and criminal conditions in Springfield and of the two crimes in particular which are offered by the mob itself as sufficient explanation why six thousand peaceful and innocent negroes should be driven by the fear of their lives from a town where some of them have lived honorably for half a hundred years. We have been assured by more cautious and indirect defenders of Springfield's populace that there *was* an exceptionally criminal element among the negroes encouraged by the bosses of both political parties. And now, after a few days of discussion, we are satisfied with these explanations, and demand only the punishment of those who took the most active part in the destruction of life and property. Assuming that there were exceptionally provocative causes for complaint against the negroes, we have closed our eyes to the whole awful and menacing truth—that a large part of the white population of Lincoln's home, supported largely by the farmers and miners of the neighboring towns, have initiated a permanent warfare with the negro race.

We do not need to be informed at great length of the character of this warfare. It is in all respects like that of the South, on which it is modeled. Its significance is threefold. First, that it has occurred in an important and historical Northern town; then, that the negroes, constituting scarcely more than a tenth of the population, in this case could not possibly endanger the "supremacy" of the whites, and, finally, that the public opinion of the North, notwithstanding the fanatical, blind and almost insane hatred of the negro so clearly shown by the mob, is satisfied that there were "mitigating

circumstances," not for the mob violence, which, it is agreed, should be punished to the full extent of the law, but for the race hatred, which is really the cause of it all. If these outrages had happened thirty years ago, when the memories of Lincoln, Garrison and Wendell Phillips were still fresh, what would not have happened in the North? Is there any doubt that the whole country would have been aflame, that all flimsy explanations and "mitigating circumstances" would have been thrown aside, and that the people of Springfield would have had to prove to the nation why they proposed to drive the negroes out, to hold a whole race responsible for a handful of criminals, and to force it to an inferior place on the social scale?

For the underlying motive of the mob and of that large portion of Springfield's population that has long said that "something was bound to happen," and now approves of the riot and proposes to complete its purpose by using other means to drive as many as possible of the remaining two-thirds of the negroes out of town, was confessedly to teach the negroes their place and to warn them that too many could not obtain shelter under the favorable traditions of Lincoln's home town. I talked to many of them the day after the massacre and found no difference of opinion on the question. "Why, the niggers came to think they were as good as we are!" was the final justification offered, not once, but a dozen times. . . .

Besides suggestions in high places of the negro's brutality, criminality and unfitness for the ballot we heard in lower ranks all the opinions that pervade the South—that the negro does not need much education, that his present education even has been a mistake, that whites cannot live in the same community with negroes except where the latter have been taught their inferiority, that lynching is the only way to teach them, etc. In fact, this went so far that we were led to suspect the existence of a Southern element in the town, and this is indeed the case. Many of the older citizens are from Kentucky or the southern part of Illinois. Moreover, many of the street railway employees are from the South. It was a street railway man's wife that was assaulted the night before the riots, and they were street railway employees, among others, that led the mob to the jail. Even the famous Kate Howard had received her inspiration, she told us, from the South. While traveling with her brother in Texas and Arkansas she had observed enviously that enforced separation of the races in cars and public places helped to teach the negro where he belonged. Returning home she had noticed the growing boycott of negroes in Springfield stores and restaurants, participated in the alarm that "no white woman was safe," etc., and in the demand for negro blood. A woman of evident physical courage, she held that it was time for the population to act up to their professions, and by the cry of "cowards" is said to have goaded the mob into some of the worst of its deeds. She exhibited to us proudly the buckshot wounds in her fleshly arms (probably Burton's) and said she relied confidently on her fellow citizens to keep her from punishment.

This was the feeling also of the half hundred whites in the hospital. It was, in fact, only three days after the first disturbance when they fully realized that the lenient public opinion of Springfield was not the public opinion of Illinois or the North, that the rioters began to tremble. Still this did not prevent them later from insulting the militia, repeatedly firing at their outposts and almost openly organizing a political and business boycott to drive the remaining negroes out. Negro employers continue to receive threatening letters and are dismissing employees every day, while the stores, even the groceries, so fear to sell the negroes goods that the State has been compelled to intervene and purchase $10,000 worth in their behalf.

The menace is that if this thing continues it will offer automatic rewards to the riotous elements and negro haters in Springfield, make the reign of terror permanent there, and offer every temptation to similar white elements in other towns to imitate Springfield's example.

If the new Political League succeeds in permanently driving every negro from office; if the white laborers get the negro laborers' jobs; if masters of negro servants are able to keep them under the discipline of terror as I saw them doing at Springfield; if white shopkeepers and saloonkeepers get their colored rivals' trade; if the farmers of neighboring towns establish permanently their right to drive poor people out of their community, instead of offering them reasonable alms; if white miners can force their negro fellow-workers out and get their positions by closing the mines, then every community indulging in an outburst of race hatred will be assured of a great and certain financial reward, and all the lies, ignorance and brutality on which race hatred is based will spread over the land. For the action of these dozen farming and four coal mining communities near Springfield shows how rapidly the thing can spread. In the little town of Buffalo, fifteen miles away, for instance, they have just posted this sign in front of the interurban station:

"All niggers are warned out of town by Monday, 12 m. sharp.
BUFFALO SHARP SHOOTERS." . . .

Either the spirit of the abolitionists, of Lincoln and of Lovejoy must be revived and we must come to treat the negro on a plane of absolute political and social equality, or Vardaman and Tillman will soon have transferred the race war to the North.

Already Vardaman boasts "that such sad experiences as Springfield is undergoing will doubtless cause the people of the North to look with more toleration upon the methods employed by the Southern people."

The day these methods become general in the North every hope of political democracy will be dead, other weaker races and classes will be persecuted in the North as in the South, public education will undergo an eclipse, and American civilization will await either a rapid degeneration or another profounder and more revolutionary civil war, which shall obliterate not only the remains of slavery but all the other obstacles to a free democratic evolution that have grown up in its wake.

Yet who realizes the seriousness of the situation, and what large and powerful body of citizens is ready to come to their aid?

• • •

Responding to the article, Mary White Ovington, a New York social worker and descendant of white abolitionists, asked Walling, Oswald Garrison Villard, editor of *The Nation*, and several other civil rights advocates—most of them white, most of them her friends—to a meeting. On February 12, 1909, the hundredth anniversary of Lincoln's birthday, the group issued "The Call" for a national conference for "the renewal of the struggle for civil and political liberty." About three hundred people, both blacks and whites, attended, including W. E. B. Du Bois and Ida Wells-Barnett. The conference led to the organization that became the National Association for the Advancement of Colored People. Through public pressure, lobbying, and legal action, the NAACP has been a major force against segregation and for justice for blacks in the United States.

CONDEMNING THE "ROPE AND FAGGOT" OF THE SOUTH, THE *CHICAGO DEFENDER* HELPS CREATE THE GREAT MIGRATION

Between 1915 and 1920, five percent of the black population left the American South. A major destination for many blacks was Chicago. Chicago's black population, between 1910 and 1920, rose from 44,103 to 109,458, an increase of 148 percent. In the eighteen months between January

1916 and June 1917—America entered World War I on April 4, 1917—more than 50,000 blacks came to Chicago, according to Emmett J. Scott, in a 1920 study of black migration. Many reasons were responsible for this migration: the often brutal treatment of blacks in the South, the desire to escape debt and sharecropping (which often was tantamount to slavery) in the South, the lure of better money in northern factories, particularly because of war production, the excitement of leaving an often poor, rural area for far more vibrant northern cities, especially Chicago.

Yet another factor in this migration was the *Chicago Defender*.

The *Defender,* a weekly selling for five cents, was founded on May 5, 1905, by Robert S. Abbott. Born on Simon's Island off the coast of Georgia, Abbott as a child lived in a black area of Savannah. He studied printing at Hampton Institute, then studied for the law. But, after a time, he decided to found his own newspaper and did so in Chicago, which, in 1905, was an expanding city. He began the *Defender,* Roland R. E. Wolseley wrote in *The Black Press, U.S.A.,* in a "rented space on State Street with a card table and a borrowed chair." He began it on credit, for his only capital was 25 cents, which he spent on paper and pencils.

The black press went back decades in America. The first was *Freedom's Journal,* published by John B. Russwurm in New York City beginning March 16, 1827. But Abbott was an especially enterprising publisher and within a decade the *Defender* was the most important black newspaper in the country. With "the exception of the *Bible*, no publication was more important among the Negro Masses," wrote Roi Ottley, an Abbott biographer, in 1955. The paper's motto, on its masthead, was "American Race Prejudice Must Be Destroyed."

Beginning in 1915, the *Defender* took up the cause of black migration from the South. In article after article, the *Defender* portrayed what it described as the difference in human dignity and economic opportunity between the South and the

North. A typical example is this story from the issue of October 7, 1916.

"Somebody Lied," by the Scrutinizer. *Chicago Defender,* October 7, 1916.

ATLANTA, GA., OCT. 6—The turmoil that the white people and the newspapers of the South are raising on account of the exodus North, is ridiculous when you remember the fact that a few years ago there was a motion on foot to legislate the Race people into a trip to Africa or some other locality, where they could work out their own destinies. They even wanted to send 1,000,000 of them to Mexico: anything to rid the South of what they called "The White Man's Burden," and the "lazy Southern Nigger."

The following paragraph is taken from the *Macon Telegraph*:

"Police officers, county or city, all over the state, all over the South, should be bending every effort to apprehend and jail the labor agents now operating everywhere about us to take the best of our Negroes North to fill the rapidly widening labor breach there. This invasion of the South for Negroes isn't just a temporary raiding of our labor market, but is part of a well thought out and skillfully executed plan to rifle the entire South of its well-behaved, able-bodied Negro labor. Unskilled labor is at a high premium in the United States just now, a premium that will increase rather than be withdrawn."

The idea that the laborers are a real necessity never seemed to come to the lynch-billies of this section until the foreign laborers had headed home to shoulder arms in defense of their flags and countries. Then again, the south has been the hot-bed of "Negro-baiting" to such an extent, especially in the past few years, that it is no wonder the men are heading for "God's country," the North. Look at this wail from the same exchange:

"We must have the Negro in the South. The Black man is fitted by nature, by centuries of living in it, to work contentedly, effectively and healthily during the long summers of semi-tropical and tropical countries. He has been with us so long that our whole industrial, commercial and agricultural structure has been built on a black foundation. It is the only labor we have—if we lose it, we go bankrupt.

"Everyone seems to be asleep about what is going on right under our noses. That is, everybody but those farmers who have wakened up of mornings recently to find every male negro over 21 on his place gone—to Cleveland, to Pittsburg, to Chicago, to Indianapolis. Better jobs, better treatment, higher pay—the bait held out is being swallowed by thousands of them all about us. And while our very solvency is being sucked out from underneath, we go about our affairs as usual—our police officers raid poolrooms for 'loafing Negroes,' bring in twelve, keep them in the barracks all night, and the next morning find that ten of them have steady, regular jobs, were there merely to spend an hour in the only indoor recreation they have; our country officers hear of a disturbance at a Negro resort and bring in fifty-odd men, women and boys and girls to spend the night in jail, to make bond at ten per cent, to hire lawyers, to mortgage half of two months' wages to get back to their jobs Monday morning—although but a bare half dozen could have been guilty of the disorderly conduct. It was the week following that several Macon employers found good Negroes, men trained to their work, secure and respected in their jobs, valuable assets to their white employers, suddenly left and gone to Cleveland, 'where they don't arrest fifty for what three have done.' Many of these men who left haven't been replaced except with those it will take years to train to do their work as well as they did it—but at as high a cost from the start.

"It is the most pressing thing before this state today. Matters of governorship and judgeships are only a bagatelle compared to the real importance of this Negro exodus going on from Georgia. There is a little lull now with winter coming on, but the spring will see it set in in full volume, unless something is done at once to stop it."

This finishing paragraph shows that *The Telegraph* does not under-estimate the seriousness, for the whites, of the situation. It is estimated that there are places for 1,500,000 working men in the cities of the North. Go to it, my Southern Brothers, the North needs you. There is an exaggerated idea, which is encouraged by the cheap hiring class of Southern whites, that when winter comes to the North, the Southern born and raised of our people will freeze to death. The *Defender* statistic department has found that in all available records there is no case of a member of our Race ever having died in the North from the effects of the weather. If Eliza, of *Uncle Tom's Cabin* fame, survived, having skidded across the Ohio river on the ice in her sock feet, the able-bodied men of our Race should not worry about cold weather. If you come North, men, and work and save one-third of the fine salaries being paid here, you will in short time be prepared for the most severe weather conditions. It is easier to spend your winters in the steam heated flats of the Northern cities than it is to eke out the bare existence and content yourselves with the rotten living facilities as most of you do in the South. Better a thousands times, even it if was true, to run chances of being nipped by the fingers of Jack Frost than to shake off this mortal coil at the end of the lynchers' rope, or to the crackling of the lyncher's fire brand.

• • •

Some critics said the *Defender*'s coverage was sensational, Juliet J. K. Walker wrote in *The Black Press in the Middle West, 1865–1985,* as the *Defender* portrayed Chicago and the rest of the North as "the promised land," which it was not. At the same time, the white press in the South was incensed by the *Defender*'s coverage. To attempt to reduce the desire of blacks to go North, white southern papers, Walker reports, wrote such stories as "Negro Woman Froze to Death Monday"

and "North Does Not Welcome Influx of South's Negroes." The somewhat more enlightened *Atlanta Constitution* said, "This loss of her [Georgia's] best labor is another penalty Georgia is paying for her indifference in suppressing mob law."

Often the *Defender* and other African-American newspapers were impounded in U.S. post offices. Blacks who read the paper could become the targets of economic and physical abuse and often were forced to bring the *Defender* in underground and read it secretly.

If the *Defender*'s coverage was sensational one way, the coverage of the migration by white newspapers in Chicago was sensational in another. Headlines such as these, Walker reports, appeared in the *Chicago Tribune,* the *Chicago Daily News,* and the *Chicago Herald Examiner.* "Negroes Arrive by Thousands—Peril to Health" and "Half a Million Darkies from Dixie Swarm North." The papers, Walker says, "dramatically overstated the volume of migration, and evoked images of a horde of blacks inundating the city, bringing their diseases, vices, and low standards of living."

The *Defender* and Abbott were unbowed by the anger they unleashed. The paper published stories, essays, poems, editorials, photographs, and cartoons all urging blacks to come North. Abbott also organized group excursions and arranged for group rates on the railroads for groups of ten to fifty. Ottley, the Abbott biographer, said that Abbott "did everything to aid and abet the migration. He argued, pleaded, shamed and exhorted Negroes to abandon the South." Nothing in the North, Abbott believed, could be worse than the "rope and faggot" of the South.

In all this, the *Defender* and Abbott were aided by a clandestine circulation and news-gathering network, the Illinois Central Railroad and the black employees, porters and waiters, who worked on the railroad. Each week, the paper was delivered to the porters and waiters, who left copies of the paper all along the railroad's route between New Orleans and Chicago. The workers, Walker wrote, also picked up copies of out-of-state newspapers and magazines that travelers left on the train, and, back in Chicago, took them to the *Defender*'s office. There, reporters and editors lifted items from the newspapers and magazines much as, decades before, Colonial and Revolutionary era editors had taken items from competitors whose publications they obtained through the mails.

The migration—and the *Defender*'s coverage of it, including its frequent public relations work—changed Chicago and changed America. It also changed the *Defender*. Between 1918 and 1920, the *Defender*'s circulation increased from 100,000 to a claimed 283,571. The Audit Bureau of Circulation did not at that time audit the circulation of black newspapers, but historians agree that the *Defender*'s circulation surely passed 230,000. More than that, thousands of papers circulated outside Chicago. Some 23,000 papers alone were sold each week in New York City. Walker says that in 1915, the *Defender* reached one-tenth of Chicago's African Americans; by 1920 it reached one-tenth of the nation's African Americans and was, Walker says, "the first black newspaper to gain extensive national circulation" and was "the premier journal of the black press." Ottley, the Abbott biographer, ranked Abbott with the black giants of his time: Booker T. Washington and W. E. B. Du Bois. Gunnar Myrdal said he considered Abbott the greatest single force in black journalism and the founder of the modern African-American press.

With the war, beginning in 1917, the authority of the *Defender* and much of the rest of the black press was recognized by the federal government. Black editors and publishers, including Abbott, were brought to Washington to discuss ways in which the papers might encourage black Americans to enlist and to support war production. Most of the black press's coverage was patriotic, but when the black press pointed out iniquities that blacks faced on the home front and in France, the government said the papers were unpatriotic.

The *Defender* and numerous other black papers, however, continued to report on the fact that

while African-American soldiers had answered the call to arms, lynching (some seventy blacks were lynched in American in 1917 alone), mob action, and guns were used against blacks in Chicago and other northern cities. In August 1919, the *Defender* under a banner headline, "Race Riots Sweep Chicago," reported on the white riot against blacks in Chicago. The Great Migration, the paper said, had filled the city's labor needs, but it had brought a bloody white reprisal. Abbott also muckraked against prostitution in black areas of Chicago and against the Ku Klux Klan.

The *Defender*—and the Great Migration—made Abbott a rich man, but he lived modestly, except for a taste for expensive automobiles. He continued to work for integration and, for his work, feared personal attack. He often, Wolseley said, traveled under an assumed name and in disguise. Abbott died in February 1940.

THE NEW YORK *WORLD* UNVEILS THE NEW KU KLUX KLAN

The first Ku Klux Klan was a reaction to the Civil War, organized by ex-Confederates in an attempt to maintain white supremacy in the face of military defeat and the emancipation of the slaves. The white-clothed Klansmen (the costume was meant to portray them as the spirits of the Confederate dead) used threats, terror, whippings, and lynchings, under the cloak of secrecy, to get their way. Their targets were blacks trying to exercise their rights, or simply to live peacefully, and those who dared to help the blacks. Klansmen became so lawless that in 1869, the Klan's Grand Wizard, Confederate General Nathan Bedford Forrest, resigned and ordered the organization's disbandonment. Local organizations, however, continued.

The second Klan had broader hates. It arose in 1915, the idea of an ex-minister and heavy drinker who had found a calling in promoting fraternal orders. Fraternal orders were big at that time, and so was a brand of militant patriotism associated with the world war. This version of the Klan hated not only blacks, but also foreigners, Catholics, and labor unions. Thus it had appeal across the country—not only in the South, but also in Maine, Oregon, and the Midwest.

Besides a general human capacity for hatred, one of the links between the two versions of the Klan was Thomas Dixon, a fiery evangelist minister who turned to fiction to spread his racist sermons to even broader audiences. His novel *The Clansman* made the Ku Klux Klan heroic. It was picked up by the pioneer filmmaker D. W. Griffith and made into the movie *The Birth of a Nation,* released in 1915. In almost every city where the movie opened, the National Association for the Advancement of Colored People protested. But millions of whites, both in the North and South, who saw the movie were enthusiastic. The movie, plus the lynching in Georgia of Leo Frank, a Jew from New York, on the grounds that he had raped a fourteen-year-old employee, created a climate in which the Klan was reborn.

The threats and violence of the first Klan soon reemerged. In 1921, the New York *World* assigned reporters to investigate; the Klan, an editor said, "has become a menace to the peace and security of every section of the United States."

"Secrets of the Ku Klux Klan Exposed by the World." New York *World,* September 6, 1921.

The Knights of the Ku Klux Klan, Inc., was organized Oct. 26, 1916, in Atlanta, Ga., by William Joseph Simmons, who at one period of his life had been an itinerant Methodist exhorter; at another, professor of Southern history at Lanier University, a small, newly organized institution in Atlanta, and at still another a solicitor of members for the Woodmen of the World. On that date Simmons and thirty-three of his friends signed a petition for a charter as a standard fraternal secret order, which charter was issued by the Superior Court of Fulton County, Ga., on July 1, 1916.

Now the organization is active in every State of the Union but three. It has a membership of more than 500,000—or 650,000, according to the boasts of its leaders.

When it was organized, its founders claimed it was a revival or legitimate rebirth of the old Ku Klux Klan of the reconstruction period in the South, and, like the original Klan, its slogan was "White Supremacy." It was directed against the negro.

Now the negro has become a side issue with it. To-day it is primarily anti-Jew, anti-Catholic, anti-alien, and it is spreading more than twice as fast through the North and West as it is growing in the South.

How has it managed to spread out so widely and rapidly?

First, by appeals to local or sectional prejudices and hatreds. On the Pacific Coast it has beckoned to Japophobes and whispered in their ears that the yellow man is plotting to incite the black man in America to rise against the white man. In the cities of the Central West it has pretended to devote itself to stamping out radicalism. On the Atlantic Coast it has preached that an alien-born man or woman, even though naturalized, has no place in America. Everywhere it has banned Jews from membership and made anti-Semitism one of its many missions. Everywhere, also, no less positively but not as frankly, it has barred and attacked Roman Catholics. Wherever a prospective member lives, he has been promised that his pet aversion will be made an object of Klan action.

Second, it owes its growth to the employment of a large number of professional salesmen, who net the country in an up-to-date sales organization and peddle memberships on a basis of $4 for every member taken into the Klan. These paid organizers, or Kleagles, are at work this summer on a membership drive directed from Atlanta and from the various cities where the State sales managers, or King Kleagles, have set up their head-quarters.

This drive is being actively pushed in scores of communities throughout the United States. The Kleagles collect no initiation fees, but each new member makes a "donation" of $10, of which the Kleagle keeps $4 and sends the rest to his King Kleagle, who pockets another $1. The remaining $5 vanishes into the "Imperial" treasury of the order.

Furthermore, the Klan itself owns the company manufacturing the regalia of cotton robe and hooded cap, which is sold to members for $6.50 and costs $1.25 to make. The whole "propaga-tion" department is in the hands of professional drive leaders, whose sole interest in Ku Kluxism is in the "split" just outlined.

In the last five years membership "donations" and sales of regalia have yielded at least $5,000,000—probably a considerably greater sum. Ku Kluxing from the inside has been a paying enterprise and its lucrative possibilities have re-cently been increased by the decision to admit women as well as men to membership. The sisters can now come on in with the brothers—at only $10 per come-on.

The original Knights of the Ku Klux Klan, Inc., modestly begun five years ago, has become a vast enterprise, doing a thriving business in the systematic sale of race hatred, religious bigotry and "100 per cent," anti-Americanism.

It has become and calls itself an "Invisible Empire," ruled by an "Emperor" and "Imperial Wizard," Col. William Joseph Simmons, who is no more legitimately a Colonel than he is an Em-peror or a wizard. Closely associated with him, and making up the triumvirate or "Big Three" which controls its affairs, are Edward Young Clarke, "Imperial Kleagle," a professional public-ity man and drive promoter, and Clarke's business partner in the management of the Southern Pub-licity Association of Atlanta, Mrs. Elizabeth Tyler, who is the principal stockholder in the *Searchlight,*

a newspaper published in Atlanta as the organ of the movement.

Efforts are being made to spread the poison of Ku Kluxism in the army and navy. For months its membership peddlers have been sending their anonymous circulars to officers on the reserve list of the military and naval forces.

Also to reach the hundreds who flew during the war and the thousands then awakened to ac-tive interest in aviation, the promoters of the Klan last spring formed in Atlanta an adjunct order headed by "Emperor" Simmons and known as "The Invisible Planet, Knights of the Air." Mem-bership in this was open to men, women and chil-dren, and Jews and Catholics were not barred. The price of admission was $10. Only Klansmen could be officers in the Knights of the Air, and every white Gentile, Protestant, native-born mem-ber was a hand-picked prospect for Klansmanship and another $10 donation.

The Klan organizers go out instructed by head-quarters to make their first drive to secure city, town and village authorities as members and to centre their efforts also on Judges of local and circuit courts and the police forces. In the weekly news letters sent out from Atlanta by Imperial Kleagle Clarke for circulation among Klansmen, the success achieved along these lines is boasted as the reason why in so many places the Klan has ventured to work openly without fear of interfer-ence and as an incentive for pushing forward the work of setting up an invisible, Klan-controlled super-government throughout the country.

What are the possibilities of such an organi-zation as the Ku Klux Klan?

A partial answer to this question lies in an an-alyzed list prepared by *The World* of outrages com-mitted by groups of masked men wearing white robes and hoods and announcing themselves to their victims as Ku Klux Klansmen. A large ma-jority of these attacks on individuals have in-volved matters of behavior along the lines of personal morality, have flagrantly violated the Bill of Rights implanted in the Federal Constitution and the charter law of every State in the Union, and have involved an assumption of the Klan's authority to impose moral censorship on communities and citizens, summarily punish any "offenses," and set up and enforce its own standards covering every incident of private life. To sum up this aspect of the case, the words of a man who knows the Klan intimately from the inside may be used. He says:

"It would be impossible to imagine an attitude more essentially lawless. Ku Kluxism, as conceived, incorporated, propagated and practised has become a menace to the peace and security of every section of the United States. Its evil and vicious possibilities are boundless. It is nothing more or less than a throwback to the centuries when terror, instead of law and justice, ruled and regulated the lives of men."

For months *The World* has been engaged in a Nation-wide investigation of the Ku Klux Klan and has uncovered a vast mass of evidence. It has learned what the Klan is, down to the last fatuous bit of verbiage tucked away in the secret ritual; what Ku Kluxism means, down to the last whispered word of its insidious propaganda, and what the propagators of Ku Kluxism, Inc., have done and have set themselves to do.

The information thus gathered *The World* now proposed to make public property in a series of articles of which this is the first. This series will constitute a complete exposure of the organization.

Specifically, here are some of the things which *The World* will lay before its readers in forthcoming articles:

Proof of the Klan's anti-Jew and anti-Catholic tenets, with definite instances of their application;

Basic extracts from the "Kloran," the ritual of the first degree of the order and the most secret of its documents;

The names and headquarters throughout the country of the Kleagles, the organizers who peddle memberships at $4 a head;

Photographs of pages and passages from the "Kloran" of initiation ceremonies in widely separated parts of the country of "Imperial" manifestoes put out by "Emperor" Simmons, of parades of Klansmen, of their chief officers, of advertisements for salesmen and members, of letters than went in and out of the Army and Navy Club in New York City and a mass of other photographic evidence;

The analyzed lists of outrages by the Klan or its imitators, and of action taken by various State and municipal authorities against the further spread of Ku Kluxism;

A blistering letter of withdrawal from one of the most active Kleagles in the South, arraigning the "Imperial Wizard" for the evil and unpatriotic things done in the name of the Klan;

Details of the efforts to widen the field of exploitation by organizing the "Invisible Plane, Knights of the Air";

Facts about efforts being made just now to "call off" the newspapers of the country by launching a $100,000 advertising campaign;

Ku Klux espionage and attempts at interference inside *The World* and other newspaper offices;

Revelations of the huge personal advantage enjoyed by the "insiders," ranging from the millions paid in commissions to the Kleagles and the establishment of a $1,500,000 "Imperial Palace" in Atlanta, to the gift of a $25,000 home to "Colonel" Simmons and the recent purchase for him of the university where he was a few years ago an inconspicuous professor of Southern history.

To gather, verify and fit together all this information concerning a movement which specializes in mystery and secrecy has been a work of months, carried on by the most highly gifted members of this paper's staff, assisted by local representatives of *The World* in more than forty cities in a score of different States.

A TABULATION OF KU KLUX KLANISM, SIMMONSISM AND OFFICIAL ACTION

WHAT HAS HAPPENED SINCE THE K.K.K., INC., BEGAN SPREADING ITS DOCTRINE

Violations of the legal rights of individuals by masked mobs wearing Ku Klux regalia	63
"Tar and feather" parties conducted by masked regulators using Klan regalia	21
Individuals seized and beaten by masked mobs in Klan regalia	25
White women stripped and maltreated by masked men wearing Klan regalia	2
Specific warnings issued to individuals in the name of the Ku Klux Klan	6
General warnings posted in name of K.K.K. to enforce moral censorship of communities	12
Killed by Ku Klux regulators	1
Ku Klux regulators killed by intended victims	2

• • •

The articles, which ran for two weeks and were syndicated in nearly twenty other newspapers across the country, introduced the Klan, and its business and "enforcement" practices, to millions of Americans. The *World* received lavish praise from other papers and from public leaders. At the same time, Klan headquarters received thousands of inquiries from potential members, some of whom filled out the membership application the paper had printed with its series.

One month later, congressional hearings were held. Grand Wizard William Simmons spent several days laying out the details of the Klan and effectively defending it. Incidents of vigilantism and violence, he said, were the work of imposters. The hearings gave the Klan further publicity, and again its membership grew.

By the mid-1920s, Klan membership was estimated at four to five million, although the numbers were hard to prove. But then the fever broke. Further scandal, including the conviction of Indiana's Grand Dragon for second-degree murder in the death of his girlfriend, led to defections.

The *World* could not stop the Klan—journalists can do only so much; then the people must take over. But the exposé put on record the nature of an organization that preferred to work in secret.

JOHN HOWARD GRIFFIN MAKES HIMSELF BLACK TO EXPERIENCE BEING A NEGRO IN THE SOUTH

At the end of the 1950s, some whites, especially northern liberals, were convinced life was getting better for blacks. At least some of the jobs opened to blacks during the worker shortages of World War II remained open. Black music and blacks in professional athletics were more common. The Supreme Court had ordered desegregation of public schools and of public buses. A U.S. Civil Rights Commission had been established.

Many blacks, especially in the South, saw things differently. They knew the law said they could vote, but local restrictions kept them from registering. They saw the pitched battles when black children tried to attend white public schools. They felt the indignity of sitting at the back of the bus.

John Howard Griffin, a Texas-born novelist

and journalist, who had specialized in race issues, set out to reconcile these two different views of southern life. Although his first intention was a sociological study, he soon concluded, "How else except by becoming a Negro could a white man hope to learn the truth?" His editors at *Sepia* magazine, a *Look*-like publication aimed at blacks, warned him of the dangers. So did three FBI agents he consulted. Griffin went ahead anyway, consulting a New Orleans dermatologist and turning himself, to all outside purposes, into "a fierce, bald and very dark Negro." Then he set out across Louisiana, Mississippi, Alabama, and Georgia on a journey of buses, hitchhiking, segregated lunch rooms, slammed doors, and daily slights.

Near the end of his five-week trip, Griffin was in Montgomery, Alabama, where the Rev. Dr. Martin Luther King Jr. had just started his civil rights activities. Griffin found a spirit of determination beginning to replace Negro hopelessness. He decided to test his observations by switching back and forth between looking white and looking black.

NOVEMBER 25

The Negroes with whom I associated feared two things. They feared that one of their own might commit an act of violence that would jeopardize their position by allowing the whites to say they were too dangerous to have their rights. They dreaded the awful tauntings of irresponsible white men, the jailing, the frames.

The white man's fears have been widely broadcast. To the Negro these fears of "intermingling" make no sense. All he can see is that the white man wants to hold him down—to make him live up to his responsibilities as a taxpayer and soldier, while denying him the privileges of a citizen. At base, though the white brings forth many arguments to justify his viewpoint, one feels the reality is simply that he cannot bear to "lose" to the traditionally servant class.

The hate stare was everywhere practiced, especially by women of the older generation. On Sunday, I made the experiment of dressing well and walking past some of the white churches just as services were over. In each instance, as the women came through the church doors and saw me, the "spiritual bouquets" changed to hostility. The transformation was grotesque. In all of Montgomery only one woman refrained. She did not smile. She merely looked at me and did not change her expression. My gratitude to her was so great it astonished me. . . .

NOVEMBER 28

I decided to try to pass back into white society. I scrubbed myself almost raw until my brown skin had a pink rather than black undertone. Yes, looking into the mirror, I felt I could pass. I put on a white shirt, but by contrast it made by face and hands appear too dark. I changed to a brown sports shirt which made my skin appear lighter.

This shift was nerve-racking. As a white man I could not be seen leaving a Negro home at midnight. If I checked into a white hotel and then got too much sun, it would, in combination with the medication still in my system, turn me too dark and I would not be able to return to the hotel.

I waited until the streets were quiet outside and I was sure everyone in the house slept. Then, taking my bags, I walked to the door and out into the night. . . .

The policeman nodded affably to me and I knew then that I had successfully passed back into white society, that I was once more a first-class citizen, that all doors and churches were suddenly open to me. After so long I could not adjust to it. A sense of exultant liberation flooded through me. I crossed over to a restaurant and entered. I took a seat beside white men at the counter and the waitress smiled at me. It was a miracle. I ordered food and was served, and it was a miracle. I went to the rest room and was not molested. No one paid me the slightest attention. No one said, "What're you doing in here, nigger?"

Out there in the night I knew the men who were exactly as I had been these past weeks roamed the streets and not one of them could go into a place and buy a cup of coffee at this time of night. Instead of opening the door into rest rooms, they looked for alleys.

To them as to me, these simple privileges would be a miracle. But though I felt it all, I felt no joy in it. I saw smiles, benign faces, courtesies—a side of the white man I had not seen in weeks, but I remembered too well the other side. The miracle was sour.

I ate the white meal, drank the white water, received the white smiles and wondered how it could all be. What sense could a man make of it?

I left the café and walked to the elegant Whitney Hotel. A Negro rushed to take my knapsacks. He gave me the smiles, the "yes, sir—yes, sir."

I felt like saying, "You're not fooling me," but now I was back on the other side of the wall. There was no longer communication between us, no longer the glance that said everything.

The white clerks registered me, surrounded me with smiles, sent me to my comfortable room accompanied by a Negro who carried my bags. I gave him his tip, received his bow and realized that already he was far from me, distant as the Negro is distant from the white. I locked the door, sat on the bed and smoked a cigarette. I was the same man who could not possibly have bought his way into this room a week ago. My inclination was to marvel at the feel of the carpet beneath my feet, to catalogue the banal miracle of every stick of furniture, every lamp, the telephone, to go and wash myself in the tile shower—or again to go out into the street simply to experience what it was like to walk into all the doors, all the joints and movies and restaurants, to talk to white men in the lobby without servility, to

look at women and see them smile courteously. . . .

DECEMBER 1

I developed a technique of zigzagging back and forth. In my bag I kept a damp sponge, dyes, cleansing cream and Kleenex. It was hazardous, but it was the only way to traverse an area both as Negro and white. As I traveled, I would find an isolated spot, perhaps an alley at night or the brush beside a highway, and quickly apply the dye to face, hands and legs, then rub off and reapply until it was firmly anchored in my pores. I would go through the area as Negro and then, usually at night, remove the dyes with cleansing cream and tissues and pass through the same area as a white man.

I was the same man, whether white or black. Yet when I was white, I received the brotherly-love smiles and the privileges from whites and the hate stares or obsequiousness from the Negroes. And when I was a Negro, the whites judged me fit for the junk heap, while the Negroes treated me with great warmth.

As the Negro Griffin, I walked up the steep hill to the bus station in Montgomery to get the schedule for buses to Tuskegee. I received the information from a polite clerk and turned away from the counter.

"Boy!" I heard a woman's voice, harsh and loud.

I glanced toward the door to see a large, matriarchical woman, elderly and impatient. Her pinched face grimaced and she waved me to her.

"Boy, come here. Hurry!"

Astonished, I obeyed.

"Get those bags out of the cab," she ordered testily, seeming outraged with my lack of speed.

Without thinking, I allowed my face to spread to a grin as though overjoyed to serve her. I carried her bags to the bus and received three haughty dimes. I thanked her profusely. Her eyebrows knitted with irritation and she finally waved me away. . . .

DECEMBER 14

Finally the photos were taken, the project concluded, and I resumed for the final time my white identity. I felt strangely sad to leave the world of the Negro after having shared it so long—almost as though I were fleeing my share of his pain and heartache.

• • •

As George Levitan, the owner of *Sepia,* had predicted, public reaction to Griffin's journey was volatile. The story ran in six monthly installments, April through September 1960. By March, the national press was aware of what Griffin had done and started calling for interviews. Thousands of letters came in, most of them favorable. Griffin's Texas neighbors started calling, too, but usually to accuse him of being a traitor to his race. Few would talk to him; he was threatened and hanged in effigy on the main street. Eventually he moved his family to Mexico.

The book held little news for most blacks, but having their story told by a white man made it more believable to other whites. Publication of *Black Like Me,** along with Griffin's own inclinations, made him a figure in the emerging civil rights movement of the 1960s. To his dismay, Griffin wrote twenty-five years later, in city after city, "it was my embarrassing task to sit in on meetings of whites and blacks, to serve one ridiculous but necessary function: I knew, and every black man there knew, that I, as a man now white once again, could say the things that needed say-

*The title comes from the Langston Hughes poem "Dream Variation": Night coming tenderly, Black like me.

ing but would be rejected if black men said them." Once, he said, he and Dick Gregory, comedian and activist, arranged to make essentially the same speech at the same school. Gregory was greeted with uncomfortable silence; Griffin got an ovation.

The book remains required reading in many schools and universities, providing for new generations a searing perspective of life on the two sides of the color line at the start of the modern civil rights movement. There are those who see similarities still.

A WHITE SOUTHERN EDITOR STANDS UP FOR JUSTICE IN RACIST SOUTH

"It would be pleasant to report that the American press as a whole distinguished itself" in coverage of racial issues during the 1950s and 1960s, wrote John Hohenberg, longtime administrator of the Pulitzer Prizes. But that would not, Hohenberg added, have been an accurate picture. Not even a majority of the country's newspapers, north or south, supported the Supreme Court's 1954 ruling that school desegregation was unconstitutional. "The wonder of it is not that there were so few," Hohenberg said, "but that a hard-bitten core of responsible journalists in every Southern state did stand up to be counted on the side of fairness in race relations."

Perhaps it is justice that it is the names of the editors in the minority at the time that made a mark in journalism history: among them, Harry Ashmore of the *Arkansas Gazette,* Ralph McGill of the *Atlanta Constitution,* Hodding Carter of the *Delta Democrat-Times* in Mississippi, and his neighboring editor, Hazel Brannon Smith of the *Lexington Advertiser.* Smith moved to Holmes County, Mississippi, in 1936, fresh out of the journalism program at the University of Alabama, and she stayed to fight.

In 1964, Smith won the Pulitzer Prize for editorial writing, including this editorial published the previous year.

"The Murder of Medgar Evers," by Hazel Brannon Smith. *Lexington (Mississippi) Advertiser,* June 13, 1963.

The shocking, hate-inspired murder of Medgar Evers, Mississippi field secretary of the NAACP, is not only a reprehensible crime against the laws of God and man. It was a vicious and dastardly act endangering the personal safety and well-being of every citizen, white and Negro, in Jackson and throughout the state. It poses a serious threat to future race relations.

The criminal should be found and punished to the fullest extent of the law.

When the unknown assailant took a position under cover of night near the victim's home and cut him down with a high-powered rifle, he did not kill the civil rights movement, as he may have supposed. He did kill a man who was a living symbol of the freedom that Mississippi Negroes are determined to achieve.

But far from killing the freedom movement in Mississippi, the perpetrator of the crime only made certain it will be increased tenfold. New leaders will arise to take Evers' place—and they will not be as moderate in their views, or as patient, reasonable, and understanding of the white man's position and views.

The murder was committed by an ignorant product of our sick, hate-filled society. Thus far it has been only a segment of our white community that has succumbed to hate. God help us when the Negro starts hating in Mississippi.

It is imperative that each of us examine our own heart and conscience and determine what part we have played, wither in things done or left undone, in acts of commission or omission, in creating a society which permits a man to be murdered because of his desire to be free and equal under the law—a man who fought Hitlerism in Germany for all our freedom.

Time is running out for us here in the Magnolia State. People of good will must act now if we are to avert total disaster in the entire field of human relations. Mayor Allen Thompson will surely recognize the urgent necessity of establishing immediately a bi-racial committee to try to achieve some degree of real understanding before it is too late—indeed, if it is not already.

• • •

Like the other progressive Southern editors, Smith had no illusions that she would quickly convince her readers to share her opinions. Her editorials led to an economic boycott that, combined with the founding of an opposition paper, broke the *Advertiser*. What Smith and others did was to offer another way of looking at Southern race relations and provide a rallying point for those who came to see that things needed to change. In addition, said Hohenberg, "They undoubtedly prepared the journalists of the North for their own ordeal by riot and firebomb when the mob spirit swept across the Mason-Dixon Line to the black ghettos beyond."

THE *DETROIT FREE PRESS* REVEALS NEEDLESS KILLINGS IN 1967 RACE RIOT

In the hot summer of 1967, Detroit's inner city, like those elsewhere in America, was simmering. Unemployment was high, housing was poor, the police were repressive, and a mood had arisen among blacks in America following riots in such cities as Los Angeles and Newark. On a steaming Saturday night, July 22, police raided a blind pig, an old-time Middle West name for an after-hours bar, and a melee ensued between police and the customers. Within hours, the word of the raid had gone out, and by Sunday morning a riot had broken out along Twelfth Street, in the heart of the city's west side black community. The riot then spread throughout much of the city. The Michigan National Guard was brought to the scene to assist Detroit police. But their efforts failed. Then President Lyndon B. Johnson sent in troops from the 82nd Airborne Division. By the time the riot ended on Thursday, forty-three people had been killed.

One of the dead was a young farm boy from Tennessee who, Detroit police said, had been shot on a stairs behind his apartment because he had a carbine in his hands and police were afraid he would shoot. Some days after the riot, a man from Tennessee walked into the *Detroit Free Press* newsroom and asked to speak to the reporter who had written the story about his son's death. The man had with him pictures of his son in his casket in the family home. The man said he had driven up from Tennessee to show the picture of his son to the reporter, and to say that his son had not been a sniper. He did not own a weapon, the father said.

Police accounts of other deaths, including those of three black youths killed in the Algiers Motel, had already troubled some *Free Press* reporters and editors. But the father's visit, and his claim of his son's innocence, was the key factor in the *Free Press*'s decision to mount a full-scale investigation into each of the riot deaths.

The reporters were Gene Goltz, William Serrin, and Barbara Stanton, who divided up the deaths and separately tracked down the circumstances. They worked under the direction of editors Neal Shine and Kurt Luedtke. The summation for the final, section-long report was written by Luedtke.

"The 43 Who Died," *Detroit Free Press*, September 3, 1967.

In the space of eight silent days and bullet-broken nights, 43 persons died or were fatally wounded on the streets of Detroit. They are explained as victims of riot, the casualties of modern civil war.

Even now, it is difficult to arrive at more satisfactory explanations. It is tempting indeed to conclude that only the riot itself can be blamed for creating the situations in which it was pathetically easy to die.

Thirty-six hours after the riot began, something more than 3,000 armed men were assigned or had access to a single 20- by 20-block area on the near West Side, a concentration of firepower paralleled only by a major military invasion force.

Hundreds of regular Army paratroopers were stationed on the East Side. In the Inner City, city and state police and National Guardsmen patrolled in scout cars, paddy wagons, expressway cruisers, jeeps, trucks, personnel carriers and tanks. The armament ranged from service revolvers and M-1 rifles to privately owned sporting arms, short-barreled repeating shotguns, carbines and machine guns of up to .50 caliber.

Numbers alone made it inevitable that confrontations would occur, that incidents would result, that mistakes would be made and that ultimately, someone would die. There were too many guns and too many people for it to be otherwise.

Now the central questions are simple, though the answers are not:

How many of the 43 deaths were necessary?

How many could have been prevented?

The answers are individual, based on more than five weeks of independent investigation by a team of *Free Press* reporters assigned to examine every non-connected death.

The conclusion reached in that investigation is inescapable:

The majority of the riot victims need not have died. Their deaths could have been—and should have been—prevented.

Fate's selection of those who would died followed no pattern and the riot victims do not fit easily into categories and classifications. Among them are the most innocent, a four-year-old girl killed by a wanton bullet, and the most guilty, a drunken sniper who died trying to take another's life. Equally various were the ways in which they died.

Eighteen of the 43 riot victims were shot and killed by Detroit police, and of that number, 14 have been confirmed as looters in the *Free Press* investigation. The other four are a sniper, a possible but unconfirmed arsonist and two of the three men shot and killed in the Algiers Motel.

At least six victims were killed by the National Guard, five of them innocent, the victims of what now seem to be tragic accidents.

In five more cases, both police and National Guardsmen were involved and it is impossible to say definitely whose bullets were fatal. Four of these five victims were innocent of any wrong-doing.

Two more persons, both looters, were shot and killed by store-owners. Three more were killed by private citizens: murder warrants have been issued in two of those cases and a warrant decision is pending in the third. And two looters died when fire swept the store from which they were stealing.

Two victims, one a fireman, the other a civilian, were killed by electric power lines.

Five deaths remain. They are a 19-year-old boy killed accidentally by a paratrooper; a 23-year-old white woman shot by an unknown gunman; a Detroit fireman killed by either a hidden sniper or a stray National Guard bullet; a policeman shot as a fellow officer struggled with a prisoner; and the third victim of the Algiers Motel slayings, whose assailant is not known.

Hindsight is easy. The fires have gone out and the streets are quiet and in the midst of normalcy, the temptation to insist that logic and order and common sense should have prevailed throughout the riot is overwhelming, but impossible to tolerate.

No one who drove those gutted streets at midnight, when the fires still burned and the shadows hung and moved in vacant doorways, when frightened voices cried "Halt" into the silence and footsteps crunched on broken glass, will contend

that men should have behaved rationally in those awful hours.

With that qualification accepted and understood, here are the general conclusions of the five-week investigation into the riot deaths:

Both the number of snipers active in the riot area and the danger that snipers presented were vastly overstated. Only one sniper is among the riot victims and only three of the victims may possibly have been killed by snipers, two of them doubtful. In all, some 31 persons were arrested and charged with sniping; none of these cases has gone to trial.

In the 43 deaths, criminal intent may possibly be an element in only seven—the three Algiers Motel deaths, three killings by civilians, and one case, that of William Dalton, still unresolved. *Free Press* investigators found no evidence of deliberate or preconceived killing in the cases remaining.

In retrospect, the performance of Michigan State and city policemen seems generally restrained and impressive. The fact that 4,000 city policemen worked for at least five days in the midst of chaos without more bloodshed is significant. There are individual incidents of poor judgment, it is true, and several regrettable instances where officers may have fired too soon, though they acted legally.

One major critical observation must be made. Both city and Army authorities acted to try to keep the death toll at a minimum, though they did so in different ways. In both cases, their efforts were not successful and permitted unnecessary death.

At 11:30 Monday night, within hours after the National Guard had come under Federal control, Lt. General John Throckmorton, the commanding officer, issued a general order commanding all troops under his control to unload their weapons and to fire only on the command of an officer.

Throckmorton's regular Army troops obeyed that order; only one person was killed in paratrooper territory in the five days that followed.

The National Guard did not obey, in many

cases because the order was improperly disseminated and was never made clear to the men on the street. As a result, the Guard was involved in a total of eleven deaths in which nine innocent people died.

Military discipline and attention to Throckmorton's order could have avoided those deaths.

Within the Detroit Police Department, authorities now say that there were no standing orders on whether looters would be shot. That may be true, but both civilians and police officers had the firm and distinct impression on Sunday, the riot's first day, that looters would not be shot.

There was reason for that impression. Police officers made no secret of the fact that they were pleased with their handling of the Kercheval incident in the summer of 1966. The tactics used in that situation included no shooting and became a model for future riot control plans.

Looting was rampant Sunday and there was no shooting. The impression in the Negro community was that looters were safe. Unhappily, that situation was to change.

As Commissioner Ray Girardin recalls it now, no specific order on whether looters could be shot was ever given. Officers were to use their discretion, nothing more.

The order that apparently changed the tide came from Superintendent Eugene Reuter, in response to a question on how to handle sniper incidents. Reuter gave permission for officers to return fire. The word quickly spread through the department and in the next several days, shooting increased.

The legal basis for shooting a looter is found in state law which permits officers to fire at fleeing felons after an order to halt is disregarded. Technically, most of those who were killed clearly fall in that category, though one is still left with a feeling that the thief who takes $5 worth of goods from a grocery store shelf and runs ought not to be required to pay with his life.

Nonetheless, the question of whether looters will be shot is a matter of public policy. No decision was ever made and announced publicly; as a result, the value of the law as a deterrent was minimal. Many looters certainly thought they were safe; many more would have stayed home had they known that death might be the result.

The official investigating agency for the riot deaths is the Detroit Homicide Bureau, which reports in turn to Wayne County Prosecutor William Cahalan, who rules on each case.

With minor exceptions, the Homicide Bureau is turning in complete and competent reports on every death. In a few cases, the investigations have been nothing short of inspired. In a few others, a reluctance to go all-out on cases involving fellow officers is understandable if not excusable.

It is not Cahalan's job to decide whether officers showed good judgment or bad, or to decide whether the deaths were necessary. Unless he finds evidence of criminal intent, Cahalan cannot act.

In most of the cases Cahalan has received so far, he has found no such evidence and where police officers are involved, has used the same citation of law over and over again. That citation reads:

"Were a man charged with crime to be held to a knowledge of all facts precisely as they are, there could be few cases in which the most innocent intention or honest zeal could justify or excuse homicide."

What that law says is simply that we cannot expect police officers to know exactly what the situation is in fact before they act. They must act as the situation appears to them at the moment and make the best judgments they can.

Forty-three are dead. In the riot's aftermath, rumor, suspicion and hatred have played equal roles in distorting the true versions of those deaths.

The report which follows is based on independent evidence and witnesses. It is as accurate as an honest regard for the facts can make it. Even now, it is impossible to arrive at complete explanations, firm conclusions or satisfactory judgments; the best that can be done is to report what is known and to suggest the probabilities that logic requires.

One conclusion must be repeated: A majority of the deaths reported here appear to be unnecessary. That price, however intolerable it may be, is part of what we have paid for eight days of insanity.

• • •

Both the Detroit police and the National Guard defended themselves from the *Free Press*'s charges. But it was clear that, as opposed to the federal troops, who conducted themselves with utmost professionalism, police officers and guardsmen lacked discipline and used their weapons with fatal recklessness. Hearings were held, and new procedures were instituted within the police department on how to handle arrests during disturbances. Change did not come quickly, but the Detroit police gradually moved to hire more black officers.

The *Free Press* report also helped to undermine the notion in America of black snipers. It had another result: The report showed that what the father had said weeks before was correct—his son had no weapon and had been wrongly killed.

GHOSTS OF MISSISSIPPI: THE JACKSON *CLARION-LEDGER* REOPENS THE CASE OF THE MEDGAR EVERS MURDER

Medgar Evers was one of the promising leaders of the NAACP when, in 1954, he was appointed Mississippi's first NAACP field secretary. He had joined the organization after a stint selling insurance to poor rural blacks in Mississippi, which made him acutely aware of the problems they faced. Evers was aggressive. He pushed the state to comply with the 1954 Brown v. Board of Education ruling by the U.S. Supreme Court on school desegregation and organized boycotts of

merchants who would not hire or serve blacks. He was also well aware of the dangers of his work, and had warned his wife, Myrlie, and their children about the possibility of violence.

On the night of June 12, 1963, as he reached his driveway in Jackson, Mississippi, on the way home from yet another meeting, Evers was shot in the back by someone hiding in nearby bushes. Byron De La Beckwith, a white supremist proud and vocal about his hatred of blacks, was twice tried for the killing, and twice all-white juries deadlocked, and Beckwith went free.

But in 1989, twenty-six years after the shooting, Jerry Mitchell, a reporter for the Jackson *Clarion-Ledger*, obtained secret files of the Mississippi Sovereignty Commission, which had worked to combat the civil rights movement. "There's something about me and secret documents," Mitchell said. "Once someone tells me I can't have something, I've got to have it." The documents included evidence that at least one of the juries in the Beckwith case might have been tampered with.

"State checked possible jurors in Evers slaying," by Jerry Mitchell. *Clarion-Ledger,* October 1, 1989.

The state Sovereignty Commission in 1964 investigated prospective jurors for Byron De La Beckwith's second trial on charges of killing black activist Medgar Evers.

The segregation spy agency responded to a request by defense lawyer Stanley Sanders of Greenwood, who is now dead, to explore the backgrounds of prospective jurors for the April 1964 trial, according to commission documents. The documents do not indicate whether prospective jurors for the first trial were investigated.

The commission had long kept an eye on Evers in hopes of catching him in an illegal act, documents show.

Beckwith was tried twice in 1964 by all-white juries for the June 12, 1963, slaying of Evers, field secretary of the Mississippi NAACP who was gunned down in the driveway of his home on Guynes Street in northwest Jackson. Both trials ended in hung juries.

Commission investigator Andy Hopkins made contact with the prospective jurors in the second trial to gather personal and biographical information, said Eric Johnston, former director of the commission, reached at his forest home last week.

Johnston speculated Hopkins, who is also dead, gathered the information through phone calls.

"It was just like looking up a committee of the Chamber of Commerce," said Johnston, who doubts the investigation influenced the makeup of the jury or the outcome of the trial.

"If they were denied service, it wasn't on account of us," Johnston said.

But the documents, which are contained in commission records that remain sealed by the state, show the commission did make apparent suggestions to the defense.

Two potential jurors are each referred to as likely to be a "fair and impartial juror." Another receives no such label. "Believed to be Jewish," a commission report says. "No further information."

Such communication with prospective jurors constitutes at least improper contact and possibly jury tampering, said Aaron Condon, professor of law at the University of Mississippi School of Law. "It's hard for me to imagine any other reason (to make contact) other than to influence the juror's decision," he said. "It could be part of a background check, but it's not proper in such a way that a juror feels he is under investigation."

Former Gov. Bill Waller, who prosecuted the case as Hinds County district attorney, said he knew the commission was interested because an investigator was "in and out of the courtroom every day."

Waller said he doesn't believe the hung jury resulted from commission contact. "I don't think so, but that's a judgment call," said Waller, who

as governor cut off the commission's funding in 1978, which led to its death. "There were sympathizers (with Beckwith) on the jury, of course."

The jury in the second trial voted 8–4 to acquit. The case was never retried and was dismissed in 1969.

Beckwith, a former Greenwood businessman, could not be reached for comment but said in a 1987 interview he is innocent of Evers' murder. He still urged "white-only, Christian rule" for the U.S.

The commission was drawn into the 1964 investigation when a person with the surname "Hopkins" appeared on a list of prospective jurors given Sanders, Johnston said.

"This lawyer asked Andy Hopkins if (the prospective juror) was any kin to him," Johnston said. "He told him he might be a distant cousin."

Hopkins then proceeded at the request of Sanders to check out potential jurors, Johnston said. "That was right in 1964 . . . everything was tense. They wondered if (jurors) in any way were connected with people coming down South."

The commission prepared a complete report on the prospective jurors. It identified them by occupation and social affiliations, Johnston said.

The commission found one prospective juror who belonged to the White Citizens Council, which strongly espoused segregationist philosophy, Johnston said. The Citizens Council sponsored a fundraising for Beckwith's defense.

"One (juror) said he was a member of the Citizens Council," Johnston said. "The rest may or may not have been." He did not know whether that person, whose name he could not recall, was selected for the final jury that heard the evidence.

The 1960s marked the heyday for the commission, created by the 1956 Legislature to guard segregation. After the commission's demise, the 1977 Legislature ordered its records closed for 50 years.

The main body of commission records is in a state Department of Archives and History vault in Jackson. U.S. District William H. Barbour Jr.

ruled July 27 that the records should be open, but they remain closed pending appeals.

In 1964, Beckwith's defense drew popular support across Mississippi, including establishing the White Citizens Legal Fund to raise money.

With the death of a prominent civil rights leader, the national spotlight shone brightly on the trial held in the Hinds County Courthouse.

The evidence against Beckwith was simple: His fingerprint was on the sight of a gun found in bushes near the slaying. Witnesses placed his car near the scene that night.

Beckwith testified his gun had been stolen.

To prove his innocence, the defense unfurled a 17-year-old newspaper to show someone might have an identical fingerprint to Beckwith's. Alibi witnesses also placed Beckwith in Greenwood.

"I think it's an outrage the state of Mississippi was prosecuting and on the other hand was trying to subvert the efforts," said Bill Minor, who covered the trial for the *Times Picayune* in New Orleans.

"It was bad enough that (former Gov.) Ross Barnett came and showed himself in front of the jury a few times," Minor said.

• • •

Twenty-six years had brought much change to Mississippi, and new law-enforcement officials in an era of integration were willing to consider going back into the civil rights crimes that had gone unpunished. In Jackson, the key convert was the assistant district attorney, Bobby Delaughter, who

was intrigued by Mitchell's story, and by a story two days later in which Myrlie Evers urged that the case be reopened. The *Clarion-Ledger,* which had been a typical Southern racist paper during the 1950s and 1960s, agreed. Within a month Delaughter's office was reinvestigating. The obstacles were many: missing court records, lost evidence, memories that had faded over three decades, public complaints that another trial for Beckwith would be divisive and stir up old hatreds. But prosecutors persevered. Beckwith was indicted in December 1990 and, in his third trial, in 1994, was found guilty. He was sentenced to life and died a prisoner in January 2001.

Mitchell said that time had to pass to allow Hinds County to reopen the Beckwith case. "What had to happen in a sense was there had to be a new generation of Southerners," said Mitchell, who grew up in Texarkana, Texas, and came to Jackson in 1986. "It's more an inside thing than an outside thing." Delaughter, who became a Hinds County, Mississippi, judge, said, "For Mississippi, it was an exorcism of sorts."

After Beckwith was indicted, Mitchell said, "The next logical question was, are there any other cases we're going to look at." There were. Mitchell and the *Clarion-Ledger* continued to explore the South's crimes of the past. In part as a result, between 1989 and early 2001, nineteen killings from the civil rights era were reexamined by authorities. That work led to twelve arrests, six convictions, one mistrial, and one acquittal.

Benjamin Franklin, a publisher in Philadelphia, was much distressed at the difficulty in getting the young English colonies to work together on almost anything, be it against the Indians, the French, or the Crown. In 1754, with the French attacking Virginians on the Ohio River, Franklin's *Pennsylvania Gazette* ran a woodcut of a dismembered snake that argued for unity among the colonies. The drawing—it is not certain whether it was by Franklin, or ordered up by him—is considered the first political cartoon in America. Franklin's arguments eventually prevailed. (*Corbis*)

Paul Revere was a silversmith, an engraver, and a Patriot, but not a journalist. On March 5, 1770, a fight broke out on King Street between a group of workers and British soldiers, leaving five colonists dead, and Revere, a Boston resident, recorded the event. Within three weeks, Revere issued an engraving of the incident, under the title "The Bloody Massacre." The engraving may have been plagiarized and was wildly inaccurate, but it was widely circulated and inflamed colonists against the British, helping to bring on the American Revolution. (*Library of Congress*)

Abraham Lincoln was considered an uncouth backwoods lawyer by many in 1860, even though his debates with Stephen A. Douglas in the senatorial campaign in 1858 had drawn national attention. But in February 1860, Lincoln agreed to speak at the Cooper Union in New York City. On the trip, Lincoln stopped by the studio of photographer Mathew Brady, who fussed with the lighting, Lincoln's hair, and Lincoln's collar before making a shot. The result gave Lincoln a seriousness and substance that surprised many. Lincoln's speech, discussing Republican options on slavery, was hugely successful. *Harper's Weekly* ran a woodcut of Brady's photograph on its front page; Brady sold thousands of prints. Later, in the White House, Lincoln told Brady that the photograph and the Cooper Union speech had made him president. (*Library of Congress*)

553.   The "Sunken Road" at Antietam.
[FOR DESCRIPTION OF THIS VIEW SEE THE OTHER SIDE OF THIS CARD.]

When the Civil War broke out, Mathew Brady determined that he and his staff would be the photographic historians of the war. The photographs of early battles were basically landscapes, taken after the fighting was over. But in September 1862, one of Brady's most accomplished assistants, Alexander Gardner, arrived at the Antietam battlefield in Maryland while the casualties of the country's bloodiest day still lay on the field. A month later, when the photographs—as pictured here—of twisted, bloated corpses were exhibited at Brady's studio at Tenth Street and Broadway in New York City, lines of silent viewers extended down the block. The *New York Times* reported that, with the exhibition, "Mr. Brady has done something to bring home to us the terrible reality and earnestness of war." (*Library of Congress*)

The Tammany Tiger Loose. —"What Are You Going To Do About It?"

As a cartoonist for *Harper's Weekly*, Thomas Nast, in the decades after the Civil War, was uniquely positioned to reach the new immigrants of New York. Even William M. "Boss" Tweed, commissioner of public works and leader of the Democratic Tammany Hall organization, conceded this: Tweed said his constituents couldn't read, so newspaper reports of corruption did not much matter, but that he could do nothing to combat Nast's pictures. The cartoons, over four years, so well portrayed Tweed that, when Tweed fled the country, he was captured by authorities in Spain after Tweed was recognized from Nast's work. (*From the Collection of Macculloch Hall Historical Museum*)

Although a number of muckraking journalists in the early twentieth century wrote about the ills of factory work and child labor in the United States, the photographs by Lewis Hine were particularly powerful. Working first for the National Child Labor Committee and then the Pittsburgh Survey, a pioneering sociological study, Hine captured the conditions of boys and girls selling newspapers, working in Pittsburgh steel mills and other factories in America, and toiling as "breaker boys" in Pennsylvania coal mines. The job as "breaker boys," often held by boys as young as twelve or fourteen, was one of the worst in the history of child labor, and Hine's photographs motivated the reformers who banned it. (*National Archives*)

What Does Mere Man Know About the Perils of Non-Stop Flying?

During his nearly half-century career (1900 to 1949), most of it based at the *Des Moines Register,* J. N. "Ding" Darling drew many editorial cartoons illustrating his concern over the damage that humans were doing to the environment. In 1934, President Franklin D. Roosevelt, a frequent Darling target on other issues, appointed Darling chief of what is now the U.S. Fish and Wildlife Service. Darling laid the groundwork for a system of National Wildlife Refuges to give shelter to migrating birds, started the Duck Stamp program to help pay for the refuges, and drew the first of the nation's duck stamps. Today there are more than 500 national wildlife refuges, including one on Sanibel Island, Florida, named for Darling. (*Courtesy the Ding Darling Foundation*)

Concerned that an upturn in factory work was causing people to believe the Depression was ending, President Franklin D. Roosevelt asked the Farm Security Administration to send its photographers to chronicle Americans not benefiting from the New Deal. In 1936, in a migrant camp in Nipomo, California, Dorothea Lange came across a family of nine who had just sold their car tires for food. Lange's shot of the mother's face became a symbol of the migrant spirit and of the Depression. At the death of the migrant family's mother, Florence Thompson, in California in 1983, the children all had good jobs and owned their own homes, according to one daughter. (MIGRANT MOTHER, NIPOMO, CALIFORNIA, *1936. Courtesy the Dorothea Lange Collection, Oakland Museum of California*)

The workers were at fault, the Chicago police and the bosses of Republic Steel said of the Memorial Day 1937 strike incident that resulted in the shooting deaths of ten marchers and the injury of scores more. But it turned out that newsreel cameras, including those from Paramount Pictures, had recorded the event. The film was regarded as incendiary and withheld, but then it was discovered and subpoenaed by congressional investigators and played. It showed that the police, not the workers, were at fault—that police had attacked workers and their family members from behind as the workers fled. (*AP/Wide World Photos*)

Margaret Bourke-White was one of the first photographers hired by *Life* magazine when it was started in 1936, with the goal of using photography to make the world a more familiar place to its readers. The magazine was instantly popular and soon reached millions. This gave Bourke-White's photographs of the liberation of Buchenwald in April 1945 an astounding impact, bringing the horror of the Holocaust into American living rooms. (*TimePix*)

"I HAVE HERE IN MY HAND—"

Herbert L. Block (Herblock) was a proudly liberal cartoonist, sharp of line and of caption, throughout his seven-decade career. In the early 1950s, at the *Washington Post,* he was appalled by the abusive tactics of Senator Joseph R. McCarthy. He coined the word "McCarthyism" and drew cartoon after cartoon pointing out McCarthy's abuses. Because McCarthy was portrayed with a heavy beard, McCarthy took to shaving several times a day. Along with the *Post* editorial page and a few other bold journalists—not many at that time—Herblock kept up the pressure that brought McCarthy's downfall. At his death in 2001, Block left most of his fortune to establish a foundation to help the poor and to promote civil rights and other causes he so long had championed. (*from* Herblock: A Cartoonist's Life, *Lisa Drew Books/Macmillan*)

Segregation became a national story when civil rights activists headed south in the early 1960s, and newspapers and network television began to cover the story. Through articles, photographs, and television pictures, people in all areas of the country could see the brutal treatment of blacks and their supporters by Southern law enforcement. The sight of dogs released on young demonstrators by Sheriff Bull Connor's officers in Birmingham, Alabama, in May 1963 helped win support and recruits for civil rights activists and strengthened the growing civil rights movement. (*AP/Wide World Photos*)

On February 1, 1968, Eddie Adams, photographer for the Associated Press, was present when South Vietnamese national police general Nguyen Ngoc Loan executed a Viet Cong officer with a pistol shot to the head. The photograph graphically captured the horror of the Vietnam War and raised questions about the South Vietnamese allies of the United States. (*AP/Wide World Photos*)

LIFE

The Faces of
The American Dead
in Vietnam

ONE WEEK'S TOLL

JUNE 27 · 1969 · 40¢

To bring home the magnitude of the Vietnam War, *Life* magazine in June 1969 gathered photographs of each American killed in one week of the war. It was a typical week: 242 dead. The yearbook-style pictures of mostly smiling young faces looking at the reader portrayed to America the tragedy of the fighting. The *Life* edition "was an issue to make men and women cry," wrote the journalist David Halberstam, and "probably had more impact on antiwar feeling than any other piece of print journalism." (*TimePix*)

SPORTS

The first college football game in America was played in 1869 between Princeton and Rutgers. The sport, an adaptation of soccer and rugby, caught on immediately, spreading first through the Ivy League and west across America. Michigan, the University of Chicago, Stanford, and other schools quickly fielded fine teams. In 1892, Amos Alonzo Stagg was hired to coach football at the University of Chicago at a salary of $6,000 and was the first coach to receive tenure and an academic appointment. The first Rose Bowl was played January 1, 1902, between Michigan and Stanford.

College football quickly became big business, popular with the alumni and profitable for the colleges. In 1905, the muckraking magazine *McClure's* carried a two-part investigation of football by Henry Beach Needham, exposing the recruitment and subsidization of college players and saying that corruption was moving into high school football as well. The motto of football, Needham said, was winning at any cost.

Winning at any cost also meant violence. Players went without helmets or pads. They routinely kicked, punched, and mangled each other; under an early rule, players could slug their opponents three times before being ejected. For several years, teams used the flying wedge formation, with players running in mass downfield and smashing into opponents. Teams could pick up their ball carrier and hurdle him over the opposition. In a game between Harvard and Yale in 1894, six players were seriously injured, one from a finger stuck in his eye, drawing blood; one with a broken collarbone after a player leapt on his shoulder; and one from a concussion that kept him unconscious for hours. Later that year a Georgetown University quarterback had a vertebrae broken and died. Deaths occurred with shocking regularity, but newspapers rarely pulled them together on a national scale. College officials and faculty members complained sporadically, but not much was done to change things.

In 1905, President Theodore Roosevelt, reacting to the violence, tried to clean up the game. Roosevelt was a football fan who thought playing the sport made young men tough and manly. He also saw football as practice for war. A number of his Rough Riders had been football players and that, he felt, helped make them so tough. But unless the game was changed, he felt, colleges and state legislatures might ban it. In October, he called representatives of three major football schools, Yale, Harvard, and Princeton, together and asked them for a pledge of reform. The pledge was made, but soon forgotten.

The next month, on November 26, 1905, the *Chicago Tribune* published an article, headlined FOOTBALL YEAR'S DEATH HARVEST, detailing the deaths in football in the 1905 season and saying that reforms must be made or the game abolished. The *Tribune* took the unusual step in journalism of sending a telegram to President Roosevelt accompanying the article. The telegram became the lead of the *Tribune's* piece, excerpts of which follow:

HON. THEODORE ROOSEVELT.

Washington, D.C., Nov. 25,

The football season practically closed today with two dead on the field of battle. Today's fatalities bring the total of slain to nineteen, and the injured (record only being made of accidents out of the ordinary) to 137.

This year's record of deaths is more than double that of the yearly average for the last five years, the total for that period being forty-five.

A significant fact is that the teams playing an open game have escaped with less than their usual quota of accidents.

THE CHICAGO TRIBUNE.

The above telegram sent last night to the man to whom the safe and sane devotees of college sport are looking to lead the way out of the bloody shambles of football as played at present summarized to date the result of the gridiron battles of 1905.

The record is not yet complete. A few games will be played next Thursday and they will swell the list of maimed. . . .

Of those slaughtered to make a touchdown, eleven were high school players and ten of the killed were immature boys of 17 and under. Three hardened, seasoned, and presumably physically fit college men were slain. The others were amateurs.

Body blows, producing internal injuries, were responsible for four deaths, concussion of the brain claimed six victims, injuries to the spine resulted fatally in three cases, blood poisoning carried off two gridiron warriors, and other injures caused four deaths.

THOSE KILLED YESTERDAY

OSBORN, CARL, 18 years old, Marshall, Ind., killed in game of Judson high school vs. Bellmore high school; injured in tackle, rib piercing heart and killing him almost instantly.

MOORE WILLAM A., right half back of Union College; killed in game with New York University; fractured skull in bucking the line; died in hospital. . . .

The death of Moore may have far reaching consequences. He may be the sacrificial victim on the altar of "sport" whose blood will cry aloud with so much insistence that even the deafest of college authorities might listen, and listening, act.

When Chancellor MacCracken of New York University was informed of the tragedy he at once sent the following telegram to President Eliot of Harvard University:

President Charles W. Eliot, Harvard University, Cambridge, Mass.—May I not request, in favor of the tragedy on Ohio field today, that you will invite a meeting of university and college presidents to undertake the reform or abolition of football?

HENRY M. MACCRACKEN.

"I am inexpressibly pained and shocked to hear of Mr. Moore's death," said Chancellor MacCracken. "I will say that within the last thirty days I said to members of the university faculty that I have only waited for some of the older and large universities to lead, to favor either the abolition or the complete reform of football. . . .

"I have not felt it to be the duty of the New York University to take the lead in this matter. We have discouraged any attempt to play football on a great scale here, and have never allowed the desire to win affect our requirement of moderation."

In an attempt to get through the New York center Moore went at the line head first like a catapult. This play was his last. No one saw what Moore's head struck, but he dropped limply to one side of the scrimmage and the ball fell from his hands. All efforts to revive him failed. . . .

Although the accident temporarily delayed the game, as soon as the unconscious half back had been carried from the field he was practically forgotten and the game proceeded to the end.

• • •

Roosevelt re-interested himself in the issue. "I demand that football change its rules or be abolished," he said. "Brutality and foul play should receive the same summary punishment given to a man who cheats at cards! Change the game or foresake it." In December the chancellor of New York University, where the Union College player had been killed, called a conference of colleges to discuss whether to ban or reform football. The idea of a ban was narrowly defeated. At a second conference in January, the Inter-Collegiate Athletic Association was formed, and it met with Walter Camp's old Rules Committee, which had been directing college football, to draft rules to reduce the violence. The organization was the beginning of the National Collegiate Athletic Association, which today governs college athletics.

The length of football games was shortened by ten minutes, and two halves of thirty minutes each were established. Hurdling was outlawed. So was the wedge formation and the kicking of rolling balls. Definitions of foul play were expanded, to include players striking other players with their fists or elbows, kneeing, kicking, and striking ball carriers in the face with the heel of a hand.

Violence, and deaths, continued. After a particularly bad year in 1909, when, according to John Sayle Watterson in *College Football* (Baltimore: Johns Hopkins University Press, 2000), ten college players were killed, additional safeguards were adopted. The number of downs a team was

given to gain ten yards was increased from three to four. Forward passes, which had been limited to twenty yards, now could be of any distance, vastly opening up the game.

The game remained tough, as it does today. But death, injuries, and general mayhem in the sport were largely eliminated. College and later professional football entered, beginning in the 1920s, what many sports writers called a golden age.

The subsidization and commercialization continued—and was expanded.

SAY IT AIN'T SO: HUGH FULLERTON CHARGES THAT THE CHICAGO WHITE SOX THREW THE 1919 WORLD SERIES

With the end of World War I, baseball in 1919 started to regain its prewar popularity. Not that the players shared in the wealth, especially after the demise of the upstart Federal League, 1914–1916, which had briefly sent player salaries from $4,000 to $12,000. With the competition gone, owners cut the pay back to previous levels.

The pinch was particularly felt on a team like the Chicago White Sox, run by Charles A. Comiskey, whom Stephen Jay Gould, anthropologist and baseball fan, later called "the meanest skinflint in baseball." No matter that Comiskey was one of the few owners to have once played ball himself. Although the White Sox drew the largest crowds in the game that year, and won the American League pennant, the players' salaries were among the lowest. The total team payroll, which included such stars as Shoeless Joe Jackson, Buck Weaver, and Eddie Cicotte, was $85,000.

"It is a hard thing to know that another man is making money off of your labor, and has no intention of dealing fairly with you," wrote Bill James, a baseball historian. That may have been particularly true in a ragtime era, when gambling was common and a dozen years of rumors about players throwing games had been overlooked and hushed up by baseball's national commission.

A few days before the World Series started, the White Sox were three-to-one favorites to beat the National League's Cincinnati Reds in an experimentally elongated series. By the time the first game started, team officials, sportswriters, and gamblers—but not most of the public—had all heard the word: the fix was in.

Hugh Fullerton, columnist for the *Chicago Herald and Examiner*, among other papers, and a fervent fan of baseball in general and the White Sox in particular, did not want to believe the possibility. But he knew something was going on. A mid-series account from the *Herald and Examiner* on October 6, 1919:

Both the Reds and the White Sox hold the advantage in the struggle for the world's championship, if we listen to the managers. In spite of the fact that each says the idle day following the deluge of last night aided their chances, there was weeping, wailing and gnashing of teeth among the athletes because they lost the chance to cut in upon the receipts of the Sunday crowd, which probably would have broken all money records.

The Sox, their confidence unshaken, but their tempers and dispositions soured by defeat, declared that the day of rest will help restore morale and aid the numerically small pitching staff. The Reds are exultant because Reuther gained a day, and a day which, according to reports, was much needed.

The Sox are sore, because they have lost two games because Moran's men seem entirely surrounded by horseshoes. They will not admit that the Reds have a license ever to win a game from them, and they claim that they have played better ball. The Reds do not have to do any talking. They can point to the three to one count in the series.

It seems to me that baseball fans quit more quickly than any other sport followers. A lot of them believe now that the White Sox have quit, and that it is over except the playing of a couple

of more games. The Sox themselves do not think so, and if anyone has seen any signs of quitting on the part of the American Leaguers, they have better eyesight than I have.

It seems to me that the White Sox have played better, cleaner and more finished ball than have the Reds, but also they appear to have lacked to a remarkable degree the spirit and confidence of Moran's crew.

There are some who profess to believe that the White Sox are tired out from their hard fight for their own pennant. They have not shown a sign of weariness; in fact, have fielded as well as they ever did. In attack the Sox have hit the ball harder, but not so fortunately, and they have not followed up the breaks as the Reds have done. . . .

There is more ugly talk and more suspicion among the fans and among others in this series than there ever has been in any world's series. The rumors of crookedness, of fixed games and plots are thick. It is not necessary to dignify them by telling what they are but the sad part is that such suspicion of baseball is so widespread.

There are three different lies going the rounds equally ridiculous. The only answer to such stories is that if any one can evolve a way of making baseball crooked without being discovered in his second crooked move he probably could peddle his secret to some owners for a million. It cannot be done.

The only reason I dignify such stories by mentioning them is to show how generally suspicion has been cast upon the sport by the actions of the magnates in the last two years.

• • •

By the time the Sox went down, five games to three, Fullerton was a convert. Since the game could not be protected, he wrote, the series should be called off. "Yesterday's, in all probability, is the last game that will ever be played in any World Series. . . . Yesterday's game also means the disruption of the Chicago White Sox ball club. There are seven men on the team who will not be there when the gong sounds next spring." Then Fullerton went fishing in Michigan. Industry publications like *Baseball Magazine* and *The Sporting News* attacked him for sullying the national pastime.

When Fullerton returned, he was angered to realize that Comiskey and other owners were doing nothing to investigate the charges of a fix. He set out to force their hand. "With a sense of outrage," wrote Eliot Asinof in his definitive *Eight Men Out,* "he began a series of articles to jolt the executive world of baseball into action. He would expose, finally, what every decent baseball writer knew, but never had the courage to write." He would name names.

His Chicago editor, citing libel laws, refused to publish what he wrote. Finally, after the stories were toned down considerably, the New York *World* took a chance. Fullerton's first story ran on December 15, 1919, in the middle of the meetings of the National Baseball Commission, with the headline, "Is Big League Baseball Being Run for Gamblers, With Ballplayers in the Deal?"

Baseball's owners still tried to keep things quiet. But Fullerton kept up the pressure. Gradually, it became clear that games were also being fixed in the 1920 season. Illinois law-enforcement officials saw a chance for political gain, convened a grand jury, and called the suspect players to testify. The owners, realizing they needed to look as if they were taking the charges of corruption seriously, reorganized baseball, hiring federal Judge Kenesaw Mountain Landis as commissioner and giving him extraordinary powers to act in the best interests of the game.

On October 22, 1920, eight White Sox players were indicted on charges of conspiracy. At the trial, the following summer, all were acquitted. But while they were still celebrating—at a restaurant where, conveniently, the jurors were also dining—Landis issued a statement banning them from baseball for life. None of the players was reinstated. Baseball began an aggressive attack on gambling. And, seeking ways to win the fans back,

the owners took note of the popularity of the new New York Yankee Babe Ruth, and took moves to make the ball livelier and beef up the number of home runs.

Fullerton's coverage of the court proceedings included an account of a young boy asking Joe Jackson, "It ain't so Joe, is it?" Jackson insisted that exchange never happened, but Fullerton's version became one of the most quoted lines of American journalism.

THE BLACK AND COMMUNIST PRESS LEAD THE WAY TO INTEGRATION OF BASEBALL

To understand America, the social critic Jacques Barzun wrote, one must understand baseball. Certainly, on the matter of integration, baseball accurately reflected the rest of American life. Most of baseball was divided into two worlds: the more heralded, organized white teams and the shoestring black teams, who moved around the country, and into Latin America, playing anyone, including whites, who could meet a payroll. Although the quality of the play varied widely, by the 1920s and 1930s, black baseball had certifiable stars, including Satchel Paige, Josh Gibson, Judy Johnson, Buck Leonard, and Cool Papa Bell. They proved their talents by regularly defeating major league players in post-season exhibition games.

Officially, Major League Baseball insisted there was no bar to black players. Baseball said they just never materialized.

Pressure to desegregate baseball, to make it truly a *national* game, began to build in the 1930s and grew with the social upheaval, and dearth of top military-age players, that accompanied World War II. Partly this came in response to the success, and wide popularity, of Joe Louis in boxing and Jesse Owens in track. Partly it came because the American Communist Party took up the issue as a way to advance civil rights and gain attention; on opening day in 1945, party members picketed

Yankee Stadium with a banner reading, "If We Can Stop Bullets, Why Not Balls?" And partly the pressure came, and stayed, because of the aggressive stance of several young black sportswriters on popular black newspapers.

After eight years of pressing the issue, Nat Low, sports editor for the *Daily Worker,* the Communist Party newspaper, took encouragement from the passage of a fair-employment practices law in New York State.

"FEPC Heralds End of Baseball Jimcrow," by Nat Low. *The Daily Worker,* March 7, 1945.

The Ives-Quinn Anti-Discrimination Bill which was passed overwhelmingly in both the State Senate and Assembly heralds the end of Jimcrow in baseball—not only in New York State, to which the bill applies—but in all states and in all baseball leagues.

The final end of the Hitler-like ban on Negro players in our great National Pastime now is only a matter of time—and short time at that. Despite all the delaying efforts that may be employed by reactionary baseball magnates, the new bill guarantees that Negro ball players, who long ago proved their rights to be in the big leagues, will take their legitimate places alongside the Dixie Walkers, Mel Otts and Hank Borowys.

Thus the eight-year-old fight of untold thousands of baseball fans is on the verge of final and complete success. No amount of hesitation or procrastination can alter the fact.

Discrimination in employment because of race, creed or color is now unlawful in New York state and punishable by heavy fines.

And the law of our great state will be carried out, have no fear of that.

The last alibi of the anti-democratic elements in baseball has now been stripped from them and they will be forced to comply with the demands of the state and the millions of fans who make baseball possible.

The next steps will be taken by Negro ball players themselves who will undoubtedly apply formally for jobs with the three New York major league teams and many other clubs in the minor leagues.

These players must be taken to the various spring training camps, must be given thorough and impartial tryouts and must, after satisfying the managers, be signed to contracts for the 1945 season.

There can be no doubt at all—especially with the manpower situation being what it is this year—that these great Negro players who have won the acclaim of major leaguers and fans alike, are good enough for the big time.

The Josh Gibsons, Dave Barnhills, Satchel Paiges, Sammy Bankheads, Roy Campanellas and others are great by any method of comparison—but when played alongside the so-called major leaguers now in baseball uniform, they tower like titans.

Their appearance in the big leagues will be heard around the world. Our fighting men, who have been spilling their blood on battlefields thousands of miles from home, will be inspired in the knowledge that while they are winning the fight for democracy overseas we are winning it here at home.

And we can be doubly proud that it was our own state—New York—that showed the way.

• • •

Although some white sportswriters would occasionally weigh in about the color bar in baseball, others, including the influential *Sporting News,* vociferously supported the status quo. It was aggressive black sportswriters who pushed the issue. "I don't think I was an advocate necessarily, just an aggressive reporter," Sam Lacy of the Baltimore *Afro-American* said in 1999, when he was ninety-five. The leaders besides Lacy were Joe Bostic of the *People's Voice* and the *Amsterdam News,* Harlem-based weeklies, and Wendell Smith of the *Pittsburgh Courier,* who, like Lacy, was not a bad ballplayer himself. They kept up the pressure with their stories, with demonstrations they helped arrange, and with demands for big-league tryouts.

"Red Sox Consider Negroes," by Wendell Smith. *Pittsburgh Courier,* April 21, 1945.

BOSTON—Here Monday on the silken turf of historic Fenway Park . . . deep in the heart of staid old Boston . . . another epochal chapter in the campaign to end racial discrimination in the major leagues was written when the Boston Red Sox gave three outstanding Negro ball players a try-out.

The three players were former Lieutenant Jackie Robinson, brilliant young Kansas City Monarchs' shortstop and former all-around star at UCLA; Sammy Jethro, outfielder of the the Cleveland Buckeyes and 1944 batting champion of the Negro American League, and Marvin Williams, smooth fielding and dangerous hitting second baseman of the Philadelphia Stars.

Sponsored by *The Pittsburgh Courier,* who paid their expenses to this tradition-steeped outpost of American liberty and freedom, the three players arrived at Fenway Park at approximately 10:30 Monday morning with Wendell Smith, *Courier* sports editor, and Boston's militant, uncompromising Councilman Isadore Muchnick.

They were greeted by Joe Cronin, Red Sox pilot, and General Manager Eddie Collins, who, after being introduced to the three players, instructed them to report to the club house and prepare for a workout. Robinson, Jethro and Williams were housed in the "visitors dressing room" and granted every courtesy by Johnny Orlando, assistant trainer of the Sox.

The players were asked if they had uniforms. Robinson had brought one from the Kansas City Monarchs, for whom he plays this year, and Jethro had his Cleveland Buckeyes' outfit with him, with the exception of the pants. Williams did not have a uniform. Assistant Trainer Orlando

gave Williams a complete Boston Red Sox uniform and Jethro a Red Sox shirt.

After they had dressed, they went to the field where seven white candidates were already in action under the supervision of Coach Hughey Duffy. The three Negro players warmed up by jogging around the field and then Duffy called for the batting cage.

At this stage of the try-out, Manager Joe Cronin came down from the Sox offices and sat beside the writer. He explained that the regulars would not appear because they were scheduled to leave for New York at one o'clock, where they were to open the season Tuesday against the New York Yankees.

"Which one of these players is Robinson," Cronin asked enthusiastically. "I saw him play football for UCLA and he was great."

I pointed to Robinson and told him that the ex-UCLA grid great was just as good a baseball player as he was a gridder.

Coach Duffy ordered batting practice and after one of the white aspirants had hit, Robinson stepped to the plate. The first pitch from an impressive, ambitious recruit was wide, but the second was "in there" and Jackie whaled it against the centerfield bleachers, 374 feet away. It was a tremendous clout and Cronin seemed to be especially impressed. Robinson proceeded to sock five more pitches with gusto and thereby made a good first impression.

Williams followed Robinson and while he did not "tear down the fence," he looked good enough for Cronin to comment: "They look like ball players all right."

Jethro followed Williams. He was not as impressive as his two sun-tanned predecessors, but he held his own against the slants of the hurling recruit, who by this time was perspiring freely and was obviously putting everything he had on the ball.

While Robinson, Jethro and Williams were batting, Coach Duffy stood at the edge of the cage checking them with a fine tooth comb. He watched every move, every swing. He told Jethro to loosen up a bit, but never said anything to Robinson or Williams. After batting practice, Coach Duffy called for infield practice and put Robinson at shortstop and Williams at second. He then proceeded to give the infielders a thorough workout. He hit every kind of ball possible—to the right, to left, hot, sizzling grounders and slow rollers to each man. Robinson and Williams fielded flawlessly. They took everything he hit in stride. He called for double play execution and Robinson and Williams, although they had never played together, teamed up perfectly. The white infield candidates playing first and third and a catcher did well, but were out-classed by the sepia players from Kansas City and Philadelphia.

Sitting beside me in the stands, Joe Cronin said: "Robinson and Williams work well together. They can field and have baseball sense. They really look good out there."

I asked him if they were good enough for the majors, or if it would be possible to farm them out.

"They're good all right," he said. "I'd have to see them in a real game before I could determine if they were good enough for the big leagues. As for the minors, I think we will run into a problem there. Most of our camps are in the South and you know how things operate down there. The only team we have in the North is Scranton (Pa.) and we only have a working agreement with that club. We do not own it. We could send them to Scranton but that club reserves the right to accept or reject any player we send there. We have no official strings on the Scranton setup."

While Robinson and Williams were going through their infield chores, Coach Larry Woodall was hitting to Jethro and three white candidates in the outfield. Jethro was by far superior to the other aspirants. Fast and shifty, he caught everything hit in his direction. He went back and got balls, he came forward and got them and was equally as good going to his right or left.

At approximately 12 o'clock, Coach Duffy called it quits. He gave the candidates information blanks to fill out. On these blanks they wrote their entire baseball history. There was only one line which they did not fill out. The particular line stated: "Recommended by . . ."

And on that line, Coach Larry Woodall wrote, "Wendell Smith, sports editor, *The Pittsburgh Courier.*"

After the workout, the three players returned to the dressing room, where they took showers and dressed. While they were dressing, Coach Woodall, whose accent indicated that he was a Southerner, came into the room and asked if any of the three were signed with any club for the season of 1945.

Robinson and Jethro said they had not signed a contract with any team, while Williams said he had a verbal contract with the Philadelphia Stars of the Negro National League.

As the players were sauntering off the field, tired and wary from the grind Coach Duffy had put them through, Manager Cronin said he would have to hurry to the station.

"I've stayed here too long now," he said, "and if I don't hurry I'll miss that one o'clock train."

I held him long enough to ask if he would give me a statement as to the ability of the men he had seen on the field for the past hour and a half.

"You can say," Cronin said, "that they looked good to me, especially Robinson and Williams. However, I can't say we will sign them. I'd like to see them in a game before going that far."

I thanked him and Eddie Collins for granting the men a try-out and then left to catch the train to New York.

I immediately cornered Coach Duffy . . . and then asked him his opinion of the Negro candidates.

"There is no doubt about it," said the energetic seventy-year-old veteran, "that they are ball players. They looked good to me."

So . . . that is the story of the three Negro players who received try-outs here Monday under the critical eyes of Manager Joe Cronin, General Manager Eddie Collins and Coaches Duffy and Woodall.

They came here last Wednesday. They were granted a try-out Monday morning . . . and they made an indelible impression.

Will they be signed by the Boston Red Sox and become the first Negroes to ever play in the major leagues? That is one question I cannot answer.

But I'm pulling for them as I never pulled for anyone in my life.

• • •

On October 23, 1945, Branch Rickey Jr. announced that he had signed Jackie Robinson to play for the Montreal Royals of the International League, the top Dodger farm team. Smith and Bostic made sure to be in the press box on opening day, April 1946, when major league baseball was officially integrated.

Notwithstanding the 1945 tryout arranged by Smith, the Boston Red Sox were the last all-white baseball team. The Red Sox did not play a black until 1959, the infielder Pumpsie Green. Robinson had retired two years before.

THE NEW YORK *HERALD TRIBUNE* STOPS BASEBALL PLAYERS' STRIKE OVER JACKIE ROBINSON

In 1946, Jackie Robinson played for the Dodgers's top farm team, the Montreal Royals, broke racial barriers, and helped the team win the minor-league championship. In 1947, he was called up to the Brooklyn Dodgers. The *Boston Chronicle*, a black newspaper, headlined: "Triumph of Whole Race Seen in Jackie's Debut in Major League Ball." But Robinson faced a horrendous ordeal. He received death threats, and some major league players, including some on the Dodgers, vowed they would not play with a black man. Many of these players were southerners who had

never dealt with black people on terms near equality.

One of the most southern teams at the time was the St. Louis Cardinals, who arrived in early May, about three weeks into the season, to play the Dodgers at Ebbets Field. The day after the series ended, Stanley Woodward, esteemed sports editor of the New York *Herald Tribune*, had an exclusive story.

"National League Averts Strike of Cardinals Against Robinson's Presence in Baseball," by Stanley Woodward. New York *Herald Tribune*, May 9, 1947.

A National League players' strike, instigated by some of the St. Louis Cardinals against the presence in the league of Jackie Robinson, Brooklyn's Negro first baseman, has been averted temporarily and perhaps permanently quashed. In recent days Ford Frick, president of the National League, and Sam Breadon, president of the St. Louis club, have been conferring with St. Louis players in the Hotel New Yorker. Mr. Breadon flew East when he heard of the projected strike. The story that he came to consult with Eddie Dyer, manager, about the lowly state of the St. Louis club was fictitious. He came on a much more serious errand.

A strike plan, formulated by certain St. Louis players, was instigated by a member of the Brooklyn Dodgers who has since recanted. The original plan was for a St. Louis club strike on the occasion of the first game in Brooklyn, May 6, in other words last Tuesday. Subsequently the St. Louis players conceived the idea of a general strike within the National League on a certain date. That is what Frick and Breadon have been combatting in the last few days.

It is understood that Frick addressed the players, in effect, as follows:

If you do this you will be suspended from the league. You will find that the friends you think you have in the press box will not support you, that you will be outcasts. I do not care if half the league strikes. Those who do it will encounter quick retribution. All will be suspended and I don't care if it wrecks the National League for five years. This is the United States of America and one citizen has as much right to play as another.

The National League will go down the line with Robinson whatever the consequences. You will find if you go through with your intention that you have been guilty of complete madness.

Several anticipatory protests against the transfer of Robinson to the Brooklyn club were forthcoming during spring training when he was still a member of the Montreal Royals, Brooklyn farm. Prejudice has been subsequently curbed except on on occasion when Ben Chapman, manager of the Phillies, undertook to ride Robinson from the bench in a particularly vicious manner.

It is understood that Frick took this matter up with the Philadelphia management and that Chapman has been advised to keep his bench comments above the belt.

It is understood that the players involved—and the recalcitrants are not all Cardinals—will say, if they decide to carry out their strike, that their object is to gain the right to have a say on who shall be eligible to play in the major leagues. As far as is known, the move so far is confined entirely to the National League. Ringleaders apparently have not solicited the cooperation of American League players.

In view of this fact it is understood that Frick will not call the matter to the attention of Happy Chandler, the commissioner. So far, it is believed, Frick has operated with the sole aid of Breadon. Other National League club owners apparently know nothing about it.

The New York *Herald Tribune* prints this story in part as a public service. It is factual and thoroughly substantiated. The St. Louis players in-

volved unquestionably will deny it. We doubt, however, that Frick or Breadon will go that far. A return of "No comment" from either or both will serve as confirmation. On our own authority we can say that both of them were present at long conferences with the ringleaders and that both probably now feel that the overt act has been averted.

It is not generally known that other less serious difficulties have attended the elevation of Robinson to the major leagues. Through it all, the Brooklyn first baseman, whose intelligence and degree of education are far beyond that of the average ball player, has behaved himself in an exemplary manner.

It is generally believed by baseball men that he has enough ability to play on any club in the majors. This ability has asserted itself in spite of the fact that he hasn't had anything resembling a fair chance. He has been so burdened with letters and telegrams from well-wishers and villifiers and efforts to exploit him that he has had no chance to concentrate.

It is almost impossible to elicit comments about Robinson's presence in the National League from any one connected with baseball. Neither club owners nor players have anything to say for publication. This leads to the conclusion that the caginess of both parties, plus natural cupidity which warns against loss of salaries or a gate attraction, will keep the reactionary element under cover.

When Robinson joined the Montreal club last year, there was resentment among some Royal players. There was also a fear on the part of league officials that trouble would be forthcoming when the Royals played in Baltimore. Both the resentment and the fear were dissipated in three months. Robinson behaved like a gentleman and was cheered as wholeheartedly in Baltimore as anywhere else. Incidentally, Baltimore had its biggest attendance in 1946 and the incidence of Negroes in the crowd was not out of proportion.

Since Robinson has played with Brooklyn many difficulties have loomed, sometimes forbiddingly, but all have been circumvented. This was in part due to the sportsmanship of the fans and in part to the intelligence and planning of the Brooklyn management.

It is understood that St. Louis players recently have been talking about staging the strike on the day that Brooklyn plays its first game in St. Louis. Publicity probably will render the move abortive.

• • •

As Woodward had predicted, Cardinal players denied that any such strike plan was afoot, and how serious the talk was remains hard to determine. Woodward defended the story in his column the next day, although he acknowledged that he had been mistaken in saying that Frick had personally talked to the Cardinal players; instead, Woodward said, Frick had given his message to Breadon, the Cardinal owner, to pass along. The exact wording of the message was clearly Woodward's, not Frick's, though Frick should have been grateful to have been given such eloquent lines, and they have often been attributed to him.

Jules Tygiel, who investigated the matter for his book, *Baseball's Great Experiment,* in 1983, concluded "the strike saga amounts to somewhat more than the denials of the players would indicate, but quite a bit less than Woodward's allegations implied." Still, Tygiel said, the story was a significant turning point in Robinson's saga. It put the baseball officialdom, which had a history of laxness when it came to supporting the chances of black players, squarely on the side of Robinson. And the negative reaction among fans and the press to the idea of a strike could not help but discourage any anti-Robinson players who thought public opinion was on their side.

No strike occurred. Robinson finished the season hitting .297 and was named Rookie of the Year. The Dodgers won the National League pennant by five games. St. Louis finished second.

"CAGE STAR'S STORY OF 'FIX'": THE NEW YORK *JOURNAL-AMERICAN* CRACKS A BASKETBALL BETTING SCANDAL AND SHOCKS AMERICAN SPORTS

Modern college basketball was pretty much invented in New York City in the 1920s and 1930s. City College, Long Island University, New York University, Columbia, Fordham—all the schools were attracted to a sport that was relatively cheap and brought the schools prestige and profits. Double- and tripleheaders in Madison Square Garden—the first was played in 1931 at the instigation of Mayor Jimmy Walker to raise money for the unemployed—were wildly successful. Basketball spread throughout the country.

An invention out of Chicago about a decade later was soon to become linked with the sport. This was the point spread, the idea of Charles McNeil, a math teacher turned bookmaker. McNeil rated each team and estimated the number of points by which the favored team would win. If a team won by less than the spread, the bet on the opponent was the bet that won. "It was in this gray area that college players and professional gamblers found common ground," wrote Randy Roberts and James S. Olson in *Winning Is the Only Thing* (Baltimore: Johns Hopkins University Press, 1989). Rumors about point-shaving became common at college games throughout the 1940s and into the 1950s.

In 1951, a Manhattan College player, a World War II veteran attending school on the GI Bill, was approached by a former teammate and asked to shave points. Everybody is doing it, the player was told. He decided not to do it and went to his coach, who went to the police.

Max Kase, sports editor of the *Journal-American,* had had reporters working on the point-shaving scandals for months. He approached District Attorney Frank S. Hogan with information, and Hogan, a man always interested in publicity, cut a deal that Kase would get an exclusive when the story broke.

"Cage Star's Story of 'Fix.' " New York *Journal-American,* January 18, 1951.

The hero of the Manhattan College basketball "fix" scandal told his own story for the first time today.

Junius Kellogg, 23, 6-foot 8-inch Negro center of the Manhattan team, told it simply and clearly, with no phony striving for the dramatic, no theatrical display of outrage.

The story of how he was offered $1,000 by Henry E. "Hank" Poppe, last season's co-captain, to throw Tuesday night's game at Madison Square Garden with DePaul University was told in the Manhattan College Dean's office in Alumni Hall.

From here on Kellogg is speaking . . .

It started last Wednesday.

I was practicing in the gym on the campus here and I saw Poppe. He gave me a big "hello." It was the first time he ever said anything to me.

After gym, I went to my room in Chrysestom Hall. I had a friend in. We were talking when Poppe walked in. He stuck around.

As soon as my friend left, Poppe said to me, "How do you think you'll do against DePaul?"

I said:

"I think we'll win. I always think we'll win."

Poppe said:

"Suppose you lose by six points?"

I said:

"What do you mean? I think we'll win."

He said:

"Well, they have a better club. They are four points favored."

Then, he said:

"Nobody will pay any attention if you lose by 10 points."

There was a long silence.

Then Poppe said:

"Are you a betting man?"

I said:

"You mean you want to bet with me?"

He said:

"No. Do you want to pick up something big, like a grand, some real dough? DePaul is going to win. Nobody will know the difference."

I was shocked. Poppe was our co-captain last year. I told him: "Get out of this room."

I went over to Smith Auditorium to do some studying. He followed me there.

He bent over my shoulder while I was reading, and he whispered in my ear:

"It's a grand. Think about it."

"It's still 'No,' " I told him.

He said:

"I'll call you Sunday."

I couldn't sleep all that night. I didn't know what to do. I figured I'd let it drop. For one thing, Poppe was a Manhattan man and this would involve the college. I didn't want to do that.

I stayed awake. I thought of other cases about athletes who had been offered bribes and didn't report them, and were punished because they kept silent. The more I thought about the deal the less I liked it.

So the next day [Thursday] about 4:30 P.M. I told coach "Kenneth" Norton.

[Norton called the police, who asked Kellogg to pretend to go along with Poppe. Poppe called Kellogg in his dorm on Sunday night.]

Poppe said:

"Did you think about it?"

I said:

"Yes, I thought about it and I'm for it. But I don't know what to do. You'll have to explain it to me."

He said:

"Well, I'll be over in 15 minutes. Meet me in the parking lot."

For the first time I was nervous. It was raining hard and I knew there were police all around the lot.

A chartreuse-colored 1950 Ford pulled up. I got in.

We drove to the Green Leaf Bar and Grill (at 242d st. and Broadway). We stood at the bar and had a beer.

I said to him:

"What about my cut? Is it going to be split?"

He said:

"No, it's all yours. How do you want it—in 50's, 20's, 10's—before or after the game?"

I told him, acting on instructions:

"Make it after."

Poppe said:

"Last year Byrnes and I pulled this. (He was speaking of John A. Byrnes, also a co-captain of the Manhattan team last season and now a co-defendant.). . . .

Poppe said:

"You know, Kellogg, this rah-rah stuff doesn't get you anywhere. This college stuff is a lot of hooey. Look at me. I've got a new car. My wife and baby are doing okay. I got plenty in the bank, and plenty of bonds. You can't get anything out of just playing ball. Other fellows are doing it."

I said:

"What fellows? Who are they?"

He said:

"Aw, forget it."

I said:

"How do I drop the game?"

He said:

"Try to do most of the shooting. Occasionally miss a shot by hooking the ball over the basket. Don't pass too much and after you get rebounds off the board don't pass it so fast. That might save two points. Fake it. Hold it, then miss it.

"If the team's going bad, you look bad right along with them. If the other team is going good, let them look good. Don't block too much. Whatever you do, don't stink up the joint."

We made a date to meet Tuesday night before the game at the Belvedere Hotel (across from Madison Square Garden). He was going to tell me what the odds were, and how much to drop the game by.

I got my first big scare when we returned to the parking lot. Coach Norton's car was there.

Poppe said:

"Is Norton here?"

I said:

"No, no. He isn't anywhere around."

Poppe didn't show up at the Belvedere. I was taking practice shots in the Garden before the people came in Tuesday night when I heard a voice say, "Put it in there, fellow."

I looked around. It was Poppe. He was sitting on a bench.

I asked him:

"Am I still in?"

He said:

"Yes, it's ten points. Make sure you lose by more. I'll see you at Gilhuly's after the game."

• • •

This is the end of Kellogg's story. After Manhattan won the game in an upset victory, Poppe did not appear at Gilhuly's. He was trailed by detectives and arrested in his home.

Suspicions turned to other teams. District Attorney Hogan made other arrests—in all, thirty-three players from seven schools, including City College, under famed coach Nat Holman, were accused of fixing forty-nine games. More than a dozen gamblers were charged, and several were convicted and received prison sentences. More charges easily could have been filed; Hogan, a Catholic, largely stayed away from investigating the Catholic schools.

The public saw the scandal as a sign that the younger generation was going to hell in a handbasket and as proof that cities bred corruption. Midwestern coaches were vocal in saying such a situation could never happen on their teams, clean living being in the air where they lived, but within months players from Bradley University, in Peoria, Illinois, the University of Toledo, in Toledo, Ohio, and from the storied University of Kentucky team of Adolph Rupp also confessed to point shaving.

Few of the players ever went to jail. But the National Basketball Association didn't want them, and those who wanted to keep on playing ended up on semipro teams. Several schools de-emphasized sports or refused to play in Madison Square Garden. New York State increased the penalty for bribing athletes from one to five years to two to ten years. Some newspapers, including the New York *Post,* said they would stop printing point spreads. For a time, news of the game-rigging caused betting on college basketball to drop. Still, Roberts and Olson found, "after all of the righteous indignation subsided, very little changed." In 1961, District Attorney Hogan announced another point-shaving scandal, this one involving players at twenty-two colleges around the country.

JIM BOUTON WRITES HONESTLY ABOUT BASEBALL AND CHANGES SPORTS AND SPORTS WRITING

Jim Bouton was not a star baseball player, but a marginal relief pitcher who kicked around and ended up on the 1969 Seattle Pilots expansion team. But he was a very funny—and irreverent—man, who kept a fan's view of the game he played. When a friend, Leonard Schechter, a sportswriter turned editor, asked him to keep a diary of a season, Bouton readily agreed, and, he said, for seven months talked into a tape recorder and scrawled notes on ticket stubs, popcorn boxes, hotel stationery, and scorecards.

The two did not think much would come of the project, given that sports books were rarely big sellers and Bouton was hardly a big name. The first printing was set for 5,000 copies. In June 1970, an excerpt appeared in *Look* magazine:

"My Love/Hate Affair with Baseball," by Jim Bouton (edited by Leonard Schechter). *Look,* **June 2, 1970.**

NOVEMBER 15, 1968

I signed a contract today to play for the new expansion-born Seattle Pilots at a salary of $22,000. It was a letdown because there was no bargaining. In the old days, before I became a 30-year-old veteran trying to hold on with a knuckleball, a freaky pitch that is almost as difficult to throw as it is to catch, signing a contract was a yearly adventure.

The biggest adventure came in the spring of 1964, after I'd won twenty-one games for the New York Yankees with an overpowering fast ball. I'd taken down a big $10,500 for that bit of work and was determined to get $20,000. The man I dealt with was Ralph Houk, the manager, who was then in his brief time as general manager. He offered me $15,500 . . .

This was around January 15. I didn't hear from Houk again until two weeks before spring training, when he came up another thousand. This was definitely final.

I said it wasn't final for me, I wanted $20,000.

"You can't make twenty," Houk said. "We never double contracts. It's a rule."

It's a rule he made up right there, I'd bet. Once again, I didn't sign.

The day before training began, Houk offered me $18,500. I told him I might have considered signing for that, except the Yankees had forced me to work for so little the year before that it had become a matter of principle. The Yankees had their rules, I had my principles. . . .

On March 8, he called me and said he was going to deduct $100 a day from his offer for every day I held out beyond March 10. It amounted to a fine for not signing. "Oh, no, it's not a fine," Houk said. "I don't believe in fining people."

Frantic, I called Joe Cronin, president of the American League. Could Houk legally fine me that way? Cronin said, "Walk around the block, then go back in and talk some more." With that encouragement, I chickened out. I signed. . . .

FEBRUARY 28

Reported to the Seattle Pilots' spring camp today in Tempe, Ariz. As soon as I got to the park, I went right over to General Manager Marvin Milkes' office, and we shook hands and he asked me if I had a nice flight. He also said:

"There's been a lot of things said about the players' strike, and I know you've said some things about it, but we're going to forget all that and start fresh. We have a new team, and everybody starts with a clean slate. I'm giving some people a new opportunity. I've got a man in the organization who is a former alcoholic. I've even got a moral degenerate that I know of. But we're going to let bygones by bygones."

As I left, I wondered where, on a scale of one to ten, a guy who talks a lot falls between a former alcoholic and a moral degenerate. . . .

MARCH 5

Mickey Mantle announced his retirement the other day, and I got to thinking about the mixed feelings I've always had about him. On the one hand, I really liked his sense of humor and his boyishness, the way he'd spend all that time in the clubhouse making up involved games of chance, and the pools he got up on golf matches and the Derby and things like that. . . .

On the other hand, there were all those times he'd push little kids aside when they wanted his autograph, and the times when he was snotty to reporters, just about making them crawl and beg for a minute of his time. I've seen him slam a bus window on kids trying to get his autograph. . . .

Like everybody else on the club, I ached with Mantle when he had one of his numerous and extremely painful injuries. I often wondered, though, if he might have healed quicker if he'd been sleeping more and loosening up with the boys at the bar less. I guess we'll never know. . . .

MARCH 6

I better explain about beaver shooting. A beaver shooter is, at bottom, a Peeping Tom. Beaver shooting can be anything from peering over the top of the dugout to look up dresses, to hanging from the fire escape on the 20th floor of some hotel to look into a window. I've seen guys chin themselves on transoms, drill holes in doors, even shove a mirror under a door.

Now, some people might look down on this sort of activity. But in baseball, if you shoot a particularly good beaver, you are a highly respected person, a folk hero of sorts. . . .

MARCH 27

Gary Bell is a funny man and, along with Tommy Davis is emerging as one of the leaders of the club. He's got an odd way of talking. Instead of saying, "Boy, that's funny," he'll wrinkle up his face and say, "How funny is that?"

Or he'll say, "How fabulous are greenies?" The answer is "very." Greenies are pep pills—dextroamphetamine sulfate—and a lot of ballplayers couldn't function without them. They need one just to get their hearts to start beating. I've taken greenies, but the trouble with them is that they make you feel so great that you think you're smoking the ball even when you're not. The result is that you get gay, throw it down the middle and get clobbered. . . .

JUNE 15

People are always asking me if it's true about stewardesses. The answer is yes. You don't have to go out hunting for a stew. They stay in the same hotels we do. Open your door, and you're liable to be invited to a party down the hall. They're on the road, same as we are, and probably just as lonely. Ballplayers are young, reasonably attractive and have more money than most men their age. Besides, baseball players often marry stews, and the stews know it. . . . A stew can come under the heading of class stuff, in comparison with some of the other creatures, who are camp followers called Baseball Annies. . . .

JULY 18

When I came in from the bullpen after we beat Minnesota a doubleheader, Joe Schultz, the manager, was patting everybody on the back, saying, "Attaway to go," and "Nice job." When he got to me, I said, "Joe, I had it out there tonight in the bullpen."

"You did?" Joe said.

"Yup. Great knuckleball. Hellacious."

"Did you throw too much?"

"Hell no."

"Good. You're starting tomorrow night. Feel up to it?" . . .

"Hell yes." Well, what do you know? It's put-up-or-shut-up time for Jim Bouton. . . .

Look at it this way: In a couple of days, two men are going to land on the moon. How the hell can I be nervous starting a baseball game?

•   •   •

"The baseball establishment went crazy," Bouton said years later. Bowie Kuhn, the baseball commissioner, reprimanded Bouton and said he had done the game "a grave disservice." Many of the players mentioned were also upset, perhaps Mickey Mantle foremost. And sportswriters of the time, many of whom had seen the same things as Bouton had, but who had never written about them, fearful of breaking the cozy alliance between players and reporters, were likewise outraged. They called Bouton, for starters, a turncoat, traitor, Judas, and a social leper. In the thirtieth anniversary edition of his book, *Ball Four*, in 2000, Bouton said that some players and baseball officials had still not forgiven him. It was not until 1998, after an open letter from his son appeared in the *New York Times*, that Bouton was invited to the Yankees' Old-Timers' Day game.

The fans reacted differently. The book sold 500,000 in hardcover, 5 million in paperback.

Ball Four opened the way for other tell-all, insider sports books, and made telling all almost a requirement. Social commentators like a *Christian Century* reviewer found that to the good, and praised the book's "contribution to the deidolizing of the American Way of Life." Bouton said, "It was no longer possible to sell the milk and cookies image" of sports.

Although much of the uproar focused on the off-field behavior of the players, team owners were particularly angered over Bouton's revelations of how hard it was to make a living in baseball and how arbitrarily owners dealt with players who could not move around under the game's reserve clause. Bouton thinks it is no coincidence that, after half a century of fighting the system, players won their free agency shortly after *Ball Four* was published. Marvin Miller, the players' union leader, called Bouton to testify in the hearing that ended up breaking the owners' power over the players.

Bouton went on to become a sportscaster, minor-league player, inventor of Big League Chew bubblegum, and motivational speaker.

ST. PAUL PIONEER PRESS REVEALS ACADEMIC CHEATING IN U-MINNESOTA BASKETBALL PROGRAM

In March 1999, fans of the University of Minnesota Gophers men's basketball were preparing to watch their team in the National Collegiate Athletic Association tournament, an occasional appearance for the Big Ten school. The Gophers flew to Seattle, site of its first-round game, on Sunday, March 7. The first game, against small but scrappy Gonzaga University, was scheduled for Thursday. Minnesota, which had won the Big Ten tournament, was feeling optimistic. Fans were setting up office pools, planning game parties, scouring for tickets, and indulging in the typical seasonal madness.

Then they picked up the March 10 edition of the *St. Paul Pioneer Press.*

"U Basketball Program Accused of Academic Fraud," by George Dohrmann. *St. Paul Pioneer Press,* March 10, 1999.

At least 20 men's basketball players at the University of Minnesota had research papers, take-home exams or other course work done for them during a five-year period, according to a former office manager in the academic counseling unit who said she did the work.

Four former players, Courtney James, Russ Archambault, Kevin Loge and Darrell Whaley, confirmed that work was prepared for them in possible violation of the student code of conduct and NCAA regulations. Another former player, Travor Winter, said he was aware of the practice.

James, Archambault and the office manager, Jan Gangelhoff, said knowledge of the academic fraud was widespread.

"These are serious allegations," University of Minnesota President Mark Yudof said Tuesday. "We've called in legal counsel. I want to look into this promptly. But they are just allegations at this point."

Gangelhoff, 50, said that from 1993 to 1998 she estimates she did more than 400 pieces of course work for players, including some starters on the 1996–97 Final Four team.

"They bring in these high-risk kids, and they know that everything they did in high school was done for them," Gangelhoff said. "It's got to stop somewhere."

Gangelhoff said she "struggled for a long time" whether to disclose the allegations. When asked to prove them, Gangelhoff provided the Pioneer Press with computer files containing more than 225 examples of course work for 19 players, dating to 1994, that she says she wrote and players turned in. Gangelhoff said she kept only about half her files.

Gangelhoff also provided printed copies of five pieces of course work that she said had been turned in by students. Some of the papers had grades and instructor's comments written on them. All five pieces also appeared in Gangelhoff's computer files.

Elayne Donahue, the retired head of the academic counseling unit, said she was unaware of the fraud but warned athletic department administrators that the office manager was tutoring players in violation of department policy and was ignored.

Coach Clem Haskins, interviewed briefly at his hotel in Seattle where the Gophers play Gonzaga in the first round of the NCAA tournament on Thursday, said the allegations were "news to me."

"I've been here 13 years, don't you know me, what I stand for as a man, as a person? I haven't changed," Haskins said. "All I'm trying to do is win a game. All I'm worrying about is beating Gonzaga. It's all I'm concentrating on. All I'll say is I will talk when the tournament is over."

Haskins referred all further comment to McKinley Boston, the vice president of student development and athletics, who questioned the credibility of Gangelhoff's allegations.

"Some of her current allegations seem to be inconsistent with statements she made in the past," he said. "We've had similar allegations made by others (about Gangelhoff), but this is new stuff."

Two former players denied Gangelhoff's allegation that she did work for them. Jermaine Stanford and Ryan Wolf said they completed all their own assignments. Three former players, Micah Watkins, Voshon Lenard and Hosea Crittenden, refused comment. Bobby Jackson said he and Gangelhoff did the work on the papers, with Gangelhoff typing them.

Gangelhoff said she did work for four players on this year's team: Kevin Clark, Miles Tarver, Antoine Broxsie and Jason Stanford. Clark and Tarver refused comment at their Seattle hotel Thursday night. Broxsie and Stanford were not made available for comment by school officials.

Normally, under the team's media policy, all inquiries for player interviews must be directed through school officials.

Five other former players could not be reached for comment.

When asked how he knew players were getting papers done, Winter, who graduated with a degree in business, attended the Carlson School of Management and now plays for the Timberwolves, said it was "common knowledge. It was just one of those things. It was unfortunate.

"If you know your teammate's getting help, if you know that somebody's helping with papers, you just (have the attitude that) 'I don't want to get involved in it.' It's like if you have a friend that's a convicted felon. You don't go around telling everybody he's a convicted felon. You just kind of let it go. It's his life. It's his choices. It's not me."

The *Pioneer Press* investigation also found these allegations:

• Gangelhoff said she was caught doing a take-home exam with Loge in November 1996 but was allowed to continue to work with players. Loge, who left the program because he wanted to play for a smaller school, confirmed the incident.

• Gangelhoff and two players, Archambault and James, said an assistant coach drove the players to Gangelhoff's Minneapolis home for tutoring sessions, a possible violation of NCAA rules. Archambault was dismissed from the team in February 1998 for rules violations, and James chose to turn pro instead of serving a season-long suspension after being convicted of fifth-degree assault in August 1997.

• Gangelhoff said she often had different players turn in the same paper for different classes, or she used excerpts from one paper in another. An analysis of the documents provided to the *Pioneer Press* revealed seven instances of duplication, including one paper that Gangelhoff said was turned in by three different players for three different classes.

• Donahue, the academic counseling chief, denied a request to allow Gangelhoff to tutor Broxsie last spring after she had been approved to tutor him during the winter quarter. But Gangelhoff said that Haskins paid her $3,000 in cash to continue tutoring the player.

"Clem Haskins absolutely denies any payment to Jan Gangelhoff for this purpose, or any other," Yudof said. "I think the world of Clem Haskins." . . .

Gangelhoff said she never was asked by a member of the coaching staff to do course work for players but said she considered it compensation when she was taken on trips to two road games, including accompanying the team when it played at the Big Island Invitational in Hawaii in the 1995–96 season. "Why else do you think I got to go to some of the places I did?" said Gangelhoff, who said she also attended team banquets and parties for the selection of the NCAA tournament field.

Boston said he was unaware Gangelhoff had gone to Hawaii.

"That's a new one on me," he said. "You will have to ask Haskins why he invited her along."

A request Monday to interview athletic director Mark Dienhart; Alonzo Newby, the team's academic counselor; and Chris Schoemann, the school's NCAA compliance director, was ignored by the school's sports information staff. And phone messages left for Newby and Schoemann were not returned. . . .

Boston said the school has self-reported one potential NCAA violation involving Gangelhoff.

On Oct. 26, Dienhart sent Gangelhoff a letter disassociating her from the program even though she had left the school the previous summer.

In the letter, obtained by the *Pioneer Press*, Dienhart wrote that the school had "recently reviewed activities in the men's basketball academic counseling unit." It said the action against her had been "reviewed and approved" by the NCAA.

Gangelhoff said after she received the letter, "I came to the conclusion that something has to change" and she decided to make the allegations public.

An NCAA official denied comment about the letter. . . .

Gangelhoff said when she left the university she never intended to reveal that she did course work for players. But the letter of disassociation angered her, she says, because she never was asked to give her side of the story.

"You look at other programs that are successful that have strong academics, and why can't [Minnesota] have that?" she said. "What are we

doing wrong that we can't get these kids to learn? . . . Something has to change or (Minnesota) will continue to bring kids in and then throw them away."

Gangelhoff said she did the course work to help academically at-risk athletes she thought were unprepared for college. Academic services' policy forbids front-office personnel from working with student-athletes. But Gangelhoff, an American Indian, said she felt a particular bond with African-American student-athletes.

"The big thing was that they trusted me. I was like a mother figure to them," Gangelhoff said. "My sisters and I, we treated them like family. We had dinners for them. We exchanged Christmas and birthday presents. And I always praised them."

James and Archambault said members of the coaching staff were aware that Gangelhoff was doing course work for players.

"The coaches knew. Everybody (in the basketball program) knew," Archambault said. "We used to make jokes about it. . . . I would go over there some night and get like four papers done. The coaches would be laughing about it."

James said, "Everybody knew we were going to see Jan."

Although Archambault said Haskins was aware of the practice, Winter said the coach may not have known.

"Clem is the basketball coach," Winter said. "When it comes to academics, there are coaches he puts in charge. If something is against the rules, he honestly, from me to you, has nothing to do with it. If there's things going on, he doesn't want to know about it. So, he has that buffer."

The buffers, he said, were assistant coaches and academic advisers.

Donahue said she was not surprised to learn from the *Pioneer Press* last week of Gangelhoff's allegations that she did course work for players.

"I believe anything is possible with Clem," she

said. "But I am surprised by how widespread (the allegations are)."

Donahue said she suspected Gangelhoff was working with basketball players in violation of department policy but did not know she was doing course work.

"I believed she was tutoring, but because I didn't know where she was doing this, I had no proof," Donahue said.

Donahue described her relationship with Haskins as "strained" and said the two often disagreed on Newby's roles and whether Newby should have reported to her. While still at the university, Donahue said she was hesitant to make accusations against Newby and Haskins for that reason.

"There was a difference of philosophies. . . . I believed that (basketball players) should do their homework," Donahue said. "I believe they are in college to become educated. And I worked toward supporting students so *they* could earn a degree. My understanding of (the basketball program) was that you enabled students to become irresponsible. 'It's OK to have someone else do the work.'"

Archambault said: "In the two years I was there, I never did a thing. Either Jan or Jeanne [Gangelhoff's sister, also a tutor] did everything."

• • •

The university, reacting quickly, barred the four named players, two of them starters, from playing in the next day's NCAA tournament opener, which the Gophers then lost to Gonzaga. University officials also reported the problem to the NCAA and contacted outside lawyers to start their own investigation.

Phone calls and E-mail messages flooded into the *Pioneer Press* newsroom, with many of the readers agreeing with Minnesota Governor Jesse Ventura that the timing of the story was "despicable." Five hundred people canceled their subscriptions. The *Pioneer Press* editor, Walker Lundy, responded that the paper had merely published when the story was ready and that Dohrmann had

been working on the reporting for more than three months. The paper sold an extra 8,000 copies that day.

Further investigation showed a larger pattern of abuse: a team academic counselor alleged that Coach Haskins had asked him to do course work; some grades were changed years after the courses; the coach was reported to have visited two professors to inquire about how players were doing. Many among the university faculty and sports programs said such infractions were common knowledge.

The university bought out Haskins's contract and did not renew his assistants. It also banned the team from post-season play after the 1999–2000 season, cut the number of athletic scholarships, recruiting trips, and campus visits allowed, and agreed to return to the Big Ten approximately $350,000 in revenue the university had earned from competing with academically ineligible players.

The university's actions enabled it to head off the anger of the NCAA investigating committee. The NCAA found that clearly Haskins was "knowledgeable about and complicit in the academic fraud" and banned him from work at another NCAA institution until 2007. Similar restrictions applied to the counselors and academic officials involved. The NCAA tightened somewhat the cuts in scholarships and recruiting activities the university had instituted, but decided, to Minnesota's pleasure, not to bar it from further post-season play.

One of the most disturbing things about the situation, the NCAA report said, was the university's lack of institutional control over the basketball team: "The widespread academic fraud involved in this case was uncovered not by the university but by a newspaper."

In April 2000, one year after the scandal broke, *Sports Illustrated* reported that the grade-point average of U-Minnesota's men's basketball team under its new coach, Dan Monson, was 2.5, up from 1.7.

CONSERVATION

WILLIAM BARTRAM JOURNEYS THROUGH THE WILDERNESS IN EARLY AMERICA

It was the writer with pencil and pen and sometimes the artist with his brushes who made America appreciate the wilderness. This effort took decades to catch on and will never be over, for America has always wavered between spoiling the wilderness and saving it. In most cases, it has spoiled it, and the despoliation continues.

Not all these men and women were journalists by name, although they were journalists by trade. Many of them preceded journalism as a profession, for modern journalism begins during the Civil War. Even when journalism as a profession was growing, many of the best nature writers were still not journalists, for the journalism profession came late to understanding the importance of writing about preservation and wild areas and wild things.

One of the first writers to understand the importance of wild areas and to write movingly about them was William Bartram. An exceptional writer, a fine illustrator, and a skilled botanist, Bartram was born in 1739 in Kingsessing, Pennsylvania, to a Quaker family that placed importance on learning. In 1773 he began a series of exploring trips on horseback, on foot, and by canoe into the wild and unsettled areas of what is now South Carolina, Georgia, and Florida. Over the next four years he traveled more than 5,000 miles in this magnificent wilderness, making keen observations and recording them in a journal.

Before Bartram, as the environmental historian Roderick Nash pointed out in his classic work, *Wilderness and the American Mind,* the few botanists who existed were "too engrossed in their studies to pay more than cursory attention to wilderness." Bartram, Nash says, "reversed this order," for Bartram marveled at wild things. In 1775 he climbed a mountain in northern Georgia and from there "enjoyed a view inexpressibly magnificent and comprehensive ... (of) the mountain wilderness through which I had lately traveled ... my imagination thus wholly engaged in the contemplation of this magnificent landscape." Bartram was so engrossed in the wilderness that, he wrote, he nearly was—a major error for a botanist—"insensible ... of ... a new species of Rhododendron."

Bartram had a keen eye and a lyrical writing style. He also saw the sublime qualities of the wilderness, and his writings, Nash writes, marked the first widespread use of that term—sublimity—in American wilderness writing.

Here is Bartram writing on two days in the wilderness of the Carolina-Georgia border. The excerpt is from his classic work, published in

1791, *Travels Through North and South Carolina, Georgia, East and West Florida, the Cherokee Country, the Extensive Territories of the Muscogulges or Creek Confederacy, and the Country of the Chactaws; Containing an account of the Soil and Natural Productions of those regions, together with observations on the Manners of the Indians.*

The day being remarkably warm and sultry, together with the labour and fatigue of ascending the mountains, made me very thirsty and in some degree sunk my spirits. Now past mid-day, I sought a cool shaded retreat, where was water for refreshment and grazing for my horse, my faithful slave and only companion. After proceeding a little farther, descending the other side of the mountain, I perceived at some distance before me, on my right hand, a level plain supporting a grand high forest and groves; the nearer I approached, my steps were the more accelerated from the flattering prospect opening to view. I now entered upon the verge of the dark forest, charming solitude! As I advanced through the animating shades, observed on the farther grassy verge a shady grove; thither I directed my steps. On approaching these shades, between the stately columns of the superb forest trees, presented to view, rushing from rocky precipices under the shade of the pensile hills, the unparalleled cascade of Falling Creek, rolling and leaping off the rocks: the waters uniting below, spread a broad, glittering sheet over a vast convex elevation of plain smooth rocks, and are immediately received by a spacious bas[i]n, where trembling in the centre through hurry and agitation, they gently subside, encircling the painted still verge; from whence gliding swiftly, they soon form a delightful little river, which continuing to flow more moderately, is restrained for a moment, gently undulating in a little lake; they then pass on rapidly to a high perpendicular steep of rocks, from when these delightful waters are hurried down with irresistible rapidity. I here seated myself on the moss-clad

rocks, under the shade of spreading trees and floriferous flagrant shrubs, in full view of the cascades. . . .

Having collected some valuable specimens at this friendly retreat, I continued my lonesome pilgrimage. My road for a considerable time led me winding and turning about the steep rocky hills; the descent of some of which were very rough and troublesome, by means of fragments or rocks, slippery clay and talc: but after this I entered a spacious forest, the land having gradually acquired a more level surface: a pretty grassy vale appears on my right, through which my wandering path led me, close by the banks of a delightful creek, which sometimes falling [over] steps of rocks, glides gently with serpentine meanders through the meadows.

After crossing this delightful brook and mead, the land rises again with sublime magnificence and I am led over hills and vales, groves and high forests, vocal with the melody of the feathered songsters; the snow-white cascades glittering on the sides of the distant hills.

It was now afternoon; I approached a charming vale, amidst sublimely high forests, awful shades! Darkness gathers around; far distant thunder rolls over the trembling hills: the black clouds with august majesty and power, move slowly forwards, shading regions of towering hills, and threatening all the destruction of a thunder storm: all around is now still as death; not a whisper is heard, but a total inactivity and silence seem to pervade the earth; the birds afraid to utter a chirrup, in low tremulous voices take leave of each other, seeking covert and safety; every insect is silenced, and nothing heard by the roaring of the approaching hurricane; the mighty cloud now expands its sable wings, extending from North to South, and is driven irresistibly on by the tumultuous winds, spreading its living wings around the gloomy concave, armed with terrors of thunder and fiery shafts of lightning. Now the lofty forests bend low beneath its fury; their limbs and wavy boughs are tossed about and catch hold of each other; the mountains tremble and seem to reel about, and the ancient hills to be shaken to their foundations: the furious storm sweeps along, smoking through the vale and over the resounding hills: the face of the earth is obscured by the deluge descending from the firmament, and I am deafened by the din of the thunder. The tempestuous scene damps my spirits, and my horse sinks under me at the tremendous peals, as I hasten on for the plain. The storm abating, I saw an Indian hunting cabin on the side of a hill, a very agreeable prospect, especially in my present condition; I made up to it and took quiet possession, there being no one to dispute it with me except a few bats and whip-poor-wills, who had repaired thither for shelter from the violence of the hurricane.

Having turned out my horse in the sweet meadows adjoining, and found some dry wood under the shelter of the old cabin, I struck up a fire, dried my clothes, and comforted myself with a frugal repast of biscuit and dried beef, which was all the food my viaticum afforded me by this time, excepting a small piece of cheese which I had furnished myself with at Charleston and kept till this time.

The night was clear, calm, and cool, and I rested quietly.

Next morning at day break I was awakened and summoned to resume my daily task . . .

I left for a little while, the stream passing swiftly and foaming over its rocky bed, lashing the steep craggy banks, and then suddenly sunk from my sight, murmuring hollow and deep under the rocky surface of the ground. On my right hand the vale expands, receiving a pretty silvery brook of water which comes hastily down from the adjacent hills, and entered the river a little distance before me. I now turn from the heights on my left, the road leading into the level lawns, to avoid the hollow rocky grounds, full of holes and cavities, arching over the river, through which the waters are seen gliding along; but the river is soon liberated from these solitary and gloomy re-

cesses, and appears waving through the green plain before me. I continued several miles, pursuing my serpentine path, through and over the meadows and green fields, and crossing the river, which is here incredibly increased in size, by the continued accession of brooks flowing in from the hills on each side, dividing their green turfy beds, forming them into parterres, vistas and verdant swelling knolls, profusely productive of flowers and fragrant strawberries, their rich juice dyeing my horse's feet and ankles.

• • •

Bartram's work was published first in England, then in Ireland, then translated into German and French. In the early 1800s, he was regarded as the dean of American natural science, and he advised a generation of naturalists whom his writings had inspired. Bartram died in 1823 in Kingsessing, Pennsylvania.

In 1976 the Bartram Trail Conference was formed, working to locate and mark the route of Bartram's journey.

THE NEW YORK *TRIBUNE* ASKS THAT THE ADIRONDACKS BE SAVED

As America moved west, a large, heavily forested, mountainous section of northeast New York State, the Adirondacks, was left largely untouched. In the middle of the nineteenth century, as some Americans, including journalists and other writers, began to call for the protection of natural areas, this splendid wild area stood out as demanding preservation. The New York *Tribune,* both its reporters and editorial writers, led this effort.

One longtime *Tribune* reporter, Joel T. Headly, wrote about the Adirondacks as early as 1849, when he published *The Adirondack: or Life in the Woods.* In his book, Headly said that a traveler equipped with strong legs, a stout heart, and a "love for the wild, and free" could spend time in the Adirondacks, which he said surpassed the Alps, and "come back to civilized life a healthier and a better man." He went on: "I love it, and I know it is better for me than the thronged city, aye, better for soul and body both."

Others joined in. In 1864, the early environmentalist George Perkins Marsh in *Man and Nature: or, Physical Geography as Modified by Human Action,* urged that a substantial portion of the Adirondacks be preserved "as far as possible, in its primitive condition." Such a preserve as the Adirondacks, Marsh said, would be "a garden for the recreation of the lover of nature: and an 'asylum' for wildlife." In 1873, *Forest and Stream,* a sportsmen's publication, said that the Adirondacks should be preserved to protect the state watersheds that rose in that area. The argument won over some people—foresters, sportsmen, and others—who would not have wanted to protect the mountains simply as wilderness. By the 1880s, wrote Roderick Nash in *Wilderness and the American Mind,* more writing had been done about preserving the Adirondacks than about preserving any other area in America.

Headly continued to urge protection of the Adirondacks in both articles and editorials. This unsigned piece appeared on the editorial page of the *Tribune* on September 2, 1883, under the headline "Saving the Adirondacks":

The State decreed last winter that Niagara Falls should be rescued from the hands of the spoiler. There seems to be good grounds for apprehending that another great natural glory of New-York is now in danger. A railroad company has acquired the right to purchase a million acres of land in the Adirondack forests. It already owns half a million acres. The road itself as contemplated will run through the heart of the great wilderness. The consulting engineer of the road has put forth a prospectus in which he says that "every possible facility is afforded not only for realizing a large immediate income from the products of these lands, but also for furnishing the road at its first opening with an immense tonnage which will always be within the entire control of the railroad company."

We believe that it will strike the majority of our citizens that this is an uncommonly good project to suppress in its initial and harmless stage. This is not to say, of course, that any rights of this company should be unjustly interfered with. But the State has the reserved right of eminent domain, and if it can be demonstrated—and it certainly looks that way—that building and operating this road means the substantial destruction of the Adirondacks, then New-York ought to step in and make effectual protest. "Everybody is of more account than anybody." The State as a whole has a greater stake in the Adirondacks than any association of individuals can have. It is one of the great safeguards of New-York, seeing that it contains the fountain-heads of the noble streams that conserve our physical and commercial prosperity. Wisdom, fortified by much experience, still advises against tampering with the goose that lays the golden egg.

The subject in all its phases and from all points of view is now being vigorously discussed by the newspapers of the interior. When discussion has exhausted itself prompt action should follow. Let the State do as well by the Adirondacks as it proposes to do by Niagara.

• • •

Others joined in the battle. The New York Chamber of Commerce and other powerful business interests demanded that the Adirondacks be saved. Not to do so, the New York State Legislature was told, would "seriously injure the internal commerce of the State."

On May 15, 1885, New York Governor David B. Hill approved a bill establishing a "Forest Preserve" of 715,000 acres in the Adirondacks that was to remain forever as "wild forest lands." In 1891 the New York State Forest Commission suggested that the state give consideration to designating the Adirondack forest preserve as a park.

This meant the argument for preserving the Adirondacks was being extended, for, the commission said, besides saving forested watersheds, a park would provide "a place where rest, recuperation and vigor may be gained by our highly nervous and overworked people." In 1892, the New York State Legislature designated some three million acres in the area as the Adirondack State Park.

In 1894, a New York State constitutional convention gave the park further protection, and in November 1894 New York state voters gave permanent protection to the park. The Adirondacks must, voters said, stay forever wild.

GEORGE BIRD GRINNELL DEFENDS BIRDS FROM THE DEMANDS OF FASHION

George Bird Grinnell was one of the nation's most important outdoorsmen, journalists, and environmentalists. He modeled himself on John James Audubon, and in fact grew up on Audubon's former estate. He was a friend of Theodore Roosevelt, had a ranch in Wyoming, and, with Roosevelt, was a founder of the Boone and Crockett Club, a sportsmen's organization devoted to hunting and preservation. Grinnell, not inconsistently, believed in both.

Grinnell, born in 1849, attended Yale University, where he became interested in paleontology under the direction of the fabled Yale scientist Othniel C. Marsh. Grinnell went dinosaur-bone gathering with Marsh in 1870 in the West. In 1872 Grinnell joined the famous U.S. Army scout Luther North on a hunting trip in the West, in 1874 he was part of General George Armstrong Custer's expedition to the Black Hills, and in 1875 he went with Custer to survey the Yellowstone area. In 1880 Grinnell received a doctorate in paleontology from Yale. He wrote his dissertation on the *Geococcyx californianus,* better known as the roadrunner.

He also was intensely interested in the American Indian, especially Pawnees, Blackfeet, and Cheyennes. He wrote *Blackfoot Lodge Tales: The Story of a Prairie People, The Fighting Cheyennes,* and *Pawnee Hero Stories and Folk Tales; with Notes on the Origins, Customs, and Character of the Pawnee People.*

In 1873 Grinnell began to write for *Forest and Stream* (a forerunner of today's *Field and Stream*). At *Forest and Stream,* Grinnell wrote numerous pieces promoting conservation in the West and campaigned, with success, for creation of Yellowstone National Park.

Grinnell was especially interested in the protection of birds and waterfowl. In 1886, he urged readers to join him in forming a group to oppose their slaughter.

"The Audubon Society," by George Bird Grinnell. *Forest and Stream,* February 11, 1886.

Very slowly the public are awakening to see that the fashion of wearing the feathers and skins of birds is abominable. There is, we think, no doubt that when the facts about this fashion are known, it will be frowned down and will cease to exist. Legislation of itself can do little against this barbarous practice, but if public sentiment can be aroused against it, it will die a speedy death.

The FOREST AND STREAM has been hammering away at this subject for some years, and the result of its blows is seen in the gradual change which has taken place in public sentiment since it began its work. The time has passed for showing that the fashion is an outrageous one, and that it results very disastrously to the largest and most important class of our population—the farmers. These are injured in two ways: by the destruction of the birds, whose food consists chiefly of insects injurious to the growing crops, and of that scarcely less important group the Rapaces, which prey upon the small rodents which devour the crop after it has matured.

The reform in America, as elsewhere, must be

inaugurated by women, and if the subject is properly called to their notice, their tender hearts will be quick to respond. In England this matter has been taken up and a widespread interest in it developed. If the women of America will take hold in the same earnest way, they can accomplish an incalculable amount of good.

While individual effort may accomplish much, it will work but slowly, and the spread of the movement will be but gradual. Something more than this is needed. Men, women and children all over our land should take the matter in hand, and urge its importance upon those with whom they are brought in contact. A general effort of this kind will not fail to awaken public interest, and information given to a right-thinking public will set the ball of reform in motion. Our beautiful birds give to many people a great deal of pleasure and add much to the delights of the country. These birds are slaughtered in vast numbers for gain. If the demand for their skins can be caused to fall off, it will no longer repay the bird butchers to ply their trade and the birds will be saved.

Statistics are as yet wanting to show the proportions to which this traffic has grown in North America, but we know that it reaches well into the hundreds of thousands. Some figures published in FOREST AND STREAM of Aug. 4, 1884, showed that in a three months' trip a single taxidermist collected bird skins to the number of 11,018, which, including specimens too badly mutilated for preservation, and skins spoiled in the making, would perhaps represent a destruction of 15,000 birds. This same person states that he handles annually about 30,000 bird skins, almost all of which are used for millinery purposes. A single middleman who collected the spoils of the shooters in one small district brought to the taxidermists in four months about 70,000 birds.

The birds of the fields, the birds of the woods, the birds of the marshes, and those of the sea, all suffer alike. It is needless to repeat the oft told story of destruction. How can we best go to work to combat this great and growing evil, what means can we best employ to awaken at once popular feeling against it?

We desire to enlist in this work every one who is interested in our birds, and we urge all such to take hold and assist us.

In the first half of this century there lived a man who did more to teach Americans about birds of their own land than any other who ever lived. His beautiful and spirited paintings and his charming and tender accounts of the habits of his favorites have made him immortal, and have inspired his countrymen with an ardent love for the birds. The land which produced the painter naturalist, John James Audubon, will not willingly see the beautiful forms he loved so well exterminated.

We propose the formation of an association for the protection of wild birds and their eggs, which shall be called the Audubon Society. Its membership is to be free to every one who is willing to lend a helping hand in forwarding the objects for which it is formed. These objects shall be to prevent, so far as possible (1) the killing of any wild birds not used for food; (2) the destruction of nests or eggs of any wild bird, and (3) the wearing of feathers as ornaments or trimming for dress.

•   •   •

Following publication of this piece, Grinnell became a leader in a nationwide campaign to abolish market hunting of wild game and to restrict the slaughter of birds. The Committee on the Protection of North American Birds, formed by Grinnell and other members of the American Ornithologists' Union, issued one of the most important documents in the history of American conservation: it distinguished between game and non-game birds, and said most non-game birds should be protected.

In three months, according to the National Audubon Society's official history, more than 38,000 people, including many notables, answered Grinnell's call to form an Audubon Society. Grinnell was overwhelmed and abandoned the group in 1898. But within a decade, women in Massachusetts who backed Grinnell's attack on bird-plume fashion formed a state Audubon society. Other states followed, and in 1905 a national organization was formed.

Audubon worked for passage of a New York state plumage law, which banned sales of plumes of all native birds in the state, in 1910, and for the 1918 Federal Migratory Bird Treaty Act.

Grinnell continued his work for the environment. He worked diligently, for example, for the passage of legislation that in 1910 led to the formation of Glacier National Park, which includes a glacier named for him.

JOHN MUIR DEMANDS PROTECTION OF THE YOSEMITE VALLEY

Carved by glaciers, marked by great mountain peaks, waterfalls, and giant trees, home to spectacular flowered meadows, named after a native word for grizzly bear, the Yosemite valley has awed centuries of visitors.

John Muir, who first visited the area in 1868, at the age of thirty, was one of them. A part-time sawyer, but mostly an outdoorsman with keen powers of observation and a solitary nature, Muir took to the mountains on lengthy solo trips. He wrote about his adventures, beginning in the New York *Tribune* in 1871, and for magazines such as *Harper's* and *Overland Monthly*. He became, said one of his biographers, "press agent for the mountains."

During the 1880s, Muir fell out of public life, newly married and devoting his attention to managing the ranch of his wife's family. Then Robert Underwood Johnson, of *Century* magazine, came to California scouting new talent, and he sought Muir out. The outdoorsman got lost in the halls

of the San Francisco Palace Hotel on the way to their meeting. He was on surer footing when he took Johnson on a pack trip to Yosemite, although saddened by the grazing, the lumbering, the farms, and the factories already defaming the valley.

Write for me, said Johnson, and we'll make this a national park.

"The Treasures of the Yosemite," by John Muir. *Century,* August 1890.

The Yosemite Valley, in the heart of the Sierra Nevada, is a noble mark for the traveler, whether tourist, botanist, geologist, or lover of wilderness pure and simple. But those who are free may find the journey a long one; not because of the miles, for they are not so many,—only about two hundred and fifty from San Francisco, and passed over by rail and carriage road in a day or two,—but the way is so beautiful that one is beguiled at every step, and the great golden days and weeks and months go by uncounted. How vividly my own first journey to Yosemite comes to mind, though made more than a score of years ago. I set out afoot from Oakland, on the bay of San Francisco, in April. It was the bloom-time of the year over all the lowlands and ranges of the coast; the landscape was fairly drenched with sunshine, the larks were singing, and the hills were so covered with flowers that they seemed to be painted. Slow indeed was my progress through these glorious gardens, the first of the California flora I had seen. Cattle and cultivation were making few scars as yet, and I wandered enchanted in long, wavering curves, aware now and then that Yosemite lay to the eastward, and that, some time, I should find it.

One shining morning, at the head of the Pacheco Pass, a landscape was displayed that after all my wanderings still appears as the most divinely beautiful and sublime I have ever beheld. There at my feet lay the great central plain of

California, level as a lake, thirty or forty miles wide, four hundred long, one rich furred bed of golden Compositae. And along the eastern shore of this lake of gold rose the mighty Sierra, miles in height, in massive, tranquil grandeur, so gloriously colored and so radiant that it seemed not clothed with light, but wholly composed of it, like the wall of some celestial city. Along the top, and extending a good way down, was a rich pearl-gray belt of snow; then a belt of blue and dark purple, marking the extension of the forests; and stretching along the base of the range a broad belt of rose-purple, where lay the miners' gold and the open foothill gardens—all the colors smoothly blending, making a wall of light clear as crystal and ineffably fine, yet firm as adamant. Then it seemed to me the Sierra should be called, not the Nevada or Snowy Range, but the Range of Light. And after ten years in the midst of it, rejoicing and wondering, seeing the glorious floods of light that fill it,—the sunbursts of morning among the mountain-peaks, the broad noonday radiance on the crystal rocks, the flush of the alpenglow, and the thousand dashing waterfalls with their marvelous abundance of irised spray,—it still seems to me a range of light. But no terrestial beauty may endure forever. The glory of wildness has already departed from the great central plain. Its bloom is shed, and so in part is the bloom of the mountains. In Yosemite, even under the protection of the Government, all that is perishable is vanishing apace.

The Sierra is about 500 miles long, 70 miles wide, and from 7000 to nearly 15,000 feet high. In general views no mark of man is visible upon it, nor anything to suggest the wonderful depth and grandeur of its sculpture. None of its magnificent forest-crowned ridges seems to rise much above the general level to publish its wealth. No great valley or river is seen, or group of well-marked features of any kind standing out as distinct pictures. Even the summit peaks, marshaled in glorious array so high in the sky, seem comparatively smooth and featureless. Nevertheless the whole range is furrowed with cañons to a depth of from 2000 to 5000 feet, in which once flowed majestic glaciers, and in which now flow and sing the bright Sierra rivers.

Though of such stupendous depth, these cañons are not raw, gloomy, jagged-walled gorges, savage and inaccessible. With rough passages here and there, they are mostly smooth, open pathways conducting to the fountains of the summit; mountain streets full of life and light, graded and sculptured by the ancient glaciers, and presenting throughout all their courses a rich variety of novel and attractive scenery—the most attractive that has yet been discovered in the mountain ranges of the world. In many places, especially in the middle region of the western flank, the main cañons widen into spacious valleys or parks of charming beauty, level and flowery and diversified like landscape gardens with meadows and groves and thickets of blooming bushes, while the lofty walls, infinitely varied in form, are fringed with ferns, flowering plants, shrubs of many species, and tall evergreens and oaks which find anchorage on a thousand narrow steps and benches, the whole enlivened and made glorious with rejoicing streams that come dancing and foaming over the sunny brows of the cliffs and through side cañons in falls of every conceivable form, to join the shining river that flows in tranquil beauty down the middle of each one of them.

The most famous and accessible of these cañon valleys, and also the one that presents their most striking and sublime features on the grandest scale, is the Yosemite, situated on the upper waters of the Merced at an elevation of 4000 feet above the level of the sea. It is about seven miles long, half a mile to a mile wide, and nearly a mile deep, and is carved in the solid granite flank of the range. The walls of the valley are made up of rocks, mountains in size, partly separated from each other by side cañons and gorges; and they are so sheer in front, and so compactly and harmoniously built together on a level floor, that the place, comprehensively seen, looks like some immense hall or temple lighted from above.

But no temple made with hands can compare with Yosemite. Every rock in its walls seems to glow with life. Some lean back in majestic repose; others, absolutely sheer or nearly so for thousands of feet, advance beyond their companions in thoughtful attitudes, giving welcome to storms and calms alike, seemingly conscious, yet heedless of everything going on about them. Awful in stern, immovable majesty, how softly these mountain rocks are adorned and how fine and reassuring the company they keep—their feet set in groves and gay emerald meadows, their brows in the thin blue sky, a thousand flowers leaning confidingly against their adamantine bosses, bathed in floods of booming water, floods of light, while snow, clouds, winds, avalanches, shine and sing and wreathe about them as the years go by! Birds, bees, butterflies, and myriads of nameless wings stir the air into music and give glad animation. Down through the midst flows the crystal Merced—river of mercy—peacefully gliding, reflecting lilies and trees and the onlooking rocks, things frail and fleeting and types of endurance meeting here and blending in countless forms, as if into this one mountain mansion Nature had gathered her choicest treasures, whether great or small, to draw her lovers into close and confiding communion with her.

Sauntering towards Yosemite up the foothills, richer and wilder become the forests and streams. At an elevation of 6000 feet above the level of the sea the silver firs are 200 feet high, with branches whorled around the colossal shafts in regular order, and every branch beautifully pinnate like a fern leaf. The Douglas spruce and the yellow and sugar pines here reach their highest development of beauty and grandeur, and the rich, brown-barked libocedrus with warm, yellow-green plumes. The majestic sequoia, too, is here, the king of conifers, "the noblest of a noble race." All these colossal trees are as wonderful in the fineness of their beauty and proportions as in stature, growing together, and assemblage of conifers surpassing all that have yet been discovered in the forests of the world. Here, indeed, is the tree-lover's paradise, the woods, dry and wholesome, letting in the light in shimmering masses half sunshine, half shade, the air indescribably spicy and exhilarating, plushy fir boughs for beds, and cascades to sing us asleep as we gaze through the trees to the stars.

These king trees, all that there are of their kind in the world, are surely worth saving, whether for beauty, science, or bald use. But as yet only the isolated Mariposa Grove has been reserved as a park for public use and pleasure. Were the importance of our forests at all understood by the people in general, even from an economic standpoint their preservation would call forth the most watchful attention of the Government. At present, however, every kind of destruction is moving on with accelerated speed. Fifteen years ago I found five mills located on or near the lower margin of the main sequoia belt, all of which were cutting big-tree lumber. How many more have been built since that time I am unable to say, but most of the Fresno group are doomed to feed the large mills established near them, and a company with ample means is about ready for work on the magnificent forests of King's River. In these mill operations waste far exceeds use. For after the young, manageable trees have been cut, blasted, and sawed, the woods are fired to clear the ground of limbs and refuse, and of course the seedlings and saplings, and many of the unmanageable giants, are destroyed, leaving but little more than black, charred monuments. These mill ravages, however, are small as yet compared with the comprehensive destruction caused by "sheepmen." Incredible numbers of sheep are driven to

the mountain pastures every summer, and desolation follows them. Every garden within reach is
trampled, the shrubs are stripped of leaves as if
devoured by locusts, and the woods are burned
to improve the pasturage. The entire belt of forests is thus swept by fire, from one end of the
range to the other; and, with the exception of the
resinous *Pinus contorta,* the sequoia suffers most of
all. Steps are now being taken towards the creation of a national park about the Yosemite, and
great is the need, not only for the sake of the
adjacent forests, but for the valley itself. For the
branching cañons and valleys of the basins of
the streams that pour into Yosemite are as closely
related to it as are the fingers to the palm of the
hand—as the branches, foilage, and flowers of a
tree to the trunk.

• • •

Johnson, a master lobbyist, set to work even before Muir's two articles, which ran in August and
September 1890, were done. He created a park
coalition that won the support of the Southern
Pacific Railroad and the powerful Hearst family.
A bill for Yosemite National Park, following
boundaries that Muir had suggested in *Century,*
was passed in September 1890 and signed by
President Benjamin Harrison the next day.

Muir was surprised by how his arguments won
favor and pleased by his new celebrity. Shedding
his loner-in-the-forests stance, with the encouragement of his wife, he resumed writing about
parks and wildlife. An article in *Atlantic* in 1897,
for example, urged federal protection of the forests; only Uncle Sam, Muir wrote, can save the
trees from fools.

In 1892, alert to the continuing pressures on
Yosemite, Muir, Johnson, and a San Francisco
lawyer, Warren Olney, formed a sort of "Yosemite Defense League." That group became the Sierra Club, one of the country's most prominent
conservation organizations. Muir was president
from its founding until his death in 1914.

PROMISING HE DOESN'T HAVE TO COME TO THE OFFICE (THAT WOULD BE LIKE "PUTTING A GRIZZLY INTO A SWALLOW-TAIL AND PATENT-LEATHER PUMPS"), THE *LADIES' HOME JOURNAL* HIRES NATURALIST ERNEST THOMPSON SETON AND THEREBY HELPS CREATE THE AMERICAN BOY SCOUTS

Born in England in 1860, Ernest Thompson Seton (he was born Seton Thompson but reversed
his name) grew up in western Canada and returned to England to study art. His stories and
wildlife paintings gave him wide attention, as did
his books, including *Wild Animals I Have Known,*
published in 1898 and republished in 1942, and
The Biography of a Grizzly Bear, published in 1900.
His works became mandatory for boys and girls
interested in wildlife.

By this time, the world had changed. Cities had
expanded. The frontier had disappeared. Many
people, including boys and girls, had lost connections with the woods and wild things. Thompson
Seton thought this was a tragedy, and that it need
not be.

In May 1902, the *Ladies' Home Journal* hired
Thompson Seton to head the magazine's "regular
department for boys." Now, the magazine said,
"boys will have months of sport and fun with the
author of *Wild Animals I Have Known.*

"It has been asked," the magazine continued,
"how is Ernest Thompson Seton to be an editor
of *The Journal* and yet live the free life of the naturalist, which is so essential to his work?"

The magazine answered, "The reply is that an
editorship in Mr. Seton's case does not mean being tied to a desk in the Philadelphia office. That
would be like putting a grizzly into a swallow-tail
and patent-leather pumps. Mr. Seton is still to live

in the woods if he chooses, being guided solely by his own bent. In other words, he is to be just what he has been; but to millions of readers of a magazine, instead of to 100,000 readers of a book, as heretofore. He will be left free in order to keep his work fresh. From wherever he may be his work for *The Journal* will be sent."

In that same number, the *Ladies' Home Journal* published Thompson Seton's first piece under the new relationship. The piece said that many animals remained in the United States that could be tracked and identified, and told how to make plaster casts of animal prints, a standard practice of young naturalists ever since. Here are excerpts from that piece.

It was written for young people, especially boys, and the language reflects that.

By Ernest Thompson Seton. *Ladies' Home Journal,* May 1902.

Most boys have the idea that wild animals are very rare now, or that you must go into the far West to find them. While this is true of some of the large kinds, it is yet safe to say that any one in the Eastern States can, within five miles, and usually much less, get into a region where he may discover some wild creatures. He may walk through a place again and again without seeing anything alive except a few birds, but he may be sure there were many bright eyes and keen ears and noses that were observing him and fully taking in the fact that their deadly enemy was passing near. Especially at night or late in the evenings is this the case, for then the wild Fourfoots are on the move, and the hundreds of these that once used to roam by daylight have either been killed off, or have learned to come out only at night when men cannot see them. There may be many of these left in our little woods, and yet, unless knowing just how to look, one may pass many times and have no idea of their existence.

————

It is unfortunate for it, though lucky for the naturalist, that wherever a Fourfoot goes it leaves behind a little written account of its visit, its name, the time, the place whence it came, what it did, and when and whither it went away. We can find these accounts and read them and thus learn of the numbers and kinds of our wild neighbors. These "manuscripts," though I should rather perhaps call them "pedoscripts," are, of course, the tracks which the animals leave in the mud, snow or dust.

Each animal makes its own kind of track; no two make exactly the same. The track of a 'Coon is never like that of a Fox, and the track of a Fox is readily distinguished from that of a Rabbit or a small Dog. And more than that, the tracks of one 'Coon may differ from that of his own brother, so that one can sometimes distinguish the tracks of a given individual, and by seeing it on different occasions get something like an insight into its life. Thus, a famous Grizzly in the West was known by his track. One of his toes had been cut off by a trap, and the difference that made in the mark was easy to see. To come nearer home, our common animals sometimes have unpleasant experiences with steel traps. The marks of these on their feet often add a peculiarity that identifies the animal; in other cases the track is extra large or small, or is crooked, but it always keeps the main features of its kind. The track of one sort of animal rarely need be mistaken for that of another, and the A B C of tracking is to learn the chief kinds of footmarks that are to be found in your region. The way to learn tracks is to draw those that you can find, always sketching them right from Nature, never from memory, and it is always best to make them exactly life-size.

The snow is the best for tracking when you wish to follow the animal a long way and see what it is doing. But the snow rarely gives a perfect individual track. The mud and the dry dust, if not too deep, are much better for details. I have tried many ways of getting records of tracks, and have some interesting results, especially among domestic animals. The Dog and Cat are the creatures whose tracks are likely to be first met with. But they are most aggravating subjects when one tries to get tracks from them. My first attempts were made with modeling-clay spread out thin on a tray; but both Dog and Cat would either bound over the tray or wriggle or squirm or scratch it in long furrows, and, in short, do anything but walk calmly across and leave a few good impressions. One cannot take the animal's paw and make an imprint. That is sure to be wrong. The creature must do it itself and in its own way, and the track is sure to be spoiled if the animal is hurt or scared. Still, patience will surely win.

A good plaster track, once secured, can be cast in plaster and kept for future use. While following tracks in Nature one soon realizes that not more than one in a thousand of those made is perfect. The accidents are so numerous that most of them are spoiled. It must be taken for granted, therefore, that a good many will be made in the modeling wax of clay before getting a perfect set showing all the details and characteristics.

A thin coat of dry flour, plaster, dust or other fine powder on a board gives a good impression, but it is difficult to make record of, sketching and photographing being the only ways. I have got a Cat to make its own records by blacking its feet, then making it trot over some papers, and these are easier to read if the ink on the hindfeet be a different color from that on the front. It is well, also, to clean the animal's feet afterward before it is allowed to enter the house.

A number of boys recently offered their help in getting a series of Cat paw prints. I gave them an idea of how to go about it. Their father kept a general country store. So while one boy mixed a bit of lampblack to the proper consistency, another helped himself to a roll of wall paper and spread it on a long corridor with the white side up, and the third went out and captured a large Tomcat. They now painted Tom's feet with the lampblack and chased him down till he was half

crazy. Whenever they could catch him they touched up his feet afresh and set him puffing and snorting over the paper. When they brought me the roll it was thickly spotted over with tracks—most of them mere smears. Some, where Tom had slipped, were six inches long. The first after each fresh painting were too dark, and the last too faint, but still among the hundreds there were one or two good ones. This trifling success aroused the boys to high enthusiasm. At the beginning their energy had far overtopped their discretion, but now discretion dropped clear out of sight. They wished to beat their record, so they fairly soaked the Cat's feet and legs in paint. Tom was, of course, thoroughly disgusted with the whole thing; he made a frantic jump and escaped through a transom, then upstairs, and so ended his troubles; but he ran over a white bedspread, where he left a beautiful train, after which the boys' troubles began.

Most Cats object strenuously to having their feet blackened, and an easier way is to lay a large piece of lampblacked or printer's-inked papers so that the Cat will walk over that first and then over the white paper. But these methods are not possible with wild animals. They will have nothing to do with your white and black papers. Even in menageries these are usually failures. It is very rarely that tracks in the mud are perfect enough or handy to be cast in plaster. As a matter of practice, I have found that sketching is the most reliable way.

Of course the first animal tracks one is likely to see are those of Dogs and Cats, and these are good to begin with. The Cat is usually taken by the scientists as an example of a perfect animal. All its muscles and bones are of the highest type for activity and strength. Its track also affords a good study of what an animal's tracks should be, and in studying it we should remember that every curve and quirk has a history and a meaning.

...The cat sneaking through the underbrush after its prey must go in silence. It can see out of one corner of one eye where to set down the front foot so as not to crush a dry stick or leaf, but it cannot watch its hindfeet. However, it does not need to do so; the hindfeet are so well trained that they go exactly into the safe places already cleared for the front feet, and thus the Cat moves in perfect silence. All wild animals that sneak after their prey do thus; no doubt the Dog did at one time, just as the Wolf does to-day, but he has lived so long in town and walked so much on sidewalks that he has forgotten the proper way, and so is a very noisy walker in the woods. The Cat is little changed in habits since it came to live with man. It is still a hunter and walks as it ought.

In studying these things one must always keep in mind the great individual variation. For example, not only is the track of a Cat never exactly like that of any other animal, but no two Cat tracks are exactly alike, and the track made by one of the Cat's feet is never exactly like that made by another of its feet.

A third striking difference between the tracks of Dog and Cat is that most Dogs drag their toes. This shows clearly if there are five or six inches of snow. A Cat lifts its feet neatly, and clear of whatever it is walking in.

In trotting, a Dog's track is usually like its walking track with the steps nearly double as long, but sometimes it goes with its body diagonally, apparently so that its feet will not interfere, and this shows another variation of the trail.

It will be seen that the [Dog's] hindfeet overreach the forefeet each time, and track farther, as is the case with all bounding animals. The right forepaw is ahead of the left at each bound. This is what I should call a right-handed gallop. Some Dogs are left-handed and always run with the left paw ahead. Then again, some Dogs will do both ways within a short distance.

One of the commonest of the truly wild animals still found generally in the Northeastern States is the Red-Squirrel. It is a remarkably hardy, active and vigorous animal. It has succeeded in maintaining itself in spite of settlement and de-

foresting, chiefly because it can live in holes in the ground. As a rule the truly forest animals are the first to fly before the settler. The ones that hold out the longest are those that cling to Mother Earth as a final refuge, and this the Red-Squirrel does very successfully.

The tracks of the common Northeastern Squirrels are alike in general features, but differ in size and details. A Red-Squirrel's hindfoot is about 2 inches long, a Gray-Squirrel's about 2½ inches and a Fox-Squirrel's nearly 3 inches....

The hind track of a Squirrel shows five toes, but the fore track only four—the thumb of the forepaw being so small that it is like a knob and does not count.

Now to go back to the woods near your city. If I were seeking for animals at such a place I should set about taking the census of the Fourfoots by looking for tracks and signs—beginning first along the bare muddy or sandy edges of the brooks or ponds, if there are any, and particularly near large old trees, because these old trees usually have hollows in them, which furnish safe homes to animals that could not otherwise live.

One day last January, finding myself with some spare hours in one of the small towns in Northern New York, I asked the hotel-keeper if there were any Squirrels to be seen about the town. He said, "No; they're all shot off long ago."

But I walked on beyond the houses, and there getting a view of some woods half a mile away I cut across fields in that direction. At a fence near the woods I found where a Dog had chased something that ran along the top rail. Some snow in a crotch showed the sign given below, and I knew that was the trail of either a small Gray or Red Squirrel, probably the creature chased by the dog.

They had one or two hollow trees of refuge, but they also had holes under the monuments and gravestones. That was what made sure they were Reds: the Grays do not make holes in the ground. A quarter of a mile off was a barn, and the snow on the fence between showed that the Squirrels ran there when they needed corn.

But the most interesting thing in that graveyard was a snowdrift playground. The Squirrels had made a labyrinth of galleries in the drift. Around the entrance I found the remains of nuts and pine cones, so maybe their Winter Palace was banquet-hall as well as gymnasium, but I could not examine it fully without destroying it, so I let it alone. This Winter Palace of the Squirrels lay between the graves of a family that had died some time before, and those of some soldiers who had been killed in the Civil War, but doubtless the Squirrels found it the merriest place on earth.

• • •

In July of 1902, Seton organized the Woodcraft Indians, later the Woodcraft League, and in 1906 he wrote *Birch Bark Roll,* as a guide to the Woodcraft Indians. The book came to the attention of a kindred spirit, Sir Robert S. S. Baden-Powell, an English hero of the Boer War, and the two met in London in October 1906. Baden-Powell incorporated many of Seton's ideas into the Boy Scout movement, which came to the United States in 1910. Seton joined with Baden-Powell in writing the first Boy Scout manual, which proposed that the boys of America lead the nation back to an emphasis on the outdoors. The book sold millions, behind only the Bible, and the movement became part of American life.

Seton also invented the merit badge system and from 1910 to 1915 was the first chief scout of the Boy Scouts of America. But Seton soon had a falling out with Baden-Powell and James E. West, a scouting executive and lawyer, and Seton was forced out of the movement in 1915. West charged that Seton was in harmony with the view of anarchists. Seton disagreed with what he regarded as the military style scouting had taken and charged that West was a bureaucrat who had no

understanding of boys and had "never seen the blue sky in his life."

Seton wrote some ninety books for young people and helped found the cub scout movement for younger boys. In 1926, Seton received the Silver Buffalo award of the Boy Scouts of America.

At the beginning of the twenty-first century, the Boy Scouts of America had some three million members, one million as Boy Scouts and two million as younger scouts.

AN URBAN PLANNER CREATES THE APPALACHIAN TRAIL

Throughout much of the 1800s, most Americans looked upon mountains as barriers to be crossed, something that stood between them and the places they wanted to go. To a small, hardy band, however, the mountains were an end in themselves.

Benton MacKaye was one of these. Growing up in Massachusetts in the late 1800s, he developed a love of the outdoors and long-distance hiking that steered him to a Harvard degree in the young field of forestry in 1905 and then a job at the new U.S. Forest Service in Washington, D.C.

Through his work, MacKaye became concerned, even at that early time, about the pressures of city living and the need for land planning. Building on an idea that was being talked out in different hiking groups, in the October 1921 *Journal of the American Institute of Architects* MacKaye laid out his plan for a project that would get more Easterners into the outdoors. He called it a skyline, or an Appalachian trail. Much of it, he argued, could be built by interested citizens; the average American adult, he calculated, could spare two weeks a year to doing whatever he or she wanted to help build the trail.

Here are excerpts from his piece.

"An Appalachian Trail, A Project in Regional Planning," by Benton MacKaye. *Journal of the American Institute of Architects,* **October 1921.**

Here is enormous undeveloped power—the spare time of our population. Suppose just one percent of it were focused upon one particular job, such as increasing the facilities for the outdoor community life. This would be more than a million people, representing over two million weeks a year. It would be equivalent to 40,000 persons steadily on the job.

Where might this imposing force lay out its camping ground?

Camping grounds, of course, require wild lands. These in America are fortunately still available. They are in every main region of the country. They are the undeveloped or under-developed areas. Except in the Central States the wild lands now remaining are for the most part among the mountain ranges—the Sierras, the Cascades, and Rocky Mountains of the West and the Appalachian Mountains of the East.

Extensive national playgrounds have been reserved in various parts of the country for use by the people for camping and kindred purposes. Most of these are in the West where Uncle Sam's public lands were located. They are in the Yosemite, the Yellowstone, and many other National Parks—covering about six million acres in all. Splendid work has been accomplished in fitting these Parks for use. The National Forests, covering about 130 million acres . . . are also equipped for public recreation purposes.

A great public service has been started in these Parks and Forests in the field of outdoor life. They have been called "playgrounds of the people." This they are for the Western people—and for those in the East who can afford time and funds for an extended trip in a Pullman car. But camping grounds to be of the most use to the people should be as near as possible to the center of population. And this is in the East.

It fortunately happens that we have throughout the most densely populated portion of the United States a fairly continuous belt of under-developed lands. These are contained in the several ranges which form the Appalachian chain of mountains. Several National Forests have been purchased in this belt. These mountains, in several ways rivalling the western scenery, are within a day's ride from centers containing more than half the population of the United States. The region spans the climates of New England and the cotton belt; it contains the crops and the people of the North and of the South.

The skyline along the top of the main divides and ridges of the Appalachians would overlook a mighty part of the nation's activities. The rugged lands of this skyline would form a camping base strategic in the country's work and play.

Let us assume the existence of a giant standing high on the skyline along these mountain ridges, his head just scraping the floating clouds. What would he see from this skyline as he strode along its length from north to south?

Starting out from Mt. Washington, the highest point in the northeast, his horizon takes in one of the original happy hunting grounds of America—the "Northwoods," a country of pointed firs extending from the lakes and rivers of northern Maine to those of the Adirondacks. Stepping across the Green Mountains and the Berkshires to the Catskills he gets his first view of the crowded east—a chain of smoky, bee-hive cities extending from Boston to Washington and containing a third of the population of the Appalachian drained area. Bridging the Delaware Water Gap and the Susquehanna on the picturesque Allegheny folds across Pennsylvania he notes more smoky columns—the big plants between Scranton and Pittsburgh that get out the basic stuff of modern industry—iron and coal. In relieving contrast he steps across the Potomac near Harpers Ferry and pushes through into the wooded wilderness of the Southern Appalachians where he finds preserved much of the primal aspects of the days of Daniel Boone. Here he finds, over on the Monongahela side, the black coal of bituminous and the white coal of water power. He proceeds along the great divide of the upper Ohio and sees flowing to waste, sometimes in terrifying floods, waters capable of generating untold hydro-electric energy and of bringing navigation to many a lower stream. He looks over the Natural Bridge and out across the battle fields around Appomattox. He finds himself finally in the midst of the great Carolina Hardwood belt. Resting now on the top of Mt. Mitchell, highest point east of the Rockies, he counts up on his big long fingers the opportunities which yet await development along the skyline he has passed.

First he notes the opportunities for recreation. Throughout the Southern Appalachians, throughout the Northwoods, and even through the Alleghenies that wind their way among the smoky industrial towns of Pennsylvania, he recollects vast areas of secluded forests, pastoral lands, and water courses, which, with proper facilities and protection, could be made to serve as the breath of a real life for the toilers in the bee-hive cities along the Atlantic seaboard and elsewhere.

Second, he notes the possibilities for health and recuperation. The oxygen in the mountain air along the Appalachian skyline is a natural resource (and a national resource) that radiates to the heavens its enormous health-giving powers with only a fraction of a percent utilized for human rehabilitation. Here is a resource that could save thousands of lives. The sufferers from tuberculosis, anemia, and insanity go through the whole strata of human society....

Next after the opportunities for recreation and recuperation our giant counts off, as a third big

resource, the opportunities in the Appalachian for employment on the land. This brings up a need that is becoming urgent—the redistribution of our population, which grows more and more top heavy.

The rural population of the United States, and of the Eastern States adjacent to the Appalachians, has now dipped below the urban....

There are in the Appalachian belt probably 25 million acres of grazing and agricultural land awaiting development. Here is room for a whole new rural population. Here is an opportunity—if only the way can be found—for that counter migration from city to country that has so long been prayed for....

Such are the outlooks—such the opportunities—seen by a discerning spirit from the Appalachian skyline.

It looks, then, as if it might be worth while to devote some energy at least to working out a better utilization of our spare time. The spare time for one percent of our population would be equivalent, as above reckoned, to the continuous activity of some 40,000 persons. If these people were on the skyline, and kept their eyes open, they would see things that the giant could see. Indeed this force of 40,000 would be a giant in itself. It could walk the skyline and develop its varied opportunities. And this is the job that we propose: a project to develop the opportunities—for recreation, recuperation, and employment—in the region of the Appalachian skyline.

The project is one for a series of recreational communities throughout the Appalachian chain of mountains from New England to Georgia, these to be connected by a walking trail. Its purpose is to establish a base for a more extensive and systematic development of outdoor community life. It is a project in housing and community architecture.

No scheme is proposed in this particular article for organizing or financing this project. Organizing is a matter of detail to be carefully worked out. Financing depends upon local public interest in the various localities affected.

> [MacKaye outlined what he saw as the four parts of the project: the trail itself, shelter camps that would be a day's walk apart, community camps, with private homes, and food and farm camps that would raise the products to support the community camps.]

The results achievable in the camp and scouting life are common knowledge to all who have passed beyond the tenderfoot stage therein. The camp community is a sanctuary and a refuge from the scramble of every-day worldly commercial life. It is in essence a retreat from profit. Cooperation replaces antagonism, trust replaces suspicion, emulation replaces competition. An Appalachian trail, with its camps, communities, and spheres of influence along the skyline, should, with reasonably good management, accomplish these achievements. And they possess within them the elements of a deep dramatic appeal.

Indeed the lure of the scouting life can be made the most formidable enemy of the lure of militarism (a thing with which this country is menaced along with all others). It comes the nearest perhaps, of things thus far projected to supplying what Professor James once called a "moral equivalent of war." It appeals to the primal instincts of a fighting heroism, of volunteer service and of work in a common cause.

These instincts are pent up forces in every human and they demand their outlet. This is the avowed object of the boy scout and girl scout movement, but it should not be limited to juveniles.

The building and protection of an Appalachian trail, with its various communities, interests, and possibilities, would form at least one outlet. Here is a job for 40,000 souls. This trail could be made to be, in a very literal sense, a battle line against fire and flood—and even

against disease. Such battles—against the common enemies of man—still lack, it is true, the "punch" of man vs. man. There is but one reason—publicity. Militarism has been made colorful in a world of drab. But the care of the country side, which the scouting life instills, is vital in any real protection of "home and country." Already basic it can be made spectacular. Here is something to be dramatized.

• • •

Although MacKaye had not been active in the hiking community of the Northeast, Guy and Laura Waterman wrote in *From Forest to Crag*, he now felt he had a "product worth pushing" and sought out others who could help him. His article was widely distributed within the planning and outdoors communities, sometimes at his own cost.

The established hiking clubs in New York and New Jersey jumped at the plan, and within two years had completed the first section of the trail, running through the Palisades Interstate Park. In a 1925 meeting of interested groups in Washington, D.C., the Appalachian Trail Conference was formed, and the route of the trail was generally set: about two thousand miles through fourteen states, from Springer Mountain in northern Georgia, through the Smoky Mountains of Tennessee and North Carolina, to the Shenandoahs of Virginia, the Adirondacks of New York, and the White Mountains of New Hampshire to end at Mt. Katahdin in northern Maine. The other parts of MacKaye's utopian vision were neglected.

Little happened, however, until the end of the 1920s, when the energetic Milton Avery became head of the trail conference. By 1934, according to the official ATC history, 1,937 miles of the trail had been blazed, apparently by fewer than one hundred volunteers. In 1937 the last two miles were opened in Maine and the trail was declared complete. Since then, the conference, mostly made up of volunteers, has worked to maintain the trail, move it when development intervened, buy up private land for its protection, and publish guidebooks and maps for users.

About three to four million people hike parts of the trail, now officially listed at 2,167 miles, each year. As of July 2001, according to the Appalachian Trail Conference, 6,006 people had hiked its entire length, either in one year or in segments.

BERNARD DEVOTO SAYS THE WEST BELONGS TO ALL

Lumbering, mining, railroading, farming, grazing—the struggle over private use of public lands has rocked the West since the earliest days of settlement. To hear the "hardworking Westerner" tell the story, the federal government was a bunch of Eastern bureaucrats whose sole purpose was to keep Westerners from earning a living. Never mind that public land, by definition, belongs to everyone in the nation. Or that the West had long paid less than market value for use of the land, was prone to ignoring the few regulations that existed, and often exploited, rather than maintained, natural resources.

In 1946, Bernard DeVoto, a historian and writer of the influential "Easy Chair" column in *Harper*'s magazine, went West to do research on what would be his trilogy on settlement of the West in the early 1800s. Although he had been born in Utah, DeVoto had not been a Western writer. But he came back from the trip "a confirmed and militant conservationist," said his colleague Wallace Stegner. DeVoto had become aware of a plan by large Western stockholders to introduce a bill in Congress to give the states greater control over public lands. Calculating that January 1947 would be about the time the bill would be introduced, he readied "The West Against Itself" as a pre-emptive move in that month's *Harper's*. In it, he first laid out the history of land and economic development in the West, then warned his readers of what was afoot.

"The West Against Itself," by Bernard DeVoto. *Harper's,* January 1947.

The national parks are composed of lands that were once part of the public domain (plus a few minute areas that had previously passed out of it). Exceedingly small in total area, they are permanently reserved and dedicated to their present uses: the preservation of wilderness areas, the protection of supreme scenic beauties, and the pleasure and recreation of the American people. By the terms of the original dedication and by policy so far kept inviolate they are to be maintained as they are, they are not to be commercially exploited at all. But they contain timber, grazing land, water, and minerals. And that, in the West's eyes, is what is wrong with them.

The Olympic National Park contains a virgin stand of Sitka spruce, which yields a wood that was once essential for airplanes. During the war a violent agitation was conducted by logging interests (unobtrusively backed by other interests . . .). There was more than enough Sitka spruce in privately owned and national forests to take care of any demand but no matter: Victory depended on our opening the Olympic National Park to logging. The persistence and power of that agitation and its accompanying propaganda (some of it conducted in the public schools, which are not supposed to be poisoned with collectivism) would be unbelievable to anyone who had not looked into them.

The National Park Service, backed by conservation associations and by other lumbering interests which have seen the light, was able to hold fast—the Olympic Park was not logged. But immediately after the war ended, the same interests, augmented by a good many others, began an even more violent campaign of agitation, commercial pressure, and political pressure. We must now house the veterans and clearly we could not do so unless we opened all the national parks to logging.

That onslaught has been held in check and it will not win this time. But it will be repeated many times and the West intends it to win.

This campaign had nothing to do with Sitka spruce, winning the war, or housing veterans. Its purpose was to make a breach in the national parks policy with the aid of war emotions, and to create a precedent. Once that precedent should be set, the rest would follow. Lumber companies could log the parks. Cattle and sheep associations could graze them. Mining companies could get at their mineral deposits. Power companies could build dams in them, water companies could use their lakes and rivers. Each of those objectives has been repeatedly attempted in the past and the sun never sets on the West's efforts to achieve them. Success would mean not only the destruction of the national parks but, as we shall see, far worse.

The parks are trivial in extent, though the destruction of their forests, many of which have critical locations, would have disproportionately destructive effect on the watersheds—the watersheds which must be preserved if the West is to continue to exist as a society. They are trivial— the main objectives of the Western assault on the natural resources are the remnants of the national domain, the Taylor Act grazing lands, and the national forests.

I have heard this assault called a conspiracy but it is in no way secret or even surreptitious; it is open and enthusiastically supported by many Westerners, by many Western newspapers, and by almost all the Western specialty press. Openly engaged in it are parts of the lumber industry (though other important parts of that industry are opposing it), some water users (though water users would be its first victims), the national associations of cattle and sheep growers and a majority of the state and local associations, large parts of the mining industry, the U.S. Chamber of Commerce (some of whose local chambers are in opposition), and those Western members of Congress who represent these interests. Obscure but blandly co-operative in the background are Eastern interests perennially hostile to the West and concerned here because they greatly desire to halt and reduce government regulation and to open additional Western wealth to liquidation— notably the power companies.

Right now the cattlemen and sheepmen are carrying the ball. We must confine ourselves to them and their principal objectives—remembering that the organized assault aims at many other objectives which would benefit other groups. Their limited objectives are:

1. Conversion of the privilege which cattlemen and sheepmen now have of grazing their stock on Taylor Act and Forest Service lands—a privilege which is now subject to regulation and adjustment and for which they pay less than it is worth—into a vested right guaranteed them and subject to only such regulation as they may impose upon themselves.

2. Distribution of all the Taylor Act grazing lands, which is to say practically all the public domain that still exists, to the individual states, as a preliminary to disposition of them by private sale. (At an insignificant price. At an inflammatory meeting of committees of the American National Livestock Association and the National Woolgrowers Association in Salt Lake City in August 1946, the price most commonly suggested was ten cents an acre.)

3. Reclassification of lands in the national forests and removal from the jurisdiction of the Forest Service of all lands that can be classified as valuable for grazing, so that these lands may be transferred to the states and eventually sold. Immediately in contemplation is the removal of all government regulation of grazing in about 27,000,000 acres of forest lands and their distribution to the states—and to stockmen and woolgrowers as soon thereafter as possible. . . .

The immediate objectives make this attempt one of the biggest landgrabs in American history.

The ultimate objectives make it incomparably the biggest. The plan is to get rid of public lands altogether, turning them over to the states, which can be coerced as the federal government cannot be, and eventually to private ownership.

This is your land we are talking about.

The attack has already carried important outposts. Regulation of the use of Taylor Act lands, the vast public range outside the national forests, was vested in the Grazing Service. Over the last few years that service was so systematically reduced in staff and appropriations that some cattlemen and sheepmen have been grazing the public range just as they see fit. Violation of the Taylor Act is widespread, flagrant, systematic, and frequently recommend to their members as policy by various local cattle and sheep associations. The Grazing Service was organized to assist grazers and to protect the public interest. When it took the latter purpose seriously it was emasculated and this year has been killed by Western members of Congress, under the leadership of Senator McCarran of Nevada. But Senator McCarran is by no means so extreme as the majority of the big stockmen whose interest he serves so brilliantly in Washington. His more limited purpose is to get the public lands away from those he calls "the swivel-chair oligarchy," that is, federal officials who cannot be coerced, and into the hands of the states. His model is his own state government, a small oligarchy dominated by stockmen. . . .

But the most revealing bill was last session's S 1945 introduced by Senator Robertson. The Senator is, it should be noted, the owner of one of the largest and finest sheep and cattle ranches in Wyoming. He holds a grazing permit in his own name in the Shoshone National Forest for 2400 sheep, has a financial interest in an association that grazes 1200 sheep there, and acts in various ways as agent for individuals and associations that graze nearly 8000 more sheep in the same forest. His bill is a sweetheart.

The Robertson Bill would transfer to thirteen Western states all unappropriated and unreserved lands, *including the minerals in them;* all oil and mineral reserves; all minerals, coal, oil, and gas and all rights related to them in the public lands; and all homestead lands that have been forfeited to the United States. It would empower the states to dispose of these lands as they might see fit—that is, to sell them—except that coal, oil, and gas lands must be leased, not sold, and the federal government would retain power to prorate production. . . .

The public lands are first to be transferred to the states on the fully justified assumption that if there should be a state government not wholly compliant to the desires of stockgrowers, it could be pressured into compliance. The intention is to free them of all regulation except such as stockgrowers might impose upon themselves. Nothing in history suggests that the states are adequate to protect their own resources, or even want to, or suggests that cattlemen and sheepmen are capable of regulating themselves even for their own benefit, still less the public's. And the regulations immediately to be got rid of are those by which the government has been trying to prevent overgrazing of the public range. Cattlemen and sheepmen, I repeat, want to shovel most of the West into its rivers.

From the states the public lands are to be transferred to private ownership. Present holders of permits are to be constituted a prior and privileged caste, to the exclusion of others except on such terms as they may dictate. They are to be permitted to buy the lands—the public lands, the West's lands, your lands—at a fraction of what they are worth. And the larger intention is to liquidate all the publicly held resources.

Everyone knows that the timber of the United States is being cut faster than replacements are being grown, that the best efforts of the government and of those private operators who realize that other generations will follow ours have not so far sufficed to balance the growth of saw timber with logging. Everyone knows that regulation of grazing is the only hope of preserving the range. . . .

But that is, by a good deal, the least of it. Most of the fundamental watersheds of the West lie within the boundaries of the Taylor Act lands, the national forests, and the national parks. And overgrazing the range and liquidating the forests destroys the watersheds. In many places in the West today property in land, irrigating systems, and crops is steadily deteriorating because the best efforts of the government to repair damage to watersheds—damage caused by overgrazing the ranges and overcutting the forests—has not been enough.

Stream beds choke with silt and floods spread over the rich fields on the slopes and in the bottoms, always impairing and sometimes destroying them. Dams and canals and reservoirs silt up, decline in efficiency, have to be repaired at great expense, cannot be fully restored. Fields gully, soil blows away. Flash floods kill productive land, kill livestock, kill human beings, sometimes kill communities. . . .

The program which is planned to liquidate the range and forests would destroy the Western watersheds. Which is to say that it would destroy the natural resources of the West, and with them so many rivers, towns, cities, farms, ranches, mines, and power sites that a great part of the West would be obliterated. It would return much of the West, most of the habitable interior West, to the processes of geology. It would make Western life as we now know it, and therefore American life as we now know it, impossible.

There you have it. A few groups of Western interests, so small numerically as to constitute a minute fraction of the West, are hellbent on destroying the West. They are stronger than they would otherwise be because they are skilfully manipulating in their support sentiments that have always been powerful in the West—the home rule which means basically that we want federal help without federal regulation, the "individualism"

that has always made the small Western operator a handy tool of the big one, and the wild myth that stockgrowers constitute an aristocracy in which all Westerners somehow share. They have managed to line up behind them many Western interests that would perish if they should succeed. And they count on the inevitable postwar reaction against government regulation to put their program over.

To a historian it has the beauty of any historical continuity. It is the Western psychology working within the pattern which its own nature has set. It is the forever recurrent lust to liquidate the West that is so large a part of Western history. The West has always been a society living under threat of destruction by natural cataclysm and here it is, bright against the sky, inviting such a cataclysm.

But if it has this mad beauty is also has an almost cosmic irony, in that the fulfillment of the great dream of the West, mature economic development and local ownership and control, has been made possible by the developments of our age at exactly the same time. That dream envisions the establishment of an economy on the natural resources of the West, developed and integrated to produce a steady, sustained, permanent yield. While the West moves to build that kind of economy, a part of the West is simultaneously moving to destroy the natural resources forever. That paradox is absolutely true to the Western mind and spirit. But the future of the West hinges on whether it can defend itself against itself.

• • •

"DeVoto's performance was a bugle call, a challenge and a declaration of war," said T. H. Watkins in his history *The Lands No One Knows*. Alerted to the plans, Western interests opposed to the stockmen began to protest, the few conservation groups rallied, and Western newspapers objected. "Everything had depended on hurrying the legislation through Congress before Congress itself and the public at large could find out what it was all about," DeVoto reflected with satisfaction. His article prevented that. Bills that had been already written were put back in the drawer, and some Western congressmen danced around their intentions; DeVoto took credit for defeating at least one western congressman and one senator. But he was also aware of how tenacious his opponents could be. (The issue of use of public lands is a continuing fight today.) Staying the course, DeVoto went on to write more than forty articles about conservation and the West, and he encouraged journalist friends to also write about the issue.

In a collection of his essays issued in 1955, DeVoto gathered some of his western land stories under the title "Treatise on the Function of Journalism."

THE WRITINGS OF MARJORY STONEMAN DOUGLAS WIN FRIENDS FOR THE EVERGLADES

For much of the twentieth century, Marjory Stoneman Douglas worked to protect the Florida Everglades. In the 1920s, she wrote pieces opposing the draining of the Everglades. In the 1930s and the 1940s, she worked in her writings and through lobbying to establish the Everglades as a national park.

Finally, results came. In 1947 she published her important, lyrical environmental work *The Everglades: River of Grass* and, that same year, saw President Harry S. Truman set aside the area as the Everglades National Park.

Still, her efforts continued to protect the Everglades, damaged by highway construction, the building of an airport, housing and commercial development, and draining for agriculture. In 1967, she wrote *Florida: The Long Frontier*, and by this time she had established her reputation as one of the nation's outstanding environmentalists and environ-

mental writers. In 1969, at age eighty, Douglas founded Friends of the Everglades to work for protection and restoration of wetlands throughout south Florida. She traveled through much of the United States, condemning, Ted Levin said in *Audubon* magazine in 1998, "foot-dragging politicians, land-hungry developers, the sugar industry, [and] the U.S. Army Corps of Engineers."

Here is an excerpt from Douglas's *The Everglades: River of Grass*, which *Audubon* magazine said in 1998, when it named Douglas one of the century's most distinguished environmentalists, "forever changed the way Americans view the Florida Everglades."

The Everglades: River of Grass, by Marjory Stoneman Douglas. New York: Rinehart & Company, 1947.

FROM THE LAST CHAPTER, "THE ELEVENTH HOUR."

The Indians, before anyone else, knew that the Everglades were being destroyed. During the war there was less and less rain, in one of those long, unpredictable, unpreventable dry spells, in which year after year the fresh water, like the soil, shrank away.

The surface of the great lake that had been so arbitrarily lowered still discharged quantities of the good water out the main canals, the Caloosahatchee and the St. Lucie. The lower Glades suffered. The land along the laterals dried and sank in deeper and wider valleys. Where there had been the flow of the river of grass, there were only drying pools, and mosquitoes.

The saw grass dried, rustling like paper. Garfish, thick in the pools where there had been watercourses, ate all the other fish, and died and stank in their thousands. The birds flew over and far south, searching for fresh water. The lower pools shrank and were brackish. Deer and raccoons traveled far, losing their fear of houses and people in their increasing thirst.

The fires began.

Cattlemen's grass fires roared uncontrolled. Cane-field fires spread crackling and hissing in the saw grass in vast waves and pillars and blowing mountains of heavy, cream-colored, purple-shadowed smoke. Training planes flying over the Glades dropped bombs or cigarette butts, and the fires exploded in the hearts of the drying hammocks and raced on before every wind, leaving only blackness. Palmetto burst in the fiery heat that spread from pine tree to pine tree in flaming brands. The flames ate down into the drying ancient saw-grass muck and smoldered and burned and glowed there for weeks, slow orange glares in the night or constant rolling smoke by day, eating down to the ultimate rock.

The acrid smoke drifted over the cities, and people choked and suffocated in it. Many left.

Men watching from fire towers got tired of counting smokes against which they could do nothing. There was not water in the canals with which to fight them. Houses, trees, groves were burned. The fires swept along the Tamiami [Tampa to Miami] Trail and burned the camps as the Indians fled from them. There were weeks when the trail and the other roads were closed to traffic, blinded by the dense covering choking smoke.

All night long the fires stood about the sky, their glare as high as the sky, the flames reflected on the churning orange pillars of their smoke. And when in the daytime they had passed slowly, burning and glowing down to the rock, behind them was only the blackness of desolation.

The whole Everglades were burning. What had been a river of grass and sweet water that had given meaning and life and uniqueness to this whole enormous geography through centuries in which man had no place here was made, in one chaotic gesture of greed and ignorance and folly, a river of fire.

Then, all the people of the cities who had not paid much attention to the Everglades were startled by another thing. The sweet water the rock had held was gone or had shrunk down far into its strange holes and cleavages. The rim of the rock, which in perfect balance had established the life of the Glades, had also held back the salty unending power of the sea. Now the tides moved easily up through the cuts and breaks men had dynamited in the rocky eastern retaining walls. The heavy salt water crept up the rivers and to their headwaters and beyond, up the canals and the least drying watercourses. . . .

In the Glades the fires raged. Up the rivers and the canals, through the rock and the soil, across the lowlands not much higher than the high tide, the salt worked.

Where the herds browsed along the old lake bottoms above the Caloosahatchee, the cattle on the burned-over fields bawled for water and there was none. There was no greenness in the dried canal beds, and little shade under the few trees. The herds began to die.

Far south, where Royal Palm State Park had kept the beauties of Paradise Key as they had been, a dark tropical jungle dominated by majestic native royal palm trees, the fires raged across the saw grass. There was no water in the old sloughs around the park. There was no one to watch the flames. In a week in which the fires spread into the drying jungles, slashed across the firebreaks, the flames worked and smoldered deep in the roots and hearts of the beautiful old live oaks. All the fine tropical trees of the jungle were eaten out. Birds, snakes, deer, small animals were caught in the flames. The delicate tree snails were burned, the orchids, the air plants, the ancient leather ferns, the butterflies. What had been unique and lovely and strange was a black monotony of destruction.

The Indians stared at the smoke, the creeping fires, with the stoic faces of fatalism. This was the end of their world.

But the white man, in all his teeming variety, men of the farms and the Glades, men of the cities and of the sea, whose inertia and pigheadedness, greed and willfulness had caused all this, as if for the first time seeing what he had done, now, when it was almost too late, the white man was aroused. For the first time in South Florida since the earliest floods, there were mass meetings and protests, editorials, petitions, letters, and excited talk. Thousands, choking in acrid smoke, saw for the first time what the drainage of the Glades had brought to pass. . . .

So that at last, with the lands drying and the smoke still drifting from the fires eating at the valuable muck, the problem of the Everglades was seen whole. . . .

It was too soon to expect that all these people would see that the destruction of the Everglades was the destruction of all. They had all cried for help in times of extreme wetness and of extreme dryness, as if they could not realize that they lived under a regular alternation of extremes. They received the help always given in emergencies. But they could not get it through their heads that they had produced some of the worst conditions themselves, by their lack of co-operation, their selfishness, their mutual distrust and their willful refusal to consider the truth of the whole situation.

Time and the destruction of the soil, the ruin of the Glades, went on surely and inevitably. It was later than they thought.

The fall rains in the year 1945 put out the fires. The people, all those diversified masses of people who lived in this still sunny and beautiful country, by the great sea, under the silken and moving airs, in a land which was still green with trees and gardens and growing groves, forgot. The old wastefulness went on. The bulldozers of new lot owners destroyed the hardwood trees of the cut-up ancient hammocks. In the Big Cypress the lumber companies were cutting out the tallest of the ancient gray trees. A new wave of hungry life, after the war, moved down into the sun and the expanding coastal cities. Again the life and death of the Everglades went unrecognized. . . .

Unless the people act the fires will come again. Overdrainage will go on. The soil will shrink and burn and be wasted and destroyed, in a continuing ruin. The salt will lie in wait.

Yet the springs of fine water had flowed again. The balance still existed between the forces of life and of death. There is a balance in man also, one which has set against his greed and his inertia and his foolishness; his courage, his will, his ability slowly and painfully to learn, and to work together.

Perhaps even in this last hour, in a new relation of usefulness and beauty, the vast, magnificent, subtle and unique region of the Everglades may not be utterly lost.

•   •   •

Douglas remained dissatisfied with efforts of local, state, and federal governmental bodies to protect the Everglades, and in 1994, at the age of 104, angry that the state was retreating from what she regarded as its responsibilities to protect the Everglades, said she wanted her name removed from the Marjory Stoneman Douglas Everglades Forever Act of 1964.

But her perseverance, and that of others, continued to cause change. In the 1990s, the federal government, after years of negotiations, announced a plan to stop agricultural development of the Everglades, reconstruct watercourses, and place major prohibitions on draining.

Douglas died in May 1998. She was 108.

SIGURD F. OLSON AND HAROLD H. MARTIN PLEA FOR PROTECTION OF THE QUETICO-SUPERIOR WILDERNESS

Shortly after World War I, Sigurd F. Olson, a high school teacher from Ely, Minnesota, began guiding canoe parties through the lakes and rivers of the Quetico-Superior wilderness along the Minnesota-Canadian border. Through this wild area more than a century before had passed the voyageurs, men of astonishing endurance who set out each summer from the western shore of Lake Superior with a year's supplies and returned after ice-out the next spring with stupendous caches of furs, to be made into top hats for fashionable men in New York, Boston, and London. Parts of this vast area were logged in the nineteenth century, and after the war cars and motorboats were becoming popular, and there was talk as well, in the northwoods and elsewhere in the United States, of constructing a "road to every lake" in the boundary waters. Chambers of Commerce began talking of developing the area into "The Playground of a Nation." There was talk, too, of constructing seven large hydroelectric dams in the region.

Those who wanted to preserve the area as wilderness were slower getting organized. Then, in the 1920s, Olson and conservationists such as Ernest C. Oberholtzer and Robert Marshall formed the Quetico-Superior Council to put together plans to protect the millions of acres of wilderness that were threatened. In 1926 the U.S. Forest Service established the Superior Primitive Area there. Later, this area, enlarged, became the Boundary Waters Canoe Area.

After World World War II, larger, more powerful motors and launches, seaplanes, plans for construction of large lodges and roads between them—and a continuing contempt for wilderness—brought new threats to the area. Olson had already written of the glories of the area in such publications as *Sports Afield* and *Field and Stream* but knew he needed a wider audience. In 1948, Olson began working with a journalist and friend, Harold H. Martin of the *Saturday Evening Post*, to get out a popular article that would alert Americans to the beauty of the Quetico-Superior area and the dangers to its lakes, streams, and forests. That summer the two, with a photographer, set out on a canoe trip into the area. No other people were on the lakes, an Olson biographer said. Early that fall this piece resulted:

"Embattled Wilderness," by Harold H. Martin. *Saturday Evening Post,* September 25, 1948.

One day last spring the bush pilots who fly their seaplanes out of the little town of Ely, Minnesota, into the wild tangle of lakes and rivers, rocks and forests along the Minnesota-Ontario border received a plaintive request from a Mr. Marshall Reinig, the operator of a mink farm.

Mr. Reinig would appreciate it very much, he said, if the pilots in their journeyings to and from the wild would refrain from flying over his establishment. His lady mink were in the process of becoming mothers and were, in consequence, in a highly nervous state. The sight and the sound of an airplane sometimes threw them into such a frenzy that they destroyed their young.

The sight and sound of seaplanes flying into the uttermost reaches of mid-continental America's last great wilderness canoe country causes more distress to many, other than Mr. Reinig's mink. It also profoundly disturbs an army of outdoorsmen who for nearly twenty-five years have fought a ceaseless, and up to now a winning battle to keep unspoiled the primeval character of one of the last remaining fragments of the original America—a lonely, wild and peaceful land of woods and waters unique upon the continent and perhaps upon the earth.

For a while it appeared that the crusade, waged with almost fanatic fervor by the Quetico-Superior Council, the Izaak Walton League, the Wilderness Society, the Minnesota Department of Conservation and many another organization with similar ideals and purposes, had finally been won. In 1933–39 the Federal government set aside 1,000,000 acres of that portion of the Superior National Forest which lay along the border lakes as a "primitive roadless area," never to be opened to commercial exploitation. Minnesota, approving, adopted the same policy on a small area of state land along the border. Canada, though she already had more wilderness than she knew what to do with, in the spirit of a good neighbor placed the same restrictions on her own magnificent canoe country, the Quetico Provincial Park, just across the line. By keeping these areas free of access roads it was hoped that the 100-odd thousand acres of private land scattered within the Federal holdings on the American side could never be developed commercially. Within 750 miles of 43,000,000 Americans, a changeless island in eternity would forever remain as wild and beautiful and serene as it was when the first *voyageur* floated his birch-bark canoe upon its waters nearly 300 years ago.

The law reckoned without the airplane and the surpassing eagerness of the American businessman to catch a fish big enough to stuff and hang upon his wall. Up until a few years ago, airplanes had gone into the wilderness only on emergency missions.

Today, in violation of the spirit if not the letter of the roadless-area order, seaplanes are dropping down on lakes once as inaccessible except by canoe as the craters of the moon, depositing thereon cargoes of happy characters wearing floppy white fishing hats. To the loneliest hinterlands of the American North country the airplane has brought such anachronisms as pretty waitresses, white napery, soft mattresses and indoor plumbing.

The appearance on the American side of hostelries ministering to the comfort of this new and softer breed of visitors to the wild has naturally caused some lifted eyebrows across the line in Canada. Ontario sees little reason why she should maintain her beautiful Quetico for the pleasure of Americans happily ensconced in hotels just across the border when by merely opening the area to airplane resorts she could be reaping a fat harvest of American dollars for herself....

Amid the encircling gloom brought on by the aerial invasion of this still essentially wild core of the proposed forest there shines, though, one recent ray of hope. The eightieth Congress passed and President Truman signed a bill authorizing the Secretary of Agriculture to spend up to $500,000 buying up private lands which might be used for commercial purposes. This will forestall further resort development. It will not affect existing resorts, a number of which lie in the heart of the wild, monopolizing for their guests some of the loneliest and most beautiful sections of the canoe country. Under the provisions of the act these resorts, developed during the war, are exempt from condemnation if their owners do not wish to sell. Nor does the bill place any controls upon the airplane, which not only serves the resorts but, for ten dollars a head, flies day parties in to isolated lakes, drops them off into a canoe carried strapped to the plane's pontoons, and picks them up at dusk, bringing ice in which to pack the fish the anglers will take home.

The canoeman's antipathy to the airplane is understandable to anyone who has ever made the journey on the border lakes in the old and simple way. It is bruising to the spirit of a man who has paddled for days seeking some sanctuary where he may commune in peace with the waters and the ancient rocks, to have a plane suddenly roar down into the silence bringing a load of jovial fishermen fresh from their paneled offices in the Chicago Loop. It is equally depressing to round some rocky headland in the gloaming and see the lights of a new fishing lodge shining from a campsite where for hundreds of years canoemen had built their cooking fires.

The airplane by its noise destroys for the man in the canoe the intangible, almost indescribably quality of the wilderness, a quality compounded of silence and solitude and a brooding sense of peace that sinks into the spirit. It also robs its user of all chance to know the magic spell the wilderness casts upon those who slowly paddle and portage their way into its heart. To the canoeman, aware of every facet of the lake country's wild beauty, the fisherman who roars down upon the wild after a fifteen-minute flight from Ely no more comprehends the land and the life about him than would a Finnish lumberjack suddenly dropped by parachute into Broadway at 42nd Street.

The spirit of the wilderness is too fragile to survive for long in a resort atmosphere. The howling of airplane engines and the sputter of outboards not only rend the veil of silence that gives to the wilderness its cathedral calm; they cause the moose, the bear and the beaver to hightail for distant parts unknown, depriving the canoe camper of the pleasure of their company. The airborne fisherman rarely sees more of that prehistoric throwback, the moose, than his head and antlers, stuffed and mounted and hung over the fireplace of a lodge. The canoeist sometimes gets close enough to some placidly browsing bull to whack him cordially on the rump with a paddle. The patron of the fishing lodge may step from his bath upon a bearskin rug. The camper hears the living bear snuffing about his tent at night, and smells his wild, rank, musty scent. The howl of a timber wolf floating over the hills sounds different to the man snug in his bed in a stout log lodge from the way it does to a camper curled in his sleeping bag on the duff beneath the trees. Both may know that the wolf does not consider people an essential item in its diet, but the man

in the open derives more comfort from that knowledge. . . .

Taking all these matters into consideration, the canoeman comes up with a simple solution. There are 11,000 lakes in Minnesota outside the wilderness area, where the scenery is beautiful and the fishing still is good. Let the resort owners now sitting in the heart of the wild sell out to the Government and move to one of these, abandoning their present locations to the wilderness. Under the law put through the last Congress by Minnesota's Senators Ball and Thye and Representative Blatnik, the Government also may exchange Federal lands in the resort areas for private holdings in the wilderness.

The answer of the resort owners to the proposal that they sell or swap is short and to the point. Said Billy Zup, whose Curtain Falls Fishing Camp sits on Crooked Lake, once a favorite stretch of canoe water: "I worked nine years to get this place going. Now I have got it. I am just like a retired man. I've got something to take care of me the rest of my life. If I sold out or traded I'd have to start all over again. If the Government wants me out of here they will have to pay me. I've got three kids to think about."

Said Martin Skala of Lac La Croix Lodge, on Lac La Croix, another body of water once highly regarded by canoe campers: "Some of my patrons are along in years. They don't have the strength to come in here by canoe. And they have just as much right to fish in these lakes as anybody."

Mr. Skala's observation brings up two of the main points of difference between the man in the canoe and the man in the resort hotel. The resort fisherman assumes that only a bull-necked athlete with the thews of a moose has the strength to make a canoe trip into the wilderness. The canoeman answers that paddling a canoe, even one heavily loaded, is as gentle a form of exercise as has yet been devised. Packs admittedly are heavy, but the portages between lakes are short, and even the sinewy *voyageur* of the fur-trade days was not ashamed to lay his burdens down for a brief rest. . . .

The canoeman also takes issues with the resort patron's view that the main lure of the wilderness is the plenitude and rapacity of its fish. . . . Too great a concentration upon fishing, he feels, causes a man to miss the myriad more subtle pleasures that the wilderness offers those who enter it with eyes and mind and heart all open to accept its mysteries.

• • •

The piece did all, and more, that Olson and Martin, one of the well-known magazine writers of the day, wished to accomplish. On December 19, 1949, President Harry S. Truman issued an executive order barring aircraft from flying over the area at altitudes of less than 4,000 feet. Olson and others continued the fight for more protection. In 1964, President Lyndon B. Johnson, acting under the Wilderness Act passed that September, designated more than nine million acres in the United States as wilderness, including the Boundary Waters Canoe Area. Similar protections exist on the Canadian side of the Minnesota border.

Olson, an affable, craggy-faced man, lived in a comfortable, unpretentious home in his beloved Ely, loved by some there, not loved by others. He worked in an old, remodeled garage, a small, narrow structure from the early days of automobiles. In the winter, outside a large window in his house, he kept a large, rough, homemade bird feeder to which were attracted many kinds of birds, including—one winter day in the 1970s when interviewed by William Serrin—a stupendous flock of pine grosbeaks.

Among Olson's books are *The Singing Wilderness* and *Listening Point*. All are movingly illustrated with handsome line drawings of canoers, birds, and animals, and scenes from the Boundary Waters wilderness area that Olson worked so long, hard, and successfully to save.

CHALLENGING THE *WASHINGTON POST*, JUSTICE WILLIAM O. DOUGLAS TAKES EDITORIAL WRITERS ON A HIKE AND SAVES THE C & O CANAL

In the early 1950s, little thought was given to conservation. Cities were spreading, dams were being constructed, and, within a few years, the nation would embark upon an almost unquestioned highway project: the construction of some 40,000 miles of interstate highways, many of them dissecting American cities. In Washington, D.C., the old Chesapeake and Ohio Canal, constructed beginning in 1828 and running 184.5 miles from Georgetown to Cumberland, Maryland, was in great disrepair. It had not been used as a working canal since 1924; the U.S. government had owned the right of way since 1938. Congress developed a proposal to construct, using the towpath and the canal as its base, a road from Washington to Maryland. Many local businesses and economic interests supported the plan.

The *Washington Post* joined these groups in an editorial on January 3, 1954.

"Potomac Parkway." *Washington Post,* January 3, 1954.

The renewal of official interest in the proposed parkway along the old C. & O. Canal between Great Falls and Cumberland will stir the enthusiasm of many Washingtonians. The purpose of such a parkway would be to open up the greatest scenic asset in this area—the Potomac River—to wider public enjoyment. Maryland is already building a 60-mile stretch of the proposed road up the river from Hancock. Local interest is largely concentrated, however, in the section of the proposed parkway that would stretch from Great Falls to Harpers Ferry.

Any fears that this project would destroy restored sections of the old canal between Washington and Great Falls can be put aside. This stretch of the river is to be opened up by the George Washington Memorial Highway. The parkway now under discussion would extend up the river from Great Falls on the bed of the abandoned C. & O. Canal or on the adjacent towpath. By utilizing the old canal—no longer either a commercial or a scenic asset—it is estimated that the parkway could be built for $100,000 a mile. The lovely Potomac Valley could thus be made available to sightseers, campers, fishermen and hikers with little detraction from its beauty. The basic advantage of the parkway is that it would enable more people to enjoy beauties now seen by very few—in the fashion, say, of the magnificent Blue Ridge parkway. Large areas of wilderness would be left and ought to be protected permanently against further encroachment.

Behind this proposal also is the hope that, with the Potomac more accessible, it would be cleaned up and made a great recreational asset. Washington has been astonishingly tardy in taking advantage of this natural playground. The famous founder of this Capital would be shocked to learn that the Potomac has become a sort of open sewer and that some of the most attractive portions of its valley are almost completely unknown even after a century and a half. By naming a committee to study the idea of a C. & O. Canal parkway, Robert M. Watkins, chairman of the Regional Planning Council, appears to have caught some of the vision of George Washington in locating the Capital here. It will take a great deal of work and practical planning, however, if this vision of a great Potomac playground is to be realized.

• • •

Not all of the readers of the *Post*'s editorial page saw the vision of George Washington in the editorial's suggestion. One of them was William O. Douglas, associate justice of the U.S. Supreme Court, a man whose passion for the outdoors sprung from his native Washington state and had never diminished, a man who believed that roadless areas were a pledge to freedom. "The editorial got under my skin," Douglas told a friend.

In a letter to the paper published on January 19, 1954, he challenged the writers of the editorial to rethink their position.

Dear Sir:

The discussion concerning the construction of a Parkway along the Chesapeake & Ohio Canal arouses many people. Fishermen, hunters, hikers, campers, ornithologists, and others who like to get acquainted with nature first-hand and on their own are opposed to making a highway out of this Sanctuary.

The stretch of 185 miles of country from Washington, D.C. to Cumberland, Maryland is one of the most fascinating and picturesque in the nation. The river and its islands are part of the charm. The cliffs, the streams, the draws, the benches and beaches, the swamps are another part. The birds and game, the blaze of color in the Spring and Fall, the cattails in the swamp, the blush of buds in late Winter—these are also some of the glory of the place.

In the early twenties Mr. Justice Brandeis travelled the canal and river by Canoe to Cumberland. It was for him exciting adventure and recreation. Hundreds of us still use this Sanctuary for hiking and camping. It is a refuge, a place of retreat, a long stretch of quiet and peace at the Capitol's back door— a wilderness area where man can be alone with his thoughts, a sanctuary where he can commune with God and with nature, a place not yet marred by the roar of wheels and the sound of horns.

It is a place for boys and girls, men and women. One can hike 15 or 20 miles on a Sunday afternoon, or sleep on high dry ground in the quiet of a forest, or just go and sit with no sound except water lapping at one's feet. It is a Sanctuary for everyone who loves woods—a Sanctuary that would be utterly destroyed by a fine two-lane highway.

I wish the man who wrote your editorial of January 3, 1954, approving the Parkway would take time off and come with me. We would go with packs on our backs and walk the 185 miles to Cumberland. I feel that if your editor did, he would return a new man and use the power of your great editorial page to help keep this Sanctuary untouched.

One who walked the Canal its full length could plead that cause with the eloquence of a John Muir. He would get to know muskrats, badgers, and fox; he would hear the roar of wind in thickets; he would see strange islands and promontories through the fantasy of fog; he would discover the glory there is in the first flower of spring, the glory there is even in a blade of grass; the whistling wings of ducks would make silence have new values for him. Certain it is that he could never acquire that understanding going 60, or even 25, miles an hour.

•   •   •

The *Post* editorial writers, Robert Estabrook and Merlo Pusey, accepted Douglas's challenge. By the time they were ready to set out, in March, they had 600 people who wanted to join them. They narrowed the group down to thirty-seven people whom they thought had serious interest in the outdoors, including the naturalist Sigurd Olson from Ely, Minnesota. Reversing Douglas's proposal, the group took a train from Washington to Cumberland and then walked back—nine of them, including Douglas, making it the whole way. Press attention was lavish. When the group got to Georgetown on the eighth day, an estimated 50,000 people were waiting for them.

The *Post,* to its credit, changed its position, in

an editorial written as a result of the walk. "It is good to renew one's contacts with nature," the editorial said. "At this point we are torn between a feeling of appreciation to Justice Douglas for luring us into this venture and irritation over the increasingly pathetic condition of our feet. But blisters heal and memories linger." Douglas said he was not surprised: "I felt that anybody who'd walk this towpath and see its beauties in the raw would never want to turn it into a highway."

Justice Douglas and other hikers organized a C & O Canal Committee to make recommendations to the Interior Department. The Park Service ordered another study, and a year later came out for a park along the canal. In January 1961, as one of his last acts in office, President Dwight D. Eisenhower designated the C & O Canal as a national monument. In 1977, the park was officially dedicated to Douglas.

Today the park draws millions of people each year and is a treasure of urban recreation.

RACHEL CARSON CREATES A FIRESTORM BY SAYING THAT PESTICIDES ARE KILLING BIRDS AND MAMMALS

It was shortly after the end of World War II that Rachel Carson, an editor with the Fish and Wildlife Service, first started seeing scientific reports that raised questions about the potential side effects of the insect spray DDT. The military had developed and made great use of the spray during the war to fight lice and other disease-carrying insects. But its effect on humans had been little tested. As the war ended, E. I. DuPont, the manufacturer, had large stocks of DDT on hand. The U.S. Department of Agriculture saw great potential and began championing DDT as a panacea. To popular acclaim, DDT was released to commercial use in August 1945.

Carson thought that the USDA was acting with undue speed, and she suggested a story to *Reader's*

Digest, then to other publications. No one was interested, and Carson turned to marine biology in her determination to, as her biographer Linda Lear put it, "write her way out of government work."

By the time Carson returned to the subject of DDT, ten years later, she was an established writer, and the United States was using about 600 million pounds of pesticide a year. *Silent Spring* was published in three parts in *The New Yorker* in 1962, and then as a book.

Silent Spring,
by Rachel Carson.
Boston: Houghton Mifflin, 1962

CHAPTER 1:
"A FABLE FOR TOMORROW"

There was once a town in the heart of America where all life seemed to be in harmony with its surroundings. The town lay in the midst of a checkerboard of prosperous farms, with fields of grain and hillsides of orchards where, in spring, white clouds of bloom drifted above the green fields. In autumn, oak and maple and birch set up a blaze of color that flamed and flickered across a backdrop of pines. Then foxes barked in the hills and deer silently crossed the fields, half hidden in the mists of the fall mornings.

Along the roads, laurel, viburnum, and alder, great ferns and wildflowers delighted the traveler's eye through much of the year. Even in winter, the roadsides were places of beauty, where countless birds came to feed on the berries and on the seed heads of the dried weeds rising above the snow. The countryside was, in fact, famous for the abundance and variety of its bird life, and when the flood of migrants was pouring through in spring and fall people came from great distances to observe them. Others came to fish the streams, which flowed clear and cold out of the hills and contained shady pools where trout lay. So it had been from the days many years ago when the first settlers raised their houses, sank their wells, and built their barns.

Then a strange blight crept over the area and everything began to change. Some evil spell had settled on the community; mysterious maladies swept the flocks of chickens; the cattle and sheep sickened and died. Everywhere was a shadow of death. The farmers spoke of much illness among their families. In the town the doctors had become more and more puzzled by new kinds of sickness appearing among their patients. There had been several sudden and unexplained deaths, not only among adults but even among children, who would be stricken while at play and die within a few hours.

There was a strange stillness. The birds, for example—where had they gone? Many people spoke of them, puzzled and disturbed. The feeding stations in the backyards were deserted. The few birds seen anywhere were moribund; they trembled violently and could not fly. It was a spring without voices. On the mornings that had once throbbed with the dawn chorus of robins, catbirds, doves, jays, and wrens, and scores of other bird voices, there was now no sound; only silence lay over the fields and woods and marsh.

On the farms the hens brooded, but no chicks hatched. The farmers complained that they were unable to raise any pigs—the litters were small and the young survived only a few days. The apple trees were coming into bloom, but no bees droned among the blossoms, so there was no pollination and there would be no fruit.

The roadsides, once so attractive, were now lined with browned and withered vegetation as though swept by fire. These, too, were silent, deserted by all living things. Even the streams were now lifeless. Anglers no longer visited them, for all the fish had died.

In the gutters under the eaves and between the shingles of the roofs, a white granular powder still showed a few patches; some weeks before it had fallen like snow upon the roofs and the lawns, the fields and streams.

No witchcraft, no enemy action had silenced the rebirth of new life in this stricken world. The people had done it themselves.

This town does not actually exist, but it might easily have a thousand counterparts in America or elsewhere in the world. I know of no community that has experienced all the misfortunes I describe. Yet every one of these disasters has actually happened somewhere, and many real communities have already suffered a substantial number of them. A grim specter has crept upon us almost unnoticed, and this imagined tragedy may easily become a stark reality we all shall know.

What has already silenced the voices of spring in countless towns in America? This book is an attempt to explain.

CHAPTER 2:
"THE OBLIGATION TO ENDURE"

The history of life on earth has been a history of interaction between living things and their surroundings. To a large extent, the physical form and the habits of the earth's vegetation and its animal life have been molded by the environment. Considering the whole span of earthly time, the opposite effect, in which life actually modifies its surroundings, has been relatively slight. Only within the moment of time represented by the present century has one species—man—acquired significant power to alter the nature of his world.

During the past quarter century this power has not only increased to one of disturbing magnitude but it has changed in character. The most alarming of all man's assaults upon the environment is the contamination of the air, earth, rivers, and sea with dangerous and even lethal materials. This pollution is for the most part irrecoverable; the chain of evil it initiates not only in the world that must support life but in living tissues is for the most part irreversible. In this now universal contamination of the environment, chemicals are the sinister and little recognized partners of radiation in changing the very nature of the world—

the very nature of its life. Strontium 90, released through nuclear explosions into the air, comes to earth in rain or drifts down as fallout, lodges in soil, enters into the grass or corn or wheat grown there, and, in time, takes up its abode in the bones of a human being, there to remain until his death. Similarly, chemicals sprayed on croplands or forests or gardens lie long in soil, entering into living organisms, passing from one to another in a chain of poisoning and death. Or they pass mysteriously by underground streams until they emerge and, through the alchemy of air and sunlight, combine into new forms that kill vegetation, sicken cattle, and work unknown harm on those who drink from once pure wells. As Albert Schweitzer has said, "Man can hardly even recognize the devils of his own creation."

It took hundreds of millions of years to produce the life that now inhabits the earth—eons of time in which that developing and evolving and diversifying life reached a state of adjustment and balance with its surroundings. The environment, rigorously shaping and directing the life it supported, contained elements that were hostile as well as supporting. Certain rocks gave out dangerous radiation; even within the light of the sun, from which all life draws its energy, there were short-wave radiations with power to injure. Given time—time not in years but in millennia—life adjusts, and a balance has been reached. For time is the essential ingredient; but in the modern world there is no time.

• • •

As Carson had expected, *Silent Spring* came under strong attack from chemical companies, food processors, agriculture groups, the U.S. Department of Agriculture establishment, a reviewer in *Time* magazine, and others. To her critics, she was a hysterical woman who loved birds more than humans. "I thought she was a spinster," a critic said. "What's she so worried about genetics for?" Her defenders, who rallied more slowly, were delighted that someone had put the issue of pesticide use—and the whole question of the appropriate use of science—in the public focus. E. B. White called her work "an 'Uncle Tom's Cabin' kind of book."

The furor Carson unleashed encouraged grass-roots groups across the country to challenge spraying programs and gave a great boost to the environmental movement. *Silent Spring* is properly credited with helping lead to the establishment of the Environmental Protection Agency in 1970 and the banning of DDT in the United States in 1972. Gradually, the levels of the pesticides in fish and birds—and humans—declined. Fish in such places as the Hudson River and Lake Erie became edible again. Birds like the peregrine falcon and the bald eagle, whose eggs had become fragile as a side effect of DDT, began a comeback. In 1999, the federal government moved to remove both from the Endangered Species list.

Other chemicals were substituted for DDT, and by the end of the century about 1.2 billion pounds of pesticide a year were being used in the United States. But rarely were they used without question, as they had been before Carson took up the cause.

Rachel Carson died of cancer in 1964. She had hidden the disease from all but a few close friends, concerned that the pesticide industry would use that knowledge to attack her scientific objectivity.

EDITOR LES LINE AND NEW REPORTERS REINVIGORATE *AUDUBON* MAGAZINE

Les Line was outdoors editor and chief photographer of the *Midland Daily News* in Midland, Michigan, in the early 1960s. He was also an ardent conservationist, a director of the Michigan Audubon Society, and a skilled wildlife photographer whose photograph of the rare Kirtland's warbler had made the cover of *Audubon,* the national society's magazine. Line seemed a perfect

fit to become editor of *Audubon,* a position he took in the autumn of 1966.

The remaking of the magazine had already begun, but Line turned *Audubon* upside down. He began publishing one splendid story after another, and soon the magazine was attracting thousands of new readers and new National Audubon Society members. He brought in new writers and commissioned new kinds of stories. Frank Graham Jr., in *The Audubon Ark,* a history of the Audubon Society, said Line developed "a handsome, well-written publication that brought the Society's members and branches into the mainstream of the modern environmental movement." The *New York Times* was more effusive. *Audubon* was, it said, under Line, "the most beautiful magazine in the world."

In March 1975, *Audubon* published a long, handsomely illustrated piece by Alvin M. Josephy Jr., a writer specializing in the West and Indian issues, about a huge water-diversion project that the U.S. Bureau of Reclamation was proposing for the northern Great Plains. The project was an outgrowth of a 1944 flood control act. The original plan called for the building of six dams on the Missouri River and the irrigation of 1.2 million acres of land in northwestern North Dakota. Twenty years of study showed that the soil of that area of North Dakota was not suitable for irrigation. Undaunted, and not about to easily give up a construction project, the federal Bureau of Reclamation proposed that water from the new Garrison Dam be diverted via canals and pipes to the central and eastern parts of the state.

"Dr. Strangelove Builds a Canal," by Alvin M. Josephy Jr. *Audubon,* March 1975.

In mid-September 1974 a huge section of the massive McClusky Canal—part of an enormous irrigation project being constructed in Dr. Strangelove fashion by the Bureau of Reclamation across half the state of North Dakota—collapsed.

It was the tenth so-called "erosion incident" to plague the building of the canal. Previous earthslides and erosion, which had carried away a total of almost half a mile of the ditch's towering slopes and had cost $750,000 to repair and restructure against new slumps, were officially blamed on inadequate cover growth and excessive rains. The September collapse, larger than all the previous ones, came after an extensive drought. It tore away 1,000 feet of bank, dumped thousands of tons of dirt into the mammoth cut, and completely blocked the canal bed lying more than 60 feet below the prairie. When winter snows brought an end to the construction season, repair operations had only begun, and much time—as well as hundreds of thousands of tax dollars—would still be needed for earthmovers to dig the canal out.

The episode was the latest in a series of engineering, environmental, human, and financial debacles that have marked this incredible but little-noticed federal project, whose ultimate cost to American taxpayers has soared from $212 million to almost a half-billion dollars (and is still rising). Its realistic benefit-cost ratio gives it the aspect of an elephant laboring to bring forth a mouse. Its pell-mell, and somewhat mad, construction activities are visiting high-handed ruin and injustice on numerous North Dakota farm families and destroying rich and productive farmland, precious wildlife habitat, and priceless natural resources. It has been called by its critics ludicrous, immoral, senseless, the biggest boondoggle in the United States, and—in the present time of inflation and the government's announced goal of cutting federal expenditures—an indefensible waste of the nation's funds.

Begun in July 1967 (and planned by the Bureau of Reclamation to go on abuilding into the 1990s), the project, known as the Garrison Diversion Unit, is a complex scheme for diverting 871,000 acre-feet of water annually from the big Missouri River reservoir, Lake Sakakawea, behind Garrison Dam in central North Dakota, 50 miles north of the capital of Bismarck. The water will be transported via a great network of more than 3,000 miles of open and pipe distribution systems—which will include 812 miles of canals and laterals, associated pumping stations, three large regulating reservoirs, and several channelized rivers and streams—for distances of up to 250 miles to different parts of northern and eastern North Dakota—all to provide irrigation for just 250,000 acres.

The immense project was initiated and is being carried out by the Bureau of Reclamation essentially as an irrigation undertaking. But its original benefit-cost ratio was so unfavorable (figured at only .76 to 1 by the Bureau of the Budget in 1960) that to gain authorization by Congress in 1965, Reclamation worked up the promise of additional "benefits." Part of the water, it said, could be used for fish and wildlife habitat, lake restoration, and recreation areas, and by 14 North Dakota municipalities and "several unidentified" industrial users. Most of these new benefits have themselves become controversial and some have been labeled hoaxes. Reclamation has continued to allocate to them 20 percent of the project's cost.

What is most startling about the Garrison Diversion Unit, however, is the balance sheet between what Reclamation is destroying and what it hopes to achieve. Unlike other irrigation projects, this one will open no new lands to agriculture and, if it creates any "new" farms, they will only be consolidated from parts of ones that are already productive. Reclamation selected seven agricultural areas in North Dakota—all currently productive and prosperous—and superimposed its project on them, the intent being to increase and diversify production on those 250,000 acres. Because of the project's host of uncertainties (even including final decisions concerning which areas will receive the water) no one can estimate with any accuracy how many farms will eventually benefit. What is certain is that it will not be many. Reclamation guesses that it will be in the neighborhood of 1,300 farms. That is the highest estimate; others have posed a figure as low as 270 farms.

But to irrigate those farms, 5,000 individual parcels of land totaling 200,000 acres, including 70,000 acres that are now being farmed productively, will be acquired by the Bureau of Reclamation, through condemnation if necessary. In addition, the government will require easements on another 28,000 acres. Altogether, in order to irrigate only six-tenths of one percent of North Dakota's 42 million acres of agricultural land, the Garrison Diversion Unit will result in a net reduction of 8,148 acres of cropland and 34,172 acres of grassland in the state.

Nor is this all. The canals will drain and alter aquifers, drying up wells and bringing trouble to nearby homes and towns. In a state famed for its nesting and feeding places for huge populations of ducks and other wildfowl, the project will destroy or seriously damage 50,000 to 80,000 acres of prairie wetlands—and ruin seven major national wildlife refuges . . . and a number of state wildlife areas. Its saline runoff waters will pollute the James, Sheyenne, Wild Rice, Souris, and Red Rivers—the last two, because they flow into Canada, in violation of the Boundary Waters Treaty made with that nation in 1909. This has prompted a protest from Canada that has unsettled the Bureau of Reclamation.

The energy cost will be high: some 157 megawatts will be used annually to power the pumping plants and sprinkler systems. Miles of tree shelter-belts, which the federal government encouraged farmers to plant and care for laboriously during the 1930s and 1940s as good conservation measures and protection against future Dust Bowls, will be cut up or bulldozed out of existence. Finally, the possibility has been raised that even the areas to be irrigated may be subjected to salinization that would ruin 250,000 acres of currently prosperous agricultural land.

Despite this array of adverse impacts, the Bureau of Reclamation has pushed the Garrison Diversion ahead with a speed that suggests a

determination to reach a stage of investment and construction at which it cannot be stopped. . . .

Since construction started, the McClusky Canal has created a swath of ecological calamities, drying up hundreds of acres of potholes, sloughs, marshes, and shallow alkali lakes everywhere along the canal; farm families testify already to the decline or disappearance of once-abundant waterfowl, although Reclamation believes the birds will return when its "enhancement" projects are developed.

Reclamation also promised that no significantly unique natural resources or resource areas will be adversely affected by the construction of Garrison Diversion Unit. One wonders how the bureau interprets "significantly unique." At the head of the McClusky Canal, the raising of the level of Lake Audubon by fifteen feet certainly will adversely affect Audubon National Wildlife Refuge, which was created to compensate for valuable wildlife habitat destroyed along the Missouri River by the building of Garrison Dam. Nesting places for waterfowl will be inundated, as will be the habitat of antelope, deer, and other upland game. Farther along the canal, John's Lake, a beautiful marshy body of water more than a mile long, a half a mile wide and considered a very important staging area for canvasback ducks, has already been drained and lies caked and barren of life. Altogether, the McClusky Canal will destroy almost 3,000 acres of wetlands, and simply as a huge, 74-mile-long ditch, it will be a disruptive and hazardous barrier to prairie wildlife. . . .

More appalling than the project's environmental injustices is the Bureau of Reclamation's high-handed treatment of landowners whose farm and property stand in the way of the Garrison Diversion Unit. "No one likes to be told that he must do something, but someone's property must be acquired in the public interest or the development of our country would come to a standstill," a bureau information booklet told the people of

North Dakota. "It is unfortunate," it added, "that a few persons must be inconvenienced for the welfare of all, but this happens to each of us, in one way or another, every day. This is the price of progress."

The booklet's warnings were understated. The "few persons inconvenienced" by the building of the McClusky Canal, for example, were to be limited to "a total of six owners or tenants" who would have to be moved out of the way, and the owners of 211 other properties whose "access" to the farm operations would be "altered." But the facts are considerably different. All along the 74-mile route and in the "take" area of the Lonetree Reservoir, Reclamation's dispossessions and "alterings" are bringing human tragedy on a wholesale scale, ruining farms, crippling the livelihood of their owners, and subjecting long-established families to nightmarish injustices....

The Bureau of Reclamation has frequently made its impact more painful than necessary by carrying out its possessions with a crudeness that bewilders its victims. Near the town of Tuirtle Klake, the McClusky Canal was routed so as to necessitate taking the entire farm of Mr. and Mrs. Leo Reiser. Compensation offered to the Reisers was not enough to allow them to relocate and they had to remain in their home after it was condemned. Late on April 2, 1973, a project foreman appeared and notified them that canal construction would begin through their farmstead the next morning. After a frantic night moving their livestock, the Reisers, together with a growing crowd of neighbors, watched at dawn as giant earth-moving machines began to cut through the prairie hills, heading steadily toward the Reisers' home.

With tempers rising amid an increasing threat of a confrontation, a television news crew drove up. Abruptly, construction halted. Soon, a Bureau of Reclamation official arrived, surveyed the tense scene, and told the Reisers that construction would be called off for at least several months because "you folks have a problem here." As soon as the television crew and the neighbors left,

however, there was another about-face. Alone, eating their lunch, the Reisers were startled by the roar of the earth-movers. Running outside, they stared in shock as bulldozers tore up the elms and apple trees in their shelterbelt and garden and pushed through a path for the canal within forty feet of their door. The Bureau of Reclamation had avoided bad publicity by the expedient of a lie.

• • •

Surprisingly, the Garrison Diversion project had not attracted that much national attention before the *Audubon* article. In North Dakota, politicians, businessmen, the universities, the newspapers were generally supportive. The Bureau of Reclamation kept its overall plans to itself, and worked piecemeal, so that at any given moment, only people in one small area were angry. The *Audubon* article brought greater public attention. The Audubon Society also threw its regional representative, Richard Madson, into the fight, and he slowly and diligently rallied farmers, outdoorsmen, and other residents to challenge the project. In 1981, the House of Representatives voted to kill the project.

Then, as had happened before within Audubon, board members and chapter representatives got into a fight, in part over whether Madson was spending too much time on Garrison. Madson was fired. While Audubon members were fighting internally, the Garrison project was kept alive by Congress. Still, concerns about economic and environmental issues grew. In 1984, construction of the Garrison project was halted and the secretary of the interior appointed a commission to restudy the project. The project was reauthorized on a smaller level.

"We stopped it," said Line in 2001, citing the Garrison article as one of the accomplishments of his editorship.

Audubon soon was receiving high notice in American magazine publishing. In 1975 and 1976, *Audubon* won the National Magazine Award for excellence in reporting, almost unheard of for a specialized magazine like *Audubon*, given that its competitors include well-known, long-standing general audience magazines like *The New Yorker, The Atlantic,* and *Harper's*. The magazine also won the highly respected Gold Medal of the Rhode Island School of Design for *Audubon*'s makeup.

Troubles lay ahead.

Line was an iconoclast, as were a number of the environmental writers he had gathered around him. He ran several articles that angered readers for being too evenhanded: a five-part series in 1979 exploring hunting in the United States and a 1982 article on fur trapping and use of the steel leg-hold trap. Both articles were by a longtime *Audubon* editor, John G. Mitchell. To many readers, the articles were too balanced when they should have been condemnatory. Each time, some members resigned.

An article on mourning doves proclaimed that no scientific reasons existed for bans on mourning dove hunting, in that hunting had no significant effect in reducing mourning dove populations. Mourning dove hunting could be opposed "only on aesthetic, not biological grounds," the article said, reflecting the national society's position. But the timing of the piece, and its position, was atrocious. A number of Audubon groups, Frank Graham wrote, had fought to have mourning doves protected as songbirds, and several Indiana chapters had recently been defeated in efforts to ban dove hunting in Indiana. Many chapters, Graham said, believed that Line and *Audubon* had betrayed them.

Many members also were distressed that *Audubon*'s advertising policies allowed almost any company to purchase paid advertisements, as a timber company did in 1978 in the magazine, saying, "Setting aside unrealistically increased areas for wilderness diminishes any chance of meeting America's growing need for forest products."

Line held that the companies had the right to state their views as long as the advertisements were clearly labeled and contained no false or misleading statements. Under attack from many members, the magazine's advertising policy was changed, and the magazine stopped accepting advertisements that advocated stands on public policy.

Then there was the matter of bird pictures. Many readers constantly wrote in that Line was not publishing enough bird pictures, as though that were *Audubon*'s most important mission.

Line and his stable of writers persevered. But so did the fights within the Audubon Society, and in March 1991 Line was dismissed as part of a shakeup for the society and the magazine. Line continued to write about nature for the *New York Times* and other publications, including *Audubon*.

AMERICA AT WAR

ISAIAH THOMAS REPORTS THE BATTLES AT LEXINGTON AND CONCORD, AND THE AMERICAN REVOLUTION BEGINS

By late winter 1775, the English government decided it must use force against American rebels in the Boston area. American "minutemen" and other troops were drilling regularly, and ammunition and arms were being collected. "The die is now cast," King George III said. "The colonies must either submit or triumph." Shortly afterward the king said, "The New England governments are in a state of rebellion. Blows must decide whether they are to be subject to this country or independent."

On the night of April 18, British General Thomas Gage ordered a force of some 1,000 English light infantrymen and grenadiers to move by boat from the Boston Common to Cambridge, Massachusetts, and then set out by foot to Concord, Massachusetts, some twenty miles from Boston. American rebels, Gage had learned through informers, had stockpiled weapons at Concord, and Gage intended to seize them.

The British troops were rowed up the Charles River, landed at Cambridge, and set out overland for Lexington. But the Americans had spies among the British, as the British had spies among the Americans. Learning of the move, Paul Revere instructed that two lanterns be hung in the tower of North Church, indicating that the English troops were moving by water. He and others then set out to warn the Americans at Lexington and Concord that the British were coming.

When the British troops, in scarlet coats and white breaches, arrived at Lexington, about sunup on April 19, they were met by some seventy armed Americans who had taken positions on the green along the Concord road. The British commander ordered the Americans to ground their arms and disperse. Instead, the Americans began an orderly withdrawal, taking their weapons with them. The British commander repeated his order for the Americans to ground their arms. The Americans refused. A shot was fired, no one knows by whom. The shot was followed by a volley by the British and then another. The British then charged with fixed bayonets. In a few minutes the Americans were routed; eight of them had been killed and ten had been wounded. The British troops, with exuberance and in good order, continued toward Concord, fifes playing and drums beating.

At Concord, however, the British met a large force of American militia. An hour or more of posturing ensued. The British searched homes. The courthouse and a blacksmith shop were set afire. The Americans began firing at the British. The British, confused, abandoned their mission and retreated down the Concord road. All the way, the Americans, from behind rocks, trees, and buildings, fired upon the British flanks and rear. The British, in haphazard formation, their men falling, reached Boston after sunset. More than 270 of the British soldiers had been killed or wounded. American losses were about a third of that.

A witness to this battle was Isaiah Thomas, a printer and in 1770 a founder in Boston of the *Massachusetts Spy,* one of the most successful newspapers in the American colonies. Under Thomas, the *Spy* first operated under Whig principles, but—as it became clear that British rule was not working, that the British garrison in Boston was to be strengthened, and that hostilities would come—soon called for independence.

Just before the fight at Concord and Lexington, Thomas moved his press to Worcester, so he could print without fear that the British would censor him or close the paper. On April 19, Thomas observed the fighting between the British and the American militiamen, and on May 3, 1775, published this detailed and, historians say, accurate story, one of the best examples of reporting of the American Revolution.

Americans! Forever bear in mind the Battle of Lexington—where British troops, unmolested and unprovoked, wantonly and in a most inhuman manner, fired upon and killed a number of our countrymen, then robbed, ransacked, and burnt their houses! Nor could the tears of defenseless women, some of whom were in the pains of childbirth, the cries of helpless babes, nor the prayers of the old age, confined to beds of sickness, appease their thirst for blood!—or divert them from their DESIGN OF MURDER AND ROBBERY!

The particulars of this alarming event will, we

are credibly informed, be soon published by authority, as a Committee of the Provincial Congress have been appointed to make special inquiry and to take the depositions, on oath, of such as are knowing in the matter. In the meantime, to satisfy the expectations of our readers, we have collected from those whose veracity is unquestioned the following account, viz.

A few days before the battle, the Grenadier and Light-Infantry companies were all drafted from the several regiments in Boston; and put under the command of an officer, and it was observed that most of the transports and other boats were put together, and fitted for immediate service. This maneuver gave rise to a suspicion that a more formidable expedition was intended by the soldiery, but what or where the inhabitants could not determine. However, town watches in Boston, Charlestown, Cambridge, etc., were ordered to look well to the landing place.

About ten o'clock on the night of the eighteenth of April, the troops in Boston were disclosed to be on the move in a very secret manner, and it was found they were embarking on boats (which they privately brought to the place in the evening) at the bottom of the Common; expresses set off immediately to alarm the country, that they might be on their guard. When the expresses got about a mile beyond Lexington, they were stopped by about fourteen officers on horseback, who came out of Boston in the afternoon of that day, and were seen lurking in by-places in the country till after dark. One of the expresses immediately fled, and was pursued two miles by an officer, who when he had got up with him presented a pistol, and told him he was a dead man if he did not stop, but he rode on till he came up to a house, when stopping of a sudden his horse threw him off, having the presence of mind to holloo to the people in the house,

"Turn out! Turn out! I have got one of them!"

The officer immediately retreated and fled as fast as he had pursued. The other express, after passing through a strict examination, by some means got clear.

The body of the troops, in the meantime, under the command of Lieutenant Colonel Smith, had crossed the river and landed at Phipp's Farm. They immediately, to the number of 1000, proceeded to Lexington, about six miles below Concord, with great silence. A company of militia, of about eighty men, mustered near the meetinghouse; the troops came in sight of them just before sunrise. The militia, upon seeing the troops, began to disperse. The troops then set out upon the run, hallooing and huzzaing, and coming within a few rods of them, the commanding officer accosted the militia, in words to this effect,

"Disperse, you damn'd rebels!—Damn you, disperse!"

Upon which the troops again huzzaed and immediately one or two officers discharged their pistols, which were instantaneously followed by the firing of four or five of the soldiers; and then there seemed to be a general discharge from the whole body. It is to be noticed they fired on our people as they were dispersing, agreeable to their command, and that we did not even return the fire. Eight of our men were killed and nine wounded. The troops then laughed, and damned the Yankees, and said they could not bear the smell of gunpowder.

A little after this the troops renewed their march to Concord, where, when they arrived, they divided into parties, and went directly to several places where the province stores were deposited. Each party was supposed to have a Tory pilot. One party went into the jailyard and spiked up and otherwise damaged two cannon, belonging to the province, and broke and set fire to the carriages. Then they entered a store and rolled out about a hundred barrels of flour, which they unheaded and emptied about forty into the river. At the same time others were entering houses and shops, and unheading barrels, chests, etc., the property of private persons. Some took possession of the town house, to which they set fire,

but was extinguished by our people without much hurt. Another party of the troops went and took possession of the North Bridge. About 150 provincials who mustered upon the alarm, coming toward the bridge, the troops fired upon them without ceremony and killed two on the spot! (Thus had the troops of Britain's king fired FIRST at two separate times upon his loyal American subjects, and put a period to two lives before one gun was fired upon them.) Our people THEN fired and obliged the troops to retreat, who were soon joined by their other parties, but finding they were still pursued the whole body retreated to Lexington, both provincials and troops firing as they went.

During this time an express from the troops was sent to General Gage, who thereupon sent out a reinforcement of about 1400 men, under the command of Earl Percy, with two fieldpieces. Upon the arrival of this reinforcement at Lexington, just as the retreating party had got there, they made a stand, picked up their dead, and took all the carriages they could find and put their wounded thereon. Others of them, to their eternal disgrace be it spoken, were robbing and setting houses on fire, and discharging their cannon at the meetinghouse.

The enemy, having halted about an hour at Lexington, found it necessary to make a second retreat, carrying with them many of their dead and wounded. They continued their retreat from Lexington to Charlestown with great precipitation. Our people continued their pursuit, firing till they got to Charlestown Neck (which they reached a little after sunset), over which the enemy passed, proceeded up Bunker's Hill, and the next day went into Boston, under the protection of the *Somerset,* man-of-war of sixty-four guns....

We have the pleasure to say that notwithstanding the highest provocations given by the enemy, not one instance of cruelty that we have heard of was committed by our militia; but, listening to the merciful dictates of the Christian religion, they "breathed higher sentiments of humanity."

The public most sincerely sympathize with the friends and relations of our deceased brethren, who sacrificed their lives in fighting for the liberties of their country. By their noble intrepid conduct, in helping to defeat the force of an ungrateful tyrant, they have endeared their memories to the present generation, who will transmit their names to posterity with the highest honor.

• • •

The fighting at Lexington and Concord was a disaster for British arms and British policy. For the Americans, the fight provided courage and the understanding that they could stand up to the British. The Second Continental Congress gathered in Philadelphia. When George Washington, a delegate to the Congress, set out for Philadelphia from his home in Mount Vernon, Virginia, he carried with him his colonial uniform he had worn in the French and Indian War a decade and more before. In June 1775, he was named commanding general of the American forces and immediately set out for Boston to assume command of the patriot forces, which had encircled the British garrison in the city.

Thomas published the *Massachusetts Spy* from Worcester throughout the war, emerging at the end of the conflict in 1783 as the leading publisher in the United States, with seven presses and 150 employees. He made Worcester his home. He went on in an illustrious career to print some 400 books on such subjects as law, medicine, and agriculture. He was the first American to print Blackstone's *Commentaries* and published the first American dictionary, a speller, and some 100 children's books, including *Mother Goose* and *Little Goody Two-Shoes*. In 1810, he published a two-volume *History of Printing in America,* a valuable work still today, and founded the American Antiquarian Society. The *Massachusetts Spy* continued until 1904.

"SUNSHINE SOLDIERS AND SUMMER PATRIOTS": THOMAS PAINE HELPS FORM A NATION

Like many who came to America, Thomas Paine was hoping to start a new, more prosperous life when he left England in October 1774. He had spent his first thirty-seven years in poverty, had worked at a succession of minor jobs that barely kept him out of debtors' prison, had no family of his own, and was thoroughly disgusted by the burdens faced by the poor and workers in English society. The new world proved good to him. Armed with a letter of introduction from Benjamin Franklin, whom he had met in London, Paine was hired by Robert Aitken, a Philadelphia printer, and became editor of Aitken's new *Pennsylvania Magazine.* Though largely self-educated, Paine showed a gift for writing clearly in words that ordinary people could seize upon. He was also a passionate believer in liberty. As it became clear to him that England and the colonies were not going to settle their differences, he took up his pen to preach the cause of independence. On January 10, 1776, he published the pamphlet *Common Sense*, which clearly laid out the arguments for independence, arguments that many other colonists were just starting to formulate.

. . . Men of passive tempers look somewhat lightly over the offences of Great Britain, and, still hoping for the best, are apt to call out, *Come, come, we shall be friends again for all this.*

But examine the passions and feelings of mankind: bring the doctrine of reconciliation to the touchstone of nature, and then tell me whether you can hereafter love, honor, and faithfully serve the power that hath carried fire and sword into your land? If you cannot do all these, then are you only deceiving yourselves, and by your delay bringing ruin upon posterity. Your future connection with Britain, whom you can neither love nor honor, will be forced and unnatural, and being formed only on the plan of present convenience, will in a little time fall into a relapse more wretched than the first. But if you say, you can still pass the violations over, then I ask, hath your house been burnt? Hath your property been destroyed before your face? Are your wife and children destitute of a bed to lie on, or bread to live on? Have you lost a parent or a child by their hands, and yourself the ruined and wretched survivor? If you have not, then you are not a judge of those who have. But if you have, and can still shake hands with the murderers, then are you unworthy the name of husband, father, friend, or lover, and whatever may be your rank or title in life, you have the heart of a coward, and the spirit of a sycophant.

This is not inflaming or exaggerating matters, but trying them by those feelings and affections which nature justifies, and without which we should be incapable of discharging the social duties of life, or enjoying the felicities of it. I mean not to exhibit horror for the purpose of provoking revenge, but to awaken us from fatal and unmanly slumbers, that we may pursue determinately some fixed object. 'Tis not in the power of Britain or of Europe to conquer America, if she doth not conquer herself by delay and timidity. The present winter is worth an age if rightly employed, but if lost or neglected the whole continent will partake of the misfortune; and there is no punishment which that man doth not deserve, be he who, or what, or where he will, that may be the means of sacrificing a season so precious and useful.

'Tis repugnant to reason, to the universal order of things, to all examples from former ages, to suppose that this continent can long remain subject to any external power. Them most sanguine in Britain doth not think so. The utmost stretch of human wisdom cannot, at this time, compass a plan, short of separation, which can promise the continent even a year's security. Reconciliation is

now a fallacious dream. Nature has deserted the connection, and art cannot supply her place. For, as Milton wisely expresses, "never can true reconcilement grow where wounds of deadly hate have pierced so deep."

Every quiet method for peace hath been ineffectual. Our prayers have been rejected with disdain; and hath tended to convince us that nothing flatters vanity or confirms obstinacy in kings more than repeated petitioning—and nothing hath contributed more than that very measure to make the kings of Europe absolute. Witness Denmark and Sweden. Wherefore, since nothing but blows will do, for God's sake let us come to a final separation, and not leave the next generation to be cutting throats under the violated unmeaning names of parent and child.

To say they will never attempt it again is idle and visionary; we thought so at the repeal of the Stamp Act, yet a year or two undeceived us; as well may we suppose that nations which have been once defeated will never renew the quarrel.

As to government matters, 'tis not in the power of Britain to do this continent justice: the business of it will soon be too weighty and intricate to be managed with any tolerable degree of convenience, by a power so distant from us, and so very ignorant of us; for if they cannot conquer us, they cannot govern us. To be always running three or four thousand miles with a tale or a petition, waiting four or five months for an answer, which, when obtained, requires five or six more to explain it in, will in a few years be looked upon as folly and childishness. There was a time when it was proper, and there is a proper time for it to cease.

Small islands not capable of protecting themselves are the proper objects for government to take under their care; but there is something absurd, in supposing a Continent to be perpetually governed by an island. In no instance hath nature made the satellite larger than its primary planet; and as England and America, with respect to each other, reverse the common order of nature, it is evident that they belong to different systems. England to Europe: America to itself.

I am not induced by motives of pride, party or resentment to espouse the doctrine of separation and independence; I am clearly, positively, and conscientiously persuaded that it is the true interest of this continent to be so; that everything short of *that* is mere patchwork, that it can afford no lasting felicity,—that it is leaving the sword to our children, and shrinking back at a time when a little more, a little further, would have rendered this continent the glory of the earth. . . .

. . . However strange it may appear to some, or however unwilling they may be to think so, matters not, but many strong and striking reasons may be given to show, that nothing can settle our affairs so expeditiously as an open and determined DECLARATION FOR INDEPENDENCE. Some of which are,

Firstly—It is the custom of nations, when any two are at war, for some other powers, not engaged in the quarrel, to step in as mediators, and bring about the preliminaries of a peace: But while America calls herself the subject of Great Britain, no power, however well disposed she may be, can offer her mediation. Wherefore, in our present state we may quarrel on for ever.

Secondly—it is unreasonable to suppose, that France or Spain will give us any kind of assistance, if we mean only to make use of that assistance for the purpose of repairing the breach, and strengthening the connection between Britain and America; because, those powers would be sufferers by the consequences.

Thirdly—While we profess ourselves the subjects of Britain, we must, in the eyes of foreign nations, be considered as Rebels. The precedent is somewhat dangerous to their peace, for men to be in arms under the name of subjects: we, on the spot, can solve the paradox; but to unite resistance and subjection, requires an idea much too refined for common understanding.

Fourthly—Were a manifesto to be published,

and despatched to foreign courts, setting forth the miseries we have endured, and the peaceful methods which we have ineffectually used for redress; declaring at the same time, that not being able any longer to live happily or safely under the cruel disposition of the British court, we had been driven to the necessity of breaking off all connections with her; at the same time, assuring all such courts of our peaceable disposition towards them, and of our desire of entering into trade with them: such a memorial would produce more good effects to this continent, than if a ship were freighted with petitions to Britain.

Under our present denominations of British subjects, we can neither be received nor heard abroad: the custom of all courts is against us, and will be so, until by an independence we take rank with other nations.

These proceedings may at first seem strange and difficult, but like all other steps which we have already passed over, will in a little time become familiar and agreeable: and until an independence is declared, the continent will feel itself like a man who continues putting off some unpleasant business from day to day, yet knows it must be done, hates to set about it, wishes it over, and is continually haunted with the thoughts of its necessity.

• • •

The fifty-page pamphlet became a best-seller and, said John C. Miller in *Origins of the American Revolution*, "Tom Paine broke the ice that was slowly congealing the revolutionary movement." George Washington was deeply impressed, said a biographer, James Thomas Flexner, and later in January began to publicly raise the possibility of independence. "By private letters which I have lately received from Virginia," Washington wrote a friend, "I find that 'Common Sense' is working a powerful change there in the minds of many men." Almost half a million copies were distributed at a time the colonies had a population of only about two and a half million people. Newspapers reprinted key paragraphs, and Paine's references, for example, to King George III as "the Royal Brute of Great Britain," were widely quoted.

With the Revolution he had sought taking place, Paine quit his editor's job to join the army. Later, in 1776, he was aide-de-camp to General Nathaniel Greene at Fort Lee, New Jersey, during the time that George Washington's army was retreating across the state after the disastrous Battle of Long Island. Morale in both the army and the civilian population was low; the feeling was spreading that perhaps the colonies had made a mistake after all and victory by England was inevitable. Paine was not about to see his cherished liberty slide by so easily. By the light of a campfire, legend has it, with a drumhead as a table, he wrote a dramatic appeal to rally the Revolutionaries. It was published in the December 19, 1776, issue of the *Pennsylvania Journal,* then as a pamphlet four days later.

American Crisis,
by Thomas Paine.

These are the times that try men's souls. The summer soldier and the sunshine patriot will, in this crisis, shrink from the service of their country; but he that stands it *now,* deserves the love and thanks of man and woman. Tyranny, like hell, is not easily conquered; yet we have this consolation with us, that the harder the conflict, the more glorious the triumph. What we obtain too cheap, we esteem too lightly; it is dearness only that gives everything its value. Heaven knows how to put a proper price upon its goods; and it would be strange indeed if so celestial an article as FREEDOM should not be highly rated. Britain, with an army to enforce her tyranny, has declared that she has a right *not only to* TAX but TO BIND us in ALL CASES WHATSOEVER, and if being *bound in that manner,* is not slavery, then is here not such a thing as slavery upon earth. Even the expression is impious; for so unlimited a power can belong only to God.

Whether the independence of the continent was declared too soon, or delayed too long, I will not now enter into as an argument; my one simple opinion is, that had it been eight months earlier, it would have been much better. We did not make a proper use of last winter, neither could we, while we were in a dependent state. However, the fault, if it were one, was all our own; we have none to blame but ourselves. But no great deal is lost yet. All that Howe [Sir William Howe, the British commander in chief in America from 1775 to 1778] has been doing for this month past, is rather a ravage than a conquest, which the spirit of the Jerseys, a year ago, would have quickly repulsed, and which time and a little resolution will soon recover.

I have as little superstition in me as any man living, but my secret opinion has ever been, and still is, that God Almighty will not give up a people to military destruction, or leave them unsupportedly to perish, who have so earnestly and so repeatedly sought to avoid the calamities of war, by every decent method which wisdom could invent. Neither have I so much of the infidel in me, as to suppose that He has relinquished the government of the world, and given us up to the care of devils; and as I do not, I cannot see on what grounds the king of Britain can look up to heaven for help against us: a common murderer, a highwayman, or a house-breaker, has as good a pretence as he.

'Tis surprising to see how rapidly a panic will sometimes run through a country. All nations and ages have been subject to them. Britain has trembled like an ague at the report of a French fleet of flat-bottomed boats; and in the fourteenth [fifteenth] century the whole English army, after ravaging the kingdom of France, was driven back like men petrified with fear; and this brave exploit was performed by a few broken forces collected and headed by a woman, Joan of Arc. Would that heaven might inspire some Jersey maid to spirit up her countrymen, and save her fair fellow sufferers from ravage and ravishment! Yet panics, in some cases, have their uses; they produce as much good as hurt. Their duration is always short; the mind soon grows through them, and acquires a firmer habit than before. But their peculiar advantage is, that they are the touchstones of sincerity and hypocrisy, and bring things and men to light, which might otherwise have lain forever undiscovered. In fact, they have the same effect on secret traitors, which an imaginary apparition would have upon a private murderer. They sift out the hidden thoughts of man, and hold them up in public to the world. Many a disguised Tory has lately shown his head, that shall penitentially solemnize with curses the day on which Howe arrived upon the Delaware....

I shall not now attempt to give all the particulars of our retreat to the Delaware; suffice it for the present to say, that both officers and men, though greatly harassed and fatigued, frequently without rest, covering, or provision, the inevitable consequences of a long retreat, bore it with a manly and martial spirit. All their wishes centred in one, which was, that the country would turn out and help them to drive the enemy back. Voltaire has remarked that King William never appeared to full advantage but in difficulties and in action; the same remark may be made on General Washington, for the character fits him. There is a natural firmness in some minds which cannot be unlocked by trifles, but which, when unlocked, discovers a cabinet of fortitude; and I reckon it among those kind of public blessings, which we do not immediately see, that God hath blessed him with uninterrupted health, and given him a mind that can even flourish upon care.

I shall conclude this paper with some miscellaneous remarks on the state of our affairs; and shall begin with asking the following question, Why is it that the enemy have left the New England provinces, and made these middle ones the seat of war? The answer is easy: New England is not infested with Tories, and we are. I have been tender in raising the cry against these men, and used numberless arguments to show them their

danger, but it will not do to sacrifice a world either to their folly or their baseness. The period is now arrived, in which either they or we must change our sentiments, or one or both must fall. And what is a Tory? Good God! What is he? I should not be afraid to go with a hundred Whigs against a thousand Tories, were they to attempt to get into arms. Every Tory is a coward; for servile, slavish, self-interested fear is the foundation of Toryism; and a man under such influence, though he may be cruel, never can be brave.

But, before the line or irrecoverable separation be drawn between us, let us reason the matter together: Your conduct is an invitation to the enemy, yet not one in a thousand of you has heart enough to join him. Howe is as much deceived by you as the American cause is injured by you. He expects you will all take up arms, and flock to his standard, with muskets on your shoulders. Your opinions are of no use to him, unless you support him personally, for 'tis soldiers, and not Tories, that he wants.

I once felt all that kind of anger, which a man ought to feel, against the mean principles that are held by the Tories: a noted one, who kept a tavern at Amboy, was standing at his door, with as pretty a child in his hand, about eight or nine years old, as I ever saw, and after speaking his mind as freely as he thought was prudent, finished with this unfatherly expression, *"Well! Give me peace in my day."* Not a man lives on the continent but fully believes that a separation must some time or other finally take place, and a generous parent should have said, *"If there must be trouble, let it be in my day, that my child may have peace,"* and this single reflection, well applied, is sufficient to awaken every man to duty. Not a place upon earth might be so happy as America. Her situation is remote from all the wrangling world, and she has nothing to do but to trade with them. A man can distinguish himself between temper and principle, and I am as confident, as I am that God governs the world, that America will never be happy till she gets clear of foreign dominion. Wars, without ceasing, will break out till that period arrives, and the continent must in the end be conqueror; for though the flame of liberty may sometimes cease to shine, the coal can never expire.

• • •

General George Washington ordered Paine's pamphlet read to his demoralized soldiers, then took them across the Delaware River on Christmas Eve, 1776, in a successful surprise attack on the Hessians at Trenton. "The opening words alone...inspired the ragged Continentals and played a crucial role in the gaining of the much-needed victory," says one historian, Philip S. Foner. "The pamphlet roused the entire continent." Fifteen equally effective *American Crisis* pamphlets followed at crucial times during the war, all signed "Common Sense."

GEORGE W. SMALLEY COVERS THE BATTLE OF ANTIETAM AND ELEVATES AMERICAN WAR REPORTING

Beginning in the early 1800s, the definition of the American newspaper was up for grabs. Papers of opinion, on which the editor was king and all content shaped by political persuasion, were challenged by genuine *news*papers, which tried to reach a new mass market by emphasizing news of the common people and giving an unbiased account of events. On this second kind of paper, the profession of reporting was born.

Although news may have trumped opinion under any circumstances, the coming of the Civil War virtually guaranteed it. With the fate of the country at stake, and millions of men off to be soldiers, fighting hundreds of miles from home, the demand for battle news was extremely high. The papers organized to provide it, sending hundreds of "specials," as the correspondents were called, to the front.

The quality of the correspondents' work varied

widely, as has the quality of war reporting ever since. Some problems were not the reporters' fault. Almost none had covered a war before. There was military censorship, difficulty in transmitting stories from the battlefield to the newsroom, difficulty in getting to remote places where battles were fought. Some of the failings, however, should be charged to the men's account. "The majority of the Northern correspondents were ignorant, dishonest, and unethical," a harsh Phillip Knightley wrote in *The First Casualty,* his history of war reporting. He added, "The dispatches they wrote were frequently inaccurate, often invented, partison, and inflammatory." Southern journalism was even weaker, he said, still regarding journalism as a matter of opinion, not facts.

But even Knightley agreed that one of the best of the reporters was George Smalley of the New York *Tribune* via Yale and Harvard Law. Smalley's future father-in-law, the abolitionist Wendell Phillips, introduced him to Sidney Gay, managing editor of the New York *Tribune,* and he was hired in the fall of 1861. He was at Sharpsburg, Maryland, on September 17, 1862, where General George McClellan and General Robert E. Lee clashed in what came to be the bloodiest day of the war. Smalley was in the thick of the battle, attaching himself to General Joseph Hooker and his staff, carrying messages between Hooker and his subordinates. But, unlike some other reporters, he remembered to keep account of what he had seen.

After the battle, Smalley rendezvoused with the other *Tribune* staffers to share information, then rode without sleep for Frederick, Maryland, where he telegraphed a short message to Baltimore, hoping it would be cleared by the military for transmission to New York. Instead, the telegraph operator first diverted it to the War Department, where Smalley's message gave Secretary of War Edwin M. Stanton and President Abraham Lincoln their first account of what had happened on Antietam Creek.

In the roundabout way that was customary for Civil War reporters, Smalley meanwhile took a train from Frederick to Baltimore, and from there to New York. He wrote the story of the battle on the way, standing under a flickering oil light. He did not know whether his first message had gotten through, nor whether other correspondents' stories were already in print. Yes to the first—after the White House had seen the story, it was forwarded to New York in time for an extra edition Friday morning. No to the second. Smalley stumbled in to the *Tribune* office about dawn. Pressmen were waiting, and an extra with the first full report of the battle of Antietam was on the street within hours.

The following dispatch has been received from one of your special correspondents.

BATTLE-FIELD OF SHARPSBURG, MD. WEDNESDAY EVENING, SEPT. 17, 1862

The Greatest battle of the war was fought to-day, lasting from daylight till dark, and closing without decisive result. The whole forces of McClellan and Lee were engaged for fourteen hours. Two hundred thousand men have fought with the utmost determination on both sides. Neither can claim a complete victory, but McClellan has partially carried the Rebel positions, holding most favorable ground for renewing the attack, and holding all the ground which was gained at any time during the fight.

All our own dead and wounded, and many of the enemy's, are in our hands.

On the left of the Rebel position, Hooker, Sumner, and Franklin have crossed Antietam Creek, and have driven the enemy from the ground they chose to cover their flanks, in front of our batteries, and troops have steadily advanced and occupy to-night a range of hills considerably beyond those first taken.

On the Rebel right, they have lost the bridge over the creek, which was carried after a hard fight, and Burnside has crossed with all his forces.

The result of the day's fight, therefore, is that the Rebels have everywhere lost ground, their position is entrenched, both flanks attacked with success, and their rear and only line of retreat seriously threatened.

After the brilliant victory on Sunday at South Mountain, near Middletown, McClellan pushed his army rapidly forward, sending cavalry and artillery out on the Hagerstown road, Burnside through Fox Gap to the Sharpsburg road, and the rest of his forces through Boonsborough to Keedysville and thence toward Sharpsburg.

On the crest of the hill this side of Sharpsburg, the enemy were discovered in great force. Their troops had been brought down from Hagerstown, up from Harper's Ferry, and part of the army held in Virginia as reserve. Lee, Jackson, Longstreet, Hill, and all the best Generals left with them were there, and with all their best troops.

Except occasional artillery contests, the armies faced each other in quiet during the rest on Monday.

On Tuesday there was no movement on our side till toward night. The Rebels had kept batteries in position, but their infantry was withdrawn from view and it was still uncertain whether they were retreating or re-enforcing.

About 4 in the afternoon of Tuesday Hooker was ordered to cross Antietam Creek, at the upper ford on the right, with his whole corps, attack the enemy's left and occupy a position on their flank. He crossed without opposition, sent forward cavalry skirmishers who were speedily driven back, and then, advancing with his whole force about 6, took possession of strong ground, close to the Rebel left, and immediately became engaged with artillery and infantry. Darkness ended the fight with slight loss on either side, Hooker carrying and holding the woods from which the enemy's fire first came.

There were constant alarms during the night,

the hostile pickets being close to each other all along the line. Early in the evening the Rebels took to fighting among themselves, and several heavy volleys were delivered there before they discovered their mistake.

At daybreak the fight was renewed suddenly and vehemently, both sides opening fire together. The number and position of the Rebel batteries the evening before had disclosed that they were in great force on the right, and word had been sent to McClellan to advance Sumner's corps during the night. It did not arrive on the field till 9 in the morning.

McClellan's plan of battle was briefly as follows: Hooker was to cross the creek on the right, as before stated; Sumner, Franklin, and Mansfield to cooperate with and sustain his attack. In front the batteries were to push forward with infantry supports, and an effort to be made to carry the hights on the left. Burnside was to cross the creek by the bridge, and attack the Rebel right, moving on Sharpsburg also, which was in their rear, and thus cut off their retreat. Porter and Sykes were held in reserve. The plan, if successful, must result not merely in the defeat but the destruction or surrender of the Rebel army. The ground is peculiar.

The Rebel line was formed on a crescent-shaped ridge, which in front slopes down into an undulating valley irregularly broken by connecting ranges of hills. Behind the crest the Rebel forces lay in uneven and strong positions, sheltered by ridges and hills, and especially strong on the flanks. Antietam Creek, a stream too deep to be forded except in very few places, sweeps by the base of their position and protected it from assault.

McClellan's forces were first formed in front, afterward thrown to the right and left. There is little or no ground on our side equal in hight to the Rebel position.

Hooker sustained, unaided, the attack on the Rebel left force nearly four hours. His line had been formed the night before and fought to-day in the same order. Ricketts's Division was on the left, Meade's Pennsylvania Reserves in the center, Doubleday's Division on the right. These terms are, of course, to be understood as referring only to Hooker's line, not to the whole field. There was artillery at all points. Meade gained ground in his first attack.

Ricketts also went forward through the woods in his front, and Doubleday, with his guns, held front against a heavy cannonade. Meade advancing, finally met a heavy body of fresh troops thrown suddenly and vigorously against him and was driven back over part of the ground he had just won. Ricketts's line was at the same hard pressed and became deserted. Mansfield, who had come over the creek the night before, was ordered into the woods to Ricketts's support, and Hartsuff's Brigade, part of Doubleday's command, was sent to sustain Meade. Mansfield took the greatest part of his troops to Ricketts's help, but they were unable to extend their line, and in the effort to push forward his men, Gen. Mansfield was mortally wounded. Gen. Hartsuff advanced to the relief of Meade with the 12th and 13th Massachusetts and another regiment. The Pennsylvania troops were retiring in haste and some confusion. Hartsuff seized a bridge in front of the field over which the Rebels were pressing, and held it in splendid style for more than half an hour against a greatly superior attack. His men behaved most gallantly, standing on this exposed ground firing steadily and never wavering once.

Gen. Hartsuff was very soon severely wounded....

The Rebels were driven through the corn field again into the woods beyond where they could not easily be dislodged without artillery. Gen. Hooker, who all the morning had kept himself under fire and generally in the hottest of it, rode forward to examine the ground in front in order to plant a battery. As he rode up the hill he became a conspicuous mark for the Rebel sharpshooters; their fire increased very suddenly and Gen. Hooker was wounded in the left foot, a bullet passing entirely through it. The wound was excessively severe and painful, and he was compelled to leave the field. Three men were shot down by his side at the same moment he was wounded. . . .

Up to 3 o'clock Burnside had made little progress. His attack on the bridge had been successful, but the delay had been so great that to the observer it appeared as if McClellan's plans must have been seriously disarranged. It is impossible not to suppose that the attacks on the right and left were meant in a measure to correspond, for otherwise the enemy had only to repel Hooker on the one hand, then transfer his troops, and hurl them against Burnside.

Here was the difference between Smith and Burnside. The former did his work at once, and lost all his men at once—that is, all whom he lost at all; Burnside seems to have attacked cautiously in order to save his men, and sending successively insufficient forces against a position of strength, distributed his loss over a greater period of time, but yet lost none the less in the end.

Finally, at 4 o'clock, McClellan sent simultaneous orders to Burnside and Franklin; to the former to advance and carry the batteries in his front, at all hazards and any cost; to the latter to carry the woods next in front of him to the right, which the Rebels still held. . . .

Attacking first with one regiment, then with two, and delaying both for artillery, Burnside was not over the bridge before 2 o'clock—perhaps not till 3. He advanced slowly up the slope in his front, his batteries in rear covering, to some extent, the movements of the infantry. A desperate fight was going on in a deep ravine on his right, the Rebel batteries were in full play and, apparently, very annoying and destructive, while heavy columns of Rebel troops were plainly visible, advancing as if careless of concealment, along the road and over the hills in the direction of Burnside's forces. It was at this point of time that McClellan sent him the order above given.

Burnside obeyed it most gallantly. Getting his troops well in hand, and sending a portion of his artillery to the front, he advanced them with rapidity and the most determined vigor, straight up the hill in front, on top of which the Rebels had maintained their most dangerous battery. The movement was in plain view of McClellan's position, and as Franklin, on the other side sent his batteries into the field about the same time, the battle seemed to open in all directions with greater activity than ever.

The fight in the ravine was in full progress, the batteries which Porter supported were firing with new vigor, Franklin was blazing away on the right, and every hill-top, ridge and woods along the whole line was crested and veiled with white clouds of smoke. All day had been clear and bright since the early cloudy morning, and now this whole magnificent, unequaled scene shone with the splendor of an afternoon September sun. Four miles of battle, its glory all visible, its horrors all veiled, the fate of the Republic hanging on the hour—could any one be insensible of its grandeur. . . .

Burnside's messenger rides up. His message is, "I want troops and guns. If you do not send them I cannot hold my position for half an hour." McClellan's only answer for the moment is a glance at the western sky: Then he turns and speaks very slowly: "Tell Gen. Burnside that this is the battle of the war. He must hold his ground till dark at any cost. I will send him Miller's battery. I can do nothing more. I have no infantry." . . .

The sun is already down; not half-an-hour of daylight is left. Till Burnside's message came it had seemed plain to every one that the battle could not be finished to-day. None suspected how near was the peril of defeat, of sudden attack on exhausted forces—how vital to the safety of the army and the nation were those fifteen thousand waiting troops of Fitz John Porter in the hollow. But the Rebels halted instead of pushing on, their vindictive cannonade died away as the light faded. Before it was quite dark the battle was over. Only a solitary gun of Burnside's thundered against the enemy and presently this also ceased and the field was still.

The peril came very near, but it has passed, and in spite of the peril, at the close the day was partly a success—not a victory, but an advantage had been gained. Hooker, Sumner, and Franklin held all the ground they had gained, and Burnside still held the bridge and his position beyond. Everything was favorable for a renewal of the fight in the morning. If the plan of the battle is sound, there is every reason why McClellan should win it. He may choose to postpone the battle to await his re-enforcements.

The Rebel army may choose to retire while it is possible. Fatigue on both sides might delay the deciding battle, yet if the enemy means to fight at all, he cannot afford to delay. His re-enforcements may be coming, his losses are enormous. His troops have been massed in woods and hollow, where artillery has had its most terrific affect. Ours have been deployed and scattered.

It is hard to estimate losses on a field of such extent, but I think ours cannot be less than six thousand killed and wounded—it may be much greater. Prisoners have been taken from the enemy—I hear of a regiment captured entire, but I doubt it. All the prisoners whom I saw agree in saying that their whole army is there.

• • •

Smalley's story was generally regarded as a masterpiece, by readers, his competitors, and military and government officials, and it was a convincing sign of the new supremacy of news in American journalism. J. Cutler Andrews, a historian of Civil War journalism, calculated that about 1,400 newspapers across the country reprinted Smalley's story. Its reputation and accuracy hold today.

Chagrined by their lagging performance, other New York papers, such as the *Herald,* which was overall the most aggressive in getting Civil War news, and the *Times,* reorganized their war coverage.

Smalley slept several hours and then took a train back to the Union army. After several months he fell ill and returned to work in the New York office. He later went to London to organize the *Tribune's* coverage of the Franco-Prussian War in 1870–1871.

News of Antietam discouraged the British from recognizing the Confederacy and encouraged President Lincoln to issue his Emancipation Proclamation.

Several months after taking his job with the *Tribune,* Smalley had written his editor, Sidney Gay, "I begin to think that if one could write for print just as he writes for private eyes his letters would be more fresh and to the point." The distinguishing marks of Smalley's report on Antietam—clear writing, a sense of being on the scene, the lack of clichés and flowery language—contributed to a new style of journalistic writing, one that prevails today.

CENTURY MAGAZINE PUBLISHES "BATTLES AND LEADERS OF THE CIVIL WAR," SAVES GENERAL GRANT FROM BANKRUPTCY, AND CREATES INTEREST IN THE CIVIL WAR THAT THE UNITED STATES HAD SEEMED IT WISHED TO FORGET

Early in 1883, Robert Underwood Johnson and Clarence Buel, editors at the *Century* magazine, were sitting in their office discussing which had been the bloodiest battle of the Civil War. Johnson said it was Cold Harbor, the gruesome battle in June 1864 between Union forces under General Ulysses S. Grant and Confederate forces under General Robert E. Lee in Grant's advance on

Richmond. Buel said it was Chickamauga, the battle in 1863 south of Chattanooga when Union forces were overrun by Confederates.

The discussion gave Buel an idea.

The Civil War had been over for nearly twenty years and already its memory was receding for many Americans. Most of the key men in the war had written almost nothing of the war. There had, it seemed, in the years following the war, almost been an effort to exclude the war, bloody and fratricidal, from the American memory.

But not long before, the *Century,* first published in 1881, had published two articles on John Brown's raid at Harper's Ferry, Virginia, in 1859. The pieces were highly successful. In July 1883, Buel suggested that the *Century* commission a series of articles on the great battles of the war by officers from both the Union and Confederate armies. Richard Watson Gilder, the magazine's editor in chief, agreed. Johnson, the associate editor, was to direct the series; Buel, the assistant editor, was to help Johnson.

Originally the idea was to publish eight to ten articles on the decisive battles of the war. But as Johnson and Buel talked to veterans of the war, and of the need for participants to recall in print what had happened, interest in the project ballooned. Scores of pieces were commissioned. Conferences were held. Ground inspections of the old battlefields occurred. Revised pieces went back and forth in the mails. The series became one of the great projects in the history of American publishing and a tour de force of magazine editing.

Johnson and Buel did most of the work, securing contributions, convincing contributors that rewriting might be needed, securing drawings and maps, editing and doing layouts. Some old officers had to be cajoled into contributing, and some had to be convinced that recasting of their pieces was necessary. Some officers, including Union General Philip A. Sheridan, wishing to publish his memories on his own, refused to contribute. Union General William Tecumseh Sherman at

first grumpily refused, then grumpily agreed to contribute a piece, "The Grand Strategy of the War." Jefferson Davis, the ex-president of the Confederacy, refused to participate, despite numerous invitations.

Among the old officers whom the *Century* worked diligently to convince to contribute—and later to recast a piece—was General Ulysses S. Grant. Grant was the first person invited to contribute to the series, for his participation was mandatory if the project was to succeed. At first Grant said no, saying he could add nothing to writings on the war or on himself that had not been included in a biography of him written by General Adam Badeau. "It is all in Badeau," Grant told the magazine. Grant was then living happily on 3 East Sixty-sixth Street in New York and was active on Wall Street in what was believed to be the prosperous banking concern of Grant and Ward. He believed his fortune exceeded a million dollars.

Then, on May 4, 1884, the Wall Street firm of Grant and Ward collapsed, due to what turned out to be the criminal management of the firm by Grant's partners, among them Ferdinand Ward, the so-called "Young Napoleon of Finance." Ward went to Sing Sing prison for ten years. Grant was absolved of wrongdoing, but he was essentially penniless. He had, at one point, he told his wife, only $180 in cash. He had, he said at another time, not enough money to pay his butcher.

Desperately needing the money, Grant agreed to contribute to the *Century.* Johnson went to Long Branch, New Jersey, then an important summer vacation destination, and a place, long a favorite of Grant's, where Grant was residing. Grant talked openly for fifteen minutes with Johnson about the collapse of his finances, exhibiting, Johnson said in his memoirs, "deep feeling, even bitterness" at what he regarded as his betrayal by his business partners.

Then the two got down to business. Grant asked how many pieces he should write. Johnson said the magazine would take as many as Grant wished to write, but that the magazine thought pieces on Grant's campaigns at Shiloh, Vicksburg, the Wilderness, and Lee's surrender at Appomattox would be most useful. Grant agreed.

The two then discussed the financial terms. The *Century* agreed to pay Grant $500 an article, an amount, Johnson wrote in his autobiography, *Remembered Yesterdays,* in 1923, then "considered a generous honorarium." Later the *Century* doubled this amount, apparently to assist Grant in his financial distress.

On July 1, 1884, Johnson received from Grant an article on Shiloh. It was, Johnson was to say, essentially a copy of Grant's dry official report of that fight. Grant, Johnson said, "did not realize the requirements of a popular publication on the war," and, Johnson said, "it was up for me to help him turn this new disaster of Shiloh into a signal success."

Johnson went to see Grant, without, Johnson said, "letting him know of its unsuitableness to the series." Johnson, a skilled editor, began by attempting to get Grant simply to talk about Shiloh. Grant, he discovered, rather than being a "silent man," was "positively loquacious." The two talked about Grant's initial opponent at Shiloh, Confederate General Albert Sidney Johnston, about the Union failure at Shiloh to entrench, whether Grant could have won without reinforcements that arrived midway through the battle. At one point, Grant told Johnson that, at night at Shiloh, after the first day of the battle, in a pouring rain, he went inside a military hospital for shelter. "I couldn't stand the amputations, and had to go out in the rain and sit for the most of the night against a tree," Grant said.

Johnson told Grant that it was these kinds of details that were necessary for a successful narrative. Grant, Johnson suggested—in the advice all editors should give their writers—should write his piece as though he were talking to friends over dinner, "some of whom should know all about the battle and some nothing at all." It was im-

portant in the writing, Johnson told Grant, *not to try too hard.* Grant, amiable, agreed to begin again.

The piece, a most admirable work, appeared about a third of the way in the series, in February 1885, and Grant continued his work (a piece on Grant's Chattanooga campaign was substituted for a piece on Lee's surrender). At one point he wrote to Johnson, "Why, I am positively enjoying the work. I am keeping at it every day and night, and Sundays."

The editors worked long and diligently on the series. They insisted upon what they described as "strict fairness to the testimony of both sides" and to "spare no pains in the interest of elucidation and accuracy." The official records of both sides in the war and documents, private and public, were consulted, as were researchers in the War Records office in Washington. The series was lovingly edited and presented. It contained numerous drawing and maps (at that time American newspapers and magazines could not, for the most part, print photographs). Wartime drawings were secured from surviving illustrators and correspondents from *Harper's* and *Leslie's Weekly* magazines, the first illustrated magazines in America. A number of drawings were prepared from war photographs taken by Mathew Brady and Alexander Gardner. The magazine collected or commissioned current drawings of the old battlefields; illustrations of naval engagements were prepared. The pieces covered all major confrontations—from the battles of Bull Run to Appomattox and campaigns in the East and West—of the Civil War, and its contributors included almost all major commanders on both sides of the conflict.

The editors made exhaustive efforts to recover the records of important cabinet meetings, to explore the life of the rank and file, and to track down the origins of the Union anthem "John Brown's Body." The remembrances of every surviving eyewitness to Lee's surrender to Grant at Appomattox were solicited, and the illustrator Winslow Homer contributed sketches of a mainstay of military transport of the time, the mule.

The series, published between November 1884 and November 1887, included contributions from, on the Union side, in addition to Grant and Sherman, General McClellan, General Henry J. Hunt, General Don Carlos Buell, Admiral David D. Porter, and General O. O. Howard. On the Confederate side contributors included General Joseph E. Johnston, General P. G. T. Beauregard, General James Longstreet, General Jubal Early, General E. P. Alexander, and General D. H. Hill. The hundreds of articles also included pieces from ordinary Union and Confederate soldiers.

Here are excerpts from Grant's Shiloh account:

While I was at breakfast . . . heavy firing was heard in the direction of Pittsburg Landing, and I hastened there . . .

On reaching the front . . . about 8 A.M., I found that the attack on Shiloh was unmistakable . . .

Shiloh was a log meeting-house, some two or three miles from Pittsburg Landing, and on the ridge which divides the waters of Snake and Lick creeks, the former entering into the Tennessee just north of Pittsburg Landing, and the latter south. Shiloh was the key to our position, and was held by [General William Tecumseh] Sherman. His division was at that time wholly raw, no part of it ever having been in an engagement, but I thought this deficiency was more than made up by the superiority of the commander. McClernand was on Sherman's left, with troops that had been engaged at Fort Donelson, and were therefore veterans so far as Western troops had become such at that stage of the war. Next to McClernand came Prentiss, with a raw division, and on the extreme left, Stuart, with one brigade of Sherman's division. Hurlbut was in rear of Prentiss, massed, and in reserve at the time of the onset. The division of General C. F. Smith was on the right, also in reserve. . . .

The position of our troops made a continuous line from Lick Creek, on the left, to Owl Creek, a branch of Snake Creek, on the right, facing nearly south, and possibly a little west. The water in all these streams was very high at the time, and contributed to protect our flanks. The enemy was compelled, therefore, to attack directly in front. This he did with great vigor, inflicting heavy losses on the National side, but suffering much heavier on his own.

The Confederate assaults were made with such disregard of losses on their own side, that our line of tents soon fell into their hands. The ground on which the battle was fought was undulating, heavily timbered, with scattered clearings, the woods giving some protection to the troops on both sides. There was also considerable underbrush. A number of attempts were made by the enemy to turn our right flank, where Sherman was posted, but every effort was repulsed with heavy loss. But the front attack was kept up so vigorously that, to prevent the success of these attempts to get on our flanks, the National troops were compelled several times to take positions to the rear, nearer Pittsburg Landing. When the firing ceased at night, the National line was all of a mile in rear of the position it had occupied in the morning.

In one of the backward moves, on the 6th, the division commanded by General Prentiss did not fall back with the others. This left his flanks exposed, and enabled the enemy to capture him, with about 2,200 of his officers and men. General [Adam] Badeau gives 4 o'clock of the 6th as about the time this capture took place. He may be right as to the time, but my recollection is that the hour was later. General Prentiss himself gave the hour as half-past five. . . . But no matter whether it was four or later, the story that he and his command were surprised and captured in their camps is without any foundation whatever: If it had been true, as currently reported at the time, and yet believed by thousands of people, that Prentiss and his division had been captured in their beds, there would not have been an all-day struggle with the loss of thousands killed and wounded on the Confederate side.

With the single exception of a few minutes after the capture of Prentiss, a continuous and un-broken line was maintained all day from Snake Creek or its tributaries on the right to Lick Creek or the Tennessee on the left, above Pittsburg. There was no hour during the day when there was not heavy firing and generally hard fighting at some point on the line, but seldom at all points at the same time. It was a case of Southern dash against Northern pluck and endurance.

Three of the five divisions engaged on Sunday were entirely raw, and many of the men had only received their arms on the way from their States to the field. Many of them had arrived but a day or two before, and were hardly able to load their muskets according to the manual. Their officers were equally ignorant of their duties. Under these circumstances, it is not astonishing that many of the regiments broke at the first fire. In two cases, as I now remember, colonels led their regiments from the field on first hearing the whistle of the enemy's bullets. In these cases the colonels were constitutional cowards, unfit for any military position. But not so the officers and men led out of danger by them. Better troops never went upon a battlefield than many of these officers and men afterward proved themselves to be who fled panic-stricken at the first whistle of bullets and shell at Shiloh . . .

So confident was I before firing had ceased on the 6th that the next day would bring victory to our arms if we could only take the initiative, that I visited each division commander in person be-fore any reenforcements had reached the field. I directed them to throw out heavy lines of skir-mishers in the morning as soon as they could see, and push them forward until they found the en-emy, following with their entire divisions in sup-porting distance, and to engage the enemy as soon as found. To Sherman I told the story of the as-sault at Fort Donelson, and said that the same tactics would win at Shiloh. Victory was assured when Wallace arrived even if there had been no other support. The enemy received no reenfor-cements. He had suffered heavy losses in killed,

wounded, and straggling, and his commander, General Albert Sidney Johnston, was dead. I was glad, however, to see the reenforcements of Buell and credit them with doing all there was for them to do. During the night of the 6th the remainder of Nelson's division, Buell's army, crossed the river, and were ready to advance in the morning, forming the left wing. Two other divisions, Crit-tenden's and McCook's, came up from the river from Savannah in the transports, and were on the west bank early on the 7th. Buell commanded them in person. My command was thus nearly doubled in numbers and efficiency.

During the night rain fell in torrents, and our troops were exposed to the storm without shelter. I made my headquarters under a tree a few hun-dred yards back from the riverbank. My ankle was so much swollen from the fall of my horse the Friday night preceding, and the bruise was so painful, that I could get no rest. The drenching rain would have precluded the possibility of sleep, without this additional cause. Some time after midnight, growing restive under the storm and the continuous pain, I moved back to the log-house on the bank. This had been taken as a hospital, and all night wounded men were being brought in, their wounds dressed, a leg or an arm ampu-tated, as the case might require, and everything being done to save life or alleviate suffering. The sight was more unendurable than encountering the enemy's fire, and I returned to my tree in the rain.

The advance on the morning of the 7th de-veloped the enemy in the camps occupied by our troops before the battle began, more than a mile back from the most advanced position of the Confederates on the day before. It is known now that they had not yet learned of the arrival of Buell's command. Possibly they fell back so far to get shelter of our tents during the rain, and also to get away from the shells that were dropped upon them by the gun-boats every fifteen minutes during the night. . . .

In a very short time the battle became general

all along the line. This day everything was favorable to the Federal side. We had now become the attacking party. The enemy was driven back all day, as we had been the day before, until finally he beat a precipitate retreat. The last point held by him was near the road leading from the landing to Corinth, on the left of Sherman and right of McClernand. About 3 o'clock, being near that point and seeing that the enemy was giving way everywhere else, I gathered up a couple of regiments, or parts of regiments, from troops near by, formed them in line of battle and marched them forward, going in front myself to prevent premature or long-range firing. At this point there was a clearing between us and the enemy favorable for charging, although exposed. I knew the enemy were ready to break, and only wanted a little encouragement from us to go quickly and join their friends who had started earlier. After marching to within musket-range, I stopped and let the troops pass. The command, Charge, was given, and was executed with loud cheers, and with a run, when the last of the enemy broke. . . .

After the rain of the night before and the frequent and heavy rains for some days previous, the roads were almost impassable. The enemy, carrying his artillery and supply trains over them in his retreat, made them still worse for troops following. I wanted to pursue, but had not the heart to order the men who had fought desperately for two days, lying in the mud and rain whenever not fighting, and I did not feel disposed positively to order Buell, or any part of his command to pursue. . . .

I rode forward several miles the day after the battle, and found that the enemy had dropped much, if not all, of their provisions, some ammunition, and the extra wheels of their caissons, lightening their loads to enable them to get off their guns. About five miles out we found their field-hospital abandoned. . . .

Shiloh was the severest battle fought at the West during the war, and but few in the East equaled it for hard, determined fighting. I saw an open field, in our possession on the second day, over which the Confederates had made repeated charges the day before, so covered with dead that it would have been possible to walk across the clearing, in any direction, stepping on dead bodies, without a foot touching the ground. On our side National and Confederate were mingled together in about equal proportions; but on the remainder of the field nearly all were Confederates. On one part, which had evidently not been plowed for several years, probably because the land was poor, bushes had grown up, some to the height of eight or ten feet. There was not one of these left standing unpierced by bullets. The smaller ones were all cut down. . . .

The criticism has often been made that the Union troops should have been intrenched at Shiloh; but up to that the pick and spade had been but little resorted to at the West. I had, however, taken this subject under consideration soon after reassuming command in the field. McPherson, my only military engineer, had been directed to lay out a line to intrench. He did so, but reported that it would have to be made in rear of the line of encampment as it then ran. The new line, while it would be nearer the river, was yet too far away from the Tennessee, or even from the creeks, to be easily supplied with water from them; and in case of attack, these creeks would be in the hands of the enemy. Besides this, the troops with me, officers and men, needed discipline and drill more than they did experience with the pick, shovel, and axe. Reenforcements were arriving almost daily, composed of troops that had been hastily thrown together into companies and regiments— fragments of incomplete organizations, the men and officers strangers to each other. Under all these circumstances I concluded that drill and discipline were worth more to our men than fortifications. . . .

Some . . . critics claim that Shiloh was won when (Confederate General Albert Sidney Johnston) fell, and that if he had not fallen the army under me would have been annihilated or captured. Ifs defeated the Confederates at Shiloh. There is little doubt that we would have been disgracefully beaten if all the shells and bullets fired by us had passed over the enemy, and if all of theirs had taken effect.... There was, in fact, no hour during the day when I doubted the eventual defeat of the enemy, although I was disappointed that reenforcements so near at hand did not arrive at an earlier hour.

• • •

The *Century*'s series (which Johnson and Buel always called The War Book) was an astonishing success—for the *Century,* Grant, and America. Within six months from publication of the first piece, the *Century*'s circulation increased from 127,000 to 225,000 copies a month, increasing its audience to two million people a month. In 1886–1887, the *Century* used the revived interest in the Civil War to publish, with much success, John G. Nicolay and John Hay's *The Life of Lincoln.*

The series also brought about a new interest in the Civil War, for, as the *Century* editors wrote, it established "a better understanding between the soldiers who were opposed in that conflict." Reunions of veterans began and a push to erect statues on battlefields was heightened. The series, published in book form by The Century Company in 1887, was also a treasure trove for American historiography. The pieces remain a most valued record on the war for historians and are consulted by all serious writers on the war.

The four pieces by Grant became the foundation of his autobiography, *Personal Memoirs of U.S. Grant,* published by Chares L. Webster and Company in 1895. The book, highly successful, "retrieved his fortunes and added a new laurel to his fame," the *Century* editors said in a preface to the book version of *Battles and Leaders.* The Grant book is widely regarded as one of the finest—and most literate—military memoirs ever published and also as an outstanding contribution to American letters.

It was Johnson who suggested to Grant that he expand upon his four articles for the *Century* and turn the material into a book.

The Century Company lost publication of Grant's autobiography. Mark Twain, a friend of Grant's, convinced Grant that Twain's publisher, Charles L. Webster and Company, a company Twain had set up to publish *The Adventures of Huckleberry Finn,* could better publish his autobiography because Webster had experience in publishing books by subscription, a method Twain and Grant favored for the Grant book. Thousands of Union veterans, some in their old blue uniforms, went door to door in numerous American cities to sell the book, saying they were doing this for their dying former commander. The two volumes were $3.50, $1 down, $2.50 on delivery. By May 1885 more than 150,000 copies had been ordered.

In writing his memoirs (Grant gave the rights to his book to his wife to provide for her financial security), Grant was as redoubtable as he had been as a soldier. Shortly after he finished his four *Century* articles in the summer of 1884, Grant developed throat cancer, "his death sentence," a biographer was to write, "written in the smoke of ten thousand cigars." But, wanting to finish, and wishing to be able to leave his family financially secure, Grant continued to write and dictate (one day he dictated 10,000 words), doing much of the work at a borrowed summer retreat at Mount McGregor, New York, in the Adirondacks.

In Grant's last days, Johnson went there to see him. Grant, Johnson wrote, "fully dressed, sat on the piazza in the sun, wearing something over his head, like a skullcap, and wrapped in a plaid shawl, looking thinner than before, and with a patient, resigned expression..." Johnson told Grant that the *Century* was relinquishing to Grant its rights to his Vicksburg piece in the *Century.* Grant could no longer talk, being able only to communicate in writing. Johnson wrote, "He smiled faintly and bowed his acknowledgement, and as I rose gave me his hand."

A week later, on July 23, 1885, cocaine and

morphine having failed to eliminate his pain, but his page proofs finished, Grant was dead. His memoirs, published later in the year, were a critical and financial success.

The *Century* went on to much brilliance. It published pieces by John Muir that led to the designation of Yosemite National Park and creation of America's national forest and continued to publish highly literary pieces. But with the beginning of the twentieth century and a changing magazine world, it was passed in circulation by the new mass market magazines and its fortunes ebbed. Not long after World War I, it was merged with the *Forum*, and then both were merged into *Current History*. It is now essentially forgotten.

JAMES CREELMAN OF THE NEW YORK *WORLD* REVEALS HORRORS IN JAPANESE CONQUEST OF PORT ARTHUR, MANCHURIA

Gifted, energetic, and much in demand as a war correspondent, James Creelman moved from paper to paper in New York in the 1890s, the time deservedly known as a golden age of reporting. Creelman broke with James Gordon Bennett's *Herald*, because Bennett wouldn't give him a byline. In 1893, Joseph Pulitzer hired Creelman and then sent him to report on the Sino-Japanese War, the first of several disputes between China and Japan over control of Korea. U.S. opinion tended to favor the Japanese, if only because it so distrusted the Chinese.

Creelman was with the Japanese as they invaded Korea and Manchuria, and wrote memorable accounts of Manchurian cavalrymen, with lances and spears, charging at Japanese troops armed with guns.

On November 21, 1894, Port Arthur in Manchuria fell to the Japanese. Creelman was the only American reporter there. But the *World* did not hear from him for several weeks, and his editors were concerned he might be dead. When his story got through—the first, cabled version was only five paragraphs—it changed the way Americans regarded the war.

"A Japanese Massacre. The *World*'s War Correspondent Reports a Butchery at Port Arthur. A Three Days' Reign of Murder," by James Creelman. New York *World,* December 12, 1894.

YOKOHAMA, JAPAN, DECEMBER 11—The Japanese troops entered Port Arthur on November 21 and massacred practically the entire population in cold blood.

The defenseless and unarmed inhabitants were butchered in their houses and their bodies were unspeakably mutilated. There was an unrestrained reign of murder which continued for three days. The whole town was plundered with appalling atrocities.

It was the first stain upon Japanese civilization. The Japanese in this instance relapsed into barbarism.

All pretense that circumstances justified the atrocities are false. The civilized world will be horrified by the details.

The foreign correspondents, horrified by the spectacle, left the army in a body.

CREELMAN

• • •

American public opinion switched from favoring Japan to opposing it. The State Department, which had received no such reports, investigated. In the Senate, an unrelated treaty that would make Americans living in Japan subject to Japanese courts was delayed.

Several days later, in Tokyo, Japan's minister of foreign affairs issued a statement to the *World* that confirmed Creelman's report and said that the country was "taking measures essential to the reputation of the empire." But the minister, following the script of officials in so many wars, cautioned against exaggeration. Japanese troops had been provoked by Chinese atrocities, he said, and most of the victims had been Chinese soldiers dressed in civilian clothes.

Creelman's full report, printed in the *World* on December 20, did not accept the Japanese defense.

FIELD MARSHAL'S HEADQUARTERS, JAPANESE ARMY OF INVASION, PORT ARTHUR, NOV. 24, via Vancouver, B.C., DEC. 19—The struggle for the emancipation of Corea has been suddenly turned into a headlong, savage war of conquest. It is no longer a conflict between civilization and barbarism. Japan has dropped her mask and for the last four days she has trampled civilization under the feet of her conquering army.

The story of the taking of Port Arthur will be one of the blackest pages of history. An easy victory over a Chinese mob and the possession of one of the most powerful strongholds in the world was too great a strain upon the Japanese character, which relapsed in a few hours back into the brutish state from which it was awakened a generation ago.

[Creelman went on for most of two full pages, with horrifying detail:]

An old man on his knees in the street was cut almost in two.

Another poor wretch was shot on a roof top. Still another fell in the street and was bayoneted through the back a dozen times.

Just below me was a hospital flying the Red Cross flag, but the Japanese fired upon the unarmed men who came out of the doorway.

A merchant in a fur cap knelt down and raised his hands in entreaty. As the soldiers shot him he put his hands over his face. I saw his corpse the next day. It was slashed beyond recognition.

Women and children were hunted and shot at as they fled to the hills with their protectors.

The town was sacked from end to end and the inhabitants were butchered in their own homes.

• • •

Japan continued to insist that Creelman's account was exaggerated. A U.S. embassy report somewhat agreed, especially since the Chinese seemed to be treated well after other battles during the two-year war.

Japan, with its better-equipped forces, was an easy victor. But under international pressure Port Arthur was returned to China, which quickly leased the site to Russia for a naval base. Japan took it again in the Japan-Russia War of 1904.

Creelman was welcomed home to New York City by one of Joseph Pulizer's favorite encomiums, a testimonial dinner. He covered the Spanish-American War in Cuba for William Randolph Hearst, who once took Creelman's dictation after Creelman was wounded while leading a charge of American soldiers. Hearst also assigned Creelman to buy a ship and scuttle it in the Suez Canal, so that the Spanish fleet could not make it to the Philippines in time to challenge Admiral George Dewey. Creelman was willing, but the fleet turned back before he had time to act. During his career, Creelman covered at least four wars, not counting the Hatfield and McCoy feud in Kentucky, and was wounded at least four times, not counting being banged up when an air ship he was riding on for an assignment crashed. He took ill and died in Berlin shortly after arriving to cover what would become the First World War.

THIS IS LONDON: EDWARD R. MURROW ON RADIO DESCRIBES THE GERMAN BLITZ

Winston Churchill was still trying to figure out how to persuade Franklin D. Roosevelt to help England, and Franklin D. Roosevelt was still trying to figure out how to persuade the American people to help, when Edward R. Murrow was making a name for himself with his broadcasts from London.

Murrow was graduated in 1930 from Washington State College, the first college in the United States to offer a course in radio broadcasting. Active in student politics, Murrow worked for the National Student Federation and then the Institute of International Education. Both positions involved traveling, particularly in Europe, making speeches and arranging student exchanges. In 1935, he became director of talks for CBS radio, which meant that he was responsible for arranging panelists for radio discussions. In 1937 he was sent to London to be in charge of broadcasting special events from Europe for CBS radio.

Murrow used radio the way it was meant to be used, as a personal medium. His resonant voice, his descriptive style, his use of natural background sound made his listeners feel that they were on the scene with him.

This was particularly effective as Murrow was pressed to describe for his U.S. listeners the bombing of London, as he did in this broadcast.

SEPTEMBER 25, 1940

This is London, 3:45 in the morning. Tonight's attack against the central London area has not been as severe as last night; less noise, fewer bombs, and not so many fires. The night is almost quiet—almost peaceful. The raid is still in progress and it is, of course, possible that we may see a repetition of last night when the weight of the attack developed in the two hours before dawn. Two and sometimes three German planes came boring in through the barrage every five minutes. I spent last night with a bomber pilot who had carried twenty-five loads of bombs over Germany. He talked about a raid over Berlin at this time last night. When we left the studio we'd gone only a few blocks when we heard one coming down. As we lay on the sidewalk waiting for

it to thump, he said, "I'd feel better up there than down here." A couple of air-raid wardens standing out in the open were discussing whether the stuff coming down was a flock of incendiaries or high explosives. The bomber pilot said: "These people are too brave. I'll feel better when I get back to my squadron. London is dangerous. I wonder how long it takes to get used to this sort of thing."

Later we went out to see a fire. A block of cheap little working-class houses had been set alight by fire bombs. As we walked toward the blaze, gusts of hot air and sparks charged down the street. We began to meet women. One clutched a blanket, another carried a small baby in her arms, and another carried an aluminum cooking pot in her left hand. They were all looking back over their shoulders at that red glow that had driven them out into the streets. They were frightened. And that bomber pilot who had been over Germany so many times stopped and said: "I've seen enough of this. I hope we haven't been doing the same thing in the Ruhr and Rhineland for the last three months."

We went back to a rooftop and stood watching, as the bombers came in. He estimated their height, the speed at which they were traveling, and the point at which they would release their bombs. And he was generally right as to the time when we would hear the bombs start coming down. He was a professional, judging the work of other professionals. But he kept talking of the firemen, the ambulance drivers, and the air-raid wardens who were out there doing their job. He thought them much braver than the boys who'd been flying over Germany every night.

At dawn we saw Londoners come oozing up out of the ground, tired, red-eyed, and sleepy. The fires were dying down. We saw them turn into their own street and look to see if their house was still standing. I shall always wonder what last night did to that twenty-one-year-old boy who had flown so many bombs over Germany but had never heard one come down before last night.

Today I walked down a long street. The gutters were full of glass; the big red buses couldn't pull into the curb. There was the harsh, grating sound of glass being shoveled into trucks. In one window—or what used to be a window—was a sign. It read: SHATTERED—BUT NOT SHUTTERED. Near by was another shop displaying a crudely lettered sign reading: KNOCKED BUT NOT LOCKED. They were both doing business in the open air. Halfway down the block, there was a desk on the sidewalk; a man sat behind it with a pile of notes at his elbow. He was paying off the staff of the store—the store that stood there yesterday.

I went to my club for lunch. A neatly lettered sign on the door informed me that the club had been temporarily closed, due to enemy action. Returning to my apartment, which is now serving as an office, I found a letter from the China Campaign Committee, informing me that during the last fifteen days they had collected the signatures of individuals and organizations representing more than one and a quarter million people. The signatures were attached to a petition. The petition read as follows: "We demand the immediate and unconditional reopening of the Burma Road." It is necessary to have lived these last fifteen days in Britain to fully appreciate that letter. Collecting signatures to a petition urging the opening of the Burma Road during fifteen days of almost constant air-raid alarms. The petition was started before the *Blitzkrieg*. Therefore, it had to be carried through. These people are stubborn. Often they are insular, but their determination must be recorded.

• • •

Murrow's broadcasts made the Battle of Britain come alive for the American public, which listened attentively to the unfolding drama. Murrow and his colleagues "put the listener in another man's shoes," wrote broadcast historian Erik Barnouw. "No better way to influence opinion has ever been found." Eric Sevareid, one of Murrow's

CBS colleagues, said Murrow was of greater influence in England than the American ambassador. "There is no doubt," Sevareid said, "of his immense aid to the President in awakening the American people to the issue before them."

Murrow had an influence in England as well. "We were a bit short on friends in those days, Ed, we weren't a very good risk by any means," a self-described "working bloke" wrote Murrow in 1965. "In the first half of this game, we were being hammered—our supporters had gone—nations stood around like a crowd round an execution—waiting for us to get the 'chop.' You didn't, though, did you? You steamed up and down that touch line yelling your head off."

THE HOLOCAUST EXPOSED: HOW COULD THE WORLD NOT KNOW?

How could the world not know about the Holocaust? How could millions of European Jews, men, women, and children, be rounded up, deported, concentrated in labor camps, starved, buried alive, machine-gunned, shotgunned, and killed in gas chambers without the American public knowing? Was it conspiracy, racism, or stupidity?

The overwhelming silence of the American press in the face of the horrific information that did come out of eastern Europe is hard to believe. "Throughout the war the regular American newspapers published comparatively few of these disclosures and nearly always relegated them to the inner pages," said David S. Wyman, in his thorough and persuasive book, *The Abandonment of the Jews* (New York: Pantheon, 1984). The deaths of hundreds of thousands of Jews were reported in articles shorter and less prominently displayed than articles about a baseball game. This continued throughout the war, even after respected refugee organizations, underground activists, and clandestine sources behind German lines started feeding reports of the horror they were seeing.

President Franklin D. Roosevelt avoided the topic when he talked to the press, Wyman found, and reporters did not ask him about it until the end of 1943. "The press's failure to arouse public interest and indignation thus handicapped efforts to build pressure for government action to aid the Jews," Wyman concluded.

The biggest exception, he said, was the Jewish press, and even its editors at first found the reports hard to believe. (He also cited two liberal publications, the *Nation* and the *New Republic*). By the fall of 1942, however, the *Jewish Frontier*, a labor Zionist monthly, was convinced. A special issue in November 1942 ran with black borders.

"Under the Axis." *Jewish Frontier,* November 1942.

In the occupied countries of Europe a policy is now being put into effect, whose avowed object is the extermination of a whole people. It is a policy of systematic murder of innocent civilians which in its dimensions, its ferocity and its organization is unique in the history of mankind.

This issue of the JEWISH FRONTIER attempts to give some picture of what is happening to the Jews of Europe. It is of necessity an incomplete picture because reports have to be smuggled out and evidence has to be pieced together. Consequently, we have hesitated to include any material whose authenticity was in any way doubtful. The information presented in this issue is vouched for by sources of unimpeachable authority. The best test of the credibility of these reports is furnished by the statements of the Nazis themselves, whose repeated public utterances make no secret of their intentions in regard to the Jewish minority. We have paid Nazi spokesmen the compliment of not believing their monstrous professions. The reports in this issue, however, substantiate the Nazi claims.

In our calculations of the holocaust that has overtaken the Jews of Europe, we do not speak of Jews fortunate enough to be able to participate in the European armies still fighting the Nazi aggressor. The fate of Jewish soldiers on the fields of battle is the fate of all who struggle bravely against the common foe. We rejoice in the opportunity given to any Jew anywhere to fight for his country and freedom. We speak here of the victims not of war, but of massacre, part of whose tragedy is that they can strike no blow in their defense.

According to conservative estimates, about one million Jewish civilians—men, women, and children—have perished through massacre and deliberate starvation since the beginning of the war. This is an infinitely higher figure proportionately than that of any other national group in Europe. The tempo of this planned slaughter is being speeded up with every new Hitler invasion. Unless it is checked, we are faced with the possibility of the murder of a whole people whose sole crime is that it is a minority that has aroused the sick blood-lust of Hitler.

We have had by now three years in which to observe the functioning of the Nazi plan for the Jews as well as for the world. The successive stages do not appear simultaneously in every occupied country because of the exigencies of time and place, but the trend is plain. Nazi savagery climbs inexorably from step to step in a well-defined pattern:

1. to deprive the Jews of civil rights;

2. to drive the Jews out of the economic life and so make it impossible for Jews to sustain themselves;

3. to segregate them in ghettos where they perish of famine and disease;

4. to exterminate those Jews who have not been killed off in the fulfillment of the previous stages.

The documents we bring as testimony in this issue reflect various stages of the master plan, but it is clear from the latest reports that Hitler has now mounted the final step of the process. The deportation of Jews from France and Poland to unknown destinations allows of only the most sinister explanation.

The annals of mankind hold no similar record of organized murder as a calculated policy of state. We publish this somber record to acquaint the free world with these facts and to call on the governments of the Allied Nations to do whatever may be done to prevent the fulfillment of this horror which broods over the blood-engulfed continent of Europe.

According to the Nazis, the very existence of the Jewish race seems to be an error of the Creator and it is the task of the Gestapo to correct that error. It is no longer a matter of pauperizing the Jews, of reducing them to the lowest social stratum conceived by the sadistic imagination of the Nazis and of segregating them from the rest of the population behind the strongly guarded walls of the ghetto. The ghetto itself seems to have been introduced by the Nazis in several countries not so much to keep the higher races of Europe from contamination by Jews as to make it easier at the proper occasion to slaughter them en masse.

We have already indicated that we cannot know exactly the number of Jews still alive in Nazi Europe. But we can get an idea about the scope of the massacres perpetrated by the Nazis on the Jews so far (with the co-operation of other Fascist armies among Hitler's satellites) by taking into consideration some odd figures that have reached us. It is thus as established fact by now that out of the 260,000 Jews driven out of Bessarabia to the part of Southern Ukraine which is not under Rumanian occupation—Bessarabia is now Judenrein—about 190,000 have been shot to death, burned alive or tortured to death on the road. What happened to the remaining seventy thousand, who reached the so-called Trans-Dniestria, we have no knowledge of. One can form an idea of the fate of many of them on reading the report of an eye-witness (an Aryan Rumanian) that in Odessa alone, on the day when a bomb exploded in the staff building, ten thousand Jews were gathered in wooden barracks and burned alive. In Kiev, the principal city of the Ukraine, the Nazis, according to the information supplied by the Soviet government, massacred forty thousand Jews. This figure was later substantiated as the minimum by other reliable sources. Hundreds of thousands of Jews were dragged out of the Polish ghettoes and driven to "an unknown destination." That they were not driven merely for forced labor can be judged by the fact that the head of the Warsaw ghetto community, Adam Czerniakow, who for three years had suffered martyrdom by "co-operating" with the Nazi authorities in supplying them with Jewish labor on a more or less regulated basis, preferred to die by his own hand rather than to give the Nazis a list of Jews for "deportation." In Prague the young poet Janus Bonn, a representative of the Kehilla, similarly refused to make up a list for "deportation," but before he had the chance to commit suicide the Nazis executed him. We have no reports about the fate of the thousands and thousands of Jews of the Protectorate (Bohemia and Moravia) and of "Independent" Slovakia who have been deported to unknown places. We know that a few Jews managed to escape from Slovakia—incidentally, the only Fascist country which officially decreed that all Jews without exception must leave the country and which elevated this decree to the dignity of a "constitutional" law—some fled to Hungary, where every Jew sheltering a refugee from Slovakia is threatened with the death penalty.

To what extent Jews are "free game" may be judged from the report obtained by Austrian refugees through underground channels that twelve hundred Dutch Jews had been deported to Vienna where they were submitted to tests on the effect of a certain poison gas, with the result that not one of them came out of the "laboratory" alive.

———————

The next article in the issue was titled "The Plan of Destruction" and written by Hayim Greenberg. An excerpt:

What is the situation today of millions of Jews on the European continent, the greater part of which is already occupied by Hitler's armies? How many of them committed suicide in a moment of extreme despair? How many Jewish parents first killed their children before settling their last accounts with the world? How large is the number of Jews who died of hunger, epidemics and lack of medical care purposely brought about by the Nazis in the larger and smaller ghettoes of Central and Eastern Europe, and of torture in concentration camps? How many Jews were executed in accordance with sentences pronounced by "legal" military tribunals and how many in mass slaughters without trial and without a show of legal procedure? How many of them died or were suffocated in the sealed railway coaches of deportations and so-called "repatriations"? How do those Jews live who have not as yet been slaughtered, and what is the source of their livelihood?

We cannot undertake to give a clear and precise answer to all these questions. We do not know nor does anyone in the world know the answer at the present moment. The object of the documents and reports with which we now come before the public is not to give a detailed picture of that which has transpired with the Jews in Europe. The material we found possible to publish is but a small part of a mass of reports which have come into our hands....

• • •

That same month, Rabbi Stephen Wise of New York held a press conference at which he revealed that the State Department had confirmed that the Nazis were embarked on an extermination campaign and that two million Jews had already been killed. From then on, the historian David Wyman said, "news of Hitler's plan to annihilate the Jews was available to everyone in the democratic world who cared to know," and certainly to news executives, who had access to all incoming reports. The *Jewish Frontier* article bore witness.

Still, Wyman said, the news media gave little prominence to the reports of the Jewish slayings. For that matter, or perhaps as a result, neither did most of President Roosevelt's administration, members of Congress, Pentagon powers, Protestant and Catholic leaders, liberals, and the vaguely anti-Semitic public.

When Allied troops went in to the extermination camps at the end of World War II, they and the war correspondents said they were shocked and overcome by what they saw.

Marguerite Higgins was in her early twenties when she went to work for the New York *Herald Tribune* in 1942. She was sent to Europe in early 1945 to cover the fighting.

"33,000 Dachau Captives Freed by 7th Army," by Marguerite Higgins. New York *Herald Tribune,* May 1, 1945.

DACHAU, Germany, April 29 (Delayed)— Troops of the United States 7th Army liberated 33,000 prisoners this afternoon at this first and largest of the Nazi concentration camps. Some of the prisoners had endured for eleven years the horrors of notorious Dachau.

The liberation was a frenzied scene. Inmates of the camp hugged and embraced the American troops, kissed the ground before them and carried them shoulder high around the place....

The Dachau camp, in which at least a thousand prisoners were killed last night before the S.S. (Elite Guard) men in charge fled, is a grimmer and larger edition of the similarly notorious Buchenwald camp near Weimar.

This correspondent and Peter Furst, of the army newspaper "Stars and Stripes," were the first two Americans to enter the inclosure at Dachau, where persons possessing some of the best brains in Europe were held during what might have been the most fruitful years of their lives.

While a United States 45th Infantry Division patrol was still fighting its way down through S.S. barracks to the north, our jeep and two others from the 42d Infantry drove into the camp inclosure through the southern entrance. As men of the patrol with us busied themselves accepting an S.S. man's surrender, we impressed a soldier into service and drove with him to the prisoners' barracks. There he opened the gate after pushing the body of a prisoner shot last night while attempting to get out to meet the Americans.

There was not a soul in the yard when the gate was opened. As we learned later, the prisoners themselves had taken over control of their inclosure the night before, refusing to obey any further orders from the German guards, who had retreated to the outside. The prisoners maintained strict discipline among themselves, remaining close to their barracks so as not to give the S.S. men an excuse for mass murder.

But the minute the two of us entered a jangled barrage of "Are you Americans?" in about sixteen languages came from the barracks 200 yards from the gate. An affirmative nod caused pandemonium.

Tattered, emaciated men, weeping, yelling and shouting "Long live America!" swept toward the gate in a mob. Those who could not walk limped or crawled. In the confusion, they were so hysterically happy that they took the S.S. man for an American. During a wild five minutes he was patted on the back, paraded on shoulders and embraced enthusiastically by prisoners. The arrival of the American soldier soon straightened out the situation.

I happened to be the first through the gate, and the first person to rush up to me turned out to be a Polish Catholic priest, a deputy of August Cardinal Hlond, Primate of Poland, who was not a little startled to discover that the helmeted, uniformed, begoggled individual he had so heartily embraced was not a man.

In the excitement, which was not the least dampened by the German artillery and the sounds of battle in the northern part of the camp, some of the prisoners died trying to pass through electrically charged barbed wire. Some who got out after the wires were decharged joined in the battle, when some ill-advised S.S. men holding out in a tower fired upon them.

The prisoners charged the tower and threw all six S.S. men out the window.

After an hour and a half of cheering, the crowd, which would virtually mob each soldier that dared to venture into the excited, milling group, was calmed down enough to make possible a tour of the camp. The only American prisoner, a flyer, with the rank of major, took some of the soldiers through. . . .

The barracks at Dachau, like those at Buchenwald, had the stench of death and sickness. But at Dachau there were six barracks like the infamous No. 61 at Buchenwald, where the starving and dying lay virtually on top of each other in quarters where 1,200 men occupied a space intended for 200. The dead—300 died of sickness yesterday—lay on concrete walks outside the quarters and others were being carried out as the reporters went through.

The mark of starvation was on all the emaciated corpses. Many of the living were so frail it seemed impossible they could still be holding on to life.

The crematorium and torture chambers lay outside the prison inclosures. Situated in a wood close by, a new building had been built by prisoners under Nazi guards. Inside, in the two rooms used as torture chambers, an estimated 1,200 bodies were piled.

In the crematorium itself were hooks on which the S.S. men hung their victims when they wished to flog them or to use any of the other torture instruments. Symbolic of the S.S. was a mural the S.S. men themselves had painted on the wall. It showed a headless man in uniform with the S.S. insignia on the collar. The man was astride a huge inflated pig, into which he was digging his spurs.

The prisoners also showed reporters the grounds where men knelt and were shot in the back of the neck. On this very spot a week ago a French general, a resistance leader under General Charles de Gaulle, had been killed.

Just beyond the crematorium was a ditch containing some 2,000 more bodies, which had been hastily tossed there in the last few days by the S.S. men, who were so busy preparing their escape they did not have time to burn the bodies.

Below the camp were cattle cars in which prisoners from Buchenwald had been transported to Dachau. Hundreds of dead were still in the cars due to the fact that prisoners in the camp had rejected S.S. orders to remove them. It was mainly the men from these cattle cars that the S.S. leaders had shot before making their escape. Among those who had been left for dead in the cattle cars was one man still alive who managed to lift himself from the heap of corpses on which he lay.

• • •

Reports like these made clear what had been happening to Jews and others under the Nazis, and finally the stories started coming. For more than a month, Wyman said, all major newspapers and news magazines talked prominently about the concentration camps. Army films were used for the newsreels that played before the features at movie theaters. And people asked, why didn't we know?

Upon encountering his first death camp, General Dwight D. Eisenhower, Allied commander, made himself tour every "nook and cranny," so that he would be prepared to testify should anyone say that reports of Nazi brutality were only propaganda. He also ordered German citizens from nearby towns to tour the camps and requested visits by members of Congress and a delegation of American newspaper editors. He did not, he said, want the correspondents' reports challenged. The editors who went said that no one could exaggerate the horror.

The image of the death camps, and journalists' belated feeling that they did too little to bring them to public attention, has shaped coverage of wars since.

Higgins stayed on to cover postwar Germany, then covered the Korean War and the fighting in Vietnam. There she contracted a rare tropical disease, which caused her death in 1966 at the age of forty-five.

AS HELICOPTERS ROUND UP A HANDFUL OF VIETCONG SOLDIERS, DAVID HALBERSTAM SEES AN "ENDLESS, RELENTLESS WAR"

In the early 1960s, much of the U.S. reporting on the fighting occurring in Vietnam was supportive of American military and state department positions. This was especially so of reporting by the older generation of U.S. reporters, many of whom had covered World War II and the Korean War, and who, on their reporting forays into Vietnam, would talk to U.S. military and state department officers and file pieces that often romanticized American fighters and said that U.S. policies would prevail.

But a new generation of younger, more aggressive, more questioning reporters was arriving in Vietnam, many willing to take the field for long periods. They began to write stories that questioned U.S. policies and the notion that the war could be won. One of these reporters was David Halberstam, then in his late twenties, a correspondent of the *New York Times*.

A graduate of Harvard, where he was managing editor of the Harvard *Crimson*, Halberstam decided that civil rights would be a major story in America and he went to work at a paper where he believed he could cover that story, in West Point, Georgia. He worked there for a year, learning journalism at the most basic level, then went to work for the *Nashville Tennessean*. Then, having come to the attention of James Reston, Halberstam was hired by the *New York Times*. He served as a correspondent in the Congo, covering the war there, and in 1962 went to Vietnam.

Along with reporters like Neil Sheehan, Charles Mohr, and Peter Arnett, Halberstam came to the view that the war was a mistake and, in the manner in which it was being fought, could not be won. His direct, bottoms-up, no-nonsense reporting brought him to national attention and, in 1964, won him the Pulitzer Prize. Once President Kennedy attempted, unsuccessfully, to get Halberstam transferred from Vietnam.

Here, from his book *The Making of a Quagmire*, published in early 1965—Halberstam by then was convinced the United States would lose the war—is Halberstam's account of a typical day in Vietnam in 1963, chasing about the countryside to round up a handful of Vietcong soldiers, in shorts or pajama-like pants, in flights of expensive, heavily armed American-flown helicopters:

The Making of a Quagmire, by David Halberstam. New York: Random House, 1965.

The first time you met a member of the Vietcong there was a sharp sense of disappointment. He was not, it turned out, very different; he was simply another Vietnamese. When you saw him he was usually either kneeling and firing at you, or he had just been captured—or, more often than not, he was dead: the bodies were always lined up, their feet in an orderly row. The guerrilla wore little, perhaps a simple peasant pajama suit, perhaps only shorts. He was slim and wiry, and his face would remind you of your interpreter or that taxi driver who drove you to My Tho. Only the haircut was different, very thin along the sides, and very long on top and in front. It was a bad haircut, and like the frailness of the uniform and the thin wallet with perhaps only a few pictures of some peasant woman, it made the enemy human. But one's sympathy did not last long; this was the same face that had been

seen by the outnumbered defenders of some small outpost before it was overrun.

There were not many operations in which the Vietcong were caught; few prisoners were taken in this war. One of the few exceptions to this that I ever observed took place in April 1963, when I accompanied the new armed-helicopter units in the upper Camau peninsula on what were known as Eagle flights. An Eagle flight was risky business; it meant that a small number of elite troops circled above the paddies in the choppers, looking for likely targets. When an objective was sighted the helicopters dropped out of the sky, virtually on top of a hamlet, and the troops made a quick search, probing and scouting. If the enemy was there, other regular units, waiting in the rear with other helicopters, would be thrown in quickly. But dropping swiftly out of the sky and exploring the unknown with a handful of troops was sometimes terrifying; the helicopters have the visibility of a press box, but you were watching a war instead of a football game. When you plunged earthward, little men sometimes rushed to different positions, kneeled and started firing at the press box while your own tracers sought them out.

On that day in April the 21st Recon Company, a particularly good outfit composed largely of troops who had fought with the Vietminh during the Indochina war, was with us. We were scouting a Vietcong battalion, moving along a line of villages which we thought the battalion had been using as its main line of communication in that region. But this was the upper Camau, almost completely enemy territory, where one could find a Vietcong squad in virtually every village.

It is perhaps deceptive to use a word like "battalion" here; when such a unit attacked a given point it might number three hundred men, but immediately afterward it would break up into small groups slipping into neighboring villages and awaiting the signal for the next operation. A single large force would make too good a target for the Government; besides, by splitting up, more men could indoctrinate more peasants, and no single village would have to take on the task of feeding three hundred extra mouths.

At about eight-thirty in the morning we saw some movement in a village below, followed by a few light crackles around us. It was ground fire; the bait had been taken. We came in low over the village and saw some men scurrying to positions. Three of the helicopters, including our own, dropped their troop load while the others circled and strafed some of the positions. We were making our advance on the treeline under fire when we saw a man in a black suit desperately running across the open field. It was the dry season and the fields were covered with sun-caked mud. Suddenly a helicopter descended almost on top of the man; he stopped and held up his hands. The Vietnamese commander ran over to him. There was no weapon on this Vietcong; neither was there any of the bowing and scraping that local guerillas posing as farmers sometimes employed.

The captured man was angry and defiant, and at first a little scared as well—until he saw me and spat at me. The commander slapped his face very hard and said something in Vietnamese. Later I was told that the captain had said to the prisoner, "The Americans are very kind. They do not kill, and they are always telling us not to kill you, but I am not so kind and I will kill you. You will see." The interpreter thought this was very funny. "You know, the enemy takes these young boys and they tell them how fierce you Americans are, and so they are all convinced that the Americans will eat their hearts for breakfast as soon as they are captured. The captain is right; you have no real taste for war." The Vietnamese commander interrogated the captured guerrilla and told us that he was well indoctrinated. "They are taught well to hate," he said a little apologetically.

It is true that the Vietcong were better at hating than our Vietnamese, though at times Government troops could be very cruel. Once, south of Bac Lieu, Vietnamese Marines had fought a particularly bitter battle but had captured a number of Vietcong prisoners. According to a Vietnamese friend of mine who was there, the enemy were very cocky and started shouting anti-American slogans and Vietnamese curses at their captors. The Marines, who had lost an officer that day and were in no mood to be called lackeys of the Americans, simply lined up the seventeen guerrillas and shot them down in cold blood. . . .

The captain said that the guerrilla was probably from an elite battalion operating in the area. "I think maybe he was a squad leader." Then the officer turned and spoke briefly and intensely to the guerrilla. He was telling the prisoner that they would kill him unless he talked—and perhaps they would kill him by throwing him out of the helicopter. "The captain is very smart," said the interpreter. "It will be the guerrilla's first helicopter ride and he will be very scared." They tied up the guerrilla and placed him in the helicopter (later we were to find out that he had indeed been frightened but did not crack), and the captain and I walked back across the open field to the village. We could hear a good deal of firing, and as always I hunched over as much as I could, but the Vietnamese officer strolled casually. He carried a small swagger stick, and he looked as if he were a large landowner inspecting his plantation. I was impressed.

By the time we reached the village the troops had rounded up two more guerrillas. They did not even pretend to be farmers; they had not surrendered until they began to take fire not only from the ground but from some of the nine other helicopters in the area. The captain was convinced that there were other Vietcong somewhere in the village, that there had been at least five or six of the enemy stationed there. But he also suspected that the others had excellent hiding places and that we would not find them. "They are probably dug in under this village somewhere," he said. He checked his watch. Time was important because the helicopters had been aloft for a long while. He told his men that they had five more minutes to search the village, then turned to the prisoners and started to talk to them. One, about nineteen years old, gave him a look of defiance and turned away, but the other, who might have been twenty-five, gave the captain a curious look. "Maybe," the captain said later, "he is a little more tired of the war and the propaganda. We shall see. The other will not talk." He was right; the next morning the elder one confessed that they were members of a battalion which had hit two outposts in the Camau the week before and had come back here to rest. This guerrilla was tired; he had been fighting too long—for seven years—and he wanted to leave the Army.

At the appointed minute the troops were back. They had found an American carbine, and the captain was surprised because it was more than he had expected. The weapon had been found in a false thatch in a roof. The captain was pleased. "Good troops," he told me. "When they search they want to find something, and when they fight they want to kill."

Then the helicopters returned and we all jumped in and prepared for the next assault.

The next two villages produced only some crude grenades made by an old farmer. "The local guerrilla," said the Vietnamese captain. These were the lowest of the three types of Vietcong; they farmed in the day and fought at night, and they had the worst weapons. When I first came to Vietnam their arms were all homemade; by the time I left they were using French equipment and even some American M-1's. But even in April 1963, in a village where there were no other weapons, a homemade grenade or a rusty rifle had great power.

The local guerrillas were a vital part of the Vietcong apparatus. They gave the village a sense of Communist continuity, they could provide intelligence on Government activities and serve as a local security force for a traveling commissar, or they could guide the professional Vietcong troops. This last was particularly important to the success and mobility of the guerrillas; everywhere they went they had trained local guides to steer them through seemingly impenetrable areas. Because of these local men the enemy's troops could often move twenty-five miles in five hours—which meant that a raiding force attacking at night was almost impossible to find by daylight. These local guerrillas were also part of the propaganda network, for in a village they might be the only ones with a radio. (Sometimes it was only the shell of a radio, but the local man could pretend he could hear news, and would give out information of Vietcong victories.)

We flew back to the base to refuel, and then returned to the area. Shortly before noon we hit pay dirt. Out of one village came a flock of Vietcong, running across the paddies, and there was intense fire from the treeline. While five of our ships emptied their troops, the rest of the choppers strafed the area. Soon the guerrillas broke from their positions and ran for a nearby canal, where they might find hiding places. We came hurtling down on them at a hundred miles an hour, just a few feet off the ground. We were still drawing fire, but it was more sporadic now.

We bore down on one fleeing Vietcong. The paddy's surface was rough and his run was staggered, like that of a good but drunken broken-field runner against imaginary tacklers. We came closer and closer; inside the helicopter I could almost hear him gasping for breath, and as we bore down I could see the heaving of his body. It was like watching a film of one of your own nightmares, but in this case we were the pursuers rather than the pursued. The copilot fired his machine guns but missed, and the man kept going. Then there was a flash of orange and a blast of heat inside the ship, and the helicopter heaved from the recoil of its rockets. When they exploded the man fell. He lay still as we went over him, but when we turned he scrambled to his feet, still making for the canal, now only about fifty yards away. While we circled and swept toward him again he was straining for the bank, like a runner nearing the finish line. We had one last shot at him. Our copilot fired one last burst of the machine gun as the guerrilla made a desperate surge. The bullets cut him down as he reached the canal, and his body skidded on the hard bank as he collapsed.

We turned and circled again. All over the paddies helicopters were rounding up Vietcong soldiers. We landed near the village which other members of the Recon company were searching. The troops were gentler with the population than most ARVN soldiers I had seen; in front of one hut a medic was giving aid to a wounded guerrilla.

"I have never taken this many prisoners before," the Vietnamese captain said. There were sixteen of them. He turned to one of his men. "Show the American the poor little farmer," he said. They brought in a wiry young man. "This one says he is a farmer," the officer said. He pushed the young man in front of me and flipped the prisoner's palms over. "He has the very soft hands for a farmer," the captain said. "He has the hands of a bar girl in Saigon. He is not a very good soldier yet. In a few months, though, he might have been very good."

The prisoner was beginning to tremble. The conversation in a foreign language obviously frightened him, and I was sure that this was why the captain was using English. I asked the captain what kind of enemy we had surprised. "Territorial," he said. This was the middle rank of Vietcong guerrillas; we called them provincial guerrillas. They operated in groups of up to one hundred and were often attached to the hard-core units to beef up their strength for a major attack; they would also hit smaller outposts.

"The leadership was not very good," the captain said. "If it had been a hard-core unit, there would have been more fighting and more dying. I think we surprised them." Before we took off again, I walked over to the canal. The little soldier's body had actually crossed the finish line; his shoulder was over the bank. His blood was still running into the canal and there was a look of agony on his face.

The helicopter pilots and the Vietnamese captain decided that they had enough fuel for one more strike. The pilots were in very good humor, pleased with the day's bag. As we skimmed over the countryside once more, they boasted of how they had made the Air Force look sick again. There was a running battle between the helicopter pilots, who were Army officers, and the Air Force over the respective merits of the helicopter and the fighter plane. In particular, the feeling was very strong between Major Ivan Slavich, commander of the armed helicopter company, and Major Bill Burgin, who was the Air Force liaison man in the Twenty-first Division. Burgin called himself "the only law south of the Mekong River," and was distinguished by his violent hatred of both the Vietcong and helicopter pilots.

"Hey," said Slavich now, "go back to BC Lieu and ask your friend Burgin if he's got a T-28 that can land in a paddy, capture some Communists and then take off again."

We hit one more village and encountered no resistance. But as I was walking toward the treeline I suddenly heard shouts and cries all around me. I was terrified, for I was unarmed and about fifty yards from the nearest soldier. Suddenly from deep bomb shelters all around me more than twenty women and children came up; they were wailing and pointing at me. Clearly, they were scared. Judging from its defensive preparations, this was a Vietcong village, and for years these people had heard propaganda about vicious Americans like me. As far as I was concerned they were dangerous, too, and we stood looking at each other in mutual fear.

I yelled out to Major James Butler, asking him what to do. Butler suggested that I try to give a good impression of Americans. "Protect our image," he said. Later he congratulated me on being the first *New York Times* correspondent ever to capture a bunch of Vietcong women. I gladly turned them over to the Vietnamese captain.

The troops were remarkably restrained in what was obviously a Vietcong village. At times the quick change in Vietnamese behavior was amazing. One moment they could be absolutely ruthless; the next, they might be talking to a prisoner as if he were an old friend. The enemy was different, however; I was told by those who had been captured by them during the Indochina war that they were not so tolerant. This was hardly surprising; much emphasis was placed in their indoctrination on teaching them to hate. They were havenots fighting the haves, and even after capture their feelings rarely changed.

We flew back to Bac Lieu. It has been a good day. There had been few government losses, and there was a chance that from all those prisoners we might learn something important. Everyone was tired and relaxed and happy. If nothing else, the day seemed to prove the value of the Eagle flights. Only Mert Perry of *Time*, who had also come along to observe the new strategy, seemed a bit depressed. It had been a good day, he agreed, and in one way the Government had done very well. But after all, he pointed out, it was a pretty limited business, and in the long run it might backfire. There was no follow-up; no one would be in those villages tonight working with the people. These peasants had seen helicopters and they knew that Americans flew the helicopters; they had seen killing and they had seen their men disappear. The conclusions that the villagers would draw were obvious—particularly if the Vietcong were there to help them. Every man taken today, Mert said, probably had a brother or a son or a brother-in-law who would take his place after today.

We listened to Perry in silence, for we knew that he was right. The Government has scored a quick victory, but in Vietnam, victories were not always what they seemed. It was an endless, relentless war to which to ordinary military rules did not apply. We went to bed that night a little less confident, knowing that although for the moment the enemy was paying a higher price, he was still out there somewhere in the darkness, living closer to the peasants and ready to seize the initiative once more.

•   •   •

Halberstam's pieces and his book—so pessimistic and prophetic and published so early in the war—began, with journalism by other reporters such as Sheehan, Bernard Fall, and Malcolm Browne, to change how America looked at the Vietnam War. What had been only a war abroad was now a revolution at home.

In 1967, Halberstam, wishing to continue writing books—and tired of occasional arguments with the often conservative *Times* foreign desk—joined *Harper's* magazine, whose new editor, Willie Morris, had impressed him immensely. At *Harper's*, Halberstam, initially making $16,000 a year (never more than $20,000), joined a crackerjack staff that included Larry L. King, John Corry, and Marshall Frady (plus numerous distinguished contributors), and wrote on such subjects as Dr. Martin Luther King Jr., the Vietnam hawk McGeorge McBundy, Chicago Mayor Richard Daley, and Eugene McCarthy. A prolific writer, Halberstam went on to write *The Best and the Brightest,* the classic examination of the Vietnam War and the brilliant, out-of-touch men responsible for taking America into that war; *The Powers That Be,* a study of the modern American media, including CBS, *Time,* and the *Los Angeles Times; The Reckoning,* an exploration of the American automobile industry; and *The Fifties,* an examination of American life in that important decade. He has always regarded his profession as that of reporter. He told Willie Morris for Morris's book *New York Days:* "The real tyranny of (newspaper) journalism has always been the lack of time and space to break away from the pack." Morris wrote, "From the beginning David Halberstam proved to be more consistently right on the inflamed issue of Vietnam than almost any of our contemporaries."

SEYMOUR M. HERSH AND THE DISPATCH NEWS SERVICE REVEAL THE KILLINGS AT MY LAI AND ANOTHER TRAGEDY OF THE VIETNAM WAR

On March 17, 1968, using official military reports released the day before in Saigon, U.S. newspapers reported the success of a movement against North Vietnamese in the coastal plain northwest of Saigon. The *New York Times* headline was G.I.'S, IN PINCER MOVE, KILL 128 IN DAYLONG BATTLE. Two American soldiers were killed, the *Times* said. The paper did not use an unusual fact from the military press report: only three enemy weapons had been captured. The disparity between the number of weapons and the number of dead was a giveaway to some with knowledge of war: Most of the dead must have been civilians.

Eighteen months later, Seymour M. Hersh, a former Pentagon reporter for the Associated Press, then working on a book, got a tip that led to the unveiling of the rest of the story, a story the military had tried hard to keep quiet.

"Officer Accused of 109 Deaths," by Seymour M. Hersh. Dispatch News Service, November 13, 1969.

FORT BENNING, GA.—Lt. William L. Calley Jr., 26, is a mild-mannered, boyish-looking Vietnam combat veteran with the nickname of "Rusty." The army says he deliberately murdered at least 109 Vietnamese civilians during a search-and-destroy mission in March 1968 in a Viet Cong stronghold known as "Pinkville."

Calley has formally been charged with six specifications of mass murder. Each specification cites a number of dead, adding up to the 109 total, and adds that Calley did "with premeditation murder ... oriental human-beings whose names and sex are unknown by shooting them with a rifle."

The army calls it murder; Calley, his counsel and others associated with the incident describe it as a case of "carrying out orders."

"Pinkville" has now become a widely known code-word among the military in a case that many officers and some well-informed congressmen believe will become far more controversial than the recent murder charges against eight Green Berets. In terms of numbers slain, "Pinkville" is by far the worst known U.S. atrocity case of the Vietnam war.

Army investigation teams spent nearly one year studying the incident before filing charges against Calley, a platoon leader of the 11th Brigade of the Americal Division at the time of the slayings.

Calley was formally charged on or about Sept. 6, 1969, with the multiple homicides, just a few days before he was due to be released from active service.

Calley has since hired a prominent civilian attorney, former Judge George W. Latimer of the U.S. Court of Military Appeals, and is now awaiting a military determination of whether the evidence justifies a general court-martial. All sources agreed that the court-martial will be ordered within a week or two. It is expected to begin early next year.

Calley, meanwhile, is being detained at Fort Benning, where his movements are sharply restricted. Even his exact location on the base is a closely held secret; neither the provost marshal, nor the army's Criminal Investigation Division, know where he is being held.

The army has steadfastedly refused to comment on the case, "in order not to prejudice the continuing investigation and rights of the accused." Similarly, Calley—although submitting to an interview—refused to discuss in detail just what did happen on that day, Mar. 16, 1968.

But many other officers and civilian officials, some angered by Calley's action and others angry that charges of murder were filed in the case, talked freely during interviews at Fort Benning and Washington.

These facts are not in dispute:

The Pinkville area, about six miles northeast of Quang Ngai, had been a Viet Cong fortress since the Vietnam war began. In early February, 1968, a company of the 11th Brigade, as part of Task Force Barker, stormed through the area and was severely shot up.

Calley's platoon suffered casualties. After the communist Tet offensive in February, 1968, a larger assault was mounted, again with high casualties and little success. A third attack was quickly mounted and it was successful.

The army claimed 128 Viet Cong dead. Many civilians also were killed in the operation. The area was a free fire zone in which all non–Viet Cong residents had been urged, by leaflet, to flee. Such zones are common throughout Vietnam.

One man who took part in the mission with Calley, in recounting what happened, said that in the earlier two attacks "we were really shot up."

"Everytime we got hit it was from the rear," he said. "So the third time in there, the order came down to go in and make sure no one was behind.

"We were told to just clear the area. It was a typical combat assault formation. We came in hot, with a cover of artillery in front of us, came down the line and destroyed the village," he said.

"There are always some civilian casualties in a combat operation. He [Calley] isn't guilty of murder," he said.

The order to "clear the area" was relayed from the battalion commander to the company commander to Calley, the source added.

Calley's attorney, Latimer, said in an interview that: "This is one case that should never have been brought. Whatever killing there was was in a firefight in connection with an operation."

"You can't afford to guess whether a civilian is a Viet Cong or not. Either they shoot you or you shoot them," Latimer said.

"This case is going to be important— To what standard do you hold a combat officer in carrying out a mission?" the attorney asked.

Adding to the complexity of the case is the fact that investigators from the army inspector general's office, which conducted the bulk of the investigation, considered filing charges against at least six other men involved in the action on that Mar. 16.

Included were Capt. Ernest Medina, Calley's company commander, and Sgt. Manuel Lopez, Calley's main non-commissioned officer. Both are now stationed at Fort Benning.

They, and at least four other men from Calley's unit, were flown to Benning sometime in late summer during the army's Article 32 hearing, the military equivalent of a grand jury proceeding. The hearing was conducted under the leadership of Lt. Col. Dwayne G. Cameron, a Fort Benning infantry officer, who concluded that Calley should be held for court-martial.

Sources report that Calley was personally accused of all of the slayings under his and Sgt. Lopez's command; the young lieutenant refused to say whether the order to fire came from Medina, his former company commander, during the Article 32 hearings.

There is another side to the Calley case, one that the army cannot reveal as yet. Interviews have brought out the fact that the investigation into the Pinkville affair was initiated six months after the incident, only after some of the men who served under Calley complained.

The army has photographs of what purports to be the incident, although these have not—thus far—been introduced as evidence in the case, and may not be.

"They simply shot up this village and he [Calley] was the leader of it," said one Washington source. "When one guy refused to do it, Calley took the rifle away and did the shooting himself."

Asked about this, Calley refused to comment.

One Pentagon officer discussed the case in a caustic manner, reaching down to tap his knee with his hand, and saying at the same time:

"Some of those kids he shot were this high. I don't think they were Viet Cong. Do you?" None of the men interviewed about the affair denied that women and children had been shot at the Pinkville incident.

· · ·

The story, so counter to America's view of itself, brought a firestorm of questions. Why had Calley and the others done it? Is "just following orders" an excuse? Was Calley being made a scapegoat? Should he and the others be punished? Should their superior officers? Why did it take the Army so long to investigate? Was the press just stirring up trouble? Why doesn't the press report about communist atrocities? Were such actions an inevitable part of the nature of war? Can anyone who hasn't seen battle understand?

At first, for all the shock the incident produced, most Americans only seized on the events of My Lai to buttress opinions they already had. But as more and more stories came out from Company C, and from other incidents in which Vietnamese civilians were killed, as the Pentagon and members of Congress investigated, as the military trial proceeded, the story of My Lai became a symbol of what the Vietnam War was doing to America.

Twenty-five officers and enlisted men were charged with wrongdoing at My Lai.

In March 1971 a military court found Calley guilty of premeditated murder, and he was sentenced to life in prison. Three years later a federal judge reversed the conviction and Calley was freed on bond. No one else was ever convicted.

THE NEW YORK TIMES PUBLISHES THE PENTAGON PAPERS AND EXPLAINS A WAR

Leslie Gelb had been in his new job in the U.S. Defense Department only three weeks in 1967 when Secretary of Defense Robert S. McNamara, increasingly discouraged by U.S. involvement in Vietnam, put him in charge of a Vietnam History Task Force. McNamara's idea was to gather together the documents upon which U.S. policy had been based, so that scholars and historians could one day—"a reasonable time after the war was over," McNamara said—have the materials needed for an examination of the roots of the war. He was determined to do this even though any such examination would surely subject some of his own decisions to harsh criticism.

The task took two years, and resulted in 7,000 pages in forty-seven volumes. Fifteen sets of the papers, rather routinely stamped "top secret," were printed and distributed. The first set went to McNamara, by then at the World Bank; a friend of his said he could never bear to read it. Two sets went to the Rand Corporation, a research institution doing considerable defense work. There they were read eagerly by Daniel Ellsberg, a defense analyst and Marine veteran of Vietnam who had done some work for Gelb's history task force. Ellsberg had become zealously antiwar and felt somewhat guilty for his earlier work on behalf of U.S. Vietnam policy. He was convinced that the material in the Pentagon Papers was explosive and that its public distribution would help end the war, and he made copies of much of the material. For more than a year, he tried to convince any antiwar members of Congress to make the documents public. Failing that, Ellsberg turned to the New York Times and Neil Sheehan, a Washington reporter who was sent to Vietnam for United Press International and made a reputation as one of the early reporters to question official U.S. accounts of how the war was going. In March of 1971, Ellsberg provided Sheehan with thousands of pages of the Pentagon Papers.

The Times worked on the stories in secret for three months. Meanwhile, its lawyers debated the legal propriety of printing top-secret material.

"Vietnam Archive: Pentagon Study Traces 3 Decades of Growing U.S. Involvement," by Neil Sheehan. *New York Times,* **June 13, 1971.**

A massive study of how the United States went to war in Indochina, conducted by the Pentagon three years ago, demonstrates that four administrations progressively developed a sense of commitment to a non-Communist Vietnam, a readiness to fight the North to protect the South, and an ultimate frustration with this effort—to a much greater extent than their public statements acknowledged at the time.

The 3,000-page analysis, to which 4,000 pages of official documents are appended, was commissioned by Secretary of Defense Robert S. McNamara and covers the American involvement in Southeast Asia from World War II to mid-1968—the start of the peace talks in Paris after President Lyndon B. Johnson had set a limit on further military commitments and revealed his intention to retire. Most of the study and many of the appended documents have been obtained by the *New York Times* and will be described and presented in a series of articles beginning today.

Though far from a complete history, even at 2.5 million words, the study forms a great archive of government decision-making on Indochina over three decades. The study led its 30 to 40 authors and researchers to many broad conclusions and specific findings, including the following:

• That the Truman Administration's decision to give military aid to France in her colonial war against the Communist-led Vietminh "directly involved" the United States in Vietnam and "set" the course of American policy.

• That the Eisenhower Administration's decision to rescue a fledgling South Vietnam from a Communist takeover and attempt to undermine the new Communist regime of North Vietnam gave the Administration a "direct role in the ultimate breakdown of the Geneva settlement" for Indochina in 1954.

• That the Kennedy Administration, though ultimately spared from major escalation decisions by the death of its leader, transformed a policy of "limited-risk gamble," which it inherited, into a "broad commitment" that left President Johnson with a choice between more war and withdrawal.

• That the Johnson Administration, though the President was reluctant and hesitant to take the final decisions, intensified the covert warfare against North Vietnam and began planning in the spring of 1964 to wage overt war, a full year before it publicly revealed the depth of its involvement and its fear of defeat.

• That this campaign of growing clandestine military pressure through 1964 and the expanding program of bombing North Vietnam in 1965 were begun despite the judgment of the Government's intelligence community that the measures would not cause Hanoi to cease its support of the Vietcong insurgency in the South, and that the bombing was deemed militarily ineffective within a few months.

• That these four succeeding administrations built up the American political, military and psychological stakes in Indochina, often more deeply than they realized at the time, with large-scale military equipment to the French in 1950; with acts of sabotage and terror warfare against North Vietnam beginning in 1954; with moves that encouraged and abetted the overthrow of President Ngo Dinh Diem of South Vietnam in 1963; with plans, pledges and threats of further action that sprang to life in the Tonkin Gulf clashes in August, 1964; with the careful preparation of public opinion for the years of open warfare that were to follow; and with the calculation in 1965, as the planes and troops were openly committed to sustained combat, that neither accommodation inside South Vietnam nor early negotiations with North Vietnam would achieve the desired result.

The Pentagon study also ranges beyond such historical judgments. It suggests that the predominant American interest was at first containment of Communism and later the defense of the power, influence and prestige of the United States, in both stages irrespective of conditions in Vietnam.

And it reveals a great deal about the ways in which several administrations conducted their business on a fateful course, with much new information about the roles of dozens of senior officials of both major political parties and a whole generation of military commanders.

The Pentagon study was divided into chronological order and thematic chapters of narrative and analysis, each with its own documentation attached. The *Times*—which has obtained all but one of nearly 40 volumes—has collated these materials into major segments of varying chronological length, from one that broadly covers the two decades before 1960 to one that deals intensively with the agonizing debate in the weeks following the 1968 Tet offensive.

The months from the beginning of 1964 to the Tonkin Gulf incident in August were a pivotal period, the study makes clear, and the *Times* begins its series with this phase.

The Pentagon papers disclose that in this phase the United States had been mounting clandestine military attacks against North Vietnam and planning to obtain a Congressional resolution that the Administration regarded as the equivalent of a declaration of war. The papers make it clear that these far-reaching measures were not improvised in the heat of the Tonkin crisis.

When the Tonkin incident occurred, the Johnson Administration did not reveal these clandestine attacks, and pushed the previously prepared resolution through both houses of Congress on Aug. 7.

Within 72 hours, the Administration, drawing on a prepared plan, then secretly sent a Canadian emissary to Hanoi. He warned Premier Pham Van Dong that the resolution meant North Vietnam must halt the Communist-led insurgencies in South Vietnam and Laos or "suffer the consequences."

The section of the Pentagon study dealing with the internal debate, planning and action in the Johnson Administration from the beginning of 1964 to the August clashes between North Vietnamese PT boats and American destroyers—portrayed as a critical period when the groundwork was laid for the wider war that followed—also reveals that the covert military operations had become so extensive by August, 1964, that Thai pilots flying American T-28 fighter planes apparently bombed and strafed North Vietnamese villages near the Laotian border on Aug. 1 and 2.

Moreover, it reports that the Administration was able to order retaliatory air strikes on less than six hours' notice during the Tonkin incident because planning had progressed so far that a list of targets was available for immediate choice. The target list had been drawn up in May, the study reports, along with a draft of the Congressional resolution—all as part of a proposed "scenario" that was to build toward openly acknowledged air attacks on North Vietnam.

Simultaneously, the papers reveal, Secretary McNamara and the Joint Chiefs of Staff also arranged for the deployment of air strike forces to Southeast Asia for the opening phases of the bombing campaign. Within hours of the retaliatory air strikes on Aug. 4 and three days before the passage of the Congressional resolution, the squadrons began their planned moves.

What the Pentagon papers call "an elaborate

program of covert military operations against the state of North Vietnam" began on Feb. 1, 1964, under the code name Operation Plan 34A. President Johnson ordered the program, on the recommendation of Secretary McNamara, in the hope, held very faint by the intelligence community, that "progressively escalating pressure" from the clandestine attacks might eventually force Hanoi to order the Vietcong guerrillas in Vietnam and the Pathet Lao in Laos to halt their insurrections.

In a memorandum to the President on Dec. 21, 1963, after a two-day trip to Vietnam, Mr. McNamara remarked that the plans, drawn up by the Central Intelligence Agency station and the military command in Saigon, were "an excellent job."

"They present a wide variety of sabotage and psychological operations against North Vietnam from which I believe we should aim to select those that provide maximum pressure with minimum risk," Mr. McNamara wrote.

President Johnson, in this period, showed a preference for steps that would remain "noncommitting" to combat, the study found. But weakness in South Vietnam and Communist advances kept driving the planning process. This, in turn, caused the Saigon Government and American officials in Saigon to demand ever more action.

Through 1964, the 34A operations ranged from flights over North Vietnam by U-2 spy planes and kidnappings of North Vietnamese citizens for intelligence information, to parachuting sabotage and psychological warfare teams into the North, commando raids from the sea to blow up rail and highway bridges and the bombardment of North Vietnamese coastal installations by PT boats.

These "destructive undertakings," as they were described in a report to the President on Jan. 2, 1964, from Maj. Gen. Victor H. Krulak of the Marine Corps, were designed "to result in substantial destruction, economic loss and harass-

ment." The tempo and magnitude of the strikes were designed to rise in three phases through 1964 to "targets identified with North Vietnam's economic and industrial well-being." . . .

The attacks were given "interagency clearance" in Washington, the study says, by coordinating them with the State Department and the Central Intelligence Agency, including advance monthly schedules of the raids from General Anthis.

The Pentagon account and the documents show that William P. Bundy, the Assistant Secretary of State for Far Eastern Affairs, and John T. McNaughton, head of the Pentagon's politico-military operations as the Assistant Secretary of Defense for International Security Affairs, were the senior civilian officials who supervised the distribution of the schedules and the other aspects of interagency coordination for Mr. McNamara and Mr. Rusk.

The analyst notes that the 34A program differed in a significant respect from the relatively low-level and unsuccessful intelligence and sabotage operations that the C.I.A. had earlier been carrying out in North Vietnam.

The 34A attacks were a military effort under the control in Saigon of Gen. Paul D. Harkins, chief of the United States Military Assistance Command there. He ran them through a special branch of his command called the Studies and Observations Group. It drew up the advance monthly schedules for approval in Washington. Planning was done jointly with the South Vietnamese and it was they or "hired personnel," apparently again mercenaries, who performed the raids, but General Harkins was in charge.

The second major segment of the Administration's covert war against North Vietnam consisted of air operations in Laos. A force of propeller-driven T-28 fighter-bombers, varying from about 25 to 40 aircraft, had been organized there. The planes bore Laotian Air Force markings, but only some belonged to that air force. The rest were manned by pilots of Air America (a pseudo-private airline run by the C.I.A.) and by Thai pilots under the control of Ambassador Leonard Unger.

Reconnaissance flights by regular United States Air Force and Navy jets, code-named Yankee Team, gathered photographic intelligence for bombing raids by the T-28's against North Vietnamese and Pathet Lao troops in Laos.

The Johnson Administration gradually stepped up these air operations in Laos through the spring and summer of 1964 in what became a kind of preview of the bombing of the North. The escalation occurred both because of ground advances by the North Vietnamese and the Pathet Lao and because of the Administration's desire to bring more military pressure against North Vietnam.

As the intensity of the T-28 strikes rose, they crept closer to the North Vietnamese border. The United States Yankee Team jets moved from high-altitude reconnaissance at the beginning of the year to low-altitude reconnaissance in May. In June, armed escort jets were added to the reconnaissance missions. The escort jets began to bomb and strafe North Vietnamese and Pathet Lao troops and installations whenever the reconnaissance planes were fired upon.

The destroyer patrols in the Gulf of Tonkin, code-named De Soto patrols, were the third element in the covert military pressures against North Vietnam. While the purpose of the patrols was mainly psychological, as a show of force, the destroyers collected the kind of intelligence on North Vietnamese warning radars and coastal defenses that would be useful to 34A raiding parties or, in the event of a bombing campaign, to pilots. The first patrol was conducted by the destroyer Craig without incident in February and March, in the early days of the 34A operations.

The analyst states that before the August Tonkin incident there was no attempt to involve the destroyers with the 34A attacks or to use the ships as bait for North Vietnamese retaliation. The patrols were run through a separate naval chain of command.

Although the highest levels of the Administration sent the destroyers into the gulf while the 34A raids were taking place, the Pentagon study, as part of its argument that a deliberate provocation was not intended, in effect says that the Administration did not believe that the North Vietnamese would dare to attack the ships.

But the study makes it clear that the physical presence of the destroyers provided the elements for the Tonkin clash. And immediately after the reprisal air strikes, the Joint Chiefs of Staff and Assistant Secretary of Defense McNaughton put forward a "provocation strategy" proposing to repeat the clash as a pretext for bombing the North.

Of the three elements of the covert war, the analyst cites the 34A raids as the most important. The "unequivocal" American responsibility for them "carried with it an implicit symbolic and psychological intensification of the U.S. commitment," he writes. "A firebreak has been crossed."

On Jan. 22, 1964, a week before the 34A raids started, the Joint Chiefs warned Mr. McNamara in a memorandum signed by the Chairman, Gen. Maxwell D. Taylor, that while "we are wholly in favor of executing the covert actions against North Vietnam . . . it would be idle to conclude that these efforts will have a decisive effect" on Hanoi's will to support the Vietcong.

The Joint Chiefs said the Administration "must make ready to conduct increasingly bolder actions," including "aerial bombing of key North Vietnam targets, using Vietnamese cover," sending American ground troops to South Vietnam and employing "United States forces as necessary in direct actions against North Vietnam."

And after a White House strategy meeting on Feb. 20, President Johnson ordered that "contingency planning for pressures against North Vietnam should be speeded up."

"Particular attention should be given to shaping such pressures so as to produce the maximum credible deterrent effect on Hanoi," the order said.

The impelling force behind the Administration's desire to step up the action during this period was its recognition of the steady deterioration in the positions of the pro-American governments in Laos and South Vietnam, and the corresponding weakening for the United States' hold on both countries. North Vietnamese and Pathet Lao advances in Laos were seen as having a direct impact on the morale of the anti-Communist forces in South Vietnam, the primary American concern.

This deterioration was also concealed from Congress and the public as much as possible to provide the Administration with maximum flexibility to determine its moves as it chose from behind the scenes.

• • •

Other news organizations around the country paid remarkably little attention to the *New York Times*'s exclusive Sunday report. In Washington, Secretary of Defense Melvin Laird and Attorney General John Mitchell, part of an administration proud of its prerogatives and distrustful of the press, conferred quickly, but did not take any action until Monday. Mitchell sent a telegram to the publisher of the *New York Times* saying that publication of the Pentagon Papers was "directly prohibited by provisions of the Espionage Law" and would "cause irreparable injury to the defense interests of the United States." The *Times* should stop publication and return the documents to the Defense Department, Mitchell said. There was internal dispute at the *Times*, but the paper went ahead with Sheehan's series. On Wednesday afternoon a federal district judge in New York City issued a restraining order halting publication—the first time in U.S. history that a newspaper was prohibited in advance from publishing an article.

By the time the case went to the U.S. Supreme Court on June 26, Daniel Ellsberg had been publicly revealed, but not by the involved newspapers, as the source of the documents. He also made

portions of the Pentagon Papers available to the *Washington Post,* the *Boston Globe*, and the *St. Louis Post-Dispatch,* which likewise faced legal challenges from the Justice Department, as well as the *Chicago Sun-Times,* the *Los Angeles Times*, the *Christian Science Monitor*, and the Knight chain of newspapers, which did not.

The court arguments were contentious, with some justices believing in the absoluteness of the First Amendment and others giving credence to the government's need to protect what it defined as national security. What probably made the difference in the decision was the historical nature of the documents in the first place; the justices examined them in secret and did not find any material that they concluded would endanger military operations or lives. By a 6–3 vote, but with nine separate opinions, the Court freed the newspapers to continue publication.

The government's effort to stop publication probably attracted more attention than the articles based on the papers themselves. Sanford Ungar, in his *The Papers and the Papers,* concluded that "relatively few Americans, in fact, read the Pentagon Papers in any detail." Certainly, contrary to what Ellsberg had expected, there was no new popular outcry against the Vietnam War. The legal decision also was ambivalent; the justices, some of whom were antagonistic to the press in their remarks, noted only that the government had not met the heavy burden of proof that would allow the court to support prior restraint of publication. The ruling clearly had not said that publication could *never* be halted.

Nonetheless, publication of the Pentagon Papers was widely regarded as a victory for the press and encouragement for more aggressive reporting about the truth behind government policy. If the results of publication were not as great as some people expected, the alternative, said Abe Rosenthal, managing editor of the *Times,* "would have changed the history of the newspaper business."

ROY GUTMAN OF *NEWSDAY* UNCOVERS BOSNIAN DEATH CAMPS

The latest war in what was once Yugoslavia had historical roots, it was certain, although it was not sure which roots were most relevant. Some traced the fighting to the Serbian defeat by the Ottomans in 1389. Some to the beginning of World War I. Some to the Versailles Treaty at the war's end. Some to the rule of Marshal Josip Tito; some to his death in 1980, with Slobodan Milosevic's rise afterward. Milosevic's authoritarian, pro-Serbian rule led the republics of Croatia, Slovenia, and Macedonia to secede from Yugoslavia in 1991, and Bosnia-Herzegovina early the next year. Serbian forces moved to seize territory and to isolate the million or so Muslims in Bosnia, then to drive journalists and international aid workers out of the country. With their actions thus hidden, Serbian officials rounded up Muslim civilians in detention centers.

From his base in Germany, where he was the *Newsday* bureau chief, Roy Gutman began to hear of the camps in July 1992. He pressured Serbian officials to take him to the camp at Omarska, an open-pit iron mine in northern Bosnia, with no success. But the reports from aid workers, refugees, and military officials were so strong that he kept on reporting. Finally, he found two men who had formerly been held at Omarska. The story ran on August 2, 1992.

"Death Camps," by Roy Gutman. *Newsday,* August 2, 1992.

The Serb conquerors of northern Bosnia have established two concentration camps in which more than a thousand civilians have been executed or starved and thousands more are being held until they die, according to two recently released prisoners interviewed by New York *Newsday.*

The testimony of the two survivors appeared to be the first eyewitness accounts of what international human rights agencies fear may be systematic slaughter conducted on a huge scale. New York *Newsday* has not been able to visit the camps. Neither has the International Red Cross or any other international agency.

In one concentration camp, a former iron-mining complex at Omarska in northwest Bosnia, more than a thousand Muslim and Croat civilians were held in metal cages, without sanitation, adequate food, exercise or access to the outside world, according to a former prisoner who asked to be identified only as "Meho." The prisoners at the camp, he said, include the entire political and cultural elite of the city of Prijedor. Armed Serbian guards executed prisoners in groups of 10 to 15 every few days, he said.

"They would take them to a nearby lake. You'd hear a volley of rifles. And they'd never come back," said Meho.

"I think if these places are not death camps, we might have access to them," said Pierre Andre Conod, head of the International Committee of the Red Cross delegation in Zagreb, which oversees conditions in northern Bosnia. "They'd have reason to show them to us if the conditions are acceptable." The Red Cross has gained access twice to what Bosnian Serbs have called a prisoner-of-war camp in Manjaca.

Yugoslavian Prime Minister Milan Panic sent word through a deputy that he could neither confirm nor deny the existence of death camps and favored the closing of all camps from all sides in the Bosnian war. The country Panic has taken over is a shadow of the former Yugoslavia and consists only of Serbia, which is accused of sponsoring the war in Bosnia, and tiny Montenegro.

Serbs, who claim the Bosnian region as their own, describe the policy of expelling Muslims and Roman Catholic Croats as "ethnic cleansing"; reports by the survivors interviewed by New York *Newsday* suggest this is a euphemism for a campaign of atrocity and brutal deportation at best.

In a second improvised camp, in a customs warehouse on the bank of the Sava River in the northwest Bosnian city of Breko, 1,350 people were slaughtered between May 15 and mid-June, according to Alija Lujinovic, 53, a traffic engineer who was imprisoned at the camp. Guards at Breko executed prisoners by slitting their throats or with firing squads, he said.

"Meho," 63, a building contractor from the nearby town of Kozarac, was coaxed out of hiding by a doctor from his hometown for a two-hour conversation with New York *Newsday* and Red Cross personnel on Friday. Meho said he was detained at Omarska for one week in June before being released, he thinks because of his age. He was held in an ore loader inside a cage roughly 700 square feet along with 300 other men awaiting processing by their captors, he said. The metal superstructure contained cages stacked four high, separated by grates. There were no toilets, and the prisoners had to live in their own filth, which dripped through the grates.

Meho said three people tried to escape by jumping through an open pipe from the top cage to the ground, but all were shot after falling 60 feet to the ground. He said he also heard from other prisoners that during his week in the camp, 35 to 40 men had died "in agony" after being beaten.

International relief agencies said his statement, given to New York *Newsday* in the presence of officials of the Bosnian Red Cross–Red Crescent, was the first confirmation of their supicions that Omarska is a death camp. They said they had heard rumors for more than a month about such camps but no one had talked to a survivor.

The International Committee of the Red Cross has been trying for more than two weeks to gain access to Omarska, Conod said, but Serb authorities in Bosnia have turned them down, saying they could not guarantee their safety. The Serb-controlled Bosnian army refused two weeks ago to take a New York *Newsday* reporter and a freelance photographer to Omarska.

The Red Cross has not yet applied to visit Breko because, after withdrawing from Bosnia in May following the killing of a Red Cross official, its staff members returned to Banja Luka, the main city in northern Bosnia, and have not yet resumed full operations in eastern Bosnia.

Meho said that while he was at Omarska, from about June 3 to 10, prisoners filled each of the four cages in the ore loader and other prisoners estimated the camp population at about 8,000. The official Bosnian War Crimes Investigation Institute, a government body set up to compile a record of war crimes, in a report last week to the UN High Commissioner for Refugees, estimated there were 11,000 prisoners at Omarska, making it the biggest of the 94 camps known to the commission. It had no estimate of prisoners killed. . . .

Like so many refugees, Meho said he was beaten regularly and witnessed atrocities while he was held at Omarska and at two other camps where he was detained briefly en route to Omarska. When interviewed here, he said he could hardly lift his left arm and he flashed a nearly toothless grin, seven teeth having been knocked out during the beatings he described.

Meho said the Bosnian Serb army had arrested him in his home town of Kozarac on May 27.

They put Red Crosses on their sleeve, and on the tanks and shouted "Give up. The Red Cross is waiting for you. You will be protected," he recalled. But as they went to buses, he said, soldiers stood at the entrance with truncheons.

"There were three armed guards in each bus. They said if you raised your head, you'd get a bullet through it." The camps had been hastily assembled. Meho was taken first to Keretem, a ceramics manufacturing plant in the town of Prijedor, and then to Ciglana, a brickworks next door, before being sent to Omarska. He said he was picked up because the authorities suspected he had two sons who had fought against the Serbs.

"The system was that they'd take you in for an

interview and would say that you'll be set free if you tell about the others. Everybody was accusing the others to save themselves. But they didn't release anyone," he said.

In the ore loader at Omarska, people were crowded so tightly that "there was nowhere to lie down. You'd drowse off and fall against the next person." Every third day, bread was distributed, a two-pound loaf for three people, and after a week, prisoners were given a small cup of weak soup once a day. . . .

• • •

Even Gutman conceded that part of the impact of his story was due not to his reporting but to the dramatic treatment *Newsday,* a tabloid, had given it. Two weeks before, Gutman had written a story focused on reports from the camps, which carried the headline, "There Is No Food. There Is No Air." This time, the front page of the paper carried the headline "The Death Camps of Bosnia" in two-inch letters. "It was a daring deci-

sion," Gutman wrote in *Witness to Genocide* (New York: Macmillan, 1993). The Holocaust reference gave Gutman's story an impact it would not otherwise have had.

There had been no official reaction to Gutman's first story, but the second one drew plenty, particularly after Britain's International Television News gained access to two Bosnian camps and emerged with harrowing, Holocaust-like photographs. Other media increased their coverage. President George Bush ordered U.S. intelligence agencies to investigate and pledged to ensure humanitarian access to the camps. Seeking to offset pressure, the Serbian leader, Radovan Karadzic, gave the Red Cross permission to visit the camps and talked of handing them over to Red Cross control.

With Bush in the midst of a reelection campaign, U.S. policy toward Bosnia did not change. But Gutman's characterization of the camps in Bosnia shaped the historical view of the Serbian regime and raised the question of genocide that became the basis of war-crime indictments.

THE PRESS

THE JOHN PETER ZENGER CASE: THE TRUTH SHALL MAKE YOU FREE

Newspaper competition came to New York in 1733, when a group of merchants and public officials discontented with the rule of William Cosby, the colonial governor, offered their backing to a young printer, John Peter Zenger. The only newspaper in the city, the *New York Gazette,* was run by William Bradford, who was also the government printer. The combination made him disinclined to criticize the establishment.

Zenger's *New-York Weekly Journal,* first printed on November 5, 1733, had no such restrictions, and it repeatedly attacked government policy. Cosby's irritation grew. Under the legal thinking of the time, printing criticism of the government that might cause public unrest—whether or not the criticism was true—was seditious libel, a crime. After twice failing in attempts to indict Zenger, Cosby succeeded. Zenger was arrested in November 1734 and held in jail on high bail until the trial started in August 1735. His wife, Anna, ran the paper in the meantime.

Theoretically, Zenger's case should have been open and shut; his attorney, the respected Andrew Hamilton of Philadelphia, even conceded that Zenger had printed the *Journal*s in question. But then Hamilton turned to the jury and urged them to break precedent and, in the cause of liberty, to lay claim to the "Right—the Liberty—both of exposing and opposing arbitrary Power (in these Parts of the World, at least) by speaking and writing—Truth."

On August 18, 1735, Zenger published this account, the only published account, of the trial:

John Peter Zenger.
New-York Weekly Journal.
Monday, August 18, 1735.

To my Subscribers and Benefactors.

Gentlemen;

I Think my self in Duty bound to make publick Acknowledgement for the many Favours received at your Hands, which I do in the Manner return you my hearty Thanks for. I very soon intend to print my Tryal at Length, that the World may see how unjust my Sufferings have been, so will only at this Time give this short Account of it.

On Monday the 4th Instant my Tryal for Printing Parts of my Journal No. 13. And 23. Came on, in the Supreme Court of this Province, before the most numerous Auditory of People, I may with Justice say, that ever were seen in that Place at once; my Jury sworn were,

1 Harmanus Rutgers,
2 Stanley Holms,
3 Edward Man,
4 John Bell,
5 Samuel Weaver,
6 Andrew Marschalk,
7 Eghert Van Borsen,
8 Thomas Hunt,
9 Benjamin Hildrith,
10 Abraham Kiteltass
11 John Goelet,
12 Hercules Wendover,

John Chambers, Esq, had been appointed the Term before by the Court as my Council, in the Place of *James Alexander* and *William Smith*, who were then silenced on my Account, and to Mr. *Chambers's* Assistance came *Andrew Hamilton*, Esq; of *Philadelphia* Barrester at Law; when Mr. Attorney offered the Information and the Proofs, Mr. *Hamilton* told him, he would acowledge my Printing and Publishing the Papers in the Information, and save him the Trouble of that Proof, and offered to prove the Facts of those Papers true, and had Witnesses ready to prove every Fact; he long insisted on the Liberty of Making Proof thereof, but was over-ruled therin. Mr. Attorney offered no Proofs of my Papers being *false, malicious* and *seditious*, as they were charged to be, but insisted that they were Lybels tho' true. There were many Arguments and Authorities on this point, and the Court were of Opinion with Mr. Attorney on that Head: But the Jury having taken the information out with them, they returned in about Ten Minutes, and found me *Not Guilty*; upon which there were immediately three Hurra's of many Hundreds of People in the presence of the Court, before the Verdict wer returned. The next Morning my Discharge was moved for and granted.

• • •

British officialdom never issued an official report on the trial, and so Zenger's account was unchallenged. Although libel law did not change until the end of the century, the journalism historians Michael Emery and Edwin Emery concluded that the Zenger case had tremendous inspirational impact. "For the trial did enunciate a principle—even if it did not establish legal precedent—and this prinicple is vital to our libertarian philosophy today in matters of free speech and press. The right to criticize officials is one of the main pillars of press freedom."

Colonial printers were emboldened by news of the Zenger decision. Nonetheless, the Emerys say, after the Zenger trial the Crown, perhaps recognizing the bent of colonial public opinion, never again tried a printer for criticizing the government.

Zenger's successful challenge of royal authority also emboldened other colonists with grievances. "The trial of Zenger in 1735 was the morning star of that liberty which subsequently revolutionized America," concluded one of the revolutionaries, Gouverneur Morris.

The first state to recognize truth as a defense in a libel trial was Pennsylvania, which included the principle in its 1790 constitution. New York followed in 1805.

THE FIRST PENNY PAPER: THE NEW YORK *SUN* ANNOUNCES A PAPER FOR ALL NEW YORKERS

In the early 1800s, newspapers were unabashedly aimed for the upper classes, the best educated and wealthiest, not for their maids and coachmen. Subscriptions were by the year, in advance, and the cost of $6 to $10 was more than even skilled workers earned in a week. Further, the papers were filled with long, discursive essays on national and foreign topics, not the kind of writing inclined to interest working people struggling with the problems of everyday life.

At the same time the lives of the so-called

common people were changing. More were living in cities. More had been educated through public schools. Their buying power had increased enough that advertisers wanted to reach them. More people were caught up in the early labor movement and in the democratic ferment of the Jacksonian era. They were ready for a newspaper aimed for them. On September 3, 1833, a printer named Benjamin H. Day started providing one.

Day announced his intentions in a front-page paragraph.

The *Sun,* New York, Tuesday, September 3, 1833 {Price One Penny}

The object of this paper is to lay before the public, at a price within the means of everyone, ALL THE NEWS OF THE DAY, and at the same time afford an advantageous medium for advertising. The sheet will be enlarged as soon as the increase of advertisements requires it—the price remaining the same.

• • •

The rest of the front page contained a column of ship advertisements, a story about a dueling Irish captain, "wonders of littleness," and a paragraph about a Vermont lad who tended to get stuck in a whistling mode, and had to be paired at work with another boy who had instructions to hit him every time he began to whistle.

The first issue hardly seems full of promise, but in fact Day was beginning a revolution in American newspapers. The *Sun* could be bought from hawkers on the street for a penny a day. It stressed local news, crime reporting, and human interest; it was highly readable and full of things the readers talked to each other about. Since it wanted to reach as many people as possible, it did not align with any political party. Day created a new class of newspaper readers. Within six months he was selling 8,000 copies a day, nearly twice that of the most successful of his more erudite competition. Naturally, the *Sun* attracted advertisers and rivals—the New York *Herald,* the New York *Tribune,* the *New York Times.*

On a building in lower Manhattan, not far from where Day had his print shop, remains a four-sided clock that marked the offices of the *Sun* for many years before it closed in 1950. On the clock is the logo that made the *Sun* a success for 117 years: "It Shines for All."

JAMES GORDON BENNETT TALKS TO A MADAM AND CREATES A JOURNALISM PRACTICE: THE INTERVIEW

One of James Gordon Bennett's biographers called him the man who invented news, and the description comes close. A Scottish immigrant who, like so many immigrants, at first moved from job to job, in the 1820s Bennett became one of the first Washington correspondents. He was a good one, pulling no punches and getting lively stories that no one else had. Upon his return to New York, he noticed the success of the New York *Sun* in reaching a new audience with a new kind of newspaper. With $500 and, legend has it, a board stretched over two barrels in a basement office on Wall Street, Bennett founded the New York *Herald* on May 16, 1835. It sold for a penny and was aimed at the masses.

The paper was a success from the beginning. Bennett stressed the importance of news and was aggressive about getting it. He covered Wall Street, Congress, and crime better than anyone. He was called a scandalous blackguard, among other names, by his more sedate opposition, but he did not mind so long as people were talking about him, and his paper.

About a year after the *Herald* was founded, a young prostitute, Helen Jewett, was killed in her room at the City Hotel and a man who had been seeing her was arrested for the crime. This was the kind of story that the more established newspapers ignored. But Bennett knew his readers wanted to hear all about it. He went personally to the scene of the crime and viewed the corpse, a bit of reporting that a critic compared to "a vampire returning to a newly found graveyard." As he continued his sleuthing, sales of the *Herald* jumped, so much that the presses strained to keep up. The case was the talk of the town; clergymen moralized. Bennett developed a theory that the wrong man had been accused. Taking another man with him for verification, he went to talk to the madam, Rosina Townsend, and then reported exactly what she told him. In doing so, he invented a new journalistic device: the interview.

New York *Herald*, June 4, 1836.

About the hour of 9 o'clock [said Rosina] on Saturday, I was called to the front door by a knock, and on enquiring "Who's there?" the reply was, "Frank Rivers." I opened the door and let him in, and he passed me with his face muffled up in his cloak, upstairs.

I went into the parlor and told Helen, Frank was there. Helen left the parlor and went out saying, "My dear Frank, I am glad to see you." They both went to Helen's room—nothing more was heard of either until about 11 o'clock, when Helen came partly down the stairs and called to me, and requested me to bring her a bottle of champagne. . . . I went downstairs and got a bottle, knocked off the rosin, and took it upstairs to Helen's door. I knocked at the door, and Helen said, "Come in." I opened the door and went in.—I saw Frank lying on the bed.

Question: What was he doing?

Answer: He was lying on his left side, with his head resting on his arm in the bed, the sheet thrown over him, and something in his other hand.

Q: What was that?

A: I can't say.

Q: Was it a book?

A: I think it was—either a book or a paper.—I saw his face.

Q: What did he say?

A: Nothing. Helen said to me, "Rosina, as you have not been well today, will you take a glass of champagne with us?" I replied, "No, I am much obliged to you, I had rather not."—I then left the room, as some of the other girls called me from below.—I neither heard nor saw anything more from that time.—The house was locked up for the night at 12 o'clock P.M.—I returned to rest.—About 3 o'clock A.M. I heard a noise at the front door, and found, on enquiring, that it was a young man who was in the habit of visiting one of the girls in the house.—I got up and let him in—after I had let him in I smelt smoke, and on going into the parlor I found the back door open, and Helen's lamp standing on the marble side table, by the door. I went directly to Helen's room, and found the door shut—I opened it, and on so doing, the smoke rushed out and nearly suffocated me.—I then raised the alarm of fire.—The watchman was called in, and he went into the room and found Helen lying on the bed and the bed on fire—she was burnt.—After the windows were opened and the smoke let out, the watchman discovered that Helen had been murdered, and then the bed set on fire.

Q: Had you ever seen Frank previous to the night after you let him in?

A: Yes—once—he was sitting in a room with me and some other girls—Helen was present, and on Frank's rising to leave the room, Helen remarked, "Rosina, don't you think my Frank very handsome?" I replied yes. . . .

Q: How did you know that the person you let in was Frank?

A: He gave his name.

Q: Did you see his face?

A: No . . . his cloak was held up over his face, I saw nothing but the eyes as he passed me—he had on a hat and cloak.

Q: Who first discovered the fire?

A: I did as I got up.

Q: On the morning of the transaction did you see Frank?

A: I did; he was in the back parlor, standing by an officer. I was called in and asked whether he was the person I had let in the night previous as Frank. I replied yes; to which he [Frank] said, "What! Me! You are mistaken!" . . . Mrs. Berry was brought in and recognized him as Frank, as he had been in the habit of visiting Helen at her house in Duane street. She said, "You villain, Frank, how could you murder Helen?" He turned pale and leaned back on the sofa; that was the only time he lost confidence or changed color; he was then carried off to prison.

[After recounting the interview, Bennett turned detective:]

Now, on this extraordinary story, we have a few remarks to make. Admitting Rosina Townsend to be a woman of virtue and integrity, is it not perceived at once that there are material contradictions in her own story?

She admits she did not see anything but the eyes of Frank, and that was in the passageway, for he did not enter the parlor. She admits that she saw him lying in bed at some distance, but although she could not tell whether he had a book or paper in his hand, she has no hesitation in asserting that it was Frank Rivers. And further, this person she is so sure of, was only once seen before, by her.

Is it not extraordinary that she should know a man so easily without seeing his face—as it was covered by his cloak? Is it not equally so that she did not know what he read—a paper or book— yet she knew the person? . . .

All the particulars related by Mrs. T. are of an extraordinary nature. There are several facts, however, we have heard, which are even more so. Mrs. T., I understand, had borrowed money of Helen; and yet it is said, she intends to administer on her property. Helen had many valuables about her—she had a large amount of jewelry—her wearing apparel was splendid, and worth probably $1,500. What has become of all this property? In

whose possession is it? At this moment many of the girls have left Mrs. Townsend's, and she herself talks of selling out, clearing out, and blowing out.

• • •

Journalism historians say that the technique of the journalistic interview was not a universal success. For a time, Louis L. Snyder and Richard B. Morris said in their *Treasury of Great Reporting*, the interview was regarded as "the most perfect contrivance yet devised to make journalism an offense, a thing of ill savor in all decent nostrils." Perhaps some of that opinion had to do with the fact that Bennett's interview was with a woman acknowledged to be involved with prostitution and at the scene of a murder, and with the fact that some people thought anything Bennett touched was scandalous.

Journalism historians also point to the importance of another early journalism interview, with a far different kind of person than Madame Townsend: Brigham Young, the Mormon leader, whom Horace Greeley interviewed and quoted directly in his New York *Tribune* in 1859. Critics then also complained at what they saw as a violation of privacy. The appeal of hearing a source's exact words won out, however; Bennett had put American journalism on the path to sound bites.

The doubts that Bennett raised were prescient. After a trial that brought out many contradictions in Townsend's statements, Frank Rivers was acquitted. Helen Jewett's killer was never apprehended.

A MUCKRAKING MAGAZINE REVEALS THE TRUTH BEHIND PATENT MEDICINES

Once sold by hustlers who traveled by wagon from town to town, by the end of the 1800s patent medicines were plentiful advertisers in the new, mass magazines. The market for these all-purpose cure-alls, hawked with testimonials and slick language, was large. In 1900, when the country had about eighty million people, estimates of the sales of patent medicines ranged from $59 million to $100 million. The medicines promised to cure pretty much anything that ailed a person, but the labels failed to disclose the alcoholic content and presence of cocaine and morphine that conveniently kept customers coming back for more.

A few courageous editors set out to raise the alarm. One was Edward Bok, who became editor of the *Ladies' Home Journal* in 1889, succeeding Louisa Curtis, wife of Cyrus Curtis, who had founded the magazine in 1883. Bok aimed his magazine at middle-class women who were interested in learning modern ways so they could better care for their homes and families. As early as 1892, Bok announced that the magazine would no longer accept patent-medicine advertisements, a decision that cost it thousands.

In 1904, he began a series of editorials urging his readers not to use the products.

"The 'Patent-Medicine' Curse," by Edward Bok. *Ladies' Home Journal,* 1904.

Every year, particularly in the springtime, tens of thousands of bottles of patent medicines are used throughout the country by persons who are in absolute ignorance of what they are swallowing. They feel "sluggish" after the all-winter indoor confinement; they feel that their systems need a "toning up," or a "blood purifier." Their eye catches some advertisement in a newspaper, or on a fence, or on the side of a barn, and from the cleverly-worded descriptions of symptoms they are convinced that this man's "bitters," or that man's "sarsaparilla," or that "doctor's" (!) "vegetable compound," or So-and-so's "pills" is exactly the thing they need as a "tonic."

"No use going to a doctor," argue these folks: "we can save that money," and instead of paying

one or two dollars for honest, intelligent medical advice they invest from twenty-five to seventy-five cents for a bottle of this, or a box of that. And what do they buy, and what do they put into their system? . . . For the sake of saving a physician's fee they pour into their mouths and into their systems a quantity of unknown drugs which have in them percentages of alcohol, cocaine and opium that are absolutely alarming. A mother who would hold up her hands in holy horror at the thought of her child drinking a glass of beer, which contains from two to five per cent of alcohol, gives to that child with her own hands a patent medicine that contains from seventeen to forty-four percent of alcohol—to say nothing of opium and cocaine! I have seen a temperance woman, who raged at the thought of whisky, take bottle after bottle of some "bitters," which contained five times as much alcohol—and compared to which sherry, port, claret and champagne were as harmless as the pink lemonade at Sunday-school picnics. I have had women rage in letters to this office because this magazine advertised a certain rootbeer, with really no alcohol in it at all, while all the time these same women were swallowing bottle after bottle of "Lydia Pinkham's Vegetable Compound," containing, by volume, 20.6 percentage of alcohol, and allowing "Baker's Stomach Bitters," with 42.6 percentage of alcohol, by volume, to be advertised on their barns! . . .

It is not by any means putting the matter too strongly to say that the patent medicine habit is one of the gravest curses, with the most dangerous results, that is inflicting our American national life. Sooner or later, the people of America must awaken to the fearful dangers that lie in these propriety preparations. The mothers of our children, in particular, must have their eye opened to the dangers that lurk in these patent medicines. Here and there a hopeful sign of an awakening is seen. Slowly but surely the best magazines are falling into line in their refusal to accept patent-medicine advertisements of any kind. Not long ago one of the insurance companies made an excellent move by requiring its medical examiners to ask of each subject for insurance, "What patent medicines have you used during the last five years?" and gradually other insurance companies are realizing the fact that the use of patent medicines is even more injurious than the use of alcoholic liquors. But much still remains: more should be done. Public interest must be more widely aroused.

... Let the officers of the Woman's Christian Temperance Union look into the advertising columns of the religious papers of the country, and see how their columns fairly reek with the advertisements of these dangerous concoctions. Yet in these very same so-called religious papers there are official Woman's Christian Temperance Union columns setting forth the "official" news of the organization and its branches. A pretty consistent picture do these two portions of the average religious paper present—advocating, with one hand, alcoholic prohibition, or temperance, and receiving, with the other hand, money for advertising—and thereby recommending to their readers—preparations filled ten times over with more alcohol than the beer which fills them with so much horror in the editorial columns! There are no papers published that are so flagrantly guilty of admitting to their columns the advertisements not only of alcohol-filled medicines but preparations and cure-alls of the most flagrantly obscene nature, as the so-called religious papers of this country.... Let the Woman's Christian Temperance Union officers counsel its members who subscribe for these people to compel their publishers to omit these advertisements, and if they refuse, let these people discontinue their patronage of the paper. Such measures would very quickly shut out from publicity the majority of these baneful patent medicines. There is vital, important work here for the Woman's Christian Temperance Union—work in a cause which is aiming with far greater danger at the very heart of American homes than the cracking of a bottle of champagne over the hull of a newly-launched craft.

Far better, ladies, that the contents of a bottle of champagne should go into the water, which it will do no one any harm, than that the contents of a bottle of "patent medicine," with forty percent of alcohol in it, by volume, should be allowed to go into the system of a child and strike at his very soul, planting the seed of a future drunkard!

• • •

Bok then hired Mark Sullivan, a young New York lawyer, to come to work for the *Journal*. Sullivan's first assignment was writing about the patent-medicine industry. Among his findings: that Lydia Pinkham, ostensibly the woman behind the Lydia Pinkham Company, who promised personally to answer letters from customers, had been dead for twenty-three years. Sullivan's completed article was 7,000 words, longer, Bok said, than the *Journal* could run. He arranged for it to be published instead in *Collier's* magazine, which had recently joined in the crusade with a series of articles called "The Great American Fraud" by Samuel Hopkins Adams.

"The Patent Medicine Conspiracy Against Freedom of the Press," anonymous [but by Mark Sullivan]. *Collier's,* November 4, 1905.

Would any person believe that there is any one subject upon which the newspapers of the United States, acting in concert, by prearrangement, in obedience to wires all drawn by one man, will deny full and free discussion? If such a thing is possible, it is a serious matter, for we rely upon the newspapers as at once the most forbidding preventive and the swiftest and surest corrective of evil. For the haunting possibility of newspaper exposure, men who know not at all the fear of God pause, hesitate, and turn back from contemplated rascality. For fear "it might get into the papers," more men are abstaining from crime and carouse to-night than for fear of arrest. But these are trite things—only, what if the newspapers fail us? Relying so wholly on the press to undo evil, how shall we deal with that evil with which the press itself has been seduced into captivity?

In the Lower House of the Massachusetts Legislature one day last March there was a debate which lasted one whole afternoon and engaged some twenty speakers, on a bill providing that every bottle of patent medicine sold in the State should bear a label stating the contents of the bottle. More was told concerning patent medicines that afternoon than often comes to light in a single day. The debate at times was dramatic—a member from Salem told of a young woman of his acquaintance now in an institution for inebriates as the end of an incident which began with patent medicine dosing for a harmless ill. There was humor, too, in the debate—Representative Walker held aloft a bottle of Peruna bought by him in a drug store that very day, and passed it around for his fellow-members to taste and decide for themselves whether Dr. Harrington, the Secretary of the State Board of Health, was right when he told the Legislative Committee that it was merely a "cheap cocktail."

In short, the debate was interesting and important—the two qualities which invariably ensure to any event big headlines in the daily newspapers. But that debate was not celebrated by big headlines, nor any headlines at all. Yet Boston is a city, and Massachusetts is a State, where the proceedings of the Legislature figure very large in public interest, and where the newspapers respond to that interest by reporting the sessions with greater fulness and minuteness than in any other State. Had that debate been on prison reform, on Sabbath observance, the early closing saloon law, on any other subject, there would have been, in the next day's papers, overflowing accounts of verbatim report, more columns of editorial comment, and the picturesque features of it would have ensured the attention of the cartoonist.

Now why? Why was this one subject tabooed? Why were the daily accounts of legislative proceedings in the next day's papers abridged to a fraction of their usual ponderous length, and all reference in the afternoon debate on patent medicines omitted? Why was it in vain for the speakers in that patent medicine debate to search for their speeches in the next day's newspapers? Why did the legislative reporters fail to find their work in print? Why were the staff cartoonists forbidden to exercise their talents on that most fallow and tempting opportunity—the members of the Great and General Court of Massachusetts gravely tippling Peruna and passing the bottle around to their encircled neighbors, that practical knowledge should be the basis of legislative action?

I take it if any man should assert that there is one subject upon which the newspapers of the United States, acting in concert and as a unit, will deny full and free discussion, he would be smiled at as an intemperate fanatic. The thing is too incredible. He would be regarded as a man with a delusion. And yet I invite you to search the files of the daily newspapers of Massachusetts for March 16, 1905, for an account of the patent medicine debate that occurred the afternoon of March 15 in the Massachusetts Legislature. In strict accuracy it must be said that there was one exception. Any one familiar with the newspapers of the United States will already have named it— the Springfield "Republican." That paper, on two separate occasions, gave several columns to the record of the proceedings of the Legislature on the patent medicine bill. Why the otherwise universal silence?

The patent medicine business in the United States is one of huge financial proportions. The census of 1900 placed the value of the annual produce at $59,611,355. Allowing for the increase of half a decade of rapid growth, it must be to-day not less than seventy-five millions. That is the wholesale price. The retail price of all the patent medicines sold in the United States in one year may be very conservatively placed at one hundred million dollars. And of this one hundred millions which the people of the United States pay for patent medicines yearly, fully forty millions goes to the newspapers. Have patience! I have more to say than merely to point out the large revenue which newspapers receive from patent medicines, and let inference do the rest. Inference has no place in this story. There are facts a-plenty. But it is essential to point out the intimate financial relation between the newspapers and the patent medicines. I was told by the man who for many years handled the advertising of the Lydia E. Pinkham Company that their expenditure was $100,000 a month, $1,200,000 a year. Dr. Pierce and the Peruna Company both advertise much more extensively than the Pinkham Company. Certainly there are at least five patent medicine concerns in the United States who each pay out to the newspaper more than one million dollars a year.... More than six years ago, Cheney, the president of the National Association of Patent Medicine Men, estimated the yearly amount paid to the newspapers by the larger patent medicine concerns at twenty million dollars—more than one thousand dollars to each daily, weekly, and monthly periodical in the United States.

Does this throw any light on the silence of the Massachusetts papers? Silence is too important a part of the patent medicine man's business to be left to the capricious chance of favor. Silence is the most important thing in his business. The ingredients of his medicine—that is nothing. Does the price of golden-seal go up? Substitute whiskey. Does the price of whiskey go up? Buy the refuse wines of the California vineyards. Does the price of opium go too high, or public fear of it make it an inexpedient thing to use? Take it out of the formula and substitute any worthless barnyard weed. But silence is the fixed quantity—silence as to the frauds he practices; silence as to the abominable stewings and brewings that enter into his nostrum; silence as to the deaths and sicknesses he causes; silence as to the drug fiends he makes, the inebriate asylums he fills. Silence he must have. So he makes silence a part of the contract.

Read the significant silence of the Massachu-

setts newspapers in the light of the following contracts for advertising. They are the regular printed form used by Hood, Ayer, and Munyon in making their advertising contracts with thousands of newspapers throughout the United States.

On the next page is shown the contract made by the J. C. Ayer Company, makers of Ayer's Sarsaparilla. At the top is the name of the firm, "The J. C. Ayer Company, Lowell, Mass.," and the date. Then follows a blank for the number of dollars, and then the formal contract: "We hereby agree, for the sum of ... Dollars per year, ... to insert in the ..., published at ..., the advertisement of the J. C. Ayer Company." Then follow the conditions as to space to be used each issue, the page the advertisement is to be on, and the position it is to occupy. Then these two remarkable conditions of the contract: "First—It is agreed in case any law or laws are enacted, either State or national, harmful to the interests of the J. C. Ayer Company, that this contract may be canceled by them from date of such enactment, and the insertions made paid for pro-rate with the contract price."

This clause is remarkable enough. But of it more later. For the present, examine the second clause: "Second—It is agreed that the J. C. Ayer Company may cancel this contract, pro-rate, in case advertisements are published in this paper in which their products are offered, with a view to substitution or other harmful motive, also in case any matter otherwise detrimental to the J. C. Ayer Company's interests is permitted to appear in the reading columns or elsewhere in the paper."

This agreement is signed in duplicate, one copy by the J. C. Ayer Company and the other one by the newspaper.

That is the contract of silence.... That is the clause which, with forty million dollars, muzzles the press of the country. I wonder if the Standard Oil Company could, for forty million dollars, bind the newspapers of the United States in a contract that "no matter detrimental to the Standard Oil

Company's interests be permitted to appear in the reading columns or elsewhere in this paper."...

I should like to ask the newspaper owners and editors of America what they think of that scheme. I believe that the newspapers, when they signed each individual contract, were not aware that they were being dragooned into an elaborately thought-out scheme to make every newspaper in the United States, from the greatest metropolitan daily to the remotest country weekly, an active, energetic, self-interested lobbyist for the patent medicine association. If the newspapers knew how they were being used as cat's-paws, I believe they would resent it. Certainly the patent medicine association itself feared this, and has kept this plan of Mr. Cheney's a careful secret. . . .

To illustrate, let me describe as typical the history of the public health bills which were introduced and defeated in Massachusetts last year. I have already mentioned them as showing how the newspapers, obeying that part of their contract which requires them to print nothing harmful to patent medicines, refused to print any account of the exposures which were made by several members of the Legislature during the debate of the bill. I wish here to describe their obedience to that other clause of the contract, in living up to which they printed scores of bitterly partisan editorials against the public health bill, and against its authors personally: threatened with political death those members of the Legislature who were disposed to vote in favor of it, and even, in the persons of editors and owners, went up to the State House and lobbied personally against the bill. And since I have already told of Mr. Cheney's authorship of the scheme, I will here reproduce, as typical of all the others (all the other large patent medicine concerns sent similar letters and telegrams), the letter which Mr. Cheney himself on the 14th day of February sent to all the newspapers in Massachusetts with which he has his lobbying contracts—practically every newspaper in the State:

"TOLEDO; OHIO, *Feb.* 14, 1905

"Publishers

—————————, Mass.

"GENTLEMEN:

"Should House bills Nos. 829, 30, 607, 724, or Senate bill No. 185 become laws, it will force us to discontinue advertising in your State. Your prompt attention regarding this bill we believe would be of mutual benefit.

"We would respectfully refer you to the contract which we have with you. Respectfully,

"CHENEY MEDICINE COMPANY" . . .

Now this seems to me a shameful thing—that a Massachusetts newspaper, of apparent dignity and outward high standing, should jump to the cracking of the whip of a nostrum-maker in Ohio; that honest and well-meaning members of the Massachusetts Legislature, whom all the money of Rockefeller could not buy, who obey only the one thing which they look upon as the expression of the public opinion of their constituents, the united voice of the press of their district—that these men should unknowingly cast their votes at the dictate of a nostrum-maker in Ohio, who, if he should deliver his command personally and directly, instead of through a newspaper supine enough to let him control it for a hundred dollars a year, would be scorned and flouted.

Any self-respecting newspaper must be humiliated by the attitude of the patent medicine association. They don't *ask* the newspapers to do it—they *order* it done. . . .

The same thing that happened in Massachusetts happened last year in New Hampsire, in Wisconsin, in Utah, in more than fifteen States. . . . In one Western State, a Board of Health officer made a number of analyses of patent medicines, and tried to have the analyses made public, that the people of his State might be warned. "Only one newspaper in the State," he says in a personal letter, "was willing to print results of these analyses, and this paper refused them after two publications in which a list of about ten was published. This paper was 'The———,' the editorial manager of which is in sympathy with the effort to restrict the sale of harmful nostrums. The business management interfered for the reason that five thousand dollars in patent medicine advertising was withdrawn within a week." . . .

"What is to be done about it?" is the question that follows exposure of organized rascality. In few cases is the remedy so plain as here. For the past, the newspapers, in spite of these plain contracts of silence, must be acquitted of any very grave complicity. The very existence of the machine that uses and directs them has been a carefully guarded secret. For the future, be it understood that any newspaper which carries a patent medicine advertisement knows what it is doing. The obligations of the contract are now public property. And one thing more, when next a member of a State Legislature arises and states, as I have so often heard: "Gentlemen, this label bill seems right to me, but I can not support it; the united press of my district is opposed to it"— when that happens, let every one understand the wires that have moved "the united press of my district."

• • •

In the same issue that *Collier's* ran the Sullivan article, it also announced it would no longer take patent-medicine advertisements. Reader response to both *Collier's* and *Ladies' Home Journal* was high. State medical societies passed resolutions, and some states, including South Carolina, moved to ban Peruna, one of the most popular medicines. In December 1905, a pure food and drug bill was reintroduced into the U.S. Senate. Conservative lawmakers stripped the bill of its ban on false advertising, and then tried to stall it in the House. Despite continuing articles by Sullivan, Bok, and Adams, the stall might have worked, except for the publication the next spring of Upton Sinclair's *The Jungle,* an exposé of Chicago packinghouse work. The resulting uproar and follow-up articles caused Congress to cave, and the Pure Food and Drug Law was passed in 1906.

COLUMNIST HEYWOOD BROUN DEMANDS FORMATION OF A NEWSPAPER UNION

Journalists have long had an image of being free-wheeling and independent, proud of their status, and no more inclined to collective action than cats are. Still, journalists were not immune to the economic unrest of the late 1920s and 1930s. Pay was low (in 1934, the government said, about half of reporters in the country made less than $36 a week), and owners were cutting that. Newspaper mergers threw people out of work and reduced the options for others. Furthermore, the ferment in other industries could not help but rub off in the newsroom, especially when reporters could look through the doors to the highly unionized back shops, where printers and pressmen often made more than they did and had some protection against management arbitrariness.

Some newswriters had tried to form unions as early as 1891, wrote the labor historian Irving Bernstein, but most of them quickly faded. Only four editorial unions were in existence in 1933, when the National Recovery Act, including its Section 7(a) guaranteeing workers the right to form a union, was passed. Publishers and editors quickly protested that reporters were professionals and that joining a union would undermine freedom of the press.

Into this situation came Heywood Broun, whom Bernstein called "the oddest union leader in American labor history." After a career as a sportswriter and drama critic, Broun became a columnist for the New York *World,* then the New York *Telegram,* then the combined New York *World-Telegram.* He was talented, popular, nationally syndicated, exceedingly well paid, and a big spender. He was also a man of enthusiasms, be it for friends, drink, poker, or, beginning in the late 1920s, socialism, the plight of the unemployed, and what he saw as the poor treatment of reporters by newspaper publishers.

"It Seems to Me," by Heywood Broun. New York *World-Telegram,* August 7, 1933.

"You may have heard," writes Reporter Unemployed, "that, although the newspapers are carrying the bulk of NRA publicity, a number of the publishers themselves are planning to cheat NRA re-employment aims.

"The newspaper publishers are toying with the idea of classifying their editorial staffs as 'professional men.' Since NRA regulations do not cover professionals, newspaper men, therefore, would continue in many instances to work all hours of the day and any number of hours of the week.

"The average newspaper man probably works on an eight-hour-a-day and six-day-week basis. Obviously the publishers, by patting their fathead employees on the head and calling them 'professionals,' hope to maintain this working week scale. And they'll succeed, for the men who make up the editorial staffs of the country are peculiarly susceptible to such soothing classifications as 'professionals,' 'journalists,' 'members of the fourth estate,' 'gentlemen of the press' and other terms which have completely entranced them by falsely dignifying and glorifying them and their work.

WHITE-COLLAR HACKS

"The men who make up the papers of this country would never look upon themselves as what they really are—hacks and white-collar slaves. Any attempt to unionize leg, rewrite, desk or makeup men would be laughed to death by these editorial hacks themselves. Union? Why, that's all right for dopes like printers, not for smart guys like newspaper men!

"Yes, and those 'dopes,' the printers, because of their union, are getting on an average some 30 per cent better than the smart fourth estaters. And not only that, but the printers, because of their union and because they don't permit themselves to be called high-faluting names, will now benefit by the new NRA regulations and have a large number of their unemployed re-employed, while the 'smart' editorial department boys will continue to work forty-eight hours a week because they love to hear themselves referred to as 'professionals' and because they consider unionization as lowering their dignity."

KEEPING HYPOCRISY OUT

I think Mr. Unemployed's point is well taken. I am not familiar with just what code newspapers publishers have adopted or may be about to adopt. But it will certainly be extremely damaging to the whole NRA movement if the hoopla and the ballyhoo (both very necessary functions) are to be carried on by agencies which have not lived up to the fullest spirit of the Recovery Act. Any such condition would poison the movement at its very roots.

I am not saying this from the point of view of self-interest. No matter how short they make the working day, it will still be a good deal longer than the time required to complete this stint. And as far as the minimum wage goes, I have been assured by everybody I know that in their opinion all columnists are grossly overpaid. They have almost persuaded me.

After some four or five years of holding down the easiest job in the world I hate to see other newspaper men working too hard. It makes me feel self-conscious. It embarrasses me even more to think of newspaper men who are not working at all. Among this number are some of the best.

I am not disposed to talk myself right out of a job, but if my boss does not know that he could get any one of forty or fifty men to pound out paragraphs as zippy and stimulating as these, then he is far less sagacious than I have occasionally assumed.

Fortunately columnists do not get fired very frequently. It has something to do with a certain inertia in most executives. They fall readily into the convenient conception that columnists are something like the weather. There they are, and nobody can do anything much about it. Of course, the editor keeps hoping that some day it will be fair and warmer, with brisk northerly gales. It never is, but the editor remains indulgent. And nothing happens to the columnist. At least, not up till now.

BOSSES I HAVE MET

It is a little difficult for me, in spite of my radical leanings and training and yearnings, to accept wholeheartedly the conception of the boss and his wage slaves. All my very many bosses have been editors, and not a single Legree in the lot. Concerning every one of them it was possible to say, "Oh, well, after all, he used to be a newspaper man once himself."

But the fact that newspaper editors and owners are genial folk should hardly stand in the way of the organization of a newspaper writers' union. There should be one. Beginning at 9 o'clock on the morning of October 1 I am going to do the best I can to help in getting one up. I think I could die happy on the opening day of the general strike if I had the privilege of watching Walter Lippmann heave half a brick through a *Tribune* window at a non-union operative who had been called in to write the current "Today and Tomorrow" column on the gold standard.

• • •

Broun's column encouraged reporters in other cities, such as Cleveland, who were already moving to form a union, and he received scores of letters of woe from reporters around the country. Broun was as good as his words. He lent his penthouse for a meeting that led to the formation of the Guild of Newspapermen and Women of New York in October 1933. The word "guild" was Broun's suggestion as being more palatable than "union" to the professional-minded reporters and copy editors. The New York group then spearheaded a national convention, which led to the founding of the American Newspaper Guild in December 1933. Broun was the first president.

In those economically tumultuous times, Broun proved to be an aggressive organizer and bargainer. Union contracts brought journalists higher wages, overtime pay, and improved benefits. In 1937, the guild reached beyond editorial workers to include the business side of newspapers. Broun remained both a columnist and guild president until his death in December 1939.

Like other labor unions, the guild has seen its fortunes decline in recent decades. The closing of big-city newspapers, especially in industrial cities of the Northeast, was particularly hurtful. In 1997, seeking additional clout, the guild merged with the Communications Workers of America. Guild membership at the start of 2001 stood at 34,000.

CHICAGO DAILY NEWS IDENTIFIES EDITORS ON STATE PAYROLL

Journalists often hold public officials and others to task for conflict of interest, but rarely do they turn a critical eye on their own profession. An exception came in 1949, when the *Chicago Daily News* and the *St. Louis Post-Dispatch* stumbled on a small, but telling, cog in the public support for Illlinois Governor Dwight H. Green, despite his scandal-ridden government. In an unusual arrangement, the two papers published the story jointly.

By George Thiem. *Chicago Daily News,*
April 14, 1949.

SPRINGFIELD, ILL.—Thirty-three editors and
publishers of downstate Illinois newspapers were
carried on the state payrolls by former Gov.
Dwight H. Green for a total of more than
$305,000, a *Daily News* search revealed Thursday.

Relatives of the editors, columnists and employees collected an additional $108,183 since
1942 while the Green gravy train was running,
records in the state auditor's office disclosed.

The actual amount paid out to journalists since
1941 to keep the Green machine oiled was considerably higher than the above figures.

The auditor's records do not include payments
made prior to 1943.

Nearly all the payrollers are connected with
weekly and semi-weekly newspapers. But at least
two labor magazines and several dailies had publishers, staff members or relatives drawing state
money.

State officials and department employees said
most of the payrollers reported little or no service
for their money except to print editorials and
news stories from the Green publicity mill.

Several, however, held responsible jobs in the
late administration and gave the major part of
their time to state work.

With few exceptions, the newspapermen went
off the payroll shortly after Green was defeated
for re-election. A few stayed on until removed by
Gov. Stevenson, who took office in January.

In his Chicago law office, Green said:

"I could not make any intelligent comment on
the story until I had contacted the heads of every
department listed to find out the facts."

Topping the list in the amount of money collected was former State Senator William R.
McCauley of Olney, co-owner and publisher of
the *Daily Mail* of that city, who drew a total of
$41,281.

McCauley went on the payroll at $4,560 a year
Feb. 1, 1941 and continued drawing an annual

salary that reached $6,072 in 1948, until he was
removed on Jan. 15, 1949.

A spokesman in the auditor's office said
McCauley also had a state car at his disposal.
McCauley's payroll card listed him as a "special
investigator" and "Statistical Clerk."

McCauley, 68, a former state commander of
the American Legion, ran second in the primaries
against Arthur C. Lueder for state auditor in 1940.

Arnold Benson, editor and publisher of the Ba-
tavia *Herald,* served as state director of agriculture
until recently, drawing a total of $22,372.22, the
auditor's record disclosed.

Harold J. Cruger, publisher of the Elmhurst
Leader and other DuPage County newspapers, and
Herschel J. Blazer, editor and publisher of the
Aledo *Times Record,* shared the post of superinten-
dent of printing in the finance department.

Among the editors and publishers listed as oil
investors in the revenue department was J. Norris
Vallow, editor of the Kinmundy *Express* in Marion County, whose pay totaled $14,378.30....

Gomer Bath, columnist on the Peoria *Star,* collected $5,811.10. He was removed from the Labor
Department payroll Nov. 30, 1948, after Green's
defeat. William F. Bridges, Vienna, brother of
Boyce Bridges, editor of the Vienna *Times,* drew
$5,508 as a state policeman.

Bridges worked in a newspaper office at Marion while holding down the state job. Another
brother, James, is a deed inspector in the Agriculture Department who drew $5,909 since Feb.
1, 1946.

Marvel Magill, sister of William D. Magill, Clinton, Ill., publisher, drew $12,675 working as a
clerk in the state auditor's office before being removed from the payroll in December.

•   •   •

In a follow-up story in May, Thiem put the count
of kept journalists at fifty-one, paid a total of
$480,000. One editor listed as a highway messen-
ger clerk later said he wrote speeches for the gov-

ernor. Another whose job was listed as checking on various state licenses said that instead he did mostly publicity work.

Green insisted that he saw nothing wrong with the practice. Perhaps not from a politician's point of view. But the country's newspaper editors rose up to condemn the practice, and to check their own state's records. The *Daily News* and the *St. Louis Post-Dispatch* won the Pulitzer Prize for public service in 1950, a step toward establishing the principle, still somewhat shakily applied, that reporters should have no financial or other arrangements with institutions they write about.

JACK GOULD FORCES THE *NEW YORK TIMES* TO STOP ITS REPORTERS AND EDITORS FROM ACCEPTING CHRISTMAS GIFTS AND JUNKETS

The *New York Times* has had since time immemorial a policy against its reporters and editors accepting gifts from people and institutions that they cover. Yet, for years, this policy was largely ignored, especially at Christmas, when public relations men and others would freely dole out gifts to reporters and editors.

The boodle would pile high at Christmas in the *Times*'s newsroom, not counting the cash and booze and fruitcakes that reporters and editors often received directly. In *The Paper's Papers: A Reporter's Journey Through the Archives of The New York Times*, by Richard Shephard, a longtime *Times* reporter and columnist, describes the Christmas scene at the paper:

"... [B]efore Christmas, the gifts—'the loot,' one reporter called it—piled up in the third-floor reception room. The job of carrying it back to our cubicle often fell to me, the youngest in the department. I usually felt like an uncomfortable ink-stained Santa Claus bearing a pile of tinsel-bound packages through the newsroom, passing by general staff reporters whose virtue was intact, perhaps by conscience, but certainly for the lack of regular corporate contacts who routinely sent gifts to everyone they did business with."

"'How do you keep honest, taking all that?' a reporter snapped at me while I was en route.

"'Easy, we throw the cards away without looking at them,' I replied.

"A flip retort, and not an entirely honest one."

In his portrait of the *Times, The Kingdom and the Power*, Gay Talese, who had been a *Times* reporter, said: "*The Times* reception room during Christmas week was stacked with newly arrived bright packages—cases of liquor, baskets of fruit, silver serving sets, movie cameras, and other tokens of affection from New York promoters and merchants."

In 1953, when a scandal arose in Washington over gift-taking by presidential assistant Sherman Adams, *Times* publisher Arthur Hays Sulzberger sent a memorandum to the paper's Women's News editor inquiring whether "any gifts are received by people who work on *The New York Times* from people who do business with the *Times*."

The editor replied that the *Times* was clean on this matter, except at Christmas, when, the editor said, "Of course at Christmas time various gifts do arrive, but most of them are of a trifling nature, and this practice has been so firmly established for long that I would not know how to eradicate it."

The practices continued.

Then, six years later, at the height of the nationwide scandal over quiz-show cheating, the paper's television columnist, Jack Gould, one of the premier writers on television as that medium emerged, decided he had had enough of the high-toned moralizing by the print media at the print media's brothers and sisters in broadcasting. On October 27, 1959, Gould wrote this column condemning gift-taking and junketeering by reporters and editors in print journalism, including the *New York Times*:

"TV: Journalists' Junkets," by Jack Gould. *New York Times,* October 27, 1959.

The television industry, for the moment somewhat bruised by the scandal over quiz shows, is nursing a small resentment against the press. Not because of the headlines that inevitably are part of the exposure of the fixed quizzes. But rather because they feel substantial elements of the Fourth Estate are not entirely qualified to don the mantle of unsullied virtue.

What many responsible individuals in TV have in mind is a practice that is prevalent in many areas of American business, not just video, but could not exist without the tacit consent and knowledge of the world of journalism. In the parlance of the newspaper trade, the practice is known as "the junket."

The junket is an arrangement whereby a business concern pays all the expenses of a newspaper man to cover an event of direct financial interest to the company. The word "expenses" is totally inclusive; de luxe transportation between the newspaper man's home office and perhaps some location thousands of miles away, the finest accommodations at the most costly hotels, the best of meals and liquors, a continuous round of parties, laundry, taxis, etc.

Tradition demands that discussion of the junket always be done in low voice. Companies that pick up substantial tabs for newspaper men cry they must give for a favorable press and a pleasant public climate. Similarly, as the economic beneficiary of the junketing era, the gentlemen of the Fourth Estate are prone to shyness in the matter.

The quiz scandal, which apparently is going to lead to fuller disclosure of many things besides prefabricated intellectualism, inevitably has affected the status of the junket.

Veteran video hands, who for weeks now have been hearing that they are the twentieth century's original sinners, are not quarreling with the duty of the Fourth Estate to champion motherhood.

They merely contend that what goes on backstage in the newspaper business is not without pertinency, in a consideration of contemporary ethics.

Lest they be drawn and quartered by writers who are inclined to insist on having the last word, people who know about junketing, which included everybody in TV, prefer that no questions be tape recorded.

But, measured by any standard, junketing is a very prevalent practice in TV. Directly involved are the scores of newspapers, trade papers, magazines and press associations that authorize employees to participate. The financing of the junkets is done not only by networks but also by sponsors, advertising agencies, individual stations, airplane lines and hotels.

One TV organization, for instance, sends upward of sixty newspaper men, which means critics, columnists, reporters and editors, to Hollywood every year. The expense-free stay is usually four or five days but this can be extended by the newspaper man if he wants to persuade a second firm to subsidize a second week. The newspaper man, incidentally, can go at his own convenience.

Another approach, which goes back to the motion picture industry's lusher days, is to import whole planeloads of newspaper men—eighty to 100 is not unusual—for several days of meeting celebrities and listening to executives reiterate the company line. The mass method not only assures saturation of the press; it also denies newspaper space to the competitors of the sponsor of a junket.

Since journalists have the usual trouble with spouses who feel they never get out of town, some junkets are designed to preserve domestic harmony. Wives and husbands—sometimes even the children, too—often may arrange a change of scene on the cuff....

In junketing, as in everything else, there are scattered exceptions to the normal practice, but TV's masters of gamesmanship are not so simply thwarted. There is, after all, the companion tradition of "the Christmas loot," the practice of showering holiday presents upon the high and low in journalism. . . .

The loot of Christmas in TV runs to substantial sums; one typical organization shells out about $25 worth of merchandise for each of 150 newspaper men. Yesterday, it was learned, an influential concern in the industry plans this season to abandon the practice.

Moreover, throughout the year, a smaller stream of gifts filters into newspaper offices; some are of fairly substantial value.

All in all, the TV folk agree their own mode of living has left much to be desired. But they just wonder whether perhaps others have not yet got around to their own fall housecleaning.

• • •

Gould's story had been submitted in advance to Orville Dryfoos, an editor at the paper, who had approved it but said Gould was opening a can of worms. On October 29, Arthur Hays Sulzberger, the paper's publisher, sent a note to Gould saying "I don't think you were fair to us." A ban "against accepting Christmas gifts," Sulzberger said, "would be impossible to enforce, because, as you pointed out, they would just be sent to the home. I get some gifts myself. The man who buys our waste paper, for instance, sends me four or six initialed handkerchiefs every Christmas. As you know, that doesn't influence our contract for the sale of waste paper and to refuse the gift would, it seems to me, be more awkward than to accept it."

In reply, Gould said that, in terms of the *Times*, "we are actually talking about thousands and thousands of dollars." Gould, according to Shephard, cited "several recent instances of misbehaving employees" and said that he had been told by "the business world that for a *Times* man you simply set up a junket to coincide with his vacation."

Almost immediately, a notice was posted in the *Times* newsroom prohibiting *Times* employees from accepting gifts or going on junkets, although this did little, Talese reported, "to enhance Gould's popularity within the office."

The *Times* has strongly enforced this policy ever since.

NEW YORK TIMES REPORTER A. H. RASKIN GETS TIMES LABOR RELATIONS NEGOTIATOR TO RESIGN

The press detests writing about itself. A. H. Raskin and his editors at the *New York Times* broke this rule in 1963, when Raskin reported and the *Times* published, running over eighteen columns, an account of the marathon newspaper strike that had silenced the city's papers for 114 days between December 1962 and March 1963.

The strike shuttered the *Times*, the *Daily News*, the *World-Telegram,* the *Journal-American*, and the *Sun*. Five other papers also closed, three in New York and two on Long Island, that had not been struck, but that had owners who reduced or suspended publication as a matter of solidarity with their fellow publishers.

Each side, publishers and unions, faced major difficulties. The papers were confronted by rising costs, television, decreasing advertising, and rising demands by the unions for wages and benefits. The unions and workers faced rising living costs and, especially, new automated publishing technologies, including automated typesetting machines that would eliminate jobs and destroy craft distinctions, some of which went back to before the Civil War.

Two men were keys in the negotiations, Bertram A. Powers, head of the New York printers union, and Amory H. Bradford, the *Times*'s general manager. Powers was an unschooled Irish-American, implacable, imperious, a skilled bargainer. Bradford was arrogant, patrician, and condescending. In his history of the *Times*, *The*

Kingdom and the Power, Gay Talese said, "When Bradford mingled with unionists, it was like the rigid proctor of a proper boys' school mingling with slum children. Bradford's smile was reminiscent of the way the Duke of Edinburgh used to smile at native chieftains while touring the African colonies: a downward-tilting, royal-eyed bonny look into the distance." Turner Catledge, the *Times*'s longtime managing editor, would write that Bradford was aloof and impatient and that he had a "don't bother me" attitude "toward subordinates, or those he took to be subordinates."

Some time after the strike began, Theodore Bernstein, a top editor at the *Times,* decided that once the strike ended, the *Times* should do a long, comprehensive piece on the strike—tell what had happened behind the scenes, what the real issues were, why it had lasted so long. To report the piece, Bernstein and other editors selected Raskin, the paper's longtime labor reporter.

Raskin, fifty, had joined the *Times* in 1931 just out of City College of New York and was a member of the American Newspaper Guild. He had immense energy, had many sources, and worked the phones well, always willing to make one more call. Still, as informed and indefatigable as he was, he faced a most difficult assignment. He had to report not only on the unions—his employers were not bothered about that, although they normally prefer not to rile such men—but on his employers and other publishers. Reporting on such people, at least in an honest manner, is rarely attempted. As Talese wrote, the assignment seemed unprecedented (Bernstein, the paper's language guardian, had banned the word *unprecedented* from the *Times,* contending that nothing in life is unprecedented). Raskin told his superiors that from what he knew, an honest piece on the strike would make a number of executives, among them Bradford, unhappy. He was told to proceed anyway. Employers, Bradford among them, did not return his telephone calls.

When the piece was finished, it was approved by Bernstein and Catledge and given to Orville Dryfoos, the paper's publisher. Dryfoos, Talese said, took the piece with him and read it alone near the reservoir in Central Park. Dryfoos returned to the newsroom, Talese said, and, although he whistled and raised his eyebrows, told Catledge to run it. Bradford also read the piece, said it was old news and inaccurate, and, seething, asked that it be spiked. Dryfoos said no.

The piece appeared April 1, a day after the strike had ended, and the first day the *Times* resumed publishing.

Here are excerpts from Raskin's piece, "A Strike: A Step-by-Step Account."

"This is a history of failure—the failure of men and machines, of politics and personalities, of miscalculated maneuvers and misjudged aspirations." That epitaph for the city's longest and costliest newspaper strike comes from a ranking official of the Publishers Association of New York City. A top unionist makes a virtually identical evaluation, then adds almost prayerfully: "This should be the strike to end all newspaper strikes. . . ."

Mr. [Bertram] Powers headed the union committee. His opposite number on the 'publishers' side was Amory H. Bradford, vice president and general manager of *The New York Times.* The two men had developed a regard for each other's intelligence and capacity while serving as co-trustees of the printers' pension and welfare funds several years before. Their mutual admiration did not last long.

The 41-year-old union president is tall, dapper, with whitish-blond hair, an earnest manner and no talent for small talk. A printer at 17 (his formal education ended after two years in high school), he served as vice president of Big Six for eight years before being elected its president by a vote of 5,080 to 3,511 in May, 1961. A year or so earlier he had contemplated quitting the local to become a Federal mediator because he saw little chance of climbing any higher on the union ladder.

One of the army of Government peacemakers who got to know him well in the endless hours of round-the-clock negotiations after Dec. 8 describes Mr. Powers as "honest, clean, democratic—and impossible."

Another Government official calls him "cold, ambitious and utterly incapable of setting any realistic priorities for himself," then observes that he was "so superior to anyone he had to negotiate against that it was like matching Sonny Liston with a Golden Glove champion. . . ."

His critics in other unions denounce him as a "rule-or-ruin" type bent on modeling himself into a counterpart of the John L. Lewis of the nineteen-thirties. They say his goal is to become head of a national fusion of all printing unions. To his defenders such ambitions do not seem excessive, though they deny they are what makes him run. . . .

Mr. Bradford, two inches taller than the union chief and nine years older, is handsome, articulate and aloof. Descendant of a distinguished New England family, he worked his way through school at Phillips Academy at Andover, Mass., Yale and Yale Law School. In the Army in World War II, he rose from private to captain. Later he served in the State Department and practiced corporation law before joining the *Times* in 1947.

One top-level mediator said Mr. Bradford brought an attitude of such icy disdain into the conference rooms that the mediator often felt he ought to ask the hotel to send up more heat. Another mediator, who called Mr. Bradford the possessor of the keenest mind on the management side, said he operates on a "short fuse."

Long in advance of the 1962 negotiations the executive committee of the Publishers Association nominated Mr. Bradford to serve as chairman of the scale committee that would bargain with Big Six in behalf of all the papers. The choice was unanimously approved by the newspaper owners. They admire his independence and assurance, although they are occasionally galled by his imperiousness. His designation to direct talks with the printers represented a mark of special trust since it was recognized that these were the year's most ticklish negotiations and that their outcome might involve life or death for some papers. . . .

Here are some . . . factors cited by mediators to explain why the strike proved so intractable:

- The submission of "pie in the sky" demands by the union developed exaggerated expectations among the strikers and helped engender the disappointment reflected in the initial rejection of the Wagner formula.

- The publishers inadvertently added to this rank-and-file disappointment by over-advertising Mr. Powers's official asking price. Long after he had cut his off-the-record figure in half, the publishers kept pointing to his formal call for a $38 package. At one stage the union chief admonished Mr. Bradford: "You've got people so convinced I want $38 that if I get $34 my members will say, 'Where's the other $4?'"

- Reversals of bargaining position by the 'Big Six' leader (Powers) caused him to lose the trust of many he had to deal with in management and labor. He was accused of making commitments one day and reneging on them the next. His written statement of what he wanted after two weeks in City Hall called for a higher cash package than he had offered to settle for at Gracie Mansion 40 days earlier.

- Miscalculations by the publishers led them astray on whether the strike would begin at the deadline and on whether they could chip other unions away from Powers's banner. The I.T.U. never had authorized a walkout immediately on expiration of a contract and this gave rise to management confidence that Big Six would stay at work after the 2 A.M. countdown. When this proved wrong, hope shifted for many weeks to the possibility that other unions could be induced to cross the printers' picket lines.

High union strike benefits, reinforced by state unemployment insurance, diminished the printing craftsmen's incentive for settling. The printers had a strike income just over $120 a week. For photoengravers the rate was $137.50 a week until two weeks ago when the parent union cut off its $25 weekly contribution. This brought the engravers stipend to $112.50. Strike insurance was a less substantial prop for the publishers because it was limited as to both amount and duration.

• The reluctance of both sides to go along with any Government fact-finding prevented the emergence early in the blackout of recommendations that might have ended the stoppage. Secretary Wirtz and the Mayor were deterred from naming such panels by objections from both groups. Governor Rockefeller was the only one with a clear statutory warrant under the 22-year-old state law authorizing the appointment of boards with subpoena power, but similar objections were addressed to him. His proposed bill for a State Commission of Public Concern was shelved, under combined fire from labor and management.

• • •

Raskin's piece caused a sensation. Powers had won much of what he wanted for the printers, Raskin said, including a wage increase of $12.63 a week over two years, a thirty-five-hour week, common expiration dates on union contracts before the large Easter advertising season. Decisions on computer-based equipment were postponed and were not made for years. The publishers, and especially Bradford, Raskin said, had blundered im-

measurably. He quoted a key member of the Publishers Association as saying, "Everytime they were unanimous, they were wrong. Always their approach was 'Give 'em nothing—and do it retroactively.' "

The piece condemned Powers and Bradford, infuriating each of them. It had praise for Mayor Robert Wagner, who finally helped mediate the strike, but quoted Wagner as saying that management and labor had lacked competence and that "both sides deserve each other."

Bradford remained furious about what he regarded as an attack not only by his colleagues but by members of his class. But his time was up. On May 25, Dryfoos died, and at the service for him at Temple Emanu-El on Fifth Avenue, attended by some 2,000 mourners, Bradford was spotted several rows back, far from the top *Times* executives in front. Harrison Salisbury, a *Times* reporter and editor and a consummate *Times* watcher, having served in the Kremlin and at other posts, saw this, and, Talese said, "immediately foresaw" that Bradford would resign.

Shortly after, he did.

A. J. Liebling, the press critic, praised Raskin's piece in *The New Yorker,* calling it "possibly the most complete and unprejudiced story of a labor dispute ever published in an American newspaper." President John F. Kennedy, who had attempted, unsuccessfully, to have the federal government mediate the strike, read the piece and, Talese wrote, said if he had been Dryfoos, he probably would not have run it.

The strike was a disaster for newspapers in New York. The *Mirror* closed not long after the strike was ended, and, in the mid-1960s, the *Herald Tribune,* the *World-Telegram and Sun,* and the *Journal-American* would also close. This reduced New York to the three mainstream papers it has today, the *Times,* the *Daily News,* and the *Post,* down from sixteen papers in 1900 and twelve in 1930.

ESQUIRE MAGAZINE PUBLISHES A NEW KIND OF NONFICTION REPORTING AND CHANGES AMERICAN MAGAZINES AND BOOKS

In the early 1960s, a revolution began in American magazine writing. It was the result of a confluence of factors: the dullness and boredom of much magazine writing in the 1950s; the rise of interesting events; the emergence of new writing talents, a number of whom had been reporters on the New York *Herald Tribune*, which had long taken in and nourished outstanding writers and reporters; and the interests of pathbreaking editors like Harold Hayes and Byron Dobell at *Esquire*.

One who flourished under this new kind of vivid, more personal journalism was Tom Wolfe, a *Herald Tribune* reporter who broke out with his articles in *Esquire*, including this imaginative and pyrotechnic piece exploring something that almost all other publications had ignored: the world of stock-car racing.

"The Last American Hero Is Junior Johnson. Yes!" by Tom Wolfe. *Esquire*, March 1965.

Ten o'clock Sunday morning in the hills of North Carolina. Cars, miles of cars, in every direction, millions of cars, pastel cars, aqua green, aqua blue, aqua beige, aqua buff, aqua dawn, aqua dusk, aqua aqua, aqua Malacca, Malacca lacquer, Cloud lavender, Assassin pink, Rake-a-cheek raspberry, Nude Strand coral, Honest Thrill orange, and Baby Fawn Lust cream-colored cars are all going to the stock-car races, and that old mothering North Carolina sun keeps exploding off the windshields. Mother dog!

Seventeen thousand people, me included, all of us driving out Route 421, out to the stock-car races at the North Wilkesboro Speedway, 17,000 going out to a five-eighths-mile stock-car track with a Coca-Cola sign out front. This is not to say there is no preaching and shouting in the South this morning. There is preaching and shouting. Any of us can turn on the old automobile transistor radio and get all we want:

"They are greedy dogs. Yeah! They ride around in big cars. Unnh-hunh! And chase women. Yeah! And drink liquor. Unnh-hunh! And smoke cigars. Oh yes! And they are greedy dogs. Yeah! Unh-hunh! Oh yes! Amen!"

There are also some commercials on the radio for Aunt Jemima which cost ten cents a pound. There are also the Gospel Harmonettes, singing: "If you dig a ditch, you better dig two...."

There are also three fools in a panel discussion on the New South, which they seem to conceive of as General Lee running the new Dulcidreme Labial Cream factory down at Griffin, Georgia.

And suddenly my car is stopped still on Sunday morning in the middle of the biggest traffic jam in the history of the world. It goes for ten miles in every direction from the North Wilkesboro Speedway. And right there it dawns on me that as far as this situation is concerned, anyway, all the conventional notions about the South are confined to ... the Sunday radio. The South has preaching and shouting, the South has grits, the South has country songs, old mimosa traditions, clay dust, Old Bigots, New Liberals—and all of it, all of that old mental cholesterol, is confined to the Sunday radio. What I was in the middle of—well, it wasn't anything one hears about in panels about the South today. Miles and miles of eye-busting pastel car on the expressway, which roar right up into the hills, going to the stock-car races. In ten years baseball—and the state of North Carolina alone used to have forty-four professional baseball teams—baseball is all over with in the South. We were all in the middle of a wild new thing, the Southern car world, and heading down the road on my way to see a breed such as sports never saw before, Southern stock-car drivers, all lined up in these two-ton mothers that go over 175 m.p.h., Fireball Roberts, Freddie Lorenzen, Ned Jarrett, Richard Petty, and—the hardest of all the hard chargers, one of the fastest automobile racing drivers in history—yes! Junior Johnson.

The legend of Junior Johnson! In this legend, here is a country boy, Junior Johnson, who learns to drive by running whiskey for his father, Johnson, Senior, one of the biggest copper-still operators of all times, up in Ingle Hollow, near North Wilkesboro, in northwestern North Carolina, and grows up to be a famous stock-car racing driver, rich, grossing $100,000 in 1963, for example, respected, solid, idolized in his hometown and throughout the rural South, for that matter. There is all this about how good old boys would wake up in the middle of the night in the apple shacks and hear a supercharged Oldsmobile, engine roaring over Brushy Mountain and say, "Listen at him—there he goes!," although that part is doubtful, since some nights there were so many good old boys taking off down the road in supercharged automobiles out of Wilkes County, and running loads to Charlotte, Salisbury, Greensboro, Winston-Salem, High Point, or wherever, it would be pretty hard to pick out one. It was Junior Johnson specifically, however, who was famous for the "bootleg turn" or "about-face," in which, if the Alcohol Tax agents had a roadblock up for you or were too close behind, you threw the car up into second gear, cocked the wheel, stepped on the accelerator and made the car's rear end skid around in a complete 180-degree arc, a complete about-face, and tore on back up the road exactly the way you came from God! The Alcohol Tax agents used to burn over Junior Johnson. Practically every good old boy in town in Wilkesboro, the county seat, got to know the agents by sight in a very short time. They would rag them practically to their faces on the subject of Junior Johnson, so that it got to be an obsession. Finally, one night they had Junior trapped on the road up toward the bridge around Millers-

ville, there's no way out of there, they had the barricades up and they could hear this souped-up car roaring around the bend, and here it comes—but suddenly they can hear a siren and see a red light flashing in the grille, so they think it's another agent, and boy, they run out like ants and pull those barrels and boards and sawhorses out of the way, and then—Ggghzzzzzzzzhhhhhgggggzzzzzzeeeeeong!—gawdam! There he goes again, it was him, Junior Johnson!, with a gawdam agent's si-reen and a red light in his grille.

I wasn't in the South five minutes before people started making oaths, having visions, telling these hulking great stories, and so forth, all on the subject of Junior Johnson. At the Greensboro, North Carolina, Airport there was one good old boy who vowed he would have eaten "a bucket of it" if that would have kept Junior Johnson from switching from a Dodge racer to a Ford. Hell yes, and after that—God-almighty, remember that 1963 Chevrolet of Junior's? Whatever happened to that car? A couple of more good old boys join in. A good old boy, I ought to explain, is a generic term in the rural South referring to a man, of any age, but more often young than not, who fits in with the status system of the region. It usually means he has a good sense of humor and enjoys ironic jokes, is tolerant and easygoing enough to get along in long conversations at places like on the corner, and has a reasonable amount of physical courage. The term is usually heard in some such form as "Lud? He's a good old boy from over at Crozet." These good old boys in the airport, by the way, were in their twenties, except for one fellow who was a cabdriver and was about forty-five, I would say. Except for the cabdriver, they all wore neo-Brummellian wardrobing such as Lacoste tennis shirts, Slim Jim pants, windbreakers with the collars turned up, "fast" shoes of the winkle-picker genre, and so on. I mention these details just by way of pointing out that very few grits, Iron Boy overalls, clodhoppers or hats with ventilation holes up near the crown enter into this story. Anyway, these good old boys are talking about Junior Johnson and how he has switched to Ford.

This they unanimously regard as some kind of betrayal on Johnson's part. Ford, it seems, they regard as the car symbolizing the established power structure. Dodge is kind of a middle ground. Dodge is at least a challenger, not a ruler. But the Junior Johnson they like to remember is the Junior Johnson of 1963, who took on the whole field of NASCAR (National Association for Stock Car Auto Racing) Grand National racing with a Chevrolet. All the other drivers, the drivers driving Fords, Mercurys, Plymouths, Dodges had millions, literally millions when it is all added up, millions of dollars in backing from the Ford and Chrysler Corporations. Junior Johnson took them all on in a Chevrolet without one cent of backing from Detroit. Chevrolet had pulled out of stock-car racing. Yet every race it was the same. It was never a question of whether anybody was going to *outrun* Junior Johnson. It was just a question of whether he was going to win or his car was going to break down, since, for one thing half the time he had to make his own racing parts. God! Junior Johnson was like Robin Hood or Jesse James or Little David or something. Every time that Chevrolet, No. 3, appeared on the track, these wild curdled yells, "Rebel" yells, they still have those, would rise up. At Daytona, at Atlanta, at Charlotte, at Darlington, South Carolina; Bristol, Tennessee; Martinsville, Virginia—Junior Johnson!

And then the good old boys get to talking about whatever happened to that Chevrolet of Junior's, and the cabdriver says he knows. He says Junior Johnson is using that car to run liquor out of Wilkes County. What does he mean? For Junior Johnson ever to go near another load of bootleg whiskey again—he would have to be insane. He has this huge racing income. He has two other

businesses, a whole automated chicken farm with 42,000 chickens, a road-grading business—but the cabdriver says he has this dream Junior is still roaring down from Wilkes County, down through the clay cuts, with the Atlas Arc Lip jars full in the back of that Chevrolet. It is in Junior's blood—and then at this point he puts his right hand up in front of him as if he is groping through fog, and his eyeballs glaze over and he looks out in the distance and he describes Junior Johnson roaring over the ridges of Wilkes County as if it is the ghost of Zapata he is describing, bounding over the Sierras on a white horse to rouse the peasants.

• • •

Wolfe's piece was electrifying and was read in newsrooms throughout the country. What was perhaps ignored, given Wolfe's style, is that he was a terrific reporter and used all his senses in reporting. Other reporters, many of them Wolfe's same age, also were doing this more personal and detailed kind of journalism. *Esquire* published Gay Talese, John Sack, Anthony Lukas, Rex Reed, and Michael Herr. *Harper's,* under Willie Morris, an émigré from Mississippi by way of the University of Texas and the maverick *Texas Observer,* published David Halberstam, John Corry, Marshal Frady, Oscar Lewis, Michael Harrington, and Nick Kotz.

As had happened earlier in the muckraking movement, other magazines saw the success of the new style of nonfiction writing and joined in. Many of these same writers turned to writing books, and turned upside down the notion of what good nonfiction book writing meant. Nonfiction books became better and more popular; advances increased; and it was now possible for a topflight journalist to make a decent living by full-time writing of nonfiction books.

THREE REPORTERS WHO LIED—
AND GOT CAUGHT

If the press is the watchdog of business, government, and the rest of society, who is the watchdog of the press? "When it comes to looking at itself, the watchdog is a lamb, timid and tame," argued Sydney Schanberg, a former reporter and columnist for the *New York Times* and *New York Newsday*. He continued, "The paper that uncovers abuses on some other publication knows it will have to quickly gird for an assault on its own dirty linen."

But sometimes a publication does take a critical look at the competition. And sometimes a publication takes a critical look at a colleague. Here are three cases.

In the spring of 1967, the city magazine *Philadelphia* investigated Harry Karafin, a top reporter for the *Philadelphia Inquirer*, on the grounds that he was bartering coverage, or lack of coverage, in the *Inquirer* for public relations contracts and cash.

Karafin, the article said, was part of a bankruptcy fraud ring; took public-relations fees from shady home-repair companies; once slanted a story about a bank hearing to persuade a bank to sign a deal with his public-relations company; and was on the payroll of a maintenance company while he wrote stories about the company's dispute with the city government, among other incidents.

The conclusion of the story follows.

"The Reporter," by Gaeton Fonzi and Greg Walter. *Philadelphia* magazine, April 1967.

There is no doubt about it: Reporter Harry Karafin became, in a few short years, one of the most successful public relations men in Philadelphia—despite the fact that a good many people now claim they did business with him reluctantly. "I don't like to deal with Harry," says one of his clients, "but he can do things for me. It's like castor oil. You don't like to take it but sometimes you have to."

Enough people took Harry Karafin to make him a relatively affluent man. (Too many, in fact, to detail in a single article.) Long conditioned to frugal survival on a reporter's modest salary, Karafin found that the rewards of public relations work could enable him to live a new style of life.

He became more popular. People showered him with gifts. (He got, for instance, more watches than he could use. His very close friend, bail bondsman Albie Schwartz, gave him an expensive set of golf clubs which, though he doesn't play the game, he keeps out ostentatiously in a corner of his den. Magistrate Dave Keiser regularly sends him cases of Scotch. He boasted that he didn't have to pay a cent for his daughter's engagement party at Palumbo's, or even for his recent hernia operation.)

He took to acquiring expensive jewelry (mostly from a store owned by the brother-in-law of a real estate man who was in the bankruptcy ring) and buying his status-conscious wife—an aggressive woman with whom, friends say, Karafin is a milquetoast—flashy clothes and fancy furs. He began vacationing in Europe and Puerto Rico. He even began dabbling in the stock market.

He has, of course, sold his modest twin home in Oxford Circle—for $1000 less than he had paid for it a decade before—and put up $19,000 cash towards a huge two-story house on a large lot in the far Northeast.

A real estate expert estimates the value of the house conservatively at $45,000. Karafin had builder Solomon Bronstein construct the house for him for $30,000. (Bronstein was one of the witnesses called in the Special Grand Jury's probe of zoning abuses in 1963.) In addition, Karafin added a host of special features to the house, including a custom-built staircase, expensive lighting fixtures, air conditioning, and an enclosed rear patio and fireplace. Then he packed more than $20,000 worth of fancy new furniture in his newly-acquired castle and surrounded it with a nursery of expensive shrubbery and a $3000 fence.

In 1964, shortly after he purchased his new home, Karafin also bought, for cash, two new cars from Wilkie Buick on North Broad Street—though at the time he was the only one in his family who knew how to drive. On one car went the license tag HK 156; on the other, 156 HK. (Harry Karafin's new house was at 156 Stratford Road.) He kept both cars for two years, and last December, bought two new Buicks, one an expensive Riviera model, and paid cash for them also.

All this despite the fact that in the last few years Harry Karafin's salary at the *Inquirer* has averaged less than $11,000 annually. Before that, it was lower.

How did he do it? He did it by prostituting the power of the press. He pimped away his legitimate rights and privileges as a reporter and pocketed the returns. He used subtle threat and coercion on those who could least afford the kind of notoriety he might give them if he were an ethical reporter. He provided public relations and other types of "services" at inflated fees because he knew that only he could give them what no other public relations counsel could give them: Alleviation from fear of exposure in the press, from fear of sensational, slanted articles. (He couldn't do it alone, of course, but that's another story.)

And yet—and this is what was particularly infuriating to those in the business who had an inkling of his activities—Harry J. Karafin went around calling himself a reporter.

He was a mouthy guy.

• • •

Even before the article was published, Karafin sued the magazine, claiming that the article was based on information "illegally obtained" from his

tax returns. His *Inquirer* bosses suspended him, investigated, and then fired him. He was, the *Inquirer*'s statement said, an unusually good liar. Karafin was sentenced to prison.

Howard Kohn, a twenty-five-year-old reporter on the *Detroit Free Press,* had a most interesting month in the spring of 1973. At the end of April, he was awarded the Paul Tobenkin award by the Columbia University Graduate School of Journalism, a tribute to his articles the previous year that had freed a Detroit man who had served eighteen years on a murder charge. Days later, a front-page article by Kohn accused Detroit police officers working in the inner city of alternately protecting and shaking down heroin dealers. Kohn's work led to indictments.

On Saturday, May 19, Kohn called in to the city desk and said he'd been shot. He told of a harrowing night in which he had been kidnapped by someone with apparent connections to the drug trade, held overnight in a shady hotel, and been fired at, escaping only because the gunman's revolver jammed and the gunman panicked and ran away. The left shoulder pad of Kohn's sport coat had what seemed to be a bullet hole. "Reporter Escapes Death in Kidnapping," the headline read Sunday. The *Free Press,* saying it would not be intimidated, offered a $25,000 award.

Thanks to reporting by Kohn's colleagues at the paper, a different picture emerged.

"Reporter Admits Kidnap Story False," by Marco Trbovich. *Detroit Free Press,* May 23, 1973.

Free Press reporter Howard Kohn, under questioning by his editors, admitted Tuesday night the kidnaping story he told Saturday was not true as he originally related it.

Kohn was immediately suspended by the *Free Press.* Managing Editor Neal Shine assigned a team of reporters to continue to check out Kohn's story and conflicting versions he related Tuesday night.

Shine issued the following statement:

"The *Free Press* regrets and apologizes for the fact that one of its reporters, Howard Kohn, has acted unprofessionally by falsifying at least part of the kidnaping story.

"We are determined to find, and intend to publish, the full truth as soon as we can determine it.

"Kohn admitted that some parts of the story of his kidnaping were false under intense questioning by his editors after other *Free Press* reporters had discovered discrepancies in his original account. . . .

"The fact that Kohn has, in the past, done important and significant investigative reporting for the *Free Press* does not mitigate nor excuse the warped judgments he made in telling a story that was not wholly true.

"Therefore, he has been suspended until the *Free Press* can establish the whole truth about his actions.

"The *Free Press* will continue to follow a policy of full disclosure in this unfortunate case."

Kohn admitted that he lied last weekend when he said that he was kidnaped at gunpoint and held captive for a night in a Detroit motel.

Kohn now says he met with an informant well known to him, who uses the name Sydel Carter, and that the two quibbled throughout the night over an alleged attempt by Carter to blackmail Kohn.

The *Free Press* immediately turned the new information over to Detroit police.

Kohn told the *Free Press* Tuesday that there was no unidentified gunman involved in the weekend incidents. He repeatedly told conflicting stories about whom he had met and why.

He first said he met the unidentified gunman and believed he was being led to Carter. Later, he said he had met only Carter.

Kohn alleged that Carter was attempting to blackmail him. He told the *Free Press* Tuesday that Carter had threatened to impugn Kohn's reputation as a journalist by using information about $500 Kohn supposedly paid an informant.

Kohn revealed the fragmented and confused versions of the weekend's events after the *Free Press* confronted him with discrepancies uncovered in its own investigation of the presumed kidnaping.

• • •

Kohn was fired from the *Free Press*. He committed himself to a psychiatric ward for several days, and county prosecutors charged him with filing a fictitious report of a crime, a misdemeanor. He left Detroit but went on to resume a successful journalism career, including several books.

Years later, Marco Trbovich, the reporter who had written both the original story about Kohn's kidnapping and the second one, discussed why he had challenged a fellow reporter's word. You know why I did it? Trbovich said, "My name was on that piece."

"Jimmy's World" made quite an impact when it was published on the front page of the *Washington Post* on September 28, 1980. The well-written, harrowing story told about an eight-year-old, third-generation heroin addict who lived a chaotic life in the city's rough neighborhoods. How can this be, readers asked in alarm. And how could the *Post* let its reporter, Janet Cooke, watch the boy being shot up with heroin, a crime, without doing anything about it? Police and youth-service officials set out to find the boy to give him help, and unsuccessfully pressured the *Post* for the name and address of the boy and his mother, who Cooke said had been given anonymity. After a three-week investigation, however, the police concluded the child did not exist.

The *Post* nominated the story for a Pulitzer Prize, and in April 1981 it won. Cooke had hoped it would not, understandably. As newspapers across the country started writing biographical sketches on the reporter, discrepancies came out.

Although she had told the Pulitzer board that she was a graduate of Vassar, she had attended only one year. She had not gone to the Sorbonne, as she had said. She did not have the master's degree from the University of Toledo she had claimed. If she lied about those things, could she have lied about the story?

Under heavy questioning, Cooke admitted there was no Jimmy. She resigned, the *Post* returned its Pulitzer, and the executive editor, Ben Bradlee, assigned the paper's ombudsman to write a full account of what had gone wrong.

Here is a part of that account.

"Janet's World," by Bill Green. *Washington Post,* April 19, 1981.

From the day "Jimmy's" story appeared, there were doubts about it. Milton Coleman (city editor) felt misgivings first when the police couldn't find the boy. Courtland Milloy (reporter) when he accompanied Janet Cooke on a trip through the area where the youngster was supposed to live.

There were others. Mayor Marion Barry was one. Dr. Alyce Gullattee, director of Howard University's Institute for Substance Abuse and Addiction, was another. She was one of the people Cooke interviewed when she was gathering her original material.

In a telephone call with Pat Tyler, then of the *Washington Post's* metro staff, Gullattee said the story had caused a panic in the community to the extent that addicts were hunkered down, afraid to go out to seek treatment out of fear that they will run afoul of swarms of police looking for the 8-year-old.

Gullattee also said she didn't believe any of those people "fired up" in front of Cooke. Junkies, she said, just don't trust reporters like that.

Elsa Walsh, Cooke's roommate, doubted. She had gone through Cooke's notes once and found nothing on "Jimmy." But there was more. "She's the kind of person who has fears for her own safety," Walsh said. "My own instincts told me it

was wrong. She would have real trouble going into the 'Jimmy' setting. And then, when I tried to put what I know of Janet together with the story itself, they wouldn't fit." She did not express these misgivings to any editors.

Among the strongest doubters was Vivian Aplin-Brownlee of the *District Weekly,* who was Janet's first editor at *The Post.* She had not been in touch with the story since it was turned over to the Metro staff.

"I had been tough on Janet. She knew it and I knew it," Aplin-Brownlee said. "But when I first read the story I was astonished. I thought it was going to be about the use of heroin that causes skin ulcers. That's what it started out to be.

"I never believed it, and I told Milton that. I knew her so well and the depth of her. In her eagerness to make a name she would write farther than the truth would allow.

"When challenged on facts in other stories, Janet would reverse herself, but without dismay or consternation with herself.

"I knew she would be tremendously out of place in a 'shooting gallery.' I didn't believe she could get access. No pusher would shoot up a child in her presence.

"Some of the language didn't ring true. What 8-year-old in 'Jimmy's' circumstances would make a connection between math and drugs?" (As the story claimed.)

On the day Cooke's Pulitzer Prize was announced, Aplin-Brownlee went to Coleman and said, "I hope she has committed the perfect crime."

When the hoax became known, Coleman went back to Aplin-Brownlee and said, "It wasn't the perfect crime after all."

In mid-November, Cooke was working on another sensational story, promising to produce the story of a 14-year-old prostitute, and when Aplin-Brownlee heard about it, she told Coleman, "She's about to do it to you again. Why would a 14-year-old hooker and her 20-year-old pimp sit down with Janet at a restaurant in Georgetown?"

Still, after she first expressed her incredulity to Coleman, she didn't go back to him. Relations between the two were strained.

"He said he believed the story," Aplin-Brownlee recalls now. "I didn't have to ask why. He believed it because he wanted to."

Aplin-Brownlee said she felt that Coleman had raided her *District Weekly* staff when Cooke was assigned to Metro after the "Jimmy" story. It was what Woodward [Bob, an editor] called a battle-field promotion.

Skepticism from people like Milloy and Aplin-Brownlee triggered newsroom rumors about "Jimmy" that wouldn't go away. Woodward didn't doubt the story, although he and Coleman talked about those who did. "I was blown away by the story," Woodward said. "Milt seemed satisfied that by now he had a name. I was also reassured by a letter to the editor *The Post* published" (on Nov. 10).

Dr. William Hamlin of Washington had written, "...The Washington metropolitan area, as well as hundreds of other large metropolitan areas around the country, are full of Jimmys. I know. I work with them...."

"Milt did think that failed trip Janet had with Courtland was bizarre," Woodward said. "That thought should have set off alarms for me. It didn't. I told Milt I believed the story."

Woodward was inclined to dismiss the doubters, attributing their skepticism to "professional jealousy."

Still, the two editors did take some precautions. As Cooke pursued the "hooker" story, they insisted that Coleman meet with the subject of the story, mainly to protect Cooke from more staff jealousies and to establish once and for all the soundness of her reporting. Cooke kept arranging times and places for such a meeting, but they were all canceled.

"I attached no particular significance to this," Woodward said, "but it was mildly troubling."

Meanwhile, something else was filtering into

The Post's reaction. It felt it was under attack. Angry words from the mayor and the police chief were reaching the staff's pride. Charges of irresponsibility from the public were tough to take. Woodward said it best, "We went into our Watergate mode: protect the source and back the reporter."

When the threat of legal action by the police department came up, publisher Don Graham went by Coleman's desk one day and asked, "Is there anything we should check out?"

Neither of them quite remembers Coleman's reply, but, in part, Coleman remembers describing Cooke's gripping account of her visit to "Jimmy's" home. Graham went away satisfied.

About three weeks after the story appeared, Simons [Howard, managing editor] called Coleman and said, "That kid is still out there and nobody's looking for him. Let's find him. Take Janet with you."

Coleman told Cooke about the plan, but they didn't get to it right away. A day later, Cooke went to Coleman and said she had gone to the house and found it vacant. The family had moved to Baltimore, she said, and there was no reason for the two of them to make a trip to "Jimmy's" house.

While Coleman had been troubled that the police were unable to find the boy, Woodward found that unremarkable. "It seemed logical," he said, "that his mother would take him away to Baltimore or wherever."

But Coleman was infuriated. He went to managing editor Simons and spilled out his anger. For the first time, Simons felt misgivings about the story. "But all I had was a hunch and the fact that she had ducked the visit. How do you prove a negative?" he said.

The faith of an editor in his reporter that is a principal connector in all the events of the episode was upheld. Skepticism was put aside.

Bradlee [Ben] says that throughout he was unaware of the skepticism. "Nobody ever came in this room and said, 'I have doubts about the story'—before or after publication—and nobody said someone else had misgivings about the story," Bradlee said.

One editor who had early misgivings was deputy Metro editor David Maraniss, who also serves as Maryland editor. He read the story on vacation and didn't feel it quite added up. Since it was not his territory and criticism might be viewed as poaching, Maraniss did not take his questions to Woodward until much later.

Uncertainties and misgivings among the newsroom staff persisted. Some of them found their way to Coleman, Woodward or Simons, but apparently made no strong impression. Looking back on it with reporters now, they seem to agree that they didn't have enough to go on. They felt they couldn't press the case without evidence, and none was available. As late as February, Metro reporters were still going to editors with their concerns, and were told that Coleman knew who "Jimmy" was.

When the hoax was exposed, their doubts about the story and their frustration with management burst out in a meeting of the Metro staff at Woodward's house last Thursday night. Coleman says now:

". . . There was undoubtedly also some degree of pride—we had published the story in the first place and stood by it. We probably put too much faith in the hope that maybe things were not the way so many indicators suggested they might be."

Woodward, likewise, feels negligent. "Questions were clearly out there," he said. "Maraniss and Coleman were my channels of information. I should have sat them down together and reviewed everything and then taken it to Simons and Bradlee. Though I had a vague idea that Coleman and Simons had talked about the questions, I never recall talking with Simons about it. I don't think I ever once took the matter up with Bradlee, who was apparently left in ignorance about the doubts swirling around."

Meanwhile, Aplin-Brownlee says that Cooke was having migraine headaches and stayed out of the office more than usual.

• • •

The incident prompted much journalistic self-searching. Although many editors were quick to say such an event could not happen in their newsrooms, many also became more questioning about reporters' anonymous sources and too-perfect quotes. The blame for "Jimmy's World" was placed on newsroom pressure at the *Post,* a push for dramatic, literary style, an acceptance of anonymous sources, and a desire to write with attitude rather than objectivity. Since Cooke is African American, some skeptics also said the story showed that unqualified blacks were being hired in a newsroom push for diversity.

Bradlee offered to resign, but the publisher, Donald Graham, refused. In *A Good Life,* an autobiography written after he retired, Bradlee said he had drawn some lessons from the incident. First, he said, "there really is no protection against a skillful liar, who has earned the trust of his or her editors." Second, "check job applications and references carefully." Third, "beware of stories you want to be true, for whatever reason." Encourage people to express their reservations. Fourth, be less accepting of anonymous sources, and require reporters to tell their editors the identity of a source granted anonymity. Fifth, if a disaster does happen, make sure to reveal it fully yourself; he did not, he said, want any other publication telling more about the Cooke mishap than the *Post* did.

Bradlee also said that the *Post* checked everything else that Cooke had written for the paper in the two years she was there. All the other stories stood up.

REPORTERS AVENGE THE KILLING OF THEIR COLLEAGUE

The irony is that Don Bolles had gone off the investigative beat. In his first thirteen years on the staff of the *Arizona Republic*, in Phoenix, beginning in 1962, he had investigated land fraud, tax commission kickbacks, a highway patrol slush fund, horse and dog racing, and the new movement of Mafia members into Arizona, a fast-growing and loosely regulated state. Bolles's work had cost people money, brought indictments, and earned him serious enemies.

Burned out, in 1975 Bolles transferred to covering the state legislature. But his investigative instinct stayed intact. Stories on the background of Kemper Marley, a onetime rancher appointed to the state racing commission, had forced Marley to resign. And in 1976, a tip from a man named John Adamson, who claimed to be able to link an Arizona congressman to land fraud, caused Bolles to set up a meeting at a downtown hotel.

The potential informant never showed at the hotel. Bolles got back in his car to head for a press club luncheon. As he backed out of his parking space, the car exploded, throwing Bolles out in a bloody heap. Before he lost consciousness, he muttered the name of the man he was planning to meet. Eleven days later, Bolles died. The same day, the police arrested Adamson for murder.

The matter might have been considered closed there, except for the impact of the killing of a reporter on his colleagues. A new group, Investigative Reporters and Editors, happened to be meeting within the week. By the time the meeting broke up, the IRE had decided to send a team of reporters to Arizona to continue the work that Bolles had been doing. Its leader was Bob Greene, the storied investigative reporter from *Newsday*. About fifty newspapers and broadcast stations around the country participated. Many re-

porters gave up vacation time to work in Arizona; newsroom collections helped pay the costs.

While the reporters were working on the project, Adamson pleaded guilty to second-degree murder and named two other men he said were involved, Max Dunlap, a building contractor, who Adamson said hired him on behalf of Marley, and James Robison, a plumber, who Adamson said helped blow up Bolles's car.

The IRE stories, collectively called the Arizona Project, were intended not to find Bolles's killer, but to continue the work that had caused his death. The twenty-three-part series started running in newspapers on March 13, 1977.

The Arizona Project: Day 15. By Investigative Reporters and Editors, Inc.

On any morning of the week, usually around 10, when the sun has burned off the remnants of the desert's dawn chill, an old man with silver hair steps out of the back door of a comfortable brick ranch house in North Tucson.

Before setting into the driver's seat of his 1976 silver-grey Cadillac Fleetwood, he whistles over to his dog, a pincer-eared Doberman that prowls the perimeter of the house at 255 Sierra Vista Drive. After a pat on the head and a fond word for "Greasy," the old man pilots his car about five blocks to the Lucky Wishbone, a fast food restaurant specializing in fried chicken.

There's a telephone booth outside the Lucky Wishbone and after carefully closing himself in, the old man fishes a handful of quarters from his pocket, drops one into the slot and begins chatting quietly. In Sicilian. Exactly what the old man says is known only to him and whomever he calls. But chances are the conversation is about narcotics, guns, girls, gambling, money, deliveries, meetings, couriers, payoffs, discipline, punishment and other elements of Arizona's biggest growth industry, organized crime.

Joseph (Joe Bananas) Bonanno Sr., senior Mafia don in the United States, is back in business.

The southwestern sunbelt, with its burgeoning wealth and population and its proximity to the narcotics warehouses of Mexico, offers a mammoth potential harvest for organized crime. Sun-bronzed, palm-fringed Arizona, the fastest growing state in the union, is the biggest plum in the Southwest. And the Mob is scooping up as much new action as it can get its hands on, growing, expanding, consolidating, diversifying.

Authorities have documented long lists of Mob-owned businesses, but these often are only front-counter operations. In the back are dummy corporations and other corporate smoke screens that effectively conceal ownership of vast amounts of land, buildings, parking lots, housing developments and other business establishments.

Already, federal investigators have documented attempts by mobsters to organize the state's garbage collection industry, to control beauty parlors throughout Tucson, to set up prepaid dental plans through trade unions.

Although a few individual cops and at least one judge are suspected of involvement with organized crime, as yet there is no widespread control of police and legal personnel.

Senior law enforcement officers worry that such control may be inevitable when the big money starts greening the police stations, and the public attitudes of some officials enhance that fear. Bernard Garmire, chief of police in Tucson for 12 years, now retired, was once asked if he had feared the Mafia incursion into his city and state. "We paid no attention to them," Garmire said. "Mafia money spends as good as anyone else's."

Garmire's nonchalance is not unusual in this state. The Sicilian Mafiosi and their Cosa Nostra compadres who have migrated from the East have done so smoothly and easily.

They have become cherished friends, good neighbors and respected citizens. They have moved in the highest circles of Arizona society, dealing and socializing with the state's business and political leaders, past and present.

Federal mob watchers estimate that 200 members of organized crime families are currently living in Arizona. And the biggest, most important man of all is Joseph Bonanno, today probably the most powerful Mafioso in America, the undisputed Boss west of the Rocky Mountains.

Today, the 72-year-old Bonanno lives quietly, comfortably, in a Tucson neighborhood, the epitome of button-down suburban respectability.

In his home, he entertains a variety of visitors, most of them spotted by federal or local investigators who keep Bonanno's home under regular surveillance. Some walk in through the front door, often prominent people like Evangelist Billy Graham. Others try to sneak in. Agents once watched Bonanno's bodyguard, Peter Notaro, meet four top mobsters at the Tucson airport, place them in a station wagon, cover them up with rugs and drive to the Bonanno house where they were unloaded around the back. . . .

The story of the Mafia's heavy encroachment into Arizona pivots on the drying up of the French Connection heroin routes in the early 1970s following the halt of Turkish poppy production.

Entrepreneurs, both Mafia and independent, looked to Mexico for an alternative supply. The Mexican Connection was quickly geared up and soon, unlimited quantities of drugs were being scooped into the wide end of a narcotics horn of plenty and funneled out at the narrow end through Arizona.

Bonanno was well-established in New York when he moved west in 1943, and the reason he set up a second home in Arizona was for nothing more sinister than his firstborn son's health.

Salvatore, known as Bill, had a mastoid in his ear and the prescribed treatment was for young Billy to sit in the sun and let his ear drain. So Bonanno moved his family west. . . .

From Tucson, Bonanno continued to run his

New York family and to oversee operation of his nationwide network of cheese outlets. With Bugsy Siegel building Las Vegas and [Peter] Licavoli setting up southwest gambling wire for horse and dog results, Bonanno moved into a house on East Elm Street and began putting roots down.

Although Bonanno's reputation preceded him to Arizona, the westerners received him openly and without prejudice. And soon, Joe Bonanno was buying up large parcels of land, appearing at the right parties, saying the proper things, donating to his church and establishing himself in the right circles. . . .

Things were going well in Arizona for Bonanno, but his heart and his principal business interests were back East. In the late 1950s and early 1960s, Bonanno began flexing his muscle in New York, strengthening alliances, making enemies and in his boldest and rashest move, calling for the assassination of Carlo Gambino.

For that he was snatched off a New York street in 1964 and was scheduled to be tried and killed. Three things saved his life: his own glib tongue, his native son Mafia status and the fact that his death would have sparked a gang war of unprecedented bloodletting.

So Bonanno was saved from the dead fish and the goodbye kiss of death. The 10-man Mob council allowed him to keep his cheese empire and retire to Arizona, presumably to lie in the sun, play with his grandchildren and grow fat on wine and pasta.

During the 1960s and early 1970s, Joe Bananas did just that, but life was far from placid.

For one thing, a lot of lesser mob figures were moving into the state grabbing off territory, jousting for pieces of the gambling, loan sharking and prostitution action, squabbling among themselves and doing a lot of indiscriminate and messy bombing, shooting and garroting.

Being the state's resident Mafia heavy put Bonanno smack in the middle of all the attention and he quickly became a favorite target for inquisitive reporters, ambitious prosecutors and federal grand juries. A further blow came in 1969 with the death of the venerable Vito Genovese, who had long been a patrone of Bonanno's.

Organized crime experts confidently predicted the end of any hopes for a Bonanno comeback, relegating him to permanent has-been status in the Mob.

And then there was the continuing problems with Bonanno's two sons, Bill and Little Joe. For one thing, one or the other kept getting indicted. Both have served time in federal prisons and currently, both are out on parole. . . .

Joe Bonanno was steadily expanding his influence and his operations throughout the West, cementing working relationships with other mobsters that are vital if business is to be transacted smoothly.

The Alaska pipeline, with its thousands of highly paid, free-spending workers, was virgin territory for the Mob and two Bonanno associates, Salvatore Spinelli and Jerry Max Pasley, who work for the Licavoli group, quickly stepped in to supply the demand for action.

A constant stream of cocaine, prostitutes and stolen goods, particularly the silver and turquoise Navajo Indian jewelry, began flowing up the AlCan Highway and today Bonanno's influence is strong in that state.

Colorado, too, with its growing population, was ripe for expansion and in early 1974, Bonanno—using the alias "Mr. Veccio"—made at least two trips to Colorado Springs and Denver to look at real estate. He apparently dropped any idea of a personal roost in Colorado after publicity about his visits in the Denver *Post*.

Today, the Bonanno organization moves kilo amounts of heroin through Pueblo, Colo., for shipment to St. Louis and other cities. Bonanno's chief contact in the state is Joe (The Ram) Salardino, for years the chief enforcer for the Smaldone organization, which has had Colorado as its turf for many years.

Now that Bonanno's two sons are established in Southern California, the old man appears to be making a concerted effort to gain control of the rackets in that state. He makes regular trips down there, and authorities are aware of at least one mini-summit meeting attended by Bonanno and Carmine Galente, the man the media here has installed as the new boss of bosses, succeeding Carlo Gambino. . . .

As a base for controlling the West, Arizona is ideal. Some 200 miles directly south is Culiacan, providing close and easy access to the heroin supplies that form a large part of the Mafia wealth. Nearby is Lake Havasu, long a spot for mob members to lay low and hide out. Pete Licavoli's sprawling Grace Ranch provides a convenient way-station for sneaking Sicilian workers and soldiers into the country from Mexico.

Las Vegas, with its vital capacity for laundering huge amounts of dirty money, is just a short drive northwest. Southern California, Colorado and Alaska are all ripe for consolidation or expansion.

How smoothly and successfully the Bonanno family is able to spread its influence depends on the effectiveness of law enforcement, which until the past two or three years has been generally weak and ineffective.

The FBI in Arizona, until recently, has served with a few notable exceptions as a comfortable retirement post for senior agents. Phoenix police have done brilliant work but have been and remain woefully undermanned. The state Department of Public Safety and the Four County Narcotics Strike Force are also understaffed and underfinanced.

The Tucson Police Department's record on organized crime is best summed up by noting that they have made only a single bookmaking arrest in 10 years. Only one.

Said William Smitherman, U.S. attorney for Arizona, in a January interview: "Organized crime is here in Arizona, and it is a tremendous problem." Law enforcement, he feels, will only be able to make a dent in the problem "when we are as well-financed and organized as they are."

• • •

Nationally, about two dozen newspapers or broadcast outlets, including *Newsday*, the *Boston Globe*, the *Kansas City Star*, the *Albuquerque Tribune*, and the *Miami Herald*, ran all or substantial parts of the series, and scores of others used wire service versions. Bolles's old paper, the *Arizona Republic*, refused, running instead a page-one statement saying that some of the material in the series had not been documented to the paper's satisfaction. To reporters who had worked on the series, to some *Republic* staffers, and to many readers in Phoenix, the paper's decision was a sign that it was under the thumb of the power structure about which Bolles had written.

Newspaper executives who had not joined the investigation, including those from the *New York Times*, the *Washington Post*, and the *Los Angeles Times*, continued to deplore what they saw as group journalism by outsiders.

Although much of the public in Arizona reacted with an everyone-knows-that attitude, some law-enforcement officials and politicians were spurred to take action. The series, Greene said, resulted in a massive overhaul of the state's penal statutes and increased financing for the state police and other regulatory agencies. At a ten-year-anniversary event of the series, Bruce Babbitt, Arizona attorney general at the time, told the reporters that their work had "dragged Arizona into the twentieth century." A number of lawsuits were filed against the reporters, but most were dropped, Greene said. In the one libel suit that went to trial, the complainant lost. "I am prouder of the Arizona project than I am of any other thing I have ever done," Greene said.

In November 1977, James Robison and Max Dunlap were convicted of murder and conspiracy to commit murder in Bolles's killing.

For the reporters who participated, the Arizona Project gave them links in other cities that led to cooperation on other investigations. For reporters as a profession, the result of the stories was an important intangible. On Bolles's down days, he was known to tell people that there was no use in exposing anything, because no one cared enough to do anything about it. The Arizona Project showed someone cared.

THE *AMERICAN JOURNALISM REVIEW* TAKES ON THE ISSUE OF REPORTERS ACCEPTING SPEAKING FEES

Criticism of the press is as old as the country: one of the reasons George Washington said he did not want to run for a third term was that he was tired of newspaper attacks. But thoughtful criticism of the press by reporters, not those being reported upon, is relatively rare. Lambert Wilmer's *Our Press Gang* in 1860, Will Irwin's "American Newspaper" articles in *Collier's* in 1911, Upton Sinclair's book *The Brass Check* in 1919, A. J. Liebling's press columns in *The New Yorker* in the 1950s, George Seldes's writings in his own *In Fact* publication for several decades until the 1980s and in twenty books throughout much of the twentieth century—these are exceptions. Other efforts to improve the media came through professional organizations, journalism schools, studies of the press, and press councils.

Beginning in 1958, with the founding of the *Montana Journalism Review*, journalism reviews began to fill the void. The *Columbia Journalism Review*, founded at the Columbia University Graduate School of Journalism in 1961, is the veteran, with the *American Journalism Review*, founded in 1977 as the *Washington Journalism Review*, also dominant. For brief times others, including *MORE*, the *Chicago Journalism Review*, and the *St. Louis Journalism Review*, enlivened the debate on journalistic standards, often with an inside-the-newsroom perspective.

Even in the reviews, however, it is rare for specific journalists to be taken to task. That may not even have been expected. Robert Karl Man-

off, once editor of the *Columbia Journalism Review*, recalls the unfriendly phone calls after he ran, in the March–April 1980 issue, a story comparing *Wall Street Journal* stories with the press releases they were based on. The stories were remarkably similar—in some cases almost identical—to what company publicists had put out.

Alicia Shepard of the *American Journalism Review* also found out how unfriendly reporters could be when reported upon. In the May 1994 issue, she tackled a subject beginning to be remarked upon in Washington and other media circles: the fees being paid to big-name reporters for speeches to groups and organizations, often groups and organizations interested in the issues that reporters covered. In January 1994, ABC's *Prime Time Live* had run a piece about a junket a group of insurance organizations had run in Key West, Florida, for about thirty congressional staffers. "The message," Shepard said, "was that once again a trade organization was trying to buy votes on Capitol Hill." But the network felt obliged to add this note: the previous year, its correspondent Sam Donaldson had been paid thousands to give a speech to the same insurance organizations. The insurance agents wondered why, if the practice of speaking to them was so bad, a top-name reporter had no problems doing the same thing. Donaldson replied that he was not a public official writing laws that would affect insurance companies.

"Talk Is Expensive," by Alicia C. Shepard. *American Journalism Review*, May 1994.

Talk doesn't come cheap.

Diane Sawyer and Sam Donaldson are said to command up to $30,000 for a speech, Cokie Roberts up to $20,000, and David Brinkley $18,000. The going rate is believed to be as high as $12,500 for George Will and $10,000 for Tim Russert. William Safire says he's gotten $20,000. Anna Quindlen has received $15,000, CNN's Judy Woodruff and NBC's Lisa Myers say they've each pulled in $7,500, and *Newsweek*'s Howard Fineman has earned $5,000.

That's according to brochures put out by speakers' bureaus, people who deal with the bureaus, published reports and, in some cases, the speakers themselves. Exact figures are often hard to pin down, since many celebrity journalists are extremely reluctant to reveal specific numbers. And often these same highly paid journalists speak for free, or charge much less than published rates.

What these journalists and a few hundred others have that the rest of us don't is "podium talent." And many have turned it into a lucrative sideline, giving one- to two-hour speeches to trade groups, colleges, corporations and conventions in return for what many other journalists may earn in a month or even a year.

Not every journalist can dip into the honoraria trough. The pool is limited to those with big names, wit and something pithy or insightful to say about politics or the media. Most of those commanding large speaking fees are the media elite of Washington. The rest come largely from the New York City media establishment. But those who collect fees are increasingly making those who don't uncomfortable. They say receiving large sums for speaking before groups with a vested interest in news coverage can give the appearance of a conflict. And it seems hypocritical for reporters to stuff their pockets with money from the same organizations they criticize for trying to buy influence on Capitol Hill.

To some, such impressive fees suggest those willing to pay want something in return. Of course, journalists who take honoraria say that isn't so. High-profile journalists say they are perceived as celebrities and entitled to capitalize on the years of work that led to stardom. And echoing members of Congress—who have been banned from taking honoraria since 1991—they insist they're not tainted by the money.

But those who decline invitations say the credibility of journalist speechmakers is compromised.

As in politics, the appearance of a conflict, they say, is just as harmful as a real one. Although evidence of a quid pro quo has never surfaced, there have been instances where it's caused embarrassment to a journalist or his or her employer.

"I think we ought not to be doing this," former CBS and NBC correspondent Roger Mudd told *AJR*. "It poses so many difficulties. Journalists as a breed hold the politicians to a certain standard of conduct and a certain standard of the appearance of conduct. When it applies to us we frequently fail our own test."

"It's not a black-and-white situation," adds Walter Cronkite, who took money for speeches while at CBS, "but I would have to agree with the critics that it probably is better avoided."

Some journalists receive honoraria for services other than speeches. Beat reporters write freelance articles for organizations that have political or social agendas that benefit from news coverage. Others give lectures in exchange for junkets aboard cruise ships.

Whatever it is, as the number of possible conflicts increases, those who may be most confused are viewers and readers. "Journalists are something like judges in society," says ethics and public affairs professor Deni Elliott of the University of Montana. "I don't know the individual journalists I'm asked to trust. Maybe they absolutely can't be co-opted but I don't know that. I don't know who to trust."

Journalists aren't the only ones collecting speech money. They're marketed in the same brochures promoting Jimmy Carter, Marilyn Tucker Quayle, F. Lee Bailey, Art Linkletter and the Amazing Kreskin. Colin Powell, the recently retired chairman of the Joint Chiefs of Staff, has 60 speeches lined up this year for $60,000 each, according to a source who has worked with the Washington Speakers Bureau. While it's unlikely that even big-name journalists rake in as much as Powell, few journalists *AJR* spoke with would disclose their earnings, saying it's not the public's business.

While print journalists aren't often considered celebrities, television has helped raise the profiles of many newspaper and magazine journalists, like Al Hunt of the *Wall Street Journal*. Hunt, the *Los Angeles Times'* Jack Nelson, *Newsweek's* Fineman, the *Washington Post's* David Broder and other print reporters became popular as public speakers by sharing inside Washington tidbits on weekly public affairs shows like *Washington Week in Review, The McLaughlin Group, This Week With David Brinkley* or CNN's *Inside Politics*.

"The ones who write about politics are most popular," says Lynn Choquette, a partner with the National Speakers Forum, which represents about 50 print and electronic journalists. She says her clients' fees range from $3,000 to $60,000, with journalists getting between $3,000 and $30,000. . . .

Whether it's $5,000 or $30,000 the fee still dazzles journalists who can't command it. The rank and file are quick to note a certain irony. "The people who tend to get these speaking gigs are the people who need it the least," says Carl Cannon, White House correspondent for Baltimore's *Sun*. Speechmaking journalists are not eager to publicize how much they do make.

Even Sam Donaldson, whose reported fee of $30,000 has been widely cited in the press, won't confirm the amount, although that's what one special interest group said it paid the anchor. Donaldson advised *AJR* to call his speakers' bureau, which won't disclose it either. "I can tell you I didn't receive $30,000 but I'm not playing games with you," Donaldson says.

"I'm not going to disclose it," echoes the *Wall Street Journal's* Al Hunt. "I don't have a standard speech fee," says the *Washington Post's* David Broder. "I don't need to discuss that," says ABC's Catherine Crier.

PBS's Robert MacNeil says he speaks "primarily to promote the *MacNeil/Lehrer NewsHour*, public television and my books" and says most of his speaking engagements are unpaid. Nonetheless, he says, "I think my fees are a private matter between me and my sponsors. But they range from honoraria of a few hundred dollars to a few that are in the upper end of current lecture scales." . . .

Cokie Roberts, a reporter for NPR and ABC, was also recently criticized when she gave a speech to the Group Health Association of America, a group with a strong interest in the outcome of President Clinton's health care reform legislation. C-SPAN wanted to cover it but was turned down by Roberts' agent, the Harry Walker Agency, which bars C-SPAN cameras because they make it difficult for its clients to command large fees.

Roberts, who did not return repeated phone calls because she was "extraordinarily busy," has never publicly disclosed her fee, but insiders say it's $20,000—minus the agent's commission.

In a March column, the *Chicago Tribune's* Washington bureau chief, James Warren, criticized Roberts and CBS's Lesley Stahl. Stahl recently took money from Cigna Corp., an insurance company with a major stake in the health care debate. Warren speculated that Stahl was paid in the $10,000 to $20,000 range.

"Taking money from such a group shouldn't be a close call for someone covering Congress's biggest issue of the year," Warren wrote, "but in Washington, the reporter-pundit class, which craves both to be on TV and subsequent speaking gigs that can bring hefty outside income, is expert at rationalizing such conflicts with a mix of sophistry and fervent self-righteousness. One line usually is, 'Oh, there's nobody who thinks that my opinions can be bought.' . . . Baloney. When money changes hands, the relationship between reporter and subject changes." . . .

Critics say that taking money from groups falling under a reporter's purview raises all sorts of potential conflicts of interest or, at the least, the appearance of one. The money also raises questions about a reporter's objectivity. "It seems to me the problem is because Sam and others take that kind of money, it precludes them from ever covering insurance scandals," Roger Mudd, who now teaches journalism at Princeton University, said on a recent radio talk show. "It puts them in an immediate conflict of interest." Mudd says while he was with the networks, he took some small fees for speeches to schools.

James D. Squires, a former editor of the *Chicago Tribune*, tells of the time the *Tribune's* movie reviewer, Gene Siskel, wanted to do some side work for the Walt Disney Co. Squires said no. "If every time Gene Siskel came on TV and says 'I'm about to review a Disney movie and I'm paid by Disney but I'll still be impartial,'" says Squires, "look how silly that would look."

Bob Steele, director of the ethics program at the Poynter Institute, believes that, in their hearts, reporters who speak for cash may be 100 percent certain of their objectivity and fairness. But there's no way to prove that to their audience. "How do we know what didn't go into the story?" he asks. "Or that a journalist would do a story and be exceptionally hard on an organization to prove they were neutral?"

There's yet to be a case, however, in which there was a proven quid pro quo. "No one for a minute who knows Sam would think he could be influenced," says Squires, who once took $5,000 from the American Petroleum Institute while at the *Tribune* and donated it to charity. "But what it does is put the credibility of brand name journalism at risk. The same kind of damage is done by *Hard Copy* and little nitwit reporters showing up on television making wild allegations."

Public figures also question the practice. At an April meeting of the American Society of Newspaper Editors, former Secretary of Defense nominee Bobby Ray Inman, who cited criticism of the media when he withdrew his name from consideration, chided columnists who take big fees for speeches.

Edward Pound, an investigative reporter for *U.S. News & World Report*, recalls asking White House adviser James Carville about speeches he gives to special interest groups. Carville de-

flected the criticism. "What he said to me was, 'What I find mostly when I go there is reporters giving speeches. I usually find myself preceding and following a reporter,'" says Pound. "There's a lot of truth to that. I don't want to sound high and mighty, but I just don't think it's good policy. When I came to Washington in 1977, it wasn't nearly at the stage it is now. It's out of control."

• • •

The reporting by Shepard, Warren, and others clearly touched a nerve. In a follow-up report in June 1995, Shepard said that *Time* magazine had banned honoraria, that ABC had banned paid speeches by reporters to trade associations and corporations (reporters could speak to such groups if the money went to charity), and that the *MacNeil/Lehrer NewsHour* had tightened its restrictions. The Washington bureau chief of the *Wall Street Journal* said he would require his reporters to make public each year their sources of outside income. NBC and *The New Yorker* said they were rewriting their policies, and press groups like the Society of Professional Journalists and the congressional press committee were debating the issue. Some reporters said their income was being hurt, in a number of cases substantially, by the crackdown.

But other organizations, like *U.S. News & World Report*, continued to encourage reporters to take speaking engagements, with the goal of increasing public visibility. And a number of reporters making speeches—Steve Roberts of *U.S. News*, Donaldson, Michael Kinsley of the *New Republic*—told Shepard that they thought the criticism was unfair and the product of cranks. Roberts went so far as to tell Shepard that Warren was "a reprehensible individual."

Still, reporters continue to make paid speeches, and even at organizations with strict policies, executives sometimes make exceptions to rules. But the issue was brought to public attention and some sense of restraint was imposed.

CRIME AND PUNISHMENT

EVERYBODY'S MAGAZINE STOPS THE LEASING OF CONVICTS FROM GEORGIA PRISONS

Facing an upsurge of crime after the Civil War, the state of Georgia adopted a unique, shameful system to avoid building additional prisons. Instead of housing the prisoners itself, the state leased them to contractors, who were then entitled to work the prisoners in return for feeding and housing them. Predictably, with the state and the contractors both making money, and with prisoners having no rights and few protectors, the system was subject to abuse. Convict leasing continued, with revisions, into the twentieth century.

When *Everybody's* magazine received a letter from a former prisoner telling about his experiences in a Georgia work camp, Charles Edward Russell was sent to investigate.

"A Burglar in the Making," by Charles Edward Russell. *Everybody's* magazine, June 1908

He had stolen the $300, there was no doubt about that, and now he sat in the Atlanta court room and listened while his lawyer pleaded in his behalf, urging his youth and inexperience and previous good record, since there was so little else to urge, and trying to break or mitigate in some way the force of the cold, pitiless, indubitable testimony that had bound chains upon him while he sat there.

Young he was, true enough; his look still ingenuous, his face fair and fresh and boyish. You could well understand that, as the lawyer said, droning on interminably and hopelessly, his antecedents and training had been good; he was no familiar and hardened criminal. But he had stole the $300; and in a place of trust. His employer's cash drawer had been in his charge, he had become fascinated with that devil's own game that is called playing the races; he had stolen again and again: with open eyes he had broke the law; now upon his head were to fall the consequences.

At last the droning lawyers ceased to drone; the judge charged briefly and in curt, keen sentences, each a slash at the young man's frail hopes; the jury retired. The young man sat there very pale, his dry lips apart, his pulses beating visibly in his neck, his fingers fumbling incessantly on his hat brim. He had not long to wait—the jurors' retirement was merely for form's sake; they gave the expected verdict, and the young man stood there, shivering, to take his sentence. Four years. . . . The sheriff's officer put his hand upon the young man's shoulder and led him gently away. He walked like one in a dream.

That afternoon they started for the farm near

Milledgeville that the State of Georgia provides for the reception of its convicted lawbreakers, for it has no penitentiary nor prison. The next day, shaved and shorn and clothed in the stripes that are the badge of the convicted wrongdoer, he found himself standing in a long line of other men similarly clad, black men and white men, placed on exhibition, while an agent for the contractors passed along and appraised their muscles and estimated their worth.

He was making selections, this man, for the forces to be drafted to a convicts' camp, where the contractor should have his will of them. For the State of Georgia, having no penitentiary nor prison nor other means of caring for its offenders, practices upon them a very strange device. It sells them for the terms of their sentences into the hands of private and irresponsible persons, and it was for these persons that the man was now going up and down the line, selecting the likeliest and choicest. Fifty years before, on another spot near at hand, another man had gone similarly up and down another line, making similar selections for service. But the service of fifty years ago had been called slavery, and the service of this day was called contract labor, and with this difference of names a great and splendid state had managed in some way to salve its conscience.

It was morning when George, with a fresh detail of purchased slaves, arrived at Gehenna. With the first glance at the camp, a chill struck to his heart; there was something most forbidding about the wild and desolate spot, made more hideous with the ragged, dirty structure and the black chimneys of the brickyard. In one corner was a high stockade with guard pens about it and men with rifles on guard, within the stockade were wretched, dark, dilapidated and most filthy huts in which other men were doomed to sleep and eat. About the factory yard were men at work, in the broad stripes of the convicts, some preparing the clay, some wheeling the yellow, damp, new bricks to the furnaces to be baked. George noticed that all these men were very badly clad, and some went almost naked. Beyond the brick kiln the land sloped into a swamp, a promising breeding place for disease.

George and the others of the new gang were led to one of the filthy sheds, where they received a breakfast of one slice of boiled salt pork and one piece of greasy corn bread. There were no knives nor forks, and George took the pork into his fingers. He felt something move under his fingers. He looked sharply at the pork. He saw what is was that had moved. It was worms.

Struggling hard with himself, he managed to swallow a little of the corn bread (after he had carefully examined it), and with the rest of the gang he was marshaled into the yard. His work was to wheel loads of those fresh, clayey, yellow bricks from the place where they had been shaped to the place where they were to be baked. When he went the first time to the place where the bricks were shaped, he was amazed to see that the persons engaged in removing the bricks from the drying belt were women. He remembered then that the State of Georgia has no prison for convicted women, and that they are rented to slave brokers just as the men slaves are rented. The work that these women were doing seemed very laborious: with bent backs they must toil hour after hour, lifting the heavy bricks and piling them. A man with a rifle stood and watched the women. They regarded him with manifest terror. If for an instant he turned away, they were wont to stand up and straighten their backs and draw in long breaths of air.

From the place where bricks were shaped to the place where bricks were burned there wound through the yard a path about four hundred feet long. George was told that by this path he must take upon the wheelbarrow each time from fifty to seventy bricks and that he must deliver at the furnaces not fewer than 105 loads in the day, sixty loads from sunrise to noon and forty-five loads from the end of the noon hour to sunset. He was also told that his work would be checked up every few hours, and that if he were found to be falling behind he would with good reason be sorry. This is the substance of the information conveyed to him: I need not quote the words. Each of the unbaked bricks weighed between five and six pounds. That made usually a wheelbarrow load of more than three hundred pounds. George weighed 110 pounds and he had been certified by the prison doctor to have heart disease.

He has not proceeded far with that first day's work when he has an opportunity to learn exactly what are the good reasons for regretting a failure to complete an apportioned task. There is a commotion in the yard, and two of the guards appear, leading forward a convict to a place where a great barrel lies on its side. A big, authoritative man comes forward and gives orders. The convict is stripped. Then he is bent over the barrel. Two Negroes hold his arms and his head. Two others hold his legs. He begs and pleads and struggles. The Negroes hold him fast. Another man stands by with an instrument. It is made of sole leather about three inches wide, three feet long, and three-eighths of an inch thick. It has a stout wooden handle. The man lifts the instrument high in the air. He brings it down, *swish!* Upon the naked man on the barrel. The man on the barrel screams aloud with sudden agony. He does not shout nor exclaim, he screams a horrible shrill scream of unutterable pain. . . .

The days that followed that first day were to George like days in a madman's dream. He must learn to face the salt pork and its animated contents; he must harden himself against the daily whippings, he must harden himself against the incessant brutality, vile smells, and abominable sights. While all else is being hardened in him, shall his soul escape? At night he crawls sore and weary into his horribly bestenched prison house, where whites and Negroes, young and old, veteran criminal and novice, decent and vile, herd together indiscriminately. Every few days his stomach, which, however his mind may fare will

not become accustomed to the salt pork and greasy corn bread, rebels and rejects the poisonous stuff, and then he works on in the sun ready to drop of weakness and weariness. . . .

The deputy warden that represented the state in charge of the camp was also in the pay of the company, which paid him three times as much as the state paid him and to which his obligation was in the same proportion. To the contracting company his use most seemed to be to extract from the convicts the most labor at the least cost. To the state his duty was much vaguer. The contracting company was obliged by its contract to feed and clothe the slaves; the function of the state seemed to be that it kept the convicts from running away. Simply that and nothing more. . . .

All the conditions seemed framed and designed to make life wretched for the victims of this terrible system. In the beginning, the contractor had bought the labor of the convicts for $11 a head for each year. Now competitive bidding had increased the price to $225 a head a year, and even more, and besides the contractor bore the expense of feeding and clothing. That he might secure a profit on such a bargain it was necessary that the men should be driven through long hours to the utmost capacity of their endurance. And that was why the deputy warden was on the contractor's payroll. . . .

The time wore by and George came to the end of his term. He had learned to be as sullen, as defiant, as hardened, as reckless as the indurate men about him. When at last the doors opened to set him free, a guard said to him:

"Well, I suppose you are going to yegg it." And George said:

"By God, I am."

He did. He went back to Atlanta and turned burglar.

And was he the only man that went forth from those gates resolved to prey upon the society that had preyed upon him? I think not. Was he the only man that ever learned at Gehenna the terrible lessons of desperation and revenge that are taught daily in that most perfect academy of crime? I think not, by some thousands. Then how shall we justify to ourselves the system that makes criminals and turns them loose to do evil among us and then catches and brands still deeper the very criminals it has made? . . .

However the thing may be named, lease or contract or what not, the fact remains that the states does give over to private unauthorized and irresponsible persons the care, control and labor, and therefore the punishment, of its offenders, and that to the private persons thus most improperly endowed with one of the most solemn and perplexing functions of state the sole interest lies in extracting the greatest possible amount of labor at the least possible cost. Under such a system the most terrible conditions, multiple and irremediable, are absolutely assured. It makes little difference and can make little that the present Prison Commissioners are honest, faithful, zealous and kindly; it makes little difference that to the very utmost of their power, and unceasingly, they strive to remedy every abuse that is brought to their attention, it makes little difference that the legislature repeatedly investigates the condition of the victims of these contracts. The whole thing is utterly and incurably and hopelessly evil. Nothing does nor can affect the great fatal fact that from the labor of the state's culprits private persons make gains, that the extent of such gains depends upon the amount of labor that the culprits can be forced to perform, and that the culprits are and must be practically at the mercy of those that buy such labor.

For the year ending May 31, 1907, the State of Georgia had 2,464 convicts, of whom 1,890 were contracted into servitude to various private persons and corporations, and 574 were employed on the county roads. In 1906 the number was 1,773 to the contractors and 571 on the county roads. From the labor of these culprits thus sold to private persons the state in 1906 received $333,463.84 and in 1907 $353,455.55. These profits are the sole returns from a system that multiplies criminals, breeds brutality, encourages crime, and puts upon one of the fairest states in the Union a hideous blot. If the profits were a thousand times as great, they would be dear at that price.

• • •

"Georgia didn't waste any time finding fault with us for calling attention to the spot on her pretty gown," *Everybody's* editorialized in its November issue. But the public exposure also embarrassed the state, and Georgia newspapers, professing surprise that the convict leasing system existed, clamored for the state's name to be redeemed. The state legislature began hearings that produced testimony more harrowing than Russell's account, but the legislators split on whether to abolish, or simply amend, the convict leasing system. It took a special session before they compromised and Governor Hoke Smith signed the bill. Under the new law, most convicts were sent to build public roads or work on state farms under state and county officers, with the expectation the prisoners would be under more humane conditions than when working for private contractors. Convicts not needed by the cities and state could still be leased to private contractors for one year. The state also added a parole system.

"All we did was to criticize," said *Everybody's*.

THE PONZI SCHEME IS EXPOSED, AND A NEW TERM IS ADDED TO THE AMERICAN VOCABULARY

To be sure, there were swindlers, fast talkers on the make, long before Charles Ponzi moved to Boston in the early 1900s. The tulip mania in the Netherlands and lotteries in the South in the nineteenth century were two examples showing that greed thrives across national and historic borders. Somehow, someone always seems ready to step forward to feed that greed. The schemes were typically called "bubbles."

The situation in New England in the early 1920s was marked by the kind of economic anxiety that prepared the ground for such a scheme to flourish. Small investors felt squeezed: urban wages and the cost of living were rising, investments in Liberty Bonds made during World War I were not very profitable, banks were reporting big profits but paying little yield.

In December 1919, Charles Ponzi opened the Security Exchange Company in Boston. Invest $1,000 with me, he said, and I will invest it in international postal reply coupons; through my knowledge of the exchange rates, I will earn you a 50 percent profit in forty-five days. By July 1920, Ponzi was taking in $1 million a week, and making all his payments. His office was crowded with people, many of them immigrants, who urged him to take their savings.

State and federal investigators grew suspicious, and one postal official swore that there were not enough postal reply coupons exchanged in the world to account for the profits Ponzi said he was making. The Boston newspapers were also investigating. In August, the *Boston Post* received word from its Montreal reporter that Ponzi was the same man who had been convicted of forgery and imprisoned in Canada. Ponzi denied the story, and so the *Post* put one of its reporters on the train with copies of recent photos of Ponzi.

"Canadian 'Ponsi' Served Jail Term," by Herbert L. Baldwin. *Boston Post,* August 11, 1920.

MONTREAL, Canada, Aug. 10—Charles Ponzi, Boston's financial wizard, and Charles Ponsi, alias Charles Bianchi, a convicted forger who spent two and a half years behind the bars of one of the Canadian jails, were pronounced one and the same man today.

A rogues' gallery expert, a police inspector who arrested Charles Ponsi (Bianchi), the warden of the penitentiary at St. Vincent de Paul; a clerk who worked in the same office where the forgeries took place, and an Italian banker, one of the best known in this city, were among those who saw photographs of Charles Ponzi of Lexington, Mass., and with one accord told a *Post* staff reporter:

"Why, that's Bianchi," or "That's Ponsi," as happened to be the name they knew him by.

"But where's his mustache?" they all wanted to know.

These photos were taken by Boston *Post* artists recently.

Eugene Laflamme, fingerprint expert and rogues' gallery chief of the Montreal police department, went even further. He declared, unqualifiedly, that photographs of Ponzi, pictures taken last week in Boston and in Lexington, Mass., and photographs that he fished from the files of the crooks in the police gallery here, were those of the same man.

"Positively, that's the same man," he told a *Post* man as he carefully checked his rogues' gallery picture of Ponsi, the forger, and Ponzi, the Hub get-rich-quick manipulator. And then he told why he made his declaration. He checked, as only an expert can check, the two photographs and pointed out what he asserted were identicalities that even 12 years could not erase.

"He's stouter and he's older, of course," said Laflamme. "But let me show you something. See that ear? Notice the lobe is eminent. Now take a squint at your photos. See that ear? Notice the lobe is eminent and exactly the same shape.

"Now take your photos. See that lower lip? Sort of a pout in the centre of it, isn't there? See the same kind of a pout on my photo? . . ."

The offense that sent Charles Ponsi to prison here and the methods of the banking office of J. Zarrossi, where the forgeries were committed, were the end of the victimizing of scores—some say hundreds—of hard-working residents of Montreal and vicinity by promising them "more percentage" than any other bank offers.

It is known here that Attorney-General Allen of Massachusetts has had in his possession for several days a complete transcript of the evidence in the case that sent him to prison. This it is believed will explain some of the moves the Bay State attorney-general has been making during the past week.

And the Charles Ponsi that Montreal knew was as mysterious in many ways as have been the methods of Boston's "financial wizard."

Twelve years have passed since Zarrossi closed his banking doors and fled to Mexico and Charles Ponsi went to jail for a term of three years. And the clerks and the friends that knew Ponsi best have scattered to many parts of Canada. Today the *Post* man saw a few of them, and bit by bit were obtained some parts of the story of how many families saw savings that they had entrusted to the company where Bianchi-Ponsi was manager, to be sent to their families in Italy, used in some other way and their money changed to useless receipts.

Vitriolic epithets were poured into the *Post* man's ears as Italian residents of Montreal and a half dozen of its suburbs were interviewed and gazed upon the photographs. There was more than a little talk of man-handling if one Charles Bianchi was ever seen by some few dozen women hereabouts.

"My money that I trusted, because I was promised more interest and told that the other banks were stealing from the poor people," said one Italian woman in the warm manner of her race. "Those dogs stole it and my poor mother never got it." . . .

Assistant Chief Inspector H. T. Cowan of Montreal's police force declared that, if events which it was intimated might be impending and that the United States government might deport an undesirable who entered the country back in 1910, Canada might have something to say about his ever again entering the Dominion.

"We should oppose Charles Ponsi-Bianchi entering Canada again," he declared.

Charles Ponsi's exploits here in Montreal were known to have extended during the years beginning in 1907, and ending in 1910, when he was released from jail. The reports at the St. Vincent de Paul penitentiary show that Charles Ponsi departed from there on July 13, 1910, having gotten some time off for good behavior. He was released on "license" and was required to report to the Dominion police each month until his time of sentence expired.

Where Charles Bianchi came from when he dropped into Montreal early in 1907, police said today that they did not know, and even among those who were his intimates as far as the *Post* man had located them today, no one knew. But they knew of Bianchi's workings in the "give you more for your money than any one else" banking game, and they'd like to hear from him again. Few of them had read of the exploits or even heard of the manipulations of Charles Ponzi of Boston. . . .

Antonio Cordasco is a steamship agent with offices at 501 St. James street, here, and one of the old-time Italian residents of the city, and his offices are almost directly opposite the corner of St. James and Inspector streets, where the Zarrossi office, of which Bianchi-Ponsi was manager, was located. This afternoon Mr. Cordasco was reticent, extremely so. He gazed at the photographs, shifted in his chair, handed them back and said:

"No, I don't know him." Then as the *Post* man started to pocket them again Mr. Cordasco snatched them and, holding them in front of him, delivered a curtain lecture.

"Ah, my fine friend," he murmured, looking at the photo of the Lexington, Mass., Ponzi, "so I see you again. You are, you are—he's Bianchi, the snake," he said as he turned to the reporter.

"Ponzi! Yes, in Boston he makes money and you praise him. Remember him? I remember him, and I remember Zarrossi, and I remember Salvia-tia and all the dogs, well do I remember. What you put in the papers is wondrous. Ponzi, great Ponzi, what I tell you is Bianchi, crooked Bianchi, and the great talks of bringing your money up to the skies that he told poor people: and their money, where did it go?—into pockets, I tell you, and I know it, too." . . .

The warden at the penitentiary smiled quietly as the *Post* man once more produced his photographs.

"Know him, warden?" asked the reporter.

"Ponsi?" queried the warden, and when the reporter disclosed that he represented the Boston *Post* the warden said:

"Yes, I should know him by that picture, and he's the same man that I knew here. I had seen pictures of your Boston Ponzi in the Montreal papers, but they didn't look like anyone I knew, but from those that you have there I should say it was the same man."

Ponsi was a model prisoner and attracted no unusual attention at the penitentiary, so far as could be learned. Records there give his height as 5 feet 2¼ inches and his age as 26 years in 1908. His occupation there is given as a bookkeeper.

Officials, both prison and police, declared that it was doubly assuring to them in their identifications of the photographs of Ponzi that in his life history, which they read with interest in last Monday morning's of the Boston *Post,* Ponzi gave his birth date as March 3, 1892. They pointed out that a man born in that year would be 26 years of age in August, 1908, when the prison and the police records show that Bianchi-Ponsi declared that he was 26. . . .

Bianchi-Ponsi at the time of his arrest declared, according to police officials here, that his mother and father were dead and that he had no relatives anywhere. Officials read with interest the details of his folks back in Parma, Italy, as supplied by Ponzi in his life story to a *Post* man last Sunday, and as they perused it they commented on the

fact that he declared he was doing private investigating during the years that Bianchi-Ponsi was doing time in the big jail 25 miles from here.

About the only thing that the extremely high and wide gray stone walls there permit of investigation to prisoners is private study of which way the uniformed guards, with rifles slung ready for action, are squinting. . . .

• • •

With his past revealed, Charles Ponzi found his attempts to calm his investors useless. He admitted bankruptcy. Investigators broke their logjam, and Ponzi served both federal time for fraud and state time for larceny. Ponzi's noteholders eventually got back a little more than a third of their original investment.

As with his previous prison terms, the lessons may not have taken. After his release, Ponzi moved to Florida to be there for the land boom. His activities there led him to be deported to Italy. He died in Brazil in 1949, in the charity ward of a hospital. But his name lives on in connection with any swindle in which the profits for the first investors are paid with the money of those lured in later. Such an activity is called a Ponzi scheme.

THE UNITED PRESS ASKS A QUESTION AND CREATES A TRADITION: THE FBI'S MOST-WANTED LIST

Under J. Edgar Hoover, who became director of the Federal Bureau of Investigation in 1924, and lasted and lasted, the FBI was alert for ways to make itself look good in the public eye. In part this may have been because Hoover got his job after an uproar over bureau investigators' collecting information on senators who were investigating the Teapot Dome scandal. In part it may have been his attempt to paper over what later was viewed as serious lapses in the FBI's view of the crime problem facing America. In part it may have been Hoover's personality, and his desire to be seen as the nation's leading crime fighter, a man above challenge.

Whatever, the bureau was more than willing to cooperate when, on a slow news day in early 1949, a United Press reporter called and asked who the FBI most wanted to capture.

James F. Donovan, United Press. February 7, 1949.

The FBI today listed 10 men as the most-wanted fugitives now at large. They are two accused murderers, four escaped convicts, a bank robber, and three confidence men.

There are about 5700 fugitives from justice in the country. Of these, the FBI said it considered these to be the 10 most potentially dangerous.

The FBI does not label any one of them as "Public Enemy No." But in response to a United Press inquiry, it compiled the list in the hope this may lead to their arrest. Anyone knowing the whereabouts of these men should communicate immediately with the nearest FBI office or the local police.

The FBI picks up an average of 9416 fugitives a year. Here are the names, pictures and records of the 10 men the FBI would like particularly to include in the 1949 Quota. . . .

• • •

Recognizing good publicity when he saw it, J. Edgar Hoover set up an official "Ten Most Wanted Fugitives" program a year later, on March 14, 1950. The first person on the list was Thomas Holden, who had robbed a mail train, then escaped from federal prison in Leavenworth, Kansas. He was wanted for the murder of his wife and her two brothers. In June of 1951, he was arrested in Oregon after the FBI was tipped by a plasterer who saw Holden's picture accompanying a newspaper story on the ten most wanted.

In March 2000, upon the fiftieth anniversary of the top-ten list, the FBI said that 429 of the 451 men and seven women who made the ten-most-wanted list had been captured, 134 of them as a result of help from people who recognized the fugitives because of stories about the list.

Although most people think of post offices when they think of the most-wanted list, the FBI has aggressively cooperated with all media. A 1953 feature article in the *Saturday Evening Post* led to three arrests. Television programs such as *America's Most Wanted* and *Unsolved Mysteries* brought twenty-one arrests by spring of 2000, the FBI said. Two people were captured after tourists at the FBI headquarters in Washington, D.C., recognized their pictures. And in May 1996, the FBI made its first Internet arrest of a top-ten fugitive: a teenager called with information on an escaped bank robber after recognizing his picture on the FBI web site, www.fbi.gov/mostwanted.htm.

RONNIE DUGGER OF THE *TEXAS OBSERVER* COVERS NIGHT-RIDER SHOOTINGS OF THREE BLACK YOUTHS AND HELPS SET THE *OBSERVER* ON ITS WAY AS A LIBERAL VOICE IN CONSERVATIVE TEXAS

In 1954, Ronnie Dugger, an iconoclastic journalist right out of the University of Texas, and others organized the *Texas Observer*. The *Observer* attracted a host of outstanding reporters and editors to cover Texas politics and Texas life. As Willie Morris was to write in his memoir, *North Toward Home,* in 1967, "The effect of Dugger's *Texas Observer* had been profound." Its circulation never exceeded 6,000, yet, as Morris said, the *Observer,* "by the sheer force of its ardor and its talent" was read by "everyone in Texas whose opinions had authority." Among the writers who wrote for the paper were William Brammer, Larry Goodwyn, J. Frank Dobie and Walter Prescott Webb (both from an older generation), Morris, Molly Ivins, Robert Sherrill, and Jim Hightower.

The *Observer* was based in a small, dark office filled with stacks of newspapers and magazines in a frame building on West Twenty-fourth Street in Austin. At times, Dugger would put out the paper himself in twenty-four hours. His delivery vehicle was a 1948 Chevrolet. A financial backer of the *Observer* for a long time was Frankie Randolph, a wealthy Texas landowner whom Morris described as a cross between Eleanor Roosevelt and the character of the newspaper owner played by Ethel Barrymore in the movie *Deadline-U.S.A.*

In November 1955, Dugger, then twenty-four, set out to do the kind of story that other Texas newspapers in those days were not doing: to cover the shooting of three black youths, and killing of one, in the small Negro community in east Texas.

"Negro Boy Murdered in East Texas," by Ronnie Dugger. *Texas Observer,* November 2, 1955.

LONGVIEW

A 16-year-old Negro boy has been murdered and two younger Negro girls shot in a rural East Texas area ridden through with race tension.

A black 1950 or 1951 Ford sped past a cafe where they were drinking soda pop and dancing and somebody in the car pumped nine bullets through the walls and a window.

The boy grabbed onto the girl he was dancing with, but she was hit too. She tried to get loose, screaming, and he let her go and fell to the floor.

The night riders sped on down Highway 149 and turned onto a farm road leading to the Negro community of Mayflower. They sprayed more bullets right and left—into a Negro school bus and the bus driver's car, a Negro's mailbox, a Negro home, and the Negro school at Mayflower.

Two of the bullets almost hit a middle-aged Negro woman who was kneeling by her bed around midnight saying her prayers. A clutch of them smashed into another room where three young children often sleep.

Police say 27 bullets were fired in all, possibly from an automatic .22 pistol.

The theory immediately developed that the killing was an expression of white resentment about a $200,000 bond issue that had been passed for a new Negro school building at Mayflower. In three separate outbursts during the six months since the election, three Negro homes, two Negro cafes, and the Negro schoolhouse in Mayflower have been shot into at night. The same school bus was fired into the night after an election confirming the bond issue.

Sheriff Noble Crawford of Gregg County called the shooting "a thing that's pretty hot."

"It's a nasty situation, I tell you for sure," he said.

He said about the killers:

"It could be whites just as well as could be niggers, no point to duck it."

Deputy Sheriff Caven Penney of Rusk County told the *Observer*:

"The lead we got we think it's white. We haven't got enough to pin 'em yet."

However, a Negro leader, J. C. Beckworth, principal of the fired-into school, said that local law enforcement agencies are working "pretty slow" and are not providing "proper protection." He said he wants the Federal Bureau of Investigation to enter the case....

The killings happened Saturday night a week ago, Oct. 22, ten miles from Longview in Gregg County on Highway 149. The rest of the shooting was along farm road 782 in Rusk County.

The boy's name was John Earl Reese. He was a good boy and had harmed no one. The morning of the day he was shot he had returned from three weeks of cotton picking and turned over $30 to his guardian grandmother. They went to town together to buy him some school clothes for Monday morning. The clothes were never unfolded.

The wounded girls were sisters, Johnnie Merl Nelson, 15, and Joyce Faye Nelson, 13. They were both shot in the arm. Joyce Faye was dancing with

352   MUCKRAKING!

the boy, who is their cousin, when the shooting occurred.

The story has been reported very briefly in the Longview paper, with no mention of the racial implication. It was distributed in a similarly cryptic Associated Press story.

The boy was buried Thursday.

Of the possible connection between the school bonds and the shootings, Beckworth, the Negro principal, said:

"I'm positive that it had to do with it. I know that's right. They don't want us to have no school. They have robbed us from the beginning and don't want us to have nothin.'"

...John Reese slept in the same room with his step-grandfather, 69-year-old Lee Hughes. His grandmother had laid his new school clothes on a couch in this room. His books were on the iron frame double bed he slept in. He had filed his old school papers and some cherished magazines in a cardboard box....

Mrs. Hughes is a stoic woman. She is the daughter of two former slaves who lived, worked, and died in the same East Texas area she has known all her life. She and her husband live in a modest but better than average Negro home on a winding red-dirt road back from the Mayflower school. A blue sign on the living room wall says: "God Bless Our Home and the People There-in."

She cried softly as she sat on the front porch and talked about her boy.

"I can't get myself reconciled," she said. "Just the one child she had. I thought a lot of him, I was partial to 'im."

She rocked a little.

"He dead. I wouldn't let them bury him with the bullet in his head even if it cost $100 to take it out. Lawda mercy, I don't think I'll ever get over it."

More she would not say.

"We ain't got no say so about nothin'. I ain't gonna say nothin' about nothin' 'cause I know I

got to go to bed and go to sleep, an' I ain't gonna talk."

• • •

The FBI came into the case, Dugger recalled, and "the local district attorney accused me of suppressing evidence even though I had identified the killers as suspects to a deputy sheriff." The killers were eventually convicted, although they received what Dugger called "Deep South justice: five years, suspended."

Still, it was this kind of reporting that challenged the status quo of the South and eventually brought greater justice to Texas.

The *Observer* continues in its journalism of commitment. Its coverage of the State Legislature is among the best in the country. A story in 2000 on a racially tainted drug sting in a Texas panhandle town, by editor Nate Blakeslee, echoed some of the points Dugger had made when the *Observer* started: "Things happen when stories make it to the top of the food chain. Corrupt politicians get dethroned. People get out of jail. Justice prevails. Sometimes."

JUSTICE AND INJUSTICE: THE REPORTER AS CRIMINAL INVESTIGATOR

Billy Sol Estes, into jail. Rubin "Hurricane" Carter, out. Richard Loeb and Nathan Leopold, into jail. Mary Katherin Hampton, out. Putting people into jail and getting the wrongly convicted out is a staple of American reporting, and there are hundreds of cases going each way. One of the finest things a reporter can do is to correct injustice, because, after all, that's what reporting is supposed to be all about.

Here are some examples, from Chicago, Houston, and Miami.

Even in a city like Chicago, accustomed to the violence of the 1920s, the kidnapping and killing of fourteen-year-old Bobby Franks, son of a wealthy watch manufacturer, in 1924 was shocking. His naked body was found stuffed into a culvert under a railroad track. Chicago police scoured the town, and Chicago's notoriously aggressive reporters likewise chased every clue. The most effective were Alvin H. Goldstein and James W. Mulroy of the *Chicago Daily News,* young reporters who helped lead the police to Richard Loeb and Nathan Leopold, two wealthy students motivated by the "thrill" of it all.

The *Daily News* explained the events in a story the day Loeb and Leopold were arrested.

"Cub Reporters Win Glory." *Chicago Daily News,* May 31, 1924.

Two "cub" reporters of the *Daily News* staff, James W. Mulroy and Alvin H. Goldstein, contributed more than most of the police force and the legions of rival newsmen combined to the solution of the Franks kidnaping mystery.

"O'Connor and Goldberg," their scornful rivals called them—a wheeze inspired by the almost fanatic zeal with which Mulroy and Goldstein wore out shoe leather in their search for clues. "O'Connor and Goldberg" they may be until they're gray and reading the copy of cubs yet unborn, but the names will be service medals, not taunts. Nobody's kidding the pair today.

It's the story of a story—a perfect realization of the dreams of all the thousands of cubs who come stumbling into the dusty local rooms of all the newspapers of the land, green and unskilled and ambitious. To jump from picture-chasing to triumph over the whole town in the biggest story of a generation sounds like the poppycock of newspaper fiction, but "O'Connor and Goldberg" did it.

They dug up the truth about the kidnaping before any one but friends of the Franks family knew about it. They accomplished a scoop which would have given most reporters glory enough for a lifetime when they brought about the identifi-

cation of the kidnaped boy's body a full jump ahead of every other newspaper in Chicago. They ran and taxied and poked about day and night through the week of frenzy that followed, turning up valuable information under the noses of the police and their rivals.

All unaided they got the evidence that broke the kidnapers' resistance today. "O'Connor and Goldberg" solved the mystery if anybody did. Without them it might have remained a mystery forever....

Mulroy was sitting in a back corner of the local room of the *Daily News* office, killing time, on the morning of Wednesday, May 21, when a tip came in about a kidnaping "that Sam Ettelson knows all about." He was sent to see Ettelson.

Now Ettelson wasn't anxious to have the newspapers get hold of the fact that the fourteen-year-old son of his old friend Jacob Franks had been kidnaped. But Mulroy has the priceless kind of personality that can't be resisted—the kind that's worth a Rolls Royce income in the bond business. He talked the story out of Ettelson.

The story wasn't printed. Publication might imperil the life of the kidnaped boy. But Mulroy didn't let that bother him. He got his pal Goldstein and they set to work.

Goldstein was sent hustling out to Hegewisch, where the body of an unidentified boy had been found crammed into a railroad culvert. Mulroy went out to the Franks home.

The description Goldstein phoned to Mulroy at the Franks house apparently didn't fit the kidnaped boy. Eyeglasses had been found near the Hegewisch body and young Franks had never worn eyeglasses.

The Frankses couldn't be interested at first, but at last Goldstein and Mulroy got an uncle of the missing boy into a taxicab, headed for the Hegewisch morgue....

Well, a kidnaping-murder was too good a story for a pair of cubs, of course. Veterans were assigned to the case. Every newspaper in town, including the *Daily News,* put its best talent to work on the mystery—big leaguers.

Goldstein and Mulroy? Oh, they just stuck. . . .

Thus they canvassed all of East 63rd Street until they located the drug store which was to have been the kidnapers' rendezvous with Franks—an important find.

Also in the course of their investigations they bumped into young Loeb and incidentally got from him a chance statement that was proved of great value later.

"If I was going to kill any kid," said Loeb to Goldstein, "I'd pick just such a fresh little——as that Franks kid."

Yesterday saw their supreme triumph. While rival reporters and detectives were pounding their skulls for a hunch on Leopold and Loeb, Goldstein and Mulroy went out to the University of Chicago campus and scouted about until they had found samples of typewriting done by Leopold on the very typewriter that produced the kidnapers' ransom letter.

They turned the stuff over to the police (after reporting their scoop, of course) and then, still forgetting sleep, they rounded up four college witnesses who popped into the case along about midnight to break down the alibis and the nerve of the two kidnapers.

They were there at the Criminal Court Building all night and they were still on the job at daybreak with volumes of exclusive material for their paper's first edition.

• • •

The typewriter proved the crucial clue. Loeb and Leopold were convicted of murder, saved from execution only by the eloquence and effectiveness of famed attorney Clarence Darrow's plea against the death penalty. Loeb was killed in a prison fight. Leopold was paroled after thirty years.

In 1963, Gene Goltz, then a reporter for the *Houston Post,* was nosing around Pasadena, Texas,

a Houston suburb, when he was told by a citizen that there was a good story in what had happened to $6 million that the residents of Pasadena had voted in a bond issue in 1959.

Goltz, thirty-three at the time he worked on this story, came relatively late to the business. He served in the U.S. Air Force and attended St. Louis University and the University of Missouri before deciding, at age twenty-seven, to become a newspaperman. He first worked at the Tama (Iowa) *News-Herald,* starting at forty-two dollars a week, and then at other newspapers in Iowa and Arizona before joining the *Houston Post* in 1961.

Goltz had solid reporting instincts. As he began his investigation, as John Hohenberg wrote in *The New Front Page* in 1966, he was "fended off, given double talk, and denied access to city records." Goltz knew he was on to something.

Here is an extract from Goltz's first article on the matter.

"City Records Hard to Get in Pasadena," by Gene Goltz. *Houston Post,* November 4, 1963.

"Abandon all hope, ye who enter here." At least, abandon hope for information.

I sometimes think this sign should be erected in front of the Pasadena City Hall. The reason is that the ordinary citizen of Pasadena is not always welcome at the City Hall if he has come to look at the public records. He is likely to get a reception that ranges from a laughing brushoff to cold hospitality.

I know. I have tried. And I am a citizen of Pasadena as well as a reporter. The right of the citizen to know how his city is being run is often flouted in Pasadena.

I found this to be true during a weary and hopeless search that lasted for six months. I was searching for the records that would show how the city of Pasadena disposed of [the] $6 million bond money that the people voted in 1959.

I started looking last April when a man pulled me aside after a commissioners' meeting and said, "if you really want a story, why don't you try to find out where that $6 million bond fund went?"

He made two points: 1) That I would not be able to find out; 2) That the city commissioners didn't know themselves. He was pretty much right on both counts.

Before I was through investigating, however, it became clear that the bond issue had receded into the background. The thing that had become increasingly disturbing was the fact that it is harder for the citizen to examine records in the Pasadena City Hall than it would be for him to break into King Saud's harem.

There is not room here for me to detail the countless journeys I made to City Hall trying to get a look at bond fund records, and later trying to get a look at the minutes of past commission meetings. There is room, though, to tell about two of those experiences.

In those first months, it was more of a joke than anything else. Often I would stick my head into one or another of the commissioners' offices and yell, "Where is that $6 million?"

After a while, of course, it ceased to be funny. One time I went into the office of George Smith, the city engineer, and asked him. "I don't know if I should tell you," he said frankly.

In the Pasadena City Hall, all roads eventually lead to the mayor. Mayor James L. Brammer told me frankly once that the city's secretary would never let anybody see any records unless the mayor gave him permission. "If he did, I'd fire him, and he knows it," the mayor said.

The bond issue was passed in 1959 and that was only four years ago. When I had some free time, I went back to Pasadena City Hall determined to get to the bottom of the bond records.

I was ushered into the mayor's office and we talked noncommittally for a while. Then I mentioned the bonds and said I still wanted to look at the minutes. The mayor got up and closed the door. Then he told me that when somebody gets after him, he never forgets it.

"You might get me, but I'll tell you one thing," Brammer said. "I'll get you. It might cost me $3,000 but I'll do it."

He told me that he had friends in high places "reaching all the way to Washington" and that they wouldn't stand for the mayor of Pasadena being harassed by any newspaper....

• • •

Goltz continued what would be a two-year investigation. He sought not only what had happened to the bond money, but who—and what—was at the bottom of the mess in Pasadena. He was treated badly for his troubles. An angry city commissioner once socked Goltz in the nose outside a grand jury room. But Goltz persevered and in 1964, because of his work, indictments were handed up against several Pasadena city officials and changes were made in how the Pasadena government handled its money. The Harris County Grand Jury report into the fraud and mismanagement that helped fritter away the $6 million said, "The fact of this case is that Gene Goltz, a *Houston Post* reporter, through his diligent and devoted efforts to report the news, was the prime factor in triggering our investigation. The information developed by the persistent Mr. Goltz has comprised the basis for a substantial part of our total investigation. We highly commend Mr. Goltz for his courage and diligent reporting and we feel that he is deserving of commendation by all citizens for his endeavor to make this community a better place in which to live."

Gene Miller of the *Miami Herald* had already gotten two people convicted of murder out of prison when he came upon the case of Freddie Pitts and Wilbert Lee. The first person he had gotten free was Mary Katherin Hampton, who had been convicted in Louisiana in 1960 for two murders. Miller proved that she had been several hundred miles away at the time of the killing, and she was set free. New evidence in the case of an airman who had been convicted of murder in Miami led to his retrial and acquittal. But those cases were relatively simple compared to the case of Freddie Pitts and Wilbert Lee, two black soldiers who had been convicted in 1963 of robbing and murdering two white service station attendants. Pitts and Lee were sentenced to death.

"Two Face Death for Murders I Committed," by Gene Miller. *Miami Herald,* February 5, 1967.

On the hot afternoon of Aug. 28, 1963, two Negro men stood before a Circuit Court judge in Gulf County. Deliberately, the judge pronounced sentence.

"And may God have mercy on your soul," said Judge W. L. Fitzpatrick.

The two Negroes had pleaded guilty. From the witness stand they had asked for mercy and "confessed" to the murders of two gasoline station attendants from Port St. Joe.

"You, Freddie L. Pitts, shall be delivered forthwith to the Florida State Prison at Raiford . . . and at the time so designated the person lawfully authorized to do so shall pass through your body a current of electricity of such intensity to cause your immediate death . . ." the judge had read.

Freddie L. Pitts said nothing.

"You, Wilbert Lee, alias Slingshot Lee," the judge began to read again. The words were identical.

"And may God have mercy on your soul."

Now, 3½ years later, there is a detailed confession to the same two murders from another man, Curtis Adams Jr.

There is substantial reason to believe this new Adams confession is totally valid. For seven weeks, Warren D. Holmes, Miami polygraph-criminologist, and this newspaper reporter have subjected the confession to hard corroboration.

Through Maurice Rosen, the appellate lawyer

for the two convicted men, the attorney general of Florida and police and prosecutor in Gulf County have been so informed. They are yet to act.

Adams is in the Broward County Jail now awaiting sentence for the 1963 murder of another gasoline station attendant, Floyd Early McFarland.

Pitts and Lee, kept alive by legal technicality, remain on Death Row at Raiford, professing to anyone who will listen that they are innocent men convicted of murders neither committed.

In the long and hot summer of 1963 it had taken only 28 days for white police, prosecutor, jury and judge to jail, indict, try, convict, sentence and deposit on Death Row two black men. . . .

Not until one night a few weeks ago in the Broward County Jail did Curtis Adams Jr. tell exactly what he knew about those murders.

Adams, 35, is a lanky crewcut man of 6 feet 2, 160 to 170 pounds. His nickname is "Boo." He is an imprisoned armed robber.

And since December 1966, he is the confessed killer of Floyd Early McFarland.

McFarland, 59, had been abducted from a gasoline station just outside Fort Lauderdale in the early hours of Aug. 16, 1965. He, too, was found shot to death in the skull on a canal bank about 12 miles from where he worked.

The murder of McFarland and those in Port St. Joe are almost identical.

Adams is from Port St. Joe. He went through the sixth grade there, and his father, a brother and a sister still live there. All, in fact, live within a few blocks of the Mo Jo station.

[In 1964, Adams was in jail in Key West for robbing a Beneficial Finance office of $547.]

To startled detectives there, Adams announced he "knowed how to clear" a murder if he could talk to Sheriff Byrd Parker in Gulf County. This conversation is verified.

He told them his mother was dying and he

wanted to go home to Port St. Joe. He was afraid he would never see her again.

Key West police allowed him to telephone Sheriff Parker.

"I told him I knew who killed Jesse Burkett and Grover Floyd and that all I wanted was for me to be took up where I could see my mother for two or three days," Adams now says.

"He told me that I didn't know what I was talking about, he already had two niggers in Raiford waiting on the chair for it, that they had confessed."

The news stunned Adams. . . .

The first indication that something might be wrong with the Port St. Joe convictions went unpursued for almost two years.

[In January 1966, an inmate who had done time with Adams told a deputy sheriff that Adams had told him he had killed McFarland and two men in Port St. Joe. Adams, questioned again, tried to put the blame on his former girlfriend and another man. A Miami polygraph expert, Warren D. Holmes, was called in to question the woman, and from what she said, Holmes and some detectives became convinced that Adams had been involved in the Port St. Joe murders. Under questioning by Holmes, Adams confessed and gave a detailed account of the killings.]

"What were your thoughts when you knew that two men had been convicted of killing Burkett and Floyd?" Holmes asked. "Did you wonder how the law could have made a mistake on this case?"

"Yeah," said Adams. "I wondered how they can take a man and punish him and all and make him confess to something that he didn't do.

"And from what the state attorney told me in Port St. Joe and what I read in the paper and all, people had to get up and swear lies on account of the men. They're just as innocent as you are."

"It must be a strange feeling to know that you killed two people and yet two other people have been convicted for what you did," said Holmes.

"Sure it is," said Adams. "It makes you wonder a lot of times, especially when you try to clear it up one time and you can't get anybody to listen to you.

"They all think you're a damn idiot or something else.

"They haven't got—I don't know how to put it. They haven't got the guts or anything to admit that they have done something wrong and try to straighten it out.

"And that's all they're doing up there, they just hate to admit that they are wrong and they have got two wrong men up there, and they're just not man enough to stand up and say it."

Told of the Adams statement in the Panhandle, Sheriffs Byrd Parker and M. J. Daffin and Deputy White responded almost identically.

"I wouldn't pay 10 cents to fly to Broward County to interview Boo Adams," said Deputy White. "There is no doubt in my mind that Boo didn't do it."

• • •

Miller's enthusiasm for reporting was infectious. On assignment with colleagues, he would review the results of a day's work and, when he thought it was appropriate, he would proclaim "Good stuff!" Thus, on assignment with Knight Ridder reporters in spring 1970, following the killings of students at Kent State protesting the U.S. invasion of Cambodia, he earned the nickname, "Good Stuff Miller."

He needed enthusiasm on the Port St. Joe story. Miller worked on freeing Pitts and Lee for eight and a half years, with the full support of his paper, which printed 130 columns on the case. Neither the sheriff nor the district attorney was helpful. At one point, Miller discovered evidence that a woman who said she had been a witness had recanted her testimony, but the state had not told the defendants' attorneys. That led to a new trial. Pitts and Lee were convicted again, and again sentenced to death. But Miller wrote on. In 1975, the new governor of Florida, Reuben Askew, took a fresh looks at the murders and granted a full pardon. Pitts and Lee walked out of prison in September 1975, twelve years and forty-eight days after they had been jailed.

At the end of the 1970s, Miller reported that all four of the people he had helped free were "well, independent, employed and, most important, lawful."

In July 1998, almost thirty-five years after the crime, the State of Florida compensated Pitts and Lee with $500,000 each for false imprisonment. "Persistence counts," Miller said.

THE *MONTGOMERY (ALABAMA) ADVERTISER* TELLS HOW EXPERIMENTAL DRUGS ARE TESTED ON PRISON INMATES

Like many state governments, the state of Alabama tried to balance punishment and cost in dealing with its prisoners. The state got its first penitentiary in 1841, but leased out convicts to build railroads, mine coal, work in timber and turpentine, work in the cotton mills, work on road camps. Leasing contracts were ended in 1893. But the idea of prisoners as a ready source of cheap labor did not.

An updated version started playing out in the 1960s, when the Board of Corrections agreed that prisoners could be used by a medical research company for drug testing.

The program came to public attention through the work of Harold E. Martin. Martin, who began his journalism career working as a printer in 1941, went back to his home state of Alabama as publisher of the *Montgomery Advertiser* in 1963. In 1969, with the help of a private investigator, and overcoming "considerable static, threats and pressures," he came to the defense of prisoners against a prominent citizen.

"Private Firm Here Uses Convicts for Drug Test," by Harold E. Martin. *Montgomery Advertiser,* January 10, 1969.

A food and drug research corporation operated by two local physicians grossed in excess of $500,000 in 1967 by conducting experiments on Alabama prisoners for major pharmaceutical companies.

In doing so, they had expenses of only $30,000 for drugs and $78,000 in salaries, while passing out $105,000 in fees to the inmates who participated in the program. (The inmates receive $1 for each blood draw and lesser amounts for taking experimental drugs.)

Southern Food and Drug Research, Inc., is located at 306 Arthur St. in Montgomery. Dr. A. R. Stough is president, Dr. Irl Long is vice president and Mrs. Elva Moore is secretary-treasurer. Dr. Long also draws $942 per month from the state as the physician at Kilby Prison.

Drs. Stough and Long have complete access to the prisoners at Draper, Kilby and Julia Tutwiler Prisons. The testing program is in the process of being expanded to Atmore.

The pharmaceutical concerns for whom the testing is conducted are among the largest in the nation, including such well-known names as Lederle, Upjohn, Merck Sharpe & Dohme, Bristol-Myers, and Wyeth Laboratories.

The minutes of the Board of Corrections show that Dr. A. R. Stough of the Oklahoma Penitentiary and Stough Research Corp. first appeared before the Alabama Board of Corrections at the October, 1962, meeting and asked for permission to start a blood plasma program similar to one Stough was operating at the State Institution at McAlister, Okla. Stough Research also operated a blood program in the Arkansas prison system.

At the November, 1962, meeting the program was adopted and the blood program was begun at Kilby, Drager and Atmore. The blood program soon was expanded to include medical research projects.

In the blood program, a quart of blood was drained from the arm of an inmate, the plasma separated from the red and white cells, the cells reconstituted with a saline solution and returned to the veins of the donor.

The process took 23 minutes and the man was sent back to work immediately.

In 1964, an outbreak of hepatitis was fatal to three prisoners. Nineteen others were hospitalized and the blood program was stopped.

Commissioner of Prisons Frank Lee said he had discontinued the plasma program for three reasons: "First, if it was causing the jaundice and was harmful to the men, we wanted it stopped; second, so many men were feeling bad from jaundice that we were short of workers; and third, the inmates were just making a little too much money."

Southern Food and Drug Research paid a total of $5 for the blood. Four dollars went to the inmate and $1 went to the Prison Welfare Fund. Estimates are that the blood was then sold for $35 to $40 per pint.

When the blood plasma program was stopped, the drug testing program was stepped up.

Last year a new building was constructed at Draper for use in the testing program. The research firm furnished the materials and prisoners did the work. The building consists of a modern laboratory facility and a room for keeping the prisoners when controlled programs are being conducted.

There are presently 30 men in the room undergoing a testing program. Several of the prisoners were playing cards when they were observed this week and some were watching television while others lay in their bunks. They appeared not to feel up to par. A prison inmate was drawing blood.

Two civilian medical technicians were at work in the laboratory. No one was in the room with the prisoners. No doctor was present.

The type of research being done at the prisons is that of testing human tolerance of dosages of new drugs, comparisons of one company's drugs against another's, blood glucose and drug level studies following doses of certain medication, etc.

A protocol (program) is set out by the pharmaceutical houses and followed in the experiments. Pills are given, injections are made, numerous blood samples, urine specimens, stool specimens, etc., are taken. Side effects are noted and graded as to their severity.

In the last few months, testicle, liver, kidney and thyroid biopsies have been performed, according to Commissioner Lee.

The experiments, though carried out for profit by a private concern, are similar to those carried out by a medical school, but with several important differences. Unlike volunteers at a medical school, prisoners who otherwise receive only 50 cents every three weeks would do almost anything for money.

Many of the protocols call for an informed consent form. The inmates sign a waiver, but they say that they have not been told of the possible effects of the tests.

According to the inmates, a physical examination is not performed before each program, as required by the protocol. A doctor is not present during many of the potentially critical periods of reaction. . . .

Dr. Stough has complete access to the inmates of Draper, Kilby and Julia Tutwiler for his firm's experimental purposes. A manifest from him is honored regardless of the need for work or training to be carried on at the institutions.

Some of the experiments leave the men too sick to perform their regular duties.

Commissioner Lee said Thursday that the Board of Corrections "leaves it up to Stough to determine the amount of money paid to the prisoners for various tests." He said they had no contract, only an oral agreement with the research firm. When asked if the prison has a record of signed waivers, he said it did not; that Dr. Stough had said he would assume any claims that might be made.

Lee said the program was discussed at the last two board meetings. "The board is thoroughly familiar with the operation and approves of the program unreservedly," he said. He added that he personally likes it because "the boys get extra money."

It is Lee's opinion that the testing program, like the blood plasma program, "is a service to the people outside (the public) that can't be fulfilled any other way." This, he said, "is the board's position."

Asked about the side effects on the prisoners, Lee answered: "To my knowledge there has been no reaction from any experiment."

Questioned about a rumor that the experimental program is going to be expanded to include foods, Commissioner Lee said that this was not true.

"The prison is going to build a new kitchen and dining room," Lee added, "and Dr. Stough is going to donate $7,000 toward the cost of equipping it."

• • •

Under pressure resulting from Martin's article, the state of Alabama canceled the drug-testing program.

THE *PHILADELPHIA INQUIRER* BREAKS POLICE SILENCE ON DUBIOUS CONFESSIONS

Frank L. Rizzo had a reputation as a tough, law-and-order police commissioner in Philadelphia, and as a man who pretty much set his own definition of law and order. With Rizzo as mayor of the city in the 1970s, the police department logically expected that it would receive full backing from city hall.

Like many big-city police departments, Phila-

delphia's was showing strains. Police were visible in the downtown, tourist area of the city. But in the poorer, minority neighborhoods, they were less often seen, and when they were, they were often feared. In particular, some neighborhood residents charged that the way the homicide squad settled its cases was by beating confessions out of suspects.

The *Philadelphia Inquirer* investigated.

"At the Roundhouse: How Detectives Compel Murder 'Confessions,' " by Jonathan Neumann and William K. Marimow. *Philadelphia Inquirer,* April 24, 1977

It can be said with certainty that two things happened in the 22 hours between Carlton Coleman's arrest and his arraignment last October.

One is that he was interrogated by homicide detectives. The other is that his health went from good to poor. When it was all over, he spent the next 28 days hospitalized for injuries of the abdomen, arms, shoulders, chest, calf, spine, and back.

Medical problems are not rare among those interrogated by the Philadelphia Police Department's 84-member homicide division. In fact, a four-month investigation by the *Inquirer* has found a pattern of beatings, threats of violence, intimidation, coercion, and knowing disregard for constitutional rights in the interrogation of homicide suspects and witnesses.

The study shows that many homicide detectives, in beating or coercing suspects and later denying it under oath, have come to accept breaking the law as part of their job.

As a result of those practices, the *Inquirer* has found, there are cases in which murders have remained unsolved, killers have gone free, and innocent men have been imprisoned.

From 1974 through this month, judges of the Common Pleas Court have been asked to rule in pretrial hearings on the legality of police investigations in 433 homicide cases. Those rulings require the judge to decide who is telling the truth—the police or the suspect. In most cases, the judge believes the police.

In 80 of those cases however, judges have ruled that the police acted illegally during homicide interrogations. The judges found in many cases that police had used either physical or psychological coercion. In some cases, the victims' injuries were documented by X-rays, medical records, and photographs.

Extensive interviews with homicide detectives and prosecutors who work with detectives every day confirm these findings. The interviews—including some with detectives who frequently have been accused of beatings—make it clear that top officials in the Police Department know of and tolerate the coercive measures.

The illegal interrogations follow a pattern:

• They are conducted by teams of detectives in tiny rooms at police headquarters—known as the Roundhouse—at Eighth and Race Streets. The suspect or witness is often handcuffed to a metal chair, which is bolted to the floor. Some of these sessions have lasted 24 hours.

• Some of the techniques used in the beating leave no severe marks. Those techniques include placing a telephone book on a suspect's head and hammering it with a heavy object; beating his feet and ankles; twisting or kicking his testicles; and pummeling his back, ribs, and kidneys.

• Other techniques do leave marks. Testimony about interrogations that judges have ruled illegal has shown that suspects have been beaten with lead pipes, blackjacks, brass knuckles, handcuffs, chairs, and table legs. One suspect was stabbed in the groin with a sword-like instrument.

• The detectives make use of one-way mirrors through which the interrogation rooms can be observed. Suspects and witnesses have testified that they were forced to watch beatings through such windows and were told that they would receive the same treatment unless they cooperated.

"What we're living in at the Roundhouse," a former homicide detective said, "is a return to the Middle Ages. All this nonsense about the 'thin blue line between society and the underworld,' it's bull——. Police are breaking the law every day, and they know it."

Why are detectives doing this?

The main reason, detectives say, is outrage—outrage at the heinousness of the crimes they investigate, and outrage at a court system that allows murderers to "walk," or go free.

"It's a fight every day," one detective said. "The homicide detective must fight the lawyers, the judges, the Supreme Court—and he must fight crime."

But there is also another reason: money.

To get a statement from a suspect, a detective often works round the clock—and that means overtime. Once he gets a statement, he becomes a court witness—and court time means more overtime.

City payroll records show that the average homicide detective got $7,575 in overtime pay last year. One, Michael Chitwood, more than doubled his base pay, earning a total of $36,293, which is higher than the salary of Police Commissioner Joseph F. O'Neill.

Do high police officials know about the crimes in the interrogation room?

They, like all citizens, have access to court records, including the 80 recent homicide cases in which interrogations have been ruled illegal. They also work extremely closely with the elite homicide division.

In one case, testimony by an assistant district attorney showed that a homicide investigation was under the direct supervision of Commissioner O'Neill and Chief Inspector Joseph Golden, who set up a temporary "command post" office at the Roundhouse.

In that case, a judge later concluded, a suspect named Larry Howard was beaten. Howard testified that he was hit with a lead pipe, punched with brass knuckles and handcuffs, and grabbed by the testicles. Another suspect, Richard Atkins, testified that he was forced to watch Howard's interrogation through a one-way mirror.

Within the Police Department, there is constant pressure to get suspects to talk. Detectives say that Chief Inspector Golden has a standing order to the homicide division: "Get a statement."

At times, the emphasis on getting statements can produce odd results.

On Jan. 19, when a North Philadelphia shopkeeper named George Lewis was murdered during a holdup, investigators determined that he had been killed by a single bullet.

Homicide detectives questioned two suspects, and by the time they emerged from their respective interrogation rooms, each had allegedly admitted firing the shot. Their cases are pending.

So far this year judges have heard 31 formal allegations of illegal interrogations and have ruled for the defendant 11 times.

One case that is expected to come up in 1977 is that of Carlton Coleman, the man who was hospitalized for 28 days after his interrogation. Coleman, 26, is charged with shooting an off-duty policeman. He allegedly signed a confession, but he is expected to argue that he was beaten and coerced.

Does the Police Department care that murder cases are lost because illegal "confessions" are thrown out?

As individuals, the police care very much. But their concern does not carry over into the department's official gauge of its effectiveness—the rate at which murder cases are "cleared." A "cleared" case is one in which someone is charged with the crime—but not necessarily convicted.

The department is proud that it has "cleared"

nearly 87 percent of its cases in recent years. But 20 percent of the homicide defendants who went to court last year were acquitted or were freed because the district attorney's office dropped the charges for lack of evidence.

An example of a murder that was "cleared," but apparently not solved, is the well-known Santiago firebombing case. As the *Inquirer* reported in November, the police rounded up seven neighbors, beat the men, threatened the women, and forced them to sign false statements implicating Robert (Reds) Wilkinson in five murders. He was convicted, but the verdict was overturned when another man, David McGinnis, confessed.

Why are homicide detectives not forced to obey the law?

No homicide detective has been prosecuted in recent years—if ever—for a crime committed during an interrogation. This apparent immunity can be explained in part by the detectives' close working relationship with the district attorney's office.

Prosecutors depend on the police for testimony and cooperation in presenting evidence. If the district attorney's office were to press criminal charges against detectives, the cooperation could collapse.

In the 80 cases in which judges have ruled interrogations illegal, the record shows that the police do not discriminate: The victims have been white and black, guilty and innocent. Women, too, have been coerced and threatened, but the *Inquirer* has seen no testimony that women have been beaten in interrogations.

Judges hearing these cases have taken extensive testimony and examined documentary evidence, including photographs, X-rays, and other medical records, before making formal findings of fact.

Based on these cases, here are several incidents from the Roundhouse interrogation rooms:

William Hoskins, 23, a black murder suspect, was handcuffed to a metal chair bolted to the floor. During an interrogation by homicide detectives Michael Chitwood, John Strohm, Daniel Rosenstein, and Rosborough McMillan, Hoskins was stabbed in the groin with a sword-like instrument and blackjacked on his feet, ankles, and legs until the blackjack broke in two.

Lawyers present on the scene that night—Nov. 5, 1975—said Hoskins was carried out of the Roundhouse and driven by police to Philadelphia General Hospital, where he was carried in on a stretcher.

Medical records show that Hoskins could not stand up when he was admitted to the hospital's emergency ward. Doctors wrote that Hoskins suffered severe injuries to his kidneys, that he was urinating blood, and that the left side of his body, from his shoulders to his buttocks, was swollen and bruised. The prisoner, handcuffed to his hospital bed, was placed on intravenous feeding and remained at the hospital for five days.

Common Pleas Court Judge Samuel Smith ruled that the Hoskins interrogation was illegal, "There is no question he was beaten," Judge Smith said in an interview. "This guy was hurt bad."

Hoskins was later convicted of murder. The verdict is being appealed.

Richard Rozanski, 28, a white murder suspect, was kicked in the testicles and beaten on the back with a wooden chair by Detective Richard Strohm. He was punched on the head and face by Detective George Cassidy until he was "numb," Rozanski testified.

That same night—Dec. 22, 1975—Detective Strohm approached Rozanski's brother-in-law, Joey Kedra, 22, who was in another interrogation room. According to court testimony, Strohm pointed a gun at Kedra's head and said: "I'm going to blow your motherf——ing brains out, Punch."

Judge James R. Cavanaugh ruled that the 17-hour interrogation of Rozanski was illegal and that the defendant had been "subjected to physical and mental threats and coercion. . . ."

Judge Cavanaugh made his ruling after reviewing photographs and hearing the testimony of Rozanski, homicide detectives, and Dr. Daniel Jacobs, who examined Rozanski a day after his interrogation.

Last July, after spending six months in prison, Rozanski was acquitted by a jury in Common Pleas Court. The murder of Joseph Lucano Jr. remains unsolved.

● ● ●

The *Inquirer* articles led the U.S. district attorney to call a grand jury to investigate. Mayor Rizzo vehemently denied the newspaper's charges and said he was sure the police would be exonerated; the police department cooperated with the grand jury only reluctantly. Within months, six officers had been indicted, and a dozen more indictments were expected. The first three officers to go to trial were acquitted by an all-white, mostly suburban jury.

REGINALD STUART IN *EMERGE* MAGAZINE WRITES OF UNFAIRNESS OF MANDATORY MINIMUM SENTENCES, AND A WOMAN IS FREED FROM PRISON

Faced with increasing drug use in the last part of the twentieth century, federal lawmakers reacted in the way politicians wary of being called soft on crime could be expected to: They built more prisons and passed mandatory minimum sentencing rules that took all discretion away from judges. Under the Omnibus Anti-Drug Abuse Act of 1986, first-time offenders involved in drug trafficking would be treated like veterans, nonviolent offenders like violent ones, and minor figures like kingpins. All that mattered was the amount of drugs involved, not the circumstances of the crime or the previous record of the defendants. Inevitably, some people got caught up in a situation where justice for all was not justice for one.

Reginald Stuart broke the story of such a case in *Emerge* magazine in May 1996.

"Kemba's Nightmare," by Reginald Stuart. *Emerge,* May 1996.

It is 6:30 A.M., and Kemba Naimbi Smith is preparing for another day in her new life, one that could go down in history books. An attractive, petite and shy 24-year-old, Kemba has received one of the nation's longest prison sentences for being a two-bit player in a drug ring: one year in prison for each of the 24 years she has lived. No chance for parole.

That amounts to tough justice, particularly for a first-time, nonviolent offender, one who even prosecutors say never handled or used the cocaine she was convicted of trafficking and one who received little benefit from its sale. Tough, tough justice, particularly when one hears of the beatings she received form the man she admired, loved and obeyed, the real player in the cocaine trafficking group. It's tough, but is it justice?

Kemba is now inmate #26370-083 and, like a growing number of intelligent, middle-class, African-American woman and men, is paying hard time for being young, naïve and running with the wrong crowd—cocaine dealers—when the "drug war" is big politics and the judicial system is on automatic pilot. Under legislative orders called mandatory minimums, judges are locking up the drug crowd for a long time, regardless of the role any one individual plays.

Kemba is part of the fastest-growing population in the U.S. prison system—the rate of criminal justice supervision for African-American women rose by 78 percent from 1989 to 1994. The number of African-American women in state prisons on drug-related charges has soared 828 percent from 1986 to 1991, according to the October 1995 report by The Sentencing Project, "Young Black Americans and the Criminal Justice System: Five Years Later."

Barring some dramatic act of mercy by the Jus-

tice Department or some miraculous change of heart by a law-and-order Congress and president, Kemba may not see freedom until at least 2016. That's five presidential elections from now, 10 congressional contests from now, 20 homecoming games from now, 20 college graduations from now. Her high school dream of becoming a business executive is but a fading memory.

It took less than three years for Kemba's life in the Tidewater area of Southeastern Virginia to change. She went from outgoing high school student in suburban Richmond, Va., to main "mule" (carrying money and weapons) for a drug dealer preying on students at Hampton University, a historically Black institution in Virginia, to near-lifetime resident of the federal prison system. How she got there is a story of tough love, too much love and no love at all.

"Even today it gives me headaches," says Kemba from the Federal Corrections Institution for Women in Danbury, Conn. She is dressed in her standard issue Army brown pants and mint green shirt. She is soft-spoken and shy, and only occasionally flashes a smile that spreads across her face. Still coming to grips with what has happened, Kemba is dismayed at her past actions. "It's unbelievable. I was part of it. Right in the middle. And all along, I'm thinking, 'I'm not doing anything wrong or wrong enough to go to jail.'"

Kemba wasn't born wealthy. But she defies the stereotype of most women imprisoned on drug charges. She was born into a solidly middle-class family. She wasn't an addict who sold drugs or committed other crimes to feed her habit. Her background was not that of a poor, inner-city youngster surrounded by the drug culture and with few life choices. She was reared in a comfortable home in the suburbs by parents who are professionals and who nurtured and loved her, gave her guidance and rules to follow. Kemba seemed to have had all the middle-class advantages that are associated with rearing a happy, successful child. Apparently, they weren't enough.

Her parents, William and Odessa Smith, native Virginians, were college sweethearts who were reared by loving parents with values rooted in the Baptist church. The law-abiding couple has worked hard and steady since their days at the Norfolk Division of Virginia State College, now Norfolk State University. . . .

After graduation in June 1989, Kemba attended the pre-college program, then enrolled in Hampton [University] that fall. Her mother and father helped her move in, making her dorm room "feel like home," stocking it with a color TV and microwave oven.

Pre-college classes had given Kemba a good head start. And indeed, there was a lot more freedom. She made new friends that summer and earned a B grade-point average. By fall, however, when regular classes started, it took only a few days for her to feel she was out of her element.

"When I went to Hampton, and you're surrounded by a bunch of pretty girls, for some reason I felt I really didn't deserve to go to Hampton," says Kemba, wondering aloud whether her father pulled strings to get her admitted. She was an average high school student who didn't blow the roof off the college admissions test.

Self-image suddenly became a problem.

"I had gone to predominantly White schools. In those settings, I thought I was pretty. When I went to Hampton, I didn't feel I was equal to the next pretty girl because I saw them as more popular. . . . I wasn't sure of myself; my self-esteem was low. I would just look in the mirror and wonder why people were not as attracted to me and why I couldn't be popular."

Kemba's look in the mirror reflected the wrong signal—that she was a loser. Lost at sea without an anchor, she became obsessed with trying to belong. It did not take long for the "bad guys" to find her.

[Kemba started going with Peter Michael Hall, a flashy dresser and partygoer from New York who was eight years older than she was. He had fancy cars and a fancy apartment, and only slowly did Kemba learn how he got them. By that time, she had basically abandoned her studies and changed schools to do whatever Hall said. In part this was because he would beat her if she didn't, but mostly it was because she loved him.]

By Christmas, Kemba had withdrawn from Johnson C. Smith and enrolled in nearby Central Piedmont Community College, trying to keep her eye on finishing school while keeping Peter and her parents happy. Kemba would spend some time at home during the Christmas break and some time in Newport News [where Hall was living].

"I fell apart a lot. I would get on my knees and ask God to help me because I didn't know what to do. I really loved Peter, but it didn't seem like I could just get up and leave. My dad [subsequently] has told me he would see my crying and on my knees. And my mother would ask what was wrong, and I would say, 'There's something going on,' but I didn't go in depth. They knew something was wrong. I was always going out to call Peter but lying to them about where I was going. I hated it. I felt alone."

In February 1993, Peter was arrrested in New York on state drug possession charges. Again, Kemba was drafted into service. A friend and a relative of Peter's contacted her in Charlotte and asked her to help get him out of jail. The next day, she was in New York and "I find out what's really going on." Peter had been arrested for carrying 10 ounces of crack in a taxicab, according to prosecutors during federal court testimony. His bail was $75,000. Kemba could help by delivering an envelope to a man in Brooklyn. She did as she was told.

"To me, I didn't know where it came from. It wasn't my money. My thing was to help Peter get out of jail. For some reason, I felt I was whole if we were together. I was crazy. I was scared of him, but I loved him. I just wanted to help. And I didn't want to be away from him. One thing you've got to understand is that Peter talked a lot and made sure he knew what you were thinking and tried to control how you thought."...

By May 1993, things got even stranger. The woman who had consoled Kemba after the bathtub incident [a time when Peter beat her] arrived in Charlotte with her belongings. So did Derrick Taylor. A few days later, Peter, Derrick and the other woman, known to others in the group as Peter's "gangsta bitch" (his partner), packed for a road trip. Kemba was not happy that the woman was going, but she dared not confront Peter about it. After all, Kemba saw the two as sister and brother, nothing more.

The next day, Peter and the woman returned without Derrick. According to the government's presentencing investigation for Kemba, Derrick was found dead in Dinwiddie County, Va., with bullet wounds in the head and neck. Peter then announced that he and the other woman were going to Atlanta.

"I don't understand what's going on. I'm scared. Peter calls later and tells me to get his two guns [also fake ID stamps, scales and other drug paraphernalia] and put them in storage. I was scared to ask what was going on. I don't know how to explain it. Then Peter tells me to come to Atlanta and check into a hotel."

As always, she complied.

"That's when he tells me what happened. [Kemba and others would testify later in federal court that Peter said he had killed Derrick Taylor]. I was shocked, upset, scared to react. I was already in confusion and that made everything a blur. He said he did it because Derrick was talking to the police, and he [Derrick] was going to rat him out and rat me out. I still managed to feel sorry for Peter because he was hurting. Peter wanted me to come home to talk to the police to see how much they knew since my parents had been talking to them. They wanted their daughter back. Their daughter wanted to be perfect, not coming home telling them her boyfriend murdered somebody."

By the summer of 1993, life for the suspected drug ring in which Kemba had been a minor player was beginning to unravel. Federal drug agents were turning up the heat on the operation, of which Kemba knew only pieces. The piece she did know about, however, was big.

According to the 16-count indictment filed with the United States Court for the Eastern District of Virginia in Norfolk, federal drug agents considered Peter Michael Hall and his brother, "Unique," leaders of a violent drug ring that moved as much as $4 million in cocaine and crack cocaine between New York and Virginia between 1989—the year Kemba finished high school—and 1993. The U.S. Marshals Service said in its December 1993 murder warrant that Peter was known to be armed and traveled "in the company of female associates who transport arms for him."

Federal drug agents believed Peter was in charge of operations in Virginia. He recruited college students, including Kemba and her girlfriends, to work as mules—some hauling hundreds of pounds of cocaine from New York to Virginia and carrying money from Virginia to New York. They were also getting cars and trucks and apartments in their names and justifying Peter's presence among college students by serving as girlfriends. Peter was also recruiting young men in and around the campuses to sell drugs, court documents say. Federal agents believed Peter was an enforcer; Derrick Taylor was one of several operatives allegedly murdered by Peter and his associates.

Kemba went home in June and was apprehended in the middle of the night by federal drug agents at her parents' home. Wanted as a material witness, Kemba was petrified, her mother was hysterical, her father was upset. Gus said federal officers had promised she would be able to turn herself in. Jailed for the first time in her life,

Kemba spent the night on the floor of the cell, scared and speechless....

• • •

Kemba refused to tell about Peter Hall and was released. In November 1993 she joined Hall in Atlanta. They went on the run, and she was out of touch with her parents for five months. During this time she became pregnant with Hall's child. Expecting a baby finally gave Kemba the incentive to leave Hall and go home. She turned herself in to federal authorities, but still wouldn't give up Peter. Then she heard word that Peter had been shot to death in Seattle. A few days later, Kemba pleaded guilty to conspiracy to distribute cocaine, lying to federal authorities, and conspiracy to launder drug money.

She gave birth to a son, William Armani, while in jail awaiting sentencing. She had some hope for leniency; a number of her girlfriends who had also been involved with Hall's activities had been released after cooperating with investigators. But the judge invoked the sentencing guidelines. Kemba was sentenced to twenty-four and a half years in jail. Stuart noted that Kemba's son, being raised by her parents, would be an adult before she was free.

The *Emerge* story sparked stories in other media and brought Kemba and her parents thousands of letters, some from young people caught up in similar situations who pledged to change their ways. The NAACP Legal Defense and Educational Fund saw the story and took her case. Kemba's parents began to tour college campuses speaking about the dangers of drugs and the unfairness of mandatory minimums. Others interested in changing mandatory minimums used Kemba's case as an example.

On December 22, 2000, after Kemba had served nearly seven years of her sentence, President Bill Clinton granted her clemency. Smith, twenty-nine, learned the news in the afternoon and was officially released at 5:29 P.M. That weekend, at church at home in Richmond, she wore a

dress for the first time since the day in April 1995 when she was sentenced.

One other thing, Stuart said. He heard from a number of parents who said they had given their children copies of his stories when they went off to college. "You never know the ripples," he said.

NORTHWESTERN UNIVERSITY STUDENT JOURNALISTS FREE AN INNOCENT MAN FROM DEATH ROW

Even people who believe in the death penalty are troubled by the idea that an innocent person might be wrongly executed. In the 1990s, nothing crystallized uncertainties about death-row convictions more than the fact that journalism students at Northwestern University in Evanston, Illinois— young people in their teens or early twenties, with no criminal investigation experience—found the evidence that cleared five people who had been convicted of murder, three of whom had been sentenced to be executed.

The Northwestern students were not naively wandering in the death-row wilderness. They were taking a class run by Professor David Protess, an experienced investigator who had uncovered fraud for Chicago's Better Government Association and checked out doubtful convictions for *Chicago Lawyer* magazine. Protess screened the cases he assigned the students, taught them about document trails and interview techniques, and worked with a private investigator and professional journalists at key points in the investigation.

In the fall of 1998, Protess assigned his students the case of Anthony Porter, who had been convicted of a 1982 double murder and had at one point been two days short of execution when the Illinois Supreme Court ruled that his mental competency (his IQ was 51) needed to be examined. "If you take that case," Protess told the students, "the stakes are going to be high, the pressure intense. . . . Anthony Porter could be dead before you reach your first final."

In established pattern, the students looked at trial testimony, court documents, and police reports; reenacted the crime, which made them doubt a key witness's testimony; interviewed the key witness, who said he had named Porter only after the police roughed him up; interviewed Porter in prison, where he gave them the name of a woman he thought might know who did it; tracked down the woman and then, with her testimony, confronted the man she named and obtained a confession.

Usually in Protess's class, the students file memos or write stories on the steps they took. This time, said one student, "things moved too fast."

A key witness, tracked down in Milwaukee, provided a handwritten affidavit that helped break the case.

My name is Margaret Inez Simon. I am over the age of twenty one year(s) old.

Being duly sworn on oath, I wish to make the following statement:

1) I currently live in the State of Wisconsin

2) In August of 1982, I was with Alstory Simon and we were living together at 5323 S. Federal, in Chicago, IL. Alstory had just recently gotten out of the penitentiary.

3) On the night of [a local] parade in August of 1982, Alstory Simon, myself, Jerry Hillard and Marilyn Green were together.

4) The four of us went to a liquor story on the corner of 55th + Garfield. We purchased some rum + Coke.

5) We then walked over to Washington Park on Garfield.

6) Upon our arrival at Washington Park the four of us Alstory, Marilyn and Jerry and I sat in the bleachers at the top, looking down at the pool.

7) The four of us were sitting there for maybe twenty minutes when Alstory and Jerry started arguing about money that Jerry had stolen from Alstory.

8) Jerry was selling drugs, crank or speed for Alstory.

9) Alstory had been complaining all day about Jerry ripping him off.

10) By the time, we got to the park Alstory was really angry.

11) Prior to getting to the park Alstory had been smoking weed and drinking rum.

12) All of a sudden I heard two gunshots.

13) I was shocked. I couldn't believe it.

14) Alstory grabbed me by the right arm by the elbow, and ripped me out of the bleachers.

15) Alstory was pulling me down the bleachers and walking and half running out of the bleacher and eventually out of the park.

16) Alstory stuffed the gun, a 38-caliber revolver into his pants pocket or waist band.

* * *

22) The next day Alstory and I left the South side of Chicago, eventually ending up in Milwaukee. We never returned.

23) I understand that this statement is being made to representatives of the defendant and journalists and not the state's attorney office or any police agency.

• • •

With the testimony from Simon, the students interviewed William Taylor, who had originally told police he had seen Porter shoot the two victims. Taylor was in the Danville Correctional Center when interviewed. He was aware that Porter was about to be executed but, he said, did not know exactly what to do about it. Then he got a letter from David Protess, whose work he was aware of. He called Protess back and was interviewed by three students. This statement was obtained:

I, William Andrew Taylor of 4128 N. Clarendon of Chicago, Illinois wish to make the following statement with regards to "The People of the State of Illinois vs. Anthony Porter."

In 1982 I was repeatedly interviewed by members of the Chicago Police Department. During the process I was threatened, harassed, and intimidated into naming Anthony Porter as a person who committed a Homicide in Washington Park in Chicago in August of 1982.

The truth is as follows:

1. I was present at the park when a shooting occurred.

2. I did not see Anthony Porter shoot anybody.

3. I never seen Anthony Porter with a gun.

4. I did not see who shot the victims that day.

I made prior statement in and out of court because that is what I know the police wanted.

I understand that this statement is being made to representatives of the defendant and not the State's Attorney office of any police agency.

•   •   •

In February 1999, after sixteen years, Porter became the tenth man freed from Illinois's death row since 1977, when the death penalty was reinstated in Illinois. In September 1999, Alstory Simon was convicted of the murders for which Porter had been about to die. "It's not that we are that good," Protess said. "Any kind of diligent effort in these cases could do what we did years later. Which is what is so outrageous about a college professor and his students solving these crimes. They were there to be solved from the start."

The students who worked on the Porter case were Shawn Armbrust, Tom McCann, Cara Rubinsky, Erica LeBorgne, Syandene Rhodes-Pitts, and Lori D'Angelo.

The work of Protess and his students, plus investigations by other Chicago media, including the *Chicago Tribune*, helped convince Governor George Ryan in January 2000 to put a moratorium on executions in Illinois. Ryan said he was a supporter of the death penalty but needed to be convinced that everyone to be executed was guilty as charged.

As of January 1, 2001, according to the Death Penalty Information Center, 3,726 prisoners were awaiting execution in the United States. As of March 2001, the center said, 701 people had been executed since the death penalty was federally reinstated in 1976. During that time, 95 people had been released with evidence of their innocence.

AMERICANA

GOLD IN CALIFORNIA

California had only two newspapers, both in San Francisco, and they were both less than two years old, when, on January 24, 1848, gold was discovered on the American River north of San Francisco. The first printed notice was in the *Californian* in March. Neither newspaper thought much of the story. "All sham," wrote E. C. Kemble, acting editor of the *California Star*, "a superb take-in, as was ever got up to guzzle the gullible." But more Californians believed the rumors of prospectors scooping up fortunes than believed the papers. The *Star,* reluctantly, changed its perspective.

"The excitement and enthusiasm of Gold Washing still continues—increases." *California Star,* June 10, 1848.

Many of our countrymen are not disposed to do us justice as regards the opinion we have at different times expressed of the employment in which over two thirds of the white population of the country are engaged. There appears to have gone abroad a belief that we should raise our voices against what some one has denominated an "infatuation." We are very far from it, and

would invite a calm recapitulation of our articles touching the matter, as in themselves amply satisfactory. We shall continue to report the progress of the work, to speak within bounds, and to approve, admonish, or openly censure whatever in our opinion, may require it at our hands.

It is quite unnecessary to remind our readers of the "prospects of California" at this time, as the effects of this gold washing enthusiasm, upon the country, through every branch of business are unmistakably apparent to every one. Suffice it that there is no abatement, and that active measures will probably be taken to prevent really serious and alarming consequences.

Every seaport as far south as San Diego, and every interior town, and nearly every rancho from the base of the mountains in which the gold has been found, to the Mission of San Luis, south, has become suddenly drained of human beings. Americans, Californians, Indians and Sandwich Islanders, men, women and children, indiscriminately. Should there be that success which has repaid the efforts of those employed for the last month, during the present and next, as many are sanguine in their expectations, and we confess to unhesitatingly believe probably, not only will witness the depopulation of every town, the desertion of every rancho, and the desolation of the once promising crops of the country, but it will also draw largely upon adjacent territories—awake

Sonora, and call down upon us, despite her Indian battles, a great many of the good people of Oregon. There are at this time over one thousand souls busied in washing gold, and the yield per diem may be safely estimated at from fifteen to twenty dollars, each individual.

We have by every launch from the embarcadera of New Helvetia, returns of enthusiastic gold seekers—heads of families, to effect transportation of their households to the scene of their successful labors, or others, merely returned to more fully equip themselves for a protracted, or perhaps permanent stay.

Spades, shovels, picks, wooden bowls, Indian baskets (for washing), etc., find ready purchase, and are very frequently disposed of at extortionate prices.

The gold region, so called, thus far explored, is about one hundred miles in length and twenty in width. These imperfect explorations contribute to establish the certainty of the placers extending much further south, probably three or four hundred miles, as we have before stated, while it is believed to terminate about a league north of the point at which first discovered. The probable amount taken from these mountains since the first of May last, we are informed, is $100,000, and which is at this time principally in the hands of the mechanical, agricultural and laboring classes.

There is an area explored, within which a body of 50,000 men can advantageously labor. Without maliciously interfering with each other, then, there need be no cause for contention and discord, where as yet, we are gratified to know, there is harmony and good feeling existing. We really hope no unpleasant occurrences will grow out of this enthusiasm, and that our apprehensions may be quieted by continued patience and good will among the washers.

• • •

"Pay up before you go," the *Star* urged its readers. "Papers can be forwarded to Sutter's Fort with all

regularity." Within days, the *Star,* acknowledging the rush of readers—and printers—to the gold claims, joined the *Californian* in temporarily suspending operation.

It is hard to believe, in this day of instant communication, but for months much of the rest of the country did not know about the gold find. News traveled between California and the East Coast in the same slow, arduous way that people did: either 3,000 miles by coach, train, horseback, and foot, or by boat around Cape Horn. Because so many sailors abandoned their posts to look for gold, it was the end of June before any ships headed for the East Coast with the news. The New York *Herald* learned of the gold strike in a letter from its California correspondent, Thomas Larkin, who had been the United States consul in Monterey when California was part of Mexico. Larkin sent along some gold flakes.

The first report in the *Herald* was on September 15, and it was a tease:

INTERESTING FROM CALIFORNIA—We have received some late and interesting intelligence from California. It is to the 1st of July. Owing to the crowded state of our columns, we are obliged to omit our correspondence. It relates to the important discovery of a very valuable gold mine. We have received a specimen of the gold.

Two days later, the *Herald* printed the letter, which had been sent from California on July 1.

"Interesting from California—The Discovery of Gold Mines."

My last to you was one month since. In that I gave you facts stronger than fiction, with the intimation that you and your thousands of *Herald* readers would not believe the statement. Were I a New Yorker, instead of a Californian, I would throw aside your paper and exclaim, Bennett had better fill his paper with, at least, probable tales and stories, and not such outrageous fictions of rivers, flowing with gold. However, for my own satisfaction, I will fall back upon the fact that the writer knows all he writes to be very near the truth and the many who know his signature, in particular the officers of the navy, will not doubt his statements of California. Oh! this California, to what will it come at last? Revolution after revolution, for years, have vacated your houses, and caused your fields to be deserted; and now, when we supposed that both houses and fields were occupied by another class of men, men whom nothing could remove—presto, a gold fever arises—strikes every one, and drives every one from his home. This writer, among others, has visited the golden country, this "Placer," in comparison to which the famous El Dorado is but a sand bank. The Arabian Nights tales of simplicity, are fit only for children; the walks of Irving's gold hunters are now brought to light which our great writer could never have dreamt of. Our territory is turned up-side down—people are leaving their wives and children and laughing at an offer of ten dollars per day to finish a contract. A mechanic says politely to his employer: "Sir, your wages were high, your conduct just and correct, but I am doing myself an injustice in remaining any longer hammering leather or jointing boards, at four or five dollars a day, when a week's ride brings me to the 'Placer', where an ounce and more of gold awaits each day's digging." The forge stops, the boards remain unplained, houses are closed, dinners uncooked, the sick recover, the plaintiff leaves his case untried, the defendant is gone, the Alcalde going, stores and hotels are closed—our newspapers stop, editors, clerks, lawyers, devils, clergymen, brickmakers, alcaldes, constables, soldiers, and sailors, some with a spade or pickaxe, others with a tin pan or wooden bowl, paid for at a thousand per cent on the former price, are forming partnerships, all bound to the American Fork and Feather River, branches of the Sacremento. Rivers whose banks and bottoms are filled with pure gold—where a Hingham bucket of dirt, with a half hour's washing in run-

ning water, produces a spoonful of black sand, containing from seven to ten dollars' worth of gold. At this minute, I can see in front of our hotel, the boarders on their last blow (the house closes to-morrow) playing in the open street with imaginary cups, bowls, pans, picks, crowbars and spades—digging gold with the highest glee; their hands and legs, heels and heads, moving in every known mode of a gold digger. The writer of this has seen, the past month, at these "diggins," fifty dollars demanded by a carpenter to leave his spade and take his plane and chisel, per day, and over a hundred dollars refused for a rough-made machine (to wash gold in) that was made by one man in a day. A spade or shovel sells for ten dollars; tin pans for the same, and flour at the rate of thirty-six dollars a barrel. A common day's work of a man turns out from five to thirty dollars; one hundred dollars has been obtained in one day. A machine put together, of a hundred feet of boards, in a day, and worked by a company of five men, some days yielded one pound of gold dust—the size of the grains differing from the point of a pin to a piece, worth six dollars. I have seen a piece worth sixteen dollars. A beer bottle will contain from fifteen to eighteen pounds, the filling of which, small as its compass is, occupied several weeks of the labor of one man. When one pound is saved, many pounds go down stream, from the imperfect mode of washing. . . . That the "Placer," of California, will bring into the country thousands and thousands of emigrants is clear.

• • •

Bennett followed his correspondent's report with other accounts picked up from other papers. After several months, he bothered to have the flakes his correspondent had sent him assayed. They turned out to be almost pure gold.

California historians say that almost half a million people from around the world flocked to the state in search of gold. They would have gone without newspaper reports, but the newspapers helped spread the word and gave a stamp of authority to the rumors. Sutter's Creek was supplemented by other finds, and by 1852 California was producing $81 million worth of gold. The Gold Rush lasted until 1864, by which time the gold from the surface and river placers had been exhausted. After that, extensive commercial mining operations were required.

HORACE GREELEY GOES WEST AND CALLS FOR CONSTRUCTION OF A TRANSCONTINENTAL RAILROAD

Journalism is a profession filled with characters, and Horace Greeley should place second to none.

Greeley was the most famous editor of his day. His New York *Tribune,* founded in 1841, was a working-class paper that avoided the sensationalism of the penny press and reached hundreds of thousands of readers with his support of causes popular to them—and some that were not popular, until Greeley started giving them an airing. Of course, if the readers did not agree with Greeley, that was all right, too—an erratic, unpredictable man, Greeley often changed his opinions nonchalantly, as though he were changing a headline between editions.

As Greeley's original New York readers moved West, they took the weekly *Tribune* with them, giving it, an 1850s traveler wrote, a place in their homes next to the Bible. This widespread circulation gave Greeley an unprecedented national influence, as did his popular lectures, books, and political forays. In addition, Greeley was distinctive: short, pudgy, bearded, disorganized, given to wearing a white duster that inevitably flapped as he bustled down the street. There was little photography then, but the work of sketch artists and cartoonists gave Greeley a familiarity few other editors obtained.

In 1859, Greeley, who for decades had been preaching the value of western migration, low-

cost homestead lands, and internal improvements, including a railroad to the Pacific, went West himself. (Greeley is still credited with having famously said, "Go West, young man, go West," but he probably never said this, at least in those words. He did, in 1851, reprint an article from the Terre Haute, Indiana, *Express,* in which the phrase was used.) Greeley now wanted to see what he had urged others to see and to look over possible western railroad routes. He also made a foray to Salt Lake City, where he interviewed the Mormon leader, Brigham Young, in one of the first interviews with direct quotes published in American newspapers.

During his three-month trip, Greeley sent back thirty-two dispatches, averaging 3,750 words each, all written in his trademark atrocious handwriting. When he was back in his office, he wrote a thirty-third letter crystallizing his arguments for a transcontinental railroad.

"Dispatch 33: A Railroad to the Pacific," by Horace Greeley. New York *Tribune,* October 1859.

New York, Oct. 20, 1859

I propose in this letter to present such considerations as seem to me pertinent and feasible, in favor of the speedy construction of a railroad, connecting at some point our Eastern network of railways with the waters of the Pacific Ocean.

Let facts be submitted to, and pondered by, considerate, reflecting men. There are thousands of usually intelligent citizens who have decided that a Pacific railroad is a humbug—the fantasy of demagogues and visionaries—without having ever given an hour's earnest consideration to the facts in the case. Let me have a patient hearing while I set forth some of the more material of those facts: and first, in answer to the question, *Is there a national need of a railroad from the Missouri to the Pacific?* Let us study the records.

The number of passengers arriving at, and departing from San Francisco by water, so far as we have official returns of them, is as follows:

YEARS	ARRIVALS	DEPARTURES
1849	91,415	No returns.
1850	36,462	No returns.
1851	27,182	No returns.
1852	66,988	22,946
1853	33,232	30,001
1854	47,531	23,508
1855	29,198	22,898
1856	28,119	22,747
1857	22,990	16,902
Total	381,107	139,002

Of course, they were not all from the Atlantic slope, via the Isthmus, or Nicaragua; but the great mass of them were. Probably most of those brought by small vessels from the Pacific ports were not reported to, or recorded at the customhouse at all. There were some immigrants to California who did not land at San Francisco, though the great mass undoubtedly did. Then there was a heavy, though capricious overland emigration. Governor Bigler stated the number in 1854 alone at sixty-one thousand four hundred and sixty-two; and there was a very large migration across the Plains in 1852. In 1857, the number was estimated at twelve thousand five hundred. This year, my estimate of the number, founded on personal observation, is thirty thousand; but others make it forty thousand to sixty thousand. . . .

Can there be any doubt that nine-tenths of these would have traveled by railroad, had such a road stretched from the Missouri or Mississippi to the Pacific, the fare being moderate, and the passage made within ten days? I estimate that twice to thrice the number who actually did go to California would have gone, had there been such a means of conveyance, and that the present Anglo-American population of the Pacific slope would have been little less that two millions—say,

California, one million five hundred thousand; Oregon, three hundred thousand; Washington, one hundred thousand; Sonora and Mexican California, one hundred thousand.

Now as to the gold crop of California. . . .

The returns for the last two years and the first three-quarters of the present are not before me, but they are known to have varied little from the rate of fifty millions of dollars per annum, making the total amount entered at the customhouse of San Francisco, as shipped at that port up to this date, rather over five hundred millions of dollars. How many more millions have been brought away in the trunks or belts of returning emigrants, or mercantile passengers, I will not attempt to guess, but the amount is certainly large. On my recent trip homeward, one of the steerage passengers was currently reported as having thirty thousand dollars in gold in his carpetbag which he kept in his hands or under his head; others were said to have their thousands each, to a very large aggregate amount. Manifestly, the export of gold from California, the current produce of her mines, has exceeded fifty millions of dollars per annum, while a considerable amount is retained in the country.

Now all this gold is sent away to pay for goods—many of them very costly in proportion to their bulk and weight—silks and other dear textile fabrics; jewelry; rare wines; expensive wares; drugs, spices, etc. Experience has amply proved that all such products take the quickest rather than the cheapest route. I believe that twenty million dollars of costly or perishable merchandise would annually seek California overland if there were a continuous line of railway from the Atlantic to the Pacific seaboard; and that this amount would steadily and rapidly increase. . . .

Now let us see how far the government would necessarily patronize such a road:

The Post Office Department is now paying at least one million and a quarter for the conveyance of mails between the Atlantic and Gulf states and California, and was recently paying one million and a half. For this, it gets a semi-monthly mail by way of the Isthmus (six thousand miles, or more than double the distance direct), and a semi-weekly mail by the Butterfield route (also very circuitous), which carries letters only. There are two or three slow mails on other routes, but they cannot be said to add anything of moment to the facilities enjoyed by California and the older states for the interchange of messages of ideas.

As to military transportation, I cannot say what is its amount, nor how far a single line of railway could reduce its proper cost. I believe, however, that the government is now paying at least six millions of dollars for the transportation of men, munitions and provisions to our various military posts between Kansas proper and California, and that fully half of this would necessarily be saved and earned by a railroad to the Pacific. . . .

The social, moral, and intellectual blessings of a Pacific railroad can hardly be glanced at within the limits of an article. Suffice it for the present that I merely suggest them:

1. Our mails are now carried to and fro California by steamships, via Panama, in twenty to thirty days, starting once a fortnight. The average time of transit from writers throughout the Atlantic states to their correspondents on the Pacific exceeds thirty days. With a Pacific railroad, this would be reduced to ten, for the letters written in Illinois or Michigan would reach their destinations in the mining counties of California quicker than letters sent from New York or Philadelphia would reach San Francisco. With a daily mail by railroad from each of our Atlantic cities to and from California, it is hardly possible that the amount of both letters and printed matter transmitted, and consequently of postage, should not be speedily quadrupled.

2. The first need of California today is a large influx of intelligent, capable, virtuous women. With a railroad to the Pacific, avoiding the miseries and perils of six thousands miles of ocean transportation, and making the transit a pleasant and interesting overland journey of ten days, at a reduced cost, the migration of this class would be immensely accelerated and increased. With wages for all kinds of women's work at least thrice as high on the Pacific as in this quarter, and with larger opportunities for honorable and fit settlement in life, I cannot doubt that tens of thousands would annually cross the Plains, to the signal benefit of California and of the whole country, as well as the improvement of their own fortunes and the profit of the railroad.

3. Thousands now staying in California, expecting to "go home" so soon as they shall have somewhat improved their circumstances, would send or come for their families and settle on the Pacific for life, if a railroad were opened. Tens of thousands who have been to California and come back, unwilling either to live away from their families or to expose them to the present hardships of migration thither, would return with all they have, prepared to spend their remaining days in the land of gold, if there were a Pacific railroad. . . .

Men and brethren! Let us resolve to have a railroad to the Pacific—to have it soon. It will add more to the strength and wealth of our country than would the acquisition of a dozen Cubas. It will prove a bond of union not easily broken, and a new spring to our national industry, prosperity and wealth. It will call new manufactures into existence, and increase the demand for the products of those already existing. It will open new vistas to national and individual aspiration, and crush our filibusterism by giving a new and wholesome direction to the public mind. My long, fatiguing journey was undertaken in the hope that I might do something toward the early construction of the Pacific railroad; and I trust that it has not been made wholly in vain.

• • •

Greeley's letters from the West were gathered in a book, *An Overland Journey,* in 1860, still a remarkable travel book that shows Greeley's skill as a reporter and writer. The book magnified Greeley's arguments in the *Tribune.*

A bill to construct a transcontinental railroad was passed by Congress in 1862, but work was stalled by the Civil War.

The war showed Greeley's contradictions. A staunch abolitionist, he also wanted the war to end, on almost any terms. In 1864, urging restoration of "the Union as it was," he went to Canada and met with Confederate agents, to what would be substantial embarrassment. President Abraham Lincoln was perplexed by the editor's inconsistencies, although he recognized Greeley's influence. During Reconstruction, Greeley called for universal amnesty and suffrage for all. In 1867, Greeley signed a bail bond for Jefferson Davis, former president of the Confederacy.

Construction of the transcontinental railroad began after the end of the war, and Greeley's dream was reality in May 1869. Although the financial machinations of the railroad companies were marked by scandal, the railroad helped, as Greeley had recognized early, bind the country together.

In 1872, Greeley broke with the Republican party and ran for president as the candidate of the Democratic and Liberal Republican parties. His platform called for civil service reform and universal amnesty for former Confederates. An unofficial campaign slogan was "Anyone but Grant."

Grant won handily. A month after the election, Greeley was dead.

SARAH JOSEPHA HALE AND *GODEY'S LADY'S BOOK* CONVINCE LINCOLN TO CREATE THANKSGIVING

Although the holiday of Thanksgiving commemorates the harvest the Plymouth colony achieved, with the help of the native Indians, in 1621, the day was not a national holiday until George Washington proclaimed it so in 1789. Then the holiday lapsed.

Sarah Josepha Hale solved that. Hale's first writings, in the 1820s, consisted of poetry, which she published under a pen name, Cornelia, because, at that time, it was not regarded as respectable for women to write and publish. In 1826 she published a novel, *Northwood, a Tale of New England.* She then became editor of *Ladies' Magazine,* in Boston.

In Boston, Hale became an activist reformer, especially for women's rights. She favored education for women and helped raise money for the Bunker Hill Monument. She is regarded to have written "Mary Had a Little Lamb."

In 1836, Hale moved to Philadelphia to become editor of *Godey's Lady's Book.* Founded in 1830 by Louis Godey, *Godey's Lady's Book* was one of the great publishing successes of the nineteenth century, featuring hand-colored engravings of clothing for men and women and also publishing fiction and poetry. In the 1850s, it had a circulation of 150,000 and was the most popular publication for women in the United States. Throughout its existence, it was a strong proponent of women's rights.

In 1846, Hale began to call for the creation of Thanksgiving as a national holiday, stressing her belief that such a holiday would help bind the country together. She continued the campaign each year, and also made sure to run recipes for dishes that could be served on a Thanksgiving.

In 1863 her editorial, which she wrote in July for publication in September, for the first time suggested a presidential proclamation could settle the issue.

"Our National Thanksgiving," by Sarah Josepha Hale. *Godey's Lady's Book,* September 1863.

Then he said unto them, Go your way, eat the fat, and drink the sweet, and send portion unto them for whom nothing is prepared; for this day is holy unto our Lord: neither be ye sorry; for the joy of the Lord is your strength.—Nehemiah viii.10.

Thus commanded the inspired leader of the Jews, when they kept the "Feast of Weeks"; in a time of national darkness and sore troubles shall we not recognize that the goodness of God never faileth, and that to our Father in heaven we should always bring the Thanksgiving offering at the ingathering of the harvest?

Wise lawgivers and great patriots have acknowledged the salutary effect of appointed times for national reunions which combine religious sentiment with domestic and social enjoyment; thus feelings of benevolence are awakened, and gratitude to the Giver of all our blessings is seen to be the great duty of life. Owing to the different economy of different churches, among Protestant denominations, except the Christian Sabbath, all our religious commemorations are partial and local.

Can we not, then, following the appointment of Jehovah in the "Feast of Weeks," or *Harvest Festival,* establish our yearly Thanksgiving as a *permanent American National Festival, which shall be celebrated on the last Thursday in November in every State of our Union?* Indeed, it has been nearly accomplished. For the last twelve or fourteen years, the States have made approaches to this unity. In 1859 *thirty States* and three Territories held the Thanksgiving Festival on the same day—the last Thursday in November. It was also celebrated that year and the following on board several of the American fleets—ships in the Indian Ocean, the Mediterranean, and on the Brazil station; by the Americans in Berlin at our Prussian Embassy; in Paris and in Switzerland; and American missionaries have signified their readiness to unite in this Festival if it should be established on a particular day which can be known as the *American Thanksgiving.*

Then, in every quarter of the globe our nationality would be recognized in connection with our gratitude to the Divine giver for all our blessings. The pious and loving thought that every American was joining in heart with the beloved family at home and with the church to which he belonged, would thrill his soul with the purest feelings of patriotism and the deepest emotions of thankfulness for his religious enjoyments.

Would it not be of great advantage, socially, nationally, religiously, to have the DAY of our American Thanksgiving positively settled? Putting aside the sectional feelings and local incidents that might be urged by any single State or isolated Territory that desired to choose its own time?

Would it not be more noble, more truly American, to become *nationally in unity* when we offer to God our tribute of joy and gratitude for the blessings of the year?

Taking this view of the case, would it not be better that the proclamation which appoints Thursday the 26th of November (1863) as the day of Thanksgiving for the people of the United States of America should, in the first instance, emanate from the President of the Republic—to be applied by the Governors of each and every State, in acquiescence with the chief executive advisors?

•   •   •

It was the last Thanksgiving editorial that Hale needed to write.

She met that year with President Abraham Lincoln, who was aware of her campaign and the influence of her magazine. On October 3, 1863, Lincoln issued a National Thanksgiving Proclamation, the first since George Washington. It reflected the North's general feeling that the fortunes of the war were turning its way, and that prosperity and good harvests were in place.

"The year that is drawing to a close has been filled with the blessings of fruitful fields and healthful skies," Lincoln wrote.

He concluded, "It has seemed to me fit and proper that they should be solemnly, reverently, and gratefully acknowledged as with one heart and one voice by the whole American people."

The day held until 1939, 1940, and 1941, when President Franklin D. Roosevelt opted for the third Thursday in November. To settle the dispute between federal and various state holidays, in 1941, Congress officially designated the fourth Thursday of November as Thanksgiving.

Hale continued to edit *Godey's Lady's Book* until 1877.

NOT WAITING FOR MILLIONAIRES, JOSEPH PULITZER ASKS HIS READERS FOR PENNIES, NICKELS, AND DIMES TO ERECT THE STATUE OF LIBERTY

The French and the American peoples had formed a special bond during their countries' respective revolutions, based on a perceived sharing of the ideals of liberty and a sharing of aid. So there was considerable enthusiasm when, in 1865, a French historian, Edouard-René Lefebvre de Laboulaye, proposed that his country give a statue to the United States in commemoration of the upcoming centennial of the Declaration of Independence. Laboulaye had another motive, too; as a republican politician, he hoped the statue would encourage republicanism in France. A theme was chosen—"Liberty Enlightening the World"—and a sculptor, Frédéric-Auguste Bartholdi.

The statue, of a woman wearing a crown and holding a torch, was to be placed on Bedloe's Island, an old Indian clamming site, in New York harbor. To emphasize the two country's partnership, the French were to provide, and pay for, the statue and the Americans to provide, and pay for, the pedestal.

Bartholdi ran behind schedule, understandable considering the skill required to place massive copper sheets on a 151-foot steel and wrought-iron structure. More embarrassing than the French delay was the fact that American fundraisers ran behind schedule on building the pedestal. Even though the city's captains of industry—this being the Gilded Age—were amassing great wealth, none stepped forward. In March of 1885, with the goddess of liberty in pieces in Paris, awaiting shipment by boat to the United States, a meeting of the American Committee of the Bartholdi Statue reported that its treasury balance was down to $2,866 and that work on the pedestal had been suspended.

A three-paragraph story about the meeting appeared on the lower part of page 6 of the New York *World* on Friday, March 13, 1885.

The headlines ran:

THE BARTHOLDI STATUE
The Committee Acknowledges its Inability
to
Proceed with the Work

By Monday, Joseph Pulitzer, the *World*'s publisher, a man "whose reverence for liberty was as powerful as his desire for circulation," as a biographer, W. A. Swanberg, was to write, had a plan. A front-page story detailing the sorry state of affairs was accompanied by a fervent editorial:

"An Appeal." New York *World,* March 16, 1885.

Money must be raised to complete the pedestal for the Bartholdi Statue. It would be an irrevocable disgrace to New York City and the American Republic to have France send us this splendid gift without our having provided even so much as a landing place for it.

Nearly ten years ago the French people set about making the Bartholdi Statue. It was to be a gift emblematical of our attainment of the first century of Independence. It was also the seal of a more serviceable gift that they made to us in 1776, when, but for their timely aid, the ragged sufferers of Valley Forge would have been disbanded and the Colonies would have continued a part of the British dominion. Can we fail to respond to the spirit that actuated this generous testimonial?

The Statue is now completed and ready to be brought to our shores in a vessel especially commissioned for the purpose by the French Government. Congress, by a refusal to appropriate the necessary money to complete preparations for its proper reception and erection, has thrown the responsibility back to the American people.

There is but one thing that can be done. We must raise the money.

The *World* is the people's paper, and it now appeals to the people to come forward and raise this money. The $250,000 that the making of the statue cost was paid in by the masses of the French people—by the workingmen, the tradesmen, the shop girls, the artisans—by all, irrespective of class or condition. Let us respond in like manner. Let us not wait for the millionaires to give this money. It is not a gift from the millionaires of France to the millionaires of America but a gift of the whole people of France to the whole people of America.

Take this appeal to yourself personally. *It is meant for every reader of* The World.... Give something, however little. Send it to us. We will receive it and see that it is properly applied. We will also publish the name of every giver, however small the sum given. Let us hear from the people. Send in your suggestions. We will consider them all. If

we all go to work together with a firm resolve and a patriotic will we can raise the needed money before the French vessel bearing us the Bartholdi Statue shall have passed the unsightly mass on Bedloe's Island that is now but a humiliating evidence of our indifference and ingratitude.

• • •

Pulitzer put a reporter, John R. Reavis, in charge of the $200,000 fund drive and contributed $250 himself. The drive touched a nerve and the outpouring was gigantic. What has become a legend is true: schoolchildren did send in their pennies, nickels, and dimes. And more. One young girl accompanied her donation with a letter: "I am a wee bit of a girl, yet I am ever so glad I was born in time to contribute my mite to the Pedestal Fund. When I am old enough I will ask my papa and mamma to take me to see the statue, and I will always be proud that I began my career by sending you $1 to aid so good a cause."

Within four months, about $75,000 had been raised; financing was completed in August. Reavis was given a bonus and a raise.

By April 1886, the pedestal was ready and the statue, which had arrived from France in 210 packing crates, began to be assembled. It was dedicated in October, after three days of celebration. Pulitzer hired two steamers to take *World* employees and their families to the island for the occasion.

Other New York newspapers had scoffed at the *World's* campaign, but they has simply misjudged the interests of the city's millions, something Pulitzer rarely did. Pulitzer added a likeness of Liberty to his paper's nameplate, and later commissioned a stained-glass window including Liberty for the *World* office building. For years the paper published anniversary issues of the statue's dedication.

THE *VILLAGE VOICE*'S RICHARD GOLDSTEIN TAKES THE NEW POP SCENE SERIOUSLY AND HELPS INTRODUCE AMERICA TO A NEW ART FORM, ROCK MUSIC, AND TO ITSELF

In the mid-1960s, a young, unknown writer, Richard Goldstein, burst on the New York music critic scene like a shooting star. God, young writers in New York City and other outposts the *Voice* served said, "Did you see what that guy is doing? I'd like to write like him."

Goldstein attended Hunter College in New York City. He was an iconoclast. He wrote "Yossarian Lives" on blackboards of classrooms, was chairman of the Cinema Society, for which he showed movies then regarded as risqué, and assisted in inviting Gus Hall, the longtime American Communist, and George Lincoln Rockwell, the American Nazi, to campus. He wore, he later wrote in the *Village Voice*, a soft beret, had a picture of Ernest Hemingway on his wall, and recited lines from the French movies of Alain Resnais. He was a fan of the pop group the Shirelles.

The *Voice* was founded in Greenwich Village in 1955, one of the first of the underground papers, as an alternative voice to the mainline New York City newspapers. Under its early leaders, such as the founding editor, Dan Wolf, and Jerry Tallmer, a writer and editor, the *Voice* took off, for New York City and the United States were changing, and the *Voice* was covering that change. A 114-day strike in 1963 at the *New York Times*, the New York *Daily News*, and, for a time, the New York *Post*, gave the *Voice* additional attention in a news-starved city.

The 1960s and the early 1970s were perhaps the paper's finest hour. It covered civil rights, the antiwar movement, the 1968 Democratic convention in Chicago, the upheaval at Columbia University that same year, the killings at Kent State University in 1970, the new feminist movement, gay liberation, hippies, Yippies, drugs, Watergate. It wrote about the city's effort to ban folk singers from Washington Square and stopped New York redeveloper Robert Moses from bulldozing a road through Washington Square. The *Voice* inaugurated a new kind of aggressive press criticism. Later it was one of the first to take seriously women's health issues and was especially effective in its coverage of New York City government. The *Voice*'s writers included Wayne Barrett, Susan Brownmiller, Teresa Carpenter, Paul Cowan, Robert Christgau, Timothy Crouse, Karen Durbin, Alexander Cockburn, Francis FitzGerald, Joe Flaherty, Michael Harrington, Murray Kempton, Norman Mailer, Jack Newfield, Mary Nichols, Lucian K. Truscott IV, James Ridgeway, and Ellen Willis.

Goldstein was the equal of any of them. He was, early on, especially interested in rock music, and when he began writing for the *Voice*, making rock music a beat for perhaps the first time at any American publication, his music pieces almost immediately began to stand out. He took rock music, rock musicians, and rock fans seriously—one of the few music writers to do that.

Here, typical of his work, is a piece on Janis Joplin and the Holding Company that Goldstein wrote in 1968.

"Next Year in San Francisco," by Richard Goldstein. *Village Voice,* April 18, 1968.

Tonight's crowd ambles languidly across the floor of Philadelphia's Electric Factory, a huge garage turned psychedelic playground. Mostly, they are straight kids come to gape at the hippies and fathom the Now. Ten years ago, they would have preened their pompadours before the cameras on *American Bandstand.* Today, they steal furtive drags on filter-tip cigarettes trying to look high. With coiled springs behind their eyes, they flash stiff South-Phillie grins at any chick who looks like she might go down. They've all had their palms read by the Wizard in the balcony, and their faces painted in the adjacent boutique. Now they stand like limp meringue, watching a local group called Edison's Electric Machine belt warm-up jive.

A real deathscene. Not a pleasant sight for Janis Joplin, who peers through a crack in the dressing room door, and scowls, "Oh, shit. It's dead out there. We'll never be able to get into those kids. Want to see death? Take a look out there. You ever played Philadelphia? No, of course not. You don't *play* anywhere."

When Janis scowls, her whole face closes up around her mouth, and even her eyelashes seem to frown. You could say she gets nervous before a set. The other members of Big Brother and the Holding Company sit guzzling beer, trying on beads, and hassling their road manager. But Janis stalks around the tiny room, her fingers drumming against a tabletop. She sips hot tea from a Styrofoam cup. She talks in gasps, and between sentences, she belts a swig of Southern Comfort, her trademark. Tonight, a knowing admirer has graced her dressing room with a fifth, in lieu of flowers. "I don't drink anything on the rocks," she explains. "Cold is bad for my throat. So, it's always straight or in tea. Tastes like orange petals in tea. I usually get about a pint and half down me, when I'm performing. Any more, I start to nod out."

Now the B-group files in, dripping sweat. The lead singer gingerly places his guitar in its plush casket and peels off an imitation-brocade jacket, sweatshirt, pullover, and drenched undershirt. "Why do you wear all that clothing if it's not so hot out there?" Janis asks.

"Because I'm freaky." And the door opens again to admit a fully-attired gorilla with rubber hands and feet. Janis glances briefly at the ground to make sure that it's still there, and then she offers the gorilla some booze and he lifts his mask to accept. His name is Gary the Gorilla, and Janis digs that, so she gives him her bottle to hold during the group's set and follows Peter the bassman through the door, while the crowd shouts for music. Gary unzips his belly and passes his feet

around, and the lead singer of Edison's Electric Machine examines a rip in his brocade, consoling himself with the B-group's prayer: Next Year In San Francisco.

I first met them last year in San Francisco. In a ranch house with an unobstructed view of ticky-tack. They were assembled for an interview on Hippy-culture, and I began with a nervous question about turning on. In answer, somebody lit up and soon the floor was hugging-warm. I glanced down at my notes as though they had become hieroglyphics (which, it later turned out, they had). When it was time to split, and everyone had boarded a paisley hearse, I muttered something like, "We shouldn't be interviewed. We should be friends." And the car drove away laughing, with long hair flying from every window.

This summer, there will be 20,000 yelpers on Haight Street, hoping to get discovered, like Janis, in some psychedelic Schwab's. But I'm afraid Big Brother and the Holding Company is the last of the great San Francisco bands. With new groups trying on serious music like a training bra, they are a glorious throwback to a time when the primary aim in rock was "to get people moving"—nothing more or less. They were nurtured in the roots of the Hip renaissance (played the Trips Festival and the first productions of the Family Dog; jammed together in a big house at 1090 Page Street, a mecca for musicians back when the only interested talent scouts were cops). Now, they are its most fragrant late-summer blossom.

In 1961, Janis and Chett Holmes (proprietor of the Family Dog) hitchhiked west. They were anonymous freaks then, newly plucked from Texas topsoil and still green. "What were the two of you like then, Janis?"

"Oh—younger."

"How were you different from today?"

"We were . . . ummm . . . just interested in being beatnicks then. Now, we've got responsibilities, and I guess you could say, ambition."

She was born in Port Arthur, Texas, in 1943.

Dropped out of four or five schools. Sang in hill-billy bars with a local bluegrass band. For the beer. "We'd do country songs, and then the band'd shut up, and I'd sing blues, 'cause that was my thing."

Her thing was no Patti Page regatta, no Connie Francis sob-along, but mangy backwoods blues, heavy with devotion to Bessie Smith. She still smears Bessie across everything she sings, making it possible for a whole generation of us to hear beyond the scratches in those old records. But she says she never really tried to sing until she joined Big Brother.

"See, Bessie, she sang big open notes, in very simple phrasing. But you can't fall back on that in front of a rock band. I mean, you can't sing loose and easy with a throbbing amplifier and drums behind you. The beat just pushes you on. So I started singing rhythmically, and now I'm learning from Otis Redding to push a song instead of just sliding over it."

It was Chett Holmes who made Janis part of the Holding Company (before that, it had been an instrumental band, one of dozens formed during the merger of folk, jazz, and rock among Bay Area youth). From the start, their music began to clothe her voice. They taught her to blast, pound, and shatter a song. She returned the favor by directing her solos inward; toward the group's rhythmic heart. In fact, Janis has made her voice into a family. It shows. People think of Big Brother as more of a commune than a group.

True, it's chic to deride the band as being unworthy of her magic, but they are certainly not lame companions. Her voice is vast enough to overwhelm any accompaniment less raucous than a bazooka, but with Big Brother behind her, freaking out like country cousins, there is no difference between voice and music—just Sound. Call that the sound of Janis Joplin and you might as well identify a fire by its smoke just because that's what hits you first.

"I have three voices," she explains. "The shouter; the husky, guttural chick; and the high wailer. When I turn into a nightclub singer, I'll probably use my husky voice. That's the one my mother likes. She says, 'Janis, why do you scream like that when you've got such a pretty voice?' "

It's not a pretty sound she makes now. A better word for it would be "primal." She plants herself onstage like a firmly rooted tree, then whips more emotion out of her upper branches than most singers can wring out of their lower depths. She slinks like tar, scowls like sunburn, stings like war. And she does one other thing that makes it all so sexy. She needs. Needs to move. Needs to feel. Needs to be screamed at. Needs to touch— and be touched back.

" 'Ball and Chain' is the hardest thing I do. I have to really get inside my head, every time I sing it. Because it's about feeling things. That means I can never sing it without really trying. See, there's this big hole in the song that's mine, and I've got to fill it with something. So, I do! And it really tires me out. But it's so groovy when you know the audience really wants you. I mean, whatever you give them, they'll believe in. And they yell back at you, call your name, and—like that."

It's always the same: at Monterey, where the nation discovered her; at the Avalon, where they know her best; at the Anderson, where the New York press corps took notes; and tonight at the Electric Factory, in Philadelphia. She begs and coaxes her audiences until they begin to holler, first in cliches like "do-it-to-it" and finally in wordless squeals. Suddenly, the room is filled with the agony in her voice. Kids surround the stage, shouting her name and spilling over with the joy of having been reached. Even the onlookers in neckties nod their heads and whisper "Shit...oh shit." Because to hear Janis sing "Ball and Chain" just once is to have been laid, lovingly and well.

Two sets later, they are back in the dressing room, flushed with sweat and applause. There is a tired hassle with the road manager. Dave the drummer changes into his third shirt that evening. And Janis is sitting on Gary the Gorilla's lap, fondling his furry knees and opening a second fifth of Southern Comfort.

"Why do I always hafta dance alone in these places?" she rasps, still recuperating from her solo. "I mean, you saw me dancing out there between sets. All those guys were standing around, panting in the corner. Finally, I had to say to one of 'em, 'Well, do you wanna dance, or not?' and he comes on waving his arms around like a fuckin' bat. Didn't even look at me. Now, why do things like that always happen?"

"Because you're so freaky looking," her road manager answers.

She nods slowly, and whispers, "Yeah."

She digs and detests her weirdness. She would like to be the freakiest chick in rock, and a gracious young lady as well. At a recent press party to celebrate the group's new contract with Columbia Records, Janis shook her hair only to confront a lady out of *Harper's Bazaar*, who covered up her drink and said, "Do you mind?" Janis answered in a tone out of *Evergreen*, "Fuck off, baby." But later she was seen pouting before a mirror, muttering, "Face it, baby, you've got ratty hair."

Now she moves out of the tiny room and surveys the remnants of this evening's scene: cigarette butts and a gaggle of local freaks. There are no pale young ladies searching for a seminal autograph in this crowd, but Peter the bassman is already making contact with a chick named Crafty. Gandalf, the wizard from the balcony, offers to read every palm in the house, whispering, "Hey—let's go up to your room and smoke."

Later, at a hamburger stand, Gandalf stops in the middle of a poem he is composing on a napkin and reflects: "Tomorrow, I'm gonna make it with Janis. I'm gonna just go up to her and say, 'Hey—let's make it.' 'Cause she's so groovy to watch. What a body she must have under that voice." He pauses to consider it, and then asks a waitress for spare whipped-cream cans.

But Gandalf the Wizard may have to wait longer than tomorrow. For this very night (while Philadelphia sleeps), Janis is with Gary the Gorilla, and they are finishing off the second fifth together.

• • •

Goldstein continues to write at the *Voice* and has broadened his interests into a number of other areas beyond music, including gay affairs and New York politics. The *Voice,* which always had its factions and often vicious in-fighting, has gone through a number of owners. It survived, while many other so-called underground papers did not, but with much less of the feistiness, timeliness, and good writing that the paper had in the 1960s and 1970s.

Joplin's lifestyle took its toll: She died in 1970, two years after this article. Rock music continues.

THE *GRAND FORKS (NORTH DAKOTA) HERALD* HOLDS ITS COMMUNITY TOGETHER AFTER A DISASTROUS FLOOD

Even for a high plains state like North Dakota, the snow in the winter of 1996–1997 had been fierce. When it started to melt in the spring, it quickly burdened the creeks and streams and then the rivers. Then came the rains, drenching downpours that strained the rivers even more. The residents of Grand Forks, a city of 50,000 on the Red River, started filling sandbags to build dikes. The Red rose to about twenty-six feet over flood level. On the night of April 18, the dikes gave way and the river won. The *Grand Forks Herald* had to stop its press run about a quarter of the way through and evacuate. So did most of the city's residents. The next day, a fire burned eleven downtown buildings, including that of the *Herald*. The paper's front-page headline: "Come hell and high water."

Catastrophe can be the test of a newspaper.

Catastrophe can also show a community a newspaper's value. The *Herald,* setting up operations in a school in a nearby town and printing at a cooperating paper in St. Paul, Minnesota, never missed a day of publication. Staff members alternated between dealing with their personal problems and those of the city. The people in Grand Forks were hungry for news, said the *Herald*'s publisher, Michael Maidenberg. "They wanted to read names, see photographs, see facts."

One of the paper's most popular features was a daily listing through which residents, cut off from their homes, their workplaces, their mailboxes, their telephones, could reach one another. A sampling from the *Herald* of April 27, 1997, underscores the concern and determination that helped the city through.

LOOKING FOR, PERSON CALLING AND MESSAGE

Employee Northwest Fabrics & Craft . . . Mary. . . . Please call for payroll information

Employees of Italian Moon. . . . Coral. . . . Please call to pick up paycheck

Patients at Sheyenne Care Center. . . . Christiansen, Craig, and Burnhast, Patty. . . . We received 27 patients/please call

U-17 Grand Forks Boys Soccer Team. . . . Pat . . . Please call for practice information

Anderson, Damon & Julie . . . Christianson, Chris. . . . Your family can stay with us—Pls call

Barry, Joshua. . . . Westover, Cheryl. . . . Please call sister

Barry, Daniel. . . . Westover, Cheryl . . . Please call sister

Barry, Seanna. . . . Westover, Cheryl . . . Please call sister

Beier, Carole. . . . Nies, Patsy. . . . Are you okay? Please call

Boulduc, Bennett . . . Boulduc, Jean. . . . Please call collect if you have to

Davidson, Lois & Morris. . . . Nielsen, Eda. . . . Pls contact she's at the three bay shelter

Garlinton, Julie. . . . Thompson, Beth. . . . Please call I am worried

Gatlin, Helen . . . Ames, Vincent & Valerie. . . . We are okay please call

Gist, Christy. . . . Rieger, Margaret . . . I am ok, please call my daughters

Hagen, Cliff. . . . Moore, Cindy. . . . 300 Block of 5th St was in a fire

Hoffman, Jake. . . . Johnson, Bob . . . Please call worried

Hoghaug, Mar. . . . Gallagher, Millie. . . . Will come and get you

Kelley, Ivy Marie. . . . Shulind, Joan & Jim . . . Call your grandparents

Lavoy, Jessica. . . . Gallagher, Millie. . . . Will come and get you

Litzinger, Jim. . . . Rochelle. . . . Ideal in Atlanta

Moe, Mike & Jean. . . . Connelly, Robin . . . Please call if you need a place to stay

Nelson, Rodney. . . . Nelson, Sally. . . . If anybody knows where he is call

Simonson, Donna. . . . Robertson, Gayle. . . . Please call regarding medical treatment

Smith, Donna. . . . McWethy, Deeann. . . . Please call you can stay with me

Smith, Glenn & Deedee. . . . Vidden, Michael & Cheryl . . . Pls call wants to know if you are OK

Alderson, Peg & Bob. . . . I am okay and I am in Fargo, ND

Foland, Ragnar . . . I am okay

Fontaine, Mary & John. . . . We're okay in Anoka, MN

Gerig, Kathleen & Paul. . . . I am at Idaho

Hunt, Janet. . . . I am okay and I am in Salt Lake City

Kilberide, Pauline, Tara & Penny. . . . Our house is gone, but we are ok

• • •

The *Grand Forks Herald* won the 1998 Pulitzer Prize for public service. Its efforts, the prize committee said, had "helped hold its community together." Peter Finley Dunne, an early Chicago columnist, would have credited the *Herald* with fulfilling one of journalism's top goals: comforting the afflicted.

AN AFTERWORD

"Journalists!" exclaimed Hildy Johnson, a Chicago reporter in *The Front Page,* the 1928 journalism parody written by Ben Hecht and Charles MacArthur. "Peeking through keyholes! Running after fire engines like a lot of coach dogs! Waking people up in the middle of the night to ask them what they think of Mussolini. Stealing pictures off old ladies of their daughters that get raped in Oak Park. A lot of lousy, daffy buttinskis, swelling around with holes in their pants, borrowing nickels from office boys! And for what? So a million hired girls and motormen's wives'll know what's going on."

The Front Page was a remarkable portrayal of American journalism and, while a parody, contained much truth, as good parody must. Still, the good journalist must ask, what's wrong with telling hired girls and motormen's wives what's going on?

This collection is about doing that: telling Americans what is going on, especially when other people—the government, the business leaders, the military, other persons of prominence and power—do not wish that this to be done.

For journalists, one of the striking lessons here is how many times over so many decades people have found stories by looking in the same places—mental hospitals, programs for the poor, jails, and prisons. Blacks could not get on the front page in the days when news was segregated,

the Rev. Martin Luther King Jr., said, so they had to write their headlines in the street. The common link here is that the people involved have no ready access to power or public attention until the press provides it.

Second, people will do things in private, or among their own kind, that they would not do in public. This is obvious for the criminal, the hateful, the corrupt, but it also applies to otherwise ordinary business people, government officials, engineers, military officers, physicians, who find privacy a convenient shield. One of his first lessons on the police beat in Baltimore, said Russell Baker, the longtime *New York Times* reporter and columnist, was that "only a fool expects the authorities to tell him what the news is." The lesson should be that the areas of society cloaked in silence are areas where abuse—and news—hides. Those are the rocks journalists should overturn.

Third, good journalism is hard. Eileen Welsome of the *Albuquerque Tribune* said that it took six years between the time she first spotted a footnote about human experiments in a technical document and the first stories naming some of the eighteen subjects injected with plutonium during the Cold War. Much of it she did on her own time, going back again and again to a topic she cared about. This is true of many of the other reporters as well and illuminates an important truth about reporting: you are responsible for what you do. A reporter has bosses, yes, and time restraints, and competing pressures, but so do the people whom reporters write about, and often expose. So reporters should stop looking for excuses for not doing good work. As Clarence Darrow, an attorney who represented many of the powerless, advised in 1916, "Chase after the truth like all hell and you'll free yourself."

Fourth, there is no other watchdog. In the United States, as the twenty-first century begins, an argument is sometimes made that society is overwhelmed by advocacy groups eager to complain and lawyers eager to sue. But not everyone has an advocacy group or a lawyer. Even for those who do, their complaints and their legal work mean nothing unless someone verifies their work and spreads the word. Those someones are journalists.

Almost any veteran journalist, even the least sentimental, can tell stories of things he or she made happen—a stoplight erected at a dangerous corner, a county commissioner defeated, a widow receiving a back payment, a worthy medical charity getting a windfall of donations. We were struck, as we started this book, by how many journalists encouraged us, as if they were almost yearning for justification for their career choices. In 1904 the publisher Joseph Pulitzer wrote in the *North American Review*: "A journalist is the lookout on the bridge of the ship of state. He notes the passing sail, the little things of interest that dot the horizon in fine weather. He reports the drifting castaway whom the ship can save. He peers through fog and storm to give warning of dangers ahead. He is not thinking of his wages or of the profits of his owners. He is there to watch over the safety and welfare of the people who trust him."

It is time to remember that journalism can be an honorable profession. The public that often condemns journalists—national polls routinely put journalists near used-car salesmen and politicians in public esteem—has its own responsibilities.

"Investigative reporting, no matter how excellent, cannot accomplish much all by itself," said J. Edward Murray, once executive editor for the *Arizona Republic,* in 1977, when accepting a posthumous award to Don Bolles, his former reporter, who had been killed after writing repeated stories on corruption in Arizona. "The people must respond to revealed scandal with popular revulsion and anger. It is this outrage which powers the whole process."

This is the bargain represented in the movie *Deadline-U.S.A.,* when a mobster phones in hopes of convincing the editor, played by Humphrey Bogart, to hold a story. Bogart holds up the phone so the caller can hear the noise of the presses. What's that noise, the caller asks. "That's the press, baby," Bogart says. "The press! And there's nothing you can do about it. Nothing!"

PERMISSIONS

Reprinted by permission of the *St. Paul Pioneer Press*.

"The West Against Itself," by Bernard DeVoto, January 1947. Reprinted by permission of *Harper's*.

Excerpt from *The Everglades: River of Grass*, by Marjory Stoneman Douglas, 50th Anniversary Edition © 1997. Used by permission of Pineapple Press, Inc.

"Embattled Wilderness," by Harold H. Martin, September 25, 1948. Reprinted by permission of the *Saturday Evening Post* © 1948 (renewed) BFL&MS, Inc.

"Potomac Parkway," January 3, 1954. Reprinted by permission of the *Washington Post*.

Excerpt from *Silent Spring*, by Rachel Carson. Copyright © 1962 by Rachel L. Carson, renewed 1990 by Roger Christie. Reprinted by permission of Houghton Mifflin Company. All rights reserved.

Excerpt from "Dr. Strangelove Builds a Canal," by Alvin Josephy Jr., *Audubon*, March 1975. Reprinted by permission of Alvin Josephy Jr.

"This Is London," Edward R. Murrow, CBS radio, September 25, 1940. Reprinted by permission of Casey Murrow.

"Under the Axis," November 1942. Reprinted by permission of the *Jewish Frontier*.

"33,000 Dachau Captives Freed by 7th Army," by Marguerite Higgins, May 1, 1945. Reprinted by permission of New York *Herald Tribune* Inc. © 1945, all rights reserved.

Excerpt from *The Making of a Quagmire*, by David Halberstam © 1965. Reprinted by permission of David Halberstam.

"Officer Accused of 109 Deaths," by Seymour M. Hersh, Dispatch News Service, November 13, 1969, © 1969. Reprinted with permission of Seymour M. Hersh.

"Vietnam Archive: Pentagon Study Traces 3 Decades of Growing U.S. Involvement," by Neil Sheehan, June 13, 1971. Reprinted by permission of the *New York Times* © 1971.

"Death Camps," by Roy Gutman, August 2, 1992. Reprinted with permission of *Newsday*, Inc. © 1992.

"Illinois Editors on State Payroll," by George Thiem, April 14, 1949. Reprinted by permission of the Chicago *Sun-Times/Daily News*.

"TV: Journalists' Junkets," by Jack Gould, October 27, 1959. Reprinted by permission of the *New York Times* © 1959.

"A Strike: A Step-by-Step Account," by A. H. Raskin, April 1, 1963. Reprinted by permission of the *New York Times* © 1963.

"The Last American Hero Is Junior Johnson. Yes!" by Tom Wolfe, March 1965. Reprinted by permission of *Esquire*.

"The Reporter," by Gaeton Fonzi and Greg Walter, April 1967. Reprinted by permission of *Philadelphia* magazine.

"Reporter Admits Kidnap Story False," by Marco Trbovich, May 23, 1973. Reprinted by permission of the *Detroit Free Press*.

"Janet's World," by Bill Green, April 19, 1981. Reprinted with permission of the *Washington Post*.

Excerpt from the Arizona Project: Day 15, by Investigative Reporters and Editors, Inc., 1977. Reprinted by permission of Bob Greene.

"Talk Is Expensive," by Alicia C. Shepard, May 1994. Reprinted by permission of the *American Journalism Review*.

"FBI's 10 Most Wanted," by James F. Donovan, February 7, 1949. Reprinted by permission of United Press International.

"Negro Boy Murdered in East Texas," by Ronnie Dugger, November 2, 1955. Reprinted by permission of the *Texas Observer*.